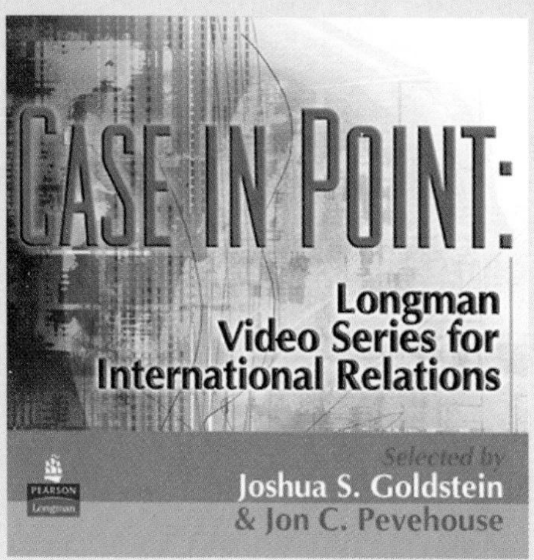

Case in Point: Longman Video Series for International Relations

Instructor Presentation Tool ISBN 0-321-36608-5

Now a 3-DVD set containing 40 video segments from *The NewsHour with Jim Lehrer* on PBS.

- Up-to-date videos from today's hot spots and on today's hot topics will engage students and bring international relations concepts to life in the classroom.
- Helps students learn using real-world examples that are tied to concepts within their textbook.
- Provides instructors with "lecture launchers" to use in the classroom.
- Available at no charge to qualified adopters of any Longman International Relations text.

Also Available

Goldstein/Pevehouse's Companion Website **www.internationalrelations.net**

Free to Students and Instructors!

This exciting Website is completely integrated with the textbook. As students read each chapter or study a topic, they are directed to the Companion Website for one-of-a-kind features that help them apply the chapter information.

Changing World Order icons lead students to discussions that examine the impact of 9/11 on international relations.

The Information Revolution icons help students explore how changes in information technologies are affecting IR.

Web Link icons direct students to relevant resources that help them answer online critical thinking questions about core IR concepts.

ONLINE PRACTICE TEST

take an online practice test at *www.internationalrelations.net*

❑ A
❑ B
☑ C
❑ D

Online Practice Tests include multiple choice, true/false, fill-in-the-blank, and essay questions. Practice tests are graded and can be emailed to instructors. For each question, text page numbers are provided for review.

Video icons provide students with current video clips from PBS's *The NewsHour with Jim Lehrer* followed by critical thinking questions tied to concepts within the textbook.

see next page for MyPoliSciLab...

International Relations

2006–2007 EDITION

Joshua S. Goldstein
American University, Washington, D.C.
University of Massachusetts, Amherst

Jon C. Pevehouse
University of Wisconsin, Madison

PEARSON
Longman

New York San Francisco Boston
London Toronto Sydney Tokyo Singapore Madrid
Mexico City Munich Paris Cape Town Hong Kong Montreal

TO OUR FAMILIES

Publisher: Priscilla McGeehon
Editor in Chief: Eric Stano
Senior Marketing Manager: Elizabeth Fogarty
Supplements Editor: Kristi Olson
Media Editor: Melissa Edwards
Production Manager: Donna DeBenedictis
Project Coordination, Text Design, and Electronic Page Makeup: Elm Street Publishing Services, Inc.
Cover Designer/Manager: Wendy Ann Fredericks
Cover Photos: *Top to bottom:* Hamas candidates in Palestinian election, Nablus, January 2006, © Alaa Badarneh/epa/Corbis. U.S. Marines patrol in Fallujah, Iraq, November 2004, © Franco Pagetti/Polaris. Cindy Sheehan leads protest near President Bush's Texas ranch, August 2005, © Jason Reed/Reuters/Corbis. Japan's Ichiro Suzuki with Cuban players after World Baseball Classic final game in San Diego, CA, March 2006, © Lucy Nicholson/Reuters/Corbis.
Photo Researcher: Julie Tesser
Manufacturing Buyer: Roy L. Pickering, Jr.
Printer and Binder: Quebecor World Taunton
Cover Printer: Phoenix Color Corporation

Library of Congress Cataloging-in-Publication Data
Goldstein, Joshua S., 1952–
International relations / Joshua S. Goldstein, Jon C. Pevehouse.—7th ed.
p. cm.
Includes bibliographical references and index.
ISBN0-321-43430-7 (alk. paper)
1. International relations—Textbooks. I. Pevehouse, Jon C. II. Title.
JZ1242.G65 2006
327—dc22

2005011528

Please visit us at www.internationalrelations.net *or* http://www.ablongman.com/goldstein

ISBN 0-321-43430-7

1 2 3 4 5 6 7 8 9 10—QWT—09 08 07 06

Brief Contents

Website: www.internationalrelations.net or *www.ablongman.com/goldstein*

Detailed Contents

Note: Each chapter ends with questions on thinking critically, a chapter summary, and a list of key terms.

Preface

"The students like it," our colleagues tell us about this book. They like it, we think, because it makes accessible such an interesting subject—International Relations (IR)—and because its coverage of that subject is up-to-date, accurate, visually appealing, and intellectually engaging. The rich complexity of international relationships—political, economic, and cultural—provides a fascinating puzzle to try to understand. The puzzle is not just intellectually challenging; it is also emotionally powerful. It contains human-scale stories in which the subject's grand themes—war and peace, tragedy and triumph, intergroup conflict and community—play out. IR also matters in our daily lives as never before; today's students will graduate into a global economy in which no nation stands alone.

This 2006–2007 edition is an update to the Seventh Edition, retaining the pagination so that syllabi do not need to change but with elements of a new edition. A new feature—"Careers in International Relations" (pp. 211, 295, and 337)—helps students think about job possibilities in the field. An extremely up-to-date photo program brings today's cases and leaders into every chapter. And of course we have updated every topic, example, and case, along with the data tables and graphs, to reflect the rapidly changing world of 2006—from a Palestinian government led by Hamas to an Iraq slipping from insurgency into sectarian conflict; from world trade talks at a deadlock to bird flu leapfrogging continents worldwide; from the end of a war in Aceh, Indonesia, to the election of women leaders in Liberia, Chile, and Germany; and from China's new global stature to Iran's confrontation with the West over nuclear weapons. We also offer new supplements with this edition, most notably a three-DVD set of short videos from PBS's *The NewsHour with Jim Lehrer*, available at no extra charge for qualified adopters, for classroom use.

Among the many effects of the "war on terrorism" is one positive: It has focused college students on international relations, especially in the United States. The September 11, 2001, attacks shattered many Americans' assumption of safety from distant international conflicts and wars. Now that young Americans are paying more attention to international affairs, we hope this textbook can help a generation to develop knowledge and critical thinking in order to find its voice and place in the evolving world order.

New to the 2006–2007 Edition

This edition adds a feature, "Careers in International Relations," to help students begin to think about careers paths in international relations. These pages, devoted to careers in nongovernmental organizations, in government and diplomacy, and to international business respectively, respond to the question "How will this class help me find a job?" and include books and Websites to further pursue the issue.

This edition also expands our new video program for the classroom and on the Internet. "Case in Point" videos—now including 14 new videos from the past year on a third DVD—illustrate concepts in the text using 10-minute reports from PBS's *The NewsHour with Jim Lehrer* focusing on issues such as the "extraordinary rendition" of terrorist suspects, the latest negotiations on global climate change, and the Iranian president's call for Israel to be "wiped off the map." A bonus track from Oxfam America, "Fair Trade on Campus," connects college students' daily lives with coffee growers in poor countries. Available at no charge on DVD to professors adopting this book, these 40 video segments (three per chapter of this book) can also be viewed by students outside class through a link on this book's

Companion Website, where students can also answer critical thinking questions about the video they have watched.

This edition updates the new feature, "Policy Perspectives," with the examples of Liberia's Ellen Johnson-Sirleaf, Germany's Angela Merkel, and Israel's Ehud Olmert. This one-page feature in each chapter places students in a particular decision-making perspective, such as Merkel's need to balance domestic economic pressures with demands by the European Union to meet criteria for the euro zone. This feature bridges international relations theory to real-world policy problems while demonstrating the tradeoffs often present in political decision making.

This edition focuses on the turbulent Middle East, where the United States is struggling to keeping a bad situation in Iraq from getting much worse, is coping with the unexpected election of the militant Hamas in Palestine, and is trying to patch together an international coalition against Iran's drive for nuclear weapons. The edition also gives new emphasis to China's continuing rise and to the difficult effort to conclude the Doha Round of world trade talks before the mid-2007 deadline. It expands the discussion of key environmental issues that have become more and more prominent in world politics, such as global warming, bird flu, and efforts to control malaria and AIDS. This edition also reflects the changing politics of Africa, where democratization in such countries as Democratic Congo and Liberia provide a counterpoint to the ongoing repression elsewhere and the genocide occurring in Darfur, Sudan.

This edition updates the examples, cases, photos, and theoretical puzzles. The quantitative data are also updated, usually to 2004 or 2005. Because the data are changing rapidly, students deserve to have access to the most recent available numbers.

The 2006–2007 edition retains but updates the full-color photos, figures, maps, and page design of the Seventh Edition. These color graphics help students both to master complex details and to connect emotionally with photos that embody key points in the text.

Students can also use a range of interactive learning resources on a multifaceted Website. The pedagogical fruits of information technology let students with different learning styles excel and let instructors and students work together in new ways.

Pedagogical Elements

This book's aim is to present the current state of knowledge in IR in a comprehensive and accessible way—to provide a map of the subject covering its various research communities in a logical order. This map is organized around the subfields of international security and international political economy.

These subfields, although separated physically in this book, are integrated conceptually and overlap in many ways. Using the concepts of power and bargaining to bridge the two subfields, this book connects both subfields to the real world by using concrete examples to illustrate theories.

Many people in the television generation find information—especially abstract concepts—easier to grasp when linked with pictures. Thus, the book uses color photographs extensively to illustrate important points. Photo captions reinforce main themes from each section of the text and link them with the scenes pictured. The new, expanded video program that accompanies this edition should further enhance the use of visual images in teaching IR.

In a subject such as IR, where knowledge is tentative and empirical developments can overtake theories, critical thinking is a key skill for college students to develop. At various points in the text, conclusions are left open-ended to let students reason their way through an issue. The questions at the end of each chapter are designed to engage students in thinking critically about the contents of the chapter.

The use of quantitative data also encourages critical thinking. Basic data, presented simply and appropriately at a global level, allow students to form their own judgments and to reason through the implications of different policies and theories. The text uses global-level data (showing the whole picture), rounds off numbers to highlight what is important, and conveys information graphically where appropriate.

Many people come to the study of IR with little background in world geography and history. The first chapter of this book presents background material on these topics. A historical perspective places recent decades in the context of the evolution of the modern international system. The global orientation of the book reflects the diversity of IR experiences for different actors, especially those in the global South.

Three levels of analysis—individual, domestic, and interstate—have often been used to sort out the multiple influences operating in international relations. This book adds a fourth, the global level. Global-level phenomena such as the United Nations, the world environment, and global telecommunications and culture receive special attention.

IR is a large subject that offers many directions for further exploration. The footnotes in this book, updated for this 2006–2007 edition, suggest further reading on various topics. Unless otherwise noted, they are not traditional source notes. (Also, to save space in the notes, major university names refer to their university presses, although this is not a correct research paper style.) Each chapter ends with questions on thinking critically, a chapter summary, a list of key terms, and a reminder to try the practice tests on the text's Companion Website. In addition, at the end of each chapter is a feature, "Let's Debate the Issue," authored by Mir Zohair Husain, giving students the chance to see charged issues from differing perspectives and understand the logic of each side's arguments.

Companion Website

Instructors and students are invited to visit this book's Companion Website at **www.internationalrelations.net** (not .com) or **www.ablongman.com/goldstein** on the World Wide Web. This online course companion provides a wealth of resources for both students and instructors using *International Relations*, 2006–2007 Edition. The site includes a custom search feature referenced by page number in the text. (When an icon appears in the book margin, just go to the Website and type in the page number to go to the content.) Students will find chapter summaries, practice tests, video clips, interactive exercises tied to the "Information Revolution" icons in the text, role-playing simulations, Web links that are referenced by marginal icons in the book, and more. Instructors, through the Companion Website, will have access to download the instructor's manual and visuals from the text in Longman's online *Instructor Resource Center* at **www.ablongman.com/irc.**

Structure of the Book

The overall structure of this book follows substantive topics, first in international security (Part One) and then in international political economy (Part Two). Parts One and Two, although convenient for organization, overlap substantively and theoretically, as noted in several places. Chapter 1 introduces the study of IR and provides some of the geographical and historical context of the subject. Chapters 2 and 3 lay out the various theoretical approaches to the subject, focusing primarily on international security but laying the groundwork for later treatments of international political economy as well. The concepts of power and bargaining, developed in Chapter 2, remain central to later discussions. They are augmented, in Chapter 3, by the important concepts of interdependence and collective goods as well as by feminist (and other) critiques of realism.

The remaining four chapters of Part One move generally from the individual to the global level of analysis. Chapter 4 examines the foreign policy process and the roles of substate actors in shaping IR. Chapter 5 introduces the main sources of international conflict, including ethnic, territorial, and economic conflicts, and terrorism. The conditions and manner in which such conflicts lead to the use of violence are discussed in Chapter 6, on military force. Chapter 7 shows how international organizations and law, especially the United Nations, have evolved to become major influences in security relations. The study of international organizations also bridges international security topics with those in international political economy.

The second part of the book similarly moves upward through levels of analysis, from microeconomic principles and national economies through trade and monetary relations, international integration, the environment, and North-South relations. Chapter 8 introduces theoretical concepts in political economy (showing how theories of international security translate into IPE issue areas) and discusses the most important topic in international political economy, namely, trade relations. Chapter 9 describes the politics of international money, banking, and multinational business operations. Chapter 10 explores the processes of international integration, telecommunications, and cultural exchange on both a regional scale—the European Union—and a global one. Chapter 11 shows how environmental politics and population growth expand international bargaining and interdependence both regionally and globally. Chapter 12 addresses global North-South relations, with particular attention to poverty in the third world. Chapter 13 then considers alternatives for third world economic development in the context of international business, debt, and foreign aid. Chapter 14—a brief postscript—reflects on the book's central themes and encourages critical thinking about the future.

Supplements

Available for Qualified College Adopters

Case in Point: Longman Video Series for International Relations (ISBN 0-321-36608-5) This 3-DVD set contains 40 video segments from *The NewsHour with Jim Lehrer* on PBS (and one Oxfam America video), selected by Joshua S. Goldstein and Jon C. Pevehouse, intended for instructor use within the classroom. Each of these up-to-date videos concerning key current events will engage students, spark discussions, and bring international relations concepts to life in the classroom.

The familiar and fair voices of *The NewsHour with Jim Lehrer* are a perfect vehicle for students to learn about real-world examples tied to concepts within their textbook and to provide instructors with "lecture launchers" to use in the classroom. Available *at no charge* to qualified adopters of any Longman international relations text.

MyPoliSciLab MyPoliSciLab is a state-of-the-art, interactive online solution for your course. Available in CourseCompass (a Blackboard platform course management system), and as a stand-alone Website free of a course management system, MyPoliSciLab offers students a wealth of assessment tools, an online e-book, 13 highly interactive simulations, interactive mapping exercises, Research Navigator (EBSCO Database), and a live feed from *The New York Times*. Instructors using the CourseCompass version of MyPoliSciLab will have access to all the *online administration features* available with the CourseCompass program. These administration features easily track students' work on the site and monitor students' progress on each activity. Both versions contain an *Instructor Gradebook* that provides maximum flexibility, allowing instructors to sort by student or activity, or to view the entire class in spreadsheet view. This program is available at no extra charge when an access code is packaged with any version of the Goldstein/Pevehouse text. Contact your local sales representative at www.ablongman.com/replocator for more details.

Instructor's Manual/Test Bank (ISBN 0-321-34203-8) Written by Robert Breckinridge of Mount Aloysius College, this resource includes chapter overviews, learning objectives, lecture outlines, teaching suggestions, ideas for student projects, and key words, in addition to numerous multiple-choice, short answer, map, and essay questions.

Transparencies (ISBN 0-321-34207-0) This acetate package is composed of images drawn from the text.

TestGen-EQ Computerized Testing Program (ISBN 0-321-34204-6) This flexible, computerized testing system includes all of the test items in the printed test bank. Instructors can easily edit, print, and expand item banks. Tests can be printed in several formats and include figures such as graphs and tables. The program also includes the Quizmaster-EQ program, which allows students to take tests on computers rather than in printed form. Quizmaster-EQ is available in a hybrid platform to accommodate both Macintosh and Windows formats.

Student Supplements for Qualified College Adopters

MyPoliSciLab MyPoliSciLab is a state-of-the-art, interactive online solution for the course. Available in CourseCompass (a Blackboard platform course management system), and as a stand-alone Website free of any course management, MyPoliSciLab offers students a wealth of assessment tools, an online e-book, 13 highly interactive simulations, interactive mapping exercises, Research Navigator (EBSCO Database), and a live feed from *The New York Times*. For each chapter of the text, students will navigate through a pre-test and post-test, both linked to the online e-book, so they can assess, review, and improve their understanding of the concepts within the chapters. Each chapter also contains a chapter exam with page references and a chapter review. In addition, students may participate in highly interactive simulations where they are given a role to play, an objective to reach, and the "Rules of the Game." How well students score depends on the decisions they make and their knowledge of the chapter content. Some roles students may play are "You Are President Kennedy during the Cuban Missile Crisis" and "You Are a Trade Advisor." This program is available at no extra charge when an access code is packaged with any version of the Goldstein/Pevehouse text. Contact your local sales representative for more details at www.ablongman.com/replocator.

Longman Atlas of World Issues (from the Penguin Atlas series) (ISBN 0-321-22465-5) Introduced and selected by Robert J. Art of Brandeis University, and sampled from the acclaimed Penguin Atlas Series, the new *Longman Atlas of World Issues* is designed to help students understand the geography and major issues facing our world today, such as terrorism, HIV/AIDS, and trade. These thematic, full-color maps examine forces shaping politics today at a global level. Explanatory information accompanies each map to help students better grasp the concepts being shown and how they affect our world today.

Companion Website Students are invited to this book's Companion Website at **www.internationalrelations.net** or **www.ablongman.com/goldstein** on the World Wide Web. This online course companion provides a wealth of resources for both students and instructors using *International Relations*, 2006–2007 Edition. The site includes a custom search feature referenced by page number in the text. Students will find chapter summaries, practice tests, video exercises, interactive exercises tied to the "Information Revolution" icons in the text, role-playing simulations, Web links that are referenced by marginal icons in the book, and more.

New Signet World Atlas (ISBN: 0-451-19732-1) From Penguin-Putnam, this pocket-sized yet detailed reference features 96 pages of full-color maps, plus statistics, key data, and much more. Available for 60 percent off the retail price when ordered packaged!

Acknowledgments

Many scholars, colleagues, and friends have contributed ideas that ultimately influenced the seven editions of this book. The book owes a special debt to the late Robert C. North, who suggested many years ago that the concepts of bargaining and leverage could be used to integrate IR theory across four levels of analysis. For help with military data issues, we thank Randall Forsberg. For suggestions, we thank Gerald Bender, our colleagues, and the students in our world politics classes. For help with footnotes and glossary, thanks to Louis Cooper and Peter Howard. For writing the "Let's Debate the Issue" boxes at the end of each chapter, we thank Mir Zohair Husain. Thanks to Mark Lilleleht for assistance on the Careers feature. Thanks also to Stephen Kucinski. The following reviewers made many useful suggestions: Philip Baumann, Minnesota State University Moorhead; Robert G. Blanton, University of Memphis; Robert E. Breckinridge, Mount Aloysius College; Brian Champion, Brigham Young University; Gregory A. Cline, Michigan State University; Myles Clowers, San Diego City College; Cynthia Combs, University of North Carolina at Charlotte; Paul D'Anieri, University of Kansas; Patricia Davis, University of Notre Dame; Elizabeth DeSombre, Colby College; June Teufel Dreyer, University of Miami; Larry Elowitz, George College and State University; George Emerson, Miami Dade Community College; Mark Everingham, University of Wisconsin–Green Bay; Jonathan Galloway, Lake Forest College; Marc Genest, University of Rhode Island; Deborah J. Gerner, University of Kansas; Emily O. Goldman, University of California, Davis; Vicki Golich, California State University, San Marcos; Robert Gregg, School of International Service, American University; Wolfgang Hirczy, University of Houston; Piper Hodson, Saint Joseph's College; Steven W. Hook, University of Missouri; Ted Hopf, Ohio State University; Mir Zohair Husain, University of South Alabama; Akira Ichikawa, University of Lethbridge; W. Martin James, Henderson State University; Matthias Kaelberer, Iowa State University; Joyce Kaufman, University of Maryland at College Park; John Keeler, University of Washington; Michael Kelley, University of Central Arkansas; Jane K. Kramer, University of Oregon; Mark Lagon, Georgetown University; William Lamkin, Glendale Community College; Wei-Chin Lee, Wake Forest University; Renée Marlin-Bennett, School of International Service, American University; James Meernick, University of North Texas; Karen Mingst, University of Kentucky; Richard Moore, Lewis-Clark State College; Layna Mosley, University of North Carolina; John W. Outland, University of Richmond; Salvatore Prisco, Stevens Institute of Technology; David Rapkin, University of Nebraska at Lincoln; Edward Rhodes, Rutgers University; Leonard Riley, Pikes Peak Community College; Henry Schockley, Boston University; Paul Vicary, Florida International University; Thomas J. Volgy, University of Arizona; and David Wilsford, Institute for American Universities, France. The errors, of course, remain our own responsibility.

JOSHUA S. GOLDSTEIN
JON C. PEVEHOUSE

To the Student

The topics studied by scholars are like a landscape with many varied locations and terrains. This textbook is a map that can orient you to the main topics, debates, and issue areas in international relations. This map divides international relations into two main territories: international security and international political economy. However, these territories overlap and interconnect in many ways. Also, the principles and concepts that apply to the interactions of states in security affairs are similar to those that apply to economic relations.

Scholars use specialized language to talk about their subjects. This text is a phrase book that can translate such lingo and explain the terms and concepts that scholars use to talk about international relations. However, IR is filled with many voices speaking many tongues. The text translates some of those voices—of presidents and professors, free traders and feminists—to help you sort out the contours of the subject and the state of knowledge about its various topics. But, ultimately, the synthesis presented in this book is that of the authors. Both you and your professor may disagree with many points. Thus, this book is only a starting point for conversations and debates.

With map and phrase book in hand, you are ready to explore a fascinating world. The great changes taking place in world politics have made the writing of this textbook an exciting project. May you enjoy your own explorations of this realm.

J. S. G.
J. C. P.

A Note on Nomenclature

In international relations, names are politically sensitive; different actors may call a territory or an event by different names. This book cannot resolve such conflicts; it has adopted the following naming conventions for the sake of consistency. The United Kingdom of Great Britain (England, Scotland, Wales) and Northern Ireland is called Britain. Burma, renamed Myanmar by its military government, is referred to as Burma. Cambodia, renamed Kampuchea by the Khmer Rouge in the 1970s, is called Cambodia. The 1991 U.S.-led multinational military campaign that retook Kuwait after Iraq's 1990 invasion is called the Gulf War. The war between Iran and Iraq in the 1980s is called the Iran-Iraq War (not the "Gulf War" as some called it at the time). The country of Bosnia and Herzegovina is generally shortened to Bosnia (with apologies to Herzegovinians). The former Yugoslav Republic of Macedonia is called Macedonia. The People's Republic of China is referred to as China. The former Zaire is Democratic Congo. Elsewhere, country names follow common usage, dropping formal designations such as "Republic of."

www.internationalrelations.net

Students are invited to use the learning resources at this book's Companion Website. There, they may take practice tests, follow links onto the Web, explore the implications of the information revolution for international relations, watch videos illustrating key concepts, and read about how world order is changing since September 11, 2001. To use these learning resources, just go to www.internationalrelations.net (not .com) and enter the page number from this book where an icon appears, to automatically bring up the indicated materials.

A Key to Icon Usage

Web Link This icon marks topics for which this book's Companion Website has links to World Wide Web sites on that topic or related theme. Critical-thinking questions accompany each of these links, so that students are inspired to think analytically about the information they encounter. Responses to those critical-thinking questions can be e-mailed directly to the instructor.

The Information Revolution These icons in each chapter refer to critical-thinking questions about the effects on IR of rapid changes in information technology. To explore these questions, students go to this book's Companion Website, follow the indicated links, and then return to the Companion Website to tie together what they have learned.

Changing World Order These icons in each chapter direct the reader to additional discussion on how world order has and has not changed since September 11, 2001. These discussions are found on the Companion Website.

Simulation These icons in each chapter direct the reader to online simulations found on MyPoliSciLab. Each simulation puts the student in the role of a political actor, such as President John F. Kennedy during the Cuban Missile Crisis, engaging them and giving them the opportunity to apply course concepts to the real world.

Video These icons in each chapter direct the reader to the book's Companion Website where they can view current video clips from PBS's *The NewsHour with Jim Lehrer*. Each of these up-to-date videos concerning key current events will engage students and bring International Relations concepts to life. In addition, critical thinking questions follow each clip to encourage students to ponder these real-world examples and how they are tied to concepts within their textbook.

Online Practice Tests This icon at the end of each chapter reminds students to take a practice test at the Companion Website.

ONLINE PRACTICE TEST
take an online practice test at
www.internationalrelations.net

❑ A
❑ B
☑ C
❑ D

North America

802374 (B01267) 5-95

Central America and the Caribbean

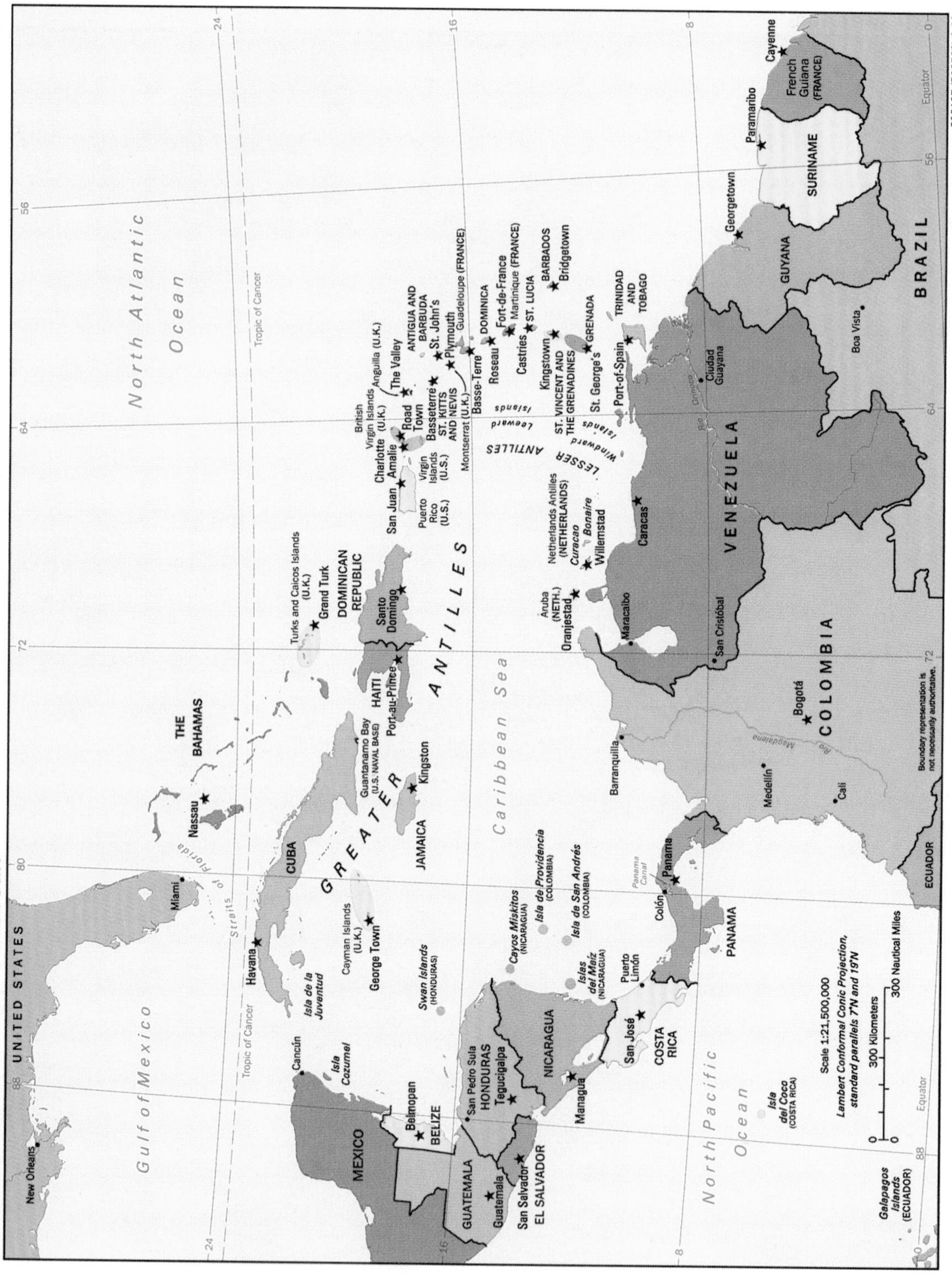

Scale 1:21,500,000

Lambert Conformal Conic Projection, standard parallels 7°N and 19°N

0 300 Kilometers

0 300 Nautical Miles

Boundary representation is not necessarily authoritative.

802107 (R00769) 8-93

South America

Africa

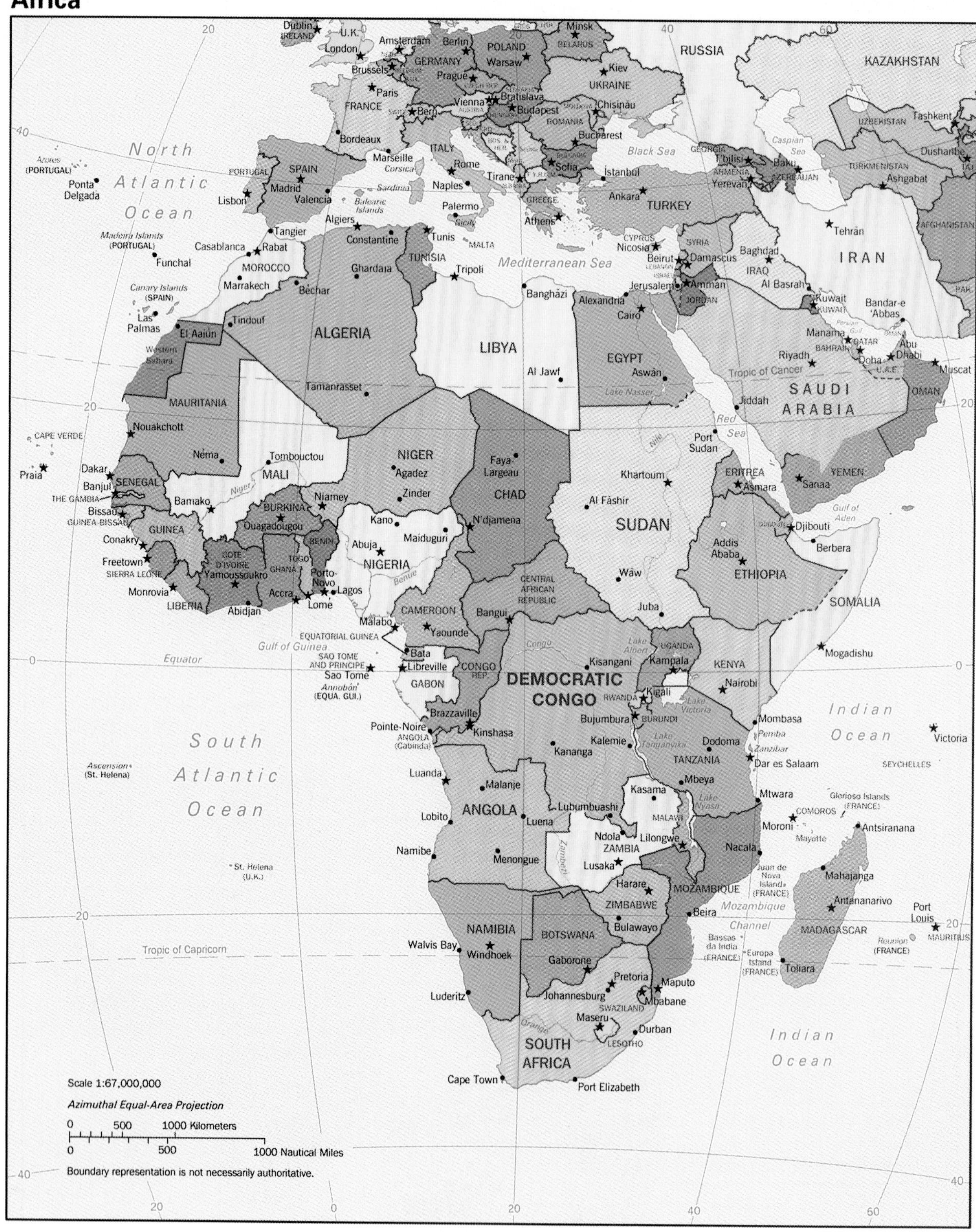

802380 (R00475) 5-95

Northern Africa and the Middle East

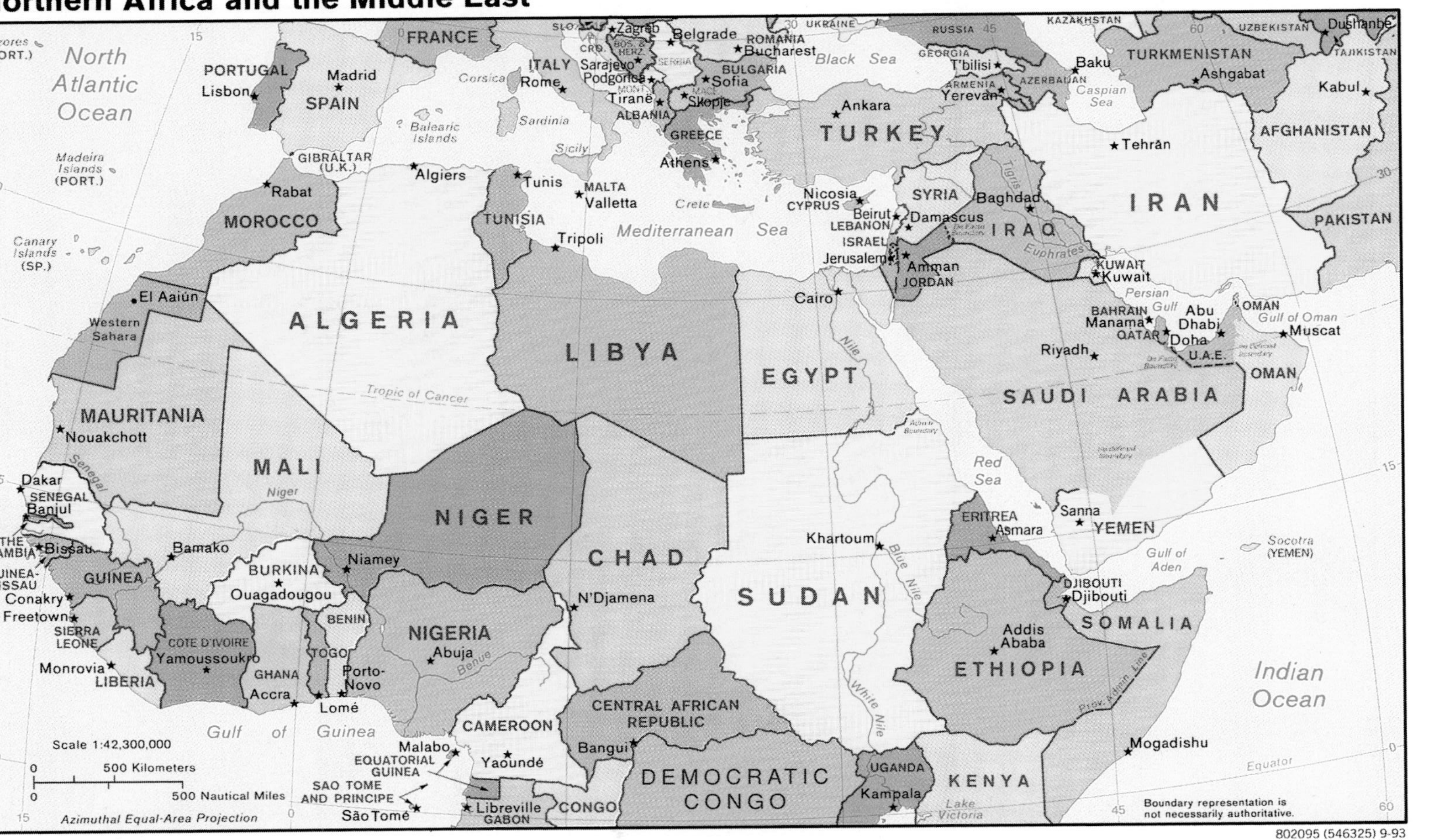

Europe

Serbia and Montenegro have asserted the formation of a joint independent state, but this entity has not been formally recognized as a state by the United States.
Greenland (DENMARK)
Jan Mayen (NORWAY)
Greenland Sea
Norwegian Sea
Barents Sea
Arctic Circle
ICELAND
Reykjavík
Hammerfest
Murmansk
Narvik
Kiruna
White Sea
Arkhangel'sk
NORWAY
Oulu
Umeå
Gulf of Bothnia
FINLAND
Lake Onega
Lake Ladoga
Trondheim
SWEDEN
Tampere
Tórshavn
Faroe Islands (DENMARK)
Shetland Islands
Helsinki
Gulf of Finland
St. Petersburg
Gävle
Rockall (U.K.)
Bergen
Oslo
Stockholm
Aland Islands
Tallinn
ESTONIA
Orkney Islands
Hebrides
RUSSIA
Skagerrak
Göteborg
Gotland
Riga
LATVIA
North Atlantic Ocean
Aberdeen
North Sea
Baltic Sea
Edinburgh
DENMARK
Öland
LITHUANIA
Smolensk
Belfast
UNITED KINGDOM
Newcastle
Copenhagen
Bornholm
Kaliningrad
RUSSIA
Vilnius
Minsk
Isle of Man (U.K.)
Dublin
Irish Sea
Gdańsk
BELARUS
IRELAND
Liverpool
Rostock
Hamburg
Berlin
Poznań
Warsaw
Brest
Amsterdam
Hannover
Kiev
Cardiff
NETHERLANDS
POLAND
London
GERMANY
Leipzig
Wrocław
Brussels
BELGIUM
Bonn
English Channel
Kraków
L'viv
UKRAINE
Guernsey (U.K.)
Jersey (U.K.)
Le Havre
Frankfurt
Prague
CZECH REPUBLIC
SLOVAKIA
Luxembourg
LUX.
Paris
Stuttgart
MOLDOVA
Chişinău
Strasbourg
Bratislava
Odesa
Nantes
Munich
Vienna
Budapest
Cluj-Napoca
FRANCE
AUSTRIA
HUNGARY
SWITZ.
LIECH.
Graz
Bay of Biscay
Bern
ROMANIA
Geneva
Ljubljana
Pécs
Lyon
SLOVENIA
Zagreb
Bucharest
Constanța
Milan
Venice
Black Sea
Bordeaux
Turin
Belgrade
Genoa
CROATIA
BOSNIA AND HERZEGOVINA
Varna
SAN MARINO
Sarajevo
Serbia
Bilbao
MONACO
BULGARIA
Florence
Sofia
Porto
Marseille
Podgorica
ITALY
Adriatic Sea
Montenegro
Skopje
İstanbul
PORTUGAL
ANDORRA
SPAIN
MACEDONIA
Barcelona
Corsica
Rome
Tirane
Madrid
VATICAN CITY
Thessaloníki
ALB.
TURKEY
Lisbon
Naples
Valencia
Sardinia
Tyrrhenian Sea
Ioánnina
Corfu
Aegean Sea
GREECE
Balearic Islands
Athens
Sevilla
Mediterranean Sea
Palermo
Ionian Sea
Málaga
Sicily
Peloponnisos
Rhodes
Strait of Gibraltar
Gibraltar (U.K.)
Ceuta (SPAIN)
Algiers
Tunis
Melilla (SPAIN)
Crete
Scale 1:19,500,000
Lambert Conformal Conic Projection, standart parallels 40°N and 56°N
Valletta
MALTA
Rabat
MOROCCO
ALGERIA
TUNISIA
0 300 Kilometers
0 300 Nautical Miles
802377 (R01083) 5-95

Asia

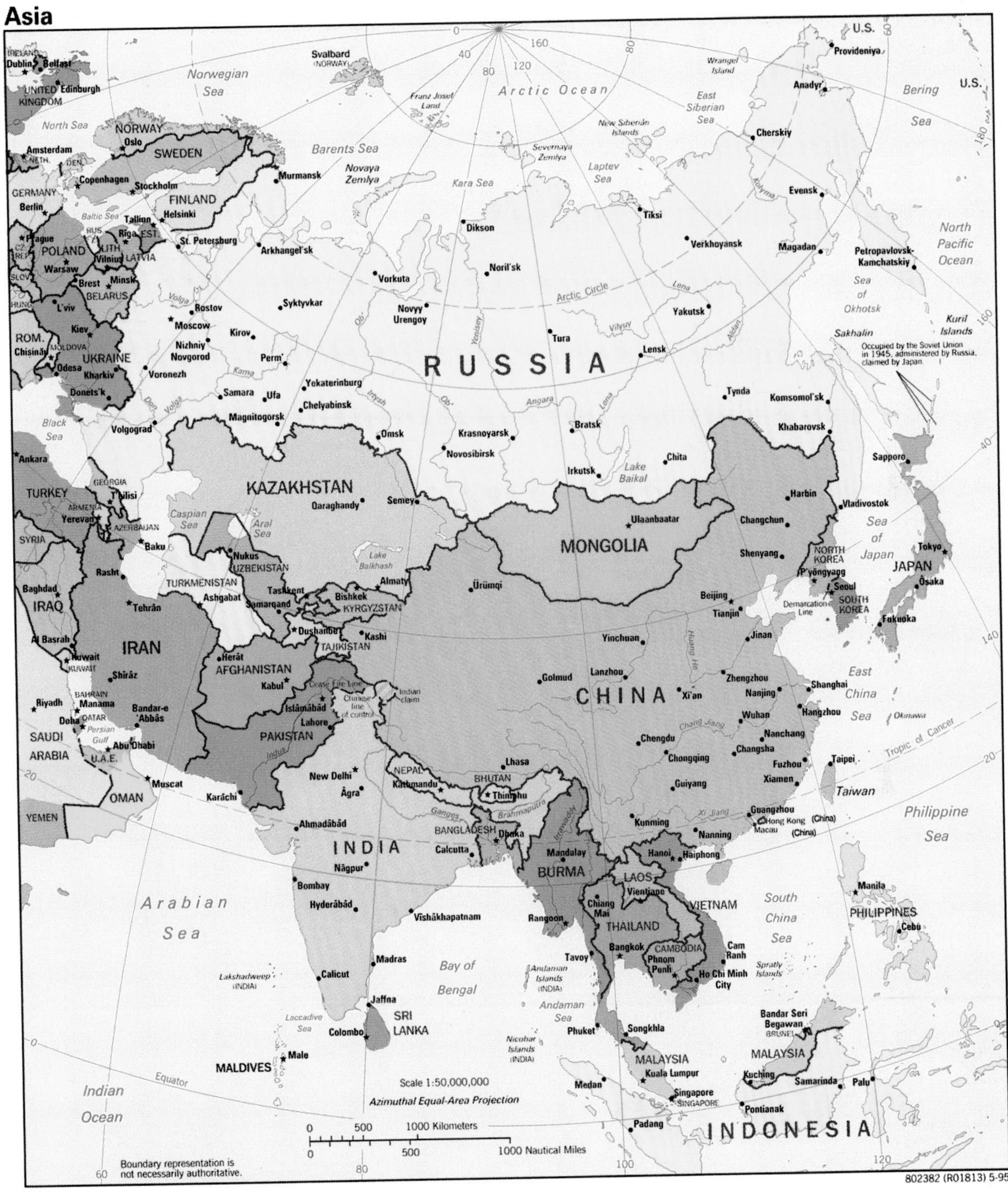
Svalbard
(NORWAY)
Norwegian Sea
Arctic Ocean
Franz Josef Land
Barents Sea
Novaya Zemlya
Kara Sea
Severnaya Zemlya
Laptev Sea
New Siberian Islands
East Siberian Sea
Wrangel Island
U.S.
Provideniya
Anadyr'
Bering Sea
U.S.
Cherskiy
Evensk
North Pacific Ocean
Magadan
Petropavlovsk-Kamchatskiy
Sea of Okhotsk
Kuril Islands
Sakhalin
Occupied by the Soviet Union in 1945, administered by Russia, claimed by Japan.
IRELAND
Dublin
Belfast
UNITED KINGDOM
Edinburgh
North Sea
NORWAY
Oslo
SWEDEN
Amsterdam
NETH.
DEN.
Copenhagen
Stockholm
GERMANY
Berlin
FINLAND
Helsinki
Baltic Sea
Tallinn
EST.
Riga
LATVIA
LITH.
Vilnius
Prague
POLAND
Warsaw
Brest
Minsk
BELARUS
L'viv
Kiev
ROM.
Chisinău
MOLDOVA
UKRAINE
Odesa
Kharkiv
Donets'k
Murmansk
St. Petersburg
Arkhangel'sk
Dikson
Noril'sk
Vorkuta
Tiksi
Verkhoyansk
Yakutsk
Syktyvkar
Rostov
Moscow
Kirov
Nizhniy Novgorod
Perm'
Novyy Urengoy
Tura
Arctic Circle
Lensk
RUSSIA
Voronezh
Samara
Ufa
Yekaterinburg
Chelyabinsk
Magnitogorsk
Volgograd
Omsk
Krasnoyarsk
Novosibirsk
Bratsk
Tynda
Komsomol'sk
Khabarovsk
Irkutsk
Lake Baikal
Chita
Sapporo
Black Sea
Ankara
GEORGIA
T'bilisi
TURKEY
ARMENIA
Yerevan
AZERBAIJAN
Baku
SYRIA
Caspian Sea
KAZAKHSTAN
Qaraghandy
Semey
Aral Sea
Lake Balkhash
MONGOLIA
Ulaanbaatar
Harbin
Vladivostok
Changchun
Shenyang
Sea of Japan
NORTH KOREA
P'yongyang
Tokyo
JAPAN
Osaka
Seoul
SOUTH KOREA
Fukuoka
Demarcation Line
Nukus
UZBEKISTAN
TURKMENISTAN
Ashgabat
Tashkent
Samarqand
Bishkek
KYRGYZSTAN
Almaty
Ürümqi
Beijing
Tianjin
Baghdad
IRAQ
Rasht
Tehrān
Dushanbe
TAJIKISTAN
Kashi
Yinchuan
Jinan
Al Basrah
Kuwait
KUWAIT
IRAN
Herāt
AFGHANISTAN
Kabul
Shīrāz
Cease Fire Line
Chinese line of control
Indian claim
Golmud
Lanzhou
CHINA
Xi'an
Zhengzhou
Nanjing
Shanghai
East China Sea
Okinawa
Riyadh
BAHRAIN
Manama
QATAR
Doha
Persian Gulf
Bandar-e 'Abbās
Islāmābād
Lahore
PAKISTAN
Wuhan
Hangzhou
SAUDI ARABIA
Abu Dhabi
U.A.E.
Chengdu
Nanchang
Changsha
Tropic of Cancer
Chongqing
Fuzhou
Taipei
Xiamen
Taiwan
Muscat
OMAN
Karāchi
New Delhi
Āgra
NEPAL
Kathmandu
BHUTAN
Thimphu
Lhasa
Guiyang
YEMEN
Ahmadābād
BANGLADESH
Dhaka
Kunming
Guangzhou
Hong Kong (China)
Macau (China)
Philippine Sea
Nanning
INDIA
Calcutta
Mandalay
BURMA
Hanoi
Haiphong
Nāgpur
LAOS
Vientiane
Bombay
Manila
Arabian Sea
Hyderābād
Vishākhapatnam
Rangoon
Chiang Mai
THAILAND
VIETNAM
South China Sea
PHILIPPINES
Cebu
Bangkok
CAMBODIA
Phnom Penh
Cam Ranh
Madras
Bay of Bengal
Tavoy
Andaman Islands (INDIA)
Ho Chi Minh City
Spratly Islands
Lakshadweep (INDIA)
Calicut
Jaffna
SRI LANKA
Andaman Sea
Laccadive Sea
Colombo
Phuket
Songkhla
Bandar Seri Begawan
BRUNEI
Nicobar Islands (INDIA)
MALAYSIA
MALAYSIA
Male
MALDIVES
Kuala Lumpur
Kuching
Samarinda
Palu
Medan
Singapore
SINGAPORE
Pontianak
Indian Ocean
Equator
Scale 1:50,000,000
Azimuthal Equal-Area Projection
Padang
INDONESIA
0 500 1000 Kilometers
0 500 1000 Nautical Miles
Boundary representation is not necessarily authoritative.
802382 (R01813) 5-95

International Relations

U.S. marine and Iraqi girl whose mother was just killed, March 2003.

CHAPTER 1

Understanding International Relations

The Study of IR

Our world is large and complex. International relations is a fascinating topic because it concerns peoples and cultures throughout the world. The scope and complexity of the interactions among these groups make international relations a challenging subject to master. There is always more to learn. This book is only the beginning of the story.

Strictly defined, the field of **international relations (IR)** concerns the relationships among the world's governments. But these relationships cannot be understood in isolation. They are closely connected with other actors (such as international organizations, multinational corporations, and individuals); with other social structures (including economics, culture, and domestic politics); and with geographical and historical influences. IR is a large subject that overlaps several other fields.

The purpose of this book is to introduce the field of IR, to organize what is known and theorized about IR, and to convey the key concepts used by political scientists to discuss relations among nations. This first chapter defines IR as a field of study, introduces the actors of interest, and reviews the geographical and historical contexts within which IR occurs.

IR and Daily Life

Sometimes international relations is portrayed as a distant and abstract ritual conducted by a small group of people such as presidents, generals, and diplomats. This is not accurate. Although leaders do play a major role in international affairs, many other people participate as well. College students and other citizens participate in international relations every time they vote in an election or work on a political campaign, every time they buy a product or service traded on world markets, and every time they watch the news. The choices we make in our daily lives ultimately affect the world we live in. Each person faces unique choices as an individual human being. Through those choices, every person makes a unique contribution, however small, to the world of international relations.[1]

---

[1] Dower, Nigel. *An Introduction to Global Citizenship*. Edinburgh, UK: Edinburgh University Press, 2003.

REFLECTIONS OF WAR

IR touches our lives in many ways. The Vietnam Veterans Memorial, 1982.

In turn, IR profoundly affects the daily lives of college students and other citizens. The prospects for getting jobs after graduation depend on the global economy and international economic competition. Those jobs also are more likely than ever to entail international travel, sales, or communication. And the rules of the world trading system affect the goods that students consume, from electronics to clothes to gasoline.

Although international economics pervades daily life, war dominates daily life only infrequently. Still, war casts a long shadow. In major wars, students and their friends and family go off to war and their lives change irreversibly. But even in peacetime, war is among the most pervasive international influences in daily life. Children play with war toys; young people go into military service; TV and films reproduce and multiply the images of war; and wars disrupt economic and social life.

As technology advances, the world is shrinking year by year. Better communication and transportation capabilities are constantly expanding the ordinary person's contact with people, products, and ideas from other countries.

VIDEO

Ground Zero Third Anniversary

This icon indicates Case in Point videos (see p. xviii).

IR as a Field of Study

As a field of study, IR has uncertain boundaries.[2] As a part of political science, IR is about *international politics*—the decisions of governments concerning their actions toward other governments. To some extent, however, the field is interdisciplinary, relating international politics to economics, history, sociology, and other disciplines. Some universities offer separate degrees or departments for IR. Most, however, teach IR in political science classes. The focus is on the *politics* of economic relationships, or the *politics* of environmental management.

Political relations among nations cover a range of activities—diplomacy, war, trade relations, alliances, cultural exchanges, participation in international organizations, and so forth. Particular activities within one of these spheres make up distinct **issue areas** on which scholars and foreign policy makers focus attention. Examples of issue areas include global trade, the environment, or specific conflicts such as the India-Pakistan and Arab-Israeli conflicts. Within each issue area, and across the range of issues of concern in any in-

[2] Carlsnaes, Walter, Thomas Risse, and Beth Simmons, eds. *Handbook of International Relations*. Sage, 2002. Hollis, Martin, and Steve Smith. *Explaining and Understanding International Relations*. Oxford, 1990. Waever, Ole. The Sociology of a Not So International Discipline: American and European Developments in International Relations. *International Organization* 52 (4), 1998: 687–727.

ternational relationship, policy makers of one nation can behave in a cooperative manner or a conflictual manner—extending either friendly or hostile behavior toward the other nation. IR scholars often look at international relations in terms of the mix of **conflict and cooperation** in relationships among nations.

One kind of politics that has an international character is not generally included in the field of IR: the domestic politics of foreign countries. That is a separate field of political science called *comparative politics*. Comparative politics overlaps with IR to the considerable extent that domestic politics influences foreign policy in many countries. Furthermore, the scholars who know about IR and foreign policies in a certain country or region often are the same people who know the most about domestic politics within that country or region. Despite these overlaps, IR as a field tends to avoid issues that concern domestic politics in the United States or other countries *except* to the extent that they affect international politics.

The scope of the field of IR may also be defined by the *subfields* it encompasses. Traditionally, the study of IR has focused on questions of war and peace—the subfield of **international security** studies. The movements of armies and of diplomats, the crafting of treaties and alliances, the development and deployment of military capabilities—these are the subjects that dominated the study of IR in the past, especially in the 1950s and 1960s, and they continue to hold a central position in the field. In the 1990s, after the Cold War, the subfield of security studies broadened beyond its traditional focus on military forces and the superpower arms race. Regional conflicts and ethnic violence began to receive more attention. Meanwhile, interdisciplinary peace studies programs, which emerged in the 1980s at many universities, sought to broaden concepts of "security" further—as did feminist scholars. While the study of war, weapons, and military forces continues to be the core concern of international security studies, these trends have expanded the boundaries of the subfield.[3]

In the 1970s and 1980s, as economics became increasingly central to international relations, the subfield of **international political economy (IPE)** grew and became the counterpoint to international security studies as a second main subfield of IR. Scholars of IPE study trade relations and financial relations among nations, and try to understand how nations have cooperated politically to create and maintain institutions that regulate the flow of international economic and financial transactions. These topics mainly relate to relations among the world's richer nations. But, since the 1990s, growing attention has been paid to global North-South relations between rich and poor nations (see pp. 17–24), including such topics as economic dependency, debt, foreign aid, and technology transfer. As the East-West confrontation of the Cold War has receded into history, North-South problems have become more salient. So are problems of international environmental management and of global telecommunications. The subfield of IPE is expanding accordingly. Of course, different professors see the scope and structure of the field of IR in different ways.[4]

The same principles and theories that help us understand international security (discussed in the first half of this book) also help us to understand IPE (discussed in the second half). Economics is important in security affairs, and vice versa. The organization of this book may seem to create a divide between the two subfields, but in reality they are interwoven.

---

[3] Terriff, Terry et al, eds. *Security Studies Today*. Cambridge, UK: Polity, 1999. Booth, Ken, ed. *Critical Security Studies and World Politics*. Boulder: Rienner, 2005. Brown, Michael E. et al, eds. *Rational Choice and Security Studies: Stephen Walt and His Critics*. MIT, 2000. Buzan, Barry, Ole Waever, Jaap de Wilde. *Security: A New Framework for Analysis*. Boulder: Rienner, 1997. Buzan, Barry. *People, States and Fear: An Agenda for International Security Studies in the Post–Cold War Era*. 2nd ed. Boulder: Rienner, 1991.

[4] Gilpin, Robert. *Global Political Economy: Understanding the International Economic Order*. Princeton, 2001. Keohane, Robert O., and Joseph S. Nye, Jr. *Power and Interdependence*. NY: Longman, 2001.

Theories and Methods

IR scholars want to understand why international events occur in the way they do. Why did a certain war break out? Why do some states sign trade agreements while others do not? Why are some countries so much richer than others? These "why" questions can be answered in several ways. One kind of answer results from tracing the immediate, short-term sequences of events and decisions that led to a particular outcome. For instance, the outbreak of war might be traced to a critical decision made by a particular leader. This kind of answer is largely *descriptive*—it seeks to describe how particular forces and actors operate to bring about a particular outcome.

Another kind of answer results from seeking general explanations and longer-term, more indirect causes. For example, a war outbreak might be seen as an instance of a general pattern in which arms races lead to war. This kind of answer is *theoretical* because it places the particular event in the context of a more general pattern applicable across many cases.

Understanding IR requires both descriptive and theoretical knowledge. It would do little good only to describe events without being able to generalize or draw lessons from them. Nor would it do much good to formulate purely abstract theories without being able to apply them to the complex world in which we live.

Different IR scholars emphasize different mixes of descriptive and theoretical work. Like other disciplines, IR includes both basic and applied research. Generally, scholars closer to the policy process are most interested in descriptive and short-term explanations that are useful for managing a particular issue area or region. Other scholars tend to be interested in more abstract, general, and longer-term explanations.

Ultimately, IR is a rather practical discipline. There is a close connection between scholars in colleges, universities, and think tanks and the policy-making community working in the government—especially in the United States. Some professors serve in the government (for instance, Professor Condoleezza Rice became President Bush's National Security Advisor in 2001 and Secretary of State in 2005), and sometimes professors publicize their ideas about foreign policy through newspaper columns or TV interviews. Influencing their government's foreign policy gives these scholars a laboratory in which to test their ideas in practice. Diplomats, bureaucrats, and politicians can benefit from both the descriptive and the theoretical knowledge produced by IR scholars.[5]

The *methods* used in developing and testing various theories can be arrayed roughly along an empirical versus theoretical axis. At one end, many scholars seek knowledge about IR by interviewing people in various places and piecing together their stories (or their memoirs, archival documents, etc.)—a method well suited to descriptive explanation or to induction (building theories from facts). At the other end, some researchers create abstract mathematical models of relationships that are all theory with no real grounding in the empirical reality of international politics—a method suited to deduction (predicting facts from a theory). Between these approaches are others that mix theory and empirical evidence in various ways. Many IR scholars try to make quantitative measurements of things such as international conflict or trade, and use statistical methods to make inferences about the relationships among those variables. All of these methods of learning about IR can be useful in different ways, though they yield different kinds of knowledge.

IR is an unpredictable realm of turbulent processes and events that catch the experts by surprise, such as the fall of the Berlin Wall in 1989. Most IR scholars are modest about their ability to make accurate predictions—and with good reason. The best theories provide only a rough guide to understanding what actually occurs in IR or to predicting what will happen next.

---

[5] George, Alexander. *Bridging the Gap: Theory and Practice in Foreign Policy*. Washington, DC: United States Institute for Peace Press, 1993.

POLICY PERSPECTIVES

Overview

International policy makers confront a variety of problems every day. Solving these problems requires difficult decisions and choices. Policy Perspectives is a box feature in each chapter that places you in a particular decision-making perspective (for example, the Prime Minister of Great Britain) and asks you to make choices concerning an important international relations issue.

Each box contains three sections. The first, "Background," provides information about a political problem faced by the leader. This background information is factual and reflects real situations faced by these decision makers.

The second section, "Scenario," suggests a new problem or crisis confronting the leader. While these crises are hypothetical, all are within the realm of possibility and would require difficult decisions for the leaders and their countries.

The third section, "Choose Your Policy," asks you to make a choice responding to the Scenario. With each decision, think about the tradeoffs between your options. What are the risks and rewards in choosing one policy over another? Are there alternative options that could effectively address the problem within the constraints that exist? Does one option pose bigger costs in the short term, but fewer in the long term? Can you defend your decision to colleagues, the public, and other world leaders?

As you consider each problem faced by the decision maker, try to reflect on the process and logic by which you have reached the decision. Which factors seem more important and why? Are domestic or international factors more important in shaping your decision? Are the constraints you face based on limited capability (for example, money or military power) or do international law or norms influence your decision as well? How do factors such as lack of time influence your decision?

You will quickly discover that there are often no "right" answers. At times, it is difficult to choose between two good options; at other times, one has to decide which is the least bad option.

Perhaps because of this complexity and unpredictability, IR scholars do not agree on a single set of theories to explain IR or even on a single set of concepts with which to discuss the field. Traditionally, the most widely accepted theories—though never unchallenged by critics—have explained international outcomes in terms of power politics or "realism."[6] But there are many theoretical disagreements—different answers to the "why" questions—both within realism and between realists and their critics. Throughout these discussions, no single theoretical framework has the support of all IR scholars.[7]

One way to look at the variety of theories is to distinguish three broad theoretical perspectives, which may be called the *conservative*, *liberal*, and *revolutionary world views* (see Figure 1.1). In some sense, each is a lens through which the world looks different and

---

[6] Shafritz, Jay M., and Phil Williams. *International Relations: The Classic Readings*. Belmont, CA: Wadsworth, 1993. Knutsen, Torbjörn, L. *The History of International Relations Theory: An Introduction*. Manchester, 1992. Clark, Ian, and Iver B. Neumann, eds. *Classical Theories in International Relations*. NY: St. Martin's, 1996.

[7] Groom, A. J. R., and Margot Light. *Contemporary International Relations: A Guide to Theory*. NY: St. Martin's, 1994. Art, Robert J., and Robert Jervis, eds. *International Politics: Enduring Concepts and Contemporary Issues*. 7th ed. NY: Longman, 2005. Dougherty, James E., Jr., and Robert L. Pfaltzgraff. *Contending Theories of International Relations: A Comprehensive Survey*. 5th ed. NY: Longman, 2001. Doyle, Michael W. *Ways of War and Peace: Realism, Liberalism, and Socialism*. NY: W. W. Norton, 1997. Viotti, Paul R., and Mark V. Kauppi, eds. *International Relations Theory: Realism, Pluralism, Globalism, and Beyond*. 3rd ed. Needham Heights, MA: Allyn & Bacon, 1999.

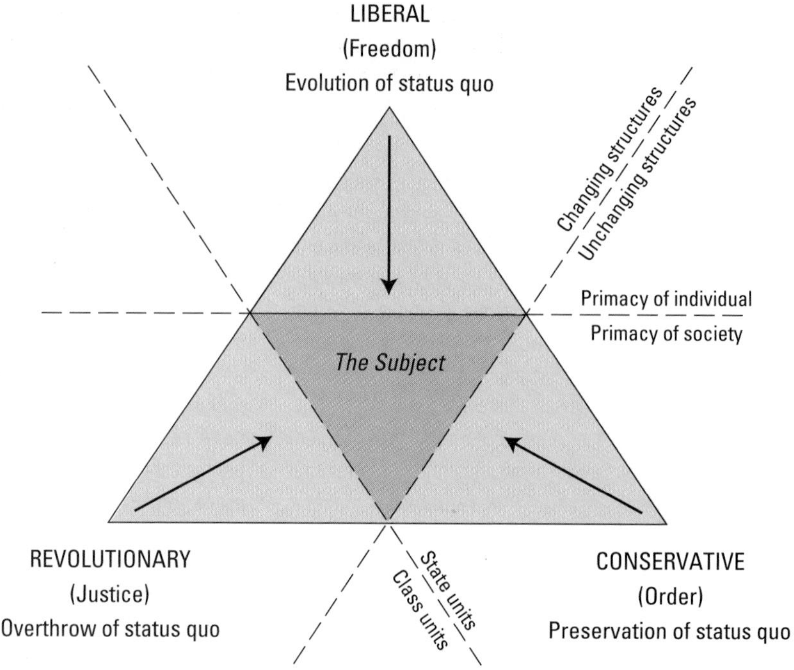

FIGURE 1.1 ■ Conservative, Liberal, and Revolutionary World Views

Source: Adapted from J. S. Goldstein, *Long Cycles: Prosperity and War in the Modern Age.* New Haven: Yale University Press, 1988.

different things seem important. At the same time, the three perspectives can complement each other, and most theories draw on all three, though in different proportions. Furthermore, each world view encompasses a variety of distinct theoretical approaches.

A *conservative* world view generally values maintenance of the status quo and discounts the element of change in IR. These perspectives focus on the laws of power politics, which are considered timeless and universal. Conservative perspectives find their most fertile ground in the subfield of international security with its logic of military power. They see states as the most important actors (largely because states control the biggest armies). Relative position with regard to other states is more important than the absolute condition of a state, because with an ever-present possibility of war, winning and losing matter above all. Conservative approaches tend to value *order*. Their advocates are prudent and not eager for change, especially rapid change or change that upsets the hierarchy of power in the international system. These perspectives tend to see war as the natural order of things, a necessary evil for which one should always be prepared. They see international trade as a potential source of national power, a view expressed in IPE as *mercantilism* (the accumulation of national war chests through the control of trade).

The Web Link icon means that interactive World Wide Web exercises are available at this book's Web site (see p. xviii).

Liberalism

A *liberal* world view values reform of the status quo through an evolutionary process of incremental change. Theories that build on the liberal tradition often focus on the mutual benefits to be gained in IR through interdependence and reciprocity. Gaining wealth in absolute terms is more important from this perspective than gaining power relative to other countries. Liberal approaches find their most fertile ground in the international political economy subfield because of the potentials for mutual gain in trade and exchange, with each nation exploiting its comparative advantage in particular products and services. Liberal approaches tend to value *freedom*, especially free trade and free exchange of ideas.

They tend to see war not as a natural tendency but as a tragic mistake, to be prevented or at least minimized by international agreements and organizations.

A *revolutionary* world view values transformation of the status quo through revolutionary and rapid change. These perspectives often focus on the unfair and exploitive aspects of international relationships, and on efforts to radically change those relationships. Revolutionary approaches have found resonance in those areas of IR scholarship dealing with North-South relations and the developing world because of the evident injustice of grinding poverty suffered by a majority of the world's people. Revolutionary approaches tend to value *justice*. They often see war as a product of underlying exploitative economic relationships, and see changes in those economic relationships as the key to solving the problem of war.

This icon indicates a simulation is available on MyPoliSciLab (see p. xviii).

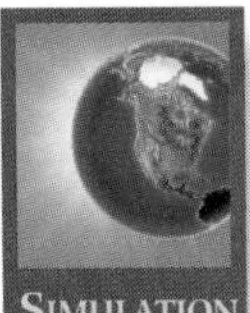

What's Your World View?

Real-world politics mixes these three perspectives in various ways. In the United States, for example, most conservative politicians adopt classically liberal positions on free trade and other economic issues, but conservative positions on military and social issues. Some European social democrats combine a liberal emphasis on freedom with a revolutionary concern for justice. Similarly, no theory or scholar in IR is purely conservative, liberal, or revolutionary.

In *international security*, a conservative world view strongly influences the contours of "realism" or power politics (taken up in Chapter 2), which holds that a nation rationally uses power to pursue its self-interest. One prominent strand of realism is "neorealism," which has attempted to make realist principles simpler and more formal. The liberal counterpoint to realism, originally called "idealism" (taken up in Chapter 3), has been less influential in scholarship concerning international security. A popular version of liberal theory is called *neoliberal institutionalism*; it grants some assumptions of neorealists but claims that the neorealists' pessimistic conclusions about international cooperation do not follow. Several new and more radical critical perspectives have emerged in recent years as serious alternatives to realism as well—feminism, postmodernism, constructivism, and peace studies (also discussed in Chapter 3).

In *international political economy*, the liberal world view dominates scholarship (and often policy). More conservative approaches such as mercantilism have been less influential than those based on liberal "free market" economics. The theoretical contrast of liberalism and mercantilism, is laid out in Chapter 8. More revolutionary theories of IPE—notably

THINKING THEORETICALLY

What Use Are Theories?

Theories provide possible explanations for events in IR. Throughout this book, these boxes on "thinking theoretically" will encourage you to think of possible theoretical (generalizable) explanations for several prominent cases. What accounts for different outcomes? Can you think of one or more (relatively) conservative, liberal, and revolutionary theoretical explanations?

Theoretical knowledge accumulates by a repeated cycle of generalizing and then testing. For a given puzzle, such as the difference between the international community's response to Kuwait and Bosnia, various theories can explain the result (though none perfectly) as a case of a more general principle or category. Each theory also logically predicts other outcomes, and these can be tested empirically. A laboratory science, controlling all but one variable, can test theoretical predictions efficiently. Obviously IR does not have this luxury and must untangle many variables that operate simultaneously. Since knowledge of IR is tenuous in this way, it is especially important to think critically about IR events and consider several different theoretical explanations before deciding which (if any) provides the best explanation.

those influenced by Marxism—are taken up in Chapter 12 ("The North-South Gap"), where they find greatest resonance.

The theoretical debates in the field of IR are fundamental, but unresolved. They leave IR scholarship in a turbulent condition, racing to try to make sense of a rapidly changing world in which old ideas work poorly. It will be up to the next generation of IR scholars—today's college students—to achieve a better understanding of how world politics works. The goal of this book is to lay out the current state of knowledge without exaggerating the successes of the discipline.

Actors and Influences

Who are the actors in IR? In one sense, this question is easy to answer. The actors in IR are the world's governments. It is the decisions and acts of those governments, in relation to other governments, that scholars of IR study.

But in reality, the international stage is crowded with actors large and small that are intimately interwoven with the decisions of governments. These actors are individual leaders and citizens. They are bureaucratic agencies in foreign ministries. They are multinational corporations and terrorist groups. The main contours of the drama are defined by the interactions of large conglomerate characters—nations—while other actors weave in and out of that drama.

State Actors

The most important actors in IR are states. A **state** is a territorial entity controlled by a government and inhabited by a population. A state government answers to no higher authority; it exercises *sovereignty* over its territory—to make and enforce laws, to collect taxes, and so forth. This sovereignty is recognized (acknowledged) by other states through diplomatic relations and usually by membership in the **United Nations (UN).** (The concepts of state sovereignty and territoriality are elaborated in Chapter 2.) The population inhabiting a state forms a *civil society* to the extent it has developed institutions to participate in political or social life. All or part of the population that shares a group identity may consider itself a *nation* (see "Nationalism, 1500–2000" later in this chapter). The state's government is a *democracy* to the extent that the government is controlled by the members of the population rather than imposed on them.[8] (Note that the word *state* in IR does not mean a state in the United States.)

In political life, and to some extent in IR scholarship, the terms *state*, *nation*, and *country* are used imprecisely, usually to refer to the decisions of state governments. It is common to discuss states as if they were people, as in "France supports the UN resolution" or "Iraq invaded Kuwait." In reality, states take such actions as the result of complex internal processes. Ultimately, only individual human beings are true actors making conscious decisions. But treating states like people makes it easier to describe and explain the relations among them.

With few exceptions, each state has a capital city—the seat of government from which it administers its territory—and often a single individual who acts in the name of the state. We may refer to this person simply as the "state leader." Often he or she is the *head of government* (such as a prime minister), or the *head of state* (such as a president, or a king or queen). In some countries, such as the United States, the same person is head of

[8] Poggi, Gianfranco. *The State: Its Nature, Development, and Prospects*. Stanford, 1991. Spruyt, Hendrik. *The Sovereign State and Its Competitors: An Analysis of Systems Change*. Princeton, 1994.

state and government. In other countries, the leadership positions of the president or royalty, or even the prime minister, have become symbolic. In any case, the most powerful political figure is the one we mean by "state leader," and these figures are the key individual actors in IR, regardless of whether these leaders are democratically elected or dictators. The state actor includes the individual leader as well as bureaucratic organizations (such as foreign ministries) that act in the name of the state.

POWERS THAT BE

States are the most important actors in IR. The United States is the world's most powerful state. A handful of others are considered great powers. Here, President Bush meets Germany's new leader, Angela Merkel, in 2006.

The **international system** is the set of relationships among the world's states, structured according to certain rules and patterns of interaction. Some such rules are explicit, some implicit. They include who is considered a member of the system, what rights and responsibilities the members have, and what kinds of actions and responses normally occur between states. The international system is discussed in detail in Chapter 2.

The modern international system has existed for less than 500 years. Before then, people were organized into more mixed and overlapping political units such as city-states, empires, and feudal fiefs. In the past 200 years the idea has spread that nations—groups of people who share a sense of national identity, usually including a language and culture—should have their own states (see "Nationalism, 1500–2000" later in this chapter). Most large states today are such **nation-states.** But since World War II, the decolonization process in much of Asia and Africa has added many new states, not all of which can be considered nation-states. A major source of conflict and war at present is the frequent mismatch between perceived nations and actual state borders (for example, in Sri Lanka or Iraq). When people identify with a nationality that their state government does not represent, they may fight to form their own state and thus to gain sovereignty over their territory and affairs. This substate nationalism is only one of several growing trends that undermine the present-day system of states. Other such trends include the globalization of economic processes, the power of telecommunications, and the proliferation of ballistic missiles.

The independence of former colonies and, more recently, the breakup into smaller states of large multinational states (the Soviet Union, Yugoslavia, and Czechoslovakia) have increased the number of states in the world. The exact total depends on the status of a number of quasi-state political entities, and it keeps changing as political units split apart or merge. There were 191 members of the UN in 2006.

Some other political entities are often referred to as states or countries although they are not formally recognized as states. Taiwan is the most important of these. It operates independently in practice but is claimed by China (a claim recognized formally by outside powers and for decades by Taiwan itself), and is not a UN member. Formal colonies and possessions still exist; their status may change in the future. They include Puerto Rico (U.S.), Bermuda (British), Martinique (French), French Guiana, the Netherlands

Antilles (Dutch), the Falkland Islands (British), and Guam (U.S.). Hong Kong reverted from British to Chinese rule in 1997, and retains a somewhat separate economic identity under China's "one country, two systems" formula. The smaller former Portuguese colony of Macau also reverted to Chinese rule in 1999. The status of the Vatican (Holy See) in Rome is ambiguous. Including various such territorial entities with states brings the world total to about 200 state or quasi-state actors.

There are also several would-be states (such as Kurdistan and Western Sahara) that do not fully control the territory they claim and are not widely recognized. Since smaller states may continue to split away from larger ones (for instance, Quebec from Canada), the number of states is likely to grow.

The size of the world's states varies dramatically, from China with more than 1 billion people to microstates such as San Marino with populations of less than 100,000. With the creation of many small states in recent decades, the majority of states now have fewer than 10 million people each, and more than half of the rest have 10 to 50 million each. Only 23 of the world's 200 states have more than 50 million people each. These 23 states contain three-quarters of the world's people. In decreasing order of population, they are China, India, the United States, Indonesia, Brazil, Pakistan, Russia, Bangladesh, Nigeria, Japan, Mexico, Germany, Vietnam, the Philippines, Turkey, Ethiopia, Egypt, Iran, Thailand, France, Britain, Italy, and Democratic Congo.

States also differ tremendously in the size of their total annual economic activity—**Gross Domestic Product (GDP)**[9]—from the $12 trillion U.S. economy to the economies of tiny states such as the Pacific island of Vanuatu ($600 million). The world economy is dominated by a few states, just as world population is. The United States alone accounts for one-fifth of the world economy; together with six other great powers it accounts for more than half (see pp. 77–80). The world's 15 largest economies—which together make up three-quarters of the world economy—are the United States, China, Japan, India, Germany, France, Britain, Italy, Brazil, Russia, Canada, Mexico, Spain, South Korea, and Indonesia.

A few of these large states possess especially great military and economic strength and influence, and are called *great powers*. They are defined and discussed in Chapter 2. The *great power system* may be defined as the set of relationships among great powers, with their rules and patterns of interaction (a subset of the international system). Great powers have special ways of behaving and of treating each other that do not apply to other states. The most powerful of great powers, those with truly global influence, have been called *superpowers*. This term generally meant the United States and the Soviet Union during the Cold War, but most IR scholars now consider the United States to be the world's only superpower (if indeed it still is one). The great powers and other *major states* (those that have large populations, large economies, or play important roles in international affairs) are the most important of the state actors in IR. Smaller and weaker states also are important in IR, but taken singly most of them do not affect the outcomes in IR nearly as much as the major states do.

---

[9] GDP is the total of goods and services produced by a nation; it is very close to the Gross National Product (GNP). Such data are difficult to compare across nations with different currencies, economic systems, and levels of development. In particular, comparisons of GDP in capitalist and socialist economies, or in rich and poor countries, should be treated cautiously. GDP data used in this book are mostly from the World Bank. GDP data are adjusted through time and across countries for "purchasing-power parity" (how much a given amount of money can buy). World total GDP is $56 trillion by this method, but only $41 trillion without it. See Summers, Robert, and Alan Heston. The Penn World Table (Mark 5): An Expanded Set of International Comparisons, 1950–1988. *Quarterly Journal of Economics* 106 (2), 1991: 327–68. GDP and population data are for 2004 unless otherwise noted.

Nonstate Actors

National governments may be the most important actors in IR, but they are strongly conditioned, constrained, and influenced by a variety of actors that are not states. These **nonstate actors** may be grouped in several categories. First there are groups and interests within states that influence the state's foreign policy. These are *substate actors*. For instance, the American automobile industry and tobacco industry have distinct interests in American foreign economic policy (to sell cars or cigarettes abroad; to reduce imports of competing products made abroad). They are politically mobilized to influence those policies through interest groups, lobbying, and other means. Substate actors need not be concerned only with economic issues—the Greek-American community tries to influence U.S. government actions toward Greece.

The actions of substate economic actors—companies, consumers, workers, investors—help to create the context of economic activity against which international political events play out, and within which governments must operate. Day in and day out, people extract natural resources, produce and consume goods, buy and sell products and services. These activities of substate actors take place in what is now clearly a world economy—a global exchange of goods and services woven together by a worldwide network of communication and culture.

IN THE ACTION

Nonstate actors participate in IR alongside states, although generally in less central roles. Nongovernmental organizations (NGOs) such as the Catholic Church are becoming increasingly active in IR. Here, Pope Benedict meets Iraq's president Jalal Talabani, 2005.

Increasingly, then, actors operating below the state level also operate across state borders, becoming *transnational actors*. Businesses that buy, sell, or invest in a variety of countries are a good example. The decision of a company to do business with or in another state changes the relationship between the two states, making them more interdependent and creating a new context for the decisions the governments make about each other.

The thousands of multinational corporations (MNCs) are important transnational actors. The interests of a large company doing business globally do not correspond with any one state's interests. Such a company may sometimes even act against its home government's policies. MNCs often control greater resources, and operate internationally with greater efficiency, than many small states. MNCs may prop up (or even create) friendly foreign governments, as the United Fruit Company did in the "banana republics" of Central America a century ago. But MNCs also provide poor states with much-needed foreign investment and tax revenues. MNCs in turn depend on states to provide protection, well-regulated markets, and a stable political environment. MNCs as international actors receive special attention in Chapters 9 and 13.

Another type of transnational actor is the **nongovernmental organization (NGO)**, thousands of which pull and tug at international relations every day. These private

Nongovernmental Organizations

organizations, some of considerable size and resources, interact with states, substate actors, MNCs, and other NGOs. Increasingly NGOs are being recognized, in the UN and other forums, as legitimate actors along with states, though not equal to them. Examples of NGOs include the Catholic Church, Greenpeace, and the International Olympic Committee. Some of these groups have a political purpose, some a humanitarian one, some an economic or technical one. Sometimes NGOs combine efforts through transnational advocacy networks.[10] There is no single pattern to NGOs.

International terrorist networks might not call themselves NGOs, but they operate in the same manner—interacting both with states and directly with relevant populations and institutions. The spectacularly destructive attacks of September 11, 2001, demonstrated the increasing power that technology gives terrorists as nonstate actors. Just as Greenpeace can travel to remote locations and beam video of its environmental actions to the world, so too could the al Qaeda network place suicide bombers in U.S. cities, coordinate their operations and finances through the Internet and global banking system, and reach a global audience with the videotaped exhortations of Osama bin Laden.[11] "Global reach," once an exclusive capability of great powers, now is available to many others, for better and worse.

Finally, states often take actions through, within, or in the context of **intergovernmental organizations (IGOs)**—organizations whose members are national governments. The UN and its agencies are IGOs. So are most of the world's economic coordinating institutions such as the World Bank and the International Monetary Fund (IMF). IGOs fulfill a variety of functions, and they vary in size from just a few states to virtually the whole UN membership. For example, the Organization of Petroleum Exporting Countries (OPEC) seeks to coordinate the production and pricing policies of its 11 member states. The World Trade Organization (WTO) sponsors negotiations on lowering trade barriers worldwide, and enforces trade rules.[12]

Military alliances such as NATO and political groupings such as the African Union (AU) are also IGOs. The hundreds of IGOs now operating on the world scene (several times more than the number of states) have been created by states to provide some function that those states find useful.

Together, IGOs and NGOs are referred to simply as international organizations (IOs). By one count there are more than 25,000 NGOs and over 5,000 IGOs. In this world of interlaced connections, of substate actors and transnational actors, states are still important. But to some extent they are being gradually pushed aside as companies, groups, and individuals deal ever more directly with each other across borders, and as the world economy becomes globally integrated (see Chapter 10). Now more than ever, IR extends beyond the interactions of national governments.

Both state and nonstate actors are strongly affected by the revolution in information technologies now under way. The new information-intensive world promises to reshape international relations profoundly. Technological change dramatically affects actors' relative capabilities and even preferences. Nobody knows where those changes will take us.

---

[10] Keck, Margaret E., and Kathryn Sikkink. *Activists Beyond Borders: Advocacy Networks in International Politics*. Cornell, 1998. Florini, Ann M., ed., *The Third Force: The Rise of Transnational Civil Society*, Washington, DC: Carnegie Endowment for International Peace, 2000.

[11] Talbot, Strobe, and Nayan Chandra, eds. *The Age of Terror: America and the World After September 11*. NY: Basic, 2001. Rose, Gideon, and James F. Hoge, Jr., eds. *How Did This Happen?: Terrorism and the New War*. NY: Public Affairs, 2001. Johnson, Chalmers. *Blowback: The Costs and Consequences of American Empire*. NY: Metropolitan, 2000. Barber, Benjamin R. *Jihad vs. McWorld: How Globalism and Tribalism Are Reshaping the World*. NY: Ballantine, 1995.

[12] Armstrong, David, et al. *International Organization in World Politics*. NY: Palgrave, 2003.

THE INFORMATION REVOLUTION

In each chapter, the "information revolution" exercises pose critical-thinking questions about the impacts that rapid changes in information technology have on IR. To explore the questions, go to this book's Web site at www.internationalrelations.net, enter the page number in this book, and follow the Information Revolution icon.

To explore the questions, go to www.internationalrelations.net

Already, information capabilities are the central motor of "globalization." Telecommunications and computerization allow economics, politics, and culture alike to operate on a global scale as never before. The ramifications of information technology for various facets of IR will be developed in each chapter of this book, with marginal icons showing where additional exercises are available on the book's website.

Levels of Analysis

The many actors involved at once in IR contribute to the complexity of competing explanations and theories. One way scholars of IR have sorted out this multiplicity of influences, actors, and processes is to categorize them into different *levels of analysis* (see Table 1.1). A level of analysis is a perspective on IR based on a set of similar actors or processes that suggests possible explanations to "why" questions. The lowest levels focus on small, disaggregated units such as individual people, whereas the highest levels focus on macro-processes such as global trends. IR scholars have proposed various level-of-analysis schemes, most often with three main levels (and sometimes a few sublevels between).[13]

The *individual* level of analysis concerns the perceptions, choices, and actions of individual human beings. Great leaders influence the course of history, as do individual citizens, thinkers, soldiers, and voters. Without Lenin, it is said, there might well have been no Soviet Union. If a few more college students had voted for Nixon rather than Kennedy in the razor-close 1960 election, the Cuban Missile Crisis might have ended differently. The study of foreign policy decision-making, which is discussed in Chapter 4, pays special attention to individual-level explanations of IR outcomes because of the importance of psychological factors in the decision-making process.

The *domestic* (or *state* or *societal*) level of analysis concerns the aggregations of individuals within states that influence state actions in the international arena. Such aggregations include interest groups, political organizations, and government agencies. These groups operate differently (with different international effects) in different kinds of societies and states. For instance, democracies and dictatorships may act differently from one another, and democracies may act differently in an election year from the way they act at other times. The politics of ethnic conflict and nationalism, bubbling up from within states, plays an increasingly important role in the relations among states. Economic sectors within states, including the military-industrial sector, can influence their governments to take actions in the international arena that are good for business. Within governments, foreign policy agencies often fight bureaucratic battles over policy decisions.

---

[13] Singer, J. David. The Level-of-Analysis Problem in International Relations. *World Politics* 14 (1), 1961: 77–92. Waltz, Kenneth. *Man, the State, and War: A Theoretical Analysis*. Rev. ed. Columbia, 2001.

TABLE 1.1 ■ Levels of Analysis

Many influences affect the course of international relations. Levels of analysis provide a framework for categorizing these influences and thus for suggesting various explanations of international events. Examples include:

Global Level	
North-South gap	World environment
World regions	Technological change
European imperialism	Information revolution
UN	Global telecommunications
Religious fundamentalism	Worldwide scientific and business communities
Terrorism	
Interstate Level	
Power	IGOs
Balance of power	Diplomacy
Alliance formation and dissolution	Summit meetings
Wars	Bargaining
Treaties	Reciprocity
Trade agreements	
Domestic Level	
Nationalism	Political parties and elections
Ethnic conflict	Public opinion
Type of government	Gender
Democracy	Economic sectors and industries
Dictatorship	Military-industrial complex
Domestic coalitions	Foreign policy bureaucracies
Individual Level	
Great leaders	Learning
Crazy leaders	Assassinations, accidents of history
Decision making in crises	Citizens' participation (voting, rebelling, going to war, etc.)
Psychology of perception and decision	

The *interstate* (or *international* or *systemic*) level of analysis concerns the influence of the international system upon outcomes. This level of analysis therefore focuses on the interactions of states themselves, without regard to their internal makeup or the particular individuals who lead them. This level pays attention to states' relative power positions in the international system and the interactions (trade, for example) among them. It has been traditionally the most important of the levels of analysis.

To these three levels can be added a fourth, the *global* level of analysis.[14] It seeks to explain international outcomes in terms of global trends and forces that transcend the interactions of states themselves. This level of analysis deserves particular attention because of the growing importance of global-level processes. The evolution of human technology, of

[14] North, Robert C. *War, Peace, Survival: Global Politics and Conceptual Synthesis*. Boulder, CO: Westview, 1990.

certain worldwide beliefs, and of humans' relationship to the natural environment are all processes at the global level that reach down to influence international relations. The global level is also increasingly the focus of IR scholars studying transnational integration through worldwide scientific, technical, and business communities (see Chapter 10). Another pervasive global influence is the lingering effect of historical European imperialism—Europe's conquest of Latin America, Asia, and Africa (see "Imperialism, 1500–2000" later in this chapter).

Levels of analysis offer different sorts of explanations for international events. For example, there are many possible explanations for the 2003 U.S.-led war against Iraq. At the individual level, the war could be attributed to Saddam Hussein's irrational gamble that he could defeat the forces arrayed against him; or to President Bush's desire to remove a leader he personally deemed threatening. At the domestic level, the war could be attributed to the rise of the powerful neoconservative faction that convinced the Bush administration and Americans that Saddam was a threat to U.S. security in a post–September 11 world. At the interstate level, the war might be attributed to the predominance of U.S. power. With no state willing to back Iraq militarily, the United States (as the largest global military power) was free to attack Iraq without fear of a large-scale military response. Finally, at the global level, the war might be attributable to a global fear of terrorism, or even a clash between Islam and the West.

Although IR scholars often focus their study mainly on one level of analysis, other levels bear on a problem simultaneously. There is no single correct level for a given "why" question. Rather, levels of analysis help to suggest multiple explanations and approaches to consider in trying to explain an event. They remind scholars and students to look beyond the immediate and superficial aspects of an event to explore the possible influences of more distant causes (recall our previous discussion of descriptive versus theoretical answers to the "why" questions). IR is such a complex process that there is rarely any single cause that completely explains an outcome. Note that the processes at higher levels tend to operate more slowly than those on the lower levels. Individuals go in and out of office often; the structure of the international system changes rarely.

An analogy can be drawn with scholars who seek to understand a disease or a pattern of automobile accidents. A careful study of a disease would consider processes operating at several levels of analysis—DNA molecules, cells, organs, the entire organism, and ecosystems. A serious attempt to understand the causes of traffic accidents could consider such factors as the individual drivers (drunk?), the kinds of vehicles (mechanically unsound?), and the road system (poorly designed?). Just as different individuals would drive the same car differently, so would they drive a state to different international outcomes. And just as the same individual would drive a Porsche differently than a school bus, so would the individual behave differently as president of Iraq than as president of Russia.

Geography

International relations takes place in the fixed context of geography. To highlight the insights afforded by a global level of analysis, this book uses a division of the world into nine regions. These *world regions* differ from each other in the number of states they contain and in each region's particular mix of cultures, geographical realities, and languages. But each represents a geographical corner of the world, and together they reflect the overall macrolevel divisions of the world. Later chapters refer back to these regions, especially in discussing the North-South gap (Chapters 12 and 13).

The global **North-South gap** between the relatively rich industrialized countries of the North and the relatively poor countries of the South is the most important geographical element at the global level of analysis. The regions used in this book have been drawn so as to separate (with a few exceptions) the rich countries from the poor ones. The North includes both the West (the rich countries of North America, Western Europe, and Japan) and the old East (the former Soviet Union and its bloc of allies).[15] The South includes Latin America, Africa, the Middle East, and much of Asia. The South is often called the "third world" (third after the West and East)—a term that is still widely used despite the second world's collapse. Countries in the South are also referred to as "developing" countries or "less-developed" countries (LDCs), in contrast to the "developed" countries of the North.

Several criteria beyond income levels help distinguish major geographically contiguous regions. Countries with similar economic levels, cultures, and languages have been kept together where possible. States with a history of interaction, including historical empires or trading zones, are also placed together in a region. Finally, countries that might possibly unify in the future—notably South Korea with North Korea, and China with Taiwan—are kept in the same region. Of course, no scheme works perfectly, and some states, such as Turkey, are pulled toward two regions.

The overall world regions are shown in Figure 1.2. The global North is divided into *North America* (the United States and Canada); *Western Europe* (mainly European Union members); *Japan/Pacific* (mainly Japan, the Koreas, Australia, and New Zealand); and *Russia and Eastern Europe* (mainly the former Soviet bloc). The South is divided into *China* (including Hong Kong and Taiwan); the *Middle East* (from North Africa through Turkey and Iran); *Latin America* (Mexico, Central America, the Caribbean, and South America); *South Asia* (Afghanistan through Indonesia and the Philippines); and *Africa* (below the Sahara desert).

Most of these regions correspond with commonly used geographical names, but a few notes may help. *East Asia* refers to China, Japan, and Korea. *Southeast Asia* refers to countries from Burma through Indonesia and the Philippines. Russia is considered a European state, although a large section (Siberia) is in Asia. The *Pacific Rim* usually means East and Southeast Asia, Siberia, and the Pacific coast of North America and Latin America.[16] *South Asia* only sometimes includes parts of Southeast Asia. Narrow definitions of the *Middle East* exclude both North Africa and Turkey. The *Balkans* are the states of southeastern Europe, bounded by Slovenia, Romania, and Greece.

Using the nine world regions as an organizing framework, the world's states and territories, whose locations are shown in Figure 1.3, are listed in Table 1.2, with an estimate of the total size of each state's economy (GDP). Reference maps with greater detail appear after the preface.

Table 1.3 shows the approximate population and economic size (GDP) of each region in relation to the world as a whole. As the table indicates, income levels per capita are, overall, more than five times higher in the North than in the South. *The North contains only 20 percent of the world's people but 60 percent of its goods and services.* The other 80 percent of the world's people, in the South, have only 40 percent of the goods and services.

Within the global North, Russia and Eastern Europe lag behind in income levels, having suffered declines in the 1990s. In the global South, the Middle East, Latin America, and (more recently) China have achieved somewhat higher income levels than have

[15] Note that geographical designations such as the "West" and the "Middle East" are European-centered. From Korea, for example, China and Russia are to the west and Japan and the United States are to the east. On world-level geography, see Kidron, Michael, Ronald Segal, and Angela Wilson. *The State of the World Atlas*. 5th ed. NY: Penguin, 1995. Boyd, Andrew. *An Atlas of World Affairs*. 9th ed. NY: Routledge, 1994.

[16] Hsiung, James C., ed. *Asia Pacific in the New World Politics*. Boulder: Rienner, 1993. Segal, Gerald. *Rethinking the Pacific*. Oxford, 1991. McDougall, Derek. *The International Politics of the New Asia Pacific*. Boulder: Rienner, 1997. Lo, Fu-Chen, and Yue-man Yeung, eds. *Emerging World Cities in Pacific Asia*. Tokyo: UN University Press, 1997.

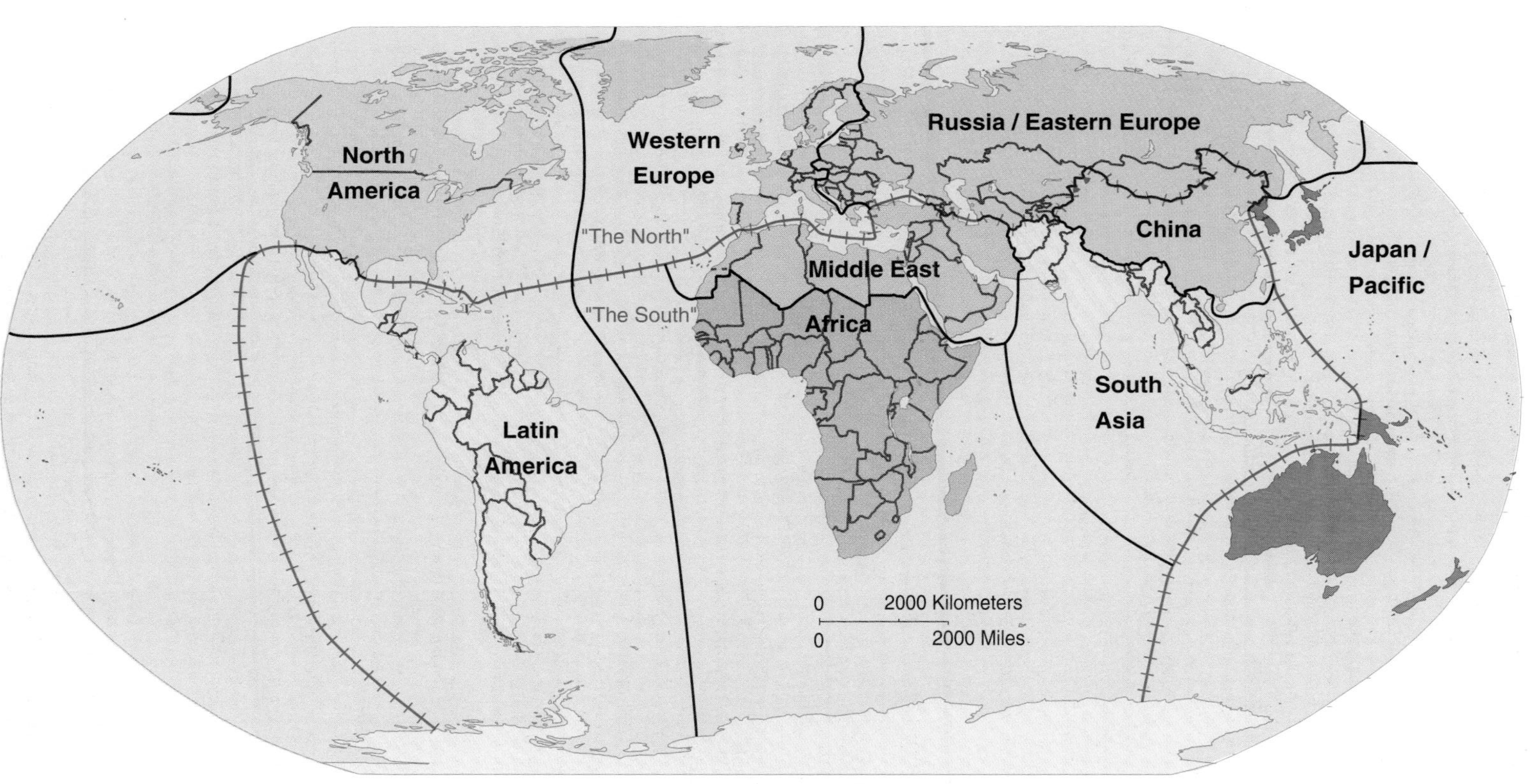

FIGURE 1.2 ■ Nine Regions of the World

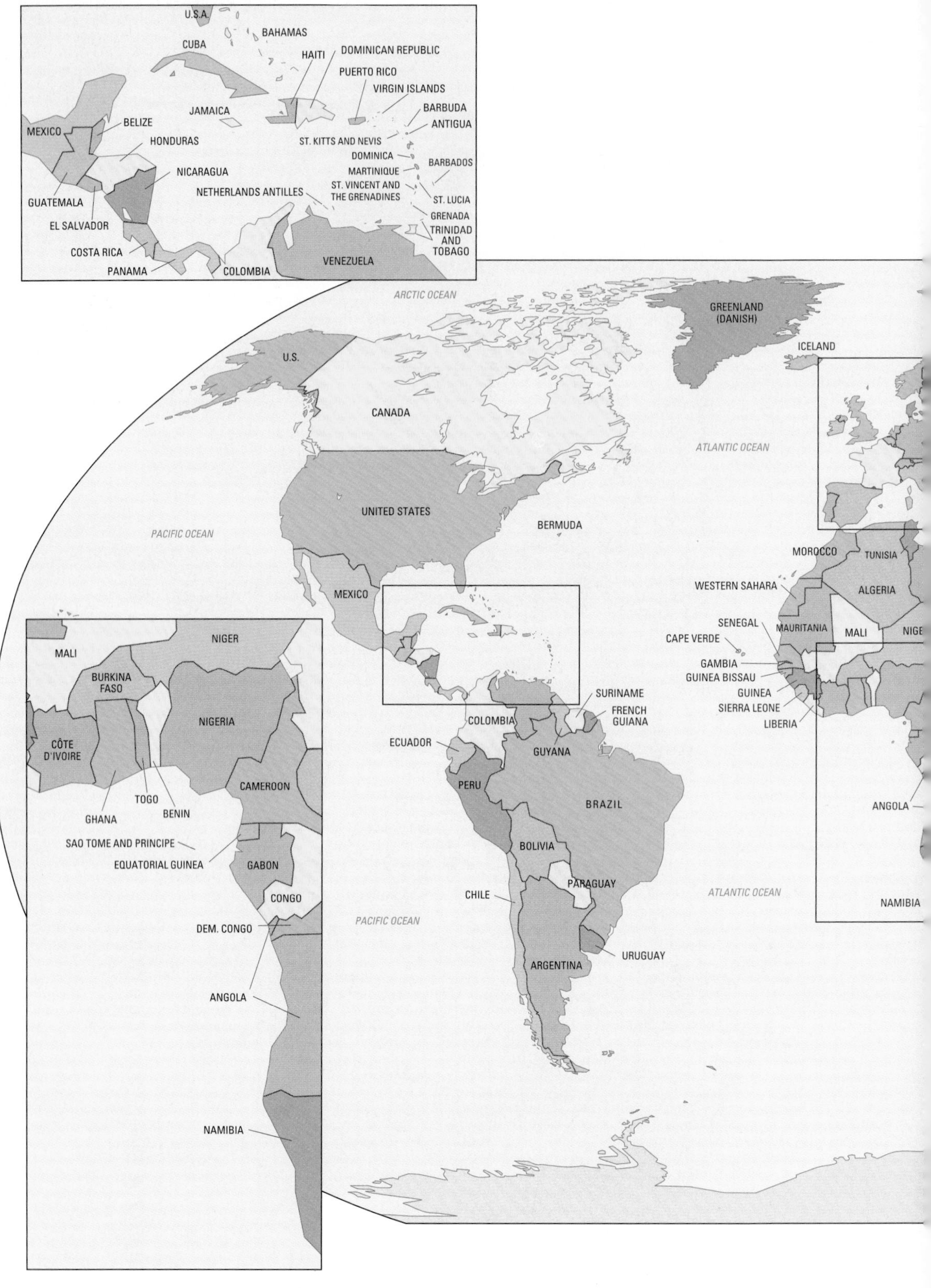
U.S.A.
BAHAMAS
CUBA
HAITI
DOMINICAN REPUBLIC
PUERTO RICO
VIRGIN ISLANDS
JAMAICA
BARBUDA
ANTIGUA
MEXICO
BELIZE
ST. KITTS AND NEVIS
HONDURAS
DOMINICA
MARTINIQUE
BARBADOS
NICARAGUA
ST. VINCENT AND THE GRENADINES
NETHERLANDS ANTILLES
ST. LUCIA
GUATEMALA
GRENADA
EL SALVADOR
TRINIDAD AND TOBAGO
COSTA RICA
VENEZUELA
PANAMA
COLOMBIA
ARCTIC OCEAN
GREENLAND (DANISH)
ICELAND
U.S.
CANADA
ATLANTIC OCEAN
UNITED STATES
PACIFIC OCEAN
BERMUDA
MOROCCO
TUNISIA
WESTERN SAHARA
ALGERIA
MEXICO
SENEGAL
MAURITANIA
MALI
CAPE VERDE
GAMBIA
GUINEA BISSAU
GUINEA
SIERRA LEONE
LIBERIA
SURINAME
FRENCH GUIANA
COLOMBIA
ECUADOR
GUYANA
PERU
BRAZIL
ANGOLA
BOLIVIA
PARAGUAY
CHILE
ATLANTIC OCEAN
NAMIBIA
PACIFIC OCEAN
URUGUAY
ARGENTINA
NIGER
MALI
BURKINA FASO
NIGERIA
CÔTE D'IVOIRE
CAMEROON
TOGO
GHANA
BENIN
SAO TOME AND PRINCIPE
EQUATORIAL GUINEA
GABON
CONGO
DEM. CONGO
ANGOLA
NAMIBIA

FIGURE 1.3 ■

World States and Territories

TABLE 1.2 ■ States and Territories with Estimated Total 2004 GDP
(In Billions of 2005 U.S. Dollars)

North America					
United States	12,000	Canada	1,000	Bahamas	5
Western Europe					
Germany[a]	2,400	Switzerland	300	Luxembourg[a]	30
Britain[a]	1,900	Austria[a]	300	Iceland	10
France[a]	1,800	Portugal[a]	200	Malta[a]	8
Italy[a]	1,700	Greece[a]	200	Andorra	1
Spain[a]	1,000	Denmark[a]	200	Monaco	1
Netherlands[a]	500	Norway	200	Liechtenstein	1
Belgium[a]	300	Finland[a]	200	San Marino	1
Sweden[a]	300	Ireland[a]	200		
Japan/Pacific					
Japan	3,900	Guam/Marianas[b]	3	Nauru	0
South Korea	1,000	Solomon Islands	1	Marshall Islands	0
Australia	600	Samoa	1	Palau	0
New Zealand	100	Vanuatu	1	Kiribati	0
North Korea	20	Tonga	1	Tuvalu	0
Papua New Guinea	20	Micronesia	0		
Fiji	5	American Samoa[b]	0		
Russia and Eastern Europe					
Russia[c]	1,400	Croatia	60	Albania	20
Poland[a]	500	Uzbekistan[c]	50	Georgia[c]	10
Ukraine[c]	300	Lithuania[a]	50	Macedonia	10
Czech Republic[a]	200	Slovenia[a]	40	Armenia[c]	10
Romania	200	Azerbaijan[c]	40	Kyrgyzstan[c]	10
Hungary[a]	200	Turkmenistan[c]	40	Tajikistan[c]	8
Kazakhstan[c]	100	Bosnia and Herzegovina	30	Moldova[c]	7
Slovakia[a]	80	Serbia-Montenegro	30	Mongolia	5
Belarus[c]	70	Latvia[a]	30		
Bulgaria	60	Estonia[a]	20		
China					
China	7,300	Hong Kong[b]	300	Macau[b]	9
Taiwan[b]	600				
Middle East					
Turkey	600	Tunisia	80	Lebanon	30
Iran	500	Iraq	70	Jordan	30
Saudi Arabia	300	Syria	70	Qatar	20
Egypt	300	United Arab Emirates	70	Yemen	20
Algeria	200	Libya	50	Cyprus[a]	20
Israel/Palestine	200	Kuwait	50	Bahrain	10
Morocco/W. Sahara	100	Oman	40		

Latin America

Brazil	1,500	Uruguay	30	Netherlands Antilles[b]	2
Mexico	1,000	Paraguay	30	Virgin Islands[b]	2
Argentina	500	Bolivia	30	Bermuda[b]	2
Colombia	300	Cuba	30	Suriname	2
Chile	200	Panama	20	French Guiana[b]	1
Venezuela	200	Honduras	20	St. Lucia	1
Peru	200	Trinidad & Tobago	20	Belize	1
Puerto Rico[b]	80	Nicaragua	20	Antigua & Barbuda	1
Dominican Republic	70	Haiti	20	Grenada	1
Guatemala	50	Jamaica	10	St. Vincent & Grenadines	1
Ecuador	50	Martinique[b]	5	St. Kitts & Nevis	1
Costa Rica	40	Barbados	5	Dominica	0
El Salvador	40	Guyana	3		

South Asia

India	3,400	Vietnam	200	Laos	10
Indonesia	800	Singapore	100	Brunei	7
Thailand	500	Sri Lanka	80	Bhutan	2
Philippines	400	Burma (Myanmar)	70	Maldives	1
Pakistan	300	Nepal	40	East Timor	0
Bangladesh	300	Cambodia	30		
Malaysia	300	Afghanistan	20		

Africa

South Africa	500	Mauritius	20	Lesotho	5
Nigeria	200	Botswana	20	Central African Republic	5
Sudan	70	Burkina Faso	20	Somalia	5
Ethiopia	60	Equatorial Guinea	20	Eritea	5
Ghana	50	Chad	20	Sierra Leone	5
Cameroon	40	Mali	10	Congo Republic	4
Democratic Congo	40	Rwanda	10	Reunion[b]	3
Kenya	40	Niger	10	Cape Verde	3
Uganda	40	Namibia	10	Liberia	3
Angola	30	Zambia	10	Gambia	3
Côte d'Ivoire (Ivory Coast)	30	Gabon	9	Djibouti	2
Zimbabwe	30	Togo	9	Guinea-Bissau	1
Tanzania	30	Benin	8	Comoros Islands	1
Mozambique	20	Malawi	7	Seychelles	1
Guinea	20	Mauritania	7	São Tomé & Principe	0
Senegal	20	Swaziland	6		
Madagascar	20	Burundi	5		

[a]European Union.

[b]Nonmember of UN (colony or territory).

[c]Commonwealth of Independent States (former USSR).

Note: GDP data are inexact by nature. Estimates for Russia and Eastern Europe, China, and other nonmarket or transitional economies are particularly suspect and should be used cautiously. Numbers below 0.5 are listed as 0.
Sources: Data are authors' estimates based on World Bank. Data are at purchasing-power parity. See footnote 9 on p. 12.

TABLE 1.3 ■ Comparison of World Regions, 2004

Region	Population (Millions)	GDP (Trillion $)	GDP per Capita (Dollars)
The North			
North America	300	$13	$43,000
Western Europe	400	12	30,000
Japan/Pacific	200	6	26,000
Russia & E. Europe	400	4	7,000
The South			
China	1,300	8	6,000
Middle East	400	2	6,000
Latin America	500	5	9,000
South Asia	2,000	7	3,400
Africa	700	2	2,400
Total North	**1,300 (21%)**	**35 (59%)**	**27,000**
Total South	**4,900 (79%)**	**25 (41%)**	**5,000**
World Total	**6,200**	**$60**	**$9,700**

Note: Data adjusted for purchasing-power parity. 2004 GDP estimates (in 2005 dollars) are from Table 1.2; those for Russia and Eastern Europe, and for China, should be treated especially cautiously.

Africa and South Asia, which remain extremely poor. Even in the somewhat higher-income regions, income is distributed quite unevenly and many people remain very poor. Note that more than half of the world's population lives in the densely populated (and poor) regions of South Asia and China.

IR scholars have no single explanation of the tremendous North-South gap in wealth and poverty (see Chapter 12). Some see it as part of a natural process of uneven growth in the world economy. Others tie it to the history of imperialism by European states, as well as by Russia, the United States, and Japan. Some see the gap as a reflection of racism—the North is predominantly white whereas most of the South is nonwhite.

Although geography provides one fixed context in which IR takes place, history provides another. The world as we perceive it developed over many years, step by step. Of special interest in IR are the past 500 years, known as the "modern age." This has been the age of the international system that we know (sovereign states). The remainder of this chapter briefly reviews the historical development of that system and its context. Special attention is given to the relations between Europe and the rest of the world, in which are found the roots of the present North-South gap.

History

The turn of the century and millennium found the world breaking free of the logic of the two world wars and the Cold War that dominated the twentieth century. New possibilities continue to emerge everywhere, some good and some bad. With so much change occurring, one might wonder whether history is still relevant to understanding the world. It is. The basic structures and principles of international relations, even in the current era, are deeply rooted in historical developments. Our discussion of these developments—

necessarily only a series of brief sketches—begins with a long-term perspective and gradually focuses on more recent history.

World Civilizations to 2000

The present-day international system is the product of a particular civilization—Western civilization, centered in Europe. The international system as we know it developed among the European states of 300 to 500 years ago, was exported to the rest of the world, and has in the last century subsumed virtually all of the world's territory into sovereign states. It is important to keep in mind that other civilizations existed in other world regions for centuries before Europeans ever arrived. These cultural traditions continue to exert an influence on IR, especially when the styles and expectations of these cultures come into play in international interactions.[17]

North American students should note that much of the world differs from North America in this regard. Before Europeans arrived, cultures in North America did not have large cities, administrative institutions, and the other trappings of states. Its indigenous cultures were largely exterminated or pushed aside by European settlers. Today's North American population is overwhelmingly descended from immigrants. In other regions, however, the European conquest followed many centuries of advanced civilization—more advanced than that of Europe in the case of China, India, Japan, the Middle East, and Central America. In most of the world (especially in Africa and Asia), European empires incorporated rather than pushed aside indigenous populations. Today's populations are descended primarily from indigenous inhabitants, not immigrants. These populations are therefore more strongly rooted in their own cultural traditions and history than are most Americans.

European civilization evolved from roots in the Eastern Mediterranean—Egypt, Mesopotamia (Iraq), and especially Greece. Of special importance for IR is the classical period of Greek city-states around 400 B.C., which exemplified some of the fundamental principles of interstate power politics (reflected in Thucydides's classic account of the Peloponnesian Wars between Athens and Sparta). By that time, states were carrying out sophisticated trade relations and warfare with each other in a broad swath of the world from the Mediterranean through India to East Asia. Much of this area came under Greek influence with the conquests of Alexander the Great (around 300 B.C.), then under the Roman Empire (around A.D. 1), and then under an Arab empire (around A.D. 600).

China remained an independent civilization during all this time. In the "warring states" period, at about the same time as the Greek city-states, sophisticated states (organized as territorial political units) first used warfare as an instrument of power politics. This is described in the classic work *The Art of War,* by Sun Tzu.[18] By about A.D. 800, when Europe was in its "dark ages" and Arab civilization in its golden age, China under the T'ang dynasty was a highly advanced civilization quite independent of Western influence. Japan, strongly influenced by Chinese civilization, flowered on its own in the centuries leading up to the Shoguns (around A.D. 1200). Japan isolated itself from Western

---

[17] Asimov, Isaac. *Asimov's Chronology of the World: The History of the World from the Big Bang to Modern Times.* NY: HarperCollins, 1991. Barraclough, Geoffrey, ed. *The Times Atlas of World History.* Maplewood, NJ: Hammond, 1978. McNeill, William Hardy. *The Pursuit of Power.* Chicago, 1982. Abu-Lughod, Janet. *Before European Hegemony: The World System, A.D. 1250–1350.* Oxford, 1989. Hodgson, Marshall G. S. *The Venture of Islam: Conscience and History in a World Civilization.* Chicago, 1974. Bozeman, Adda. *Politics and Culture in International History.* Princeton, 1960. Cohen, Raymond, and Raymond Westbrook, eds. *Amarna Diplomacy: The Beginnings of International Relations.* Johns Hopkins, 1999.

[18] Sun Tzu. *The Art of War.* Translated by Samuel B. Griffith. Oxford, 1963.

World Civilizations, 1000–2000

	Before A.D. 1000	A.D. 1000 – 1250	1250 – 1500	1500 – 1750	1750 – 2000
Japan	Korean and Chinese influences	samurai; shoguns →	→	Tokugawa isolation →	→ Meiji restoration; WW II; prosperity
China	Dynasties; Great Wall begun; Taoism; Buddhism; paper, gunpowder	Sung dynasty	Mongol dynasty; Ming dynasty	Manchu dynasty	European dominance; People's Republic
S. Asia	Emergence of Hinduism, Buddhism; Ancient India; Arab conquest	Turkish period		Taj Mahal built; European colonialism →	→ independence
Africa	Kingdom of Ghana	Yoruba, Mali, Benin (kingdoms)	Congo; Zimbabwe; slave trade →	Buganda; Ashanti →	→ European colonialism; independence
Middle East	Mesopotamia, Egypt, Persia; Jews, Christians; Greeks/Romans; Islam	Crusades; Arab empire →	→	Ottoman Empire →	→ Arab nationalism; European colonialism; Islamic rev.
W. Europe	Ancient Greece; Roman Empire; Vikings; Feudalism	"Dark Ages"	Venice; Renaissance	Protestantism; Empires →	→ French Revolution; German/Italian unifica-tions; WW I/II; loss of empires
Russia & E. Europe	Khazars		Genghis Khan	Ivan the Terrible; czars →	→ Lenin; USSR; WW II; CIS
N. America	(Preagricultural)			Columbus; European colonization	American Revolution; U.S. Civil War; westward expansion; WW II; Cold War
Latin America	Mayans	Aztec & Inca Empires →	→	Portuguese & Spanish conquest; colonialism →	→ independence; European & U.S. interventions; wars, debts, dictators, revolutions

influence under the Tokugawa shogunate for several centuries, ending after 1850 when the Meiji restoration began Japanese industrialization and international trade. Latin America also had flourishing civilizations—the Mayans around A.D. 100 to 900 and the Aztecs and Incas around 1200—independent of Western influence until conquered by Spain around 1500. In Africa, the great kingdoms flowered after about A.D. 1000 (as early as A.D. 600 in Ghana) and were highly developed when the European slave traders arrived on the scene around 1500.

The Arab empire of about A.D. 600 to 1200 plays a special role in the international relations of the Middle East. Almost the whole of the region was once united in this empire, which arose and spread with the religion of Islam. European invasions—the Crusades—were driven out. In the sixteenth to nineteenth centuries, the eastern Mediterranean came under the Turkish-based Ottoman Empire, which gave relative autonomy to local cultures if they paid tribute. This history of empires continued to influence the region in the twentieth century. For example, *Pan-Arabism* (or Arab nationalism), especially strong in the 1950s and 1960s, saw the region as potentially one nation again, with a single religion, language, and identity. Iraq's Saddam Hussein during the Gulf War likened himself to the ruler who drove away Crusaders a thousand years ago. The strength of Islamic fundamentalism throughout the region today, as well as the emotions attached to the Arab-Israeli conflict, reflect the continuing importance of the historic Arab empire.

Europe itself began its rise to world dominance around 1500, after the Renaissance (when the Greek and Roman classics were rediscovered). The Italian city-states of the period also rediscovered the rules of interstate power politics, as described by an adviser to Renaissance princes named Niccolò Machiavelli. Feudal units began to merge into large territorial nation-states under single authoritarian rulers (monarchs). The military revolution of the period created the first modern armies.[19] European monarchs put cannons on sailing ships and began to "discover" the world. The development of the international system, of imperialism, of trade and war, were all greatly accelerated by the *Industrial Revolution* after about 1750. Ultimately the European conquest of the world brought about a single world civilization, albeit with regional variants and subcultures.[20]

In recent decades, the world regions formerly dominated by Europe have gained independence, with their own sovereign states participating in the international system. Independence came earlier in the Americas (around 1800). In Latin America, most of the nineteenth century was absorbed with wars, border changes, the rise and fall of dictatorships and republics, a chronic foreign debt problem, revolutions, and recurrent military incursions by European powers and the United States to recover debts.

The Great-Power System, 1500–2000

The modern international system is often dated from the *Treaty of Westphalia* in 1648, which established the principles of independent, sovereign states that continue to shape the international system today. These rules of state relations did not, however, originate at

---

[19] Howard, Michael. *War in European History*. Oxford, 1976. Parker, Geoffrey. *The Military Revolution: Military Innovation and the Rise of the West, 1500–1800*. 2nd ed. Cambridge, 1996. Black, Jeremy, ed. *The Origins of War in Early Modern Europe*. Edinburgh: J. Donald, 1987. Thomson, Janice E. *Mercenaries, Pirates, and Sovereigns: State-Building and Extraterritorial Violence in Early Modern Europe*. Princeton, 1994.

[20] Barraclough, Geoffrey. *An Introduction to Contemporary History*. NY: Penguin, 1964. Cipolla, Carlo M. *Guns, Sails and Empires*. NY: Pantheon, 1965. Anderson, Perry. *Lineages of the Absolutist State*. London: N.L.B., 1974. Braudel, Fernand. *Civilization and Capitalism, 15th–18th Century*, 3 vols. NY: Harper & Row, 1984. Bull, Hedley, and Adam Watson, eds. *The Expansion of International Society*. Oxford, 1984.

The Great-Power System, 1500–2000

	1500–1600	1600–1700	1700–1800	1800–1900	1900–2000
Wars	Spain conquers Portugal; Spanish Armada	**30 Years' War**	War of the Spanish Succession; 7 Years' War	**Napoleonic Wars**; Franco-Prussian War	**World War I**; **World War II**; Cold War
Major Alliances	Turkey (Muslim) vs. Europe (Christian)	Hapsburgs (Austria-Spain) vs. France, Britain, Netherlands, Sweden	France vs. Britain, Spain	France vs. Britain, Netherlands	Germany (& Japan) vs. Britain, France, Russia, United States, China; Russia vs. U.S., W. Eur., Japan
Rules & Norms	Nation-states (France, Austria)	Dutch independence; Grotius on int'l law; **Treaty of Westphalia 1648**	Treaty of Utrecht 1713; Kant on peace	Congress of Vienna 1815; Concert of Europe	League of Nations; Geneva conventions; Communism; UN Security Council 1945-; Human rights
Rising Powers	Britain, France; Netherlands	Russia; **Netherlands hegemony**	Prussia →	United States, Germany, Japan, Italy; **British hegemony**	China; **U.S. hegemony**
Declining Powers	Venice	Spain	Netherlands; Sweden; Ottoman Empire		Britain, France, Austria, Italy; Russia

Westphalia; they took form in Europe in the sixteenth century. Key to this system was the ability of one state, or a coalition, to balance the power of another state so that it could not gobble up smaller units and create a universal empire.

This power-balancing system placed special importance on the handful of great powers with strong military capabilities, global interests and outlooks, and intense interactions with each other. (Great powers are defined and discussed on pp. 77–80.) A system of great-power relations has existed since around A.D. 1500, and the structure and rules of that system have remained fairly stable through time, although the particular members change. The structure is a balance of power among the six or so most powerful states, which form and break alliances, fight wars, and make peace, letting no single state conquer the others.

The most powerful states in sixteenth-century Europe were Britain (England), France, Austria-Hungary, and Spain. The Ottoman Empire (Turkey) recurrently fought with the European powers, especially with Austria-Hungary. Today, that historic conflict between the (Islamic) Ottoman Empire and (Christian) Austria-Hungary is a source of ethnic conflict in the former Yugoslavia (the edge of the old Ottoman Empire).

Within Europe, Austria-Hungary and Spain were allied under control of the Hapsburg family, which also owned the territory of the Netherlands. The Hapsburg countries (which were Catholic) were defeated by mostly Protestant countries in northern Europe—France, Britain, Sweden, and the newly independent Netherlands—in the *Thirty Years' War* of 1618–1648.[21] The 1648 Treaty of Westphalia established the basic rules that have defined the international system ever since—the sovereignty and territorial integrity of states as equal and independent members of an international system. Since then, states defeated in war might be stripped of some territories but were generally allowed to continue as independent states rather than being subsumed into the victorious state.

In the eighteenth century, the power of Britain increased as it industrialized, and Britain's great rival was France. Sweden, the Netherlands, and the Ottoman Empire all declined in power, but Russia and later Prussia (the forerunner of modern-day Germany) emerged as major players. In the *Napoleonic Wars* (1803–1815), which followed the French Revolution, France was defeated by a coalition of Britain, the Netherlands, Austria-Hungary, Spain, Russia, and Prussia. The *Congress of Vienna* (1815) ending that war reasserted the principles of state sovereignty in reaction to the challenges of the French Revolution and Napoleon's empire.[22] In the *Concert of Europe* that dominated the following decades, the five most powerful states tried, with some success, to cooperate on major issues to prevent war—a possible precedent for today's UN Security Council. In this period, Britain became a balancer, joining alliances against whatever state emerged as the most powerful in Europe.

By the outset of the twentieth century, three new rising powers had appeared on the scene: the United States (which had become the world's largest economy), Japan, and Italy. The great-power system became globalized instead of European. Powerful states were industrializing, extending the scope of their world activities and the might of their militaries. After Prussia defeated Austria and France in wars, a larger Germany emerged to challenge Britain's position.[23] In *World War I* (1914–1918), Germany, Austria-Hungary, and the Ottoman Empire were defeated by a coalition that included Britain, France, Russia, Italy, and the United States. After a 20-year lull, Germany, Italy, and Japan were defeated in *World War II* (1939–1945) by a coalition of the United States, Britain, France, Russia (the Soviet Union), and China. Those five winners of World War II make up the permanent membership of today's UN Security Council.

---

[21] Rabb, Theodore K., ed. *The Thirty Years' War*. NY: University Press of America, 1981.

[22] Kissinger, Henry A. A *World Restored*. Boston: Houghton Mifflin, 1973 [1957].

[23] Langer, William L. *European Alliances and Alignments, 1871–1890*. NY: Knopf, 1931.

Imperialism, 1500–2000

	1500–1600	1600–1700	1700–1800	1800–1900	1900–2000
North America	Columbus	British & French colonization	U.S. independence	War of 1812; Canada →	
Latin America	Brazil (Portuguese); Central & S. America (Spanish)			Independence; European & U.S. interventions →	Mexican Revolution
East Asia		Russian conquest of Siberia	(China) →	Opium Wars; T'ai P'ing Rebellion; Boxer Rebellion	Taiwan & Korea (Japanese); Japanese empire; Korea split; Taiwan autonomous; Communist China; Hong Kong to China
South Asia	European explorers	Dutch East Indies Company; Indonesia (Dutch) →		India (British)	Philippines (U.S.); Indian independence; Vietnam War
Africa	Slave trade →; Angola, Mozambique (Portuguese)			Scramble for colonies (Brit., Fr., Ger.)	Independence
Middle East	Ottoman Empire →				British & French mandates (Palestine); Algerian independence

After World War II, the United States and the Soviet Union, which had been allies in the war against Germany, became adversaries for 40 years in the Cold War. Europe was split into rival blocs—East and West—with Germany itself split into two states. The rest of the world became contested terrain where each bloc tried to gain allies or influence, often by sponsoring opposing sides in regional and civil wars. The end of the Cold War around 1990, when the Soviet Union collapsed, returned the international system to a more cooperative arrangement of the great powers somewhat similar to the Concert of Europe in the nineteenth century. However, new strains emerged among the European-American-Japanese "allies" once they no longer faced a common threat from the Soviet Union.[24]

Imperialism, 1500–2000

European imperialism (described more fully in Chapter 12) got its start in the fifteenth century with the development of oceangoing sailing ships in which a small crew could transport a sizable cargo over a long distance. Portugal pioneered the first voyages of exploration beyond Europe. Spain, France, and Britain soon followed. With superior military technology, Europeans gained control of coastal cities and of resupply outposts along major trade routes. Gradually this control extended further inland, first in Latin America, then in North America, and later throughout Asia and Africa.

In the sixteenth century, Spain and Portugal had extensive empires in Central America and Brazil, respectively. Britain and France had colonies in North America and the Caribbean. The imperialists bought slaves in Africa and shipped them to Mexico and Brazil, where they worked in tropical agriculture and in mining silver and gold. The wealth produced was exported to Europe, where monarchs used it to buy armies and build states.

These empires decimated indigenous populations and cultures, causing immense suffering. Over time, the economies of colonies developed with the creation of basic transportation and communication infrastructure, factories, and so forth. But these economies were often molded to the needs of the colonizers, not the local populations.

Decolonization began with the British colonists in the United States who declared independence in 1776. Most of Latin America gained independence a few decades later. The new states in North America and Latin America were, of course, still run by the descendants of Europeans, to the disadvantage of Native Americans and African slaves.

New colonies were still being acquired by Europe through the end of the nineteenth century, culminating in a scramble for colonies in Africa in the 1890s (resulting in arbitrary territorial divisions as competing European armies rushed inland from all sides). India became Britain's largest and most important colony in the nineteenth century. Latecomers such as Germany and Italy were frustrated to find few attractive territories remaining in the world when they tried to build overseas empires in the late nineteenth century. Ultimately, only a few non-European areas of the world retained their independence: Japan, most of China, Iran, Turkey, and a few other areas. Japan began building its own empire, as did the United States, at the end of the nineteenth century. China became weaker and its coastal regions fell under the domination, if not the formal control, of European powers.

In the wave of decolonization after World War II, it was not local colonists (as in the Americas) but indigenous populations in Asia and Africa who won independence. Decolonization continued through the mid-1970s until almost no European colonies

---

[24] Unger, Daniel, and Paul Blackburn, eds. *Japan's Emerging Global Role*. Boulder: Rienner, 1993. Akaha, Tsuneo, and Frank Langdon, eds. *Japan in the Posthegemonic World*. Boulder: Rienner, 1993. Inoguchi, Takashi, and Daniel I. Okimoto, eds. *The Political Economy of Japan*. Vol. 2: *The Changing International Context*. Stanford, 1988.

remained. Most of the newly independent states have faced tremendous challenges and difficulties in the postcolonial era. Because long-established economic patterns continue despite political independence, some refer to the postcolonial era as being *neocolonial*. Although the global North no longer imports slave labor from the South, it continues to rely on the South for cheap labor, for energy and minerals, and for the products of tropical agriculture. However, the North in turn makes vital contributions to the South in capital investment, technology transfer, and foreign assistance (see Chapter 13). The collapse of the Soviet Union and its bloc, which reduced Russia to its size of a century earlier, can be seen as an extension of the post–World War II wave of decolonization and self-determination.

Nationalism, 1500–2000

Many people consider **nationalism**—devotion to the interests of one's nation—to be the most important force in world politics in the past two centuries. A nation is a population that shares an identity, usually including a language and culture. For instance, most of the 60 million inhabitants of France speak French, eat French cuisine, learn French history in school, and are represented (for better or worse) by the national government in Paris. But nationality is a difficult concept to define precisely. To some degree, the extension of political control over large territories like France created the commonality necessary for nationhood—states created nations. At the same time, however, the perceived existence of a nation has often led to the creation of a corresponding state as a people win sovereignty over their own affairs—nations created states.

Around A.D. 1500, countries such as France and Austria began to bring entire nations together into single states. These new nation-states were very large and powerful; they overran smaller neighbors. Over time, many small territorial units were conquered and incorporated into nation-states.[25] Eventually the idea of nationalism itself became a powerful force and ultimately contributed to the disintegration of large, multinational states such as Austria-Hungary (in World War I), the Soviet Union, and Yugoslavia.

The principle of *self-determination* implies that people who identify as a nation should have the right to form a state and exercise sovereignty over their affairs. Self-determination is a widely praised principle in international affairs today (not historically). But it is generally secondary to the principles of sovereignty (noninterference in other states' internal affairs) and territorial integrity, with which it frequently conflicts. Self-determination does not give groups the right to change international borders, even those imposed arbitrarily by colonialism, in order to unify a group with a common national identity. Generally, though not always, self-determination has been achieved by violence. When the borders of (perceived) nations do not match those of states, conflicts almost inevitably arise. Today such conflicts are widespread—in Northern Ireland, Quebec, Israel-Palestine, India-Pakistan, Sri Lanka, Tibet, Sudan, and many other places.[26]

The Netherlands helped to establish the principle of self-determination when it broke free of Spanish ownership around 1600 and set up a self-governing Dutch republic. The struggle over control of the Netherlands was a leading cause of the Thirty Years'

---

[25] Gellner, Ernest. *Nations and Nationalism*. Cornell, 1983. Tilly, Charles. *Coercion, Capital and European States, A.D. 990–1990*. Oxford, UK: Blackwell, 1990. Hobsbawm, E. J. *Nations and Nationalism Since 1780: Programme, Myth, Reality*. NY: Cambridge, 1990. Mayall, James. *Nationalism and International Society*. Cambridge, 1990. Greenfeld, Liah. *Nationalism: Five Roads to Modernity*. Harvard, 1992.

[26] Lake, David A. and Donald Rothchild, eds. *The International Spread of Ethnic Conflict: Fear, Diffusion, and Escalation*. Princeton, 1998.

War (1618–1648), and in that war states mobilized their populations for war in new ways. For instance, Sweden drafted one man out of ten for long-term military service, while the Netherlands used the wealth derived from global trade to finance a standing professional army.

This process of popular mobilization intensified greatly in the French Revolution and the subsequent Napoleonic Wars, when France instituted a universal draft and a centrally run "command" economy. Its motivated citizen armies, composed for the first time of Frenchmen rather than mercenaries, marched longer and faster. People participated in part because they were patriotic. Their nation-state embodied their aspirations, and brought them together in a common national identity.

The United States meanwhile had followed the example of the Netherlands by declaring independence from Britain in 1776. The U.S. nation held together in the Civil War of the 1860s and developed a surprisingly strong sense of nationalism, considering how large and diverse the country was. Latin American states gained independence early in the nineteenth century, and Germany and Italy unified their nations out of multiple political units (through war) later in that century.

Before World War I, socialist workers from different European countries had banded together as workers to fight for workers' rights. In that war, however, most abandoned such solidarity and instead fought for their own nation; nationalism proved a stronger force than socialism. Before World War II, nationalism helped Germany, Italy, and Japan to build political orders based on *fascism*—an extreme authoritarianism girded by national chauvinism. And in World War II it was nationalism and patriotism (not communism) that rallied the Soviet people in order to sacrifice by the millions to turn back Germany's invasion.

Understanding Fascism

In the past 50 years, nations by the dozens have gained independence and statehood. Jews worked persistently in the first half of the twentieth century to create the state of Israel, and Palestinians have aspired in the second half to create a Palestinian state. While multinational states such as the Soviet Union and Yugoslavia have fragmented in recent years, ethnic and territorial units such as Ukraine, Slovenia, and East Timor have established themselves as independent nation-states. Others, such as Kosovo and Kurdistan, are seeking to do so. The continuing influence of nationalism in today's world is evident. More than ever, it is a major factor in international conflict and war.

National identity is psychologically reinforced on a daily basis by symbols such as the national flag, by rituals such as the U.S. Pledge of Allegiance, and by other practices designed to reinforce the identification of a population with its nation and government. In truth, people have multiple identities, belonging to various circles from their immediate family through their town, ethnic or religious group, nation or state, and humanity as a whole (see pp. 185–188). Nationalism has been remarkably successful in establishing national identity as a people's primary affiliation in much of the world.

Nationalism harnesses the energies of large populations based on their patriotic feelings toward their nation. The feeling of "we the people" is hard to sustain if the people are excluded from participating in their government. This participation is so important that even authoritarian governments often go through the motions of holding elections (with one candidate or party). Democracy can be a force for peace, constraining the power of state leaders to commit their nations to war. But popular influence over governments can also increase conflict with other nations, especially when ethnic tensions erupt.

Over time, democratic participation has broadened to more countries and more people within those countries (nonlandowners, women, etc.). The trend toward democracy seems to be continuing in most regions of the world in recent years—in Russia and Eastern Europe, Africa, Latin America, and Asia. Both nationalism and democracy remain great historical forces exerting strong influences in IR.

The World Economy, 1750–2000

	1750–1800	1800–1850	1850–1900	1900–1950	1950–2000
Production	industrialization →			WW I; world depression; WW II; assembly line; Soviet industrialization	postwar prosperity; globalization; Cold War arms race; Japanese & German growth; Soviet collapse
Energy	coal →			oil →	nuclear power → nat. gas →
Leading Sectors	steam engine; cotton gin	iron & steam →; textiles →	steel →	electricity →; motor vehicles →	electronics →; computers →; plastics →; biotech →
Transportation	(wooden sailing ships)	iron steamships →; railroads →	Suez Canal	airplanes →; Trans-Siberian Railroad; automobiles →; Panama Canal	jets →; freeways →; high speed rail →
Trade		British dominance	(free trade)	protectionism	U.S. dominance; GATT →; WTO; European integration; NAFTA
Money		sterling (British) as world currency →		post-WW I inflation; Keynes	U.S. dollar as world currency; Marshall Plan; U.S. drops gold standard; Russia joins IMF; IMF →; Bretton Woods; debt crises
Communication		telegraph →	telephone invented	transoceanic cables; radio →	communication satellites; information revolution →; Internet; fax, modem, cellular, etc.

The World Economy, 1750–2000

In 1750, Britain, the world's most advanced economy, had a GDP of about $1,200 per capita (in today's dollars). That is less than the present level of most of the global South. However, today Britain produces more than ten times that much per person (and with a much larger population than in 1750). This accomplishment was due to **industrialization**—the use of energy to drive machinery and the accumulation of such machinery along with the products created by it. The Industrial Revolution started in Britain in the eighteenth century (notably with the inventions of a new steam engine in 1769, a mechanized thread-spinner in 1770, and the cotton gin in America in 1794). It was tied to Britain's emerging leadership role in the world economy. Industrialization—a process at the world level of analysis—spread to the other advanced economies.[27]

By around 1850, the wooden sailing ships of earlier centuries had been replaced by larger and faster coal-powered iron steamships. Coal-fueled steam engines also drove factories producing textiles and other commodities. The great age of railroad building was taking off. These developments not only increased the volume of world production and trade, but also tied distant locations more closely together economically. The day trip across France by railroad contrasted with the same route a hundred years earlier, when it took three weeks to complete. In this period of mechanization, however, factory conditions were extremely harsh, especially for women and children operating machines.

Britain dominated world trade in this period. Because Britain's economy was the most technologically advanced in the world, its products were competitive worldwide. Thus British policy favored **free trade.** In addition to its central role in world trade, Britain served as the financial capital of the world, managing an increasingly complex world market in goods and services in the nineteenth century. The British currency, pounds sterling (silver), became the world standard. International monetary relations were still based on the value of precious metals, as they had been in the sixteenth century when Spain bought its armies with Mexican silver and gold.

By the outset of the twentieth century, however, the world's largest and most advanced economy was no longer Britain but the United States. The industrialization of the U.S. economy was fueled by territorial expansion throughout the nineteenth century, adding vast natural resources. The U.S. economy was attracting huge pools of immigrant labor from Europe as well. The United States led the world in converting from coal to oil and from horse-drawn transportation to motor vehicles. New technical innovations, from electricity to airplanes, also helped push the U.S. economy into a dominant world position.

In the 1930s, the U.S. and world economies suffered a severe setback in the Great Depression. The protectionist Hawley-Smoot Act adopted by the United States in 1930, which imposed tariffs on imports, contributed to the severity of the depression by provoking retaliation and reducing world trade. Adopting the principles of *Keynesian economics*, the U.S. government used deficit spending to stimulate the economy, paying itself back from new wealth generated by economic recovery. The government role in the economy intensified during World War II.

Following World War II, the capitalist world economy was restructured under U.S. leadership. Today's international economic institutions, such as the World Bank and International Monetary Fund (IMF), date from this period. The United States provided massive assistance to resuscitate the Western European economies (through the Marshall

[27] North, Douglass C., and Robert Paul Thomas. *The Rise of the Western World: A New Economic History*. Cambridge, 1973. Hobsbawm, E. J. *Industry and Empire: From 1750 to the Present Day*. Harmondsworth, UK: Penguin-Pelican, 1969. Tracy, James D., ed. *The Political Economy of Merchant Empires: State Power and World Trade, 1350–1750*. NY: Cambridge, 1991.

Plan) as well as Japan's economy. World trade greatly expanded, and the world market became ever more closely woven together through air transportation and telecommunications. Electronics emerged as a new leading sector, and technological progress accelerated throughout the twentieth century.

Standing apart from this world capitalist economy in the years after World War II were the economies of the Soviet Union and Eastern Europe, organized on communist principles of central planning and state ownership. The Soviet economy had some notable successes in rapidly industrializing the country in the 1930s, surviving the German assault in the 1940s, and developing world-class aerospace and military production capability in the 1950s and 1960s. The Soviet Union launched the world's first satellite (*Sputnik*) in 1957, and in the early 1960s its leaders boasted that communist economies would outperform capitalist ones within decades. Instead, the Soviet bloc economies stagnated under the weight of bureaucracy, ideological rigidity, environmental destruction, corruption, and extremely high military spending. In the 1990s, the former Soviet republics and their Eastern European neighbors tried—with mixed success—to make a transition to some form of capitalist market economy, but found it difficult.

Today there is a single integrated world economy that almost no country can resist joining. At the same time, the imperfections and problems of that world economy are evident in the periodic crises and recessions of recent years—in Russia and Eastern Europe, Japan and other Asian economies, and even periodically in the mature industrialized countries of North America and Western Europe. Above all, the emergence of a global capitalist economy has sharpened disparities between the richest and poorest world regions. While the United States enjoys unprecedented prosperity, Africa's increasing poverty has created a human catastrophe on a continental scale.

Just as the world economy climbed out of previous depressions in the 1890s and 1930s, it appears that a new wave of technological innovation is pulling the advanced industrialized countries, especially the United States, into a new phase of growth—possibly one that is more information-intensive and resource-efficient. Much less clear is whether technological change will bypass or empower the global South (see Chapters 12 and 13).

The Two World Wars, 1900–1950

World War I (1914–1918) and World War II (1939–1945) occupied only 10 years of the twentieth century. But they shaped the character of the century. Nothing like those wars has happened since, and they remain a key reference point for the world in which we live today. With perhaps just two other cases in history—the Thirty Years' War and the Napoleonic Wars—the two world wars were global or hegemonic wars in which almost all major states participated in an all-out struggle over the future of the international system.[28]

For many people, World War I symbolizes the tragic irrationality of war. It fascinates scholars of IR because it was a catastrophic war that seems unnecessary and perhaps even accidental. After a century of relative peace, the great powers marched off to battle for no good reason. There was even a popular feeling that Europe would be uplifted and reinvigorated by a war—that young men could once again prove their manhood on the battlefield in a glorious adventure. Such ideas were soon crushed by the immense pain and evident pointlessness of the war.

---

[28] Dockrill, Michael. *Atlas of Twentieth Century World History*. NY: HarperCollins, 1991. Ferguson, Niall. *The Pity of War: Explaining World War I*. NY: Basic, 1999. Keegan, John, ed. *The Times Atlas of the Second World War*. NY: HarperCollins, 1989. Weinberg, Gerhard L. *A World at Arms: A Global History of World War II*. Cambridge, 1994.

The previous major war had been the Franco-Prussian war of 1870–1871, when Germany executed a swift offensive using railroads to rush forces to the front. That war had ended quickly, decisively, and with a clear winner (Germany). People expected that a new war would follow the same pattern. All the great powers made plans for a quick railroad-borne offensive and rapid victory—what has been called the *cult of the offensive*. The one to strike first would win, it was believed. Under these doctrines, one country's mobilization for war virtually forced its enemies to mobilize as well. Thus, when a Serbian nationalist assassinated Archduke Ferdinand of Austria in 1914 in Sarajevo, a minor crisis escalated and the mobilization plans pushed Europe to all-out war.[29]

Contrary to expectations, the war was neither short nor decisive, and certainly not glorious. It bogged down in *trench warfare* along a fixed front. For example, in 1917 at the Battle of Passchendaele (Belgium), the British in three months fired five tons of artillery shells per yard of front line, over an 11-mile-wide front, and then lost 400,000 men in a failed ground attack. The horrific conditions were worsened by chemical weapons and by the attempts of Britain and Germany to starve each other's population into surrender.

Russia was the first state to crumble. Revolution at home removed Russia from the war in 1917 (and led to the founding of the Soviet Union). But the entry of the United States into the war on the anti-German side that year quickly turned the tide. In the *Treaty of Versailles* of 1919, Germany was forced to give up territory, pay reparations, limit its future armaments, and admit guilt for the war. German resentment against the harsh terms of Versailles would contribute to Adolf Hitler's rise to power in the 1930s. After World War I, U.S. President Woodrow Wilson led the effort to create the **League of Nations,** a forerunner of today's United Nations. But the U.S. Senate would not approve U.S. participation, and the League did not prove effective. U.S. isolationism between the world wars, along with declining British power and a Russia crippled by its own revolution, left a power vacuum in world politics.

In the 1930s, Germany and Japan stepped into that vacuum, embarking on aggressive expansionism that ultimately led to World War II. Japan had already occupied Taiwan and Korea, after defeating China in 1895 and Russia in 1905. In World War I, Japan gained some German colonies in Asia. In 1931, Japan occupied Manchuria (northeast China) and set up a puppet regime there. In 1937, Japan invaded the rest of China and began a brutal occupation that continues to haunt Chinese-Japanese relations.

Meanwhile, in Europe in the 1930s, Nazi Germany under Hitler had rearmed, intervened to help fascists win the Spanish Civil War, and grabbed territory from its neighbors under the rationale of reuniting ethnic Germans in those territories with their homeland. Hitler was emboldened by the weak response of the international community and League of Nations to aggression by fascist regimes in Italy and Spain. In an effort to appease German ambitions, Britain and France agreed in the **Munich Agreement** of 1938 to let Germany occupy part of Czechoslovakia (known as the Sudetenland). Appeasement has since had a negative connotation in IR, because the Munich Agreement seemed only to encourage Hitler's further conquests.

In 1939, Germany invaded Poland, leading Britain and France to join the war against Germany. Hitler signed a nonaggression pact with his archenemy Joseph Stalin of the Soviet Union and threw his full army against France, occupying most of it quickly. Hitler then double-crossed Stalin and invaded the Soviet Union in 1941. This offensive ultimately bogged down and was turned back after several years. But the Soviet Union took

[29] Van Evera, Stephen. The Cult of the Offensive and the Origins of the First World War. *International Security* 9 (1), 1984: 58–107. Snyder, Jack Lewis. *The Ideology of the Offensive: Military Decision Making and the Disasters of 1914*. Cornell, 1984. Kahler, Miles. Rumors of War: The 1914 Analogy. *Foreign Affairs* 58 (2), 1979/80: 374–96.

The Two World Wars, 1900–1950

	1900–1910	1910–1920	1920–1930	1930–1940	1940–1950
Europe	mobilization plans developed; Balkan crises	**World War I**; Sarajevo; U.S. enters war		Italy invades Ethiopia; Munich Agreement	**World War II**; U.S. enters war; D Day
Germany	naval arms race with Britain ⟶	Defeat	Weimar Republic; hyperinflation	Hitler wins power; rearm- ament; occupation of Austria, Czech.; invasion of Poland	occupation of Europe; The Holocaust; strategic bombing; Defeat; occupied by Allied forces
Russia		Russian Revolution; USSR formed	(civil war)	(industrialization); pact with Hitler	German invasion; Victory
Asia	U.S. in Philippines; Russo-Japanese War	Japan neutral in WW I		Japan occupies Manchuria (China); Japan invades China	Pearl Harbor; island battles; Japan occupies S.E. Asia; Hiroshima; Occupied by U.S.
International Norms & Law	Hague Peace Conferences	Versailles treaty	League of Nations ⟶; Washington Naval Treaty	U.S. isolationism; Japan quits League of Nations	Nuremberg Tribunal; United Nations ⟶
Technology	destroyers	trench warfare; chemical weapons; tanks; submarines		mechanized armor	air war; radar; nuclear weapons

the brunt of the German attack and suffered by far the greatest share of the 60 million deaths caused by World War II. This trauma continues to be a powerful memory that shapes views of IR in Russia and Eastern Europe.

The United States joined World War II against Germany in 1942. The U.S. economy produced critically important weapons and supplies for allied armies. The United States played an important role with Britain in the strategic bombing of German cities—including the firebombing of Dresden in February 1945, which caused 100,000 civilian deaths. In 1944, after crossing the English Channel on June 6 (*D-Day*), British-American forces pushed into Germany from the west while the Soviets pushed from the east. A ruined Germany surrendered and was occupied by the allied powers.

At its peak, Nazi Germany and its allies occupied virtually all of Europe, except Britain and part of Russia. Under its fanatical policies of racial purity, Germany rounded up and exterminated 6 million Jews and millions of others, including homosexuals, Gypsies, and communists. The mass murders, now known as the Holocaust, along with the sheer scale of war unleashed by Nazi aggression, are considered among the greatest *crimes against humanity* in history. Responsible German officials faced justice in the *Nuremberg Tribunal* after the war (see pp. 287–288). The pledges of world leaders after that experience to "never again" allow **genocide**—the systematic extermination of a racial or religious group—have been found wanting as genocide recurred in the 1990s in Bosnia and Rwanda, and more recently in Sudan.

Remembering Auschwitz

While the war in Europe was raging, Japan fought a war over control of Southeast Asia with the United States and its allies. Japan's expansionism in the 1930s had only underscored the dependence on foreign resources that it was intended to solve: the United States punished Japan by cutting off U.S. oil exports. Japan then destroyed much of the U.S. Navy in a surprise attack at *Pearl Harbor* (Hawaii) in 1941, and seized desired territories (including Indonesia, whose oil replaced that of the United States). The United States, however, built vast new military forces and retook a series of Pacific islands in subsequent years. The strategic bombing of Japanese cities by the United States culminated in the only historical use of nuclear weapons in war—the destruction of the cities of *Hiroshima* and *Nagasaki* in August 1945—which triggered Japan's quick surrender.

The lessons of the two world wars seem contradictory. From the failure of the Munich Agreement in 1938 to appease Hitler, many people have concluded that only a hard-line foreign policy with preparedness for war will deter aggression and prevent war. Yet in 1914 it was just such hard-line policies that apparently led Europe into a disastrous war, which might have been avoided by appeasement. Evidently the best policy would be sometimes harsh and at other times conciliatory, but IR scholars have not discovered a simple formula for choosing (see "The Causes of War" in Chapter 5).

The Cold War, 1945–1990

The United States and the Soviet Union became the two superpowers of the post–World War II era.[30] Each had its ideological mission (capitalist democracy versus communism), its networks of alliances and clients, and its deadly arsenal of nuclear weapons. Europe was divided, with massive military forces of the United States and its *North Atlantic*

[30] Gaddis, John Lewis. *We Now Know: Rethinking Cold War History*. Oxford, 1997. Zubok, Vladislav, and Constantine Pleshakov. *Inside the Kremlin's Cold War: From Stalin to Krushchev*. Harvard, 1996. Garthoff, Raymond. *Détente and Confrontation: American-Soviet Relations from Nixon to Reagan*. Washington, DC: Brookings, 1985. Larson, Deborah Welch. *Anatomy of Mistrust: U.S.-Soviet Relations During the Cold War*. Cornell, 1997. Trachtenberg, Marc. A *Constructed Peace: The Making of the European Settlement, 1945–1963*. Princeton, 1999.

The Cold War, 1945–1990

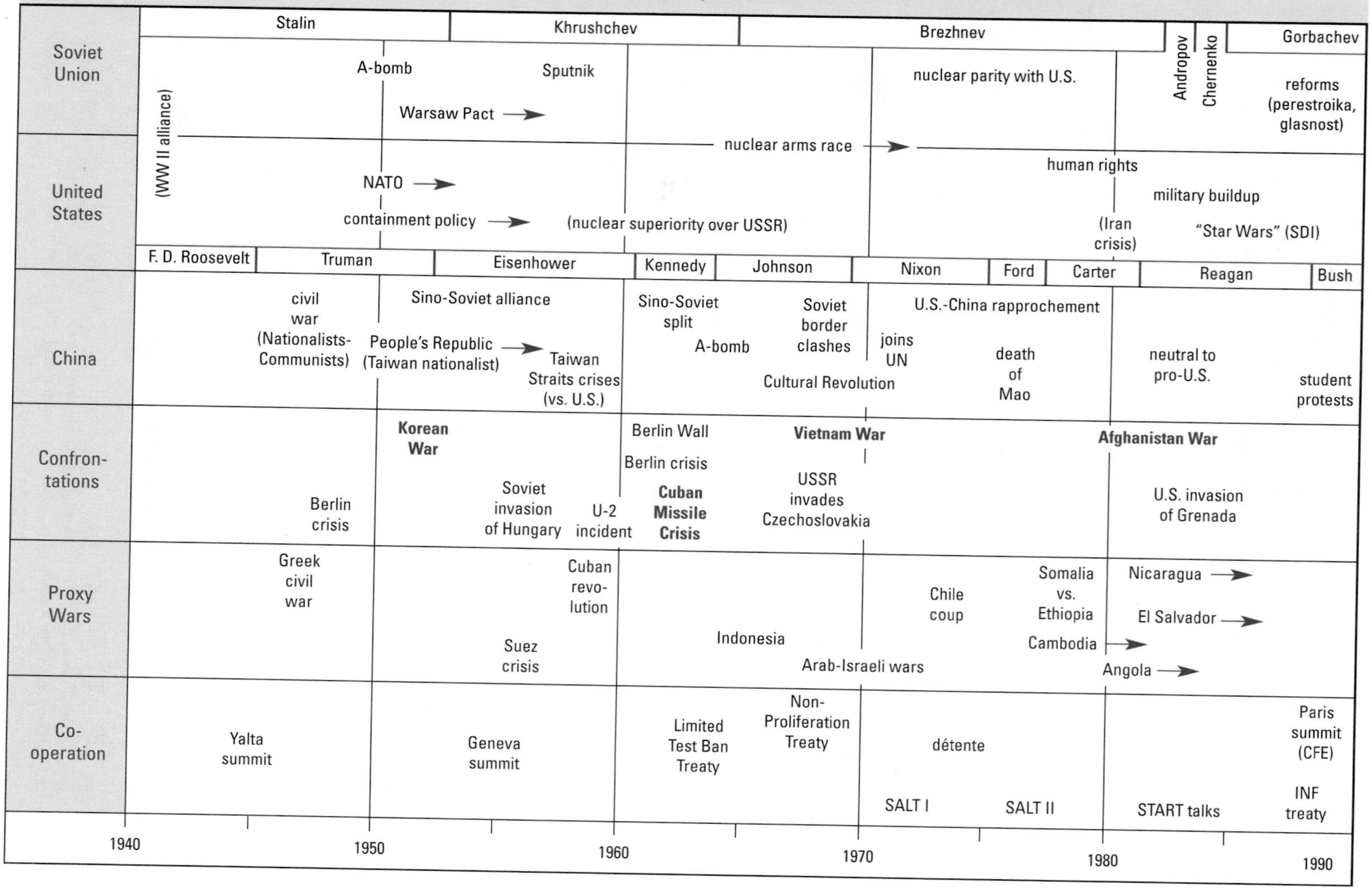

	1940	1950	1960	1970	1980–1990
Soviet Union (leaders)	Stalin	Stalin; Khrushchev	Khrushchev; Brezhnev	Brezhnev	Brezhnev; Andropov; Chernenko; Gorbachev
Soviet Union	(WW II alliance)	A-bomb; Warsaw Pact →; Sputnik	nuclear arms race →	nuclear parity with U.S.	reforms (perestroika, glasnost)
United States	(WW II alliance)	NATO →; containment policy →; (nuclear superiority over USSR)	(nuclear superiority over USSR); nuclear arms race →	human rights; (Iran crisis)	military buildup; "Star Wars" (SDI)
United States (presidents)	F. D. Roosevelt; Truman	Truman; Eisenhower	Kennedy; Johnson	Nixon; Ford; Carter	Reagan; Bush
China	civil war (Nationalists-Communists)	People's Republic (Taiwan nationalist) →; Sino-Soviet alliance; Taiwan Straits crises (vs. U.S.)	Sino-Soviet split; A-bomb; Soviet border clashes; Cultural Revolution	joins UN; U.S.-China rapprochement; death of Mao	neutral to pro-U.S.; student protests
Confrontations	Berlin crisis	**Korean War**; Soviet invasion of Hungary; U-2 incident	Berlin Wall; Berlin crisis; **Cuban Missile Crisis**; **Vietnam War**; USSR invades Czechoslovakia		**Afghanistan War**; U.S. invasion of Grenada
Proxy Wars	Greek civil war	Suez crisis; Cuban revolution	Indonesia; Arab-Israeli wars	Chile coup; Somalia vs. Ethiopia; Cambodia →	Nicaragua →; El Salvador →; Angola →
Co-operation	Yalta summit	Geneva summit	Limited Test Ban Treaty; Non-Proliferation Treaty	détente; SALT I; SALT II	START talks; Paris summit (CFE); INF treaty

Treaty Organization (NATO) allies on one side and massive forces of the Soviet Union and its *Warsaw Pact* allies on the other. Germany itself was split, with three-quarters of the country—and three-quarters of the capital city of Berlin—occupied by the United States, Britain, and France. The remainder, surrounding West Berlin, was occupied by the Soviet Union. Crises in Berlin in 1947–1948 and 1961 led to armed confrontations but not war. In 1961, East Germany built the Berlin Wall separating East from West Berlin. It symbolized the division of Europe by what Winston Churchill had called the "iron curtain."

Despite the hostility of East-West relations during the **Cold War,** a relatively stable framework of relations emerged, and conflicts never escalated to all-out war. At a U.S.-Soviet-British meeting at *Yalta* in 1945, when the defeat of Germany was imminent, the Western powers acknowledged the fact of the Soviet army's presence in Eastern Europe, allowing that area to remain under Soviet influence. Although the Soviet bloc did not join Western economic institutions such as the IMF, all the world's major states joined the UN. The United Nations (unlike the ill-fated League of Nations) managed to maintain almost universal membership and adherence to basic structures and rules throughout the Cold War era.

The central concern of the West during the Cold War was that the Soviet Union might gain control of Western Europe—either through outright invasion or through communists' taking power in war-weary and impoverished countries of Western Europe. This could have put the entire industrial base of the Eurasian landmass (from Europe to Siberia) under one state. The *Marshall Plan*—U.S. financial aid to rebuild European economies—responded to these fears, as did the creation of the NATO alliance. Half of the entire world's military spending was devoted to the European standoff. Much spending was also devoted to a superpower nuclear arms race, in which each superpower produced tens of thousands of nuclear weapons (see pp. 244–245).

Through the policy of **containment,** adopted in the late 1940s, the United States sought to halt the expansion of Soviet influence globally on several levels at once—military, political, ideological, economic. The United States maintained an extensive network of military bases and alliances worldwide. Virtually all of U.S. foreign policy in subsequent decades, from foreign aid and technology transfer to military intervention and diplomacy, came to serve the goal of containment.

The *Chinese communist revolution* in 1949 led to a Sino-Soviet alliance (*Sino* means "Chinese"). But China became fiercely independent in the 1960s following the **Sino-Soviet split,** when China opposed Soviet moves toward *peaceful coexistence* with the United States.[31] In the late 1960s, young radicals, opposed to both superpowers, ran China during the chaotic and destructive *Cultural Revolution*. But feeling threatened by Soviet power, China's leaders developed a growing affiliation with the United States during the 1970s, starting with a dramatic visit to China by U.S. President Nixon in 1972. This visit led to U.S.-Chinese diplomatic relations in 1979. During the Cold War, China generally tried to play a balancer role against whichever superpower seemed most threatening at the time.

In 1950, the *Korean War* broke out when communist North Korea attacked and overran most of U.S.-allied South Korea. The United States and its allies (under UN authority obtained after the Soviets walked out of the Security Council in protest) counterattacked and overran most of North Korea. China sent masses of "volunteers" to help North Korea, and the war bogged down near the original border until a 1953 truce ended the fighting.

---

[31] Mayers, David Allan. *Cracking the Monolith: U.S. Policy Against the Sino-Soviet Alliance, 1949–1955.* Louisiana State, 1986. Kim, Ilpyong J., ed. *Beyond the Strategic Triangle.* NY: Paragon, 1992.

The Korean War hardened U.S. attitudes toward communism and set a negative tone for future East-West relations, especially for U.S.-Chinese relations in the 1950s.

The Cold War thawed temporarily after Stalin died in 1953. The first **summit meeting** between superpower leaders took place in Geneva in 1955. This thaw in relations led both sides to agree to reconstitute Austria, which had been split into four pieces like Germany. But the Soviet Union sent tanks to crush a popular uprising in Hungary in 1956 (an action it repeated in 1968 in Czechoslovakia), and the Soviet missile program that orbited *Sputnik* in 1957 alarmed the United States. The shooting down of a U.S. spy plane (the *U-2*) over the Soviet Union in 1960 scuttled a summit meeting between superpower leaders Nikita Khrushchev and Dwight D. Eisenhower. Meanwhile in Cuba, after Fidel Castro's communist revolution in 1959, the United States attempted a counterrevolution in the botched 1961 *Bay of Pigs* invasion.

Cuban Missile Crisis

These hostilities culminated in the **Cuban Missile Crisis** of 1962, when the Soviet Union installed medium-range nuclear missiles in Cuba. The Soviet aims were to reduce the Soviet Union's strategic nuclear inferiority, to counter the deployment of U.S. missiles on Soviet borders in Turkey, and to deter another U.S. invasion of Cuba. U.S. leaders, however, considered the missiles threatening and provocative. As historical documents revealed years later, nuclear war was quite possible. Some U.S. policy makers favored military strikes before the missiles became operational, when in fact some nuclear weapons in Cuba were already operational and commanders were authorized to use them in the event of a U.S. attack.[32] Instead, President John F. Kennedy imposed a naval blockade to force their removal. The Soviet Union backed down on the missiles, and the United States promised not to invade Cuba in the future. Leaders on both sides were shaken, however, by the possibility of nuclear war. They signed the *Limited Test Ban Treaty* in 1963, prohibiting atmospheric nuclear tests, and began to cooperate in cultural exchanges, space exploration, aviation, and other areas.

The two superpowers often jockeyed for position in the global South, supporting **proxy wars** in which they typically supplied and advised opposing factions in civil wars. The alignments were often arbitrary. For instance, the United States backed the Ethiopian government and the Soviets backed next-door rival Somalia in the 1970s; when an Ethiopian revolution caused the new government to seek Soviet help, the United States switched to support Somalia instead.

Vietnam War

One flaw of U.S. policy in the Cold War period was to see all regional conflicts through East-West lenses. Its preoccupation with communism led the United States to support unpopular pro-Western governments in a number of poor countries, nowhere more disastrously than during the *Vietnam War* in the 1960s. The war in Vietnam divided U.S. citizens and ultimately failed to prevent a communist takeover. The fall of South Vietnam in 1975 appeared to signal U.S. weakness, especially combined with U.S. setbacks in the Middle East—the 1973 Arab oil embargo against the United States and the 1979 overthrow of the U.S.-backed Shah of Iran by Islamic fundamentalists.

In this period of apparent U.S. weakness, the Soviet Union invaded Afghanistan in 1979. But, like the United States in Vietnam, the Soviet Union could not suppress rebel armies supplied by the opposing superpower. The Soviets ultimately withdrew after almost a decade of war that considerably weakened the Soviet Union. Meanwhile, President Ronald Reagan built up U.S. military forces to record levels and supported rebel armies in the Soviet-allied states of Nicaragua and Angola (and one faction in Cambodia) as well as Afghanistan. Superpower relations slowly improved after Mikhail Gorbachev, a reformer, took power in the Soviet Union in 1985. But some of the battlegrounds of the global South

---

[32] Nathan, James A., ed. *The Cuban Missile Crisis Revisited.* NY: St. Martin's, 1992. May, Ernest, and Philip Zelikow, eds. *The Kennedy Tapes: Inside the White House During the Cuban Missile Crisis.* Harvard, 1997.

(notably Afghanistan and Angola) continued to suffer from brutal civil wars (fought with leftover Cold War arms) into the new century.

In retrospect, it seems that both superpowers exaggerated Soviet strength. In the early years of the nuclear arms race, U.S. military superiority was absolute, especially in nuclear weapons. The Soviets managed to match the United States over time, from A-bombs to H-bombs to multiple-warhead missiles. By the 1970s the Soviets had achieved strategic parity, meaning that neither side could prevent its own destruction in a nuclear war. But behind this military parity lay a Soviet Union lagging far behind the West in everything else—sheer wealth, technology, infrastructure, and citizen/worker motivation.

In June 1989, massive pro-democracy demonstrations in China's capital of Beijing (Tiananmen Square) were put down violently by the communist government. Hundreds were shot dead in the streets. Around 1990, as the Soviet Union stood by, one after another Eastern European country replaced its communist government under pressure of mass demonstrations. The toppling of the Berlin Wall in late 1989 symbolized the end of the Cold War division of Europe. Germany formally reunified in 1990. The Soviet leader, Gorbachev, allowed these losses of external power (and more) in hopes of concentrating on Soviet domestic restructuring under his policies of *perestroika* (economic reform) and *glasnost* (openness in political discussion). In 1991, however, the Soviet Union itself broke apart. Russia and many of the other former republics struggled throughout the 1990s against economic and financial collapse, inflation, corruption, war, and military weakness, although they remained political democracies. China remained a communist, authoritarian government but liberalized its economy and avoided military conflicts. In contrast to the Cold War era, China developed close ties with both the United States and Russia, and joined the world's liberal trading regime.

Scholars do not agree on the important question of why the Cold War ended.[33] One view is that U.S. military strength under President Reagan forced the Soviet Union into bankruptcy as it tried to keep up in the arms race. A different position is that the Soviet Union suffered from internal stagnation over decades and ultimately imploded because of weaknesses in its system of governance that had little to do with external pressure. Indeed, some scholars think the Soviet Union might have fallen apart earlier without the United States as a foreign enemy to bolster the Soviet government's legitimacy with its own people.

The Early Post–Cold War Era, 1990–2006

The post–Cold War era began with a bang, while the Soviet Union was still disintegrating. In 1990, perhaps believing that the end of the Cold War had left a power vacuum in its region, Iraq occupied its neighbor Kuwait in an aggressive grab for control of Middle East oil. Western powers were alarmed—both about the example that unpunished aggression could set in a new era, and about the direct threat to energy supplies for the world economy. The United States mobilized a coalition of the world's major countries (with almost no opposition) to oppose Iraq. Working through the UN, the U.S.-led coalition applied escalating sanctions against Iraq—from condemnation, to embargoing Iraq's oil exports, to threats

[33] Koslowski, Rey, and Friedrich Kratochwil. Understanding Change in International Politics: The Soviet Empire's Demise and the International System. *International Organization* 48 (2), 1994: 215–48. Brooks, Stephen G., and William C. Wohlforth. Power, Globalization, and the End of the Cold War: Reevaluating a Landmark Case for Ideas. *International Security* 25 (3), 2000/2001: 5–53. Herrmann, Richard K. and R. Ned Lebow. *Ending the Cold War: Interpretations, Causation, and the Study of International Relations*. NY: Palgrave, 2004.

CHANGE IN THE AIR

Peaceful trends mark the post–Cold War era, but war and terrorism continue. The uneasy relationship of Islam with the West will influence the directions of the unfolding era. Here, women begin to remove the burqa covering after the liberation of Kabul, Afghanistan, December 2001.

and ultimatums. The first President Bush received authorization from the U.S. Congress to use force against Iraq.

When Iraq did not withdraw from Kuwait by the UN's deadline, the United States and its allies easily smashed Iraq's military and evicted its army from Kuwait in the *Gulf War*. But the coalition did not occupy Iraq or overthrow its government. The costs of the Gulf War were shared among the participants in the coalition, with Britain and France making military commitments while Japan and Germany made substantial financial contributions. The pass-the-hat financing for this war was an innovation, one that worked fairly well.[34]

The final collapse of the Soviet Union followed only months after the Gulf War. The 15 republics of the Soviet Union—of which Russia under President Boris Yeltsin was just one—had begun taking power from a weakened central government, declaring themselves as sovereign states. This process, which is still working itself out, raised complex problems ranging from issues of national self-determination to the reallocation of property. The Baltic republics (Estonia, Latvia, and Lithuania), which had been incorporated into the Soviet Union only in the 1940s, were leaders in breaking away. The others held long negotiations under Gorbachev's leadership to restructure their confederation, with stronger republics and a weaker center.

The *Union Treaty* outlining this new structure provoked hard-liners in the old central government to try to seize control of the Soviet Union in a military coup in 1991.[35] The failure of the coup—and the prominent role of Russian President Yeltsin in opposing it—accelerated the collapse of the Soviet Union. The Communist party was banned, and soon both capitalism and democracy were adopted as the basis of the economies and political systems of the former Soviet states. (In reality, the daily workings of society change somewhat more slowly; the old guard tends to retain power wearing new hats.) The republics became independent states and formed a loose coordinating structure—the **Commonwealth of Independent States (CIS)**—whose future, if any, is still unclear. Of the former Soviet republics, only the three small Baltic states are nonmembers. Russia and Belarus formed a quasi-union in 2000.

Western relations with Russia and the other republics have been mixed since the 1990s. Because of their own economic problems, and because of a sense that Russia needed internal reform more than external aid, Western countries provided only limited aid for the region's harsh economic transition, which had drastically reduced living standards. Russia's brutal suppression of its secessionist province of Chechnya in 1995 and 1999 provoked Western fears of an expansionist, aggressive Russian nationalism, especially after success of ultranationalists in Russian parliamentary elections earlier in the decade. Russian leaders

[34] Freedman, Lawrence, and Efraim Karsh. *The Gulf Conflict: 1990–1991*. Princeton, 1993.

[35] McFaul, Michael. *Russia's Unfinished Revolution: Political Change from Gorbachev to Putin*. Cornell, 2001. Billington, James H. *Russia Transformed: Breakthrough to Hope: Moscow, August 1991*. NY: Free Press, 1992. Goldman, Marshall I. *What Went Wrong with Perestroika*. NY: W. W. Norton, 1994.

feared that NATO expansion into Eastern Europe would place threatening Western military forces on Russia's borders, creating a new division of Europe. Russian President Yeltsin warned of a "Cold Peace." Meanwhile, Japan and Russia could not resolve a lingering, mostly symbolic, territorial dispute.[36]

Despite these problems, the world's great powers overall increased their cooperation after the Cold War. Russia was accepted as the successor state to the Soviet Union and took its seat on the Security Council. Russia and the United States agreed to major reductions in their nuclear weapons, and carried them out in the 1990s.

U.S. leaders had hoped that the Gulf War would set valuable precedents for the future—the punishment of aggression, the reaffirmation of sovereignty and territorial integrity (of both Kuwait and Iraq), the utility of the UN Security Council, and the willingness of the United States to lead the post–Cold War order, which President Bush named the "New World Order." The prime architect of the "New World Order" of the early 1990s was, in many ways, Franklin D. Roosevelt—the U.S. president during most of World War II in the 1940s. His vision was of a great power collaboration through a new United Nations after the defeat of Germany and Japan in the war. Included would be the winners of the war—the United States, the Soviet Union, and Britain, along with France and (for the first time) China. The five would hold permanent seats on the UN Security Council. Germany and Japan would be reconstructed as democracies, and the United States would take a strong leadership role in world affairs. Roosevelt's vision was delayed by 40 years while the Soviet Union and United States contested the world order. But then, surprisingly, it came into existence in the early 1990s in something close to the original vision.

Hopes for a "New World Order" after the Gulf War quickly collided with less pleasant realities, however. In Bosnia-Herzegovina (hereafter called Bosnia for short), the UN mounted its largest peacekeeping mission, yet the gap between the international community's words and deeds took years to close. Just after the Gulf War in 1991, the former Yugoslavia broke apart, with several of its republics declaring independence. Ethnic Serbs, who were minorities in Croatia and Bosnia, seized about a third of Croatia and two-thirds of Bosnia as territory to form a "Greater Serbia" with the neighboring republic of Serbia. In those territories, with help from Serbia, which controlled the Yugoslav army, the Serb forces massacred hundreds of thousands of non-Serb Bosnians and Croatians and expelled millions more, to create an ethnically pure state. Croatian militias in Bosnia emulated these tactics, though on a smaller scale.

The international community recognized the independence of Croatia and Bosnia, admitting them to the UN and passing dozens of Security Council resolutions to protect their territorial integrity and their civilian populations. But in contrast to the Gulf War, the great powers showed no willingness to bear major costs to protect Bosnia. Instead they tried to contain the conflict by assuming a neutral role as peacekeeper and intermediary. An arms embargo was imposed on unarmed Bosnia and heavily armed Serbia alike, despite the UN resolutions declaring Serbia the aggressor.[37] In 1995, Serbian forces overran two UN-designated

---

[36] Ikenberry, G. John. *After Victory*. Princeton, 2000. Garthoff, Raymond L. *The Great Transition: American-Soviet Relations and the End of the Cold War*. Washington, DC: Brookings, 1994. Gaddis, John Lewis. *The United States and the End of the Cold War: Implications, Reconsiderations, Provocations*. NY: Oxford, 1992. Jervis, Robert, and Seweryn Bialer, eds. *Soviet-American Relations After the Cold War*. Duke, 1991. Ramberg, Bennett, ed. *Arms Control Without Negotiation: From the Cold War to the New World Order*. Boulder: Rienner, 1993. Fukuyama, Francis. *The End of History and the Last Man*. NY: Free Press, 1992.

[37] Gow, James. *Triumph of the Lack of Will: International Diplomacy and the Yugoslav War*. Columbia, 1997. Rieff, David. *Slaughterhouse: Bosnia and the Failure of the West*. NY: Simon & Schuster, 1995. Malcolm, Noel. *Bosnia: A Short History*. New York University, 1994. Gutman, Roy. *A Witness to Genocide*. NY: Macmillan, 1993. Burg, Steven L., and Paul S. Shoup. *The War in Bosnia-Herzegovina: Ethnic Conflict and International Intervention*. Armonk, NY: M.E. Sharpe, 1999.

"safe areas" in eastern Bosnia, expelling the women and slaughtering thousands of the men, but then the tide of battle turned and Serb forces lost ground. Two weeks of NATO air strikes (the alliance's first-ever military engagement) induced Serb forces to come to terms. U.S. negotiators pushed through the *Dayton Agreement*, which formally held Bosnia together as a single country, but granted Serb forces great autonomy on half of Bosnia's territory. Sixty thousand heavily armed troops, mostly from NATO (with 20,000 from the United States withdrawn by 2004), went to Bosnia and established a stable cease-fire.

Kosovo War

In contrast to their indecision early in the Bosnia crisis, the Western powers acted quickly in 1999 when Serbian forces carried out "ethnic cleansing" actions in the Serbian province of Kosovo, predominantly populated by ethnic Albanians. NATO launched an air war against Serbia that escalated over ten weeks as the Serbian government intensified its campaign in Kosovo. Serbian strongman Slobodan Milosevic was indicted for war crimes by the UN tribunal for the former Yugoslavia, delivered to the tribunal in 2001 after losing power, and died in 2006 near the end of a lengthy trial.[38] NATO came under criticism—notably from Russia and China—for acting without explicit UN authorization and interfering in Serbia's internal affairs. (The international community and the UN considered Kosovo, unlike Bosnia, to be a part of Serbia.) In the end, Serbian forces withdrew from Kosovo and the UN has controlled the province since.

In Somalia, a U.S.-led coalition sent tens of thousands of troops to suppress factional fighting and deliver relief supplies to a large population that was starving. However, when those forces were drawn into the fighting and sustained casualties, the United States abruptly pulled out, with the UN following by 1995.[39] In Rwanda in 1994, the genocide of more than half a million civilians—massacred in just a few weeks—was virtually ignored by the international community. The great powers, burned by failures in Somalia and Bosnia, decided that their vital interests were not at stake. In 1997, the Rwanda conflict spilled into neighboring Zaire (now the Democratic Congo), where rebels overthrew a corrupt dictator. Neighboring countries were drawn into the fighting but the international community steered clear even as living conditions worsened and millions of civilians died. The U.S. military intervened in Haiti to restore the elected president, but the situation there remains bleak. In 2004, rebels forced Jean-Bertrand Aristide from office and a U.S.- and French-led force moved in to provide stability temporarily, but after they left political violence resumed.

Russian-American relations faced continuing challenges. Not only has the West provided precious little aid, in Russia's perspective, but it is pushing NATO's boundaries eastward. The United States built new pipelines to bypass Russian territory in moving oil from former Soviet republics to Western consumers. It criticized the conduct of the war in Chechnya, a province of Russia, yet conducts its own military attacks around the world unilaterally when it so chooses. And it plans to rapidly deploy ballistic missile defenses, having withdrawn from the ABM Treaty (see p. 244).

While these U.S.-Russian conflicts reflect lingering problems from earlier times, new rifts opened in 2001 between the United States and both China and Europe—possibly signaling a realignment against U.S. predominance in world affairs. In President George W. Bush's first year, the United States stood nearly alone against the rest of the international

---

[38] Bacevich, Andrew J., and Eliot A. Cohen. *War over Kosovo*. Columbia, 2002. Prifti, Peter R. *Confrontation in Kosovo: The Albanian-Serb Struggle, 1969–1998*. Columbia, 1999. Mertus, Julie A. *Kosovo: How Myths and Truths Started a War*. California, 1999. Vickers, Miranda. *Between Serb and Albanian: A History of Kosovo*. Columbia, 1998.

[39] Clarke, Walter S., and Jeffrey I. Herbst, eds. *Learning from Somalia: The Lessons of Armed Humanitarian Intervention*. Boulder, CO: Westview, 1997. Fogarassy, Helen. *Mission Improbable: The World Community on a UN Compound in Somalia*. Lanham, MD: University Press of America, 1999.

community on a range of issues—missile defenses, the Kyoto treaty on global warming, a treaty to enforce the prohibition on biological weapons, a proposal to curb international small-arms sales, a proposed International Criminal Court (to replace the ad hoc war crimes tribunals of the 1990s), and a proposal to curb tobacco marketing in poor countries. Signaling aspects of this shifting alignment, Russia and China signed a treaty of friendship in 2001, and European countries helped vote the United States off two important UN commissions.

This icon indicates a Changing World Order discussion is available on the Companion Website (see p. xviii).

A New Era?

These divisive issues receded when the United States was attacked by terrorists on September 11, 2001. The attack destroyed the World Trade Center in New York and a wing of the Pentagon in Washington, DC, killing thousands of Americans and citizens of about 60 other countries. The attacks mobilized support for the United States by a very broad coalition of states, out of a realization that terrorism threatens the interstate system itself. President Bush declared a "war on terrorism" that was expected to last years and span continents, employing both conventional and unconventional means. In late 2001, U.S. and British forces and their Afghan allies ousted the Taliban regime in Afghanistan, which had harbored and supported the al Qaeda network (led by Osama bin Laden) responsible for attacks on the United States.

The great-power divisions reappeared, however, as the United States and Britain tried to assemble a coalition to oust Iraq's Saddam Hussein by force in early 2003. France and Germany (along with Russia and China) bitterly opposed the war, as did millions of protesters around the world and European public opinion. As the U.S. secretary of defense called France and Germany "old Europe"—in contrast to the more pro-American "new Europe" states of Eastern Europe just joining NATO—the dispute brought the Atlantic alliance to a low point and wrecked France's dream of leading a unified European foreign policy. The war on Iraq also weakened the UN's post–Cold War security role, since the U.S.-led coalition went forward despite its failure to win explicit authorization for war from the Security Council.

The invasion itself was brief and decisive. Although the United States had lost friends, Iraq had not made any, and it was overpowered in three weeks by a regional U.S. military force of 250,000 troops with advanced technology. Many Iraqis welcomed the end of a dictatorial regime, as had most Afghans in late 2001, but the war inflamed anti-American sentiment especially in Muslim countries such as Egypt and Pakistan. Insurgent forces in Iraq gained strength in the first three years of the U.S. occupation, and by early 2006 U.S. public opinion had turned against the war as violence continued with seemingly no end in sight. Sectarian violence between Shi'ite and Sunni communities (rival wings of Islam) pushed the country to the brink of all-out civil war, despite several successful elections for a new government. Estimates of Iraqi deaths caused by the war ranged from tens of thousands to more than 100,000. With many scenes of the destruction in Iraq broadcast regionally and worldwide, anti-Americanism exploded in Muslim countries. Following several other coalition partners, Italy announced it would withdraw its 3,000 troops from Iraq in 2006, leaving the United States and Britain increasingly alone in their efforts.[40]

At the same time, the United States faced new crises involving nuclear weapons programs. North Korea restarted its program, producing possibly a half dozen nuclear bombs in 2003. Iran, in an agreement with Europe, suspended enriching uranium that could be used to build nuclear weapons, but then in 2006 began enrichment again—causing the UN Security Council to take up the issue.

---

[40] Gordon, Michael R. and Gen. Bernard E. Trainor. *Cobra II: The Inside Story of the Invasion and Occupation of Iraq*. NY: Pantheon, 2006. Packer, George. *The Assassins' Gate: America in Iraq*. NY: Farrar, Straus, and Giroux, 2005.

The post–Cold War era may seem a conflict-prone period in which savage wars flare up with unexpected intensity around the world, in places such as Bosnia and Rwanda—even New York City. It is true that the era is complex and unpredictable, leaving some U.S. policy makers susceptible to Cold War nostalgia—longing for a time when world politics followed simpler rules based on a bipolar world order. Despite these new complexities, however, *the post–Cold War era has been more peaceful than the Cold War*. World military spending decreased by about one-third from its peak in the 1980s, although it has risen partway back since 2001. Old wars have ended faster than new ones have begun.[41] Latin America and Russia/Eastern Europe have nearly extinguished interstate war in their regions, joining a zone of peace already encompassing North America, Western Europe, Japan/Pacific, and China.

Warfare is diminishing even in the arc of conflict from Africa through the Middle East to South Asia. Long, bloody wars ended in South Africa, Mozambique, Angola, Democratic Congo, southern Sudan, and Ethiopia-Eritrea, as did the Cold War conflicts in Central America. More recent wars in Sri Lanka, Ivory Coast, Rwanda, Indonesia, and the Philippines have also largely wound down. After the Cold War, world order did not spiral out of control with rampant aggression and war. However, the Israeli-Palestinian conflict, which saw rising expectations of peace in the 1990s, worsened again in 2000 after a proposed deal fell through. With the 2006 Palestinian election victory of the militant Islamist party Hamas, responsible for many terrorist bombings in Israel, hopes for a durable peace faded. And the continuing war in Iraq threatened the broader stability of the Middle East. Tensions between Muslim and Western countries heightened in 2006 after the publication of anti-Muslim cartoons in a Danish newspaper sparked riots from Africa to South Asia.

Hamas Wins Palestinian Election

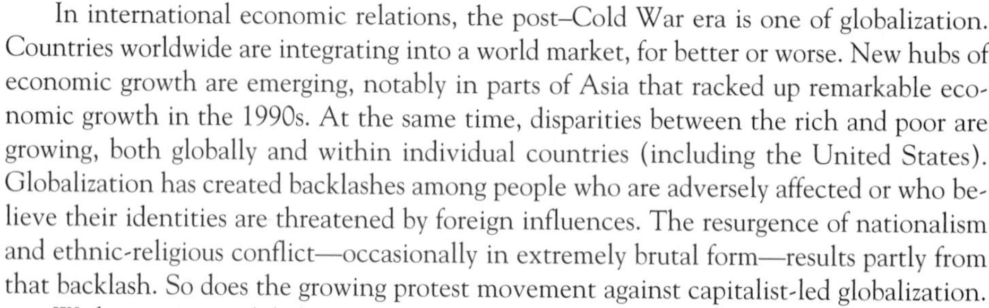

In international economic relations, the post–Cold War era is one of globalization. Countries worldwide are integrating into a world market, for better or worse. New hubs of economic growth are emerging, notably in parts of Asia that racked up remarkable economic growth in the 1990s. At the same time, disparities between the rich and poor are growing, both globally and within individual countries (including the United States). Globalization has created backlashes among people who are adversely affected or who believe their identities are threatened by foreign influences. The resurgence of nationalism and ethnic-religious conflict—occasionally in extremely brutal form—results partly from that backlash. So does the growing protest movement against capitalist-led globalization.

With increasing globalization, transnational concerns such as environmental degradation and disease have become more prominent as well. Global warming looms as an ever more present danger, underscored in 2005 by the toll of Hurricane Katrina on New Orleans and the accelerating melting of arctic ice. In early 2006, a virulent bird flu spread worldwide, faster than expected, and triggered panicky efforts to prepare for a possible human pandemic if the flu virus mutates and spreads person-to-person.

China is becoming more central to world politics as the twenty-first century begins. Its size and rapid growth make China a rising power—a situation that some scholars liken to Germany's rise a century earlier. Historically, such shifts in power relations have caused instability in the international system. China is the only great power that is not a democracy. Its poor record on human rights—symbolized dramatically by the killing of hundreds of peaceful demonstrators in Tiananmen Square (Beijing) in 1989—makes it a frequent target of Western criticism from both governments and NGOs.

China holds (but seldom uses) veto power in the UN Security Council, and it has a credible nuclear arsenal. China adjoins several regional conflict areas (Korea, Southeast Asia, India, and Central Asia) and affects the global proliferation of missiles and nuclear

[41] Human Security Centre. *Human Security Report 2005: War and Peace in the 21st Century*. Oxford, 2006.

weapons. It claims disputed territory in the resource-rich South China Sea, but has not fought a military battle in 25 years. With the transfer of Hong Kong from Britain in 1997, China acquired a valuable asset and turned to hopes of someday reintegrating Taiwan as well, under the Hong Kong formula of "one country, two systems."

China is the only great power from the global South. Its population size and rapid industrialization from a low level make China a big factor in the future of global environmental trends such as global warming. All these elements make China an important actor in the coming decades of international relations. Western policy makers argue about whether a harsh policy of containment or a mild policy of engagement will best get China to cooperate on a range of issues such as trade, human rights, weapons sales, and intellectual property rights.

It remains to be seen whether, in the coming years, the international system can provide China with appropriate status and respect to reflect its rising power and historical importance, and whether China in turn can come to conform with international rules and norms. The 2008 Olympic games in Beijing may clarify these long-term processes. So will the Chinese leadership's decisions about whether to encourage or discourage the rising tide of nationalism among China's young people as communist ideology loses its hold.

The transition into the post–Cold War era has been a turbulent time, full of changes and new possibilities (both good and bad).[42] It is likely, however, that basic rules and principles of IR—those that scholars have long struggled to understand—will continue to apply even though their contexts and outcomes may change. Most central to those rules and principles is the concept of power, to which we now turn.

THINKING CRITICALLY

1. Pick a current area in which interesting international events are taking place. Can you think of possible explanations for those events from each of the four levels of analysis? (See Table 1.1, p. 16.) Do explanations from different levels provide insights into different aspects of the events?
2. For a given nation-state that was once a *colony*, can you think of ways in which the state's current foreign policies might be influenced by its history of having been a colony?
3. In what ways do international economics shape our daily lives? Is this true for all people in all places? Or do economic processes like globalization affect some regions more than others?
4. Given the contradictory lessons of World Wars I and II, can you think of situations in today's world where appeasement (a conciliatory policy) would be the best course? Situations where hard-line containment policies would be best? Why?
5. What do you expect will be the character of the twenty-first century? Peaceful? War-prone? Orderly? Chaotic? Why do you have the expectations you do, and what clues from the unfolding of events in the world might tell you whether your guesses were correct?

---

[42] Singer, Max, and Aaron B. Wildavsky. *The Real World Order: Zones of Peace, Zones of Turmoil*. Chatham, NJ: Chatham House, 1996. Hoffmann, Stanley. *World Disorders: Troubled Peace in the Post–Cold War Era*. Lanham, MD: Rowman & Littlefield, 1998. Booth, Ken, and Tim Dunne, eds. *Worlds in Collision: Terror and the Future of Global Order*. NY: Palgrave, 2002.

CHAPTER SUMMARY

- IR affects daily life profoundly; we all participate in IR.
- IR is a field of political science, concerned mainly with explaining political outcomes in international security affairs and international political economy.
- Theories complement descriptive narratives in explaining international events and outcomes, but scholars do not agree on a single set of theories or methods to use in studying IR.
- States are the most important actors in IR; the international system is based on the sovereignty of (about 200) independent territorial states.
- States vary greatly in size of population and economy, from tiny microstates to great powers.
- Nonstate actors such as multinational corporations (MNCs), nongovernmental organizations (NGOs), and intergovernmental organizations (IGOs) exert a growing influence on international relations.
- The worldwide revolution in information technologies will profoundly reshape the capabilities and preferences of actors in IR, in ways that we do not yet understand.
- Four levels of analysis—individual, domestic, interstate, and global—suggest multiple explanations (operating simultaneously) for outcomes observed in IR.
- The global level of analysis—a recent addition—draws attention especially to technological change and the global gap in wealth between the industrialized North and the poor South.
- A variety of world civilizations were conquered by Europeans over several centuries and forcefully absorbed into a single global international system initially centered in Europe.
- The great-power system is made up of about half a dozen states (with membership changing over time as state power rises and falls).
- Great powers have restructured world order through recurrent wars, alliances, and the reign of hegemons (states that temporarily gain a preponderance of power in the international system). The most important wars have been the Thirty Years' War, the Napoleonic Wars, World War I, and World War II. Periods of hegemony include Britain in the nineteenth century and the United States after World War II.
- European states colonized most of the rest of the world during the past five centuries.
- Latin American countries gained independence shortly after the United States did (about 200 years ago), while those in Africa, Asia, and the Middle East became independent states only in the decades after World War II.
- Nationalism strongly influences IR; conflict often results from the perception of nationhood leading to demands for statehood or for the adjustment of state borders.
- Democracy is a force of growing importance: more states are becoming democratically governed, and democracies rarely fight each other in wars.
- The world economy has generated wealth at an accelerating pace in the past two centuries and is increasingly integrated on a global scale, although with huge inequalities.
- World Wars I and II dominated the twentieth century, yet they seem to offer contradictory lessons about the utility of hard-line or conciliatory foreign policies.
- For nearly 50 years after World War II, world politics revolved around the East-West rivalry of the Cold War. This bipolar standoff created stability and avoided great-power wars, including nuclear war, but turned states in the global South into proxy battlegrounds.

- The post–Cold War era that began in the 1990s holds hope of general great-power cooperation despite the appearance of new ethnic and regional conflicts.
- A "war on terrorism"—with broad international support but uncertain scope and duration—began in 2001 after terrorist attacks on the United States.
- The U.S. military campaign in Iraq overthrew a dictator, but divided the great powers and heightened anti-Americanism worldwide.

KEY TERMS

international relations (IR) 3
issue areas 4
conflict and cooperation 5
international security 5
international political economy (IPE) 5
state 10
United Nations (UN) 10
international system 11
nation-states 11
Gross Domestic Product (GDP) 12
nonstate actors 13
nongovernmental organization (NGO) 13
intergovernmental organization (IGO) 14
North-South gap 17
nationalism 32
industrialization 35
free trade 35
League of Nations 37
Munich Agreement 37
genocide 39
Cold War 41
containment 41
Sino-Soviet split 41
summit meeting 42
Cuban Missile Crisis 42
proxy wars 42
Commonwealth of Independent States (CIS) 44

ONLINE PRACTICE TEST

Take an online practice test at *www.internationalrelations.net*

❑ A
❑ B
☑ C
❑ D

LET'S DEBATE THE ISSUE

Globalization: Vanishing State Sovereignty?

by Mir Zohair Husain

Overview People live in a globally interdependent system where events occurring thousands of miles away affect them. This shrinking of the world is "globalization," an economic, political, technological, and sociocultural process where the importance of state boundaries decreases, and the countries and their people live in an integrated global system. However, nonstate actors, both governmental and nongovernmental, are challenging the dominance of states and their sovereignty. This erosion of state boundaries and the loss of state sovereignty is a critical issue because this is what makes states unique.

Many organizations regularly operate across the borders of numerous countries, such as Microsoft, an American multinational corporation, which assists customers calling from all over the world with technical support, to the Red Cross, whose nongovernmental professionals and volunteers from a variety of countries deliver humanitarian aid worldwide.

If states lose their sovereignty and influence within their borders, will it be more difficult for states to solve problems within their borders? What consequences might lie ahead for the world if states were to lose their sovereignty?

Argument 1 States Have Lost Their Sovereignty

Globalization is eroding state sovereignty. Globalization permits the interests of influential individuals, nongovernmental organizations, and intergovernmental organizations to override the national interests of states. For example, multinational corporations pressure governments to lower environmental standards, grant tax breaks, and provide a low-wage labor force—or risk the company moving its jobs to another country that *will* sacrifice the health of its people for new corporate jobs and tax revenues.

> Every . . . national economy and every kind of public good is today vulnerable to the inroads of transnational commerce. Markets abhor frontiers as nature abhors a vacuum. Within their expansive and permeable domains, interests are private, trade is free, currencies are convertible, access to banking is open, contracts are enforceable, and the laws of production and consumption are sovereign, trumping the laws of legislatures and courts. In Europe, Asia, and the Americas such markets have already eroded national sovereignty and given birth to a new class of institutions—international banks, trade associations, transnational lobbies like OPEC, world news services like CNN and BBC, and multinational corporations—institutions that lack distinctive national identities and neither reflect nor respect nationhood as an organizing or a regulative principle. While mills and factories sit somewhere on sovereign territory under the eye and potential regulation of nation-states, currency markets and the Internet exist everywhere, but nowhere in particular. Without an address or a national affiliation, they are altogether beyond the devices of sovereignty. (Benjamin R. Barber. *Jihad vs. McWorld.* New York: Times Books/Random House, 1995, pp. 13–14.)

Global environmental problems ignore international borders and state sovereignty. One country's pollution affects people beyond its borders, which makes environmental degradation a global issue. So, individuals (such as environmentalists), intergovernmental organizations (such as the UN Environmental Program), and nongovernmental organizations (such as Greenpeace) constantly pressure states to change their environmental and business regulations with differing degrees of success.

> Even the most developed, supposedly self-sufficient nations can no longer pretend to genuine sovereignty. That is the meaning of *ecology,* a term that marks the final obsolescence of all manmade boundaries. When it comes to acid rain or oil spills or depleted fisheries or tainted groundwater or fluorocarbon propellants or radiation leaks or toxic wastes or sexually transmitted diseases, national frontiers are simply irrele-

vant. Toxins don't stop for customs inspections and microbes don't carry passports. North America became a water and air free-trade zone long before NAFTA loosened up the market in goods. (Benjamin R. Barber. *Jihad vs. McWorld.* New York: Times Books/Random House, 1995, pp. 12–13.)

Globalization fosters cultural homogenization, which threatens indigenous values and languages. As people are exposed to international cultures and values, they assimilate these new ideas, ultimately replacing many aspects of their indigenous culture. This blending of diverse cultures is known as "cultural homogenization." For example, Hollywood continues to produce films with new sights and typical Western values, some materialistic and hedonistic, that make deep impressions on its global audience.

> The spread of technology, easy access to the international media, the availability of standardized foods and products, and the pervasive influence of American popular culture are changing how people in different parts of the world think and act. This process of change is hard to control, and its inroads are often difficult to gauge or regulate. (Patrick O'Meara et al. *Globalization and the Challenges of a New Century.* Indiana University Press, 2000, p. 417.)

Argument 2 Predictions of State Sovereignty's Demise Are Premature

States remain the preeminent actors and the driving force in world affairs. Many international organizations are touted as panaceas for the world's ills. However, powerful states (such as the United States and Britain), not international organizations, are the ones responsible for producing real results, such as uprooting al Qaeda from Afghanistan and forcing regime change in Iraq.

> Of course, even enthusiastic multilateralists now concede that international entities like the United Nations, NATO, the European Union, and nongovernmental health and environmental organizations have all been relegated to the sidelines in recent months.
>
> "All the most important agreements were made on a state-by-state basis," said Christopher Hill, a lecturer in international affairs at Yale, pointing to assistance offered the United States after September 11 by Britain, Italy, Germany, Russia, Pakistan, and other nations. "Pick any problem out there [such as] AIDS, the environment or terrorism," he added, "if the state isn't effective in its jurisdiction, then the problem isn't going to get solved." (Alexander Stille. "What Is America's Place in the World Now?" *The New York Times,* January 12, 2002.)

States dictate to nonstate actors what will occur within their borders. Regardless of the pressure from interest groups, international organizations, and nongovernmental organizations, states retain final policy decisions. States can choose to relinquish some sovereignty in exchange for other benefits, but states retain the power of sovereignty.

> Some scholars argue that globalization erodes the sovereignty of nation-states because national sovereignty has been transferred from governments to capital markets. Governments and markets, however, are not mere abstractions, and governments are far from surrendering political power to capital markets. In fact, think about who ultimately enables capital to move freely across national borders. Is it governments or capital markets? Is it possible that governments who now allow capital to move in and out of their national borders will someday impose capital controls? Capital moves freely across the globe because governments have made a choice to allow this to happen. (Rosa Gomez Dierks. *Introduction to Globalization.* Rowman and Littlefield Publishers, Inc., 2001, pp. 98–101.)

States, state borders, and state sovereignty remain intact despite globalization. Although globalization has profoundly affected much of the world, its effect on state sovereignty has been surprisingly minimal. Since 1971, only four states (Pakistan, Czechoslovakia, the Soviet Union, and Yugoslavia) of nearly 200 have fragmented, resulting in the emergence of several sovereign states, while two formerly divided states actually united (Germany and Yemen in 1990). The roots of "state sovereignty" can be traced to the end of the Thirty Years War and the Treaty of Westphalia (1648). So, despite predictions of the end of state sovereignty, the UN, its member states, and international law recognize and respect the concept of state sovereignty.

> The Treaty of Westphalia . . . established principles, that have endured and remain at the heart of contemporary international politics. Many . . . now maintain that "globalization" has rendered the traditional nation-state redundant. [This] modern assault on the treaty is unlikely to prove more accurate [than past ones]. ("State and Sovereignty." *The Times (London),* December 30, 1999.)

Questions

1. Think about your family, friends, and schoolmates, your personal possessions, and what you continue to learn about world events. How many different languages, cultures, religions, and nationalities are present in your life alone? How does globalization affect your life in these areas on a daily basis?

Globalization

2. Does globalization contribute to the promise of a more peaceful world, or does it contribute to a more turbulent and perilous global system? Do the promises of globalization outweigh its perils?

Selected Readings

Robert O. Keohane and Joseph S. Nye. *Power and Interdependence,* 3rd edition. NY: Longman, 2001.

Jagdish Bhagwati. *In Defense of Globalization.* NY: Oxford University Press, 2004.

U.S. Marines in Fallujah, Iraq, November 2004.

CHAPTER 2

Power Politics

Realism

No single theory reliably explains the wide range of international interactions, both conflictual and cooperative. But there is a theoretical framework that has traditionally held a central position in the study of IR. This approach, called realism, is favored by some IR scholars and vigorously contested by others, but almost all take it into account. It is a relatively conservative theoretical approach; liberal and revolutionary alternatives will be reviewed in Chapter 3.

Realism (or *political realism*) is a school of thought that explains international relations in terms of power (see "Defining Power," pp. 57–58). The exercise of power by states toward each other is sometimes called *realpolitik*, or just *power politics*. Realists are often pessimistic concerning human nature. Realism has a long history, and it dominated the study of IR in the United States during the Cold War.

Realism as we know it developed in reaction to a liberal tradition that realists called **idealism** (of course, idealists themselves do not consider their approach unrealistic). Idealism emphasizes international law, morality, and international organizations, rather than power alone, as key influences on international events. Idealists think that human nature is basically good. With good habits, education, and appropriate international structures, human nature can become the basis of peaceful and cooperative international relationships. Idealists see the international system as one based on a community of states with the potential to work together to overcome mutual problems (see Chapter 3). For idealists, the principles of IR must flow from morality.

Idealists were particularly active in the period between World War I and World War II, following the painful experience of World War I. U.S. President Woodrow Wilson and other idealists placed their hopes for peace in the League of Nations as a formal structure for the community of nations.

Those hopes were dashed when that structure proved helpless to stop German, Italian, and Japanese aggression in the 1930s. Since World War II, realists have blamed idealists for looking too much at how the world *ought* to be instead of how it *really* is. Sobered by the experiences of World War II, realists set out to understand the principles of power politics without succumbing to wishful thinking. Realism provided a theoretical foundation for the Cold War policies of containment and the determination of U.S. policy makers not to appease the Soviet Union and China as the West had appeased Hitler at Munich in 1938.

Aggression in the 1930s

Realists ground themselves in a long tradition. The Chinese strategist *Sun Tzu*, who lived two thousand years ago, advised the rulers of states how to survive in an era when war had become a systematic instrument of power for the first time (the "warring states" period). Sun Tzu argued that moral reasoning was not very useful to the state rulers of the day, faced with armed and dangerous neighbors. Sun Tzu showed rulers how to use power to advance their interests and protect their survival.[1]

At roughly the same time, in Greece, *Thucydides* wrote an account of the Peloponnesian War (431–404 B.C.) focusing on relative power among the Greek city-states. He stated that "the strong do what they have the power to do and the weak accept what they have to accept."[2] Much later, in Renaissance Italy (around 1500), *Niccolò Machiavelli* urged princes to concentrate on expedient actions to stay in power, including the manipulation of the public and military alliances. Today the adjective *Machiavellian* refers to excessively manipulative power maneuvers.[3]

English philosopher *Thomas Hobbes* in the seventeenth century discussed the free-for-all that exists when government is absent and people seek their own self-interest. He called it the "state of nature" or "state of war"—what we would now call the "law of the jungle" in contrast to the rule of law. Hobbes favored a strong monarchy (which he labeled a *Leviathan*) to tame this condition. Realists see in these historical figures evidence that the importance of power politics is timeless and cross-cultural.

After World War II, scholar *Hans Morgenthau* argued that international politics is governed by objective, universal laws flowing from the idea that national interests are defined in terms of power (not psychological motives of decision makers). He reasoned that no nation had "God on its side" (a universal morality) and that all nations had to base their actions on prudence and practicality. He opposed the Vietnam War, arguing in 1965 that a communist Vietnam would not harm U.S. national interests.

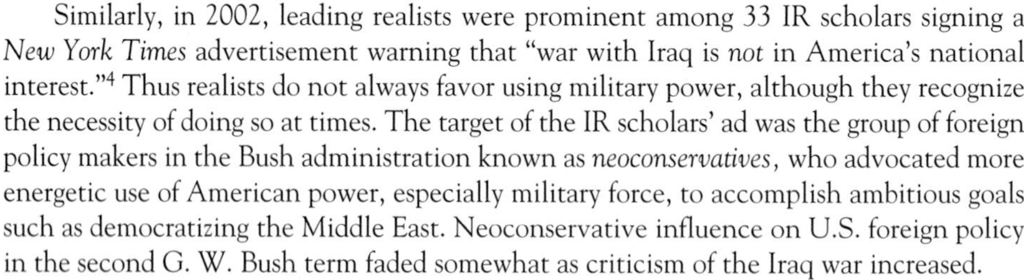

Power Politics

Similarly, in 2002, leading realists were prominent among 33 IR scholars signing a *New York Times* advertisement warning that "war with Iraq is *not* in America's national interest."[4] Thus realists do not always favor using military power, although they recognize the necessity of doing so at times. The target of the IR scholars' ad was the group of foreign policy makers in the Bush administration known as *neoconservatives,* who advocated more energetic use of American power, especially military force, to accomplish ambitious goals such as democratizing the Middle East. Neoconservative influence on U.S. foreign policy in the second G. W. Bush term faded somewhat as criticism of the Iraq war increased.

Realists tend to treat political power as separate from, and predominant over, morality, ideology, and other social and economic aspects of life. For realists, ideologies do not matter much, nor do religions or other cultural factors with which states may explain their actions. Realists see states with very different religions or ideologies or economic systems as quite similar in their actions with regard to national power.[5]

Today realists share several assumptions about how IR works. They assume that IR can be best (though not exclusively) explained by the choices of states operating as autonomous actors rationally pursuing their own interests in a system of sovereign states. Sometimes the realist framework is summarized in three propositions: (1) *states* are the most important actors (the state-centric assumption); (2) they act as *rational* individuals in

---

[1] Sun Tzu. *The Art of War*. Translated by Samuel B. Griffith. Oxford, 1963, p. 22.

[2] Thucydides. *History of the Peloponnesian War*. Translated by R. Warner. NY: Penguin, 1972, p. 402.

[3] Machiavelli, Niccolò. *The Prince, and the Discourses*. Translated by Luigi Ricci. Revised by E. R. P. Vincent. NY: Modern Library, 1950. Meinecke, Friedrich. *Machiavellism: The Doctrine of Raison d'État and Its Place in Modern History*. Translated by D. Scott. Yale, 1957.

[4] Morgenthau, Hans. We Are Deluding Ourselves in Vietnam, *The New York Times Magazine*, Apr. 18, 1965; Advertisement, *The New York Times*, Sept. 26, 2002.

[5] Morgenthau, Hans J., and Kenneth W. Thompson. *Politics Among Nations: The Struggle for Power and Peace*. 6th ed. NY: Knopf, 1985. Carr, Edward Hallett. *The Twenty Years' Crisis, 1919–1939: An Introduction to the Study of International Relations*. London: Macmillan, 1974 [1939]. Aron, Raymond. *Peace and War: A Theory of International Relations*. Translated by R. Howard and A. B. Fox. NY: Doubleday, 1966.

TABLE 2.1 ■ Assumptions of Realism and Idealism

Issue	Realism	Idealism
Human Nature	Selfish	Altruistic
Most Important Actors	States	States and others including individuals
Causes of State Behavior	Rational pursuit of self-interest	Psychological motives of decision makers
Nature of International System	Anarchy	Community

pursuing national interests (the unitary rational-actor assumption); and (3) they act in the context of an international system lacking central government (the *anarchy* assumption).

Table 2.1 summarizes some major differences between the assumptions of realism and idealism. We will return to the realism-liberalism debate at the start of Chapter 3.

Power

Power is a central concept in international relations—the central one for realists—but one that is surprisingly difficult to define or measure.

Defining Power

Power is often defined as the ability to get another actor to do what it would not otherwise have done (or not to do what it would have done).[6] A variation on this idea is that actors are powerful to the extent that they affect others more than others affect them.[7] These definitions treat power as influence. If actors get their way a lot, they must be powerful.

One problem with this definition is that we seldom know what a second actor would have done in the absence of the first actor's power. There is a danger of circular logic: power explains influence, and influence measures power. Thus it is hard to use power to explain why international events occur (the aim of realism). A related problem is that common usage treats power as a thing rather than a process: states "have" power.

These problems are resolved if we recall that power is not influence itself, but the ability or potential to influence others. Many IR scholars believe that such potential is based on specific (tangible and intangible) characteristics or possessions of states—such as their sizes, levels of income, armed forces, and so forth. This is power as *capability*. Capabilities are easier to measure than influence and less circular in logic.

Measuring capabilities to explain how one nation influences another is not simple, however. It requires summing up various kinds of potentials. States possess varying amounts of population, territory, military forces, and so forth. *The best single indicator of a state's power may be its total GDP*, which combines overall size, technological level, and wealth. But even GDP is at best a rough indicator. An alternative method, compared to the method followed in this book, gives GDP estimates that are on average about 50 percent higher for countries in the global North and about 50 percent lower for the global

[6] Dahl, Robert A. *Modern Political Analysis*. 2nd ed. Englewood Cliffs, NJ: Prentice Hall, 1970.

[7] Waltz, Kenneth. *Theory of International Politics*. Reading, MA: Addison-Wesley, 1979.

POWER AS INFLUENCE

Power is the ability to influence the behavior of others. Military force and economic sanctions are among the various means that states and nonstate actors use to try to influence each other. In 2006, the Western powers contemplated various means, ranging from promises of aid to sanctions to military force, to try to get Iran to give up its nuclear program. Iran appeared poised to acquire nuclear weapons in the coming years, and its leaders apparently thought such weapons, and missiles to carry them, would enhance Iran's power. Here, Iran's assertively anti-Western president, Mahmoud Ahmadinejad, reviews ballistic missiles in a parade, 2005.

South (see Chapter 1, footnote 9, p. 12). In particular, this alternative method reduces China's GDP substantially from the figures reported in this book. So GDP is a useful estimator of material capabilities but not a precise one. These tangible capabilities (including military forces) are often referred to as material power.

Furthermore, power depends on nonmaterial elements. Capabilities give a state the potential to influence others only to the extent that political leaders can mobilize and deploy them effectively and strategically. This depends on national will, on diplomatic skill, on popular support for the government (its legitimacy), and so forth. Some scholars emphasize the *power of ideas*—the ability to maximize the influence of capabilities through a psychological process. This process includes the domestic mobilization of capabilities—often through religion, ideology, or (especially) nationalism. International influence is also gained by forming the rules of behavior, to change how others see their own national interests. If a state's own values become widely shared among other states, it will easily influence others. For example, the United States has influenced many other states to accept the value of free markets and free trade. This has been called *soft power*.[8]

Because power is a relational concept, a state can have power only relative to other states. *Relative power* is the ratio of the power that two states can bring to bear against each other. It matters little to realists whether a state's capabilities are rising or declining in absolute terms, only whether they are falling behind or overtaking the capabilities of rival states. Most realists, moreover, emphasize material power.

Even realists recognize the limits to explanations based solely on power. At best, power provides a general understanding of typical or average outcomes. In actual IR there are many other elements at work, including an element of accident or luck. The more powerful actor does not always prevail. Power provides only a partial explanation.[9]

[8] Nye, Joseph S., Jr. *Bound to Lead: The Changing Nature of American Power*. NY: Basic Books, 1990.

[9] Barnett, Michael and Raymond Duvall. Power in International Politics. *International Organization* 59 (1), 2005: 1–37. Baldwin, David. Power in International Relations. In Carlsnaes, Walter, Thomas Risse, and Beth Simmons, eds. *Handbook of International Relations*. Sage, 2002, pp. 177–91. Rothgeb, John M., Jr. *Defining Power: Influence and Force in the Contemporary International System*. NY: St. Martin's, 1992. Guzzini, Stefano. *Realism in International Relations and International Political Economy*. Routledge, 1998. Cox, Robert W. *Production, Power, and World Order: Social Forces in the Making of History*. Columbia, 1987.

Estimating Power

Sun Tzu's first chapter advises rulers to accurately estimate their own power—ranging from money to territory to popular domestic support—and that of their potential enemies. "Know the enemy and know yourself," he wrote. Any estimate of an actor's overall power must combine diverse elements and will therefore be inexact. But such estimates are nonetheless useful. The logic of power suggests that in wars the more powerful state will generally prevail. Thus, estimates of the relative power of the two antagonists should help explain the outcome of each war. These estimates could take into account the nations' relative military capabilities and the popular support for each one's government, among other factors. But most important is the total size of each nation's economy—the total GDP—which reflects both population size and the level of income per person (per capita). With a healthy enough economy, a state can buy a large army, buy popular support (by providing consumer goods), and even buy allies.

For example, the United States that invaded Iraq in 2003 was the most powerful state in world history, and Iraq had been weakened by two costly wars and a decade of sanctions. The power disparity was striking. In GDP, the United States held an advantage of more than a hundred to one; in population, more than ten to one. U.S. forces were larger and much more capable technologically. In 2003, the United States lacked some of the power elements it had possessed during the 1991 Gulf War—the moral legitimacy conferred by the UN Security Council, a broad coalition of allies (including the most powerful states regionally and globally), and partners willing to pay for most of the costs of the war. Despite these shortfalls, U.S. military power was able to carry out the objective of regime change in Iraq, within a month and with low U.S. casualties. When the war began, the U.S.-led coalition established its dominance within hours and went on to systematically crush Iraq's military power and drive Saddam Hussein's regime from Baghdad.

So the GDP ratio—nearly one hundred to one—would seem to reflect accurately the power imbalance between the United States and Iraq. (In the short term, of course, other factors ranging from political strategies to military forces to weather play a role.)

And yet, three years later, the U.S. forces' grip on Iraq remained tenuous as an anti-American insurgency proved far stronger than expected and religious violence threatened to tear Iraq apart. At the same time, the war in Iraq weakened support for American policies around the world. The difficulties encountered by the world's superpower in trying to establish stable political control in Iraq demonstrate that power—getting others to do what you want—includes many elements beyond just military might. GDP does not always predict who will win a war, as shown by the U.S. loss in the Vietnam War. Nonetheless, despite its lack of precision, GDP is probably the best single indicator of power.

Counterinsurgency Warfare in Iraq

Elements of Power

State power is a mix of many ingredients, such as natural resources, industrial capacity, moral legitimacy, military preparedness, and popular support of government. All these elements contribute to an actor's power. The mix varies from one actor to another, but overall power does relate to the rough quantities of the elements on which that power is based.

Power resources are elements that an actor can draw on over the *long term*. The power measure used earlier—total GDP—is in this category. So are population, territory, geography, and natural resources. These attributes change only slowly. Less tangible long-term power resources include political culture, patriotism, education of the population, and strength of the scientific and technological base. The credibility of its commitments (reputation for keeping its word) is also a power resource that a state can nurture over time. So is the ability of one state's culture and values to consistently shape the thinking of other states (the power of ideas). Power resources shape an actor's potential power.

The importance of long-term power resources was illustrated after the Japanese surprise attack on the U.S. fleet at Pearl Harbor in 1941, which decimated U.S. naval capabilities in the Pacific. In the short term, Japan had superior military power and was able to occupy territories in Southeast Asia while driving U.S. forces from the region. In the longer term, the United States had greater power resources due to its underlying economic potential. It built up military capabilities over the next few years that gradually matched and then overwhelmed those of Japan.

Power capabilities allow actors to exercise influence in the *short term*. Military forces are such a capability—perhaps the most important kind. The size, composition, and preparedness of two states' military forces matter more in a short-term military confrontation than do their respective economies or natural resources. Another capability is the military-industrial capacity to quickly produce tanks, fighter planes, and other weapons. The quality of a state's bureaucracy is another type of capability, allowing the state to gather information, regulate international trade, or participate in international conferences.

As with power resources, some power capabilities are intangible. The *support* and *legitimacy* that an actor commands in the short term from constituents and allies are capabilities that the actor can use to gain influence. The *loyalty* of a nation's army and politicians to its leader (in the short term) is in effect a capability available to the leader. Although capabilities come into play more quickly than power resources, they are narrower in scope. In particular, military capabilities are useful only when military power can be effective in gaining influence. Likewise, economic capabilities are of little use in situations dominated by a military component.

THE ECONOMICS OF POWER

Military power such as tanks rests on economic strength, roughly measured by GDP. The large U.S. economy supports U.S. military predominance. In the 2003 U.S. Iraq War, the United States could afford to send a large and technologically advanced military force to the Middle East. Here, U.S. forces enter Iraq, March 2003.

Given the limited resources that any actor commands, there are always trade-offs among possible capabilities. Building up military forces diverts resources that might be put into foreign aid, for instance. Or buying a population's loyalty with consumer goods reduces resources available for building up military capabilities. To the extent that one element of power can be converted into another, it is *fungible*. Generally money is the most fungible capability because it can buy other capabilities.

Realists tend to see *military force* as the most important element of national power in the short term, and they see other elements such as economic strength or diplomatic skill or moral legitimacy as being important to the extent that they are fungible into military power. Such fungibility of nonmilitary elements of power into military ones is considerable, at least in the long term. Well-paid soldiers fight better, as do soldiers imbued with moral fervor for their cause, or soldiers using higher-technology weapons. Skilled diplomats can avoid unfavorable military confrontations or provoke favorable ones. Moral foreign policies can help sway public opinion in foreign countries and cement alliances that increase military strength. Realists tend to treat these dimensions of power as important mainly because of their potential military impact. Indeed, realists share this emphasis on material (usually military) power with revolutionaries such as communist leaders during the Cold War. Chairman Mao Zedong of China said: "All power grows out of the barrel of a gun."

The different types of power capabilities can be contrasted by considering the choice to possess tanks or gold. One standard power capability that states want is battle tanks. In land warfare to control territory, the tank is arguably the most powerful instrument available, and the leading defense against it is another tank. One can assess power on this dimension by counting the size and quality of a state's tank force (an imprecise but not impossible exercise). A different power capability of time-honored value is the stockpile of *gold* (or its modern-day equivalent in hard currency reserves; see Chapter 9). Gold represents economic power and is a power resource, whereas tanks represent military power and are a power capability.

In the long term, the gold is better because one can always turn gold into tanks (it is fungible), but it might be hard to turn tanks into gold. However, in the short term the tanks might be better because if an enemy tank force invades one's territory, gold will not stop them; indeed they will soon take the gold for themselves. For example, in 1990, Iraq (which had gone for tanks) invaded its neighbor Kuwait (which had gone for gold). In the short term, Iraq proved much more powerful: it occupied Kuwait and plundered it.

Morality can contribute to power, by increasing the will to use power and by attracting allies. States have long clothed their actions, however aggressive, in rhetoric about their peaceful and defensive intentions. For instance, the 1989 U.S. invasion of Panama was named "Operation Just Cause." Of course, if a state overuses moralistic rhetoric to cloak self-interest too often, it loses credibility even with its own population.

The use of geography as an element of power is called **geopolitics.** It is often tied to the logistical requirements of military forces (see Chapter 6). Frequently, state leaders use maps in thinking about international power positions and alignments. In geopolitics, as in real estate, the three most important considerations are location, location, location. States increase their power to the extent they can use geography to enhance their military capabilities, such as by securing allies and bases close to a rival power or along strategic trade routes, by controlling key natural resources, or by enjoying separation from potential adversaries by large bodies of water. In general, power declines as a function of distance from a home state, although technology seems to be making this decline less steep.

A recurrent geopolitical theme for centrally located, largely landlocked states such as Germany and Russia is the threat of being surrounded. Militarily, centrally located states often face a *two-front problem*. Germany had to fight France to the west and Russia to the east simultaneously in World War I—a problem reduced early in World War II by Hitler's pact with Stalin (until Hitler's disastrous decision to invade the Soviet Union).

For states less centrally located, such as Britain or the United States, different geopolitical problems appear. These states have been called "insular" in that bodies of water protect them against land attacks.[10] Their geopolitical problem in the event of war is to move soldiers and supplies over long distances to reach the scene of battle. This capability was demonstrated in the U.S. participation in World War I, World War II, the Cold War, and the Gulf War.

---

[10] Dehio, Ludwig. *The Precarious Balance: Four Centuries of the European Power Struggle*. Translated by Charles Fullman. NY: Vintage Books, 1962 [from the German version of 1948]. Modelski, George, and William R. Thompson. *Seapower in Global Politics, 1494–1993*. Washington, 1988. Goldstein, Joshua S., and David P. Rapkin. After Insularity: Hegemony and the Future World Order. *Futures* 23 (9), 1991: 935–59.

Bargaining

The exercise of power involves two or more parties, each trying to influence the other more than it is itself influenced. The mutual attempts to influence others constitute a bargaining process. Bargaining is important in various theoretical perspectives (not just realism), though different theories emphasize different motivations, tactics, and outcomes.

Bargaining and Leverage

U.S. Influence on Iran's Nuclear Program

Bargaining may be defined as tacit or direct communication in an attempt to reach agreement on an exchange of value—that is, of tangible or intangible items that one or both parties value. Bargaining need not be explicit. Sometimes the content is communicated through actions rather than an exchange of words.[11]

A bargaining process has two or more *participants* and sometimes has *mediators* whose participation is nominally neutral. Participants have a direct stake in the outcome; mediators do not. There are one or more *issues* on which each participant hopes to reach agreement on terms favorable to itself, but the participants' *interests* diverge on these issues, creating conflicts. These conflicts define a *bargaining space*—one or more dimensions, each of which represents a distance between the positions of two participants concerning their preferred outcomes. The bargaining process disposes of these conflicts by achieving agreement on the distribution of the various items of value that are at stake. The end result is a position arrived at in the bargaining space.

Such agreements do not necessarily represent a *fair* exchange of value; many agreements are manifestly one-sided and unfair. But in a broad sense, bargains whether fair or unfair contain an element of *mutual gain*. This is possible because the items of value being exchanged have different value to the different parties.

Participants bring different means of *leverage* to the bargaining process.[12] Leverage derives from power capabilities that allow one actor to influence the other to reach agreements more favorable to the first actor's interests. Leverage may operate on any of three dimensions of power: the *promise* of positive sanctions (rewards) if the other actor gives one what one wants; the *threat* of negative sanctions (damage to valued items) if not; or an *appeal* to the other's feeling of love, friendship, sympathy, or respect for oneself.[13] For instance, Cuba during the Cold War could obtain Soviet oil by purchasing the oil with hard currency, by threatening to cut its alliance with the Soviet Union unless given the oil at subsidized prices, or by appealing to the Soviet leaders' sense of socialist solidarity.

Bringing bargaining leverage into play generally opens up a new dimension in the bargaining space, allowing outcomes along this new dimension to be traded off against those on the original dimension (the main issue at stake). Leverage thus helps to get deals done—albeit not always fair ones. One-sided agreements typically result when one side has a preponderance of leverage relative to the other.[14]

---

[11] Synder, Glenn H., and Paul Diesing. *Conflict Among Nations: Bargaining, Decision Making, and System Structure in International Crises*. Princeton, 1977. Morgan, T. Clifton. *Untying the Knot of War: A Bargaining Theory of International Crises*. Michigan, 1994. Telhami, Shibley. *Power and Leadership in International Bargaining: The Path to the Camp David Accords*. Columbia, 1990.

[12] North, Robert C. *War, Peace, Survival: Global Politics and Conceptual Synthesis* (see footnote 14 on p. 16).

[13] Boulding, Kenneth E. *Three Faces of Power*. Newbury Park, CA: Sage, 1990. Hayward, Clarissa Rile. *De-Facing Power*. Cambridge, 2000.

[14] Art, Robert J., and Patrick M. Cronin, eds. *The United States and Coercive Diplomacy*. Herndon, VA: United States Institute of Peace Press, 2003.

The use of violence can be a means of settling conflicts. The application of violent negative leverage can force an agreement that ends a conflict. (Again, the agreement may not be fair.) Because such violence may also create new sources of conflict, agreements reached through violence may not last. Nonetheless, from a realist perspective violence is just another leverage—an extension of politics by other means. Politics itself has been described as the process of deciding "who gets what, when, how."[15]

BARGAINING PROCESS

Bargaining includes both indirect moves and explicit negotiations. The Israeli-Palestinian relationship has seen plenty of both types. In 2000, President Clinton convened the Camp David II peace talks over the objections of Palestinian leader Yasser Arafat, who did not think conditions were ripe for a settlement. Here, as the talks convened, Arafat had to be pushed through the door by Israeli leader Ehud Barak. The failure of the talks led to a new and more vicious round of violence. By 2006, despite some temporary advances, the peace process remained deadlocked.

The same principles of bargaining apply to both international security affairs and international political economy. In both cases power and leverage matter. Also in both cases structures and institutions have been designed to aid the bargaining process. In international security such institutions as diplomatic missions and international organizations facilitate the bargaining process. Realists studying international security focus on political-military bargaining more than economic bargaining because they consider it more important. The economic framework is elaborated in Chapter 8.

Bargaining that takes place formally—usually at a table with back-and-forth dialogue—is called **negotiation.** Because the issues in IR are important and the actors are usually sophisticated players in a game with long-established rules and traditions, most issues of contention reach a negotiating table sooner or later. Often bargaining takes place simultaneously at the negotiating table and in the world (often on the battlefield). The participants talk in the negotiation hall while manipulating instruments of leverage outside it.

Negotiating styles vary from one culture or individual to another. In international negotiations on major political and military issues, problems of cultural difference may become serious obstacles. For example, straight-talking Americans might misunderstand negotiators from Japan, where saying "no" is rude and is therefore replaced by phrases such as "that would be difficult." A good negotiator will take time to understand the other party's culture and bargaining style, as well as its interests and available means of leverage.

[15] Lasswell, Harold D. *Politics: Who Gets What, When, How*. NY: Meridian, 1958. Starkey, Brigid, Mark A. Boyer, and Jonathan Wilkenfeld. *Negotiating a Complex World: An Introduction to International Negotiation*. 2nd ed. Lanham, MD: Rowman & Littlefield.

Strategies

Power strategies are plans actors use to develop and deploy power capabilities to achieve goals. A key aspect of strategy is choosing the kinds of capabilities to develop, given limited resources, in order to maximize international influence. This requires foresight because the capabilities required to manage a situation may need to be developed years before that situation presents itself. Yet the capabilities chosen often will not be fungible in the short term. Central to this dilemma is what kind of standing military forces to maintain in peacetime—enough to prevent a quick defeat if war breaks out, but not so much as to overburden one's economy (see pp. 214–219). Strategies also include choices about how capabilities are used in situations—sequences of actions designed for maximum effect; the creation of alliances; the use of contingency plans; and so forth. Depending on the situation, most power strategies mix economic instruments (trade, aid, loans, investment, boycotts) with military ones. (In the short term, within a given situation such plans are called *tactics*.)

Strategies include whether (and in which situations) a state is willing to use its power capabilities. For example, in the Vietnam War the United States had overall power capabilities far superior to those of the Vietnamese communists but lost the war because it was unwilling or unable to commit the resources necessary or use them effectively. The *will* of a nation or leader is hard to estimate. Even if leaders make explicit their intention to fight over an issue, they might be bluffing.

AMPLIFYING POWER

Coherent strategy can help a state to make the most of its power. China's foreign policy is generally directed toward its most important regional interests, above all preventing Taiwan's formal independence. Despite conflicts with a number of its neighbors, China has had no military engagements for 25 years. Here, China uses its veto in the UN Security Council for only the fifth time ever, to end a peacekeeping mission in Macedonia, which had just established ties with Taiwan, 1999.

The strategic actions of China in recent years exemplify the concept of strategy as rational deployment of power capabilities. China's central foreign policy goal is to prevent the independence of Taiwan, which China considers an integral part of its territory (as does the United Nations and, at least in theory, the United States). Taiwan's government was set up to represent all of China in 1949, when the nationalists took refuge there after losing to the communists in China's civil war. Since 1949, Taiwan has operated more and more independently, and many Taiwanese favor independence. China may not have the military power to invade Taiwan successfully, but it has declared repeatedly that it will go to war if Taiwan declares independence. So far, even though such a war might be irrational on China's part, the threat has deterred Taiwan from formally declaring independence. China might lose such a war, but would certainly inflict immense damage on Taiwan. In 1996, China held war games near Taiwan, firing missiles over the sea. The United States sent two aircraft carriers to signal China that its exercises must not go too far.

Not risking war by declaring independence, Taiwan instead has engaged in diplomacy to gain influence in the world. It lobbies the U.S.

Congress, asks for admission to the UN and other world organizations, and grants foreign aid to countries that recognize Taiwan's government (25 mostly small, poor countries worldwide as of 2006).

China has used its own diplomacy to counter these moves. It breaks diplomatic relations with countries that recognize Taiwan, and it punishes any moves in the direction of Taiwanese independence. Half the countries that recognize Taiwan are in the Caribbean and Central America, leading to a competition for influence in the region. China has tried to counter Taiwanese ties with those countries by manipulating various positive and negative leverages. For example, in Panama, where China is a major user of the Panama Canal (which reverted to Panama from U.S. ownership in 1999), Taiwan has cultivated close relations, invested in a container port, and suggested hiring guest workers from Panama in Taiwan. But China has implicitly threatened to restrict Panama's access to Hong Kong, or to reregister China's many Panamanian-registered ships in the Bahamas instead. (Bahamas broke with Taiwan in 1997 after a Hong Kong conglomerate, now part of China, promised to invest in a Bahamian container port.) Similarly, when the Pacific microstate of Kiribati recognized Taiwan in late 2003, to gain Taiwanese aid, China broke off relations and removed a Chinese satellite-tracking station from Kiribati. Since the tracking station played a vital role in China's military reconnaissance and growing space program—which had recently launched its first astronaut—its dismantling underscored China's determination to give Taiwan priority even at a cost to other key national goals. In 2005, China threatened to retaliate against Vanuatu for recognizing Taiwan, leading Vanuatu to reverse its decision. And in 2004 China gave more than $100 million in aid to Dominica for breaking relations with Taiwan.

Two of the five vetoes China has ever used in the UN Security Council were to block peacekeeping forces in countries that extended recognition to Taiwan. These vetoes demonstrate that if China believes its Taiwan interests are threatened, it can play a spoiler role on the Security Council. When the former Yugoslav republic of Macedonia recognized Taiwan in 1999 (in exchange for $1 billion in aid), China vetoed a UN peacekeeping mission there at a time of great instability in next-door Kosovo. By contrast, when its Taiwan interests are secure, China cooperates on issues of world order. For example, although China opposed the 1991 Gulf War, it did not veto the UN resolution authorizing it.

Chinese President's U.S. Visit

These Chinese strategies mobilize various capabilities, from missiles to diplomats to industrial conglomerates, in a coherent effort to influence the outcome of China's most important international issue. Strategy thus amplifies China's power. Similarly, during the Cold War, China used strategy to amplify power, by playing a balancer role between two superpowers and by playing up the importance of the global South, which it claimed to lead.[16]

Camp David

Some individual actors too are better than others at using their capabilities strategically. For instance, in the 1970s U.S. President Jimmy Carter used the great-power capabilities available to him, but his own strategic and interpersonal skills seem to have been the key to success in the Camp David agreements (which achieved the U.S. foreign policy goal of an Egyptian-Israeli treaty). Good strategies bring together power capabilities for maximum effect, but poor strategies make inefficient use of available capabilities. Of course, even the most skillful leader never has total control of an international situation, but can make best use of the opportunities available while minimizing the effects of bad luck.

---

[16] Rohter, Larry. Taiwan and Beijing Duel for Recognition in Central America. *The New York Times*, Aug. 5, 1997: A7. Zhao, Quansheng. *Interpreting Chinese Foreign Policy: The Micro-Macro Linkage Approach*. Oxford, 1996. Swaine, Michael and Ashley Tellis. *Interpreting China's Grand Strategy: Past, Present, and Future*. Santa Monica: Rand, 2000.

In the context of bargaining, actors use various strategies to employ leverage in an effort to move the final agreement point closer to their own positions. One common bargaining strategy is to start with extreme demands and then gradually compromise them in an effort to end up close to one's true (but concealed) position. Another strategy is to "drive a hard bargain" by sticking closely to one's original position in the belief that the other participant will eventually accept it. U.S. Secretary of State Henry Kissinger in the 1970s, however, used a policy of preemptive concessions to induce movement on the other side and get to a middle-ground agreement quickly in few steps.[17]

Another common bargaining strategy is *fractionation*—splitting up a complex issue into a number of small components so that progress may be sought on solvable pieces. For instance, the Arab-Israeli negotiations that began in 1991 had many sets of talks concurrently working on various pieces of the problem. The opposite approach, which some bargainers prefer, is to lump together diverse issues—called *linkage*—so that compromises on one can be traded off against another in a grand deal. This was the case, for instance, in the Yalta negotiations of 1945 among the United States, Britain, and the Soviet Union. On the table simultaneously were such matters as the terms of occupation of Germany, the Soviet presence in Eastern Europe, the strategy for defeating Japan, and the creation of the United Nations.

Reciprocity, Deterrence, and Arms Races

To have the best effect, strategic bargaining over IR outcomes should take into account the other actor's own goals and strategies. Only then can one predict which forms of leverage may induce the other actor to take the actions one desires. But this can be a problem: often states do not know each others' true intentions but can only observe each others' actions and statements (which may be lies).

One very effective strategy for influencing another actor whose plans are not known is **reciprocity**—a response in kind to the other's actions, often referred to as a "tit-for-tat" strategy.[18] A strategy of reciprocity uses positive forms of leverage as promises of rewards (if the actor does what one wants); simultaneously it uses negative forms of leverage as threats of punishment (if the actor does not refrain from doing what one does not want). Reciprocity is effective because it is easy to understand. After one has demonstrated one's ability and willingness to reciprocate—gaining a reputation for consistency of response—the other actor can easily calculate the costs of failing to cooperate or the benefits of cooperating.

Reciprocity can be an effective strategy for achieving cooperation in a situation of conflicting interests. If one side expresses willingness to cooperate and promises to reciprocate the other's cooperative and conflictual actions, the other side has great incentive to work out a coöperative bargain. And because reciprocity is relatively easy to interpret, the vow of future reciprocity often needs not be stated explicitly.[19] For example, in 1969 China's relations with the United States had been on ice for 20 years. A total U.S. economic embargo against China was holding back the latter's economic development.

---

[17] Kissinger, Henry. *White House Years*. Boston: Little, Brown, 1979, pp. 179–80.

[18] Keohane, Robert O. Reciprocity in International Relations. *International Organization* 40 (1), 1986: 1–27. Rock, Stephen R. *Why Peace Breaks Out: Great Power Rapprochement in Historical Perspective*. North Carolina, 1989. Downs, George W., and David M. Rocke. *Optimal Imperfection? Domestic Uncertainty and Institutions in International Relations*. Princeton, 1995.

[19] Goldstein, Joshua S., and John R. Freeman. *Three-Way Street: Strategic Reciprocity in World Politics*. Chicago: University of Chicago Press, 1990. Goldstein, Joshua S., and Jon C. Pevehouse. Reciprocity, Bullying, and International Cooperation: Time-Series Analysis of the Bosnia Conflict. *American Political Science Review* 91 (3), 1997: 515–29.

China's support of North Vietnam was costing many American lives. The two states were not on speaking terms. President Nixon (and adviser Kissinger) decided to try a signal to China in hopes of improving relations (splitting China away from North Vietnam and further away from the Soviet Union). Nixon slightly relaxed the U.S. trade embargo against China. Three days later, with no explicit connection to the U.S. move, China released three U.S. citizens whose boat had earlier drifted into Chinese waters.[20] China reciprocated other U.S. initiatives in the following months, and the two states resumed formal talks within six months. By 1972, Nixon visited China in a spirit of rapprochement.

Reciprocity can also help achieve cooperation in the sense of refraining from an undesired action. This is the intent of the strategy of **deterrence**—the threat to punish another actor if it takes a certain negative action (especially attacking one's own state or one's allies). The slogan "peace through strength" reflects this approach. If deterrence works, its effects are almost invisible; its success is measured in attacks that did not occur.[21]

Generally, advocates of deterrence believe that conflicts are more likely to escalate into war when one party to the conflict is weak. In this view, building up military capabilities usually convinces the stronger party that a resort to military leverage would not succeed, so conflicts are less likely to escalate into violence. A strategy of **compellence,** sometimes used after deterrence fails, refers to the use of force to make another actor take some action (rather than refrain from taking an action).[22] Generally it is harder to get another state to change course (the purpose of compellence) than it is to get it to refrain from changing course (the purpose of deterrence).

One strategy used to try to compel compliance by another state is *escalation*—a series of negative sanctions of increasing severity applied in order to induce another actor to take some action. In theory, the less severe actions establish credibility—showing the first actor's willingness to exert its power on the issue—and the pattern of escalation establishes the high costs of future sanctions if the second actor does not cooperate. These should induce the second actor to comply, assuming that it finds the potential costs of the escalating punishments to be greater than the costs of compliance.

Escalation

U.S. actions against Saddam prior to the Gulf War illustrate the strategy of escalation. First came statements of condemnation, then UN resolutions, then the formation of an alliance with power clearly superior to Iraq's. Next came the application of economic sanctions, then a military buildup with an implicit threat to use force, then explicit threats of force, and finally ultimatums threatening force after a specific deadline. In this case the strategy did not induce compliance, and only military defeat induced Iraq to accept U.S. terms.

Escalation can be quite dangerous. During the Cold War, many IR scholars worried that a conventional war could lead to nuclear war if the superpowers tried to apply escalation strategies. In fact, side by side with the potential for eliciting cooperation, reciprocity in general contains a danger of runaway hostility. When two sides both reciprocate but never manage to put relations on a cooperative footing, the result can be a drawn-out, nasty, tit-for-tat exchange of punishments. This characterizes Israeli relations with Palestinian militants, for instance.[23]

---

[20] Kissinger, Henry. *White House Years*. Boston: Little, Brown, 1979: 179–80.

[21] Zagare, Frank C. *Perfect Deterrence*. Cambridge, 2000. Goldstein, Avery. *Deterrence and Security in the 21st Century*. Stanford, 2000. Morgan, Patrick. *Deterrence Now*, Cambridge, 2003. Huth, Paul K. *Extended Deterrence and the Prevention of War*. Yale, 1988. Jervis, Robert, Richard Ned Lebow, and Janice Gross Stein. *Psychology and Deterrence*. Johns Hopkins, 1985. George, Alexander L., and Richard Smoke. *Deterrence in American Foreign Policy: Theory and Practice*. Columbia, 1974.

[22] Schelling, Thomas C. *The Strategy of Conflict*. Harvard, 1960.

[23] Goldstein, Joshua, Jon Pevehouse, Deborah Gerner, and Shibley Telhami. Reciprocity, Triangularity, and Cooperation in the Middle East, 1979–1997. *Journal of Conflict Resolution* 45 (5), 2001: 594–620.

An **arms race** is a reciprocal process in which two (or more) states build up military capabilities in response to each other. Since each wants to act prudently against a threat (often a bit overblown in the leaders' perceptions), the attempt to reciprocate leads to a runaway production of weapons by both sides. The mutual escalation of threats erodes confidence, reduces cooperation, and makes it more likely that a crisis (or accident) could cause one side to strike first and start a war rather than wait for the other side to strike. The arms race process was illustrated vividly in the U.S.-Soviet nuclear arms race, which created arsenals of tens of thousands of nuclear weapons on each side.[24]

Rationality

Consistent with the bargaining framework just outlined, most realists (and many nonrealists) assume that those who wield power behave as **rational actors** in their efforts to influence others.[25]

First, the assumption of rationality implies that states and other international actors can identify their interests and put priorities on various interests: A state's actions seek to advance its interests. The assumption is a simplification, because the interests of particular politicians, parties, economic sectors, or regions of a country often conflict. Yet realists assume that the exercise of power attempts to advance the **national interest**—the interests of the state itself.

But what are the interests of a state? Are they the interests of domestic groups (see Chapter 4)? The need to prevail in conflicts with other states (see Chapter 5)? The ability to cooperate with the international community for mutual benefit (see Chapter 7)? There is no simple answer. Some realists simply define the national interest as maximizing power—a debatable assumption.[26]

Second, rationality implies that actors are able to perform a **cost-benefit analysis**—calculating the costs incurred by a possible action and the benefits it is likely to bring. Applying power incurs costs and should produce commensurate gains. As in the problem of estimating power, one has to add up different dimensions in such a calculation. For instance, states presumably do not initiate wars that they expect to lose, except in cases where they stand to gain political benefits, domestic or international, that outweigh the costs of losing the war. But it is not easy to tally intangible political benefits against the tangible costs of a war. Even victory in a war may not be worth the costs paid. Rational actors can miscalculate costs and benefits, especially when using faulty information (although this does not mean they are irrational). Finally, human behavior and luck can be unpredictable.

The ancient realist Sun Tzu advised that the best general was not the most courageous or aggressive one, but the one who could coolly calculate the costs and benefits of alternative courses. The best war was a short one, in Sun Tzu's view, because wars are costly. Better yet was to take another state intact without fighting—by intimidation, deception, and the disruption of enemy alliances. Capturing an enemy army was better than fighting

---

[24] Isard, Walter, and Charles H. Anderton. Arms Race Models: A Survey and Synthesis. *Conflict Management and Peace Science* 8, 1985: 27–98. Plous, S. The Nuclear Arms Race: Prisoner's Dilemma or Perceptual Dilemma? *Journal of Peace Research* 30 (2), 1993: 163–79. Glaser, Charles. When are Arms Races Dangerous? Rational versus Suboptimal Arming. *International Security* 28 (4), 2004: 44–84.

[25] Brown, Michael E., Owen R. Cote, Sean M. Lynn-Jones, and Steven E. Miller, eds. *Rational Choice and Security Studies*. MIT, 2000. Lake, David A., and Robert Powell, eds. *Strategic Choice and International Relations*. Princeton, 1999. Fearon, James. Rationalist Explanations for War. *International Organization* 49 (3), 1995: 379–414. Friedman, Jeffrey, ed. *The Rational Choice Controversy: Economic Models of Politics Reconsidered*. Yale, 1996.

[26] Morgenthau and Thompson, *Politics Among Nations* (see footnote 5 in this chapter). Mearsheimer, John J. *The Tragedy of Great Power Politics*. NY: Norton, 2001.

THINKING THEORETICALLY

Costs and Benefits of Combating Terrorism

Conservative, revolutionary, and liberal world views all make use of cold cost-benefit calculations. When terrorists destroyed the World Trade Center, the damage seemed immeasurable, and no price seemed too high to prevent a recurrence. Yet analysts soon tallied up the damage—human deaths representing lost future income—and estimated the cost of the attack and its aftermath to be of the magnitude of $100 billion. This is a very large number, but not infinite. It roughly equals the cost of fighting the Gulf War or Iraq War, one-quarter of U.S. annual military spending, or 1 percent of the annual U.S. GDP.

A rational state, seemingly, should pay up to $100 billion annually to prevent a recurrence, or $50 billion a year to reduce the chances by half. The initial allocations of the U.S. government to fight the war on terrorism were on this level. Congress passed $29 billion in emergency funding to combat terrorism, and President Bush proposed a $45 billion increase in the annual defense budget. The funds primarily supported military and law-enforcement efforts.

However, there are other ways to spend funds. A rational actor considers a variety of options in making a cost-benefit analysis. The idea of world views (conservative, revolutionary, liberal) helps generate alternatives. From a conservative world view, the importance of national security makes cost a secondary factor. Also, the more seriously one takes the threat of weapons of mass destruction against American cities, the higher a price it would be worth paying to fight terrorism. This perspective helps explain the rapid increase in U.S. spending on national security since September 11, 2001, on the order of almost $200 billion a year including the wars in Iraq and Afghanistan, increases in the regular Pentagon budget, and homeland security spending.*

From a more revolutionary perspective, such funds could be better spent. The War Resisters' League argues: "The best way to improve our national security is to redirect money from the military and arms trade to social programs at home and massive humanitarian aid abroad." And $50 billion a year would go a long way; for example, the UN is trying to raise $7 billion for a world AIDS fund, and total U.S. foreign aid is below $10 billion a year. Now think: Which would be more likely to reduce the frequency of major terrorist attacks on the United States—more military and law enforcement to stop terrorists from succeeding, or more foreign aid to alleviate the poverty and despair that breeds terrorism? One can make a good case either way, but how you answer will strongly affect your cost-benefit calculations.

Yet another alternative—perhaps appealing from a liberal perspective—is no dramatic response at all. Of course, law enforcement and international coordination can be improved incrementally, but suppose the United States put its funds and energies elsewhere and "took the hit" from time to time as terrorists destroyed people and property? This may seem callous, but economic liberals believe in rationality and cost-benefit just as much as realists do. Money spent fighting terrorism might be more rationally used for debt reduction and tax cuts, or possibly in such areas as public health, education, or other economically productive programs. A major terrorist attack even once a year would slow the economy by just 1 percent, whereas successful economic policies could raise the growth rate by more than that amount. You will find the do-nothing option less attractive, however, if you think future terrorist attacks could be even more costly (for example, by using nuclear weapons), or more frequent.

Theories should help us clarify our thinking. Considering multiple perspectives helps avoid "blind spots." If you were trying to reduce the future incidence of major terrorist attacks, how would you allocate $200 billion per year among the three options—military campaigns and law enforcement; foreign aid and social programs; or unrelated areas such as tax cuts or health research?

*Goldstein, Joshua S. *The Real Price of War: How You Pay for the War on Terror*. New York University Press, 2004.

INTERNAL DIVISIONS

The unitary actor assumption holds that states make important decisions as though they were single individuals able to act in the national interest. In truth, factions and organizations with differing interests put conflicting pressures on state leaders. Iraq is badly split among Shi'ite, Sunni, and Kurdish factions, which could not agree on the shape of a government for months after the elections of December 2005. Here, one faction campaigns in the election. Rivalries within the Shi'ite community, and the presence of both U.S. forces and foreign jihadist fighters, further complicate Iraqi politics. With Sunni and Shi'ite militias sliding towards civil war and Kurdish regions bent on autonomy if not total independence, the very concept of Iraq as a state seemed in jeopardy in 2006.

it. If fighting was necessary, it should occur on another state's territory so the army could live off the land. Attacking cities was too destructive and thus reduced the benefits of war.

In addition to rationality, many realists make an additional assumption that the actor (usually states) exercising power is a single entity that can "think" about its actions coherently and make choices. This is called the *unitary actor* assumption, or sometimes the *strong leader* assumption, and it is used to describe the nature of states as international actors. Although useful, this simplification does not capture the complexity of how most states actually arrive at decisions (see Chapter 4).

These three assumptions about rationality and the actors in IR are simplifications that not all IR scholars accept. But realists consider these simplifications useful because they allow scholars to explain in a general way the actions of diverse actors. Power in IR has been compared with money in economics—a universal measure. In this view, just as firms compete for money in economic markets, states compete for power in the international system.[27]

Despite these criticisms of these assumptions, realists argue that rational actor models capture not all but the most important aspects of IR. These simplified models provide the foundations for a large body of IR research that represents international bargaining relationships mathematically. By accepting the limitations of the assumptions of rationality, IR scholars can build very general and abstract models of international relationships.

Game Theory

Game theory is a branch of mathematics concerned with predicting bargaining outcomes. A game is a setting in which two or more players choose among alternative moves, either once or repeatedly. Each combination of moves (by all players) results in a set of payoffs (utility) to each player. The payoffs can be tangible items such as money or any intangible items of value. Game theory aims to deduce likely outcomes (what moves players will make), given the players' preferences and the possible moves open to them. Games are sometimes called formal models.

[27] Waltz, *Theory of International Politics* (see footnote 7 in this chapter).

Game theory was first used extensively in IR in the 1950s and 1960s by scholars trying to understand U.S.-Soviet nuclear war contingencies. Moves were decisions to use nuclear weapons in certain ways, and payoffs were outcomes of the war. The use of game theory to study international interactions has become more extensive among IR scholars in recent years, especially among realists, who accept the assumptions about rationality. To analyze a game mathematically, one assumes that each player chooses a move rationally, to maximize its payoff.

Different kinds of situations are represented by different classes of games, as defined by the number of players and the structure of the payoffs. One basic distinction is between **zero-sum games,** in which one player's gain is by definition equal to the other's loss, and *non-zero-sum games*, in which it is possible for both players to gain (or lose). In a zero-sum game there is no point in communication or cooperation between the players because their interests are diametrically opposed. But in a non-zero-sum game, coordination of moves can maximize the total payoff to the players, although each may still maneuver to gain a greater share of that total payoff.

A *two-person game* has only two players; because it is simple and easy to analyze mathematically, this is the most common type of game studied. An *N-person* game has more than two players, and the moves typically result in coalitions of players, with the members of the winning coalition dividing the payoff among themselves in some manner. In most games, all the players make a move simultaneously. They may do so repeatedly, in a *repeated game* (or an *iterated game*, a *sequential game*, or a *supergame*). In a few games, the players alternate moves so each knows the other's move before deciding on its own.

Analysis of a game entails searching for a *solution* (or equilibrium)—a set of moves by all the players such that no player can increase its payoff by changing its move. It is the outcome at which rational players will arrive. Some simple games have one solution, but many games have multiple solutions.

A category of games with a given structure—in terms of the relationships between moves and payoffs—is sometimes given a name that evokes a story or metaphor representing the nature of the game. Each such game yields an insight or lesson regarding a category of international bargaining situations.[28]

The game called *Prisoner's Dilemma (PD)* is the one most commonly studied. It is a situation in which rational players will choose moves that produce an outcome in which all players are worse off than under a different set of moves. They all could do better, but as individual rational actors they are unable to achieve this outcome. How can this be?

The original story tells of two prisoners questioned separately by a prosecutor. The prosecutor knows they committed a bank robbery but has only enough evidence to convict them of illegal possession of a gun unless one of them confesses. The prosecutor tells each prisoner that if he confesses and his partner doesn't confess, he will go free. If his partner confesses and he doesn't, he will get a long prison term for bank robbery (while the partner goes free). If both confess, they will get a somewhat reduced term. If neither confesses, they will be convicted on the gun charge and serve a short sentence. The story assumes that neither prisoner will have a chance to retaliate later, that only the immediate outcomes matter, and that each prisoner cares only about himself.

This game has a single solution: both prisoners will confess. Each will reason as follows: "If my partner is going to confess, then I should confess too, because I will get a slightly

[28] O'Neill, Barry. A Survey of Game Theory Models on Peace and War. In R. Aumann and S. Hart, eds. *Handbook of Game Theory*. Vol. 2. Amsterdam: North-Holland, 1994. Powell, Robert. *In the Shadow of Power: States and Strategies in International Politics*. Princeton, 1999. Morrow, James D. *Game Theory for Political Scientists*. Princeton, 1995. Myerson, Roger B. *Game Theory: Analysis of Conflict*. Harvard, 1991.

shorter sentence that way. If my partner is not going to confess, then I should still confess because I will go free that way instead of serving a short sentence." The other prisoner follows the same reasoning. The dilemma is that by following their individually rational choices both prisoners will end up serving a fairly long sentence when they could have both served a short one by cooperating (keeping their mouths shut).

In IR, the PD game has been used to gain insight into arms races. Consider the decisions of India and Pakistan about whether to build sizable nuclear weapons arsenals. Both have the ability to do so. In 1998, when India detonated underground nuclear explosions to test weapons designs, Pakistan promptly followed suit. Neither side can know whether the other is secretly building up an arsenal, unless they reach an arms control agreement with strict verification provisions. To analyze the game, we assign values to each possible outcome—often called a *preference ordering*—for each player. This is not simple: if we misjudge the value a player puts on a particular outcome, we may draw wrong conclusions from the game.

The following preferences regarding possible outcomes are plausible: the best outcome would be that oneself but not the other player had a nuclear arsenal (the expense of building nuclear weapons would be worth it because one could then use them as leverage); second best would be for neither to go nuclear (no leverage, but no expense); third best would be for both to develop nuclear arsenals (a major expense without gaining leverage); worst would be to forgo nuclear weapons oneself while the other player developed them (and thus be subject to blackmail).

The game can be summarized in a *payoff matrix* (see Table 2.2). The first number in each cell is India's payoff, and the second number is Pakistan's. To keep things simple, 4 indicates the highest payoff, and 1 the lowest. As is conventional, a decision to refrain from building nuclear weapons is called "cooperation," and a decision to proceed with nuclear weapons is called "defection." The dilemma here parallels that of the prisoners just discussed. Each state's leader reasons: "If they go nuclear, we must; if they don't, we'd be crazy not to." The model seems to predict an inevitable Indian-Pakistani nuclear arms race, although both states would do better to avoid one. And, indeed, a costly and dangerous arms race has unfolded since this book first discussed that prediction ten years ago. Both sides now have dozens of nuclear missiles, and they nearly went to war in 2002, with estimated war deaths of up to 12 million.

The model can be made more realistic by allowing the players to play the game repeatedly; as in most IR contexts, the same actors will bargain over an issue repeatedly over a sustained time period. Game theorists have shown that in a *repeated* PD game, the possibility of reciprocity can make it rational to cooperate. Now the state leader reasons: "If we defect now, they will respond by defecting and both of us will lose; if we cooperate they might cooperate too; and if we are suckered once we can defect in the future." The keys to

TABLE 2.2 ■ Payoff Matrix in India-Pakistan PD Game

		Pakistan	
		Cooperate	Defect
India	Cooperate	(3,3)	(1,4)
	Defect	(4,1)	(2,2)

Note: First number in each group is India's payoff, second is Pakistan's. The number 4 is highest payoff, 1 lowest.

cooperation are the non-zero-sum nature of the PD game and the ability of each player to respond in the future to present moves.[29]

IR scholars have analyzed many other games beyond PD. For example, *Chicken* represents two male teenagers speeding toward a head-on collision. The first to swerve is "chicken." Each reasons: "If he doesn't swerve, I must; but if he swerves, I won't." The player who first commits irrevocably not to swerve (for example, by throwing away the steering wheel or putting on a blindfold while behind the wheel) will win. Similarly, in the 1962 Cuban Missile Crisis, some scholars argued that President John F. Kennedy "won" by seeming ready to risk nuclear war if Soviet Premier Nikita Khrushchev did not back down and remove Soviet missiles from Cuba. (There are, however, alternative explanations of the outcome of the crisis.)

Through analysis of these and other games, IR researchers try to predict what rational actors would do in various situations. Games can capture and simplify the fundamental dynamics of various bargaining situations. However, a game-theoretic analysis is only as good as the assumptions that go into it. In particular, the results of the analysis depend on the preferences that players are assumed to have about outcomes. Of course, it is difficult to know what the exact preferences of players (such as state leaders) are, since this requires intimate knowledge of a player's goals and desires.

The International System

States interact within a set of well-defined and long-established "rules of the game" governing what is considered a state and how states treat each other. Together these rules shape the international system as we know it.[30]

Anarchy and Sovereignty

Realists emphasize that the rules of the international system create **anarchy**—a term that implies not complete chaos or absence of structure and rules, but rather the lack of a central government that can enforce rules.[31] In domestic society within states, governments can enforce contracts, deter citizens from breaking rules, and use their monopoly on legally sanctioned violence to enforce a system of law. Both democracies and dictatorships provide central government enforcement of a system of rules. If a law is broken, there is a police force and courts to punish the lawbreaker. Realists contend there is no such central authority to enforce rules and ensure compliance with norms of conduct. Lack of such a central authority among states is what realists mean by anarchy. The power of one state is countered only by the power of other states. States must rely on *self-help*, which they supplement with allies and the (sometimes) constraining power of international norms.

The Bush Doctrine

[29] Snidal, Duncan. Coordination vs. Prisoner's Dilemma: Implications for International Cooperation and Regimes. *American Political Science Review* 79 (4), 1985: 923–42.

[30] Buzan, Barry, and Richard Little. *International Systems in World History: Remaking the Study of International Relations*. Oxford, 2000. Luard, Evan. *Conflict and Peace in the Modern International System: A Study of the Principles of International Order*. London: Macmillan, 1988. Wight, Martin. *Systems of States*. Leicester, 1977.

[31] Bull, Hedley. *The Anarchical Society: A Study of Order in World Politics*. Columbia, 2002 [1977]. Taylor, Michael. *Anarchy and Cooperation*. NY: Wiley, 1976. Starr, Harvey. *Anarchy, Order, and Integration: How to Manage Interdependence?* Michigan, 1997.

SOVEREIGN TERRITORY

Sovereignty and territorial integrity are central norms governing the behavior of states. They give states control within established borders. Terrorism and other recent developments challenge these norms. Here, the Coast Guard enforces U.S. sovereignty near New York, 2003.

Some people think that only a world government can solve this problem. Others think that adequate order can be provided by international organizations and agreements, short of world government (see Chapter 7). But most realists think that IR cannot escape from a state of anarchy and will continue to be dangerous as a result.[32] In this anarchic world, realists emphasize prudence as a great virtue in foreign policy. States should pay attention not to the intentions of other states but rather to their capabilities. As Sun Tzu advised, do not assume that other states will not attack but rather be ready if they do.

Despite its anarchy, the international system is far from chaotic. The great majority of state interactions closely adhere to **norms** of behavior—shared expectations about what behavior is considered proper.[33] Norms change over time, slowly, but the most basic norms of the international system have changed little in recent centuries.

WEB LINK
Sovereignty

Sovereignty—traditionally the most important norm—means that a government has the right, at least in principle, to do whatever it wants in its own territory. States are separate, are autonomous, and answer to no higher authority (due to anarchy). In principle, all states are equal in status if not in power. Sovereignty also means that states are not supposed to interfere in the internal affairs of other states. Although states do try to influence each other (exert power) on matters of trade, alliances, war, and so on, they are not supposed to meddle in the internal politics and decision processes of other states. For example, it would be inappropriate for Russia or Britain to endorse a candidate for U.S. president. (This rule is often bent in practice.)[34]

Putting together the concepts of anarchy and sovereignty illustrates a key realist concern about IR—the prospect of *enforcing* agreements. Since there is no "world police" to punish states if they break an agreement, parties to agreements will be concerned that states carry through with their obligations. The norm of sovereignty, however, can be used to forbid external "meddling" in internal affairs, making enforcement of international agreements difficult. Ultimately, states must rely on each other to allow inspections and enforcement.

---

[32] Mearsheimer. *The Tragedy of Great Power Politics* (see footnote 26 in this chapter).

[33] Franck, Thomas M. *The Power of Legitimacy Among Nations*. Oxford, 1990. Finnemore, Martha, and Kathryn Sikkink. International Norm Dynamics and Political Change. *International Organization* 52 (4), 1998: 887–917.

[34] Finnemore, Martha. *Purpose of Intervention*. Cornell, 2004. Krasner, Stephen D. *Sovereignty: Organized Hypocrisy*. Princeton, 1999. Kegley, Charles W., and Gregory A. Raymond. *Exorcising the Ghost of Westphalia: Building World Order in the New Millennium*. Prentice Hall, 2002.

For example, in the 1990s, North Korea announced it would no longer allow inspections of its nuclear facilities by other states, which put it in violation of the Non-Proliferation Treaty (NPT). The international community used a mix of positive incentives and threats to convince North Korea to stop production of nuclear material. But in 2002 North Korea withdrew from the NPT and proceeded to build perhaps a half-dozen nuclear bombs. Similarly, in 2006, Iran brushed aside world concerns and asserted its sovereign right to enrich uranium (potential nuclear bomb fuel). These examples show the difficulty of enforcing international norms in the sovereignty-based international system.

In practice, most states have a harder and harder time warding off interference in their affairs. Such "internal" matters as human rights or self-determination are, increasingly, concerns for the international community. For example, election monitors increasingly watch internal elections for signs of fraud (as in the Ukraine in 2004), while international organizations monitor ethnic conflicts for signs of genocide (as in the Sudan in 2004). Also, the integration of global economic markets and telecommunications (such as the Internet) makes it easier than ever for ideas to penetrate state borders.

States are based on territory. Respect for the territorial integrity of all states, within recognized borders, is an important principle of IR. Many of today's borders are the result of past wars (in which winners took territory from losers), or were imposed arbitrarily by third parties such as colonizers. The territorial nature of the interstate system reflects the origins of that system in an age when agrarian societies relied on agriculture to generate wealth. In today's world, where trade and technology rather than land create wealth, the territorial state may be less important. Information-based economies are linked across borders instantly, and the idea of the state as having a hard shell now seems archaic. The accelerating revolution in information technologies may dramatically affect the territorial state system in the coming years.

Cyberspace versus Sovereignty?

Membership in the international system rests on general recognition (by other states) of a government's sovereignty within its territory. This recognition is extended formally through diplomatic relations and by membership in the UN. It does not imply that a government has popular support but only that it controls the state's territory and agrees to assume its obligations in the international system—to accept internationally recognized borders, to assume the international debts of the previous government, and to refrain from interfering in other states' internal affairs.

States have developed norms of diplomacy to facilitate their interactions. An embassy is considered to be territory of the home state, not the country where it is located (see pp. 281–283). The U.S. embassy in China, for instance, harbored a wanted Chinese dissident for two years after the Tiananmen Square crackdown of 1989, and Chinese troops did not simply come in and take him away. To do so would have been a violation of U.S. territorial integrity. Yet the norms of diplomacy can be violated. In 1979, Iranian students took over the U.S. embassy in Tehran, holding many of its inhabitants hostage for 444 days.

Diplomatic norms recognize that states try to spy on each other. It is up to each state to keep others from successfully spying on it. In 2002, China discovered that its new presidential aircraft—a Boeing 767 refurbished in Texas—was riddled with sophisticated listening devices. But China did not make an issue of it (the plane had not gone into service), and a U.S.-China summit the next month went forward. In the post–Cold War era, spying continues, even between states that are not openly hostile (Russia and the United States) or are openly friendly (Israel and the United States).

Realists acknowledge that the rules of IR often create a **security dilemma**—a situation in which states' actions taken to assure their own security (such as deploying more military forces) tend to threaten the security of other states.[35] The responses of those other states (such as deploying more of their own military forces) in turn threaten the first state. The dilemma parallels the Prisoner's Dilemma game discussed earlier. It is a prime cause of arms races in which states waste large sums of money on mutually threatening weapons that do not ultimately provide security. The current debate over developing U.S. missile defenses hinges in part on whether such defenses would cause a worried China to deploy more nuclear weapons against the United States—another case of a security dilemma.

The security dilemma is a negative consequence of anarchy in the international system. Realists tend to see the dilemma as unsolvable, whereas liberals think it can be solved through the development of norms and institutions (see Chapters 3 and 7).

As we shall see in later chapters, changes in technology and in norms are undermining the traditional principles of territorial integrity and state autonomy in IR. Some IR scholars find states to be practically obsolete as the main actors in world politics, as some integrate into larger entities and others fragment into smaller units.[36] Other scholars find the international system quite enduring in its structure and state units.[37] One of its most enduring features is the balance of power.

Balance of Power

Balance of Power

In the anarchy of the international system, the most reliable brake on the power of one state is the power of other states. The term **balance of power** refers to the general concept of one or more states' power being used to balance that of another state or group of states. The term is used in several ways and is imprecisely defined. Balance of power can refer to any ratio of power capabilities between states or alliances, or it can mean only a relatively equal ratio. Alternatively, balance of power can refer to the process by which counterbalancing coalitions have repeatedly formed in history to prevent one state from conquering an entire region.[38]

The theory of balance of power argues that such counterbalancing occurs regularly and maintains the stability of the international system. The system is stable in that its rules and principles stay the same: state sovereignty does not collapse into a universal empire. This stability does not, however, imply peace; it is rather a stability maintained by means of recurring wars that adjust power relations.

Alliances (to be discussed shortly) play a key role in the balance of power. Building up one's own capabilities against a rival is a form of power balancing, but forming an alliance against a threatening state is often quicker, cheaper, and more effective. When such a counterbalancing coalition has a geopolitical element—physically hemming in the threatening state—the power-balancing strategy is called containment. In the Cold War, the United States encircled the Soviet Union with military and political alliances to prevent Soviet territorial expansion.

Sometimes a particular state deliberately becomes a balancer (in its region or the world), shifting its support to oppose whatever state or alliance is strongest at the moment.

---

[35] Herz, John. Idealist Internationalism and the Security Dilemma. *World Politics* 2 (2), 1950: 157–80. Jervis, Robert. Cooperation Under the Security Dilemma. *World Politics* 30 (2), 1978: 167–214.

[36] Aydinli, Ersel and James N. Rosenau, eds. *Globalization, Security, and the Nation State: Paradigms in Transition*. SUNY, 2005. Rosenau, James N. *Distant Proximities: Dynamics beyond Globalization*. Princeton, 2003. Ferguson, Yale H., and Richard W. Mansbach. *Polities: Authority, Identities, and Change*. South Carolina, 1996.

[37] Weiss, Linda. *The Myth of the Powerless State*. Cornell, 1998.

[38] Gulick, Edward V. *Europe's Classical Balance of Power*. Cornell, 1955. Niou, Emerson M. S., Peter C. Ordeshook, and Gregory F. Rose. *The Balance of Power: Stability and Instability in International Systems*. Cambridge, 1989. Vasquez, John, and Colin Elman, eds. *Realism and the Balance of Power: A New Debate*. Prentice Hall, 2002.

Britain played this role on the European continent for centuries, and China played it in the Cold War. But states do not always balance against the strongest actor. Sometimes smaller states "jump on the bandwagon" of the most powerful state; this has been called bandwagoning as opposed to balancing. For instance, after World War II a broad coalition did not form to contain U.S. power; rather most major states joined the U.S. bloc. States may seek to balance threats rather than raw power; U.S. power was greater than Soviet power but was less threatening to Europe and Japan (and later to China as well).[39] Furthermore, small states create variations on power-balancing themes when they play off rival great powers against each other. For instance, Cuba during the Cold War received massive Soviet subsidies by putting itself in the middle of the U.S.-Soviet rivalry.

In the post–Cold War era of U.S. dominance, balance-of-power theory would predict closer relations among Russia, China, and even France—great powers that are not close U.S. military allies. These predictions appear to be on the mark. Russian-Chinese relations have improved dramatically in such areas as arms trade and demilitarization of the border. France contested U.S. positions vigorously in global trade negotiations and discussions of NATO's command structure, and sometimes sided with Russia and China in the UN Security Council, notably before the 2003 Iraq War. French leaders have complained repeatedly of U.S. "hyperpower." Europe and Japan opposed U.S. positions on a range of proposed treaties in 2001, on such subjects as missile defense, biological weapons, small arms trade, and global warming. (Public opinion in European countries disapproved of Bush administration international policies by large majorities in mid-2001 and even larger majorities in 2003.)[40] Only the appearance of a common enemy—international terrorists—brought the great powers back together temporarily after September 2001. But the 2003 Iraq War brought back a power-balancing coalition of great powers (except Britain)—along with most other countries and world public opinion—against U.S. predominance. In 2003, as America used military force in Iraq, world public opinion revealed widespread anti-American sentiment. In Indonesia, Pakistan, Turkey, and Nigeria—containing half of all the world's Muslims—more than 70 percent worried that the United States could become a threat to their own country, a worry shared by 71 percent of Russians. In Indonesia, Pakistan, Turkey, and Jordan, less than a quarter of the population supported the U.S. war on terrorism. A survey of 38,000 people in 44 nations showed a dramatic drop in support for the United States from 2002 to 2003.

Great Powers and Middle Powers

Power, of course, varies greatly from one state to another. The *most powerful* states in the system exert most of the influence on international events and therefore get the most attention from IR scholars. By almost any measure of power, a handful of states possess the majority of the world's power resources. At most a few dozen states have any real influence beyond their immediate locality. These are called the great powers and middle powers in the international system.

Although there is no firm dividing line, **great powers** are generally considered the half dozen or so most powerful states. Until the past century the great power club was exclusively European. Sometimes great powers' status is formally recognized in an international structure such as the nineteenth-century Concert of Europe or the UN Security Council.

[39] Walt, Stephen M. *The Origins of Alliances*. Cornell, 1987. Schweller, Randall. Bandwagoning for Profit. *International Security* 19 (1), 1994: 72–107.

[40] Sweig, Julia E. *Friendly Fire: Losing Friends and Making Enemies in the Anti-American Century*. NY: Public Affairs, 2006. O'Connor, Brendon and Martin Griffiths, eds. *The Rise of Anti-Americanism*. NY: Routledge, 2006. Walt, Stephen M. *Taming American Power: The Global Response to U.S. Primacy*. NY: Norton, 2005.

CHINA RISING

Realists emphasize relative power as an explanation of war and peace. The modernization of China's military—in conjunction with China's rapidly growing economy—will increase China's power over the coming decades. Some observers fear instability in Asia if the overall balance of power among states in the region shifts rapidly. Here, China's air force, whose inventory of combat aircraft still lags in terms of techology, conducts training exercises in 2005.

In general, great powers may be distinguished by the criterion that they can be defeated militarily only by another great power. Great powers also tend to share a global outlook based on national interests far from their home territories.[41]

The great powers generally have the world's strongest military forces and the strongest economies to pay for military forces and other power capabilities. These large economies in turn rest on some combination of large populations, plentiful natural resources, advanced technology, and educated labor forces. Because power is based on these underlying resources, membership in the great-power system changes slowly. Only rarely does a great power—even one defeated in a massive war—lose its status as a great power, because its size and long-term economic potential change slowly. Thus Germany and Japan, decimated in World War II, are powerful today and Russia, after gaining and then losing the rest of the Soviet Union, is still considered a great power.

What states are great powers today? Although definitions vary, seven states appear to meet the criteria. Certainly the United States is one. In total GDP, a measure of potential power, the United States ranks highest by far at $12 trillion per year (2004 data). Because of its historical role of world leadership (especially in and after World War II), and its predominant military might, the United States is considered the world's only superpower.[42]

China, with a total GDP exceeding $7 trillion, is or soon will be the world's second largest economy. China's GDP is especially hard to estimate, and another method would put it below $2 trillion. In any case, China's sheer size (more than 1 billion people) and its rapid economic growth (8–10 percent annually since the 1990s) make it a powerful state. China has a large but not a very modern military, and its orientation is regional rather than global. But, with a credible nuclear arsenal and a seat on the UN Security Council, China qualifies as a great power. It is expected to play a central role in world politics in the twenty-first century. Japan ranks third (or perhaps second), with a GDP of nearly $4 trillion. Along with Germany (over $2 trillion GDP), Japan is an economic great power, but both countries' military roles in international security affairs have been curtailed since World War II. Nonetheless, both Japan and Germany have very large and capable military forces, and recently both have begun using military forces beyond their own territories.

Russia, even after the breakup of the Soviet Union, has a GDP above $1 trillion—again a hard one to estimate—and very large (though rundown) military forces including a massive nuclear arsenal. France and Britain finish out the list, each nearing $2 trillion

[41] Levy, Jack S. *War in the Modern Great Power System, 1495–1975*. Kentucky, 1983.

[42] Perito, Robert M. *Where Is the Lone Ranger When We Need Him? America's Search for a Postconflict Stability Force*. Herndon, VA: United States Institute of Peace Press, 2004.

GDP each. With Russia, they were winners in World War II and have been active military powers since then. Although much reduced in stature from their colonial heydays, they still qualify as great powers by most standards.

The great powers thus include the five permanent members of the UN Security Council: the United States, Russia, France, Britain, and China. The same five states are also the members of the "club" possessing large nuclear weapons arsenals (there are also several recent smaller-scale nuclear states). In world political and economic affairs, Germany and Japan are also great powers (they would like Security Council seats, too; see p. 264).

These seven great powers account for about half of the world's total GDP—and hence, presumably, about half of the total power in the world. This concentration of power is especially strong in practice because the remaining half of the world's power is split up among nearly 200 other states (see Figure 2.1).

The slow change in great-power status is evident. Britain and France have been great powers for 500 years, Russia and Germany for more than 250 years, the United States and Japan for about 100 years, and China for 50 years. Only six other states were ever (but no longer are) considered great powers: Italy, Austria (Austria-Hungary), Spain, Turkey (the Ottoman Empire), Sweden, and the Netherlands.

Middle powers rank somewhat below the great powers in terms of their influence on world affairs. Some are large but not highly industrialized; others have specialized capabilities but are small. Some aspire to regional dominance, and many have considerable influence in their regions.

A list of middle powers (not everyone would agree on it) might include states such as Canada, Italy, India, Brazil, Mexico, South Korea, Australia, Iran, and Turkey. Middle powers have not received as much attention in IR as have great powers. These states do, however, often come into play in the specific regional conflicts that dominate the day-to-day flow of

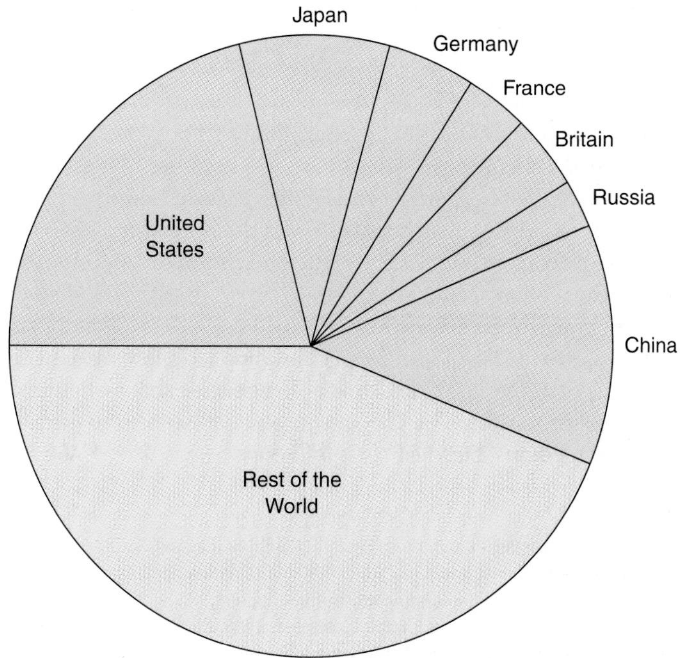

FIGURE 2.1 ■ Great Power Shares of World GDP, 2004 (purchasing-power method)

international news.[43] Smaller, weaker states (not even of middle-power strength) also are often at the center of specific conflicts and crises. But their own actions have only minor influence on world politics; the actions of great powers and middle powers in those conflicts and crises have more impact.

Power Distribution

With each state's power balanced by other states, the most important characteristic of an international system in the view of many realists is the *distribution* of power among states in an international system. Power distribution as a concept can apply to all the states in the world or to just one region, but most often it refers to the great-power system (with most of the world's total power capabilities).

Neorealists (so called because they have adopted and refined realism) try to explain patterns of international events in terms of the system structure—the international distribution of power—rather than the internal makeup of individual states.[44] **Neorealism** is thus also called structural realism. Neorealists often use game theory and related models in such analyses.[45] Compared to traditional realism, neorealism is more scientific in the sense of proposing general laws to explain events, but neorealism has lost some of the richness of traditional realists who took account of many complex elements (geography, willpower, diplomacy, etc.).

Sometimes an international power distribution (world or regional) is described in terms of polarity (a term adopted from physics), which refers to the number of independent power centers in the system. This concept encompasses both the underlying power of various participants and their alliance groupings.

In a **multipolar system** there are typically five or six centers of power, which are not grouped into alliances. Each state participates independently and on relatively equal terms with the others. They may form a coalition of the whole for mutual security through coordination of efforts. Some IR researchers think that multipolarity provides a context for smooth interaction. There are always enough actors present to prevent one from predominating. But to other IR scholars a multipolar system is particularly dangerous, lacking the discipline that predominant states or alliance blocs impose. In a sense, both are correct: in the classical multipolar balance of power, the great-power system itself was stable but wars were frequently used as power-adjusting mechanisms.

At the other extreme, a unipolar system has a single center of power around which all others revolve. This is called hegemony, and will be discussed shortly. The predominance of a single state tends to reduce the incidence of war; the hegemonic state performs some of the functions of a government, somewhat reducing anarchy in the international system.

A bipolar system has two predominant states or two great rival alliance blocs. Tight bipolar systems, such as the East-West standoff in the 1950s, may be distinguished from looser ones such as those that developed when China and (to a lesser extent) France split off from their alliance blocs in the 1960s. IR scholars do not agree about whether bipolar systems are relatively peaceful or warlike. The U.S.-Soviet standoff seemed to provide stability and peace to great-power relations, but rival blocs in Europe before World War I did not.

---

[43] Cohen, Stephen P. *India: Emerging Power*. Washington, DC: Brookings, 2001. Otte, Max. *A Rising Middle Power? German Foreign Policy in Transformation, 1989–1999*. NY: Palgrave, 2000.

[44] Waltz, *Theory of International Politics* (see footnote 7 in this chapter).

[45] Keohane, Robert O., ed. *Neorealism and Its Critics*. Columbia, 1986. Buzan, Barry, Charles Jones, and Richard Little. *The Logic of Anarchy: Neorealism to Structural Realism*. Columbia, 1993. Vasquez, John. The Realist Paradigm and Degenerative versus Progressive Research Programs: An Appraisal of Neotraditional Research on Waltz's Balancing Proposition. *American Political Science Review* 91 (4), 1997: 899–912.

In a tripolar system there are three great centers of power. Such a configuration is fairly rare; there is a tendency for a two-against-one alliance to form. Aspects of tripolarity can be found in the "strategic triangle" of the United States, the Soviet Union, and China during the 1960s and 1970s.[46] Some scholars imagine that in the coming decades a tripolar world will emerge, with rival power centers in North America, Europe, and East Asia.

These various polarities can be conceptualized as a pyramid or hierarchy of power in an international system. At the top is the most powerful state, with other great powers and middle powers arrayed below. Such a pyramid is similar to the dominance (or status) hierarchies that many animals use to regulate access to valuable resources such as food. (We often call this a "pecking order.") A multipolar system, then, is one with a relatively flat pyramid—relative equality of status among actors. A unipolar system has a relatively steep pyramid with unequal status. The steepness of the pyramid represents the concentration of power in the international system.

Status Hierarchies in IR

Some IR scholars have argued that peace is best preserved by a relatively equal power distribution (multipolarity) because then no country has an opportunity to win easily. The empirical evidence for this theory, however, is not strong. The opposite proposition has more support: peace is best preserved by hegemony, and next best by bipolarity.

Such is the thrust of power transition theory.[47] This theory holds that the largest wars result from challenges to the top position in the status hierarchy, when a rising power is surpassing (or threatening to surpass) the most powerful state. At such times, power is relatively equally distributed, and these are the most dangerous times for major wars. Status quo powers that are doing well under the old rules will try to maintain them, whereas challengers that feel locked out by the old rules may try to change them.[48] Status disequilibrium refers to a difference between a rising power's status (formal position in the hierarchy) and its actual power. In such a situation, the rising power may suffer from relative deprivation—the feeling that it is not doing as well as others or as well as it deserves, even though its position may be improving in absolute terms. The classic example is Germany's rise in the nineteenth century, which gave it great-power capabilities even though it was left out of colonial territories and other signs of status.

If the challenger does not start a war to displace the top power, the latter may provoke a "preventive" war to stop the rise of the challenger before it becomes too great a threat.[49] Germany's intensive arms race with Britain (the top power) led to increasing hostility and the outbreak of World War I. After the war there was again a disparity between Germany's actual power (still considerable) and its harsh treatment under the terms of the Versailles Treaty. That disparity may have contributed to World War II.

According to power transition theory, then, peace among great powers results when one state is firmly in the top position, and the positions of others in the hierarchy are clearly defined and correspond with their actual underlying power. Such a situation usually results only from a great war, when one state predominates in power because its rivals and allies alike have been drained. Even then, the different rates of growth among great powers lead to a slow equalization of power and eventually the emergence of challengers: the system becomes more multipolar.

---

[46] Schweller, Randall. *Deadly Imbalances: Tripolarity and Hitler's Strategy of World Conquest*. Columbia, 1998.

[47] Organski, A. F. K. *World Politics*. NY: Knopf, 1958. Organski, A. F. K., and Jacek Kugler. *The War Ledger*. Chicago, 1980. Kugler, Jacek, and Douglas Lemke, eds. *Parity and War: Evaluations and Extensions of the War Ledger*. Michigan, 1996.

[48] Mansfield, Edward D. The Concentration of Capabilities and the Onset of War. *Journal of Conflict Resolution* 36 (1), 1992: 3–24. Thompson, William R., and Karen Rasler. War and Systemic Capability Reconcentration. *Journal of Conflict Resolution* 32 (2), 1988: 335–66. Doran, Charles F. *Systems in Crisis: New Imperatives of High Politics at Century's End*. Cambridge, 1991.

[49] Levy, Jack S. Declining Power and the Preventive Motivation for War. *World Politics* 40 (1), 1987: 82–107.

Hegemony

Hegemony is the holding by one state of a preponderance of power in the international system, so that it can single-handedly dominate the rules and arrangements by which international political and economic relations are conducted.[50] Such a state is called a *hegemon*. (Usually hegemony means domination of the world, but sometimes it refers to regional domination.) The Italian Marxist theorist Antonio Gramsci used the term hegemony to refer to the complex of *ideas* that rulers use to gain consent for their legitimacy and keep subjects in line, reducing the need to use force to accomplish the same goal.[51] By extension, such a meaning in IR refers to the hegemony of ideas such as democracy and capitalism, and to the global predominance of U.S. culture (see pp. 400–402).

Most studies of hegemony point to two examples: Britain in the nineteenth century and the United States after World War II. Britain's predominance followed the defeat of its archrival France in the Napoleonic Wars. Both world trade and naval capabilities were firmly in British hands, as "Britannia ruled the waves." U.S. predominance followed the defeat of Germany and Japan (and the exhaustion of the Soviet Union, France, Britain, and China in the effort). In the late 1940s, the U.S. GDP was more than half the world's total; U.S. vessels carried the majority of the world's shipping; the U.S. military could single-handedly defeat any other state or combination of states; and only the United States had nuclear weapons. U.S. industry led the world in technology and productivity, and U.S. citizens enjoyed the world's highest standard of living.

As the extreme power disparities resulting from major wars slowly diminish (states rebuild over years and decades), hegemonic decline may occur, particularly when hegemons have overextended themselves with costly military commitments. IR scholars do not agree about how far or fast U.S. hegemonic decline has proceeded, if at all, and whether international instability will result from such a decline.[52] And beyond the U.S. and British cases, IR scholars do not agree on which historical cases were instances of hegemony. Some see the Netherlands in the early seventeenth century, or Spain in the sixteenth, as cases of hegemony.

The theory of hegemonic stability (see pp. 105–106) holds that hegemony provides some order similar to a central government in the international system: reducing anarchy, deterring aggression, promoting free trade, and providing a hard currency that can be used as a world standard. Hegemons can help to resolve or at least keep in check conflicts among middle powers or small states.

From the perspective of less powerful states, of course, such hegemony may seem an infringement of state sovereignty, and the order it creates may seem unjust or illegitimate. For instance, China chafed under U.S.-imposed economic sanctions for 20 years after 1949, feeling itself encircled by U.S. military bases and hostile alliances led by the United States. To this day, Chinese leaders use the term *hegemony* as an insult, and the theory of hegemonic stability does not impress them.

---

[50] Kapstein, Ethan B., and Michael Mastanduno. *Unipolar Politics*. Columbia, 1999. Rupert, Mark. *Producing Hegemony: The Politics of Mass Production and American Global Power*. Cambridge, 1995. Nye, Joseph S. *Paradox of American Power: Why the World's Only Superpower Can't Go it Alone*. Oxford, 2002.

[51] Gramsci, Antonio. *The Modern Prince and Other Writings*. NY: International Publishers, 1959. Gill, Stephen, ed. *Gramsci, Historical Materialism and International Relations*. Cambridge, 1993.

[52] Kennedy, Paul. *The Rise and Fall of the Great Powers: Economic Change and Military Conflict from 1500–2000*. NY: Random House, 1987. Posen, Barry R. Command of the Commons: The Military Foundations of U.S. Hegemony. *International Security* 28 (1), 2003: 5–46. Ikenberry, G. John, ed. *America Unrivaled: The Future of the Balance of Power*. Cornell, 2002.

Even in the United States itself there is considerable ambivalence about U.S. hegemony. U.S. foreign policy has historically alternated between *internationalist* and *isolationist* moods.[53] It was founded as a breakaway from the European-based international system, and its growth in the nineteenth century was based on industrialization and expansion within North America. The United States acquired overseas colonies in the Philippines and Puerto Rico but did not relish a role as an imperial power. In World War I, the country waited three years to weigh in and refused to join the League of Nations afterward. U.S. isolationism peaked in the late 1930s when polls showed 95 percent of the public opposed to participation in a future European war, and about 70 percent against joining the League of Nations or joining with other nations to stop aggression.[54]

Internationalists, such as Presidents Theodore Roosevelt and Woodrow Wilson, favored U.S. leadership and activism in world affairs. These views seemed vindicated by the failure of isolationism to prevent or avoid World War II. U.S. leaders after the war feared Soviet (and then Chinese) communism and pushed U.S. public opinion towards a strong internationalism during the Cold War. The United States became an activist, global superpower. In the post–Cold War era, U.S. internationalism was tempered by a new cost consciousness, and by the emergence of a new isolationist camp born in reaction to the displacements caused by globalization and free trade.[55] However, the terrorist attacks of September 2001 renewed public support for U.S. interventionism in distant conflicts that no longer seemed so distant. Recently, though, opposition to the Iraq war spurred a new isolationist trend, manifest in the outcry in 2006 against a proposed sale of some U.S. port operations to an Arab-owned company from Dubai.

A second area of U.S. ambivalence is *unilateralism* versus *multilateralism* in U.S. internationalism. Multilateral approaches—working through international institutions—augment U.S. power and reduce costs, but they limit U.S. freedom of action. For example, the United States cannot always get the UN to do what it wants. Polls in the 1990s showed that a majority of U.S. citizens supported working through the UN

PRICE OF HEGEMONY

The United States is the world's most powerful single actor. Its ability and willingness to resume a role as hegemon—as after World War II—are important factors that will shape world order, but the U.S. role is still uncertain. America's willingness to absorb casualties will affect its role. Here, soldiers return from Afghanistan, 2004.

[53] Zakaria, Fareed. *From Wealth to Power: The Unusual Origins of America's World Role*. Princeton, 1998. Holsti, Ole R. Public Opinion and Foreign Policy: Challenges to the Almond-Lippmann Consensus. *International Studies Quarterly* 36 (4), 1992: 439–66.

[54] Free, Lloyd A., and Hadley Cantril. *The Political Beliefs of Americans*. Rutgers, 1967.

[55] Brown, Michael E., Owen R. Cote, Jr., Sean M. Lynn-Jones, and Steven E. Miller, eds. *America's Strategic Choices* (revised edition). MIT, 2000. Haass, Richard N. *The Reluctant Sheriff: The United States After the Cold War*. Washington, DC: Brookings, 1997. Ruggie, John G. *Winning the Peace*. Columbia, 1996. Lieber, Robert J. *Eagle Rules? Foreign Policy and American Primacy in the 21st Century*. Prentice Hall, 2002.

and other multilateral institutions.[56] However, members of the U.S. Congress, skeptical of the UN and international agencies, often favored a more unilateralist approach, in which the United States dictated terms and expected the world to comply. In the 1990s, Congress slipped more than $1 billion behind in paying U.S. dues to the UN. Similarly, in the late 1990s Congress passed the *Helms-Burton Act,* which provides for sanctions against countries that do business in Cuba, and the *Iran-Libya Sanctions Act,* which imposes sanctions on countries that invest in Iran or Libya. These unilateralist U.S. policies were resisted by European states and Canada. In 2001, the new Bush Administration declined to participate in such international efforts as a treaty on global warming (see pp. 418–419), a conference on racism, and an International Criminal Court (see p. 284). The international community's united front against terrorism pushed these disputes to the back burner, but they soon reemerged.

A third aspect of ambivalent U.S. hegemony is that of *morality* versus *realism*. Should the United States be a moral guiding light for the world—pursuing goals such as democracy and human rights—or should it concentrate on its own national interests, such as natural resources and geostrategic position? Most U.S. citizens do not want to be "the world's policeman," and some resent paying for the security of allies such as Japan and Europe. After the collapse of the Soviet Union, efforts to win congressional approval of foreign aid for Russia had to be couched in terms of U.S. interests (avoiding a return to costly Russian aggression), not humanitarian assistance or a moral obligation to help a nation achieve freedom and democracy. Yet the U.S. people also think of themselves as a caring nation and a beacon of hope for the world. Presidents continue to say things such as "where people are hungry, we will help. We are the United States!"[57]

Alliances

An *alliance* is a coalition of states that coordinate their actions to accomplish some end. Most alliances are *formalized* in written treaties, concern a *common threat* and related issues of international security, and *endure* across a range of issues and a period of time. If actors' purposes in banding together were shorter-term, less formal, or more issue-specific (such as the occupation of Iraq), the association is usually called a *coalition* rather than an alliance. Informal but enduring strategic *alignments* in a region are discussed shortly. But all these terms are somewhat ambiguous. Two countries may have a formal alliance and yet be bitter enemies, such as the Soviet Union and China in the 1960s or NATO members Greece and Turkey today. Or, two countries may create the practical equivalent of an alliance without a formal treaty.

Purposes of Alliances

Alliances generally have the purpose of augmenting their members' power relative to other states. By pooling their power capabilities, two or more states can exert greater leverage in their bargaining with other states. For smaller states, alliances can be their most important power element, and for great powers the structure of alliances shapes the con-

---

[56] Kull, Steven, and I. M. Destler. *Misreading the Public: The Myth of a New Isolationism*. Washington, DC: Brookings, 1999.

[57] President George Bush, June 1992, speech on Sarajevo. Ferguson, Niall. *Colossus: The Price of America's Empire*. NY: Penguin, 2004. Daalder, Ivo H. and James M. Lindsay. *America Unbound: The Bush Revolution in Foreign Policy*. NY: Wiley, 2005.

figuration of power in the system. Of all the elements of power, none can change as quickly and decisively as alliances.

Most alliances form in response to a perceived threat. When a state's power grows and threatens to overmatch that of its rivals, the latter often form an alliance to limit that power. Thucydides attributed the outbreak of the Peloponnesian Wars more than 2,000 years ago to the growing power of Athens, and to the fear that caused in Sparta. Sparta turned to its neighbors in the Peloponnesian League, and that alliance managed to defeat Athens.

Alliances are an important component of the balance of power. Except in the rare circumstance of hegemony, every state is weaker than some combination of other states. If states overstep norms of international conduct they may face a powerful alliance of opposing states. This happened to Iraq when it invaded Kuwait in 1990, as it had to Hitler's Germany in the 1940s and to Napoleon's France in the 1800s.

MARRIAGE OF CONVENIENCE

Alliances generally result from a convergence of practical interests, not sentimental or ideological reasons. Here, a U.S. general gets rival Afghan warlords to patch up relations, 2002.

Realists emphasize the fluidity of alliances. They are not marriages of love, but marriages of convenience. Alliances are based on national interests, and can shift as national interests change. This fluidity helps the balance-of-power process to operate effectively.

Still, it is not simple or costless to break an alliance: one's reputation may suffer and future alliances may be harder to establish. There is an important norm that says that written treaties should be honored—in Latin, *pacta sunt servanda*. So states often do adhere to alliance terms even when it is not in their short-term interest to do so. Nonetheless, recall that because of the nature of international anarchy, there is no mechanism to enforce contracts in IR, so the possibility of turning against a friend is always present. Realists would agree with the British statesman Lord Palmerston, who told Parliament in 1848 that "We have no eternal allies and we have no perpetual enemies. Our interests are perpetual and eternal and those interests it is our duty to follow." French president Charles de Gaulle said in 1963, "Treaties are like roses and young girls. They last while they last."[58]

Examples are many. Anticommunist Richard Nixon could cooperate with communist Mao Zedong in 1972. Joseph Stalin could sign a nonaggression pact with a fascist, Adolph Hitler, and then cooperate with the capitalist West against Hitler. The United States could back the Islamic militants in Afghanistan against the Soviet Union in the 1980s, then attack them in 2001. Every time history brings another such reversal in international alignments, many people are surprised or even shocked. Realists are not so surprised.

[58] Remarks in the House of Commons, March 1, 1848; *Time*, July 12, 1963.

The fluidity of alliances deepens the security dilemma. Recall that the dilemma is that one state's efforts to ensure its own security (building up military capabilities) reduce the security of another state. If there were only two states, it would be possible to match capabilities so that both have adequate defense but cannot attack. But if a third state is free to ally with either side, then each state has to build adequate defenses against the potential alliance of its enemy with the third state. The threat is greater and the security dilemma is harder to escape.

The nightmare of being overpowered looms large when a state faces a potential hostile alliance that could form overnight. For example, in a war Israel alone could defeat any of its neighbors. But Israeli leaders believe they must arm against the worst contingency—an attack by all their neighbors together. Because the neighbors are not very aligned (and the most important, Egypt and Jordan, are at peace with Israel), Israel's military capabilities appear excessive to those neighbors, deepening the security dilemma between these states.

Alliance cohesion is the ease with which the members hold together an alliance.[59] Cohesion tends to be high when national interests converge and when cooperation within the alliance becomes institutionalized and habitual. When states with divergent interests form an alliance against a common enemy, the alliance may come apart if the threat subsides (as with the U.S.-Soviet alliance in World War II, for instance). Even when alliance cohesion is high, as in NATO during the Cold War, conflicts may arise over who bears the costs of the alliance (**burden sharing**).[60]

The credibility with which an alliance can deter an enemy depends on the alliance's cohesion as well as its total power capabilities. If an alliance is successful at displaying a common front and taking a unified line on issues, a potential enemy is more likely to believe that members will honor their alliance commitments (such as their promise to fight if an ally is attacked). An enemy may try to split the alliance by finding issues on which the interests of the members diverge. For instance, the United States subtly encouraged the Sino-Soviet split, and the Soviet Union subtly tried to turn European members of NATO away from the United States.

Great powers often form alliances with smaller states, sometimes called client states.[61] In the Cold War, each superpower extended a security umbrella over its allies. The issue of credibility in such an alliance is whether (and under what circumstances) the great power will assist its clients in a war. Extended deterrence refers to a strong state's use of threats to deter attacks on weaker clients—such as the U.S. threat to attack the Soviet Union if it invaded Western Europe.

Great powers face a real danger of being dragged into wars with each other over relatively unimportant regional issues if their respective clients go to war. If the great powers do not come to their clients' protection, they may lose credibility with other clients, but if they do, they may end up fighting a costly war.[62] The Soviet Union worried that its commitments to China in the 1950s, to Cuba in the 1960s, and to Syria and Egypt in the 1970s (among others) could result in a disastrous war with the United States.

---

[59] Kegley, Charles W., and Gregory A. Raymond. *When Trust Breaks Down: Alliance Norms and World Politics*. South Carolina, 1990. Martin, Pierre and Mark R. Brawley, eds. *Alliance Politics, Kosovo, and NATO's War: Allied Force or Forced Allies?* NY: Palgrave, 2000.

[60] Oneal, John R. The Theory of Collective Action and Burden Sharing in NATO. *International Organization* 44 (3), 1990: 379–402. Sandler, Todd and Keith Hartley. *The Political Economy of NATO: Past, Present, and into the 21st Century*. Cambridge, 1999.

[61] David, Steven R. *Choosing Sides: Alignment and Realignment in the Third World*. Johns Hopkins, 1991.

[62] Snyder, Glenn H. *Alliance Politics*. Cornell, 1997. Leeds, Brett Ashley. Do Alliances Deter Aggression? The Influence of Military Alliances on the Initiation of Militarized Interstate Disputes. *American Journal of Political Science* 47 (3), 2003: 427–40.

NATO and the U.S.-Japanese Security Treaty

NATO

At present, two important formal alliances dominate the international security scene. By far the more powerful is the **North Atlantic Treaty Organization (NATO),** which encompasses Western Europe and North America. Using GDP as a measure of power, the 26 NATO members possess nearly half the world total (roughly twice the power of the United States alone). Members are the United States, Canada, Britain, France, Germany, Italy, Belgium, the Netherlands, Luxembourg, Denmark, Norway, Iceland, Spain, Portugal, Greece, Turkey, Poland, the Czech Republic, Hungary, Lithuania, Estonia, Latvia, Slovenia, Slovakia, Bulgaria, and Romania. At NATO headquarters in Brussels, Belgium, military staffs from the member countries coordinate plans and periodically direct exercises in the field. The NATO "allied supreme commander" has always been a U.S. general. In NATO, each state contributes its own military units—with its own national culture, language, and equipment specifications.

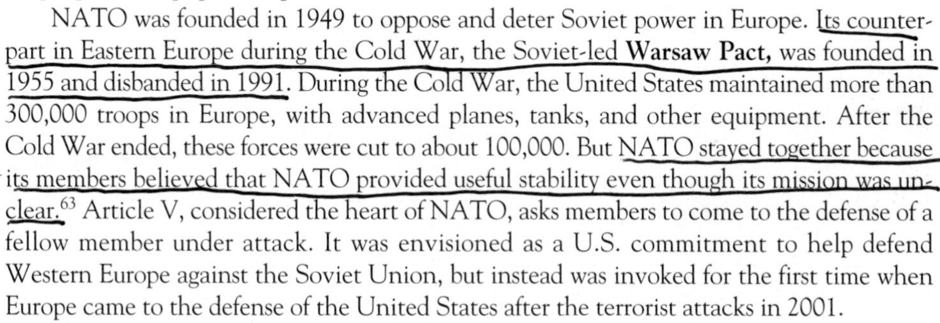

NATO was founded in 1949 to oppose and deter Soviet power in Europe. Its counterpart in Eastern Europe during the Cold War, the Soviet-led **Warsaw Pact,** was founded in 1955 and disbanded in 1991. During the Cold War, the United States maintained more than 300,000 troops in Europe, with advanced planes, tanks, and other equipment. After the Cold War ended, these forces were cut to about 100,000. But NATO stayed together because its members believed that NATO provided useful stability even though its mission was unclear.[63] Article V, considered the heart of NATO, asks members to come to the defense of a fellow member under attack. It was envisioned as a U.S. commitment to help defend Western Europe against the Soviet Union, but instead was invoked for the first time when Europe came to the defense of the United States after the terrorist attacks in 2001.

The first actual use of force by NATO was in Bosnia in 1994, in support of the UN mission there. A "dual key" arrangement gave the UN control of NATO's actions in Bosnia, and the UN feared retaliation against its lightly armed peacekeepers if NATO attacked the Serbian forces to protect Bosnian civilians. As a result, NATO made threats, underlined by symbolic airstrikes, but then backed down after UN qualms; this waffling undermined NATO credibility. More extensive NATO airstrikes in 1995, however, alarmed Russian leaders who were already concerned by NATO's expansion plans. These problems, along with tensions between the American and European NATO members over Bosnia policy, dogged the first major NATO mission of the post–Cold War era. Later NATO actions in the Balkans (the air war for Kosovo in 1999 and peacekeeping in Macedonia in 2001) went more smoothly in terms of alliance cohesion.

The European Union has formed its own rapid deployment force, outside NATO. The decision grew in part from European military weaknesses demonstrated in the 1999 Kosovo war, in which the United States contributed the most power by far. Although this Eurocorps generally works *with* NATO, it also gives Europe more independence from the United States. In 2003, the European Union sent military forces as peacekeepers to Democratic Congo—the first multinational European military operation to occur outside NATO. In 2004, NATO and U.S. forces withdrew from Bosnia after nine years, turning over peacekeeping there to the European Union (as they had in Macedonia). But NATO forces including U.S. soldiers remain next door in Kosovo.

The biggest issue for NATO is its recent eastward expansion, beyond the East-West Cold War dividing line. In 1999, former Soviet-bloc countries Poland, the Czech Republic, and Hungary joined the alliance. Joining in 2004 were Estonia, Latvia, Lithuania,

---

[63] Yost, David S. *NATO Transformed: The Alliance's New Roles in International Security*. Washington, DC: U.S. Institute of Peace Press, 1999. Goldgeier, James M. *Not Whether But When: The Decision to Enlarge NATO*. Washington, DC: Brookings, 1999. Wallander, Celeste. Institutional Assets and Adaptability: NATO After the Cold War. *International Organization* 54 (4), 2000: 705–35.

ALLIANCE OF THE STRONG

The NATO alliance has been the world's strongest military force since 1949; its mission in the post–Cold War era is somewhat uncertain. Here, President Kennedy reviews U.S. forces in Germany, 1963.

Slovakia, Slovenia, Romania, and Bulgaria. Making the new members' militaries compatible with NATO is a major undertaking, requiring increased military spending by existing and new NATO members. NATO expansion was justified by liberals as a way to solidify new democracies while keeping Europe peaceful, and by conservatives as protection against possible future Russian aggression. NATO forces have participated in the war in Afghanistan, but the 2003 Iraq War bypassed and divided NATO members. France and Germany strongly opposed the war, and Turkey refused to let U.S. ground forces cross into Iraq. At the same time, U.S. leaders began shifting some operations (and money) to new members in Eastern Europe such as Romania—with lower prices and a location closer to the Middle East—while drawing down forces based in Germany.

Russian leaders oppose NATO's expansion into Eastern Europe as aggressive and anti-Russian. They view NATO expansion as reasserting dividing lines on the map of Europe, but pushed closer to Russia's borders. These fears strengthen nationalist and anti-Western political forces in Russia. To mitigate the problems, NATO created a category of symbolic membership—the Partnership for Peace—which almost all Eastern European and former Soviet states including Russia joined. However, the 1999 NATO bombing of Serbia heightened Russian fears regarding NATO's eastward expansion.[64]

The second most important alliance is the **U.S.-Japanese Security Treaty,** a bilateral alliance. Under this alliance the United States maintains nearly 50,000 troops in Japan (with weapons, equipment, and logistical support). Japan pays the United States several billion dollars annually to offset about half the cost of maintaining these troops. The alliance was created in 1951 (during the Korean War) against the potential Soviet threat to Japan.

Because of its roots in the U.S. military occupation of Japan after World War II, the alliance is very asymmetrical. The United States is committed to defend Japan if it is attacked, but Japan is not similarly obligated to defend the United States. The United States maintains troops in Japan, but not vice versa. The United States belongs to several other alliances, but Japan's only major alliance is with the United States. The U.S. share of the total military power in this alliance is also far greater than its share in NATO.

Japan's constitution (written by U.S. General Douglas MacArthur after World War II) renounces the right to make war and maintain military forces, although interpretation has loosened this prohibition over time. Japan maintains military forces, called the Self-Defense Forces, strong enough for territorial defense but not for aggression. It is a powerful

[64] Moens, Alexander, et al., eds. *NATO and European Security: Alliance Politics from the End of the Cold War to the Age of Terrorism*. Westport, CT: Praeger, 2003.

NATO Expansion

army by world standards but much smaller than Japan's economic strength could support. Japanese public opinion restrains militarism in general and precludes the development of nuclear weapons in particular after Japanese cities were destroyed by nuclear weapons in World War II.

Japan is as dependent as ever on natural resources from foreign countries, but Japanese leaders generally believe that economic and diplomatic (rather than military) capabilities can best assure a smooth flow of resources to Japan and export markets for Japanese goods. The security alliance with the United States—Japan's largest trading partner—provides a stable security framework conducive to business. Japan need not worry that in a dispute over trade barriers the U.S. Navy will arrive to pry Japan's doors open (as it did in 1854). Nonetheless, some Japanese leaders believe that Japan's formal security role should now expand commensurate with its economic power. Japanese troops participated in Afghanistan in 2001 and Iraq in 2004 (though not in combat roles), and Japan seeks a seat on the UN Security Council. The UN in turn is pressing Japan to participate fully in peacekeeping missions.

For its part, the United States has used the alliance with Japan as a base to project U.S. power in Asia, especially during the wars in Korea (1950–1953) and Vietnam (1965–1975) when Japan was a key staging area for U.S. war efforts. The continued U.S. military presence in Japan (as in Europe) symbolizes the U.S. commitment to remain engaged in Asian security affairs. However, these U.S. forces have been drawn down somewhat in the past decade in response to high costs, reduced threats, and some opposition by local residents (especially on Okinawa island). As the U.S. begins to focus more on the Middle East, more cuts in troops could follow in the coming years.[65]

Parallel with the U.S.-Japan treaty, the United States maintains military alliances with several other states, including South Korea and Australia. Close U.S. collaboration with militaries in other states such as Pakistan make them de facto U.S. allies.

The Former Soviet Republics

The 12 members of the *Commonwealth of Independent States (CIS)* comprise the former Soviet republics except the Baltic states (Estonia, Latvia, and Lithuania). Russia is the leading member and Ukraine the second largest. Officially, CIS headquarters is in the city of Minsk, in Belarus, but in practice there is no strong center and meetings rotate around. After its first decade, the CIS remains a loose coordinating institution for states to solve practical problems in economic and (sometimes) military spheres.

When the Soviet Union disintegrated in 1991, a chaotic situation emerged. Power for several years had been shifting from the center in Moscow to the 15 constituent Soviet republics. The Warsaw Pact had collapsed. The Soviet army itself began to break up, and several republics began forming their own military forces using Soviet forces, bases, and equipment located on their territories. At the same time, other former Soviet forces located outside Russia remained in a chain of command centered in Moscow, effectively under Russian control. Until 1997, Russia and Ukraine debated ownership of the Black Sea fleet, whose port was in Ukraine but whose history was distinctly Russian. (Russia and Ukraine are the two largest and most important members of the CIS; see this chapter's "Policy Perspectives" feature, p. 91.) One reason for forming the CIS was simply to speed the death of the old Soviet Union and ease the transition to full independence for its republics. After the formation of the CIS at the end of 1991, the Soviet Union quickly dissolved. The extensive property of the Soviet Union (including state-owned industry and military forces) went to the individual republics, especially to Russia, which became the USSR's successor state.

The disposition of the Soviet Union's property and armed forces was negotiated by CIS members. Although some military coordination takes place through the CIS, plans for a joint military force instead of 12 independent armies did not succeed. Among the largest CIS members, Kazakhstan and Belarus are the most closely aligned with Russia, while Ukraine is the most independent. In 1999, Russia and Belarus formed a confederation that might lead to future economic integration or even an anti-Western military alliance, but currently remains merely symbolic.

---

[65] Vogel, Steven K. *U.S.-Japan Relations in a Changing World.* Washington, DC: Brookings, 2002. Marquand, Robert. U.S. Redeployments Afoot in Asia. *Christian Science Monitor* November 18, 2003: 6.

POLICY PERSPECTIVES

President of Russia, Vladimir Putin

PROBLEM *How do you confront a fluid security environment in which the balance of power could shift quickly?*

BACKGROUND Imagine that you are the president of Russia. Since the breakup of the Soviet Union in 1991, your relations with your most powerful and important neighbor, Ukraine, have been tense, but with periods of cooperation. You share a nearly 1,000-mile border, and Ukraine maintains an army of 300,000 troops. Ukraine owns a very modern military, including a nearly 3,000-plane air force.

Your country and Ukraine were able to reach an agreement to divide the Soviet Navy's Black Sea Fleet, left in Ukrainian ports when the Soviet Union collapsed. Ukraine agreed to return nuclear weapons placed in its territory, and you have signed an agreement to establish a free trade area. Still, tensions have recently arisen concerning the drawing of borders and the implementation of the free trade agreement. Moreover, Ukraine claims you have not abided by the agreement on the Black Sea Fleet.

Since the end of the Cold War, several of your neighbors, including Ukraine, have cooperated with the North Atlantic Treaty Organization (NATO). To date, no CIS members have joined NATO, but many are members of NATO's Partnership for Peace (PfP) program. Your own country, Russia, does not anticipate NATO membership but has cooperated with NATO through the PfP program. In addition, you receive large amounts of aid from NATO member states, including $1 billion a year from the United States.

NATO expansion is not popular within Russia. Voices from within your parliament (the Duma) are demanding you take efforts to ensure Russian security. Nearly 20 percent of the Duma is now controlled by Communist or nationalist parties that oppose NATO expansion. Public opinion polls consistently show 60 percent of the public believes that NATO expansion threatens Russia.

Ukraine depends heavily on you for fuel and relies on your market to export more than 17 percent of its economic output. In 2006, Russia temporarily cut natural gas supplies to Ukraine to apply pressure in a price dispute. The fuel issue is a double-edged sword, however, since you rely on Ukrainian ports to export oil and Ukrainian pipelines to ship gas to Western Europe. In the 2006 dispute, Ukraine cut these trans-shipments and you had to back down.

SCENARIO Imagine that Ukraine announces it will accept an invitation to join NATO. You could quietly allow this to happen without making any objections. Such a course would keep Western donor states happy, but place you in a strategically vulnerable position. Moreover, NATO may ask you to remove your portion of the Black Sea Fleet from Ukraine once military integration begins. At this time, however, you have no reason to expect military conflict between your country and Ukraine (or any other NATO member).

You could also cease cooperation with NATO while pressuring Ukraine to leave. This signal of hostility could place your aid from NATO states in jeopardy, but would be quite popular domestically. This option would also place strain on your trade relationships with Ukraine.

CHOOSE YOUR POLICY Do you object to Ukraine's admission to NATO? Do you cease cooperation with NATO? What relative weight do factors such as international aid play in your decision? How do you address security concerns arising from an alliance that may or may not be hostile to you in the future?

It is to the CIS's credit that in the post-Soviet chaos no major war erupted between major CIS member states. Substantial warfare did occur between some of the smaller members (notably Armenia and Azerbaijan), and there was civil violence within several other CIS states (Russia, Georgia, Moldova, and Tajikistan); CIS forces were drawn into a few small clashes. But the large members were not drawn into wars. The outcome could have been much worse.

One of the first problems facing CIS military forces was what position to take in inter-republic warfare, such as that between Armenia and Azerbaijan, secessionist wars as in Georgia, or civil wars to control republics' governments as in Tajikistan. In the mid-1990s, the CIS operated a 24,000-person peacekeeping force in Tajikistan, generally supporting the government in a civil war there. A 1,500-person force in Moldova and a 500-person force in Georgia, both acting as buffer forces to monitor cease-fires, operated under joint commands of Russia and the governments and rebel forces in each of those countries.

Another pressing military problem for the CIS was the disposition of the tens of thousands of nuclear weapons of the former Soviet Union. As the Soviet successor state, Russia assumed control of the weapons and within a year moved all the tactical nuclear weapons out of the other republics and into Russian territory. This was a very touchy operation because of the danger of theft or accident while so many weapons were in transit. The United States provided specially designed railroad cars for use in moving the weapons. Still, there were reports that nuclear materials (or perhaps even warheads) had been stolen and sold on the international market by corrupt CIS officers or officials (see pp. 238–242 on proliferation).

The strategic nuclear weapons—those on long-range missiles—presented another kind of problem. These weapons were located in four republics—Russia, Ukraine, Belarus, and Kazakhstan—under control of Russian commanders. They were not easily moved, and the three republic leaders expressed some ambivalence about losing them to Russia. At a minimum they wanted assurances that the nuclear weapons would be destroyed, not retargeted on their own republics. Ukraine toyed with using the missiles as bargaining chips in negotiations with Russia or with the Western powers. But in the end all the former Soviet republics except Russia agreed to become nonnuclear states.

Overall, the CIS is a marriage of convenience. For now the members find it a necessary marriage—especially because of the tight economic integration of the member states—if not always a happy one. A divorce could occur quickly.

Regional Alignments

Beyond the three alliances just discussed and the regional IGOs mentioned earlier, most international alignments and coalitions are not formalized in alliances. Among the great powers, a close working relationship (through the UN) developed among the United States, Western European powers, Japan, and Russia after the Cold War. By the mid-1990s new strains had appeared in great-power relations, including economic conflicts among the former Western allies, differences over policy in Bosnia, Kosovo, and Iraq, as well as Western alarm at Russia's war in the secession-minded Chechnya province. Of the great powers, China continues to be the most independent, but prudently avoids conflict with the others unless China's immediate security interests are at stake.

Nonaligned Movement

In the global South, many states joined a **nonaligned movement** during the Cold War, standing apart from the U.S.-Soviet rivalry. This movement, led by India and Yugoslavia, was undermined by the membership of states such as Cuba that were clearly clients of one superpower. In 1992, the nonaligned movement agreed to stay in business, though its future is unclear. One vestige of past centuries is the Commonwealth—a group of countries with historical ties to Britain (including Canada and Australia) working together for mutual economic and cultural benefit. France also maintains ties (including regular summit meetings) with its former colonies in Africa. France had troops stationed in six African countries in the late 1990s. But France reduced its African ties in the 1990s, and in 1997 it stood by while friendly governments in Zaire (Democratic Congo) and the Republic of Congo were overthrown.

At the turn of the century, the 53-member Organization of African Unity, an IGO with few powers, reformed as the African Union (AU), a stronger organization with a continentwide parliament, central bank, and court. The African Union's first real test came with allegations of genocide in the Darfur region of Sudan in 2004. In response, the AU deployed 3,000 troops, but their effectiveness remained limited as of early 2006.

In Asia, China used to have conflicts with most of its major neighbors: between 1940 and 1979, it engaged in military hostilities with Japan, South Korea, the United States, India, Russia, and Vietnam. In 1965, China lost its only major regional ally (Indonesia) after a violent change of government there. China has long been loosely aligned with Pakistan in opposition to India (which was aligned with the Soviet Union). The United States tended to favor the Pakistani side as well (especially when Pakistan supported anti-Soviet rebels in Afghanistan in the 1980s), and Pakistan remains a U.S. ally depite strongly anti-American public opinion there. But both U.S.-Indian and U.S.-Chinese relations have improved since the Cold War ended. Vietnam slowly normalized relations with the United States after the wars in Vietnam and Cambodia. The United States has 35,000 troops stationed in South Korea under terms of a formal bilateral alliance dating to the Korean War (North Korea is vaguely aligned with China). Australia is also a U.S. military ally. Other long-standing U.S. friends in Asia include the Philippines (where joint antiterrorist operations began in 2002), the Chinese Nationalists on Taiwan (only informally since the 1970s), Singapore, Thailand. In late 2005, the first East Asia Summit included 16 states from India to Russia to New Zealand, with the notable exception of the United States. With China and Japan still squabbling about World War II, the unity of this new grouping appeared doubtful.[66]

In the Middle East, the Arab-Israeli conflict created a general anti-Israel alignment of the Arab countries for decades, but that alignment broke down as Egypt in 1978 and then Jordan in 1994 made peace with Israel. As the Israeli-Palestinian peace process moves forward and backward year by year, Arab countries continue to express varying degrees of solidarity with each other and opposition to Israel. Meanwhile, Israel and Turkey formed a close military relationship that amplifies Israeli power and links it to the oil-rich Caspian Sea region (see pp. 434–435). Also, despite its small size, Israel has been the largest recipient of U.S. foreign aid since the 1980s (about $3 billion per year).[67]

The United States has close relations with Egypt (since 1978), and cooperates closely with Turkey (a NATO member), Kuwait and Saudi Arabia (cemented by the 1991 Gulf War), and Morocco. U.S.-Iranian relations remain chilled 25 years after the 1979 revolution. But, oddly, Iran with its Shi'ite population has close ties with Iraq's new U.S.-backed government, dominated by Shi'ite religious parties. The United States had very hostile relations with Iraq before the 2003 war, and faced stronger antipathy in the region thereafter. U.S. relations with Libya were also hostile for decades until a 2003 agreement normalized Libya's place in the international system in return for Libya's reformed behavior. President Bush's second term began with an emphasis on spreading democracy and isolating what Secretary of State Condoleezza Rice called "outposts of tyranny"—Cuba, Burma, North Korea, Iran, Belarus, and Zimbabwe.

---

[66] Hemmer, Christopher and Peter Katzenstein. Why is there no NATO in Asia? Collective Identity, Regionalism, and the Origins of Multilateralism. *International Organization* 56 (3), 2002: 575–607.

[67] Fawcett, Louise, ed. *International Relations of the Middle East*. NY: Oxford, 2004. Telhami, Shibley. *The Stakes: America and the Middle East*. Boulder: Westview, 2002.

It is unclear what new international alignments may emerge in the years to come. The fluidity of alliances makes them a wild card for scholars to understand and for policy makers to anticipate. For the present, international alignments center on the United States; although several independence-minded states such as China, Russia, and France keep U.S. hegemony in check, there is little sign of a coherent or formal rival power alignment emerging to challenge the United States. Although U.S. leadership in international security affairs has fluctuated, the leading U.S. role is central to the course of world politics in the early twenty-first century.

This chapter has focused on the concerns of realists—the interests of states, distribution of power among states, bargaining between states, and alliances of states. The chapter has treated states as unitary actors, much as one would analyze the interactions of individual people. The actions of state leaders have been treated as more or less rational in terms of pursuing definable interests through coherent bargaining strategies. But realism is not the only way to frame the major issues of international security. Chapter 3 reexamines these themes critically, from more liberal and more revolutionary theoretical perspectives.

THINKING CRITICALLY

1. Using Table 1.3 on pp. 22–23 (with GDP as a measure of power) and the maps at the front of the book, pick a state and speculate about what coalition of nearby states might form with sufficient power to oppose the state if it became aggressive.
2. Choose a recent international event and list the power capabilities that participants used as leverage in the episode. Which capabilities were effective, and which were not? Why?
3. Given the distinction between zero-sum and non-zero-sum games, can you think of a current international situation that is a zero-sum conflict? One that is non-zero-sum?
4. If you were the leader of a small state in Africa, bargaining with a great power about an issue where your interests diverged, what leverage and strategies could you bring into play to improve the outcome for your state?
5. Given recent changes in international power distribution and the end of the Cold War order, where do you think the threats to peace will come from in the future? Is the international system moving from one power distribution (unipolarity) to another (tripolarity, bipolarity, etc.)?
6. The modern international system came into being at a time when agrarian societies relied primarily on farmland to create wealth. Now that most wealth is no longer created through farming, is the territorial nature of states obsolete? How might the diminishing economic value of territory change the ways in which states interact?

CHAPTER SUMMARY

- Realism explains international relations in terms of power.
- Realists and idealists differ in their assumptions about human nature, international order, and the potential for peace.
- Power can be conceptualized as influence or as capabilities that can create influence.
- The most important single indicator of a state's power is its GDP.
- Short-term power capabilities depend on long-term resources, both tangible and intangible.
- Realists consider military force the most important power capability.

- International affairs can be seen as a series of bargaining interactions in which states use power capabilities as leverage to influence the outcomes.
- Bargaining outcomes depend not only on raw power but also on strategies and luck.
- Reciprocity can be an effective strategy for reaching cooperation in ongoing relationships but carries a danger of turning into runaway hostility or arms races.
- Rational-actor approaches treat states as though they were individuals acting to maximize their own interests. These simplifications are debatable but allow realists to develop concise and general models and explanations.
- Game theory draws insights from simplified models of bargaining situations.
- International anarchy—the absence of world government—means that each state is a sovereign and autonomous actor pursuing its own national interests.
- The international system traditionally places great emphasis on the sovereignty of states, their right to control affairs in their own territory, and their responsibility to respect internationally recognized borders.
- Seven great powers account for half of the world's GDP as well as the great majority of military forces and other power capabilities.
- Power transition theory says that wars often result from shifts in relative power distribution in the international system.
- Hegemony—the predominance of one state in the international system—can help provide stability and peace in international relations, but with some drawbacks.
- States form alliances to increase their effective power relative to another state or alliance.
- Alliances can shift rapidly, with major effects on power relations.
- The world's main alliances, including NATO and the U.S.-Japanese alliance, face uncertain roles in a changing world order.

KEY TERMS

ONLINE PRACTICE TEST

Take an online practice test at *www.internationalrelations.net*

❑ A
❑ B
☑ C
❑ D

LET'S DEBATE THE ISSUE

The Bush Doctrine: Will It Eliminate or Increase Terrorism?

by Mir Zohair Husain

Overview Less than a week after September 11, 2001, President George W. Bush revealed his plan for America's new "war on terrorism," known as the Bush doctrine. This proactive and preemptive strategy was to aggressively pursue "terrorists" wherever they are in the world and warn America's enemies to desist from harboring or sponsoring terrorists, or face the same fate as the Afghan and Iraqi regimes. However, following Bush's second inaugural address, he promised to tone down this rhetoric and place even greater emphasis on encouraging friendly governments to assist the United States in their continuing anti-terrorist efforts.

This global war on terrorism continues a heated debate in the United States and abroad. The supporters of the Bush doctrine argue that the only way for the United States to defend its national interests and prevent future terrorist attacks is by using America's enormous military and economic capabilities. However, critics believe that terrorism cannot be solved with violence alone and the world may view such U.S. unilateral actions as "vigilante justice." These critics would like the United States to adopt a multilateral approach toward terrorism that includes winning allies, going through the UN, adhering to international law, and fighting world poverty.

The Bush doctrine raises several key questions: Will the Bush doctrine effectively combat terrorism, reestablish national security, and usher in a new world order? Or will the Bush doctrine rapidly broaden and deepen anti-Americanism, thereby breeding more terrorism, producing more sanctuaries for terrorists, and isolating the United States further in the global community?

Argument 1 Bush Doctrine Proponents

The Bush doctrine shifted American foreign policy from containment to preemption. The containment of the Soviet Union and communism was the hallmark of U.S. foreign policy during the Cold War (1947–1989). However, targeting of terrorist cells is far more difficult than containing and deterring traditional states.

> For much of the last century America's defense relied on the cold war doctrines of deterrence and containment. In some cases those strategies still apply. But new threats also require new thinking. . . . Deterrence, the promise of massive retaliation against nations, means nothing against shadowy terrorist networks with no nation or citizens to defend. Containment is not possible when unbalanced dictators with weapons of mass destruction can deliver those weapons on missiles or secretly provide them to terrorist allies. . . . We cannot defend America and our friends by hoping for the best. We cannot put our faith in the word of tyrants who solemnly sign nonproliferation treaties and then systematically break them. If we wait for threats to fully materialize we will have waited too long. ("Text of Bush's Speech at West Point Military Academy." *The New York Times,* June 1, 2002.)

The U.S. desires multilateralism, but will do what is necessary to defend its national interests. The United States would prefer to fight the war on terrorism multilaterally. However, the United States cannot remain passive while terrorism spreads and endangers U.S. interests throughout the world.

> While the U.S. will constantly strive to enlist the support of the international community, we [Americans] will not hesitate to act alone, if necessary, to exercise our right of self-defense by acting preemptively against such terrorists, to prevent them from doing harm against our people and our country; and denying further sponsorship, support, and sanctuary to terrorists by convincing or compelling states to accept their sovereign responsibilities. ("Bush's National Security Strategy. President Bush's Speech at the National Cathedral in Washington, DC, on September 14, 2001." *The New York Times,* September 20, 2002.)

The U.S. is indispensable in maintaining a peaceful and stable international system. The international system is anarchic because it lacks a world government to maintain law and order. According to the hegemonic stability theory, a hegemon (dominant actor in a system) is necessary to maintain world order and prevent other states from destabilizing the international system. In the post-September 11 world, the United States is the indispensable hegemon. Therefore, the woes the world suffers with U.S. preeminence, which many view as imperialism, would be much worse without America's stabilizing presence.

> "Whatever else you can say about empire, it had the advantage of maintaining order and suppressing anarchy," Mr. [John Lewis] Gaddis said. "We may need some kind of structure we wouldn't call it empire, call it spheres of influence, to deal with these problems."
>
> . . . [For] scholars like John Mearsheimer, a political scientist at the University of Chicago, Sept. 11 shows that old-fashioned power politics still operates in this new world. Power is the currency of the international system, Mr. Mearsheimer argues, and the United States should use it when it sees fit. (Alexander Stille. "What Is America's Place in the World Now?" *The New York Times,* January 12, 2002.)

Argument 2 Bush Doctrine Opponents

International cooperation is more effective than the Bush doctrine. Despite America's unrivaled power, the Bush doctrine is making the United States an unpopular and lonely superpower in geopolitics. The United States should find greater success by working the national interests and opinions of other countries into its vision for peace and stability as proposed by the second term of the Bush administration.

> . . . [A] superpower cannot protect itself without the help of other countries. Much of the world already resents the United States because of its size and wealth. Even our allies hate being made to feel as if they live on a planet in which only one country's opinion matters. The biggest challenge for the U.S. is not how to win the next military encounter, but how to conduct itself so that other nations willingly accept its leadership.
>
> The most effective way to make other countries comfortable with American military power is to demonstrate that the United States has their best interests at heart, too. ("The Uses of American Power." *The New York Times,* March 2, 2002.)

The Bush doctrine is provoking more volatile and dangerous anti-Americanism. The central problem with the Bush doctrine is that it encourages the view that the United States is a bully that meddles in the affairs of other countries. Moreover, in the very country the United States argues it is liberating, Iraq, al Qaeda and other terrorist organizations have enjoyed surging levels of new recruits by using the U.S. presence as a selling point.

> The architects of America's national security policy at once grasp this crosscultural interdependence and don't. They see that prosperous and free Muslim nations are good for America. But they don't see that the very logic behind this goal counsels against pursuing it crudely, with primary reliance on force and intimidation.
>
> With hatred becoming Public Enemy No. 1, a successful war on terrorism demands an understanding of how so much of the world has come to dislike America. When people who are born with the same human nature as you and I grow up to commit suicide bombings or applaud them there must be a reason. And it's at least conceivable that their fanaticism is needlessly encouraged by American policy or rhetoric. (Robert Wright. "Two Years Later, a Thousand Years Ago." *The New York Times,* September 11, 2003.)

Other states will emulate America's example of preemption with catastrophic results. The United States is not the only country in the world to fear that international actors threaten its national security interests. Mimicking the United States, other countries could justify similar preemptive attacks on their adversaries labeling them an imminent threat to their national security interests.

> . . . [O]ther nations could immediately follow the American lead and twist a policy of pre-emption to their advantage. Israel could use it to justify harder strikes into Palestinian territory; India could use it to pre-empt any Pakistani nuclear threat; China could use it to justify an attack on Taiwan.
>
> "Consistency poses problems," said Peter W. Galbraith, a former ambassador to Croatia. Mr. Galbraith said he is a supporter of pre-emptive action against Iraq, yet he worries about what happens if the new American doctrine spreads uncontrolled. "No place is the risk greater than in South Asia," he said. "If India adopted the American doctrine of pre-emption, it risks a nuclear war, with devastating consequences for the world. It's a tricky business." (David E. Sanger. "Bush to Formalize a Defense Policy of Hitting First." *The New York Times,* June 17, 2002.)

Questions

1. Reflecting on recent events: Is the Bush doctrine succeeding in its goals of diminishing global terrorism? Has the Bush doctrine strengthened or weakened U.S. national security?
2. If preemption is adopted by other states, do you think we will live in a safer or more dangerous world?

The Bush Doctrine

Selected Readings

Benjamin R. Barber. *Fear's Empire: War, Terrorism, and Democracy.* NY: W. W. Norton, 2003.

Mark Hertsgaard. *The Eagle's Shadow: Why America Fascinates and Infuriates the World.* NY: Farrar, Straus and Giroux, 2003.

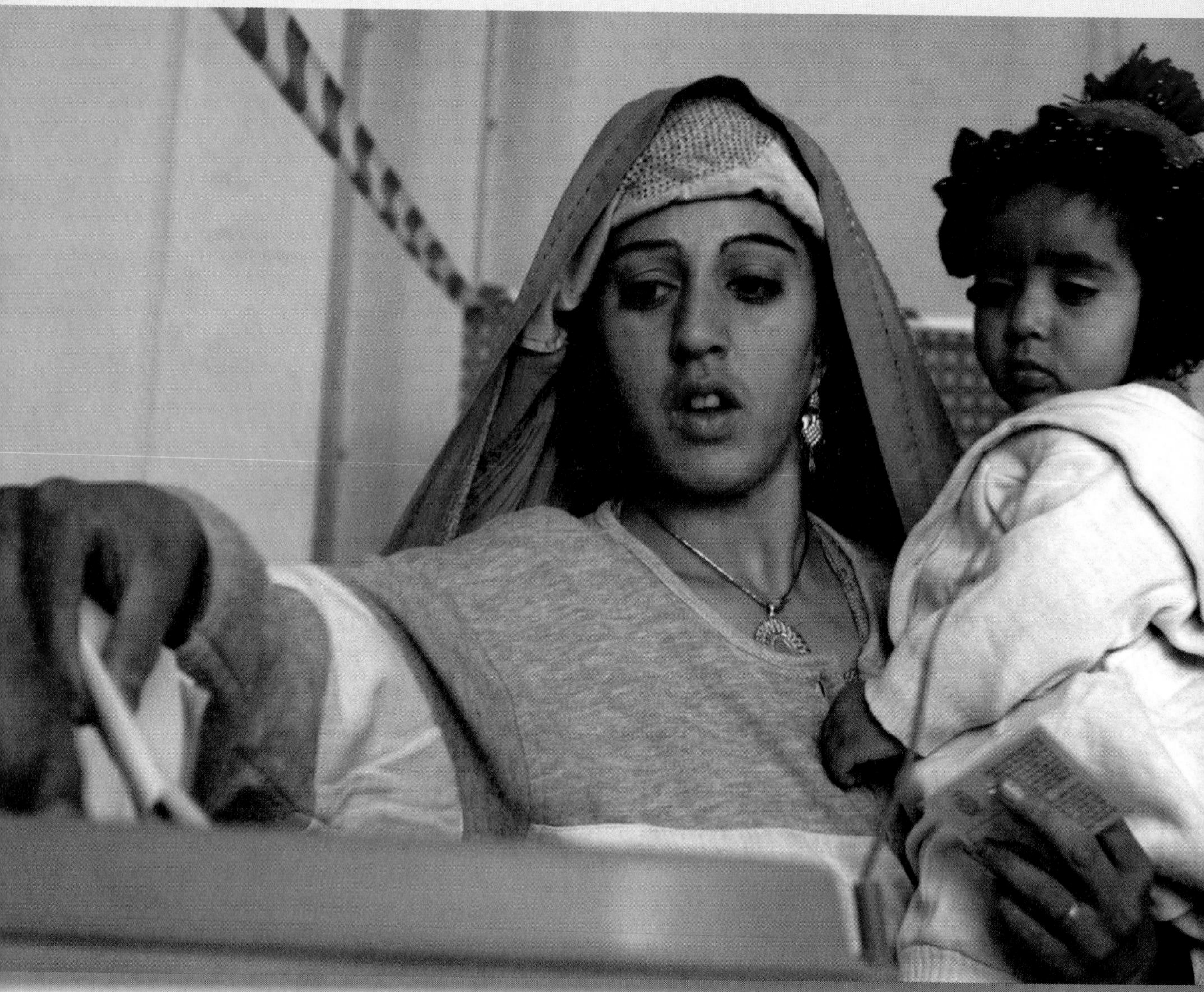

■ Afghanistan's first presidential election, 2004.

Liberalism
Traditional Liberal Critiques • What Is Rationality? • Neoliberalism • Collective Goods • International Regimes • Hegemonic Stability • Collective Security

Feminism
Why Gender Matters • The Masculinity of Realism • Gender in War and Peace • Women in IR • Balancing the Feminist Arguments

Constructivism

Postmodernism
Deconstructing Realism • Postmodern Feminism

Peace Studies
Conflict Resolution • War and Militarism • Positive Peace • Peace Movements • Nonviolence

CHAPTER 3

Alternatives to Power Politics

Liberalism

How well do the assumptions of realism capture what is important about IR? Where are the problems in the realist framework—the places where abstractions diverge too much from the reality of IR, where realism is "unrealistic" in its portrayal?[1]

This chapter revisits the realism-idealism debate, discusses current liberal approaches to international security, and then considers several broader and more interdisciplinary alternatives to the realist framework—feminism, constructivism, postmodernism, and peace studies. Each of these research communities seeks to radically recast the terms of reference in which we see IR.

Traditional Liberal Critiques

Since the time of Mo Ti and Sun Tzu in ancient China, idealism has provided a counterpoint to realism. This long tradition of idealism in IR holds that: morality, law, and international organization can form the basis for relations among states; human nature is not evil; peaceful and cooperative relations among states are possible; and states can operate as a community rather than merely as autonomous self-interested agents.[2]

To review the core concepts of realism, states (the central actors in IR) use power to pursue their own interests in the context of an anarchic system lacking central enforcement mechanisms. Power capabilities come into play as leverage in bargaining among states over the outcomes of conflicts. Leverage can be positive (rewards) or negative (punishments); in both cases the purpose is to influence the rational decisions and actions of another state so as to bring about a more favorable outcome for the actor using the leverage. Military force is an important form of leverage—emphasized by realists over all other forms—because of the inherent insecurity of living in an anarchic world.[3]

Traditionally, liberals have offered four major lines of criticism against these assumptions of realism. First, the key assumption of international *anarchy* is no more than a partial

[1] Sterling-Folker, Jennifer, ed. *Making Sense of International Relations Theory*. Boulder: Rienner, 2005. Guzzini, Stefano. *Realism in International Relations and International Political Economy: The Continuing Story of a Death Foretold*. NY: Routledge, 1998.

[2] Nardin, Terry, and David R. Mapel, eds. *Traditions of International Ethics*. Cambridge, 1992. Long, David, and Peter Wilson, eds. *Thinkers of the Twenty Years' Crisis: Inter-War Idealism Reassessed*. Oxford, 1995.

[3] Vasquez, John A. *The Power of Power Politics: From Classical Realism to Neotraditionalism*. Cambridge, 1999.

truth. Of course, international interactions are structured by power relations, a position the realists are happy to accept. But order also evolves through norms and institutions based on reciprocity and cooperation, even on law. Realists have a harder time reconciling the ever-expanding scope of international interdependence and cooperation with the assumptions of anarchy, of the inevitability of security dilemmas, and of the primacy of military leverage.

Second, liberals criticize the notion of states as *unitary actors*, each with a single set of coherent interests. As the study of foreign policy reveals (Chapter 4), state actions often do not reflect a single individual set of preferences. Rather, state behavior is shaped by internal bargaining among and within bureaucracies, interest groups, and other actors with divergent goals and interests. Nonstate actors—individuals, NGOs, IGOs, and ethnic groups, among others—further confound the idea that IR can be reduced to the interactions of a small number of well-defined state actors pursuing national interests.

Third, the concept of *rationality* is problematical. If states are single actors with coherent interests, they often seem to do a poor job in maximizing those interests. Of course, it is hard to tell from an actor's unexpected behavior whether the actor was irrational or merely pursued a goal, interest, or value that *we* would not consider normal or productive. Central to the debate over rationality is the notion of *preferences*. Most realists are happy to assume states desire power. Critics contend that we need not assume these desires but rather investigate why actors in IR value the things they do.

Fourth, *military force* as a form of leverage does not seem nearly as all-important as realism implies. It is a costly way to influence other actors (see Chapter 6), as compared with diplomacy, conflict resolution, peacekeeping, and other nonmilitary means. Its outcome is also uncertain; even powerful states lose wars. International organizations, laws, and norms create stable contexts for bargaining, making nonmilitary leverage increasingly effective as international organization develops (see Chapter 7). This criticism of realism applies even more to international political economy (Chapters 8 through 13) than to security affairs.

In addition to these general criticisms of realism, some liberals have argued that changes in the way IR works have made realist assumptions obsolete. Realism may once have been realistic, when European kings and queens played war and traded territories as property. But states are now interconnected, a reality contradicting the assumptions of autonomy and sovereignty. Borders are becoming fluid, making territorial integrity increasingly untenable. The evolution of norms regarding the use of force has substantially changed the ways in which military force contributes to international power. This line of argument has been prominent in liberal interdependence approaches to IR since the 1970s.

What Is Rationality?

Rationality

At the core of the liberal approach is a concept of *rationality* that differs sharply from the realist concept. Realists see rationality as an individual actor's attempt to maximize its own short-term interests. Liberals believe that rational actors are capable of forgoing short-term individual interests in order to further the long-term well-being of a community to which they belong. Such actions are rational because they contribute to the actor's individual well-being, indirectly or over the long term. The German philosopher Immanuel Kant argued, 200 years ago, that states, although autonomous, could join a worldwide federation like today's UN and respect its principles even at the cost of forgoing certain short-term individual gains. To Kant, international cooperation was a more rational option for states than resorting to war. Thus, in realist conceptions of rationality, war and violence appear rational (because they often advance short-term state interests), but liberals tend to see war and violence as irrational deviations that result from defective reasoning and that harm the (collective, long-term) well-being of states.[4]

Liberals argue that trade increases wealth, cooperation, and global well-being—all while making conflict less likely in the long-term since governments will not want to disrupt any process that adds to the wealth of their state. Realists are skeptical, however, arguing that one state's reliance on another creates *more* tensions in the short-term because states are nervous that another actor has an important source of leverage over them.[5]

Liberal and realist approaches to *power* reflect the distinction between rationality as seeking narrow self-interest and rationality as seeking to share in long-term collective benefits. Realists define power as the ability to get another actor to do something—or as the capabilities required to so influence an actor (see pp. 57–58). This is power *over* others—a concept that some liberals consider inherently oppressive, rooted in a need to control or dominate other people. This is the power of the bully, to make others comply. But are bullies really the most powerful actors? Do they achieve the best outcomes? And do we really live in an international world populated by bullies?

An alternative definition of power is based not on power over others but on power to accomplish desirable ends. This kind of power often derives from capitalizing on common interests rather than gaining an edge in bargaining over conflicting interests. Such empowerment often entails the formation of coalitions and partnerships, or the mobilization of the resources of multiple actors for a common purpose. For many liberals, this is a truer, more useful concept of power.

HAPPY FAMILY

Liberals emphasize the potential for rivalries to evolve into cooperative relationships as states recognize that achieving mutual benefits is most cost-effective in the long run. For example, the U.S. and Soviet/Russian space programs began cooperating in the 1960s, and today many countries participate in building the International Space Station. Here, U.S. shuttle commander Eileen Collins says goodbye to Space Station commander Sergei Krikalev while astronauts from the United States, Japan, and Australia look on, 2005.

Neoliberalism

In the 1980s, a new liberal critique of realism emerged. The approach stressed the importance of international institutions in reducing the inherent conflict that realists assume in an international system. The reasoning is based on the core liberal idea that seeking long-term mutual gains is often more rational than maximizing individual short-term gains. The approach became known as "neoliberal institutionalism" or **neoliberalism** for short.

The neoliberal approach differs from earlier liberal approaches in that it concedes to realism several important assumptions—among them, that states are unitary actors

[4] Angell, Norman. *The Foundations of International Polity*. London: William Heinemann, 1914.

[5] Mansfield, Edward, and Brian Pollins. The Study of Interdependence and Conflict: Recent Advances, Open Questions, and Directions for Future Research. *Journal of Conflict Resolution* 45 (6), 2001: 834–59.

rationally pursuing their self-interests in a system of anarchy. Neoliberals say to realists, "Even if we grant your assumptions about the nature of states and their motives, your pessimistic conclusions do not follow." States achieve cooperation fairly often because it is in their interest to do so, and they can learn to use institutions to ease the pursuit of mutual gains and the reduction of possibilities for cheating or taking advantage of another state.

Despite the many sources of conflict in IR, states do cooperate most of the time. Neoliberal scholars ask how this is possible in an anarchic world.[6] They try to show that even in a world of unitary rational states the neorealists' pessimism about international cooperation is not valid. States can create mutual rules, expectations, and institutions to promote behavior that enhances (or at least doesn't destroy) the possibilities for mutual gain.

Neoliberals use the *Prisoner's Dilemma (PD)* game (see pp. 71–72) to illustrate their argument that cooperation is possible. Each actor can gain by individually defecting, but both lose when both defect. The narrow, self-serving behavior of each player leads to a bad outcome for both, one they could have improved by cooperation. Similarly, in IR states often have a mix of conflicting and mutual interests. The dilemma can be resolved if the game is played over and over again—an accurate model of IR, where states deal with each other in repeated interactions.

A strategy of strict reciprocity after an initial cooperative move (nicknamed **tit for tat**) can bring about mutual cooperation in a repeated PD game, because the other player must conclude that any defection will merely provoke a like defection in response.[7] The strategy parallels just war doctrine (see pp. 286–287), which calls for states never to initiate war but to use war in response to war. In international trade, such a strategy calls for opening one's markets but selectively closing them in response to another state closing its markets (see pp. 320–322).

Reciprocity is an important principle in IR that helps international cooperation emerge despite the absence of central authority. Through reciprocity, not a world government, norms and rules are enforced. In international security, reciprocity underlies the gradual improvement of relations sought by arms control agreements and peacekeeping missions. In international political economy (IPE), where cooperation can create great benefits through trade, the threat to restrict trade in retaliation for unfair practices is a strong incentive to comply with rules and norms. The World Trade Organization (WTO) and its predecessor, the General Agreement on Trade and Tariffs (GATT), function on this principle—states that defect on their obligations by increasing tariffs must suffer punishment by allowing other states to place tariffs on their goods.

Although reciprocity is an important norm, it is just one among many norms that mediate states' interactions. For example, diplomatic practices and participation in international organizations (IOs) are both strongly governed by shared expectations about the rules of correct behavior. As dilemmas such as the Prisoner's Dilemma crop up in IR, states rely on a context of rules, norms, habits, and institutions that make it rational for all sides to avoid the self-defeating outcomes that would result from pursuing narrow, short-term self-interest. Neoliberals study historical and contemporary cases in IR to see how in-

---

[6] Baldwin, David A., ed. *Neorealism and Neoliberalism: The Contemporary Debate*. Columbia, 1993. Nye, Joseph S., Jr., Neorealism and Neoliberalism [review article]. *World Politics* 40 (2), 1988: 235–51. Milner, Helen. International Theories of Cooperation Among Nations: Strengths and Weaknesses [review article]. *World Politics* 44 (3), 1992: 466–94. Oye, Kenneth A., ed. *Cooperation Under Anarchy*. Princeton, 1986. Keohane, Robert O., and Lisa Martin. The Promise of Institutionalist Theory. *International Security* 20 (1), 1995: 39–51.

[7] Axelrod, Robert. *The Evolution of Cooperation*. NY: Basic, 1984. Axelrod, Robert, and Robert O. Keohane. Achieving Cooperation Under Anarchy: Strategies and Institutions. In Oye, ed. *Cooperation Under Anarchy* (see footnote 6 in this chapter), pp. 226–54. Axelrod, Robert. *The Complexity of Cooperation: Agent-Based Models of Competition and Collaboration*. Princeton, 1997.

stitutions and norms affected the possibilities for overcoming dilemmas and achieving international cooperation. Thus, for neoliberals the emergence of international institutions is key to understanding how states achieve a superior rational outcome that includes long-term self-interest and not just immediate self-interest.

Collective Goods

The problem of the security dilemma (p. 75), which helps explain costly arms races, is an example of a PD-like dilemma in international security. Such examples are even more common in IPE, where protectionism and other forms of economic nationalism attempt to increase national wealth (relative to other states), at some cost to global wealth (see Chapter 8). The overall efficiency of the world economy is reduced, but the distribution of gains from trade shifts toward one's own state or groups within it. The problem is that if other states take similar actions, global efficiency decreases and the distribution of benefits remains about the same. So all states end up worse off than they could be.

All these situations are examples of the **collective goods problem.** A collective good is a tangible or intangible good available to all members of a group, regardless of their individual contributions, and difficult to withhold from those who do not contribute to providing it. As in the security dilemma or Prisoner's Dilemma, participants can gain by lowering their own contribution to the collective good, but if too many participants do so the good cannot be provided.

For example, it costs less to drive a polluting car than to pay for emission controls, and the air that the car owner breathes is hardly affected by his or her own car. The air quality is a collective good. If too many car owners pollute, all will breathe dirty air. But if just a few pollute, they will breathe fairly clean air; the few who pollute are **free riders,** because they benefit from someone else's provision of the collective good. Moreover, we cannot make the free riders breathe only their dirty air while others breathe clean air. These important concepts in IPE come up again in later chapters, especially in discussions of the global environment (Chapter 11) and of international organization and law (Chapter 7).

Within domestic society, many collective goods problems are solved by governments, which enforce rules for the common good. Governments can punish free riders who are tempted to avoid contributing. Governments can pass laws against polluting cars or force citizens to pay taxes to support collective goods such as national defense, highways, or schools. In the anarchic international system, the

COLLECTIVE EFFORT

Collective goods are provided to all members of a group regardless of their individual contributions. Liberal theorists see the community of nations as similarly interdependent. However, the provision of collective goods presents difficult dilemmas as players seek to maximize their own share of benefits. Prevention of a bird flu pandemic—here discussed by the World Health Organization in 2005—benefits all countries regardless of contribution.

absence of central government sharpens the difficulties created by collective goods. It is difficult to maintain multilateral cooperation when each government is tempted by its own possibility of free riding.

In general, collective goods are easier to provide in small groups than in large ones.[8] In a small group, the defection (free riding) of one member is harder to conceal, has a greater impact on the overall collective good, and is easier to punish. The advantage of small groups helps explain the importance of the great-power system in international security affairs. And it is one reason why the G7 (Group of Seven) industrialized countries have frequent meetings to try to coordinate their economic policies, instead of relying only on groups such as the World Bank or WTO (each of which has more than a hundred member states). Small groups do not solve the problem entirely, however. Whether in small groups or large, the world's states lack a government to enforce contributions to collective goods; states must look elsewhere.

International Regimes

International Regimes

Because of the contradictory interpretations that parties to a conflict usually have, it is difficult to resolve such conflicts without a third party to arbitrate or an overall framework to set common expectations for all parties. These considerations underlie the creation of IOs in the international security field (see Chapter 7). Norms of behavior are at least as important in international economics as in international security because of the great gains to be realized from maintaining a stable framework for smoothly carrying on large economic transactions.

An **international regime** is a set of rules, norms, and procedures around which the expectations of actors converge in a certain issue area (whether arms control, international trade, or Antarctic exploration).[9] The convergence of expectations means that participants in the international system have similar ideas about what rules will govern their mutual participation: each expects to play by the same rules. (This meaning of regime is not the same as that referring to the domestic governments of states, especially governments considered illegitimate or in power for only a short time.)

Regimes can help solve collective goods problems by increasing transparency—because everyone knows what everyone is doing, cheating is more costly. The current revolution in information technologies is strengthening regimes particularly in this aspect. Also, with better international communication, states can identify conflicts and negotiate solutions through regimes more effectively.

Regimes are an important and widespread phenomenon in IR. Several will be discussed in the remaining chapters on international security. For example, the Ballistic Missile Technology Control Regime (see p. 236) is a set of rules and expectations governing the international trade in missiles. In IPE, regimes are even more central. The frameworks within which states carry on trade and monetary relations, communications, and environmental protection policies are key to realizing the benefits of mutual cooperation in these areas.

IR scholars conceive of regimes in several different ways, and the concept has been criticized as too vague. But the most common conception of regimes combines elements of realism and liberalism. States are considered the important actors, and states are seen as

[8] Sandler, Todd. Global Collective Action. Cambridge, 2004. Olson, Mancur. *The Logic of Collective Action*. Harvard, 1971 [1965].

[9] Krasner, Stephen D., ed. *International Regimes*. Cornell, 1983. Hasenclever, Andreas, Peter Mayer, and Volker Rittberger. *Theories of International Regimes*. Cambridge, 1997.

autonomous units maximizing their own interests in an anarchic context. Regimes do not play a role in issues where states can realize their interests directly through unilateral applications of leverage. Rather, regimes come into existence to overcome collective goods dilemmas by coordinating the behaviors of individual states. Although states continue to seek their own interests, they create frameworks to coordinate their actions with those of other states if and when such coordination is necessary to realize self-interest (that is, in collective goods dilemmas). Thus, regimes help make cooperation possible even within an international system based on anarchy—exactly the point neoliberals focus on.

Empowering Regimes?

Regimes do not substitute for the basic calculations of costs and benefits by states; they just open up new possibilities with more favorable benefit-cost ratios. Regimes do not constrain states, except in a very narrow and short-term sense. Rather they facilitate and empower national governments faced with issues where collective goods or coordination problems would otherwise prevent governments from achieving their ends. Regimes can be seen as *intervening variables* between the basic causal forces at work in IR—for realists, the relative power of state actors—and the outcomes such as international cooperation (or lack thereof). Regimes do not negate the effects of power: more often they codify and normalize existing power relations. For example, the ballistic missile regime just mentioned (see p. 104) protects the status quo in which only a few states have such missiles. If the regime works, it will keep less-powerful states from gaining leverage they could use against more-powerful states.

Hegemonic Stability

Since regimes depend on state power for their enforcement, some IR scholars argue that regimes are most effective when power in the international system is most concentrated—when there is a hegemon to keep order (see "Hegemony" on pp. 82–84). This theory is known as **hegemonic stability theory.**[10] When one state's power is predominant, it can enforce rules and norms unilaterally, avoiding the collective goods problem. In particular, hegemons can maintain global free trade and promote world economic growth, in this view.

Hegemony and Stability

This theory attributes the peace and prosperity of the decades after World War II to U.S. hegemony, which created and maintained a global framework of economic relations supporting relatively stable and free international trade, as well as a security framework that prevented great-power wars. By contrast, the Great Depression of the 1930s and the outbreak of World War II have been attributed to the power vacuum in the international system at that time—Britain was no longer able to act as hegemon, and the United States was unwilling to begin doing so.[11]

Why should a hegemon care about enforcing rules for the international economy that are in the common good? According to hegemonic stability theory, hegemons as the largest international traders have an inherent interest in the promotion of integrated world markets (where the hegemons will tend to dominate). As the most advanced state in productivity and technology, a hegemon does not fear competition from industries in other states; it fears only that its own superior goods will be excluded from competing in other states. Thus hegemons favor free trade and use their power to achieve free trade.

[10] Keohane, Robert O. The Theory of Hegemonic Stability and Change in International Economic Regimes, 1967–1977. In Holsti, Ole R., R. M. Siverson, and A. L. George, eds. *Change in the International System*. Boulder, CO: Westview, 1980.

[11] Kindleberger, Charles P. *The World in Depression, 1929–1939*. California, 1973. Lake, David A. *Power, Protection, and Free Trade: International Sources of U.S. Commercial Strategy, 1887–1939*. Cornell, 1988.

Hegemony, then, provides both the ability and the motivation to maintain regimes that provide a stable political framework for free international trade, according to hegemonic stability theory. This theory is not, however, accepted by all IR scholars.[12]

What happens to regimes when hegemons lose power and decline? Regimes do not always decline with the power of hegemons that created them. Rather, they may take on a life of their own. Although hegemony may be crucial in *establishing* regimes, it is not necessary for *maintaining* them.[13] Once actors' expectations converge around the rules embodied in a regime, the actors realize that the regime serves their own interests. Working through the regime becomes a habit, and national leaders may not give serious consideration to breaking out of the established rules.

This persistence of regimes was demonstrated in the 1970s, when U.S. power declined following the decades of U.S. hegemony since 1945. Diminished U.S. power was evident in the loss of the Vietnam War, the rise of OPEC, and the malaise of the U.S. economy. Some IR scholars expected that the entire framework of international trade and monetary relations established after World War II would collapse once the United States was no longer able to enforce the rules of that regime. But that did not happen. The international economic regimes adjusted somewhat and survived.

In part, that survival is attributable to the embedding of regimes in permanent *institutions* such as the UN, NATO, and the International Monetary Fund. As the rules of the game persist over time and become habitual, formal institutions develop around them. These institutions become the tangible manifestation of shared expectations as well as the machinery for coordinating international actions based on those expectations. In international security affairs, the UN and other IOs provide a stable framework for resolving disputes (Chapter 7). IPE is even more institutionalized, again because of the heavier volume of activity and the wealth that can be realized from cooperation.[14]

Institutions gain greater stability and weight than do noninstitutionalized regimes. With a staff and headquarters, an international institution can actively promote adherence to the rules in its area of political or economic life. Important institutions in international security and IPE are discussed in Chapters 7 and 8, respectively.

Collective Security

A major application of liberal conceptions of international security affairs is the concept of **collective security**—the formation of a broad alliance of most major actors in an international system for the purpose of jointly opposing aggression by any actor. The rationale for this approach was laid out by Immanuel Kant. Since past treaties ending great-power wars had never lasted permanently, Kant proposed a federation (league) of the world's states. Through such a federation, Kant proposed, the majority of states could unite to punish any

---

[12] Gruber, Lloyd. *Ruling the World: Power Politics and the Rise of Supernational Institutions*. Princeton, 2000. Gowa, Joanne. Rational Hegemons, Excludable Goods, and Small Groups: An Epitaph for Hegemonic Stability Theory? *World Politics* 41 (3), 1989: 307–24. Eichengreen, Barry. Hegemonic Stability Theories of the International Monetary System. In Cooper, R. N. et al., eds, *Can Nations Agree? Issues in International Economic Cooperation*. Washington, DC: Brookings, 1989.

[13] Keohane, Robert O. *After Hegemony: Cooperation and Discord in the World Political Economy*. Princeton, 1984. Gowa, Joanne. Bipolarity, Multipolarity, and Free Trade. *American Political Science Review* 83 (4), 1989: 1227–44.

[14] Taylor, Paul, and A. J. R. Groom, eds. *International Institutions at Work*. NY: St. Martin's, 1988. Keohane, Robert O. International Institutions: Two Approaches. *International Studies Quarterly* 32 (4), 1988: 379–96. Mansfield, Edward. The Proliferation of Preferential Trading Arrangements. *Journal of Conflict Resolution* 42 (5), 1998: 523–43.

one state that committed aggression, safeguarding the collective interests of all the nations while protecting the self-determination of small nations that all too easily became pawns in great-power games.[15]

After the horrors of World War I, the *League of Nations* was formed. But it was flawed in two ways. Its membership did not include all the great powers (including the most powerful one, the United States), and its members proved unwilling to bear the costs of collective action to oppose aggression when it did occur in the 1930s, starting with Japan and Italy. After World War II, the United Nations was created as the League's successor to promote collective security (see Chapter 7).

Several regional IGOs also currently perform collective security functions (deterring aggression) as well as economic and cultural ones. In Latin America and the United States, there is the *Organization of American States (OAS)*. In the Middle East (including North Africa), there is the *Arab League*. In Africa (also including North Africa), there is the *African Union (AU)*.

The success of collective security depends on two points. First, the members must keep their alliance commitments to the group (that is, members must not free ride on the efforts of other members). When a powerful state commits aggression against a weaker one, it often is not in the immediate interest of other powerful states to go to war over the issue. It can be very costly to suppress a determined aggressor.

A second requisite for collective security is that enough members must agree on what constitutes aggression. The UN Security Council is structured so that aggression is defined by what all five permanent members, in addition to at least four of the other ten members, can agree on (see "The Security Council" on pp. 262–264). This collective security system does not work against aggression by a great power. When the Soviet Union invaded Afghanistan, or the United States mined the harbors of Nicaragua, or France blew up the Greenpeace ship *Rainbow Warrior*, the UN could do nothing—because those states can veto Security Council resolutions.[16]

Collective security worked in the 1990 Iraqi case because the conquest of Kuwait brought all the great powers together and because they were willing to bear the costs of confronting Iraq. It was the first time since the founding of the UN that one member state had invaded, occupied, and annexed another—attempting to erase it as a sovereign state. The invasion was so blatant a violation of Kuwaiti sovereignty and territorial integrity that the Security Council had little trouble labeling it aggression, and authorizing the use of force by a multinational coalition.[17]

In the case of Bosnia, the aggression was somewhat less clear-cut, since it followed on the disintegration of what had been a single state, Yugoslavia. What would have been an internal matter became an international one when Croatia and Bosnia were recognized as separate states independent of Serbia. But members of the UN (especially the great powers) were reluctant to pay a high price to reverse aggression when their own vital national interests were not threatened. Eventually they patched together an international response that contained the conflict at a modest cost.

In 2002–2003, the Security Council repeatedly debated Iraq's failure to keep the agreements it had made at the end of the Gulf War, in particular the promise to disclose and destroy all its weapons of mass destruction. In late 2002 the Council unanimously

---

[15] Kant, Immanuel. *Perpetual Peace*. Edited by Lewis White Beck. Indianapolis: Bobbs-Merrill, 1957 [1795].

[16] Lepgold, Joseph, and Thomas G. Weiss, eds. *Collective Conflict Management and Changing World Politics*. SUNY, 1998.

[17] Sutterlin, James S. *The United Nations and the Maintenance of International Security: A Challenge to Be Met*. Westport, CT: Praeger, 2003.

passed Resolution 1441, faulting Iraq's compliance and providing a final chance to disarm, with UN weapons inspectors sent back into Iraq (they had left in 1998). The great powers split, however, on the question of what to do next. In early 2003, a proposed U.S.-British resolution authorizing military force was withdrawn after France promised to veto it; Germany, Russia, and China had all strongly opposed it, and the war. Public opinion around the world, especially in predominantly Muslim countries, unified against the war, making governments wary of backing the U.S. position. When the UN did not act, the United States, Britain, and Australia sent military forces and overthrew Saddam Hussein by force, accusing the UN of acting like the toothless League of Nations (see p. 37).

The concept of collective security has been broadened in recent years. For example, *failed states* have very weak control of their territory, making them potential havens for drugs trafficking, money laundering, and terrorist bases. Essentially, domestic politics look rather like international anarchy. In these cases, there is a duty for the international community to intervene in such states in order to restore law and order and thus provide collective security for the international system.[18]

Liberals have sought to reform rather than radically reshape the international system as we know it. Liberal scholars and liberal state leaders alike have argued that international cooperation and the avoidance of violence are ultimately better for states themselves and more rational for state leaders to pursue.

The remainder of this chapter considers more revolutionary critiques of realism. These approaches broadly reject the terms of reference—issues, assumptions, language—that realists use to discuss IR. As a result, there has not been much productive debate between realism and these schools of thought. Yet, with growing numbers of IR scholars taking these critiques seriously, they provide perspectives that compete with realist and even liberal approaches.

Feminism

Feminism

Feminist scholarship has cut a broad swath across academic disciplines, from literature to psychology to history. In recent years, it has made inroads in international relations, once considered one of the fields most resistant to feminist arguments. Feminist scholarship in IR has produced a rapidly growing literature in the past two decades.[19]

Why Gender Matters

Feminist scholarship encompasses a variety of strands of work, but all have in common the insight that gender matters in understanding how IR works—especially in issues relating to war and international security. Feminist scholarship in various disciplines seeks to uncover hidden assumptions about gender in how we study a subject such as IR. What scholars traditionally claim to be universal often turns out to be true only of males.

---

[18] Rotbert, Robert. Failed States in a World of Terror. *Foreign Affairs* 81 (4), 2002: 127–141.

[19] Goldstein, Joshua S. *War and Gender: How Gender Shapes the War System and Vice Versa*. Cambridge, 2001. Peterson, V. Spike, and Anne Sisson Runyan. *Global Gender Issues*. 2nd ed. Boulder, CO: Westview, 1999. Tickner, J. Ann. *Gendering World Politics: Issues and Approaches in the Post–Cold War Era*. Columbia, 2001. Steans, Jill. *Gender and International Relations: An Introduction*. Rutgers, 1998. Whitworth, Sandra. *Feminism and International Relations*. NY: St. Martin's, 1994. Tickner, J. Ann. *Gender in International Relations: Feminist Perspectives on Achieving Global Security*. Columbia, 1992.

Some feminists have argued that the core assumptions of realism—especially of anarchy and sovereignty—reflect the ways in which *males* tend to interact and to see the world. In this view, the realist approach simply assumes male participants when discussing foreign policy decision making, state sovereignty, or the use of military force.

A GUY THING

Feminists from various theoretical traditions agree that the gender makeup of international summits is important. Here, leaders of the G8 states—the United States, Canada, France, Japan, Britain, Italy, Russia, and Germany—meet with the leaders of Nigeria, Senegal, Ethiopia, Tanzania, and South Africa, along with the heads of the World Bank, UN, African Union, and European Union in 2005. All twenty are men. (In 2006, a woman was elected leader of Germany.)

This is a somewhat complex critique. Because in fact the vast majority of heads of state, of diplomats, and of soldiers *are* male, it may be realistic to study them as males. What the feminist critics then ask is that scholars explicitly recognize the gendered nature of their subject (rather than implicitly assuming all actors are male). In this view, our understanding of male actors in IR can be increased by considering how their gender identity affects their views and decision processes. And females also influence IR (more often through nonstate channels than males do)—influences often ignored by realism. Feminist scholars argue that we can better understand IR by including the roles and effects of women. Some feel that women scholars tend to be more interested in these roles and effects than are their male colleagues. Yet, when a survey in 2005 listed the 25 most influential IR scholars, all 25 were male.[20]

Women and AIDS

Beyond revealing the hidden assumptions about gender in a field of scholarship, feminists often *challenge traditional concepts of gender* as well. In IR, these traditional concepts revolve around the assumptions that males fight wars and run states, whereas females are basically irrelevant to IR. Such gender roles are based in the broader construction of masculinity as suitable to *public* and political spaces, whereas femininity is associated with the sphere of the *private* and domestic. An example of this gendered construction was provided by White House Chief of Staff Donald Regan's comment at a 1985 Reagan-Gorbachev summit meeting that women do not care about throw weights of ICBMs (see p. 233) and would rather watch Nancy Reagan. Feminists call into question, at a minimum, the stereotypes of women as caring more about fashion than arms control.

Beyond a basic agreement that gender is important, there is no single feminist approach to IR but several such approaches—*strands* of scholarship and theory. Although they are interwoven (all paying attention to gender and to the status of women), they often run in different directions. On some core issues, the different strands of feminism have conflicting views, creating interesting debates *within* feminism.

---

[20] Meyer, Mary K., and Elisabeth Prügl, eds. *Gender Politics in Global Governance*. NY: Rowman & Littlefield, 1999. Peterson, Susan, Michael J. Tierney, and Daniel Maliniak. Inside the Ivory Tower. *Foreign Policy* 151, Nov./Dec. 2005: 58-64.

Viewing Gender Issues in Sub-Saharan Africa

One strand, **difference feminism,** focuses on valorizing the feminine—that is, valuing the unique contributions of women *as* women. Difference feminists do not think women do all things as well as men or vice versa. Because of their greater experience with nurturing and human relations, women are seen as potentially more effective than men (on average) in conflict resolution as well as in group decision making. Difference feminists believe there are real differences between the genders that are not just social constructions and cultural indoctrination (although these contribute to gender roles, too). Some difference feminists believe there is a core biological essence to being male or female (sometimes called *essentialism*), but the majority think women's difference is more culturally than biologically determined. In either case, feminine perspectives create a *standpoint* from which to observe, analyze, and criticize the traditional perspectives on IR.[21]

Another strand, **liberal feminism,** rejects these claims as being based on stereotyped gender roles. Liberal feminists see the "essential" differences in men's and women's abilities or perspectives as trivial or nonexistent—men and women are equal. They deplore the exclusion of women from positions of power in IR but do not believe that including women would change the nature of the international system. Liberal feminists seek to include women more often as subjects of study—such as women state leaders, women soldiers, and other women operating outside the traditional gender roles in IR.

A third approach combines feminism with postmodernism, discussed later in this chapter. **Postmodern feminism** tends to reject the assumptions about gender made by both difference and liberal feminists. Where difference feminists consider gender differences to be important and fixed, and liberal feminists consider those differences to be trivial, postmodern feminists find them important but arbitrary and flexible.

To some extent the divergent views of feminist strands—difference, liberal, and postmodern—overlap with the general themes of conservative, liberal, and revolutionary world views, respectively. But these parallels are only rough.

The Masculinity of Realism

Difference feminism provides a perspective from which to reexamine the core assumptions of realism—especially the assumption of autonomy, from which flow the key realist concepts of sovereignty and anarchy. To realists, the international system consists of autonomous actors (states) that control their own territory and have no right to infringe on another's territory. Do these concepts rest on a "masculine" view of the world? If so, what would a "feminine" approach to international security be like? Some difference feminists have argued that realism emphasizes autonomy and separation because men find separation easier to deal with than interconnection.

This view rests on a psychological theory that boys and girls grow up from a young age with different views of separateness and connection.[22] In this theory, because a child's primary caretaker is almost always female in the early years, girls form their gender identity around the perception of *similarity* with their caretaker (and by extension the environment in which they live), but boys perceive their *difference* from the caretaker. From this experience, boys develop social relations based on individual *autonomy*, but girls' relations are based on *connection*. As a result, women are held to be more likely than men to fear abandonment, whereas men are more likely to fear intimacy.

---

[21] Keohane, Robert O. International Relations Theory: Contributions of a Feminist Standpoint. *Millennium* 18 (2), 1989: 245–53.

[22] Gilligan, Carol. *In a Different Voice: Psychological Theory and Women's Development*. Harvard, 1982. Chodorow, Nancy. *The Reproduction of Mothering*. California, 1978.

In *moral* reasoning, according to this research, boys tend to apply abstract rules and stress individual rights (reflecting their sense of separation from the situation), but girls pay more attention to the concrete contexts of different situations and to the responsibility of group members for each other. In playing *games*, boys tend to resolve disputes through arguments about the rules and then keep playing, but girls are more likely to abandon a game rather than argue over the rules and risk the social cohesion of their group. In *social relations*, boys form and dissolve friendships more readily than girls, who are more likely to stick loyally with friends. All these gender differences in children reflect the basic concept that for girls connection matters more than independence, but for boys the reverse is true.

HER ROLE AND HIS

Feminist scholars emphasize the importance of gender roles in IR, especially the traditional distinction between males in the political-military roles and females in the domestic-family roles. Here, a UN soldier in Sarajevo provides cover as a Bosnian citizen runs along "sniper's alley," 1994.

Realism, of course, rests on the concept of states as separate, autonomous actors that make and break alliances freely while pursuing their own interests (but not interfering in each other's internal affairs). Such a conception of autonomy parallels the masculine psyche just described. Thus, some feminists find in realism a hidden assumption of masculinity. Furthermore, the sharp distinction that realists draw between international politics (anarchic) and domestic politics (ordered) parallels the distinction in gender roles between the public (masculine) and private (feminine) spheres. Thus, realism constructs IR as a man's world.

By contrast, an international system based on *feminine* principles might give greater importance to the *interdependence* of states than to their autonomy, stressing the responsibility of people to care for each other with less regard for states and borders. In the struggle between the principles of human rights and of sovereignty (noninterference in internal affairs), human rights would receive priority. In the choice of forms of leverage when conflicts arise between states, violence might be less prevalent. The concept of national security might be based on common security (see p. 108) rather than narrow self interest.

The realist preoccupation with the interstate level of analysis presumes that the logic of war itself is autonomous and can be separated from other social relationships such as economics, domestic politics, sexism, and racism. Difference feminism, however, reveals the *connections* of these phenomena with war. It suggests new avenues for understanding war at the domestic and individual levels of analysis—underlying causes that realists largely ignore.

From this difference-feminist perspective, neoliberalism has gone backward from traditional liberalism, by accepting the realist assumption of separate unitary states as the important actors, and downplaying substate and transnational actors including women. Neoliberalism's conception of cooperation as rule-based interactions among autonomous actors also reflects masculinist assumptions.

THINKING THEORETICALLY

Manhood and the Decision for War

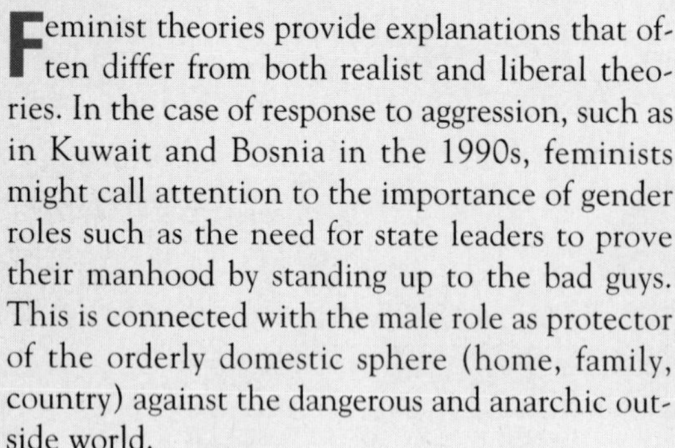

Feminist theories provide explanations that often differ from both realist and liberal theories. In the case of response to aggression, such as in Kuwait and Bosnia in the 1990s, feminists might call attention to the importance of gender roles such as the need for state leaders to prove their manhood by standing up to the bad guys. This is connected with the male role as protector of the orderly domestic sphere (home, family, country) against the dangerous and anarchic outside world.

In the case of Kuwait, the first President Bush had long been criticized as being a "wimp" (an insult to his manhood), and his determination to respond to Iraq's aggression became a personal battle with Saddam Hussein. A key moment in Bush's decision process was said to be when Britain's prime minister, Margaret Thatcher—a woman—urged him to act firmly, saying, "Don't go all wobbly on us, George." By the time of the Bosnia war, Thatcher was no longer the British prime minister, and Bush (after the Gulf War) perhaps no longer had to prove his manhood.

Gender in War and Peace

In addition to its emphasis on autonomy and anarchy, realism stresses military force as the key form of leverage in IR. Here, too, many difference feminists see in realism a hidden assumption of masculinity. They see war as not only a male occupation, but also the quintessentially male occupation. In this view, men are inherently the more warlike gender, and women the more peaceful. Thus, although realism may accurately portray the importance of war and military force in IR as we now know it, this merely reflects the male domination of the international sphere to date—not a necessary, eternal, or inescapable logic of relations among states.[23]

Difference feminists find plenty of evidence to support the idea of war as a masculine pursuit. Anthropologists have found that in all known cultures, males are the primary (and usually the only) combatants in warfare, despite the enormous diversity of those cultures in so many other ways. (Of course, voting and political leadership were also male domains for most of history, yet feminists would hardly call those activities essentially masculine.)

One supposed link between war and masculinity is the male sex hormone testosterone (along with related hormones), which some biologists have connected with aggressive behavior in animals. However, testosterone does not *cause* aggression. Rather, social interactions "feed back" to affect testosterone levels (winners' testosterone levels rise while losers' levels fall). Thus testosterone is a link in a complex system of relationships between the organism and the social environment. Complex behaviors such as aggression and war cannot be said to be biologically *driven* or predetermined, because humanity's most striking biological capability is flexibility.

Even some feminists who see gender differences as strictly cultural, and not biological at all, view war as a masculine construction. In one theory, for example, war may fill a void left for men by their inability to give birth; war provides a meaning to life and gives men an opportunity through heroism to transcend their individual isolation and

[23] Lorentzen, Lois Ann, and Jennifer Turpin, eds. *The Women and War Reader*. New York University, 1998. Elshtain, Jean Bethke, and Sheila Tobias, eds. *Women, Militarism, and War: Essays in History, Politics, and Social Theory*. Lanham, MD: University Press of America, 1989.

overcome their fear of death—opportunities that women potentially get through childbirth. In addition, heroism on the battlefield, especially before modern mechanized war, promised men a form of immortality, as their deeds would live on in collective memory.[24]

By contrast, women are usually portrayed by difference feminists as more peaceful creatures than men—whether because of biology, culture, or (most likely) both. These feminists emphasize women's unique abilities and contributions as *peacemakers*. They stress women's roles as *mothers* and potential mothers. Because of such caregiving roles, women are presumed to be more likely than men to oppose war and more likely to find alternatives to violence in resolving conflicts.[25]

CRITICAL MASS

Difference feminists see women as inherently less warlike than men and more adept at making peace because of their potential and actual experiences as mothers. Low representation of women in governments makes this theory hard to test. In an exception, Chile's first woman president, Michelle Bachelet, appointed women as half the members of her cabinet in 2006.

Both biologically and anthropologically, there is no firm evidence connecting women's caregiving functions (pregnancy and nursing) with any particular kinds of behavior such as reconciliation or nonviolence—although females have been studied less than males. The role of women varies considerably from one society to another. Although they rarely take part in combat, women sometimes provide logistical support to male warriors and sometimes help to drive the men into a war frenzy by dancing, shaming nonparticipating males, and other activities supportive of war. Yet in other cultures, women restrain the men from war or play special roles as mediators in bringing wars to an end.

The idea of women as peacemakers has a long history. In ancient Athens, the (male) playwright Aristophanes speculated about how women might end the unpopular Peloponnesian War with Sparta, then in progress. (His play, *Lysistrata,* was read in 1,000 locations in 56 countries on March 3, 2003, to protest the coming Iraq War.) In the play, a young woman named Lysistrata organizes the Athenian and Spartan women to withhold sex from the men until the latter stop the war (the women also make off with the war treasury). In short order, the men come to their senses and make peace.[26]

Women have formed their own organizations to work for peace on many occasions. In 1852, *Sisterly Voices* was published as a newsletter for women's peace societies. Bertha von Suttner in 1892 persuaded Alfred Nobel to create the Nobel peace prize (which Suttner

[24] Hartsock, Nancy C. M. Masculinity, Heroism, and the Making of War. In Harris, Adrienne, and Ynestra King, eds. *Rocking the Ship of State: Toward a Feminist Peace Politics*. Boulder, CO: Westview, 1989, pp. 133–52.

[25] Woolf, Virginia. *Three Guineas*. London: Hogarth, 1977 [1938]. Pierson, Ruth Roach. *Women and Peace: Theoretical, Historical and Practical Perspectives*. London: Croom Helm, 1987. Burguieres, M. K. Feminist Approaches to Peace: Another Step for Peace Studies. *Millennium* 19 (1), 1990: 1–18. Brock-Utne, Birgit. *Educating for Peace: A Feminist Perspective*. NY: Pergamon, 1985. Reardon, Betty. *Sexism and the War System*. NY: Teachers College, 1985. Di Leonardo, Micaela. Morals, Mothers, and Militarism: Antimilitarism and Feminist Theory [review article]. *Feminist Studies* 11 (3), 1985, 599–617.

[26] Aristophanes. *Lysistrata*. Edited by Jeffrey Henderson. Oxford, 1987.

won in 1905). During World War I, in 1915, Jane Addams and other feminists convened an international women's peace conference at the Hague. They founded the Women's Peace Party (now called the Women's International League for Peace and Freedom).[27]

After World War I, the *suffrage* movement won the right for women to vote. Difference feminists thought that women would vote for peace and against war, changing the nature of foreign policy, but women generally voted as their husbands did. Similarly, decades later when women participated in liberation struggles against colonialism in the global South, some feminists thought such participation would change foreign policies in the newly independent countries, but in general such changes did not materialize (partly because women were often pushed aside from political power after the revolution).

Nonetheless, U.S. public opinion on foreign policy issues since the 1930s partially vindicates difference feminists. A **gender gap** in polls shows women to be about 10 percentage points lower than men on average in their support for military actions. This gender gap shrinks, however, when there is broad consensus on a military action, as when U.S. forces attacked terrorist supporters in Afghanistan in late 2001.

WEB LINK
Greenham Common

Meanwhile, feminists in recent decades have continued to organize women's peace organizations.[28] In the 1980s, Women's Action for Nuclear Disarmament (WAND) opposed the nuclear arms buildup, and women encamped for years at Britain's Greenham Common air base. In 1995, the UN-sponsored Beijing conference on women brought together women activists from around the world, and helped deepen feminists' engagement with global issues such as North-South inequality. In 2000, the UN Security Council passed Resolution 1325 mandating greater inclusion of women and attention to gender in UN peacekeeping and reconstruction. In Bahrain, women won the right to vote and to run for office in 2002, but none were elected.

Through these various actions, difference feminists began developing a feminist practice of international relations that could provide an alternative to the masculine practice of realism. The motto of the UN Educational, Scientific, and Cultural Organization (UNESCO) is, "Since war begins in the minds of men, it is in the minds of men that the foundations for peace should be sought." For difference feminists, war does indeed begin in the minds of men but the foundations for peace would better be sought in the minds of women.

Women in IR

Liberal feminists are skeptical of difference-feminist critiques of realism. They believe that when women are allowed to participate in IR, they play the game basically the same way men do, with similar results. They think that women can practice realism—based on autonomy, sovereignty, anarchy, territory, military force, and all the rest—just as well as men can. Liberal feminists therefore tend to reject the critique of realism as masculine. (In practice, many feminists draw on both difference and liberal feminists views in various proportions.)[29]

Liberal feminism focuses on the integration of women into the overwhelmingly male preserves of foreign policy making and the military. In most states, these occupations are typically at least 90 percent male. For instance, in 1995 the world's diplomatic delegations

[27] Degen, Marie Louise. *The History of the Woman's Peace Party*. NY: Burt Franklin Reprints [1939 edition, Johns Hopkins], 1974.
[28] Swerdlow, Amy. Pure Milk, Not Poison: Women Strike for Peace and the Test Ban Treaty of 1963. In Harris and King, eds. *Rocking the Ship of State* (see footnote 24 in this chapter), pp. 225–37. Stephenson, Carolyn M. Feminism, Pacifism, Nationalism, and the United Nations Decade for Women. In Stiehm, Judith, ed. *Women and Men's Wars*. Oxford: Pergamon, 1983, pp. 341–48. Kirk, Gwyn. Our Greenham Common: Feminism and Nonviolence. In Harris and King, eds. *Rocking the Ship of State* (see footnote 24 in this chapter), pp. 115–30.
[29] Kelly, Rita Mae, et al., eds. *Gender, Globalization, and Democratization*. NY: Rowman & Littlefield, 2001.

to the UN General Assembly were 80 percent male overall, and the heads of those delegations were 97 percent male. The U.S. military, with one of the highest proportions of women anywhere in the world or in history, is still 85 percent male.[30]

For liberal feminists, the main effect of this gender imbalance on the nature of IR—that is, apart from effects on the status of women—is to waste talent. Since liberal feminists think that women have the same capabilities as men, the inclusion of women in traditionally male occupations (from state leader to foot soldier) would bring additional capable individuals into those areas. Gender equality would thus increase national capabilities by giving the state a better overall pool of diplomats, generals, soldiers, and politicians.

In support of their argument that, on average, women handle power just as men do, liberal feminists point to the many examples of women who have served in such positions. No distinctly feminine feature of their behavior in office distinguishes these leaders from their male counterparts. Rather, they have been diverse in character and policy. Of course, women in traditionally male roles may have been selected (or self-selected) on the basis of their suitability to such roles: they may not act the way "average" women would act. Still, they do show that individuals cannot be judged accurately using group characteristics alone.

FLOWER GIRLS

Consistent with liberal feminism's premises, the first two female U.S. secretaries of state, Madeleine Albright and Condoleezza Rice, were at least as hardline as their male colleagues. Albright advocated the use of force in Bosnia and the expansion of NATO in Eastern Europe, and Rice supported the invasion of Iraq in 2003. Here, however, in 1997, Albright told refugee girls from Afghanistan (where the Taliban faction harshly restricted women) that women worldwide "are all the same, and we have the same feelings"—a line more consistent with difference feminism.

Female state leaders do not appear to be any more peaceful, or any less committed to state sovereignty and territorial integrity, than are male leaders. It has even been suggested that women in power tend to be more warlike to compensate for being females in traditionally male roles.

Only one female has led a great power in the past century—Britain's Margaret Thatcher in the 1980s. She went to war in 1982 to recover the Falkland Islands from Argentina (at issue were sovereignty and territorial integrity). Among middle powers, Indira Gandhi led India in war against Pakistan in 1971, as did Israel's Golda Meir against Egypt and Syria in 1973. But Benazir Bhutto of Pakistan and Corazón Aquino of the Philippines struggled to control their own military forces in the late 1980s. Turkey's Tansu Çiller led a harsh war to suppress Kurdish rebels in the mid-1990s. But Violetta Chamorro of Nicaragua kept the peace between factions that had fought a brutal civil war in the 1980s. The former president of Sri Lanka and her mother, the prime minister, tried to

[30] Seager, Joni. *The Penguin Atlas of Women in the World*. NY: Penguin, 2003.

make peace with separatists, but returned to war when that initiative failed. Indonesia's president Megawati Sukarnoputri struggled to keep calm in that country and was defeated in 2004 after just one term in office. Other states, such as Finland, Norway, and Iceland, have had female leaders when war and peace were not major political issues in those countries. Overall, women state leaders, like men, seem capable of leading in war or in peace as circumstances demand.[31]

Within the U.S. foreign policy establishment, the record of women leaders similarly does not show any particular soft or hard tendency relative to their male counterparts. Madeleine Albright, the first female secretary of state, was considered one of the tougher foreign policy makers in the Clinton administration, as were Condoleezza Rice (national security advisor and secretary of state for George W. Bush) and Jeane Kirkpatrick (UN ambassador in the Reagan administration). But Republican Senator Nancy Kassebaum was a voice for compassion who led efforts to increase humanitarian aid to Africa in the 1990s.

Women in IR

In the U.S. Congress, it is hard to compare men's and women's voting records on foreign policy issues because there have been so few women. The U.S. Senate, which approves treaties and foreign policy appointments, was 98 to 99 percent male until 1992 (but has dropped to 86 percent male in 2006). Women have never chaired the key foreign policy committees (Armed Services and Foreign Relations/International Relations) in the Senate or House—although a woman, Nancy Pelosi, has been the minority (Democratic) leader in the House of Representatives since 2002.

Liberal feminists believe that women soldiers, like women politicians, have a range of skills and abilities comparable to men's. Again the main effect of including more women would be to improve the overall quality of military forces.[32] About 200,000 women soldiers serve in the U.S. military (15 percent of the total) and more than 1 million women are veterans. Women perform well in a variety of military roles from logistical and medical support to training and command. Women have had success in other countries that have allowed them into the military (or, in a few cases, drafted them).

Although women have served with distinction in military forces, they have been excluded from combat roles in almost all those forces. (It is a myth that women in the Israeli army serve in combat infantry roles.) In some countries, military women are limited to traditional female roles such as nurses and typists. Even where women may hold nontraditional positions such as mechanics and pilots (as in the United States), most women remain in the traditional roles. And certain jobs still remain off-limits; for instance, women cannot serve on U.S. submarines or in combat infantry. Thus there are relatively few cases to judge women's abilities in combat.

Those cases include historical examples of individual women who served in combat (sometimes disguised as men, sometimes not). In the fifteenth century, Joan of Arc rallied French soldiers to defeat England, turning the tide of the Hundred Years' War. (The English burned her at the stake as a witch after capturing her.) In recent years, U.S. women soldiers have found themselves in combat (present-day mobile tactics and fluid front lines make it

---

[31] D'Amico, Francine, and Peter R. Beckman, eds. *Women in World Politics: An Introduction*. Westport, CT: Bergin & Garvey, 1995. Nelson, Barbara J., and Najma Chowdhury, eds. *Women and Politics Worldwide*. Yale, 1994. Genovese, Michael A., ed. *Women as National Leaders: The Political Performance of Women as Heads of Government*. Thousand Oaks, CA: Sage, 1993. McGlen, Nancy E., and Meredith Reid Sarkees. *Women in Foreign Policy: The Insiders*. NY: Routledge, 1993.

[32] De Pauw, Linda Grant. *Battle Cries and Lullabies: Women in War from Prehistory to the Present*. Oklahoma, 1998. Francke, Linda Bird. *Ground Zero: The Gender Wars in the Military*. NY: Simon & Schuster, 1997. Stiehm, Judith Hicks, ed. *It's Our Military, Too!* Temple, 1996. Fraser, Antonia. *The Warrior Queens*. NY: Knopf, 1989. Addis, Elisabetta, Valerie E. Russo, and Lorenza Ebesta, eds. *Women Soldiers: Images and Realities*. NY: St. Martin's, 1994. Isaksson, Eva, ed. *Women and the Military System*. NY: St. Martin's, 1988.

hard to separate combat from support roles). Women helicopter pilots flew in combat zones during the 1991 Gulf War (in which tens of thousands of U.S. women served, 13 were killed, and 2 were captured as POWs). In the late 1990s, women began serving on some U.S. combat ships and airplanes, but not in ground combat units. In the 2003 Iraq War, women flew all manner of airplanes and helicopters, and one woman was in the first group of U.S. POWs captured early in the war. Women have also repeatedly participated in combat in rebel forces fighting guerrilla wars in Vietnam, Nicaragua, and elsewhere, as well as in terrorist or paramilitary units in countries such as Peru, Germany, Italy, and Palestine. Women in Eritrea's guerrilla forces became part of that country's regular army after independence and then served in front-line combat units during the Eritrea-Ethiopia war in the late 1990s. All these cases suggest that (at least some) women are able to hold their own in combat.

FIGHTING FEMALES

Women soldiers have performed as well as men in military tasks, as predicted by liberal feminists. But in state armies, women are barred from virtually all infantry combat units worldwide. Guerrilla forces more often include women, such as these soldiers of the Tamil Tigers rebels in Sri Lanka, 2002.

Some argue that women are more vulnerable (that is, to rape) if taken as POWs. Again liberal feminists disagree. All POWs are vulnerable, and both men and women POWs can be sexually abused.

The main reason that military forces exclude women from combat is fear about what effect their presence might have on the male soldiers, whose discipline and loyalty have traditionally been thought to depend on male bonding and single-minded focus. Opponents of women in the military claimed vindication, ironically, from a series of high-profile cases of sex discrimination, harassment, adultery, and rape in the U.S. military in the mid-1990s. The presence of females in the ranks, they said, was breaking down discipline and morale. Liberal feminists reject such arguments and argue that group bonding in military units does not depend on gender segregation. (After all, similar rationales were once given for racial segregation in U.S. military forces.)[33]

The effects of war on noncombatant women has also received growing attention.[34] Attacks on women in Algeria, Rwanda, Bosnia, Afghanistan, Democratic Congo, and Sudan pointed to a possible new trend toward women as military targets. Systematic rape was used as a terror tactic in Bosnia and Rwanda, and the Japanese army in World War II operated an international network of sex slaves known as "comfort women." Rape has long been treated as a normal if regrettable by-product of war, but recently certain instances of rape were declared war crimes (see p. 284) by the international tribunal for the former Yugoslavia.

---

[33] Katzenstein, Mary Fainsod, and Judith Reppy, eds. *Beyond Zero Tolerance: Discrimination in Military Culture*. Lanham, MD: Rowman & Littlefield, 1999.

[34] Enloe, Cynthia. *Maneuvers: The International Politics of Militarizing Women's Lives*. California, 2000.

In sum, liberal feminists reject the argument that women bring uniquely feminine assets or liabilities to foreign and military affairs. They do not critique realism as essentially masculine in nature but do criticize state practices that exclude women from participation in international politics and war.

Balancing the Feminist Arguments

The arguments of difference and liberal feminists may seem totally at odds. Difference feminists argue that realism reflects a masculine perception of social relations, whereas liberal feminists think that women can be just as realist as men. Liberal feminists believe that female participation in foreign policy and the military will enhance state capabilities, but difference feminists think women's unique abilities can be put to better use in transforming (feminizing) the entire system of international relations rather than in trying to play men's games.

The evidence in favor of both positions can be reconciled to some extent by bearing in mind that the character and ability of an individual are not the same as that of his or her group. Rather, the qualities of individuals follow a bell curve distribution, with many people clustered in the middle and fewer people very high or low on a given capability.

Gender differences posited by difference feminists mean that one bell curve is shifted from the other, even though the two may still overlap quite a bit (see Figure 3.1). To take a simple example, a few women are physically larger than almost all men, and a few men are smaller than almost all women. But on average men are somewhat larger than women. On various dimensions of capability, the women's curve is above or below the men's on average, but there is still much overlap.

Liberal feminist arguments emphasize the overlap of the two bell curves. They say that individual women—*most* women on most relevant dimensions—are well within the male curve and thus can perform equally with the men. Indeed, women in nontraditional gender roles may well perform better than their male counterparts, because presumably women who self-select into such roles (such as joining the military) are near the high end of the female bell curve, whereas the men are closer to the middle of the male curve (because more of them join). Similarly, women who become state leaders are presumably more adept at

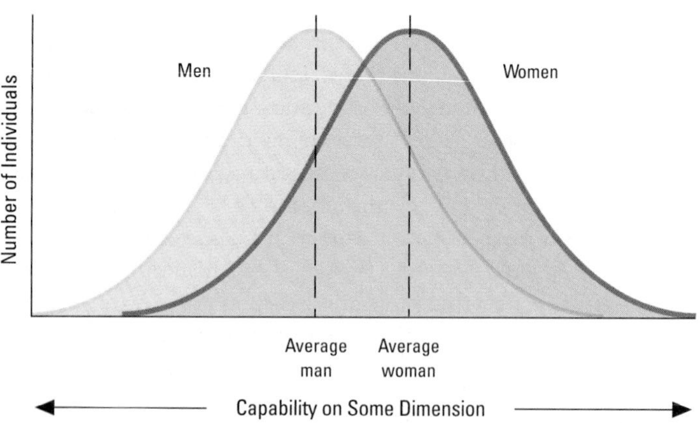

FIGURE 3.1 ■ Overlapping Bell Curves

Bell curves show that individuals differ in capabilities such as physical strength or peacemaking ability. Although the genders differ on average, for most individuals (in the area of overlap) such differences do not come into play. Liberal feminists emphasize the area where the curves overlap; difference feminists emphasize the overall group differences.

foreign policy making than most women (or men), because political processes tend to select women at the high end of the curve in terms of their affinity for realism.

Difference feminists are more interested in the shift in the two bell curves, not their overlap. On average, in this perspective, women tend to see international relations in a somewhat different way from that of men. So, although *individuals* selected to participate in foreign policy and the military may not differ from their male counterparts, women as a group differ. Women voters display different concerns regarding IR than men (as shown by the gender gap in opinion polls and voting patterns).

By this logic, then, profound differences in IR—and a shift away from the utility of realism in explaining state behavior—would occur only if many women participated in key foreign policy positions. That is, a *few* women politicians or women soldiers do not change the masculine foundations of IR. Women foreign policy makers today are surrounded by males (advisers, military officers, political leaders, and foreign state leaders). But a world in which *most* politicians or soldiers were female might be a different story. Then, instead of the selection of women for their ability to fit into men's games, the rules of the game might themselves change to reflect the fact that "average" women would be the main actors in the traditionally important IR roles. Of course, these theories of difference feminists have never been tested, because women have never attained predominance in foreign policy making in any country—much less in the international system as a whole.

Thus, the difference feminist critique of realism is intriguing but hard to demonstrate empirically. It may be, as this critique claims, that realism and neoliberalism alike put too much emphasis on the aspects of IR that fit a typical masculine view of the world—particularly autonomy, sovereignty, and anarchy. If so, realism and neoliberalism miss many important aspects that could help provide fuller explanations of events in IR.

In addition to the liberal and difference strands of feminism, the third strand, postmodern feminism, is connected with the rise of postmodernism in the social sciences.

Constructivism

An alternative approach to the study of IR, called **constructivism,** has grown immensely in popularity in the past 20 years. Constructivism is best described as an approach rather than a theory. Like feminism and postmodernism, its origins lie in other disciplines. When stripped to its core, it says nothing about IR per se, but its lessons about the nature of norms, identity, and social interaction can provide powerful insights into the world of IR.

Constructivism

Constructivism is interested in how actors define their national interests, threats to those interests, and their relationships to one another. Realists (and neoliberals) tend to simply take state interests as given. Thus, constructivism puts IR in the context of broader social relations.[35]

There are many strands of constructivist research. One prominent line examines how states' interests and identities are intertwined, as well as how those identities are shaped by interactions with other states.[36] For example, why is the United States con-

---

[35] Legro, Jeffrey W. *Rethinking the World: Great Power Strategies and International Order*. Cornell, 2005. Hopf, Ted. *Social Construction of International Politics: Identities and Foreign Policies, Moscow, 1955 and 1999*. Cornell, 2002. Crawford, Neta C. *Argument and Change in World Politics: Ethics, Decolonization, and Humanitarian Intervention*. Cambridge, 2002.

[36] Hall, Rodney Bruce. *National Collective Identity: Social Constructs and International Systems*. Columbia, 1999. Reus-Smit, Christian. *The Moral Purpose of the State: Culture, Social Identity, and Institutional Rationality in International Relations*. Princeton, 1999. Barnett, Michael. *Dialogues in Arab Politics*. Columbia, 1998.

cerned when North Korea builds nuclear weapons, but not when Great Britain does? Realists would quickly answer that North Korea poses a bigger threat, yet from a pure military power perspective, Great Britain is a *far* superior military force to North Korea. Yet, no one would argue that Great Britain is a threat to the U.S. no matter how many nuclear weapons it builds. Constructivist scholars would point out that there is a shared history, shared alliances, and shared norms that tell Americans and the British they are not a threat to one another although they are very powerful militarily. Identity of the potential adversary matters, not just its military capabilities and interests. This is a rejection of the realist assumption that states always want more rather than less power and wealth and of the assumption that state interests exist independently of a context of interactions among states.[37]

Constructivists hold that these state identities are complex, changing, and arise from interactions with other states—often through a process of *socialization*. Some constructivist scholars contend that over time, states can conceptualize one another in such a way that there is no danger of a security dilemma, arms races, or the other effects of anarchy. They point to Europe as an example—a continent that was the center of two military conflicts in the first half of the twentieth century that killed millions. By the end of that century, war had become unthinkable. European identities are now intertwined with the European Union, not with the violent nationalism that led to two World Wars. For constructivists, power politics, anarchy, and military force cannot explain this change. Institutions, regimes, norms, and changes in identity are better explanations.[38]

States may also come to value and covet something like status or reputation, which are social, not material concepts. Switzerland, for example, values its role as a neutral, nonaligned state (it belongs to neither the European Union nor NATO, and joined the UN only in 2002). This status as a neutral gives Switzerland prestige and power—not a material power like money or guns—but a normative power to intervene diplomatically in important international affairs. Similarly, Canada's foreign policy contains its own identity-driven imperatives and limits.

Another field of constructivist research also relies heavily on international norms and their power to constrain state action. While realists (and neoliberals) contend states make decisions based on a *logic of consequences* (what will happen to me if I behave a certain way), constructivist scholars note there is a powerful *logic of appropriateness* (how should I behave in this situation).[39] For example, some cases of humanitarian intervention—military intervention by a state or states to protect citizens or subjects of another—seem difficult to explain in realist or liberal terms. Why, for example, did the United States in 1992 send troops to Somalia—a country of minimal strategic and economic importance to the United States—as Somalia descended into political chaos and faced the possibility of mass starvation (see p. 46)? A constructivist explanation might point to changing norms about which kinds of people are worthy of protection. In the nineteenth century, European powers occasionally intervened to protect Christian subjects of the Ottoman Empire from massacres, but generally ignored non-Christian victims. However, as decolonization enshrined the principle of self-determination and as human rights became

---

[37] Wendt, Alexander. *Social Theory of International Politics*. Cambridge, 1999. Wendt, Alexander. Anarchy Is What States Make of It: The Social Construction of Power Politics. *International Organization* 46 (2), 1992: 391–426.

[38] Checkel, Jeffrey. Social Learning and European Identity Change. *International Organization* 55 (3), 2000: 553–88.

[39] March, James G., and Johan Olsen. The Institutional Dynamics of International Political Orders. *International Organization* 52 (4), 1998, 943–69.

widely valued, the scope of humanitarian intervention expanded. Although the international community does not always respond effectively to humanitarian crises, it is no longer acceptable to view only Christians as deserving protection.[40] The United States in this example tried to act in an appropriate fashion rather than according to the dictates of cost-benefit calculations.

Examples can be found in the developing world as well. Some constructivists have argued that countries in Latin America, Africa, and the Middle East have adopted or changed policies in response to international norms—not because it provided large benefits, but rather because it was perceived as the appropriate course of action. For example, many developing states have raced to create science bureaucracies and/or begin technological modernization of their militaries. Constructivists point out that the reason developing states chose to spend their limited resources on such projects is their desire to be perceived as "modern" by the international system. "Modern" states have science bureaucracies and advanced militaries. Ironically, many states that build science bureaucracies have few scientists while many states who build advanced militaries have few enemies.[41] Thus, constructivists emphasize that identities and norms must be used to explain this seemingly puzzling behavior.

How are these international norms spread around the world? In an age of global communication and relative ease of transportation, there are many possibilities. Constructivists emphasize different sets of actors who spread norms. Some contend that individuals, labeled *norm entrepreneurs*, through travel, writing, and meeting with elites change ideas and encourage certain types of norms. Some point to broad-based social movements and nongovernmental organizations, such as the anti-Apartheid movement encouraging the development of a global norm of racial equality. Others show how international organizations (such as the UN or NATO) can diffuse norms of what is appropriate and inappropriate behavior. In each case, however, it is new ideas and norms, rather than power and self-interest driving state behavior.[42]

Constructivism is still a controversial approach to the study of IR, but cannot be ignored. Some suggest that a melding of realist-oriented and constructivist-oriented scholarship may develop, but others are less hopeful.[43]

Postmodernism

Postmodernism, like feminism and constructivism, is a broad approach to scholarship that has left its mark on various academic disciplines, especially the study of literature. Because of their literary roots, postmodernists pay special attention to *texts* and to

---

[40] Finnemore, Martha. *Purpose of Intervention*. Cornell, 2004.

[41] Finnemore, Martha. International Organizations as Teachers of Norms: The United Nations Education, Scientific, and Cultural Organizations and Science Policy. *International Organization* 47 (4), 1993, 565–97. Eyre, Dana, and Mark Suchman. Status, Norms, and the Proliferation of Conventional Weapons: An Institutional Theory Approach. In Katzenstein, P., ed. *The Culture of National Security*. Columbia, 1996.

[42] Keck, Margaret, and Kathryn Sikkink. *Activists Beyond Borders: Advocacy Networks in International Politics*. Cornell, 1998. Klotz, Audie. *Norms in International Relations: The Struggle Against Apartheid*. Cornell, 1995. Finnemore, Martha. *National Interests in International Society*. Cornell, 1996. Johnston, Alastair Iain. Treating Institutions as Social Environments. *International Studies Quarterly* 45 (3), 2001: 487–516. Finnemore, Martha, and Kathryn Sikkink. International Norm Dynamics and Political Change. *International Organization* 52 (4), 1998: 887–917.

[43] Fearon, James, and Alexander Wendt. Rationalism v. Constructivism: A Skeptical View. In Carlsnaes, W., T. Risse, and B. Simmons, eds. *Handbook of International Relations*. Sage, 2002. Jupille, Joseph, James Caporaso, and Jeffrey Checkel. Integrating Institutions. *Comparative Political Studies* 36 (1/2), 2003: 7–41.

discourses—how people talk and write about their subject (IR).[44] Postmodern critiques of realism thus center on analyzing realists' words and arguments.[45]

Deconstructing Realism

A central idea of postmodernism is that there is no single, objective reality but a multiplicity of experiences and perspectives that defy easy categorization. For this reason, postmodernism itself is difficult to present in a simple or categorical way. This section will merely convey some important postmodern themes, necessarily oversimplified, and show how postmodernism can help illuminate some problems of realism.

From a postmodern perspective, realism cannot justify its claim that states are the central actors in IR and that states operate as unitary actors with coherent sets of objective interests (which they pursue through international power politics). Postmodern critics of realism see nothing objective about state interests, and certainly nothing universal (in that one set of values or interests applies to all states).

More fundamentally, postmodernism calls into question the whole notion of states as actors. States have no tangible reality; they are "fictions" that we (as scholars and citizens) construct to make sense of the actions of large numbers of individuals. For postmodernists, the stories told about the actions and policies of states are just that—stories. From this perspective, it is an arbitrary distinction that leads bookstores to put spy novels on the fiction shelf whereas biographies and histories go on the nonfiction shelf. None of these is an objective reality, and all are filtered through an interpretive process that distorts the actual experiences of those involved.[46]

Contrary to realism's claim that states are unitary actors, postmodernists see multiple realities and experiences lurking below the surface of the fictional entities that realists construct (states). The Soviet Union, for example, was treated by realists as a single actor with a single set of objective interests. Indeed, it was considered the second most important actor in the world. Realists were amazed when the Soviet Union split into 15 pieces, each containing its own fractious groups and elements. It became clear that the "unitary state" called the Soviet Union had masked (and let realists ignore) the divergent experiences of constituent republics, ethnic groups, and individuals.

Postmodernists seek to "deconstruct" such constructions as states, the international system, and the associated stories and arguments (texts and discourses) with which realists portray the nature of international relations. To *deconstruct* a text—a term borrowed from literary criticism—means to tease apart the words in order to reveal hidden meanings, looking for what might be omitted or included only implicitly. The hidden meanings not explicitly addressed in the text are often called the **subtext.**[47]

---

[44] Rosenau, Pauline Marie. *Post-Modernism and the Social Sciences: Insights, Inroads, and Intrusions*. Princeton, 1992.

[45] Ashley, Richard K., and R. B. J. Walker. Speaking the Language of Exile: Dissident Thought in International Studies [Introduction to special issue]. *International Studies Quarterly* 34 (3), 1990: 259–68. Lapid, Yosef. The Third Debate: On the Prospects of International Theory in a Post-Positivist Era. *International Studies Quarterly* 33 (3), 1989: 235–54. Der Derian, James. *On Diplomacy: A Genealogy of Western Estrangement*. NY: Basil Blackwell, 1987.

[46] Shapiro, Michael J. Textualizing Global Politics. In Der Derian, James, and Michael J. Shapiro, eds. *International/Intertextual Relations: Postmodern Readings of World Politics*. NY: Lexington, 1989, pp. 11–22. Shapiro, Michael J., and Hayward R. Alker, eds. *Challenging Boundaries: Global Flows, Territorial Identities*. Minnesota, 1996.

[47] Campbell, David. *Politics Without Principle: Sovereignty, Ethics, and the Narratives of the Gulf War*. Boulder, CO: Lynne Rienner, 1993. Stephanson, Anders. *Kennan and the Art of Foreign Policy*. Harvard, 1989. Chaloupka, William. *Knowing Nukes: The Politics and Culture of the Atom*. Minnesota, 1992.

What is subtext in the stories realists tell about IR? What does realism omit from its accounts of IR? We have just discussed one major omission—women and gender. Furthermore, in its emphasis on states, realism omits the roles of individuals, domestic politics, economic classes, MNCs, and other nonstate actors. In its focus on the great powers, realism omits the experiences of countries in the global South. In its attention to military forms of leverage, it omits the roles of various nonmilitary forms of leverage.

Realism focuses so narrowly because its aim is to reduce IR down to a simple, coherent model. The model is claimed to be objective, universal, and accurate. To postmodernists, the realist model is none of these things: it is a biased model that creates a narrow and one-sided story for the purpose of promoting the interests of powerful actors. Postmodernists seek to destroy this model along with any other model (including neoliberalism) that tries to represent IR in simple objective categories. Postmodernists instead want to celebrate the diversity of experiences that make up IR without needing to make sense of them by simplifying and categorizing.[48]

Postmodern Feminism

One line of criticism directed at realism combines feminism and postmodernism.[49] *Postmodern feminism* seeks to deconstruct realism with the specific aim of uncovering the pervasive hidden influences of gender in IR while showing how arbitrary the construction of gender roles is. Feminist postmodernists agree with difference feminists that realism carries hidden meanings about gender roles but deny that there is any fixed inherent meaning in either male or female genders. Rather, feminist postmodernists look at the interplay of gender and power in a more open-ended way. Postmodern feminists criticize liberal feminists for trying merely to integrate women into traditional structures of war and foreign policy. They criticize difference feminists as well, for glorifying traditional feminine virtues.

In studying war, postmodern feminists have challenged the archetypes of the (male) "just warrior" and the (female) "beautiful soul." They argue that women are not just passive bystanders or victims in war, but active participants in a system of warfare tied to both genders. Women act not only as nurses and journalists at the "front" but as mothers, wives, and girlfriends on the "home front."[50] These scholars believe that stories of military forces should not omit the roles of prostitutes at military bases, nor should stories of diplomacy omit the roles of diplomats' wives.[51]

Postmodern feminists reject not only realism but also some of the alternative approaches that emphasize the protection of women and other noncombatants. Just war doctrine (see pp. 286–287) is considered too abstract—a set of concepts and rules that does

---

[48] Walker, R. B. J., and Saul H. Mendlovitz, eds. *Contending Sovereignties: Redefining Political Community*. Boulder, CO: Lynne Rienner, 1990. Walker, R. B. J. *Inside/Outside: International Relations as Political Theory*. Cambridge, 1993. Weber, Cynthia. *Simulating Sovereignty: Intervention, the State and Symbolic Exchange*. Cambridge, 1995. Sjolander, Claire Turenne, and Wayne S. Cox, eds. *Beyond Positivism: Critical Reflections on International Relations*. Boulder, CO: Lynne Rienner, 1994. George, Jim. *Discourses of Global Politics: A Critical (Re)Introduction to International Relations*. Boulder, CO: Lynne Rienner, 1994.

[49] Peterson, V. Spike, ed. *Gendered States: Feminist (Re)Visions of International Relations Theory*. Boulder, CO: Lynne Rienner, 1992. Sylvester, Christine. *Feminist Theory and International Relations in a Postmodern Era*. Cambridge, 1994.

[50] Elshtain, Jean Bethke. *Women and War*. 2nd ed. Chicago, 1995. Braybon, Gail, and Penny Summerfield. *Out of the Cage: Women's Experiences in Two World Wars*. NY: Pandora, 1987.

[51] Enloe, Cynthia. *Bananas, Beaches, and Bases: Making Feminist Sense of International Politics*. California, 1989. Pettman, Jan Jindy. *Worlding Women: A Feminist International Politics*. NY: Routledge, 1996. Moon, Katherine H. S. *Sex Among Allies: Military Prostitution in U.S.–Korea Relations*. Columbia, 1997.

SEX IN THE SUBTEXT

Feminist postmodernists try to reveal hidden subtexts connecting gender with IR, such as the roles of sex and death in the constructions of masculinity by U.S. airmen in England, 1944.

not do justice to the richness of each historical context and the varied roles of individual men and women within it.[52]

Postmodern feminists have tried to deconstruct the language of realism, especially where it reflects influences of gender and sex. For instance, the first atomic bombs had male gender (they were named "Fat Man" and "Little Boy"); the coded telegram informing Washington, DC, that the first hydrogen bomb had worked said simply, "It's a boy" (presumably being born a girl would have indicated a failure). The plane that dropped the atomic bomb on Hiroshima (the *Enola Gay*) had female gender; it was named after the pilot's mother. Likewise the French atom-bomb test sites in the South Pacific were all given women's names.[53] Similarly, pilots have pasted pinup photos of nude women onto conventional bombs before dropping them. In all these cases, postmodern feminists would note that the feminine gender of vehicles, targets, or decorations amplifies the masculinity of the weapon itself.

These efforts find sex and gender throughout the subtext of realism. For example, the terms *power* and *potency* refer to both state capability and male virility. Military force depends on phallic objects—weapons designed to shoot projectiles, penetrate targets, and explode. In basic training, men chant: "This is my rifle [holding up rifle], this is my gun [pointing to crotch]; one's for killing, the other's for fun."[54] Nuclear weapons are also repeatedly spoken of in sexual terms, perhaps due to their great "potency." Female models are hired to market tanks, helicopter missiles, and other "potent" weapons to male procurement officers at international military trade shows.[55] The phallic character of weapons has seemingly persisted even as technology has evolved from spears to guns to missiles.

Realism and liberalism ignore all the sexual aspects of weaponry, limiting themselves to such issues as a weapon's explosive power, its range, and other technical information about its use as state leverage. But if sexual drives enter (perhaps unconsciously) into decisions about whether and when to use bombs or other military forces, then realism and liberalism cannot adequately explain those decisions.[56] Postmodernism thus reveals another reality—the sexual gratification of male politicians and soldiers—which competes with the realities of realism and neoliberalism, with their focus on maximizing national interests (narrowly or broadly construed). By radically shifting the focus and approach of IR scholarship, postmodernists hope to increase our understanding of IR in general and of the notion of rationality in particular.

---

[52] Elshtain. *Women and War* (see footnote 50 in this chapter). Ruddick, Sara. *Maternal Thinking: Towards a Politics of Peace*. London: The Women's Press, 1989.

[53] Cohn, Carol. Sex and Death in the Rational World of Defense Intellectuals. *Signs* 12 (4), 1987: 687–718.

[54] Dyer, Gwynne. *War*. NY: Crown, 1985.

[55] Center for Defense Information [Washington, DC]. Weapons Bazaar [slide show], 1985.

[56] Trexler, Richard C. *Sex and Conquest: Gendered Violence, Political Order, and the European Conquest of the Americas*. Cornell, 1995.

Peace Studies

Another approach of growing importance that challenges some fundamental concepts behind both realism and liberalism is peace studies. Many colleges have created interdisciplinary peace studies programs through which scholars and students organize discussions and courses about peace.[57] Typically, such programs include not only political scientists but also psychologists who have studied conflict, physicists who have studied nuclear weapons, religious scholars who have studied practical morality, and so forth. With these various disciplinary backgrounds, scholars of peace studies tend to be more eclectic than political scientists and much more broad-ranging in the topics they consider worthy of study in international security affairs. In particular, peace studies seeks to shift the focus of IR away from the interstate level of analysis and toward a broad conception of social relations at the individual, domestic, and global levels of analysis. Peace studies connects war and peace with individual responsibility, with economic inequality, with gender relations, with cross-cultural understanding, and with other aspects of social relationships. Peace studies seeks the potentials for peace not in the transactions of state leaders but in the transformation of entire societies (through social revolution) and in transnational communities (bypassing states and ignoring borders to connect people and groups globally).[58]

Peace in Northern Ireland

Another way in which peace studies seeks to broaden the focus of inquiry is to reject the supposed objectivity of traditional (realist and liberal) approaches. Most scholars of peace studies think that a good way to gain knowledge is to participate in action—not just to observe objectively. This lack of objectivity has been criticized as **normative bias** because scholars impose their personal norms and values on the subject. Scholars in peace studies respond, however, that realism itself has normative biases and makes policy prescriptions.

Conflict Resolution

The development and implementation of peaceful strategies for settling conflicts—using alternatives to violent forms of leverage—are known by the general term **conflict resolution.** These methods are at work, competing with violent methods, in virtually all international conflicts. Recently the use of conflict resolution has been increasing, becoming more sophisticated, and succeeding more often.[59]

Most conflict resolution uses a third party whose role is **mediation** between two conflicting parties.[60] Most of today's international conflicts have one or more mediating parties working regularly to resolve the conflict short of violence. There is no hard-and-fast rule saying what kinds of third parties mediate what kinds of conflicts. Presently the UN is the most

[57] Barash, David P. *Introduction to Peace Studies*. Belmont, CA: Wadsworth, 1991. Klare, Michael T., ed. *Peace and World Security Studies: A Curriculum Guide*. 6th ed. Boulder, CO: Lynne Rienner, 1994. Smoker, Paul, Ruth Davies, and Barbara Munske, eds. *A Reader in Peace Studies*. NY: Pergamon, 1990. Lopez, George A., ed. Peace Studies: Past and Future. *Annals of the American Academy of Political and Social Science*, no. 504, Newbury Park, CA: Sage, 1989.
[58] Cancian, Francesca M., and James William Gibson. *Making War/Making Peace: The Social Foundations of Violent Conflict*. Belmont, CA: Wadsworth, 1990. Rapoport, Anatol. *Peace: An Idea Whose Time Has Come*. Michigan, 1992. Galtung, Johan. *Peace by Peaceful Means: Peace and Conflict, Development and Civilization*. Sage, 1996.
[59] Kurtz, Lester R., ed. *Encyclopedia of Violence, Peace, and Conflict*. 3 vols. San Diego: Academic, 1999. Jeong, Ho-Won. *Conflict Resolution: Dynamics, Process, and Structure*. Brookfield, VT: Ashgate, 2000. Chayes, Antonia Handler, and Abram Chayes. *Planning for Intervention: International Cooperation in Conflict Management*. Cambridge, MA: Kluwer Law International, 1999. Lund, Michael S. *Preventing Violent Conflicts: A Strategy for Preventive Diplomacy*. Washington, DC: U.S. Institute of Peace, 1996. Väyrynen, Raimo, ed. *New Directions in Conflict Theory: Conflict Resolution and Conflict Transformation*. Sage, 1991. Burton, John W. *Conflict Resolution and Prevention*. NY: St. Martin's, 1990. Hauss, Charles. *International Conflict Resolution*, NY: Continuum, 2001.
[60] Bercovitch, Jacob, ed. *Resolving International Conflicts: The Theory and Practice of Mediation*. Boulder, CO: Lynne Rienner, 1996. Princen, Thomas. *Intermediaries in International Conflict*. Princeton, 1992.

STEPS TOWARD PEACE

Conflict resolution offers an alternative avenue for settling conflicts short of violence. The UN plays a central role in conflict resolution worldwide. Here, UN peacekeepers from Bangladesh operate a checkpoint in Ivory Coast in November 2004, during a long negotiated transition from civil war.

important mediator on the world scene. Some regional conflicts are mediated through regional organizations, single states, or even private individuals. For instance, the former president of Costa Rica, Oscar Arias, won the 1987 Nobel peace prize for mediating a multilateral agreement among Central American presidents to end several brutal wars in the region.[61]

The involvement of the mediator can vary. Some mediation is strictly *technical*—a mediator may take an active but strictly neutral role in channeling communication between two states that lack other channels of communication.[62] For example, Pakistan secretly passed messages between China and the United States before the breakthrough in U.S.-Chinese relations in 1971. Such a role is sometimes referred to as offering the mediator's *good offices* to a negotiating process. In facilitating communication, a mediator listens to each side's ideas and presents them in a way the other side can hear. The mediator works to change each side's view of difficult issues. In these roles, the mediator is like the translator between the two sides, or a therapist helping them work out psychological problems in their relationship.[63]

If both sides agree in advance to abide by a solution devised by a mediator, the process is called *arbitration*. In that case, both sides present their arguments to the arbitrator, who decides on a "fair" solution. For example, when Serbian and Bosnian negotiators could not agree on who should get the city of Brcko, they turned the issue over to arbitration rather than hold up the entire 1995 Dayton Agreement. Arbitration often uses a panel of three people, one chosen by each side unilaterally and a third on whom both sides agree. In 2002, such a panel (with the UN choosing the third member) delineated the Ethiopian-Eritrean border following a costly war.

Why should a state settle nonviolently a conflict that might be settled by military means? It must see that doing so would be in its better interest. To get national leaders to come to this conclusion one must create conditions to bring into play mutual interests that already exist or create new mutual interests.

---

[61] Child, Jack. *The Central American Peace Process, 1983–1991: Sheathing Swords, Building Confidence*. Boulder, CO: Lynne Rienner, 1992.

[62] Stein, Janice Gross, ed. *Getting to the Table: The Processes of International Prenegotiation*. Johns Hopkins, 1989.

[63] Crocker, Chester A., Fen Osler Hampson, and Pamela Aall. *Taming Intractable Conflicts: Mediation in the Hardest Cases*. Herndon, VA: United States Institute of Peace Press, 2004. Kremenyuk, V.A., ed. *International Negotiation: Analysis, Approaches, Issues*. 2nd ed. San Francisco: Jossey-Bass, 2002.

In many situations, two conflicting parties could benefit from a solution other than war but lack the trust and communication channels to find such a solution.[64] Neutral mediation with various degrees of involvement can bring about awareness of the two parties' common interests. For example, Egypt and Israel had a common interest in making peace in the late 1970s, but they also had a high level of mistrust. U.S. President Jimmy Carter invited the two heads of state to a private and relaxed setting—his Camp David retreat—where they could go through the issues without the restrictions of formal negotiations.

When heads of state do not see their common interests, ordinary citizens might try to raise awareness of such mutual interests on both sides. Travel and discussion by private individuals and groups toward this end has been called *citizen diplomacy*, and it occurs fairly regularly (though not very visibly) when conflicting states are stuck in a cycle of hostility.[65] Sometimes a private trip takes on historical significance, as when the U.S. wrestling team visited Iran in 1998.

Conflicting parties (and mediators) can also work to *restructure* the terms of bargaining—in effect extending the possible solutions for one or both sides so that their interests overlap. Often a mediator can come up with a win-win solution.[66] A win-win solution often trades off two disputed items on which the states place different priorities. Each side can then prevail on the issue that it considers important while yielding on an issue it does not care about as much.

Another way to create mutual interests is to break a conflict into pieces (fractionation) and start with those pieces in which a common interest and workable solution can be found. These may be largely symbolic *confidence-building* measures at first but can gather momentum as the process proceeds. A gradual increase in trust reduces the risks of nonviolent settlements relative to their costs and creates an expectation that the issues at stake can be resolved nonviolently.

Confidence-Building Measures

A mediator who is in a position to apply positive or negative leverage to the two parties can use that leverage to influence each side's calculation of interests (again opening up new mutual interests). For instance, the promise of future U.S. aid to both Israel and Egypt was an important sweetener in bringing them to a substantive agreement at Camp David. Likewise, the reluctance of states in the Middle East to incur U.S. displeasure played a role in bringing parties in the Arab-Israeli conflict into peace talks in 1991–2000.

War and Militarism

Peace studies resonates with Benjamin Franklin's observation that "there never was a good war or a bad peace."[67] Peace studies scholars argue that war is not just a natural expression of power, but one closely tied to militarism in (some) cultures.[68] **Militarism** is the glorification of war, military force, and violence through TV, films, books, political speeches, toys, games,

[64] Walter, Barbara. *Committing to Peace: The Successful Settlement of Civil Wars*. Princeton, 2002. Fortna, V. P. *Peace Time: Cease-Fire Agreements and the Durability of Peace*. Princeton, 2004.

[65] Agha, Hussein, Shai Feldman, Ahmad Khalidi, and Ze'ev Schiff. *Track II Diplomacy: Lessons from the Middle East*. MIT, 2003.

[66] Fisher, Roger, and William Ury, with Bruce Patton. *Getting to Yes: Negotiating Agreement Without Giving In*. NY: Penguin, 1983.

[67] Letter to Josiah Quincy, Sept. 11, 1773.

[68] Bacevich, Andrew J. *The New American Militarism: How Americans Are Seduced by War*. Oxford, 2005. Grossman, Lt. Col. Dave. *On Killing: The Psychological Cost of Learning to Kill in War and Society*. Boston: Little, Brown, 1995.

SHADOW OF WAR

Militarism in a culture, or the lack thereof, can influence foreign policy. In societies at war, children's psychological trauma contributes to intergroup conflicts decades later. Generations of Palestinians have grown up in a society permeated by violent conflict with Israel. This boy holds a Palestinian gunman's assault rifle during fighting in Bethlehem, 2001.

sports, and other such avenues. Militarism also refers to the structuring of society around war—for example, the dominant role of a military-industrial complex in a national economy, the dominance of national security issues in domestic politics, and so forth. Militarism is thought to underlie the propensity of political leaders to use military force. Historically, militarism has had a profound influence on the evolution of societies. War has often been glorified as a "manly" enterprise that ennobles the human spirit (especially before World War I, which changed that perspective). Not only evil acts but also exemplary acts of humanity are brought forth by war—sacrifice, honor, courage, altruism on behalf of loved ones, and bonding with a community larger than oneself.

The culture of modern states celebrates and rewards these qualities of soldiers, just as hunter-gatherer cultures created rituals and rewards to induce participation in warfare. We have holidays in honor of warriors, provide them (or their survivors) with veterans' benefits, and bury them in special cemeteries where their individual identities are symbolically submerged into a larger collective identity. Because militarism seems so pervasive and so strongly associated with the state, many scholars in peace studies question whether the very nature of states must change before lasting peace will be possible. In this regard, peace studies differs from both realism and neoliberalism.

Examples of less-militarized cultures show that realism's emphasis on military force is not universal or necessary. Costa Rica has had no army for 50 years (just lightly armed forces), even during the 1980s when wars occurred in neighboring Nicaragua and Panama. Japanese culture since World War II has developed strong norms against war and violence. Public opinion, even more than Japan's constitution, prevents political leaders from considering military force a viable instrument of foreign policy.

Anthropologists have tried to connect the domestic characteristics of hunter-gatherer societies with their external propensity to engage in warfare. There is some evidence that war occurs more frequently in societies with internal (especially gender) inequalities, with harsh child-rearing practices, and with fathers who are absent from child rearing. By contrast, relatively peaceful societies are more likely to have open decision-making processes, relative gender equality, and permissive and affectionate child rearing.[69] But all these societal attributes could as well be *effects* of war as causes. And since all kinds of society seem to have the potential for warfare under some conditions (see Chapter 5), distinctions such as "warlike" are only relative.

[69] Ross, Marc Howard. A Cross-Cultural Theory of Political Conflict and Violence. *Political Psychology* 7, 1986: 427–69. Ember, Carol R. A Cross-Cultural Perspective on Sex Differences. In Munroe, Ruth H. et al., eds. *Handbook of Cross-Cultural Human Development*. NY: Garland, 1980, pp. 531–80. Whiting, Beatrice B., and John W. M. Whiting. *Children of Six Cultures: A Psycho-Cultural Analysis*. Harvard, 1975.

POLICY PERSPECTIVES

President of the United States, George W. Bush

PROBLEM *How do you balance security needs against domestic political concerns?*

BACKGROUND Imagine that you are the president of the United States. The fight in the war on terror has taken a toll on U. S. armed forces. In 2005, more than 150,000 troops were deployed in Iraq, with thousands more placed in Afghanistan. More than 25 percent of reservists were already deployed, and more than 10,000 had been held on duty beyond their initial deployment. Military recruitment had slowed dramatically despite increased financial incentives, with the National Guard missing its recruitment goals for the first time in a decade and Army recruiting down 30 percent. These factors combined to stretch U.S. military forces thin.

A continued threat to the United States is North Korea, which maintains an army of an estimated 700,000 troops within 90 miles of the demilitarized zone (DMZ) between North and South Korea. North Korean reserve forces number over 7 million troops. The nearly 100,000 U.S. troops presently in the East Asia/Pacific region could offer staunch resistance to an initial North Korean attack, but more troops would be needed in an extended war.

During the 2004 presidential election campaign, the issue of the draft received attention. Many military advisors suggest that a draft is not a solution to a short-term problem, since it would take six months from a draft order until the first draftees reported to training. Moreover, career military officers prefer the current all-volunteer force, where all personnel choose to enter. Still, in the words of one Army colonel, "If the president decided we needed to go somewhere other than Iraq, it doesn't take a mental giant to figure out we don't have the people to do that."*

Military conscription (the draft), ended in the United States in 1973, as the Vietnam War wound down. Congress then reformed the draft's deferment system to eliminate the "higher education shelter," meaning a new draft would include college students (who could finish their current semester). This makes any draft proposal especially unpopular in public opinion. Furthermore, Congress would decide whether to include women or limit a new draft to men as was the case in the past.

SCENARIO Now imagine that along with continued instability in Iraq and Afghanistan, a new crisis emerges. North Korea makes preparations for an attack across the DMZ, and daily reports of large-scale incursions into the DMZ flood into American intelligence channels. Clearly, a major land force would be necessary to repel any North Korean invasion, especially if force is required to retake lost territory.

CHOOSE YOUR POLICY As president of the United States, do you support a new draft, which would include college students and possibly women? Facing the prospect of an extended conflict in Iraq, Afghanistan, and North Korea, a draft would provide much-needed personnel.

If a draft is not an option, how do you choose to confront possible shortages of personnel? Do you ask your allies to contribute troops to the war effort? Can you trust they will do so in sufficient numbers?

How do you balance the domestic pressures of public opinion with a need for more troops to meet security concerns?

*Ricks, Thomas E. Small Minority Says Draft Could Happen; New Conflict Would Further Strain Troop Levels. *Washington Post.* October 27, 2004: A3.

Positive Peace

Just as war is seen in peace studies as a pervasive aspect of society as a whole, so can peace be reconceptualized in a broader way.[70] According to peace studies scholars, peace should be defined as more than just the absence of war. The mere absence of war does not guarantee that war will not recur. As Kant pointed out, each peace treaty ending a European great-power war in the sixteenth through eighteenth centuries merely set the stage for the next war. Nor can the absence of great-power war in the Cold War be considered true peace: proxy wars killed millions of people while a relentless arms race wasted vast resources. Because realism assumes the normalcy of military conflicts, it recognizes only a negative kind of peace—the temporary absence of war.

By contrast, **positive peace** refers to a peace that resolves the underlying reasons for war—peace that is not just a cease-fire but a transformation of relationships. Under positive peace, not only do state armies stop fighting each other, they stop arming, stop forming death squads against internal protest, and reverse the economic exploitation and political oppression that scholars in peace studies believe are responsible for social conflicts that lead to war.

Proponents of this approach see broad social and economic issues—assumed by realists to be relatively unimportant—as inextricably linked with positive peace. Some scholars define poverty, hunger, and oppression as forms of violence—which they call **structural violence** because it is caused by the structure of social relations rather than by direct actions such as shooting people. Structural violence in this definition kills and harms many more people each year than do war and other forms of direct political violence. Positive peace is usually defined to include the elimination of structural violence because it is considered a source of conflict and war.

Advocates of positive peace also criticize militaristic culture. The "social construction of war"—a complex system of rules and relations that ultimately supports the existence of war—touches our lives in many ways: from children's war toys to patriotic rituals in schools; from teenagers' gender roles to military training for young men; from the taxes we pay to the sports we play. The positive peace approach seeks to change the whole system, not just one piece of it.

Confronting the Past in Chile

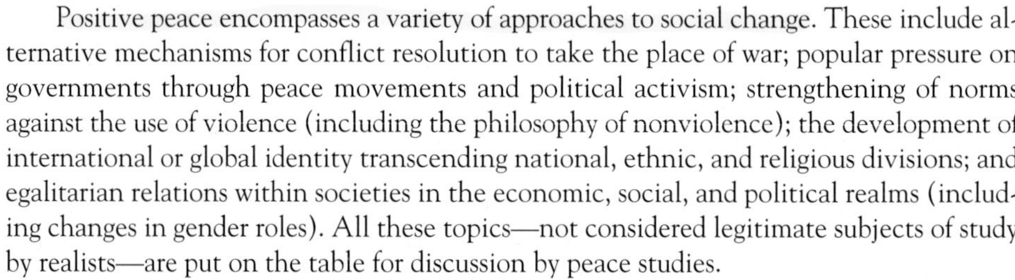

Positive peace encompasses a variety of approaches to social change. These include alternative mechanisms for conflict resolution to take the place of war; popular pressure on governments through peace movements and political activism; strengthening of norms against the use of violence (including the philosophy of nonviolence); the development of international or global identity transcending national, ethnic, and religious divisions; and egalitarian relations within societies in the economic, social, and political realms (including changes in gender roles). All these topics—not considered legitimate subjects of study by realists—are put on the table for discussion by peace studies.

Many people think that positive peace would depend on overcoming ethnic conflict, racism, xenophobia, and other sources of tension between groups with different cultures, languages, and religions—tensions that may contribute to war and violence (see "Ethnic Conflict" on pp. 185–192).[71] One approach explores travel, tourism, cultural exchanges (concerts, films), and citizen diplomacy as means of overcoming intergroup conflicts.

---

[70] Lipschutz, Ronnie D. and Mary Ann Tétreault. *Global Politics as if People Mattered*. Lanham, MD: Rowman & Littlefield, 2005. Elias, Robert, and Jennifer Turpin, eds. *Rethinking Peace*. Boulder: Rienner, 1994. Kende, Istvan. The History of Peace: Concept and Organizations from the Late Middle Ages to the 1870s. *Journal of Peace Research* 26 (3), 1989: 233–47.

[71] Smock, David R., ed. *Interfaith Dialogue and Peacebuilding*. Herndon, VA: U.S. Institute of Peace Press, 2003.

Some decades ago, a world language called *Esperanto* was created in hopes of encouraging worldwide communication and global identity; the results have been disappointing overall.

Another approach to intergroup conflict is reform in the educational system. For example, Western European countries revised textbooks after World War II to remove nationalistic excesses and promote respect for neighboring countries (see p. 190). Japan's failure to fully include in textbooks its own World War II misdeeds fuels continuing tension with Korea and China.

Positive peace is usually defined to include political equality and human rights as well. When a small ruling group or dictator holds political power, fewer checks on government violence operate than when democratic institutions exist (see pp. 160–163). And when avenues of legitimate political participation are open, citizens are less likely to turn to violence.

More controversial within peace studies is the question of whether positive peace requires that states' authority be subordinated to a **world government.**[72] The creation of a world government has long been debated by scholars and pursued by activists; many plans have been drawn up, though none has yet succeeded. Some scholars believe progress is being made (through the UN) toward the eventual emergence of a world government. Others think the idea is impractical or even undesirable (merely adding another layer of centralized control, when peace demands decentralization and freedom).

Peace Movements

Peace Movements

Scholars in peace studies also study how to achieve the conditions for positive peace. Most peace studies scholars share a skepticism that state leaders left to themselves would ever achieve positive peace. Rather, they believe the practice of IR will change only as a result of pressures from individuals and groups.

The most commonly studied method of exerting such pressure is through **peace movements**—people taking to the streets in protest against war and militarism.[73] Such protests occur in many, though not all, states involved in wars. In peace studies it is believed that people all over the world want peace more than governments do. As U.S. President Eisenhower once said, "People want peace so much that one of these days governments had better get out of their way and let them have it."[74]

In addition to mass demonstrations, common *tactics* of peace movements include getting antiwar messages into the media, participating in civil disobedience (nonviolently breaking laws and inviting arrest to show one's beliefs), and occasionally organizing consumer boycotts. Favorite *targets* of peace movements include the draft, government buildings, taxes, and nuclear test sites. Like other interest groups, peace movements also participate in elections and lobbying (see pp. 152–154). And peace movements try to educate the public by spreading information about a war or arms race that the government may be suppressing or downplaying.

Peace activists often disagree on goals. In the U.S. peace movement since World War I, an *internationalist* wing has seen international organizations (today, the UN) as the best hope for peace and has supported wars against aggression. A *pacifist* wing has opposed all wars, distrusted international organizations whose members are state

[72] Wooley, Wesley T. *Alternatives to Anarchy: American Supranationalism Since World War II*. Indiana, 1988.
[73] Breyman, Steve. *Why Movements Matter: The West German Peace Movement and U.S. Arms Control Policy*. SUNY, 2001. Lynch, Cecelia. *Beyond Appeasement: Interpreting Interwar Peace Movements in World Politics*. Cornell, 1999. Carter, April. *Peace Movements: International Protest and World Politics Since 1945*. White Plains, NY: Longman, 1992.
[74] Eisenhower, Dwight D. *Ike's Letters to a Friend, 1941–1958*. Edited by Robert Griffith. Kansas, 1984.

STANDING FOR PEACE

Peace demonstrators play a role in many international conflicts. Here, activist Cindy Sheehan (whose son died in Iraq) leads a demonstration near President Bush's ranch in Texas as the president's motorcade passes, 2005.

governments, and favored more radical social change to achieve positive peace.[75] In other countries, peace movements vary greatly in their goals and character. In Japan, peace movements are extremely broad-based (enjoying wide popular support) and are pacifist in orientation (as a result of reaction against militarism before and during World War II).These divergent tendencies in peace movements come together at peak times in opposition to particular wars or arms races, as happened worldwide before the 2003 Iraq War. But beyond this reactive mode of politics, peace movements often have had trouble defining a long-term direction and agenda. Scholars of peace studies are interested in studying the successes and failures of peace movements to understand how popular influence on foreign policy can affect state decisions. (The 2003 demonstrations seemed to have little effect on U.S. policy.)

Nonviolence

The philosophies of **nonviolence** and **pacifism** are based on a unilateral commitment to refrain from using any violent forms of leverage in bargaining. No state today follows such a strategy; indeed, it is widely believed that in today's world, a state that adopted a nonviolent philosophy would risk exploitation or conquest.[76]

Pacifism nonetheless figures prominently in debates concerning the peaceful solution of conflicts and the achievement of positive peace. Many states contain substantial numbers of citizens, often organized into popular movements, who believe that only pacifism—an ironclad commitment to renounce violence—can change the nature of IR so as to avoid future wars. Japan has a sizable pacifist movement, and pacifists have historically formed the hard core of the peace movement in the United States and Western Europe as well.

The term *pacifism* has fallen into disfavor because it has been taken to imply passivity in the face of aggression (a charge leveled at U.S. isolationists in the 1930s). The more popular term, nonviolence, reflects especially the philosophy and practice of *Mahatma Gandhi*, who led India's struggle for independence from the British empire before 1948. Gandhi emphasized that nonviolence must be *active* in seeking to prevent violence, to resolve conflicts without violence, and especially to stand up against injustice enforced violently. Gandhi organized Indians to resist the British colonial occupation without resorting to violence, even when British troops shot down unarmed Indian protesters.

Proponents of nonviolence emphasize the *practical* side of nonviolence in addition to its morality. As a tactic in bargaining, it uses moral norms as leverage. Furthermore, reassuring the other side that one will not employ violent leverage makes it easier for the

[75] De Benedetti, Charles. *Origins of the Modern American Peace Movement, 1915–1929*. Milwood, NY: KTO, 1978.
[76] Miller, Richard B. *Interpretations of Conflict: Ethics, Pacifism, and the Just-War Tradition*. Chicago, 1991.

other side to put such options aside as well (by eliminating the security dilemma). As a tool of the *powerless* standing up against injustices by the powerful, nonviolence is often the most cost-effective approach—because the costs of violent resistance would be prohibitive.[77] In the United States, the philosophy of nonviolence spread widely in the 1960s in the civil rights movement, especially through the work of Martin Luther King, Jr. The dilemma of nonviolence is how to respond to violence.[78] Gandhi believed that there was always a third alternative to passivity or response in kind. Nonviolence does not always succeed when faced with violence, but then neither does violent response. However, political leaders may believe they have done their duty if they respond violently without success, but not if they respond nonviolently without success. Within peace studies, scholars emphasize different aspects of peace and how to achieve it. These differences are deepened by the multidisciplinary nature of peace studies (sociologists, political scientists, psychologists, anthropologists, etc.).

Peace studies tends to be inclusive and tolerant, hoping that different scholars (and activists) can find a core of agreement on the meaning of peace. This tolerance can mask incompatibilities within peace studies, however. With this chapter and the previous one as theoretical background, the next four chapters will cover the major topics in international security studies, broadly defined. These chapters move through all four levels of analysis, from foreign policy processes (individual and domestic levels) through conflict and military force (domestic and interstate levels), to international law and organization (interstate and global levels).

Beginning at the bottom levels of analysis means turning now to what happens inside the state. How do states decide on actions? What kinds of bargaining go on *within* a state that is engaged in international bargaining? How do individual and group psychology affect the decision process, pulling it away from rationality? These questions, the domain of foreign policy studies, are the subject of Chapter 4.

THINKING CRITICALLY

1. U.S.-Canadian relations seem better explained by liberalism than realism. What other (one or more) interstate relationships have this quality? Discuss the contrasting tenets of realism and liberalism, showing how each applies to the relationship(s).
2. Would IR operate differently if most leaders of states were women? What would the differences be? What evidence (beyond gender stereotypes) supports your answer?
3. In what ways do the explanations of IR events change if women are considered primary players rather than peripheral ones? Which women, in which roles, would you consider important?
4. Deconstruct this book by identifying implicit themes, subjects not covered, and hidden biases.
5. Peace studies claims that internal characteristics of states (at the domestic level of analysis) strongly affect the propensity for war or potential for lasting peace. For one society, show how internal characteristics—social, economic, and/or cultural—influence that society's external behavior.

---

[77] Ackerman, Peter, and Jack DuVall. *A Force More Powerful: A Century of Nonviolent Conflict*. NY: St. Martin's, 2001. Wehr, Paul, Heidi Burgess, and Guy Burgess, eds. *Justice Without Violence*. Boulder, CO: Lynne Rienner, 1994. Crow, Ralph, Philip Grant, and Saad E. Ibrahim, eds. *Arab Nonviolent Political Struggle in the Middle East*. Boulder, CO: Lynne Rienner, 1990.

[78] Sharp, Gene. *Civilian-Based Defense: A Post-Military Weapons System*. Princeton, 1990.

CHAPTER SUMMARY

- The central claims of realism—regarding anarchy, state actors, rationality, and the utility of military force—have been challenged on a variety of grounds.
- Liberals dispute the realist notion that narrow self-interest is more rational than mutually beneficial cooperation.
- Neoliberalism argues that even in an anarchic system of autonomous rational states, cooperation can emerge through the building of norms, regimes, and institutions.
- Collective goods are benefits received by all members of a group regardless of their individual contribution. Shared norms and rules are important in getting members to pay for collective goods.
- International regimes—convergent expectations of state leaders about the rules for issue areas in IR—help provide stability in the absence of a world government.
- Hegemonic stability theory suggests that the holding of predominant power by one state lends stability to international relations and helps create regimes.
- In a collective security arrangement, a group of states agrees to respond together to aggression by any participating state; the UN and other IGOs perform this function.
- Feminist scholars of IR agree that gender is important in understanding IR but diverge into several strands regarding their conception of the role of gender.
- Difference feminists argue that real (not arbitrary) differences between men and women exist. Men think about social relations more often in terms of autonomy (as do realists), but women think in terms of connection.
- Difference feminists argue that men are more warlike on average than women. They believe that although individual women participants (such as state leaders) may not reflect this difference, the participation of large numbers of women would change the character of the international system, making it more peaceful.
- Liberal feminists disagree that women have substantially different capabilities or tendencies as participants in IR. They argue that women are equivalent to men in virtually all IR roles. As evidence, liberal feminists point to historical and present-day women leaders and women soldiers.
- Constructivists reject realist assumptions about state interests, tracing those interests in part to social interactions and norms.
- Postmodern critics reject the entire framework and language of realism, with its unitary state actors. Postmodernists argue that no simple categories can capture the multiple realities experienced by participants in IR.
- Postmodern feminists seek to uncover gender-related subtexts implicit in realist discourse, including sexual themes connected with the concept of power.
- Peace studies programs are interdisciplinary and seek to broaden the study of international security to include social and economic factors ignored by realism.
- Peace studies acknowledges a normative bias—that peace is good and war is bad—and a willingness to put theory into practice by participating in politics.
- Mediation and other forms of conflict resolution are alternative means of exerting leverage on participants in bargaining. Increasingly, these means are succeeding in settling conflicts without (or with no further) use of violence.
- For scholars in peace studies, militarism in many cultures contributes to states' propensity to resort to force in international bargaining.
- Positive peace implies not just the absence of war but addressing conditions that scholars in peace studies connect with violence—especially injustice and poverty.
- Peace movements try to influence state foreign policies regarding military force; such movements are of great interest in peace studies.

- Nonviolence—the renunciation of force—can be an effective means of leverage, especially for poor or oppressed people with few other means available.

KEY TERMS

neoliberalism 101
tit for tat 102
collective goods problem 103
free riders 103
international regime 104
hegemonic stability theory 105
collective security 106
difference feminism 110
liberal feminism 110
postmodern feminism 110
gender gap 114
constructivism 119
postmodernism 121
subtext 122
normative bias 125
conflict resolution 125
mediation 125
militarism 127
positive peace 130
structural violence 130
world government 131
peace movements 131
nonviolence/pacifism 132

ONLINE PRACTICE TEST

Take an online practice test at *www.internationalrelations.net*

❑ A
❑ B
☑ C
❑ D

LET'S DEBATE THE ISSUE

The Arab-Israeli Conflict: What Are the New Obstacles to Peace?

by Mir Zohair Husain

Overview Jews and Palestinian Arabs have fought over the same small geographical area for 100 years because the land has immense religious significance for both nations. Since the creation of Israel in 1948, the Arab-Israeli conflict has intensified and received worldwide attention. The central problem is Israel's loosely defined borders and Israeli-occupied territories—the predominantly Palestinian West Bank that belonged to Jordan, the predominantly Palestinian Gaza Strip that belonged to Egypt, and the Golan Heights that belonged to Syria. Since 1993, Palestinian-Israeli peace agreements advanced Palestinian autonomy in parts of the West Bank and Gaza Strip in fits and starts until President Bill Clinton's effort to craft a final settlement failed at the July 2000 Camp David II Summit. The two parties could not agree on the major issues: Jerusalem (how to divide and share the city that is steeped in historical and religious significance), Jewish settlements in the West Bank and Gaza Strip (how many were going to be dismantled and over what time period), and the return of Palestinian refugees to the West Bank, Gaza Strip, and some parts of Israel.

After the failure of Camp David II, the visit of Israel's Likud party leader Ariel Sharon to the al-Aqsa Mosque—one of the most venerated mosques in Islam—on September 28, 2000, triggered the second Palestinian *intifadah* (uprising), also known as the al-Aqsa intifadah. The cycle of violence between suicide bombers and the Israeli military that followed Sharon's visit and his landslide election victory in February 2001 contributed to more than 3,000 Palestinian deaths and 1,000 Israeli deaths.[a]

The latest peace proposal, President George W. Bush's "Roadmap to Peace," is a three-year peace plan with a scheduled series of steps for both sides, culminating in an independent Palestinian state by 2005.[b] But the refusal of the Sharon and Bush administrations to negotiate with President Yasser Arafat of the Palestine National Authority (PNA) and Israel's building of a security fence to stave off Palestinian suicide bombers greatly increased the cycle of violence. However, Arafat's death on November 11, 2004; the election of Mahmoud Abbas (Abu Mazen) as President of the PNA on January 9, 2005; Sharon's commitment to dismantle the Jewish settlements in Gaza comprising more than 8,000 Jewish settlers (along with dismantling four Jewish settlements in the West Bank) by late July 2005; the marked decrease in the cycle of Palestinian-Israeli violence; and the Bush administration's new vigor in mediating the Palestinian-Israeli conflict in its second four-year term have resurrected the Palestinian peace process. The big question is: Can the "new" obstacles to peace be overcome?

Argument 1 Palestinian Perspective

Today's intifadah is the result of Palestinian hopelessness, humiliation, and anger in the face of Israeli occupation and militarism. The second Palestinian intifadah began in October 2000, characterized by suicide bombings and Israeli military actions.

> [Early in the second intifadah], Palestinians increasingly demanded an armed response to the continuous Israeli killing and it was during this period that . . . suicide bombings began . . . against civilians and others . . . against military targets . . . (Ghassan Khatib. "Where Are We Now?" *Palestinian-Israeli Crossfire,* Edition 37, September 29, 2003. www.bitterlemons.org)

[a]Steven Erlanger. "Hope, Skepticism and Fear: Back on the Road to Civility." *The New York Times,* February 8, 2005, p. 14.

[b]David K. Shipler. "On the Path to Peace, the Process Gets in the Way." *The New York Times,* May 4, 2003.

Israel's wall in the disputed West Bank is an obstacle to peace. Palestinians and the international community in a UN resolution have criticized Israel's building of the wall intended to seal off Israel from the West Bank.

> The fence will put 14.5 percent of West Bank land on the Israeli side, the [UN] report said, adding, "This land, some of the most fertile in the West Bank, is currently the home for more than 274,000 Palestinians."
>
> The [UN] made a rough estimate that an additional 400,000 Palestinians would be adversely affected. In some instances, the barrier is going up between Palestinian villages and nearby farmland. In many small Palestinian communities, employees and students must cross the barrier to reach larger cities and towns where they work or study. (Greg Myre. "UN Estimates Israeli Barrier Will Disrupt Lives of 600,000." *The New York Times,* November 12, 2003.)

Abbas must overcome Palestinian extremists. In addition to addressing external threats to Palestinian interests, President Abbas must also overcome Palestinian extremists (such as the revolutionary Islamists of Hamas and Islamic Jihad) that oppose any peace settlements that entail major concessions by Palestinians. Similar to extremist groups in Israel, these groups will continue to be a major impediment to making progress on a negotiated compromise where both sides must make concessions.

> I do not believe that these militant messianists can actually win in Iraq, Israel or Palestine, but they can prevent the majorities in each country from forging any new pragmatic, tolerant power-sharing arrangements—and in the case of Israelis and Palestinians, new borders. (Thomas L. Friedman. "Remapping the Middle East, Maybe." *The New York Times,* January 9, 2005.)

Argument 2 Israeli Perspective

Israeli military reprisals are necessary responses to the Palestinian intifadah and terrorism. Regardless of how the intifadah began, Israelis must use military force to defend themselves from Palestinian attacks and to make clear that terrorism will not be tolerated.

> The need for Israel to act directly against the terrorists became clear after the suicide bombing on March 27 in a hotel in Netanya. That bombing ended a bloody month in which 130 Israelis died at the hands of terrorists, a proportion of the Israeli population twice as large as that of Americans killed on September 11. These killings occurred despite Israeli compliance with the efforts of Anthony Zinni, the United States emissary, to achieve a cease-fire and in the context of the Palestinian Authority's use of terror as an alternative to negotiations. . . .
>
> There are no illusions that there can be a purely military solution to the Israeli-Palestinian conflict. However, the recent operation has already had a very real effect in disrupting terrorist plans and degrading terrorist capabilities. In human terms, that will translate into many Israeli lives saved. (Nitsan Alon. "Why Israel's Mission Must Continue." *The New York Times,* April 12, 2002.)

The security fence along the West Bank is to protect Israelis. Three years of Palestinian intifadah have prompted Israel to build a security fence. This barrier, which includes an electronic fence, concrete walls, trenches, and other obstacles, is intended to block Palestinian attackers, and not act as a political border.

> [In response to the U.N. report that Israelis security fence would disrupt the lives of 600,000 Palestinians, Israel Defense Ministry Spokeswoman Rachel Niedak-Ashkenazi counters,] "We do have one number: the 6.5 million Israelis will be better protected when the fence is finished. . . . [We are also] building gates and taking other steps to minimize disruptions." "To say that we are not taking humanitarian issues into account is misleading." (Greg Myre. "UN Estimates Israeli Barrier Will Disrupt Lives of 600,000." *The New York Times,* November 12, 2003.)

Sharon must overcome Israeli extremists. Similar to his counterpart's situation in the PNA, Sharon is challenged by Israeli extremists largely over the issue of withdrawing Israeli settlers from their settlements in Gaza and the West Bank. Once considered the architect and guardian of the Israeli settlement movements, Sharon faces stiff opposition in delivering on Israeli withdrawal from the settlements.

> In Israel the theocratic-nationalist settler movement has already begun to make its move. Last Thursday, four battalion commanders and 30 other officers, all residents of West Bank Jewish settlements, published a statement in the Israeli daily Yediot Aharonot, declaring that they would not obey any orders to evacuate Jewish enclaves in Gaza or the West Bank. This is an open rebuke of Prime Minister Ariel Sharon's cabinet-approved plan to withdraw all Israeli forces and settlements from Gaza and a small part of the West Bank. (Thomas L. Friedman. "Remapping the Middle East, Maybe." *The New York Times,* January 9, 2005.)

Questions

The Arab-Israeli Conflict

1. Besides the controversial, enduring, and difficult issues of Jerusalem, Jewish settlements on the West Bank and Gaza Strip, and the return of Palestinian refugees, which of these recent issues—the intifadah (perceived as a legitimate uprising by Palestinians and terrorism by Israelis), the Israeli security fence, or extremists on both sides—poses the greatest obstacle to a peace settlement? Why?
2. What role should the United States, the European Union, and the United Nations play in resolving the Arab-Israeli conflict? Will the "Roadmap to Peace" bring about a peace settlement? Why or why not?

Selected Readings

Auriana Ojeda, ed. *The Middle East: Current Controversies.* Detroit, MI: Greenhaven Press, 2003.

Neil Alger, ed. *The World Hot Spots: Palestinians and the Disputed Territories.* Detroit, MI: Greenhaven Press, 2004.

■ Secretary of State Condoleezza Rice at confirmation hearings, 2005.

Making Foreign Policy

Decision Making

Models of Decision Making • Individual Decision Makers • Group Dynamics • Crisis Management

Substate Actors

Bureaucracies • Interest Groups • The Military-Industrial Complex • Public Opinion • Legislatures

Democracy and Foreign Policy

CHAPTER 4

Foreign Policy

Making Foreign Policy

Looking at states as though they were unitary actors is useful up to a point, but not very accurate. A state is not a single conscious being; its actions are a composite of individual human choices—by its citizenry, its political leaders, its diplomats and bureaucrats—aggregated through the state's internal structures. This chapter looks at the state from inside out, trying to understand the processes and structures *within* states that make them take the actions they do toward other states.

Foreign policies are the strategies used by governments to guide their actions in the international arena. Foreign policies spell out the objectives state leaders have decided to pursue in a given relationship or situation as well as the general means by which they intend to pursue those objectives. Day-to-day decisions made by various arms of government are guided by the goal of implementing foreign policies.

Every day, states take actions in international affairs. Diplomats are appointed to posts, given instructions for their negotiations, or recalled home. Trade negotiators agree to reduce their demands by a few percent. Military forces are moved around and occasionally sent into battle. Behind each of these actions are decisions by a host of foreign policy decision makers, ranging from top state leaders to bureaucrats. In general, IR scholars are less interested in specific policies than in the **foreign policy process**—how policies are arrived at and implemented.[1]

States establish various organizational structures and functional relationships to create and carry out foreign policies. Officials and agencies collect information about a situation through various channels; they write memoranda outlining possible options for action; they hold meetings to discuss the matter; some of them meet privately outside these meetings to decide how to steer the meetings. Such activities, broadly defined, are what is meant by "the foreign policy process." IR scholars are especially interested in exploring whether certain kinds of policy processes lead to certain kinds of decisions—whether certain processes produce better outcomes (for the state's self-defined interests) than do others.

WEB LINK

Comparative Foreign Policy

Foreign policy outcomes result from multiple forces at various levels of analysis. The outcomes depend on individual decision makers, on the type of society and government they are working within, and on the international and global context of their actions. Since the study of foreign policy concentrates

[1] Neack, Laura. *The New Foreign Policy: U.S. and Comparative Foreign Policy in the 21st Century*. Lanham, MD: Rowman & Littlefield, 2003. Snow, Donald M. *United States Foreign Policy: Politics Beyond the Water's Edge*. NY: Longman, 2003. Meyer, William H. *Security, Economics, and Morality in American Foreign Policy: Contemporary Issues in Historical Context*. Upper Saddle River, NJ: Pearson Prentice Hall, 2004.

FRESH LEADERSHIP

Foreign policy outcomes result from processes at several levels of analysis. For example, the sudden change in Palestinian leadership after Yasser Arafat's death in 2004 tested the importance of the individual level (which changed radically) versus larger social structures and conflicts (which did not). Here, Mahmoud Abbas votes in fair elections in 2005 that elected him president. Abbas opposes violence against Israel and hoped to restart peace talks to establish a Palestinian state. But legislative elections in 2006 brought to power the violently anti-Israeli party Hamas, halting peace talks and suggesting that the domestic and interstate levels of analysis can trump the individual level.

on forces within the state, its main emphasis is on the individual and domestic levels of analysis.

Comparative foreign policy is the study of foreign policy in various states in order to discover whether similar types of societies or governments consistently have similar types of foreign policies (comparing across states or across different time periods for a single state). Such studies have focused on three characteristics in particular: size, wealth, and extent of democratic participation in government.[2] Unfortunately, no simple rule has been found to predict a state's warlike tendencies based on attributes such as size, wealth, and type of government. There is great variation among states, and even within a single state over time. For example, both capitalist and communist states have proven capable of naked aggression or peaceful behavior, depending on circumstances.

Some political scientists have tried to interpret particular states' foreign policies in terms of each one's *political culture and history*. For example, the Soviet Union (Russia) had experienced repeated devastating land invasions over the centuries (culminating in World War II) while the United States had experienced two centuries of safety behind great oceans. Thus the military might of the Soviet Union, and its control of buffer states in Eastern Europe, seemed defensive in nature to Soviet leaders but appeared aggressive to U.S. leaders.

Most studies of foreign policy have not focused on the comparison of policies of different states, however; they have instead tried to probe the effects of foreign policy processes on the behavior of states, as well as the resulting outcomes. The study of foreign policy processes runs counter to realism's assumption of a unitary state actor.

Decision Making

The foreign policy process is a process of *decision making*. States take actions because people in governments—*decision makers*—choose those actions. Decision making is a *steering* process in which adjustments are made as a result of feedback from the outside world. Decisions are carried out by actions taken to change the world, and then information from the world is monitored to evaluate the effects of

[2] Hook, Steven W. *Comparative Foreign Policy*. Upper Saddle River, NJ: Prentice Hall, 2002. Beasley, Ryan K. et al., eds. *Foreign Policy in Comparative Perspective: Domestic and International Influences on State Behavior*. Washington DC: CQ Press, 2002.

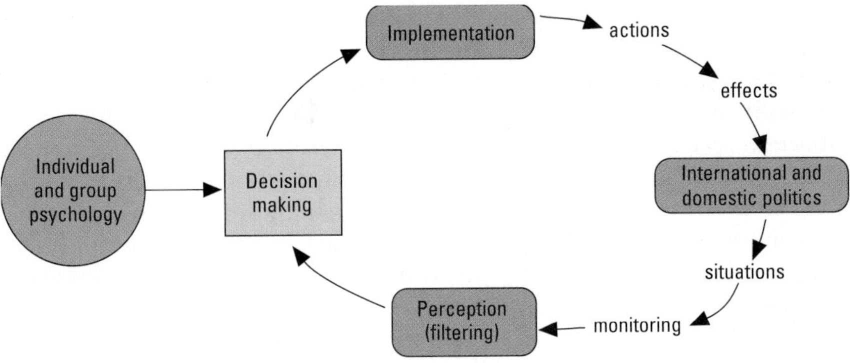

FIGURE 4.1 ■ Decision Making as Steering

actions. These evaluations—along with information about other, independent changes in the environment—go into the next round of decisions (see Figure 4.1).

Decision Making

Models of Decision Making

A common starting point for studying the decision-making process is the **rational model.**[3] In this model, decision makers set goals, evaluate their relative importance, calculate the costs and benefits of each possible course of action, then choose the one with the highest benefits and lowest costs:

1. *Clarify goals* in the situation.
2. *Order them* by importance (in case different goals conflict).
3. *List the alternatives* available to achieve the goals.
4. *Investigate the consequences* (probable and possible outcomes) of those alternatives.
5. *Choose* the course of action that will produce the best outcome (in terms of reaching one's goals).

The choice may be complicated by *uncertainty* about the costs and benefits of various actions. In such cases, decision makers must attach probabilities to each possible outcome of an action. For example, will pressuring a rival state to give ground in peace talks be persuasive or will it backfire? Will signing a free trade agreement lead to more trade with the partner state or will jobs leave the country as a result of the agreement (or both)? Some decision makers are relatively *accepting of risk*, whereas others are *averse to risk*. These factors affect the importance that decision makers place on various alternative outcomes that could result from an action. The rational model may imply that decision making is simpler than is actually the case. A decision maker may hold different conflicting goals simultaneously. The goals of different individuals involved in making a decision may diverge, as may the goals of different state agencies. For example, the U.S. secretary of state may have a different goal than the secretary of defense, just as the Central Intelligence Agency may view a situation differently than the National Security Council. The rational model of decision making thus is somewhat complicated by uncertainty and the multiple goals of decision makers.

[3] The rational model, along with the organizational process and bureaucratic politics models discussed later, derives from Graham Allison; see Allison, Graham T., and Philip Zelikow. *Essence of Decision: Explaining the Cuban Missile Crisis*. 2nd ed. NY: Longman, 1999. Bernstein, Barton J. Understanding Decisionmaking, U.S. Foreign Policy and the Cuban Missile Crisis. *International Security* 25 (1), 2000: 134–164.

An alternative to the rational model of decision making is the **organizational process model.** In this model, foreign policy decision makers generally skip the labor-intensive process of identifying goals and alternative actions, relying instead for most decisions on standardized responses or *standard operating procedures*. For example, the U.S. State Department every day receives more than a thousand reports or inquiries from its embassies around the world and sends out more than a thousand instructions or responses to those embassies. The vast majority of those cables are never seen by the top decision makers (the secretary of state or the president); instead, they are handled by low-level decision makers who apply general principles—or who simply try to make the least controversial, most standardized decision. These low-level decisions may not even reflect the high-level policies adopted by top leaders, but rather have a life of their own. The organizational process model implies that much of foreign policy results from "management by muddling through."[4]

Governmental Bargaining

Another alternative to the rational model is the **government bargaining** (or *bureaucratic politics*) **model,** in which foreign policy decisions result from the bargaining process among various government agencies with somewhat divergent interests in the outcome.[5] In 1992, the Japanese government had to decide whether to allow sushi from California to be imported—a weakening of Japan's traditional ban on importing rice (to maintain self-sufficiency in its staple food). The Japanese Agriculture Ministry, with an interest in the well-being of Japanese farmers, opposed the imports. The Foreign Ministry, with an interest in smooth relations with the United States, wanted to allow the imports. The final decision to allow imported sushi resulted from the tug-of-war between the ministries. Thus, according to the government bargaining model, foreign policy decisions reflect (a mix of) the interests of state agencies.

Although the rational model is the usual starting point for thinking about foreign policy decision making, there are many reasons to question whether decisions can be considered rational, even beyond the influences of organizational inertia and government bargaining. These nonrational elements in decision making are best understood from a *psychological* analysis of individual and group decision-making processes.[6]

Individual Decision Makers

Individuals are the only true actors in IR. Every international event is the result, intended or unintended, of decisions made by individuals. IR does not just happen. President Harry Truman, who made the decision to drop U.S. nuclear bombs on two Japanese cities in 1945, understood this. He had a sign on his desk: "The buck stops here." As leader of the world's greatest power, he had nobody to pass the buck to. If he chose to use the bomb (as he did), more than 100,000 civilians would die. If he chose not to, the war might drag on for months with tens of thousands of U.S. casualties. Truman had to choose. Some people applaud his decision; others condemn it. But for better or worse, Truman as an individual had to decide, and to take responsibility for the consequences. Similarly, the decisions of individual citizens, although they may not seem important when taken one by one, are what create the great forces of world history.

---

[4] Avant, Deborah D. *Political Institutions and Military Change: Lessons from Peripheral Wars*. Cornell, 1995. Levy, Jack S. Organizational Routines and the Causes of War. *International Studies Quarterly* 30 (2), 1986: 193–222.
[5] Welch, David A. The Organizational Process and Bureaucratic Politics Paradigms: Retrospect and Prospect. *International Security* 17 (2), 1992: 112–46. Rhodes, Edward. Do Bureaucratic Politics Matter? Some Disconfirming Findings from the Case of the U.S. Navy. *World Politics* 47 (1), 1994: 1–41.
[6] Stein, Janice Gross. Psychological Explanations of International Conflict. In Carlsnaes, Walter, Thomas Risse, and Beth A. Simmons, eds. *Handbook of International Relations*, 292–308. Sage, 2002. Snyder, Richard C., H. W. Bruck, and Burton Sapin. *Foreign Policy Decision Making (Revisited)*. London: Palgrave, 2002.

THINKING THEORETICALLY

Policy Continuity in the Balkans

As a candidate for president, George W. Bush promised to withdraw U.S. troops from the Balkans, where President Clinton had sent them for peacekeeping duties in Bosnia, Kosovo, and Macedonia. He argued that peacekeeping missions overextended the U.S. military and left too few resources for the main missions of deterring and fighting wars. As president, however, Bush in 2001 postponed indefinitely the idea of withdrawing after considering the range of issues at stake. He decided that an abrupt U.S. departure could undermine NATO cohesion, and might reignite Balkan wars, perhaps destabilizing nearby countries. What theories might help explain Bush's switch? A variety of explanations might be drawn from the three world views. Consider one liberal and one realist approach.

One theory, the organizational process model, holds that government bureaucracies churn out policy in a routine manner, with only incremental change as political leaders come and go. (Liberal elements in this model include its emphasis on substate actors and its view of change as incremental.) This reasoning could explain the continuity in U.S. Balkan policy even when a new leader came in with new ideas. The State Department and Pentagon "educated" Bush, and policy remained relatively unchanged.

A different theoretical approach, drawing on realist themes, explains military interventions as actions taken rationally (benefits exceed costs) in pursuit of national interests. These interests for realists tend to be defined rather narrowly, as access to tangible power resources such as territory, energy supplies, strategic military bases, and the like. By this line of reasoning, Bush did not change the U.S. posture in the Balkans because U.S. interests there had not changed. For realists, neither political rhetoric nor changes in government matter as much as basic national interests and capabilities. Bush and Clinton made roughly the same cost-benefit calculation as had the first President Bush: that Balkan peace was worth money and effort (how much depending on various pressures and dangers), but not worth taking substantial U.S. casualties.

How could we begin testing these theories against each other? We need an "experiment" in which the two theories make opposite predictions. Seemingly, the war on terrorism after September 11, 2001, provides something of an experiment, because it dramatically changed the global demands on U.S. military forces. For the realist theory, this change should have altered the cost-benefit calculation regarding the effects of far-flung peacekeeping missions. Bush would have pulled forces out of the Balkans to use in the war on terrorism instead. As it turned out, this prediction would have been a good one. With U.S. forces stretched thin by the unexpectedly difficult war in Iraq, the United States pulled its forces out of Bosnia by 2004, leaving Europe to carry on the remaining work.

A good experiment keeps certain factors the same (such as the nature of the U.S. foreign policy bureaucracy) while others change (the demands on U.S. military forces). Then the influence of each factor on the outcome can be assessed. Nonetheless, these assessment are usually far from conclusive. "Experiments" in IR are very imperfect because we do not control the conditions in a laboratory, and no single experiment can prove or invalidate a theory. •

The study of individual decision making revolves around the question of rationality. To what extent are national leaders (or citizens) able to make rational decisions in the national interest—if indeed such an interest can be defined—and thus to conform to a realist view of IR? Individual rationality is not equivalent to state rationality: states might filter individuals' irrational decisions so as to arrive at rational choices, or states might distort individually rational decisions and end up with irrational state choices. But realists tend to assume that both states and individuals are rational and that the goals or interests of states correlate with those of leaders.

The most simplified rational-actor models go so far as to assume that interests are the same from one actor to another. If this were so, individuals could be substituted for each

MADMAN?

Foreign policies often deviate from rationality as a result of the misperceptions and biases of decision makers and populations. Saddam Hussein's rule of Iraq was marked by many mistakes, and in his last years he apparently became even more irrational, possibly delusional. Here, a bearded, dazed Saddam appears after his capture in late 2003.

other in various roles without changing history very much. And states would all behave similarly to each other (or rather, the differences between them would reflect different resources, geography, and similar features, not differences in the nature of national interests). This assumption is at best a great oversimplification.[7] In truth, individual decisions reflect the *values* and *beliefs* of the decision maker.

How can IR scholars characterize an individual's values and beliefs? Sometimes beliefs and values are spelled out in ideological autobiographies. Other times IR researchers try to infer beliefs through a method called *content analysis*—analyzing speeches or other documents to count the number of times key words or phrases are repeated, and in what contexts. Scholars of IR have also described *operational codes*—routines and methods that mediate between beliefs and practical actions.[8] Other scholars have created computer-based models of beliefs.[9]

The goals of individuals differ, as do the ways in which they pursue those goals. Individual decision makers not only have differing values and beliefs, but also have unique personalities—their personal experiences, intellectual capabilities, and personal styles of making decisions. Some IR scholars study individual psychology to understand how personality affects decision making. Psychoanalytic approaches hold that personalities reflect the subconscious influences of childhood experiences. For instance, Bill Clinton drew much criticism in his early years as president for a foreign policy that seemed to zigzag. A notable Clinton personality trait was his readiness to compromise. Clinton himself has noted that his experience of growing up with a violent, alcoholic stepfather shaped him into a "peacemaker, always trying to minimize the disruption."[10]

---

[7] Farnham, Barbara. *Roosevelt and the Munich Crisis: A Study of Political Decision-Making*. Princeton, 1997. Greenstein, Fred I. The Changing Leadership of George W. Bush: A Pre- and Post-9/11 Comparison. In Wittkopf, Eugene R., and James M. McCormick, eds. *The Domestic Sources of American Foreign Policy*, 353–362. Lanham, MD: Rowman & Littlefield, 2004.

[8] Walker, Stephen G., Mark Schafer, and Michael D. Young. Presidential Operational Codes and Foreign Policy Conflicts in the Post-Cold War Era. *Journal of Conflict Resolution* 43 (5), 1999: 610-625.

[9] Taber, Charles S. POLI: An Expert System Model of U.S. Foreign Policy Belief Systems. *American Political Science Review* 86 (4), 1992: 888–904. Hudson, Valerie M., ed. *Artificial Intelligence and International Politics*. Boulder, CO: Westview, 1991.

[10] Collins, Nancy. A Legacy of Strength and Love [Interview with President Clinton]. *Good Housekeeping* 221 (5), 1995: 113–115.

Beyond individual *idiosyncrasies* in goals or decision-making processes, there are at least three *systematic* ways in which individual decision making diverges from the rational model. First, decision makers suffer from **misperceptions** and **selective perceptions** (taking in only some kinds of information) when they compile information on the likely consequences of their choices.[11] Decision-making processes must by necessity reduce and filter the incoming information on which a decision is based; the problem is that such filtration often is biased. **Information screens** are subconscious filters through which people put the information coming in about the world around them. Often they simply ignore any information that does not fit their expectations. Information is also screened out as it passes from one person to another in the decision-making process. For example, prior to the September 2001 terrorist attacks, U.S. intelligence agencies failed to adequately interpret available evidence because too few analysts were fluent in Arabic. Similarly, Soviet leaders in 1941 and Israeli leaders in 1973 ignored evidence of pending invasions of their countries.

Misperceptions can affect the implementation of policy by low-level officials as well as its formulation by high-level officials. For example, in 1988, officers on a U.S. warship in the Persian Gulf shot down a civilian Iranian jet that they believed to be a military jet attacking them. The officers were trying to carry out policies established by national leaders, but because of misperceptions their actions instead damaged their state's interests.

Second, the rationality of individual cost-benefit calculations is undermined by emotions that decision makers feel while thinking about the consequences of their actions—an effect referred to as *affective bias*. (Positive and negative affect refer to feelings of liking or disliking someone.) As hard as a decision maker tries to be rational in making a decision, the decision-making process is bound to be influenced by strong feelings held about the person or state toward which a decision is directed. (Affective biases also contribute to information screening, as positive information about disliked people or negative information about liked people is screened out.)

Third, *cognitive biases* are systematic distortions of rational calculations based not on emotional feelings but simply on the limitations of the human brain in making choices. The most important seems to be the attempt to produce *cognitive balance*—or to reduce *cognitive dissonance*. These terms refer to the tendency people have to try to maintain mental models of the world that are logically consistent (this seldom succeeds entirely). For instance, after deciding whether to intervene militarily in a conflict, a state leader will very likely adjust his or her mental model to downplay the risks and exaggerate the gains of the chosen course of action.[12]

One implication of cognitive balance is that decision makers place greater value on goals that they have put much effort into achieving—the *justification of effort*. This is especially true in a democracy where politicians must face their citizens' judgment at the polls and so do not want to admit failures. The Vietnam War trapped U.S. decision makers in this way in the 1960s. After sending half a million troops halfway around the world it was difficult for U.S. leaders to admit to themselves that the costs of the war were greater than the benefits.

Decision makers also achieve cognitive balance through *wishful thinking*—an overestimate of the probability of a desired outcome. A variation of wishful thinking is to

---

[11] Jervis, Robert. *Perception and Misperception in International Politics*. Princeton, 1976.

[12] Vertzberger, Yaacov Y. I. *The World in Their Minds: Information Processing, Cognition, and Perception in Foreign Policy Decisionmaking*. Stanford, 1990. Sylvan, Donald A. and James F. Voss. *Problem Representation in Foreign Policy Decision Making*. Cambridge, 1998. Renshon, Stanley A., and Deborah W. Larson, eds. *Good Judgement in Foreign Policy: Theory and Application*. Lanham, MD: Rowman & Littlefield, 2003.

assume that an event with a *low probability* of occurring will *not* occur. This could be a dangerous way to think about catastrophic events such as accidental nuclear war.

Cognitive balance often leads decision makers to maintain a hardened image of an *enemy* and to interpret all of the enemy's actions in a negative light (since the idea of bad people doing good things would create cognitive dissonance).[13] Obviously, this cognitive bias overlaps with the affective bias felt toward such enemies. The enemy-image problem is especially important today in ethnic conflicts (see pp. 188–190).

A *mirror image* refers to two sides in a conflict maintaining very similar enemy images of each other ("we are defensive, they are aggressive," etc.). A decision maker may experience psychological *projection* of his or her own feelings onto another actor. For instance, if (hypothetically) Indian leaders wanted to gain nuclear superiority over Pakistan but found that goal inconsistent with their image of themselves as peaceful and defensive, the resulting cognitive dissonance might be resolved by believing that Pakistan was trying to gain nuclear superiority (the example works as well with the states reversed).

Another form of cognitive bias, related to cognitive balance, is the use of *historical analogies* to structure one's thinking about a decision. This can be quite useful or quite misleading, depending on whether the analogy is appropriate.[14] As each historical situation is unique in some way, when a decision maker latches onto an analogy and uses it as a shortcut to a decision, the rational calculation of costs and benefits may be cut short as well. In particular, decision makers often assume a solution that worked in a past instance will work again—without fully examining how similar the situations really are. For example, U.S. leaders used the analogy of Munich in 1938 to convince themselves that appeasement in the Vietnam War would lead to increased communist aggression in Asia. In retrospect, the differences between North Vietnam and Nazi Germany made this a poor analogy (largely because of the civil war nature of the Vietnam conflict). During Vietnam, leaders then used the analogy of the Korean War to warn against using too much force, since this might risk direct Chinese involvement. After Vietnam, that war then became a potent analogy that helped convince U.S. leaders to avoid involvement in certain overseas conflicts, including Bosnia; this was called the "Vietnam syndrome" in U.S. foreign policy.

All these psychological processes—misperception, affective biases, and cognitive biases—interfere with the rational assessment of costs and benefits in making a decision.[15] Two specific modifications to the rational model of decision making have been proposed to accommodate psychological realities.

First, the model of *bounded rationality* takes into account the costs of seeking and processing information. Nobody thinks about every single possible course of action when making a decision. Instead of **optimizing,** or picking the very best option, people usually work on the problem until they come up with a "good enough" option that meets some minimal criteria; this is called **satisficing,** or finding a satisfactory solution.[16] The time constraints faced by top decision makers in IR—who are constantly besieged with crises requiring their attention—generally preclude their finding the very best response to a situation. These time constraints were described by U.S. Defense Secretary William Cohen

---

[13] Herrmann, Richard K. and Michael P. Fischerkeller. Beyond the Enemy Image and the Spiral Model: Cognitive-Strategic Research After the Cold War. *International Organization* 49 (3), 1995: 415–50. Mercer, Jonathan L. *Reputation and International Politics*. Cornell, 1996,

[14] Khong, Yuen Foong. *Analogies at War: Korea, Munich, Dien Bien Phu, and the Vietnam Decisions of 1965*. Princeton, 1992. Neustadt, Richard E. and Ernest R. May. *Thinking In Time: The Uses of History for Decision Makers*. New York: Free Press, 1986.

[15] Tuchman, Barbara W. *The March of Folly: From Troy to Vietnam*. NY: Knopf/Random House, 1984. Parker, Richard B. *The Politics of Miscalculation in the Middle East*. Indiana, 1993. Bennett, Andrew. *Condemned to Repetition? The Rise, Fall, and Reprise of Soviet-Russian Military Interventionism, 1973–1996*. MIT, 1999.

[16] Simon, Herbert A. *Models of Bounded Rationality*. MIT, 1982.

in 1997: "The unrelenting flow of information, the need to digest it on a minute-by-minute basis, is quite different from anything I've experienced before. . . . There's little time for contemplation; most of it is action."[17]

Second, **prospect theory** provides an alternative explanation (rather than simple rational optimization) of decisions made under risk or uncertainty.[18] According to this theory, decision makers go through two phases. In the editing phase, they frame the options available and the probabilities of various outcomes associated with each option. Then, in the evaluation phase, they assess the options and choose one. Prospect theory holds that evaluations take place by comparison with a *reference point*, which is often the status quo but might be some past or expected situation. The decision maker asks if she or he can do better than that reference point, but the value placed on outcomes depends on how far from the reference point they are. The theory also holds that individuals *fear losses* more than they relish gains. Decision makers are therefore often willing to forgo opportunities rather than risk a setback.

Individual decision making thus follows an imperfect and partial kind of rationality at best. Not only do the goals of different individuals vary, but decision makers face a series of obstacles in receiving accurate information, constructing accurate models of the world, and reaching decisions that further their own goals. The rational model is only a simplification at best and must be supplemented by an understanding of individual psychological processes that affect decision making.

Not even an absolute dictator, however, makes decisions all alone. State decisions result from the interactions of groups of people. Decision-making bodies—from committees and agency task forces to legislatures and political parties—all rely on the interactions of relatively small groups of people reasoning or arguing together. The psychology of group dynamics thus has great influence on the way foreign policy is formulated.

Group Dynamics

What are the implications of group psychology for foreign policy decision making? In one respect, groups promote rationality by balancing out the blind spots and biases of any individual. Advisers or legislative committees may force a state leader to reconsider a rash decision. And the interactions of different individuals in a group may result in the formulation of goals that more closely reflect state interests rather than individual idiosyncrasies. However, group dynamics also introduce new sources of irrationality into the decision-making process. These fall into two general categories: the psychological dynamics that occur within groups, and the ways that the structure of group decision-making processes can bias the outcomes.

Group Psychology The most important psychological problem is the tendency for groups to reach decisions without accurately assessing their consequences, since individual members tend to go along with ideas they think the others support. This is called **groupthink.**[19] The basic phenomenon is illustrated by a simple psychology experiment. A group of six

---

[17] *Washington Post*, March 5, 1997: A22.

[18] Davis, James W. *Threats and Promises: The Pursuit of International Influence*. Johns Hopkins, 2000. McDermott, Rose. *Risk-Taking in International Politics: Prospect Theory in American Foreign Policy*. Michigan, 1998. Levy, Jack. Prospect Theory, Rational Choice, and International Relations. *International Studies Quarterly* 41 (1), 1997: 87–112.

[19] Janis, Irving L. *Victims of Groupthink: A Psychological Study of Foreign-Policy Decisions and Fiascoes*. Boston: Houghton Mifflin, 1972. Hart, Paul, Eric K. Stern, and Bengt Sundelius, eds. *Beyond Groupthink: Political Group Dynamics and Foreign Policy-Making*. Michigan, 1997.

people is asked to compare the lengths of two lines projected onto a screen. When five of the people are secretly instructed to say that line A is longer—even though anyone can see that line B is actually longer—the sixth person is likely to agree with the group rather than believe her or his own eyes.

Unlike individuals, groups tend to be overly optimistic about the chances of success and are thus more willing to take risks. Doubts about dubious undertakings are suppressed by participants because everyone else seems to think an idea will work. Also, because the group diffuses responsibility from individuals, nobody feels accountable for actions.

In a spectacular case of groupthink, President Ronald Reagan's close friend and director of the U.S. Central Intelligence Agency (CIA), William Casey, bypassed his own agency and ran covert operations spanning three continents using the National Security Council (NSC) staff in the White House basement. The NSC sold weapons to Iran in exchange for the freedom of U.S. hostages held in Lebanon, and then used the Iranian payments to illegally fund Nicaraguan Contra rebels. The **Iran-Contra scandal** resulted when these operations, managed by an obscure NSC aide named Oliver North, became public. Because the operation was secret, the small group involved was cut off from skeptical views, and its few participants seem to have talked themselves into thinking that the operation was a smart idea. They discounted risks such as being discovered and exaggerated the benefits of opening channels to Iranian moderates (who proved elusive). The involvement of a top authority figure surely reassured other participants.

VICTIM OF GROUPTHINK?

Small groups isolated from outsiders may blind themselves to risks and reach poor decisions, a process known as groupthink. Critics of President George W. Bush blame him for relying too closely on a small circle of close advisors, vulnerable to groupthink in formulating policies such as decisions about Iraq. To counter these critics, Bush invited a bipartisan group of former Secretaries of State and Defense to meet with him in early 2006. But Bush—sittting closest to his own inner circle of Donald Rumsfeld, Dick Cheney, and Condoleezza Rice—talked *to* the group for forty minutes and left only five to ten minutes for an exchange of views.

WEB LINK

Iran-Contra Scandal

Decision Structure The *structure of a decision-making process*—the rules for who is involved in making the decision, how voting is conducted, and so forth—can affect the outcome, especially when a group has *indeterminate preferences* because no single alternative appeals to a majority of participants. Experienced participants in foreign policy formation are familiar with the techniques for manipulating decision-making processes to favor outcomes they prefer. A common technique is to control a group's formal *decision rules*. These rules include the items of business the group discusses and the order in which proposals are considered (especially important when participants are satisficing). Probably most important is the ability to *control the agenda* and thereby structure the terms of debate.

The structure of decision making also reflects the composition of a decision group. Who is represented? Often the group is composed of individuals cast in particular *roles* in the group. (Some IR scholars treat role as a distinct level of analysis between the individual and domestic levels.) Roles can be institutional—a participant representing a viewpoint shared by her or his particular group, for example, an intelligence agency. Different sorts of roles within particular groups can be based on factions, mediators, swing voters, and so forth. One adviser might often play the role of introducing new ideas, another the role of defending the status quo, and a third the role of staying neutral so as to gain the leader's ear last.

State leaders often rely on an inner circle of advisers in making foreign policy decisions. The composition and operation of the inner circle vary across governments. For instance, President Lyndon Johnson had "Tuesday lunches" to discuss national security policy with top national security officials. Some groups depend heavily on *informal* consultations in addition to formal meetings. Some leaders create a "kitchen cabinet"—a trusted group of friends who discuss policy issues with the leader even though they have no formal positions in government. For instance, Israel's Golda Meir held many such discussions at her home, sometimes literally in the kitchen. Russian President Boris Yeltsin relied on the advice of his bodyguard, who was a trusted friend.

Informal settings may be used in another way—to shake up formal decision groups and draw participants away from their usual bureaucratic roles. Soviet Premier Leonid Brezhnev in 1972 took President Richard Nixon on a speedboat ride before settling down for discussions at Brezhnev's dacha (villa) in the countryside.

Crisis Management

The difficulties in reaching rational decisions, both for individuals and for groups, are heightened during a crisis.[20] *Crises* are foreign policy situations in which outcomes are very important and time frames are compressed. (In the United States, crises are accompanied by a severalfold increase in pizza deliveries to government agencies, as decision makers work through mealtimes.) Crisis decision making is harder to understand and predict than is normal foreign policy making.

In a crisis, decision makers operate under tremendous time constraints. The normal checks on unwise decisions may not operate. Communications become shorter and more stereotyped, and information that does not fit a decision maker's expectations is more likely to be discarded simply because there is no time to consider it. In framing options there is a tendency to restrict the choices, again to save time, and a tendency to overlook creative options while focusing on the most obvious ones.

You Are President Kennedy

Groupthink occurs easily during crises. During the 1962 Cuban Missile Crisis, President John Kennedy created a small, closed group of advisers who worked together intensively for days on end, cut off from outside contact and discussion. Even the president's communication with Soviet leader Nikita Khrushchev was rerouted through Kennedy's brother Robert and the Soviet ambassador, cutting out the State Department. Recognizing the danger of groupthink, Kennedy would leave the room from time to time—removing the authority figure from the group—to encourage free discussion. Through this and other means, the group managed to identify an option (a naval blockade) between their first two choices (bombing the missile sites or doing nothing). Sometimes, leaders will purposefully designate someone in the group (known as a *devil's advocate*) to raise objections to ideas.

[20] Brecher, Michael, and Jonathan Wilkenfeld. *A Study of Crisis*. Michigan, 2000. Houghton, David. *U.S. Foreign Policy and the Iran Hostage Crisis*. Cambridge, 2001. Gelpi, Christopher. *The Power of Legitimacy: Assessing the Role of Norms in International Crisis Bargaining*. Princeton, 2003.

WORKING UNDER STRESS

Crisis management takes a high toll psychologically and physiologically. President Eduard Shevardnadze of Georgia seems to show this strain in 1992—just the beginning of years of civil war and perpetual crisis in that country. Shevardnadze, formerly Gorbachev's foreign minister, returned to lead his native Georgia when the Soviet Union dissolved. He left office in 2003 after a popular uprising against corruption.

Participants in crisis decision making are not only rushed, they experience severe psychological *stress*. As most of us have experienced personally, people usually do not make decisions wisely when under stress. Stress amplifies the biases just discussed. Decision makers tend to overestimate the hostility of adversaries and to underestimate their own hostility toward those adversaries. Dislike easily turns to hatred, and anxiety to fear. More and more information is screened out in order to come to terms with decisions being made and to restore cognitive balance. Crisis decision making also leads to physical exhaustion. *Sleep deprivation* sets in within days as decision makers use every hour to stay on top of the crisis. College students who have "pulled an all-nighter"—or several in a row—know that within days people deprived of sleep lose touch with reality, experience everything as exaggerated, and suffer from depression and even hallucinations. Unless decision makers are careful about getting enough sleep, these are the conditions under which vital foreign policy decisions may be made.

Because of the importance of sound decision making during crises, voters pay great attention to the psychological stability of their leaders. Before Israeli Prime Minister Yitzhak Rabin won election in 1992, he faced charges that he had suffered a one-day nervous breakdown when he headed the armed forces just before the 1967 war. Not so, he responded; he was just smart enough to realize that the crisis had caused both exhaustion and acute nicotine poisoning; he needed to rest up for a day in order to go on and make good decisions.

Whether in crisis mode or normal routines, individual decision makers do not operate alone. Their decisions are shaped by the government and society in which they work. Foreign policy is constrained and shaped by substate actors ranging from government agencies to political interest groups and industries.

Substate Actors

Foreign policy is shaped not only by the internal dynamics of individual and group decision making but also by the states and societies within which decision makers operate.

Bureaucracies

The substate actors closest to the foreign policy process are the state's bureaucratic agencies maintained for developing and carrying out foreign policy. Different states maintain different foreign policy bureaucracies but share some common elements.

Diplomats

Diplomats Virtually all states maintain a *diplomatic corps*, or *foreign service*, of diplomats working in *embassies* in foreign capitals (and in *consulates* located in noncapital foreign cities), as well as diplomats who remain at home to help coordinate foreign policy. States appoint *ambassadors* as their official representatives to other states and to international organizations. Diplomatic activities are organized through a *foreign ministry* or the equivalent (for example, the U.S. State Department).

In many democracies, some diplomats are *political appointees* who come and go with changes in government leaders (often as patronage for past political support). Others are *career diplomats*, who come up through the ranks of the foreign service and tend to outlast changes in administration. Skilled diplomats are assets that increase a state's power.

Diplomats provide much of the information that goes into making foreign policies, but their main role is to carry out rather than create policies. Nonetheless, foreign ministry bureaucrats can often make foreign relations so routine that top leaders and political appointees can come and go without greatly altering the country's relations. The national interest is served, the bureaucrats believe, by the stability of overall national goals and positions in international affairs.

Tension is common between state leaders and foreign policy bureaucrats. Career diplomats try to orient new leaders and their appointees, and to control the flow of information they receive (creating information screens). Politicians for their part struggle to exercise power over the formal bureaucratic agencies because the latter can be too "bureaucratic" (cumbersome, routinized, conservative) to easily control. Also, these agencies are often staffed (at lower levels) mostly by career officials who may not owe loyalty to political leaders.

Size alone does not guarantee power for a bureaucracy. For example, the U.S. Trade Representative (USTR) and the National Security Council (NSC) each have staffs of only about 200 people, compared with 5,000 people with responsibilities for similar matters in the Commerce and State Departments. The power of these agencies is their proximity to the U.S. president. It is the NSC chief who traditionally briefs the president every morning on international security issues.

Sometimes, state leaders appoint a close friend or key adviser to manage the foreign policy bureaucracy. The first President Bush did this with his closest friend, James Baker, as did President George W. Bush in his second term with his former NSC chief and confidante Condoleezza Rice. Chinese leader Mao Zedong put his loyal ally, Zhou Enlai, in charge of foreign policy.

At times, frustration with the bureaucracy leads politicians to bypass normal channels of diplomacy. For example, during the 1962 Cuban Missile Crisis, President Kennedy demanded to be put in direct contact with military personnel in the Caribbean overseeing the blockade of Cuba, bypassing the secretary of defense and high-ranking officers.

Interagency Tensions Tensions between top political leaders and foreign policy bureaucracies are only one form of *interagency* tension in the formulation of foreign policy. Certain agencies traditionally clash, and an endless tug-of-war shapes the foreign policies that emerge. In an extreme example of interagency rivalry, the U.S. State Department and the CIA backed opposite sides in a civil war in Laos in 1960. In the United States and the Soviet Union during the Cold War, the defense ministry was usually more hawkish (favoring military strength) and the foreign ministry or State Department more dovish (favoring diplomacy), with the president or premier holding the balance.

In general, bureaucracies promote policies in which their own capabilities would be effective and their power would increase. There is a saying that "where you stand" on an issue "depends on where you sit" (in the bureaucratic structure). One can often predict just from the job titles of participants how they will argue on a policy issue. The government bargaining model pays special attention to the interagency negotiations that result from conflicts of interest between agencies of the same government. For example, after Americans were taken hostage in Iran in 1979, military and CIA officials pushed President Carter to attempt a military rescue, while the State Department vehemently opposed such a mission. After days of debate, the president decided to go ahead with the rescue mission (which proved disastrous), but did not invite the secretary of state to the meeting where the final decisions were made.

Although representatives of bureaucratic agencies usually promote the interests of their own bureaucracies, sometimes heads of agencies try to appear loyal to the state leader by forgoing the interests of their own agencies. Also, the preferences of leaders of bureaucratic agencies cannot always be predicted given the goal of their institution. For example, in the Cuban Missile Crisis, defense officials were hesitant to commit to a military solution to the crisis, while some diplomatic officials favored a preemptive military strike.

Units within agencies have similar tensions. In many countries, the different military services (army, navy, air force) pull in somewhat different directions, even if they ultimately unite to battle the foreign ministry. Bureaucrats working in particular units or projects become attached to them. Officials responsible for a new weapon system will lose bureaucratic turf, and perhaps their jobs, if the weapon's development is canceled.

Of special concern in many poor states is the institutional interest that military officers have in maintaining a strong military. If civilian state leaders allow officers' salaries to fall or the size of the military forces to be cut, they may well face institutional resistance from the military—in the extreme case a military takeover of the government (see pp. 222–224). These issues were factors in attempted military coups in the Philippines, Venezuela, and Paraguay in the 1990s.[21]

In general, bureaucratic rivalry as an influence on foreign policy challenges the notion of states as unitary actors in the international system. Such rivalries suggest that a state does not have any single set of goals—a national interest—but that its actions may result from the bargaining of subunits, each with its own set of goals.[22] Furthermore, such a perspective extends far beyond bureaucratic agencies because other substate actors have their own goals, which they seek to advance by influencing foreign policy.

Interest Groups

Interest Groups

Foreign policy makers operate not in a political vacuum but in the context of the political debates in their society. In all states, societal pressures influence foreign policy, although these are aggregated and made effective through different channels in different societies. In pluralistic democracies, interested parties influence foreign policy through interest groups and political parties. In dictatorships, similar influences occur but less visibly. Thus foreign policies adopted by states generally reflect some kind of

[21] Feaver, Peter D., and Christopher Gelpi. *Choosing Your Battles: American Civil-Military Relations and the Use of Force*. Princeton, 2004. Aguero, Felipe. Democratic Consolidation and the Military in Southern Europe and South America. In Gunther, Richard, P. Nikiforos Diamandouros, and Hans J. Puhle, eds. *The Politics of Democratic Consolidation*, 124–65. Johns Hopkins, 1995.

[22] Kaarbo, Juliet. Power Politics in Foreign Policy: The Influence of Bureaucratic Minorities. *European Journal of International Relations* 4 (1), 1998, 67–97.

process of domestic coalition formation.[23] Of course, international factors also have strong effects on domestic politics.[24]

Interest groups are coalitions of people who share a common interest in the outcome of some political issue and who organize themselves to try to influence the outcome. For instance, French farmers have a big stake in international negotiations on the European Community (which subsidizes agriculture) and in world trade talks (which set agricultural tariffs). The farmers exert political pressure on the French government through long-established and politically sophisticated associations and organizations. They lobby for desired legislation and contribute to politicians' campaigns. More dramatically, when their interests are threatened—as during a U.S.-European trade dispute in 1992—French farmers have turned out in large numbers across the country to block roads, stage violent street demonstrations, and threaten to grind the national economy to a halt unless the government adopts their position. Similarly (but often less dramatically), interest groups form around businesses, labor unions, churches, veterans, senior citizens, members of an occupation, or citizens concerned about an issue such as the environment.

MAKING THEMSELVES HEARD

Foreign policies are affected by the pulling and tugging of various domestic interest groups. European farmers and truckers have tried to influence policies by repeatedly blocking rail and road traffic. Here, Belgian truckers block a border crossing to Germany, 2000.

Lobbying is the process of talking with legislators or officials to influence their decisions on some set of issues. Three important elements that go into successful lobbying are the ability to gain a hearing with busy officials, the ability to present cogent arguments for one's case, and the ability to trade favors in return for positive action on an issue. These favors—legal and illegal—range from campaign contributions through dinners at nice restaurants and trips to golf resorts to securing illicit sexual liaisons and paying bribes. In many states, corruption is a major problem in governmental decision making (see pp. 513–514), and interest groups may induce government officials by illegal means to take certain actions.

Ethnic groups within one state often become interest groups concerned about their ancestral nation outside that state. Many members of ethnic groups feel strong emotional ties to their relatives in other countries; because the rest of the population generally does not care about such issues one way or the other, even a small ethnic group can have

[23] Smith, Tony. *Foreign Attachments: The Power of Ethnic Groups in the Making of American Foreign Policy*. Harvard, 2000. Solingen, Etel. *Regional Orders at Century's Dawn: Global and Domestic Influences on Grand Strategy*. Princeton, 1998. Bueno de Mesquita, Bruce, and David Lalman. *War and Reason: Domestic and International Imperatives*. Yale, 1992. Snyder, Jack. *Myths of Empire: Domestic Politics and International Ambition*. Cornell, 1991.

[24] Gourevitch, Peter. The Second Image Reversed: International Sources of Domestic Politics. *International Organization* 32 (4), 1978: 881–911. Rogowski, Ronald. *Commerce and Coalitions: How Trade Affects Domestic Political Alignments*. Princeton, 1989.

considerable influence on policy toward a particular country. Such ethnic ties are emerging as a powerful foreign policy influence in various ethnic conflicts in poor regions. The effect is especially strong in the United States, which is ethnically mixed and has a pluralistic form of democracy. For example, Cuban Americans organize to influence U.S. policy toward Cuba, as do Greek Americans on Greece, Jewish Americans on Israel, and African Americans on Africa. In a 1996 U.S. Senate election in South Dakota, one candidate raised large contributions from the Pakistani-American community and the other from the rival Indian-American community.

Whether or not a foreign country has a large constituency of ethnic nationals within another country, it can set about lobbying that country's government, as other interest groups do. Israel and Taiwan have strong lobbying presences in the U.S. Congress, and many less visible states have hired U.S. public relations firms to represent their interests in Washington, DC.

Cotton Subsidies

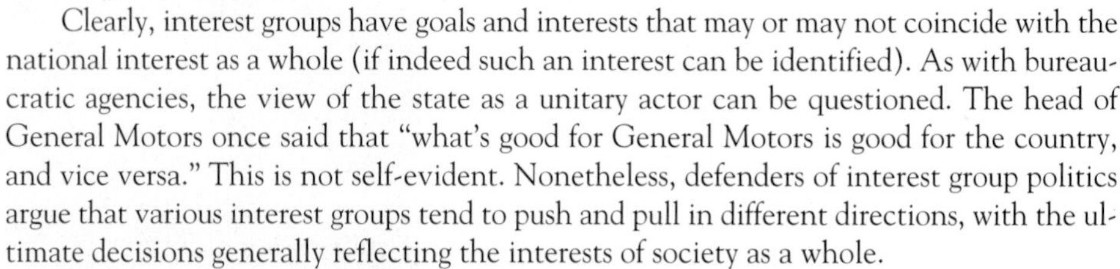

Clearly, interest groups have goals and interests that may or may not coincide with the national interest as a whole (if indeed such an interest can be identified). As with bureaucratic agencies, the view of the state as a unitary actor can be questioned. The head of General Motors once said that "what's good for General Motors is good for the country, and vice versa." This is not self-evident. Nonetheless, defenders of interest group politics argue that various interest groups tend to push and pull in different directions, with the ultimate decisions generally reflecting the interests of society as a whole.

According to *Marxist* theories of international relations (see Chapter 12), the key domestic influences on foreign policy in capitalist countries are rich owners of big businesses. For instance, European imperialism benefited banks and big business, which made huge profits from exploiting cheap labor and resources in overseas colonies. This is the official view (if not always the operative one) of the Chinese government toward Western industrialized states. During the Cold War, Marxists frequently argued that U.S. foreign policy and that of its Western allies were driven by the profit motive of arms manufacturers.[25]

The Military-Industrial Complex

Military-Industrial Complex

A **military-industrial complex** is a huge interlocking network of governmental agencies, industrial corporations, and research institutes, working together to supply a nation's military forces. Because of the domestic political clout of these actors, the complex was a very powerful influence on foreign policy in *both* the United States and the Soviet Union during the Cold War. Some of that influence remains, though it has diminished. The military-industrial complex was a response to the growing importance of technology (nuclear weapons, electronics, and others) and of logistics in Cold War military planning.

States at war have long harnessed their economic and technological might for the war effort. But during the Cold War military procurement occurred on a massive scale in "peacetime," as the superpowers raced to develop new high-technology weapons. This race created a special role for scientists and engineers in addition to the more traditional role of industries that produce war materials. In response to the Soviet satellite *Sputnik* in 1957, the United States increased spending on research and development and created new science education programs. By 1961, President Dwight Eisenhower warned in his farewell speech that the military-industrial complex (a term he coined) was gaining "unwarranted influence" in U.S. society and that militarization could erode democracy in the United States. The threat to democracy was that the interest of the military-

[25] Konobeyev, V. The Capitalist Economy and the Arms Race. *International Affairs* [Moscow] 8, 1982: 28–48.

industrial complex in the arms race conflicted with the interest of ordinary citizens in peace, while the size of the complex gave it more political clout than ordinary citizens could muster.

The complex encompasses a variety of constituencies, each of which has an interest in military spending. *Corporations* that produce goods for the military profit from government contracts. So do military *officers* whose careers advance by building bureaucratic empires around new weapons systems. And so do universities and scientific institutes that receive military research contracts—a major source of funding for scientists in Russia and the United States.

Subcontractors and parts suppliers for big U.S. weapons projects are usually spread around many states and congressional districts, so that local citizens and politicians join the list of constituents benefiting from military spending. Early funding for the Strategic Defense Initiative (or Star Wars) was given to each military service branch, the Department of Energy, NASA, and hundreds of private contractors. Recently, a similar phenomenon has emerged in the European Community, where weapons development programs have been parceled out to several European states. A new fighter jet is less likely to be canceled if one country gets the contract for the wings, another for the engines, and so forth.

FLYING PORK-BARREL?

In the 1990s, the military-industrial complex was hit hard in the United States, and harder in the former Soviet Union, by cuts in military spending. B-2 long-range stealth bombers, here being built by Northrop Grumman in southern California (1988), survived the end of the Cold War despite their enormous cost and disappearing mission. Defense manufacturers have an interest in high military spending—one link in the military-industrial complex. The boost in military spending after September 2001 has made such companies much more profitable.

Executives in military industries, as the people who best understand their industries, are often appointed as government officials responsible for military procurement decisions and then return to their companies again—a practice called the *revolving door*. In democracies, military industries also try to influence public opinion through *advertising* that ties their products to patriotic themes. Finally, U.S. military industries give generous *campaign contributions* to national politicians who vote on military budgets, and sometimes bribes to Pentagon officials as well. Military industry became an important source of *political action committee (PAC)* money raised by members of Congress. In the 1996 elections, for example, one company alone (Lockheed Martin) contributed more than $2 million to congressional campaigns.[26]

When the Cold War ended, the military-industrial complex in both superpowers endured cutbacks in military budgets. In Russia, military industries formed the backbone of a

[26] Der Derian, James. *Virtuous War: Mapping the Military-Industrial-Media-Entertainment Network*. Boulder, CO: Westview, 2001. Jones, Christopher M. Roles, Politics, and the Survival of the V-22 Osprey. *Journal of Political and Military Sociology* 29 (1), 2001: 46–72.

political faction seeking to slow down economic reforms and continue government subsidies to state-owned industries. They succeeded in replacing Russia's reformist prime minister with an industrial manager in late 1992. In the United States, meanwhile, the lingering influence of the military-industrial complex may help to explain why Congress kept funding certain Cold War weapons (such as the Seawolf submarine and B-2 bomber) after their purpose seemingly disappeared.

Public Opinion

Military industries and other substate actors seek to influence **public opinion**—the range of views on foreign policy issues held by the citizens of a state. Public opinion has greater influence on foreign policy in democracies than in authoritarian governments. But even dictators must pay attention to what citizens think. No government can rule by force alone: it needs legitimacy to survive. It must convince people to accept (if not to like) its policies, because in the end policies are carried out by ordinary people—soldiers, workers, and bureaucrats.

Because of the need for public support, even authoritarian governments spend great effort on *propaganda*—the public promotion of their official line—to win support for foreign policies. States use television, newspapers, and other information media in this effort. For instance, when China invited President Nixon to visit in 1972, the Chinese government mounted a major propaganda campaign to explain to its people that the United States was not so bad after all. In many countries, the state owns or controls major mass media such as television and newspapers, mediating the flow of information to its citizens; however, new information technologies with multiple channels make this harder to do.

In democracies, where governments must stand for election, public opinion is even more important. An unpopular war can force a leader or party from office, as happened to U.S. President Johnson in 1968 during the Vietnam War. Or a popular war can help secure a government's mandate to continue in power, as happened to Margaret Thatcher in Britain after the 1982 Falkland Islands War. A key influence on public opinion is the content of scenes appearing on television: U.S. soldiers were sent to Somalia to assist in relief efforts in 1992 after TV news showed the heartrending results of civil war and famine there. But after TV news showed an American soldier's body being dragged through the streets by members of a Somali faction after a deadly firefight that killed 18 U.S. soldiers, public opinion shifted quickly against the Somalia operation. During the war in Bosnia, officials in the U.S. State Department said privately that the main goal of U.S. policy was often just to keep the conflict there off of the front pages of U.S. newspapers (an elusive goal, as it turned out).

Reporting on the Iraq War

Journalists serve as the gatekeepers of information passing from foreign policy elites to the public. The media and government often conflict, because of the traditional role of the press as a watchdog and critic of government actions and powers. The media try to uncover and publicize that which the government wants to hide, especially in situations such as the Iran-Contra scandal. Foreign policy decision makers also rely on the media for information about foreign affairs.

Yet the media also depend on government for information; the size and resources of the foreign policy bureaucracies dwarf those of the press. These advantages give the government great power to *manipulate* journalists by feeding them information, in order to shape the news and influence public opinion. Government decision makers can create dramatic stories in foreign relations—through summit meetings, crises, actions, and so forth. Bureaucrats can also *leak* secret information to the press in order to support their own point of view and win bureaucratic battles. Finally, the military and the press have

POLICY PERSPECTIVES

President of the Philippines, Gloria Arroyo

PROBLEM *Deciding what foreign policy tools best balance domestic and international concerns.*

BACKGROUND Imagine that you are the president of the Philippines, a state composed of more than 7,000 islands. Since the late 1960s, various separatists groups on the smaller islands have rebelled against the central government in Manila. Guerrilla warfare has raged for years on these islands, with rebels carrying out bombings, kidnappings, and hijackings, while the government responds with repression of the rebel movements.

Some of these rebels groups are organized around their religious faith. The Moro Islamic Liberation Front (MILF) was active on the island of Mindanao against the central government but signed a cease-fire agreement in 2003. Abu Sayyaf and Jemaah Islamiah have continued to fight on the islands of Jolo and Mindanao, carrying out attacks against civilians, especially Western aid workers and missionaries.

Meanwhile, the United States has pledged support for your efforts against the rebels. Abu Sayyaf has been linked with al Qaeda and you have pledged your support to the United States in the war on terror. U.S. special forces have been training Filipino units, but your closeness with the U.S. in not popular domestically. In fact, in July 2004, you withdrew Philippine troops from Iraq to save the life of a kidnapped hostage there. This move was very popular domestically, in part due to the massive public opposition to your support for the Iraq war.

Unfortunately, you have doubts concerning the loyalty of your army. In July 2003, 300 soldiers rebelled and seized control of a shopping center, which was to serve as a headquarters for a coup attempt. In January 2004, five officers were arrested for "inciting rebellion" against the government. In March 2006, you declared a state of emergency in response to an alleged coup plot.

Despite U.S. assistance, rebel attacks continue. In 2002, several bombs exploded in Manila and nearby cities. In 2003, bombs on Mindanao killed 38, while injuring hundreds. Increasingly, the rebels are bringing their attacks to the main island and to large cities, including Manila.

SCENARIO Now imagine that your military is pressuring you to escalate the fight against the rebellion. Additional assistance to fight the rebels would be helpful, especially given the tensions between you and the armed forces. Unfortunately, U.S. troops would be very unpopular with the voting public. When the United States maintained two large naval bases in the Philippines, there were considerable tensions between U.S. troops and your citizens.

You could negotiate with the rebels. This strategy was successful in bringing peace with the MILF. If successful, this strategy could bring long-term peace to your country. Yet, this move would certainly anger the United States, a key ally. It might also appear as if you are giving in to terrorist threats, a charge you are sensitive to after the withdrawal from Iraq.

CHOOSE YOUR POLICY Should you ask for U.S. troops to participate in fighting the rebels? Do you attempt to negotiate with the remaining rebel groups?

How do you adopt a foreign policy that generates public support, yet also pleases key domestic and international constituencies?

a running battle about journalists' access to military operations, but both sides gained from the open access given to journalists "embedded" with U.S. forces in Iraq in 2003.

Occasionally a foreign policy issue is decided directly by a referendum of the entire citizenry (the United States lacks such a tradition, which is strong in Switzerland and Denmark, for example).[27] In 2005, referendums in France and the Netherlands rejected a proposed constitution for the European Union, despite the support of major political leaders for the change (see p. 392). The defeat did not jeopardize the EU itself, but slowed the pace of integration and put leaders on notice that citizens were not behind them.

Even in the most open democracies, states do not merely *respond* to public opinion. Decision makers enjoy some autonomy to make their own choices, and they are pulled in various directions by bureaucracies and interest groups, whose views often conflict with the direction favored by public opinion at large. Furthermore, public opinion is seldom unified on any policy, and sophisticated polling can show that particular segments of the population (regions of the country, genders, income groups, races, etc.) often differ in their perceptions of foreign policy issues. So a politician may respond to the opinion of one constituency rather than the whole population. Public opinion varies considerably over time on many foreign policy issues. States use propaganda (in dictatorships) or try to manipulate the media (in democracies) to keep public opinion from diverging too much from state policies.

In democracies, public opinion generally has *less effect on foreign policy than on domestic policy*. National leaders traditionally have additional latitude to make decisions in the international realm. This derives from the special need of states to act in a unified way to function effectively in the international system, as well as from the traditions of secrecy and diplomacy that remove IR from the realm of ordinary domestic politics. In the case of Japan, public opinion is a major political force restraining the military spending of the government, its commitment of military forces beyond Japan's borders, and especially the development of nuclear weapons (which is within Japan's technical abilities). The ruling party—under pressure from the United States to share the burden of defense and to shoulder its responsibilities as a great power—has slowly but steadily pushed to increase Japan's military spending and allow Japanese military forces to expand their role modestly (in the 1980s, to patrol Asian sea lanes vital to Japanese trade; in the 1990s, to participate in UN peacekeeping operations). Repeatedly, these efforts have been slowed or rebuffed by strong public opinion against the military. In Japan, people remember the horrible consequences of militarism in the 1930s and World War II, culminating in the nuclear bombings of 1945. They are suspicious of any increase in the size or role of military forces, and dead set against Japan's having nuclear weapons. In this case, public opinion constrains the state's conduct of foreign policy, and has slowed the pace of change.

The *attentive public* in a democracy is that minority of the population that stays informed about international issues. This segment varies somewhat from one issue to another, but there is also a core of people who care in general about foreign affairs and follow them closely. The most active members of the attentive public on foreign affairs constitute a foreign policy *elite*—people with power and influence who affect foreign policy. This elite includes people within governments as well as outsiders such as businesspeople, journalists, lobbyists, and professors of political science. Public opinion polls show that elite opinions sometimes (but not always) differ considerably from those of the general population, and sometimes from those of the government as well.[28]

---

[27] Rourke, John T., Richard P. Hiskes, and Cyrus Ernesto Zirakzadeh. *Direct Democracy and International Politics: Deciding International Issues Through Referendums*. Boulder, CO: Lynne Rienner, 1992.

[28] Sobel, Richard. *The Impact of Public Opinion on U.S. Foreign Policy Since Vietnam*. Oxford, 2001. Holsti, Ole R. *Public Opinion and American Foreign Policy (Revised)*. Michigan, 2004. Murray, Shoon. *Anchors Against Change: American Opinion Leaders' Beliefs After the Cold War*. Michigan, 1996. Nincic, Miroslav, Steven Kull, and I. M. Destler. *Misreading the Public: The Myth of a New Isolationism*. Washington DC: Brookings, 1999.

Governments sometimes adopt foreign policies for the specific purpose of generating public approval and hence gaining domestic legitimacy.[29] This is the case when a government undertakes a war or foreign military intervention at a time of domestic difficulty, to distract attention and gain public support—taking advantage of the **rally 'round the flag syndrome** (the public's increased support for government leaders during wartime, at least in the short term). Citizens who would readily criticize their government's policies on education or health care will often refrain from criticism when the government is at war and the lives of the nation's soldiers are on the line. Policies of this sort are often labeled diversionary foreign policy. Unfortunately, it is always difficult to tell whether a state adopts a foreign policy to distract the public, since leaders would never admit to trying to divert public attention.

However, wars that go on too long, or are not successful, can turn public opinion against the government and even lead to a popular uprising to overthrow the government. In Argentina, the military government in 1982 led the country into war with Britain over the Falkland Islands. At first Argentineans rallied around the flag, but after losing the war they rallied around the cause of getting rid of the military government, and they replaced it with a new civilian government that prosecuted the former leaders. In 2006, President Bush's popularity, which had soared early in the Iraq war, plummeted as the war dragged on for three years with mounting costs.

Legislatures

One conduit through which interest groups and public opinion may wield influence is legislatures. Some democracies, such as the United States, have presidential systems, where legislative bodies are elected apart from the president (also referred to as *executives*). In these systems, legislatures play a direct role in making foreign policy by passing budgets, regulating bureaucratic rules, creating trade law, even controlling immigration policy. While an executive may attend summits and talks, any agreement they sign must be approved by their domestic legislature.[30]

While few would argue that legislatures in presidential democracies do not influence foreign policy generally, different rules may apply to the use of military force. Some contend that legislatures, like public opinion, rally around the flag during times of international crises. For example, three days after the September 11, 2001, attacks, the U.S. Congress voted to give President Bush full authority to prosecute a war in Afghanistan. In October 2002, Congress passed a resolution authorizing the use of force in Iraq. Thus, legislatures rarely if ever challenge an executive on important military matters.

Others point to a different dynamic in which legislatures do stand up to executive power regarding military force. For example, because legislatures hold the "purse strings" (the ability to approve or reject new spending), they have the ability to stop a war in its tracks. In the United States, the War Powers Act, enacted during the close of the Vietnam War, requires the president to notify Congress when U.S. troops are deployed for combat. After this notification, the president has 60 days (plus a possible 30-day extension) to recall the troops unless Congress explicitly approves the military action.

---

[29] Richards, Diana, T. et al. 1993. Good Times, Bad Times, and the Diversionary Use of Force. *Journal of Conflict Resolution* 37 (3), 1993: 504–36. Baum, Matthew. The Constituent Foundations of the Rally-Round-the-Flag Phenomenon. *International Studies Quarterly* 46 (2), 2002: 263–298.

[30] Milner, Helen. *Interests, Institutions, and Information: Domestic Politics and International Relations*. Princeton, 1997. Evans, Peter B., Harold K. Jacobson, and Robert D. Putnam, eds. *Double-Edged Diplomacy: International Bargaining and Domestic Politics*. California, 1993.

Finally, some evidence from the United States suggests that presidents are more likely to use military force when their own political party is in power in Congress, suggesting that politics do not stop "at the water's edge."[31]

In parliamentary systems, such as Great Britain, executives (for example, prime ministers) are chosen by the political parties that hold a dominant position in the legislative bodies. Often, parliamentary executives do not need to submit treaties or policies for formal approval by the legislature. Yet, legislatures in parliamentary systems still hold power regarding foreign policy. In Great Britain, for example, Parliament is not required to vote on international agreements negotiated by the prime minister, but it must approve any change to British laws that such agreements entail. Since most international agreements do involve these types of changes, Parliament effectively exercises a right of ratification over international agreements.

In many parliamentary systems, if a policy is particularly controversial, parties that do not have a majority in the legislature can attempt to call elections—meaning that the country votes again on which parties will hold seats in the legislature. If a different group of parties wins a majority of seats, a new executive is appointed. Thus, in parliamentary systems, legislatures play a key role in the design and implementation of foreign policy.

Democracy and Foreign Policy

Authoritarian Governments: Hindrance or Help?

Overall, the differences in the foreign policy process from one state to another are more influenced by a state's type of government than by the particular constellation of bureaucracies, interest groups, or individuals within it. Government types include military dictatorship, communist party rule, one-party (noncommunist) rule, and various forms of multiparty **democracy.** Relatively democratic states tend to share values and interests, and hence to get along better with each other than with nondemocracies.[32]

In practice, most states lie along a spectrum with some mix of democratic and authoritarian elements. For example, because of campaign contributions, even democracies in North America and Japan give greater influence to rich people than to poor people. In many states, governments control TV and radio stations, putting opposition politicians at a disadvantage in elections. In Angola, relatively fair elections were held in 1992, but the losing side rejected the results and resorted to military attacks. In Burma, a military government held elections, lost them, and then simply refused to step aside or allow the newly elected parliament to meet. In Algeria, the military canceled elections midway as Islamic parties were winning. Although there are certain basic elements that most would consider necessary for democracy (free elections, free press, free speech), coming up with a perfect definition of democracy can be very difficult.

The Democratic Peace How do the foreign policies of democracies differ from those of authoritarian governments? We have already referred to a number of differences in the nature of internal decision making, the effects of interest groups, the importance of pub-

[31] Howell, Will and Jon C. Pevehouse. *While Dangers Gather: Congressional Checks on Presidential War Powers.* Princeton, forthcoming. Gowa, Joanne. Politics at the Water's Edge: Parties, Voters and the Use of Force Abroad. *International Organization* 52 (2), 1998: 307–24. Fisher, Louis. *Congressional Abdication on War and Spending.* Texas A&M, 2000. Fordham, Benjamin. Partisanship, Macroeconomic Policy, and the U.S. Uses of Force, 1949–1994. *Journal of Conflict Resolution* 42 (4), 1998: 418–39.

[32] Gartzke, Erik. Kant We All Just Get Along: Opportunity, Willingness, and the Origins of the Democratic Peace. *American Journal of Political Science* 42 (1), 1998: 1–27. Peceny, Mark, Caroline C. Beer, and Shannon Sanchez-Terry. Dictatorial Peace? *American Political Science Review* 96 (1), 2002: 15–27.

lic opinion, and the presence of effective legislatures. Although public opinion, interest group activism, and legislatures operate in some form in virtually all states, they are more influential in democracies.

Democracy

Some 200 years ago, philosopher Immanuel Kant argued that lasting peace would depend on states' becoming republics, with legislatures to check the power of monarchs (or presidents) to make war. He thought that checks and balances in government would act as a brake on the use of military force—as compared to autocratic governments where a single individual (or small ruling group) could make war without regard for the effect on the population.

IR scholars have examined data for the idea that democracy is linked with a kind of foreign policy fundamentally different from that of authoritarianism.[33] One theory they considered was that democracies are generally *more peaceful* than authoritarian governments (fighting fewer, or smaller, wars). This turned out to be not true. Democracies fight as many wars as do authoritarian states. Indeed, the three most war-prone states of the past two centuries (according to political scientists who count wars) were France, Russia, and Britain. Britain was a democracy throughout, France for part of the period, and Russia not at all.

What *is* true about democracies is that although they fight wars against authoritarian states, *democracies almost never fight each other*. No major historical cases contradict this generalization, which is known as the **democratic peace.** Why this is so is not entirely clear. As there have not been many democracies for very long, the generalization could be just a coincidence, though this seems unlikely. It may be that democracies do not tend to have severe conflicts with each other, as they tend to be capitalist states whose trade relations create strong interdependence (war would be costly since it would disrupt trade). Or, citizens of democratic societies (whose support is necessary for wars to be waged) may simply not see the citizens of other democracies as enemies. By contrast, authoritarian governments of other states can be seen as enemies. Note that the peace among democracies gives empirical support to a long-standing liberal claim that, because it is rooted in the domestic level of analysis, contradicts realism's claim that the most important explanations are at the interstate level.

Informed or Brainwashed?

Over the past two centuries, democracy has become more and more widespread as a form of government, and this trend is changing the nature of the foreign policy process worldwide. Many states do not yet have democratic governments (the most important of these is China). And existing democracies are imperfect in various ways—from political apathy in the United States and corruption in Japan to autocratic traditions in Russia. Nonetheless, the trend is toward democratization in most of the world's regions.

President Bush on Democracy and Peace

In the past two decades the trend has accelerated in several ways. New democracies emerged in several (though not all) states of the old Soviet bloc. Military governments were replaced with democratically elected civilian ones throughout most of Latin America as well as in several African and Asian countries. South Africa, the last white-ruled African country, adopted majority rule in 1994. In several of these cases (for instance, in the Philippines in 1986), long-standing dictatorships were ended by nonviolent popular

---

[33] Kinsella, David. No Rest for the Democratic Peace. *American Political Science Review* 99, 2005: 453–57. Reiter, Dan and Allan C. Stam. *Democracies at War*. Princeton, 2002. Huth, Paul and Todd Allee. *The Democratic Peace and the Territorial Conflict in the Twentieth Century*. Cambridge, 2003. Lipson, Charles. *Reliable Partners: How Democracies Have Made a Separate Peace*. Princeton, 2003. Bueno de Mesquita, Bruce et al. *The Logic of Political Survival*. MIT, 2003. Schultz, Kenneth A. *Democracy and Coercive Diplomacy*. Cambridge, 2001. Russett, Bruce, and John Oneal. *Triangulating Peace: Democracy, Interdependence, and International Organizations*. NY: Norton, 2000. Gowa, Joanne. *Ballots and Bullets: The Elusive Democratic Peace*. Princeton, 1999. Rummel, R.J. *Power Kills: Democracy as a Method of Nonviolence*. New Brunswick, NJ: Transaction, 1997. Doyle, Michael W. Liberalism and World Politics. *American Political Science Review* 80 (4), 1986: 1151–70.

ELECTORAL UPSET

Upsurges of democratic movements throughout the world in recent years testify to the power of the idea of democracy. Since democracies rarely fight each other, worldwide democratization might lead to lasting peace. But democratization also brings surprises. In free elections in 2006, Palestinians fed up with a corrupt administration elected the militant and violent Islamic party Hamas, whose candidates here campaign with green crescents, a symbol of Islam.

movements. Elsewhere (for instance, in Nicaragua) civil wars ended with internationally supervised democratic elections. In the late 1990s, long-standing dictatorships or military governments were replaced peacefully by democratic governments in Indonesia and Nigeria, both regional giants. In late 2004 and early 2005, pro-democracy forces won a string of victories in Ukraine, Palestine, Afghanistan, Iraq, and Kyrgyzstan. In 2006 in Nepal, massive popular protests forced the king to reverse his seizure of absolute power and reinstate the Parliament. However, movement in the other direction still occurs. Military governments took over Pakistan and Ivory Coast in 1999, an extra-constitutional seizure of power took place in Togo in 2005, and Russia's government has constrained democracy in recent years while China's communist party has maintained its iron grip on politics.

We do not know where these trends toward democracy will lead, but because it is now conceivable that someday all or most of the world's states will be democratically governed, wars may become less frequent. As Kant envisaged, an international community based on peaceful relations may emerge. However, although mature democracies almost never fight each other, a period of *transition* to democracy may be more prone to war than either a stable democracy or a stable authoritarian government.[34] Therefore the process of democratization does not necessarily bode well for peace in the short term. This theory gained support in early 2006 when first Iraqi elections were followed by a rise in sectarian violence and then Palestinian elections brought to power the militant faction Hamas, which rejects Israel's right to exist. The Bush Administration's vision of bringing democracy to the Middle East appeared to backfire, at least in the short term.

A further caution is in order. The generalization about democracies almost never fighting each other is historically valid but not necessarily applicable in the future. By way of analogy, there was a generalization during the Cold War that communist governments never yield power peacefully. That generalization held up beautifully until suddenly a series of communist governments did just that around 1990. As the world has more democracies for a longer time, the generalization about their almost never fighting each other might not hold up.

The attempt to explain foreign policy in a general and *theoretical* way has met only limited success. This is one reason realists continue to find simple unitary actor models of

---

[34] Mansfield, Edward D. and Jack Snyder. *Electing to Fight: Why Emerging Democracies Go to War*. MIT, 2005. Snyder, Jack. *From Voting to Violence: Democratization and Nationalist Conflict*. NY: Norton, 2000.

the state useful; the domestic and individual elements of the foreign policy process add much complexity and unpredictability. One area of foreign policy where knowledge stands on a somewhat firmer basis is the *descriptive* effort to understand how particular mechanisms of foreign policy formation operate in various states. Such approaches belong to the field of comparative politics.

To summarize, foreign policy is a complex outcome of a complex process. It results from the struggle of competing themes, competing domestic interests, and competing government agencies. No single individual, agency, or guiding principle determines the outcome. Yet, foreign policy does achieve a certain overall coherence. States do form foreign policy on an issue or toward a region; it is not just an incoherent collection of decisions and actions taken from time to time. Out of the turbulent internal processes of foreign policy formation come relatively coherent interests and policies that states pursue.

Of course, those aggregate state interests and policies frequently come into conflict with the interests and policies of other states. Such conflicts are the subject of the next chapter.

THINKING CRITICALLY

1. India and Pakistan are neighbors and enemies. Given the problems of misperception and bias in foreign policy decision making, what steps could you propose that each government adopt to keep these problems from interfering in the rational pursuit of national interests?
2. Sometimes aggressive international actions are attributed to a "madman" such as Iraq's Saddam Hussein or Nazi Germany's Adolf Hitler. Do you agree that such leaders (each of whose actions severely damaged his state's well-being) must be "mad"? What other factors could account for their actions? How do you think such people achieve and maintain national leadership?
3. Imagine a sudden, unexpected crisis caused by an event such as the explosion of a nuclear weapon (of unknown origin) in Moscow. Given the dangers inherent in crisis decision making, what steps could the leaders of affected states take to prevent the situation from spinning out of control? Which of these steps might be taken *before* any crisis occurred, to prepare for a future crisis?
4. Inasmuch as democracies almost never fight wars with each other, do existing democracies have a national security interest in seeing democratization spread to China and other authoritarian states? If so, how can that interest be reconciled with the longstanding norm of noninterference in the internal affairs of other sovereign states?
5. Traditionally, foreign policy elites have faced only sporadic pressure from mass public opinion. Is the role of television changing this relationship? If you were a top foreign policy maker, what steps could you take to keep TV news from shaping the foreign policy agenda before you could define your own goals and directions?

CHAPTER SUMMARY

- Foreign policies are strategies governments use to guide their actions toward other states. The foreign policy process is the set of procedures and structures that states use to arrive at foreign policy decisions and to implement them.
- In the rational model of decision making, officials choose the action whose consequences best help to meet the state's established goals. By contrast, in the organizational process model, decisions result from routine administrative procedures, and in the government bargaining (or bureaucratic politics) model, decisions result from negotiations among governmental agencies with different interests in the outcome.
- The actions of individual decision makers are influenced by their personalities, values, and beliefs as well as by common psychological factors that diverge from rationality. These factors include misperception, selective perception, emotional biases, and cognitive biases (including the effort to reduce cognitive dissonance).
- Foreign policy decisions are also influenced by the psychology of groups (including "groupthink"), the procedures used to reach decisions, and the roles of participants. During crises, the potentials for misperception and error are amplified.
- Struggles over the direction of foreign policy are common between professional bureaucrats and politicians, as well as between different government agencies.
- Domestic constituencies (interest groups) have distinct interests in foreign policies and often organize politically to promote those interests.
- Prominent among domestic constituencies—especially in the United States and Russia, and especially during the Cold War—have been military-industrial complexes consisting of military industries and others with an interest in high military spending.
- Public opinion influences governments' foreign policy decisions (more so in democracies than in authoritarian states), but governments also manipulate public opinion.
- Democracies have historically fought as many wars as authoritarian states, but democracies have almost never fought wars against other democracies. This is called the democratic peace.

KEY TERMS

foreign policy process 139
rational model 141
organizational process model 142
government bargaining model 142
misperceptions, selective perceptions 145
information screens 145
optimizing 146
satisficing 146
prospect theory 147
groupthink 147
Iran-Contra scandal 148
interest groups 153
military-industrial complex 154
public opinion 156
rally 'round the flag syndrome 159
democracy 160
democratic peace 161

ONLINE PRACTICE TEST

Take an online practice test at
www.internationalrelations.net

❑ A
❑ B
☑ C
❑ D

LET'S DEBATE THE ISSUE

The War on Terrorism: Should Public Opinion Influence Foreign Policy in Democracies?

by Mir Zohair Husain

Overview Foreign policy decision making in democracies is a complex process. Political leaders in democracies are constantly ascertaining the needs, interests, and fears of the masses—the public's opinion. Hence, polls are regularly taken and analyzed by those leaders.

Realism asserts that states make rational decisions to promote their national interests. However, democratic norms and values pose challenges to such a claim. In democracies, political leaders represent their citizens' diverse desires concerning domestic and foreign policies. The policies of America's war on terrorism illustrate the potential for public opinion to influence state decision makers.

Studies show no significant link between public opinion and the formulation of public policy. However, September 11, 2001, unified American public opinion, creating a unique mandate. Indeed, just six weeks later, when the American public was feeling most vulnerable, President George W. Bush declared war on terrorism, and an overwhelming majority in Congress passed the Patriot Act. Subsequently, Congress established the Department of Homeland Security. This war on terrorism has taken on "worldwide dimensions, playing out from Washington to Kabul, Baghdad to Tehran, and Cairo to Manila. It is weaving itself into the fabric of American life, altering how we travel, revolutionizing our foreign policy, and affecting how we think about freedom."[a]

Policies born out of crises can have far-reaching implications. Therefore many question the prudence of permitting public opinion, even in a democracy, to play a significant role in foreign policy decision making. Is there a place for public opinion, the foundation of democracies, in crafting foreign policy decisions? Or should political leaders ignore public opinion to facilitate more rational decisions?

Argument 1 Public Opinion Can Facilitate Beneficial Policies

Public opinion is a key principle of democracies. Citizens in democracies feel outraged when their governments enact policies and laws in opposition to their views. Unlike authoritarian governments, democracies belong to the people and political leaders represent their opinions; therefore, political decisions should conform to the majority's public opinion.

> . . . American democracy belongs to its citizens and America might therefore be called a "citizens' democracy." The country is formally considered a representative democracy, but the representatives are supposed to be guided by the citizenry, through voting and participating in other ways. Elected officials from the president on down may ultimately make the decisions, but they are still seen as doing the citizens' bidding: acting as surrogates for them between elections. (Herbert J. Gans. "Democracy and the News." *The New York Times,* March 16, 2003.)

Public opinion and rational decisions are not mutually exclusive. Democratically elected officials view public opinion polls as reflective of their constituents' attitudes and desired policies. Moreover, if political leaders did not believe that such input had value, they would not continuously study polls to evaluate public attitudes.

[a]"Are We Winning?" *The St. Louis Post-Dispatch,* December 28, 2003: B2.

> . . . public opinion is essentially rational in nature, and when it changes, it tends to do so in sensible ways and for good reason. Although . . . Americans know very little about government and policy specifics, . . . public opinion, overall, is basically stable and coherent. (Regina Dougherty Rodgers. "Playing Their Part: Public Opinion in American Democracy." *The Public Perspective,* 11 (2) March/April 2000: pp. 24+.)

Public opinion was instrumental in making necessary changes. Since the early 1990s experts had warned government officials of terrorist threats against America, but little was done to address the problem. Following September 11, 2001, U.S. leaders, realizing that Americans would hold them accountable for another terrorist attack, quickly took strong measures to address the problem and attained immediate results.

As of Spring 2004, the U.S. Department of Justice had captured or killed nearly two-thirds of al Qaeda's known senior leadership and incapacitated more than 3,000 al Qaeda operatives worldwide. Over 515 individuals linked to the September 11 investigation have been removed from the United States.

Argument 2 Public Opinion Facilitates Unsound Policies

The public does not possess sufficient information to precipitate sound policies. While key leaders have access to a considerable amount of classified information on vital issues, the public lacks such an advantage to form their opinions. As a result, policy makers are typically in a better position to make vitally important decisions.

This is supported by the results of the University of South Alabama's Polling Group's National Survey that was taken in February 2002. . . . As many as 64 percent knew that Muslims believed in Muhammad as a prophet, and 75 percent knew Islam's holy book is called the Qur'an. However, respondents did not fare as well on other key policy topics. Only 25 percent were aware that there are more than 1 billion Muslims worldwide. On the most significant issue, only 11 percent knew that jihad entailed the nonviolent spiritual struggle to be a more righteous individual, while 49 percent of the public believed that jihad mainly meant a violent "holy war."[b]

The Patriot Act demonstrates the fallacies of public opinion in policy making. September 11, 2001, was a watershed event in which Americans rallied around their government and new national security policies. The Patriot Act was designed to prevent another act of terrorism and included measures that did not coincide with America's democratic values, which the American public would not have tolerated prior to September 11.

> The U.S.A. Patriot Act, rushed into law six weeks after 9/11, has given government agencies wide latitude to invoke the Foreign Intelligence Surveillance Act and get around judicial restraints on search, seizure and surveillance of American citizens. FISA, originally intended to hunt international spies, permits the authorities to wiretap virtually at will and break into people's homes to plant bugs or copy documents. Last year, surveillance requests by the federal government under FISA outnumbered for the first time in U.S. history all of those under domestic law. (Matthew Brzezinski. "Fortress America." *The New York Times,* February 23, 2003.)

Additional War on Terrorism policies have international ramifications. The overwhelming public support for anti-terrorism policies affected both the domestic and foreign policies of the United States. While policies such as the Patriot Act may appease and better secure the public, such policies have a trickle-down effect that has caused the United States to lose ground on the foreign policy front. Indeed, War on Terrorism policies are creating further problems. So, even for the sake of pleasing their constituents, leaders in democracies cannot ignore that such policies have too many far-reaching national and international implications.

> . . . (in Pakistan,) there's no getting away from the ratcheting up of anti-American sentiment during George Bush's first term. It is a mistake to assume that sentiment is based primarily on Muslim extremism. In most cases it is directly linked to the wars in Afghanistan and Iraq, the camps at Guantanamo Bay, and the innumerable accounts by Muslims in America of being treated as criminals by immigration and police officials for no discernable reason but their religion. Still, the fact remains that in George Bush, those who use Islam as a political tool have found their most powerful rallying cry. (Kamila Shamsie. "Prosperity vs. Peace." *The New York Times,* November 8, 2004.)

Questions

1. Should political leaders represent their constituents' views in foreign policy? Explain.
2. What should be the most important factor in states making foreign policy decisions? In contrast, what do you believe is the most important factor that influences your state's foreign policy?

The War on Terrorism

Selected Readings

Richard Sobel. *The Impact of Public Opinion in U.S. Foreign Policy Since Vietnam.* NY: Oxford University Press, 2001.

Robert M. Entman. *Projections of Power: Framing News, Public Opinion, and U.S. Foreign Policy.* Chicago: University of Chicago Press, 2004.

[b] Nicholls, Keith, and Mir Zohair Husain, "Nationwide Poll on the Impact of 9/11 on Islam and Muslims." University of South Alabama's Polling Group. February 7–February 21, 2002.

Israeli security wall under construction, 2002.

CHAPTER 5

International Conflict

The Causes of War

The Roman writer Seneca said nearly 2,000 years ago: "Of war men ask the outcome, not the cause."[1] This is not true of political scientists. They ask two fundamental questions: Why do international actors (states and nonstate actors alike) come into conflict with each other? And why do those conflicts sometimes lead to violence and war? This chapter addresses both questions.

Conflict among states is not an unusual condition but an ordinary one. **Conflict** may be defined as a difference in preferred outcomes in a bargaining situation. International conflicts will always exist. In such conflict bargaining, states develop capabilities that give them leverage to obtain more favorable outcomes than they otherwise would achieve. Whether fair or unfair, the ultimate outcome of the bargaining process is a **settlement** of the particular conflict.

Violence is an effective form of leverage in some bargaining situations (see p. 62). So states develop capabilities for using violence in international conflicts (these military capabilities are discussed in Chapter 6). But these capabilities only sometimes come into play in international conflicts. In fact, the great majority of international conflicts do not lead to war, but are resolved in other ways. The study of the causes of war, then, is really an effort to understand the *outbreak of war*—the resort to violence as a means of leverage in international conflicts. But understanding the outbreak of war requires studying the underlying conflicts as well.

The question of why war breaks out can be approached in different ways. More descriptive approaches, favored by historians, tend to focus narrowly on specific direct causes of the outbreak of war, which vary from one war to another.[2] For example, one could say that the assassination of Archduke Franz Ferdinand in 1914 "caused" World War I. More general, theoretical approaches, favored by many political scientists, tend to focus on the search for general explanations, applicable to a variety of contexts, about why wars break

---

[1] Seneca, Hercules Furens. In *Seneca's Tragedies*. vol. 1. Translated by Frank Justus Miller. London: Heinemann, 1917.

[2] Howard, Michael. *The Invention of Peace: Reflections on War and the International Order*. Yale, 2001. Rotberg, Robert I., and Theodore K. Rabb, eds. *The Origin and Prevention of Major Wars*. Cambridge, 1989. Blainey, Geoffrey. *Causes of War*. 3rd ed. NY: Free Press, 1988.

out.[3] For example, one can see World War I as caused by shifts in the balance of power among European states, with the assassination being only a catalyst.

Theories about War

Broad generalizations about the causes of war have been elusive. Wars do not have a single or simple cause. Some scholars distinguish *necessary* causes (conditions that must exist for a war to occur, but might not trigger one) from *sufficient* causes (conditions that will trigger war but are responsible for only some wars).[4] Many theories about war have been put forward, but few have universal validity. Levels of analysis can help us organize these theories.[5] Wars have been viewed as resulting from forces and processes operating on all the levels.

Individual Level

The Individual Level On the *individual* level of analysis, the question of why conflicts turn violent revolves around the familiar issue of rationality. One theory, consistent with realism, holds that the use of war and other violent means of leverage in international conflicts is normal and reflects *rational* decisions of national leaders: that "wars begin with conscious and reasoned decisions based on the calculation, made by *both* parties, that they can achieve more by going to war than by remaining at peace."[6]

An opposite theory holds that conflicts often escalate to war because of *deviations* from rationality in the individual decision-making processes of national leaders. These potentials were discussed in Chapter 4—information screens, cognitive biases, groupthink, and so forth. A related theory holds that the education and mentality of whole populations of individuals determine whether conflicts become violent. In this view, public nationalism or ethnic hatred—or even an innate tendency toward violence in human nature—may pressure leaders to solve conflicts violently. Some IR researchers and activists alike believe that the reeducation of populations can result in fewer conflicts turning violent.

Neither of these theories holds up very well. Some wars clearly reflect rational calculations of national leaders, whereas others clearly were mistakes and cannot be considered rational. Certainly some individual leaders seem prone to turn to military force to try to settle conflicts on favorable terms. But no reliable guide has been discovered that yet predicts who will be a more warlike or more peaceful leader. A man of war can become a man of peace, as did Egypt's Anwar Sadat, for example. Individuals of many cultural backgrounds and religions lead their states into war, as do both male and female leaders.

The Domestic Level The *domestic* level of analysis draws attention to the characteristics of states or societies that may make them more or less prone to use violence in resolving

---

[3] Vasquez, John A., ed. *What Do We Know About War?* Lanham, MD: Rowman Littlefield, 2000. Maoz, Zeev, and Azar Gat, eds. *War in a Changing World*. Michigan, 2001. Copeland, Dale C. *The Origins of Major War*. Cornell, 2001. Schneider, Gerald, Katherine Barbieri, and Nils Petter Gleditsch, eds. *Globalization and Armed Conflict*. Lanham, MD: Rowman Littlefield, 2003. Van Evera, Stephen. *Causes of War: Power and the Roots of Conflict*. Cornell, 1999. Brown, Michael E., Owen R. Coté Jr., Sean M. Lynn-Jones, and Steven E. Miller, eds. *Theories of War and Peace*. MIT, 1998. Suganami, Hidemi. *On the Causes of War*. Oxford, 1996. Holsti, Kalevi J. *Peace and War: Armed Conflicts and International Order*. Cambridge, 1991.

[4] Most, Benjamin A., and Harvey Starr. *Inquiry, Logic and International Politics*. South Carolina, 1989.

[5] Levy, Jack S. The Causes of War: A Review of Theories and Evidence. In Tetlock, P. E. et al., eds. *Behavior, Society, and Nuclear War*. vol. 1. Oxford, 1989, pp. 209–333. Waltz, Kenneth N. *Man, the State, and War: A Theoretical Analysis*. Columbia, 2001.

[6] Howard, Michael. *The Causes of Wars, and Other Essays*. Harvard, 1983, p. 22. Emphasis in original. For a related argument see, Fearon, James, Rationalist Explanations for War, *International Organization* 49 (3), 1995: 379–414.

conflicts. During the Cold War, Marxists frequently said that the aggressive and greedy *capitalist* states were prone to use violence in international conflicts, whereas Western leaders claimed that the expansionist, ideological, and totalitarian nature of *communist* states made them especially prone to using violence. In truth, both types of society have used violence regularly in international conflicts.

Likewise, rich industrialized states and poor agrarian ones both use war at times. In fact, anthropologists have found that a wide range of *preagricultural* hunter-gatherer societies were prone to warfare under certain circumstances.[7] Thus the potential for warfare seems to be universal across cultures, types of society, and time periods—although the importance and frequency of war vary greatly from case to case.

Some argue that domestic political factors shape a state's outlook on war and peace. For example, the democratic peace suggests that democracies almost never fight other democracies (see Chapter 4), although both democracies and authoritarian states fight wars. Others claim that domestic political parties, interest groups, and legislatures play an important role in whether international conflicts become international wars.[8]

Few useful generalizations can be made about which societies are more prone or less prone to war (given that all are war-prone to some extent). The same society may change greatly over time. For example, Japan was prone to using violence in international conflicts before World War II, but averse to such violence since then. The !Kung bush people in Angola and Namibia—a hunter-gatherer society—were observed by anthropologists in the 1960s to be extremely peaceful. Yet anthropologists in the 1920s had observed them engaging in murderous intergroup violence.[9] If there are general principles to explain why some societies at some times are more peaceful than others and why they change, political scientists have not yet identified them.

The Interstate Level The theories at the *interstate* level explain wars in terms of power relations among major actors in the international system. Some of these theories are discussed in Chapter 2. For example, power transition theory holds that conflicts generate large wars at times when power is relatively equally distributed and a rising power is threatening to overtake a declining hegemon in overall position. At this level, too, there are competing theories that seem incompatible. Deterrence, as we have seen, is supposed to stop wars by building up power and threatening its use. But the theory of arms races holds that wars are caused, not prevented, by such actions. As is noted in Chapter 2, no general formula has been discovered to tell us in what circumstances each of these principles holds true.

Lacking a reliable method for predicting what power configurations among states will lead to war, some political scientists have tried to estimate statistically the *probabilities* that one or another type of interstate relationship might lead to war.[10] Current research

---

[7] Keeley, Lawrence H. *War Before Civilization: The Myth of the Peaceful Savage*. Oxford, 1996. O'Connell, Robert L. *Ride of the Second Horseman: The Birth and Death of War*. Oxford, 1995. Ehrenreich, Barbara. *Blood Rites: Origins and History of the Passions of War*. NY: Metropolitan/Henry Holt, 1997. Ember, Carol R., and Melvin Ember. Resource Unpredictability, Mistrust, and War: A Cross-Cultural Study. *Journal of Conflict Resolution* 36 (2), 1992: 242–62.

[8] Shultz, Kenneth. Domestic Opposition and Signaling in International Crises. *American Political Science Review* 92 (4), 1998: 829–44. Fearon, James. Domestic Political Audiences and the Escalation of International Disputes, *American Political Science Review* 88 (3), 1994: 577–92.

[9] Eibl-Eibesfeldt, Irenaus. *The Biology of Peace and War: Men, Animals, and Aggression*. NY: Viking, 1979.

[10] Wright, Quincy. *A Study of War*. Chicago, 1965 [1942]. Richardson, Lewis F. *Arms and Insecurity*. Pittsburgh: Boxwood, 1960. Geller, Daniel S., and J. David Singer. *Nations at War: A Scientific Study of International Conflict*. Cambridge, 1998. Midlarsky, Manus I., ed. *Handbook of War Studies II*. Michigan, 2000. Diehl, Paul F., ed. *The Scourge of War: New Extensions of an Old Problem*. Michigan, 2004.

WHY WAR?

Political scientists do not agree on a theory of why great wars like World War II occur and cannot predict whether they could happen again. The city of Stalingrad (Volgograd) was decimated during Germany's invasion of the Soviet Union, 1943.

focuses on the effects of democracy, government structure, trade, international organizations, and related factors in explaining the escalation or settlement of "militarized interstate disputes."[11]

Scholars use quantitative and statistical methods to test various ideas about international conflict, such as analyzing data about wars, weapons, and arms races. The quality of data, however, is a major problem for statistical studies of infrequent occurrences such as wars.

The Global Level At the *global* level of analysis, a number of theories of war have been proposed. Of the several variations on the idea that major warfare in the international system is *cyclical*, one approach links large wars with *long economic waves* (also called *Kondratieff cycles*) in the world economy, of about 50 years' duration. Another approach links the largest wars with a 100-year cycle based on the creation and decay of world orders (see "Hegemony" on pp. 82–84). These **cycle theories** at best can explain only general tendencies toward war in the international system over time.[12]

An opposite approach in some ways is the theory of linear long-term change—that war as an outcome of conflict is becoming less likely over time due to the worldwide development of both technology and international norms. Some IR scholars argue that war and military force are becoming *obsolete* as leverage in international conflicts because these means of influence are not very effective in today's highly complex, interdependent world. A parallel line of argument holds that today's military technology is too powerful to use in most conflicts; this is especially applicable to nuclear weapons.

A possibly complementary theory traces the obsolescence of war to the evolution of international norms against the use of force. War once was seen as a normal way to resolve disputes but now is considered distasteful. An analogy has been drawn to the practices of slavery and dueling—once considered normal but now obsolete.[13] However, all these arguments about the linear evolution of warfare in the international system rest on mixed empirical evidence. In truth, although major wars have become shorter and less frequent,

---

[11] Bremer, Stuart A., and Thomas R. Cusack. *The Process of War: Advancing the Scientific Study of War*. Newark, NJ: Gordon & Breach, 1995. Singer, J. David, and Paul F. Diehl, eds. *Measuring the Correlates of War*. Michigan, 1990. Ghosn, Faten, Glenn Palmer, and Stuart Bremer. The Militarized Interstate Dispute 3 Data Set, 1993–2001: Procedures, Coding Rules, and Description. *Conflict Management and Peace Science* 21 (2), 2004: 133–154.

[12] Goldstein, Joshua S. *Long Cycles: Prosperity and War in the Modern Age*. Yale, 1988. Modelski, George. *Long Cycles in World Politics*. Washington, 1987.

[13] Mueller, John. *Retreat from Doomsday: The Obsolescence of Major War*. NY: Basic, 1989.

they are now more destructive than ever. And even in the absence of major wars, smaller wars around the world have not yet evolved out of existence. War may be obsolete, but it still occurs with great frequency.[14]

Thus, although the levels of analysis suggest many explanations for why conflicts lead to war, few such generalizations hold up. On all the levels of analysis, competing theories offer very different explanations for why some conflicts become violent and others do not. For these reasons, political scientists cannot yet predict with any confidence which of the world's many international conflicts will lead to war. Still, thinking about conflicts through the levels of analysis approach is helpful since it reminds us that the simple explanations we give to wars are probably incomplete.

We can gain insight, however, by studying various types of conflicts to understand better what it is that states are fighting about. We can also examine some of the alternative forms of leverage, violent and nonviolent, that states use in conflicts.

Conflicts of Interest

One way of looking at international conflicts is to assume that all states want maximum power relative to other states. Conflict then becomes a universal condition among states, and they fight about power, status, and alliances in the international system. This realist approach offers insights into power rivalries that sometimes become detached from underlying conflicts over territory, religion, or other specific causes. China attacked Vietnam in 1979 to "teach Vietnam a lesson" after Vietnam invaded Cambodia and overthrew the Chinese-aligned Khmer Rouge government there. (China perhaps learned the greater lesson—its military was less effective than expected, and China has not fought a battle in the 25 years since.) In this case, China did not want Vietnamese territory; it just wanted to administer punishment for an act it disapproved of. In such cases the struggle for power in an abstract sense takes on its own logic.

But why do states want power? Power gives states specific benefits—the ability to gain better outcomes in bargaining over particular issues that matter to their well-being. Most international conflicts—including those behind the dozens of wars going on at present—are disputes about concrete grievances and demands. They are about territorial borders, ethnic hatreds, revolutions, and so forth. To understand the nature of international conflicts, including their potential for becoming violent, one must study the underlying interests and goals of the actors involved.

The following sections discuss six types of international conflict. Three are conflicts over tangible material interests:

1. Territorial border disputes, including secession attempts
2. Conflicts over who controls national governments
3. Economic conflicts over trade, money, natural resources, drug trafficking, and other economic transactions

The other three types of conflict concern less-tangible clashes of ideas:

4. Ethnic conflicts
5. Religious conflicts
6. Ideological conflicts

---

[14] Brogan, Patrick. *The Fighting Never Stopped: A Comprehensive Guide to World Conflict Since 1945*. NY: Random/Vintage, 1991. Delmas, Phillipe. *The Rosy Future of War*. Translated by C. Atamian and C. Hewitt. NY: Free Press, 1997.

These six types of conflict are not mutually exclusive, and they overlap considerably in practice. For example, the conflicts between Russia and Ukraine after the 1991 Soviet breakup were complex. The two new states had a *territorial* dispute over the Crimean peninsula, which Soviet leader Nikita Khrushchev had transferred to Ukraine in the 1950s. In addition, *ethnic* Russians living in Ukraine, and ethnic Ukrainians in Russia, experienced ethnic conflict. There are *religious* differences between Ukrainian and Russian forms of Christianity. The two states also had *economic* conflicts over trade and money after the Soviet breakup, which created new borders and currencies. These multiple conflicts did not lead to the use of military force, however. In 2005, the opposition took control of Ukraine's government (after a flawed election was rerun in response to weeks of mass street protests). Russian President Putin, who had campaigned for the incumbent party in Ukraine, protested vigorously but did not seriously consider military force. Thus, conflicts of interest lie at the heart of all international bargaining, from trade negotiations to arms control, but only sometimes do they turn violent.

Territorial Disputes

Among the international conflicts that concern tangible "goods," those about territory have special importance because of the territorial nature of the state (see "Anarchy and Sovereignty" on pp. 73–76). Conflicts over control of territory are really of two varieties: territorial disputes (about where borders are drawn) and conflicts over control of entire states within existing borders (discussed next under "Control of Governments"). Consider first differences over where borders between two states should be drawn—that is, who controls a disputed piece of land.

Because states value home territory with an almost fanatical devotion, border disputes tend to be among the most intractable in IR. States will seldom yield territory in exchange for money or any other positive reward. Nor do states quickly forget territory that they lose involuntarily. For example, in 2002, Bolivian public opinion opposed a gas export pipeline through Chile to the sea because Chile had seized the coastline from Bolivia in 1879. The goal of regaining territory lost to another state is called **irredentism.** This form of nationalism often leads directly to serious interstate conflicts.[15]

Because of their association with the integrity of states, territories are valued far beyond any inherent economic or strategic value they hold. For example, after Israel and Egypt made peace in 1978, it took them a decade to settle a border dispute at Taba, a tiny plot of beachfront on which Israeli developers had built a hotel just slightly across the old border. The two states finally submitted the issue for binding arbitration, and Egypt ended up in possession. For Egypt, regaining every inch of territory was a matter of national honor and a symbol of the sovereignty and territorial integrity that defined Egyptian statehood.

The value states place on home territory seems undiminished despite the apparent reduction in the inherent value of territory as technology has developed. Historically, territory was the basis of economic production—agriculture and the extraction of raw materials. Even in Sun Tzu's time, it was said that "land is the foundation of the state." It was in these agrarian societies that the international system developed. Winning and losing wars meant gaining or losing territory, which meant increasing wealth and hence long-term power. Today, however, much more wealth derives from trade and technology than from agriculture. The costs of most territorial disputes appear to outweigh any economic benefits that

---

[15] Diehl, Paul F., ed. A *Road Map to War: Territorial Dimensions of International Conflict*. Vanderbilt, 1999. Diehl, Paul F., and Gary Goertz. *Territorial Changes and International Conflict*. NY: Routledge, 1992. Kacowicz, Arie Marcelo. *Peaceful Territorial Change*. South Carolina, 1994. Ambrosio, Thomas. *Irredentism: Ethnic Conflict and International Politics*. Westport, CT: Praeger, 2001.

the territory in question could provide. There are exceptions, however, such as the capture of diamond-mining areas in several African countries by rebels who use the diamond revenues to finance war. (In 2002, 40 states created a program of UN certification for legitimate diamonds, trying to keep the "conflict diamonds" off the international market.)

Means of Controlling Territory Historically, military means have been the most effective leverage for controlling territory, and wars have often redrawn the borders of states. Military forces can seize control on the ground in a way that is hard to contest by any means except other military forces. For example, when Saddam Hussein invaded Kuwait, his opponents found no better means to dislodge him (economic sanctions, diplomatic isolation, negotiations, and so on) than to use military force themselves. Nor was his regime toppled except by military force in 2003.

Since World War II, however, there has been a strong norm in the international system *against* trying to alter borders by force. Such attempts are considered grave matters by the international community. Thus, when Iraq annexed Kuwait and erased its borders, most states treated the act as not merely distasteful but intolerable. By contrast, it is considered a lesser offense for one state merely to topple another's government and install a puppet regime, even if done violently. The principle is: Governments come and go; borders remain.

Secession Efforts by a province or region to secede from an existing state are a special type of conflict over borders—not the borders of two existing states but the efforts by a substate area to draw international borders around itself as a new state. Dozens of secession movements exist around the world, of varying sizes and political effectiveness, but they succeed in seceding only rarely. The existing state almost always tries to hold onto the area in question. For instance, the mainly Muslim republic of Chechnya, one of the republics of Russia (the Russian Federation), tried to split away from Russia in the early 1990s after the Soviet Union collapsed. In 1994–1995, Russia sent in a huge military force that destroyed the Chechen capital, but faced fierce resistance from Chechen nationalist guerrillas, and withdrew in defeat. In 1999–2000, another destructive Russian campaign won a tentative grip on power in the province. Today, Chechen guerrillas continue to fight Russian control and have taken their fight to Russian territory, including airline hijackings, hostage taking, and suicide bombings. In 2004, hundreds of children died after Chechen terrorists took over a school and held them hostage. In 2005, Russian forces killed the Chechen separatist leader they held responsible. Russian leaders portray the Chechen war as parallel to, and allied with, the U.S. war on terrorism.

As this example suggests, wars of secession can be large and deadly, and they can easily spill over international borders or draw in other countries. This spillover is particularly likely if members of an ethnic or a religious group span two sides of a border, constituting the majority group in one state and a majority in a nearby region of another state, but a minority in the other state as a whole. This pattern occurs in Bosnia-Serbia, Moldova-Russia, and India-Pakistan. In some cases, secessionists want to merge their territories with the neighboring state (as in the effort to carve out a "greater Serbia"), which amounts to redrawing the international border. International norms frown on such an outcome. (Ethnic and religious conflict are discussed later in this chapter.)

The strong international norms of sovereignty and territorial integrity treat secession movements as domestic problems that are of little concern to other states. In the case of Chechnya, the Western governments objected not to Russia's goal of maintaining control of the republic, but only to Russia's methods of waging the war—which included indiscriminate bombing and shelling of civilian areas. These actions violated standards of human rights, which are a weaker set of norms than those promoting state sovereignty. Ironically,

GOING SEPARATE WAYS

Efforts by a region to secede from a state are a frequent source of international conflict, but international norms generally treat such conflicts as internal matters unless they spill over borders. Increasingly, autonomy agreements are resolving secession conflicts. Here, Indonesian troops leave Aceh province in 2005 after separatists disarmed under a limited self-rule agreement.

as Chechen rebels have begun their own indiscriminate acts of violence against Russian civilians and in the aftermath of the September 2001 terrorist attacks, Western objections have lessened. Even at their loudest, however, these objections did not disrupt political relations with Russia.

Even when secession conflicts occasionally spill over international borders, the international community tends to treat the matter lightly as long as the cross-border incursion is temporary. The general principle seems to be: "We existing states all have our own domestic problems and disaffected groups or regions, so we must stick together behind sovereignty and territorial integrity."

Messy border problems can be created when multinational states break up into pieces. In such cases, borders that had been internal become international; since these borders are new they may be more vulnerable to challenge. This was the case in the former Yugoslavia, where ethnic groups had intermingled and intermarried, leaving mixed populations in most of the Yugoslav republics. When Yugoslavia broke up in 1991–1992, several republics declared their independence as separate states. Two of these, Croatia and Bosnia, contained minority populations of ethnic Serbs. Serbia seized effective control of significant areas of Croatia and Bosnia that contained Serbian communities or linked such populations geographically. Non-Serbian populations in these areas were driven out or massacred—**ethnic cleansing.** Then, when Croatia reconquered most of its territory in 1995, Serbian populations in turn fled. Ethnic nationalism proved stronger than multiethnic tolerance iboth Serbia and Croatia.

The breakup of a state need not lead to violence, however. Czechoslovakia split into the Czech Republic and Slovakia in a cooperative manner. And the breakup of the Soviet Union did not lead to violent territorial disputes between republics in *most* cases, even where ethnic groups were split across new international borders (such as Ukraine-Russia).

The norm against forceful redrawing of borders does not apply to cases of decolonization. Only the territorial integrity of existing, recognized states is protected by international norms. Colonies and other territorial possessions historically were valued only as property to be won, lost, sold, or traded in political deals and wars. For example, when Portugal's empire crumbled in 1975, its colony of East Timor was brutally invaded and annexed by neighboring Indonesia. Because East Timor was not a UN member state (most states did not recognize its independence), and because the United States saw Indonesia but not East Timor as strategically important, Indonesia got away with this move. As with Chechnya, the problem was treated mainly as one of human rights. However, several decades later, East Timor achieved independence, joining the UN in 2003.

The transfer of Hong Kong from British to Chinese control in 1997 also illustrates how colonial territory is dispensable (Britain's perspective) while home territory is nearly sacred (China's perspective). From neither perspective do the views of the inhabitants carry much weight. The peaceful transfer of Hong Kong is one of the few recent cases in which territory has changed hands in the international system.

Increasingly, autonomy for a region has become a realistic compromise between secession and full control by a central government. In 2005, spurred partly by the devastating tsunami a year earlier, separatists in Aceh province, Indonesia, disbanded, giving up on independence and instead participating in regional elections in 2006. The Indonesian government withdrew its 24,000 troops from Aceh and offered the province limited self-rule along with 70 percent of the oil, gas, and mineral wealth earned there.

Interstate Borders Border disputes between existing states are taken more seriously by the international community, but are less common than secessionist conflicts. Because of the norm of territorial integrity, few important border conflicts remain among long-established states. At one time, huge chunks of territory were passed between states at the stroke of a pen (on a peace treaty or marriage contract). However, this kind of wholesale redrawing of borders has not occurred among established states for 50 years. Since the end of World War II, only a minuscule amount of territory has changed hands between established states through force (this does not apply to the formation of new states and the fragmenting of old ones). Such efforts have been made, but have failed. For instance, when Iraq attacked Iran in 1980, one objective was to control the Shatt-al-Arab waterway (with access to the Persian Gulf) because of its commercial and strategic value. But ten years and a million deaths later, the Iran-Iraq border was back where it started.

Furthermore, when territorial disputes do occur between established states, they *can* sometimes be settled peacefully, especially when the involved territory is small compared with the states disputing it. The Soviet Union simply agreed to China's boundary preferences in 1986 after the two states had disputed ownership of some minor river islands for years (including military skirmishes in 1969). El Salvador and Honduras got the World Court to adjudicate their border disputes in 1992. And in 1994 a panel of Latin American judges settled a century-long border dispute between Argentina and Chile over some mountainous terrain that both claimed. The 3 to 2 ruling, after the countries submitted the dispute for judicial arbitration, awarded the territory to Argentina and provoked howls of protest from Chile—even a hair-pulling fight between the Chilean and Argentine contestants in the Miss World beauty contest two months later. But despite the strong feelings evoked by the loss of territory, Argentina and Chile settled 22 of 24 remaining border disputes peacefully over the previous ten years (after nearly going to war in 1978 over disputed islands).

At the end of 2003, Nigeria transferred sovereignty over 33 villages to Cameroon under terms of a World Court ruling. A joint delegation of officials, with UN experts and observers, traveled by dirt road and canoe to oversee the flag lowering and raising in each village. Why would Nigeria—a country with nine times Cameroon's population, more than triple its GDP, and a much stronger military—voluntarily cede territory? Doing so would seem to run counter to the predictions of realism. Rather, as neoliberals might emphasize, Nigeria acted in its own self-interest since turning the dispute over to the World Court and bringing in the UN to assist with implementation brought the kind of stability needed for foreign investment to develop the area's resources, primarily oil. Nigeria cares more about economic development than about a few remote villages in contested territory. A harder test came in 2004 when, under the same ruling, Nigeria was to hand over the Bakassi peninsula on the coast, thought to be rich in oil. As of early 2006, Nigeria had delayed the turnover repeatedly, leaving the outcome in doubt, but had stated that it intended to relinquish the territory.

Lingering Disputes Today, only a few of the world's interstate borders are disputed. Nonetheless, those that persist are important sources of international conflict. Among the most difficult are the borders of *Israel*, which have never been firmly defined and recognized by its neighbors. The 1948 cease-fire lines resulting from Israel's war of independence expanded in the 1967 war, then contracted again on the Egyptian border with the Camp David peace treaty of 1978. The remaining territories occupied in 1967—the *West Bank* near Jordan, the *Gaza Strip* near Egypt, and the *Golan Heights* of Syria—are central to the Arab-Israeli conflict. Israeli-Palestinian agreements since 1993 tried to move toward Palestinian autonomy in parts of the West Bank and Gaza Strip, and negotiations seemed headed toward creation of a state of Palestine in all or most of the occupied territories. However, the U.S. effort to craft a final settlement at the 2000 "Camp David II" summit failed—over how to divide Jerusalem, and other emotional issues—and a new phase of violence and hate began, with each side blaming the other for failing to make peace.

Another major border dispute is in the *Kashmir* area where India, Pakistan, and China intersect. The Indian-held part of Kashmir is predominantly inhabited by Muslims, a group that is the majority in Pakistan but a minority in India. A *Line of Control* divides the disputed province. Pakistan accuses India of oppressing Kashmiris and thwarting an international agreement to decide Kashmir's future by a popular referendum. India accuses Pakistan of aiding and infiltrating Islamic radicals who carry out attacks in Indian-occupied Kashmir. The two countries went to war twice before over the issue, and nearly did so again in 2002—but that time with both sides holding dozens of nuclear-armed missiles that some experts estimated would kill more than 10 million people in an India-Pakistan war. Perhaps chastened by this experience, the two countries improved relations in 2003 and began a cease-fire that stopped the incessant low-level fighting along the Line of Control, although not the fighting between Indian authorities and insurgents. In 2004, India agreed to begin a slow withdrawal of troops from the region, and in 2005 a major earthquake in the region led to improved relations owing to the need to coordinate relief efforts.

Peru and Ecuador fought border skirmishes in 1995 over a nearly inaccessible stretch of mountainous terrain. The conflict, which involved no tangible assets worth fighting over, illustrated once again the almost mystical power of territory as a symbol of national honor, and the continuing usefulness of nationalism in generating political support for state leaders (the popularity of both presidents increased as the conflict heated up).

Many of the world's other remaining interstate territorial disputes—and often the most serious ones—concern the control of small islands, which often provide strategic advantages, natural resources (such as offshore oil), or fishing rights. China asserts a right to the tiny disputed *Spratly Islands* in the South China Sea. The islands and the surrounding waters, which may hold substantial oil reserves, are closer to Vietnam, the Philippines, Malaysia, and Brunei than to China, and are claimed in part or in full by all those countries and by Taiwan (see Figure 5.1). All of those states except Brunei have resorted to military occupation at times to stake their claims, but in 2002 the countries agreed to avoid conflicts over the islands, and they remain calm. About half of the world's trade tonnage passes near the Spratly Islands, including Persian Gulf oil and other key resources headed for Japan, China, South Korea, and Taiwan. The Spratly Islands conflict has importance beyond the immediate dispute since it may signal China's intentions as a rising great power.

Japan and China also dispute tiny islands elsewhere, as do Japan and South Korea. These disputes involve low economic stakes, but have become a focus of nationalist sentiments on both sides, fueled partly by memories of World War II, when Japan occupied China and Korea. In 2005, after Japan spent half a billion dollars preserving Okinotori—an uninhabited coral reef with two tiny protrusions smaller than a house and just inches above sea level—China declared it not an "island" (with a surrounding economic zone) but just a "rock" (which, without economic activity, does not quality for such a zone).

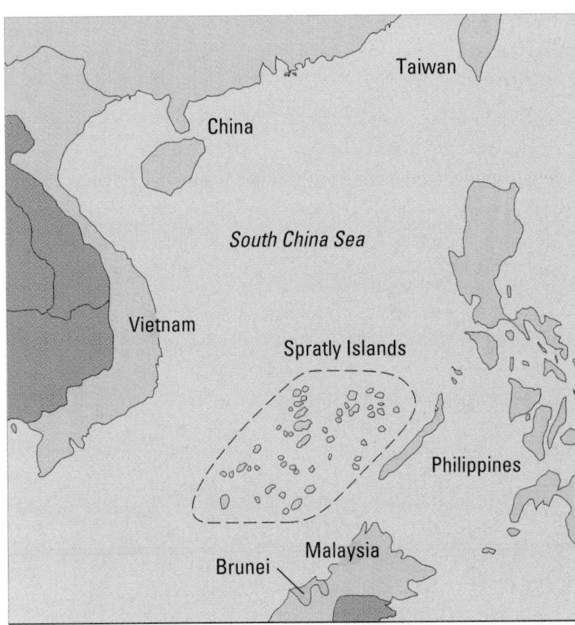

FIGURE 5.1 ■ Disputed Islands

The Spratly Islands exemplify contemporary conflicts over territory and natural resources around islands. All or part of the Spratlys are claimed by China, Vietnam, Malaysia, Brunei, the Philippines, and Taiwan.

A number of smaller conflicts exist around the globe. In the Middle East, Iran and the United Arab Emirates dispute ownership of small islands near the mouth of the Persian Gulf. In 2002, Spain sent soldiers to oust a handful of Moroccan troops from islands off Morocco's coast. In South America, Argentina and Britain still dispute control of the *Falkland Islands (Islas Malvinas)*, over which they fought a war in 1982. And the major bone of contention in Russian-Japanese relations is the ownership of the small but strategically located *Kuril Islands* occupied by the Soviet Union in 1945. In 2001, Japan objected when Russia granted South Korea fishing rights near the islands (a provisional settlement was reached). With islands now bringing control of surrounding economic zones, international conflicts over islands will undoubtedly continue in the coming years.

Territorial Waters States treat **territorial waters** near their shores as part of their national territory. Definitions of such waters are not universally agreed upon, but norms have developed in recent years, especially after the *UN Convention on the Law of the Sea (UNCLOS)* (see pp. 426–428). Waters within three miles of shore have traditionally been recognized as territorial, but beyond that there are disputes about how far out national sovereignty extends and for what purposes. UNCLOS generally allows a 12-mile limit for shipping, and a 200-mile *exclusive economic zone (EEZ)* covering fishing and mineral rights (but allowing for free navigation by all). The EEZs together cover a third of the world's oceans.

It is because of the EEZs that sovereignty over a single tiny island can now bring with it rights to as much as 100,000 square miles of surrounding ocean. But these zones overlap greatly, and shorelines do not run in straight lines; thus numerous questions of interpretation arise about how to delineate territorial and economic waters. For example, Libya claims ownership of the entire Gulf of Sidra, treating it as a bay; the United States treats it as a curvature in the shoreline and insists that most of it is international waters. In 1986, the United States sent warships into the Gulf of Sidra to make its point. U.S. planes shot down two Libyan jets that challenged the U.S. maneuvers.

LOCATION, LOCATION, LOCATION

Control of islands, and of the large exclusive economic zone (EEZ) that surrounds them under the law of the sea, has created a number of complicated interstate conflicts. Japan claims Okinotori, shown here in 2005, as an island with an EEZ, but China calls it merely a "rock" without surrounding economic rights.

Canada in 1994–1995 sent its navy to harass Spanish fishing boats just *beyond* the 200-mile zone (but affecting fish stocks within the zone). In the Sea of Okhotsk, Russia's EEZ includes all but a small "doughnut hole" of international waters in the middle (see p. 428). Non-Russian boats have fished intensively in the "hole," which of course depletes fish stocks in Russia's EEZ.

Airspace **Airspace** above a state is considered the territory of the state. Any airplane that wants to fly over a state's territory must have the state's permission. For example, in a 1986 raid on Libya, U.S. bombers based in Britain had to fly a long detour over the Atlantic Ocean because France (between Britain and Libya) would not grant permission for U.S. planes to use its airspace during the mission.

Outer space, by contrast, is considered international territory like the oceans. International law does not define exactly where airspace ends and outer space begins. However, orbiting satellites fly higher than airplanes, move very fast, and cannot easily change direction to avoid overflying a country. Also, very few states can shoot down satellites, though many can shoot airplanes. Since satellites have become useful to all the great powers as intelligence-gathering tools, and since all satellites are extremely vulnerable to attack, a norm of demilitarization of outer space has developed. No state has ever attacked the satellite of another, and doing so would be a severe provocation.

Control of Governments

Control of Governments

Despite the many minor border disputes that continue to plague the world, most of the struggles to control territory do not involve changing borders. Rather, they are conflicts over which governments will control entire states.

In theory, states do not interfere in each other's governance, because of the norm of sovereignty. In practice, states often have strong interests in the governments of other states and use a variety of means of leverage to influence who holds power in those states. When one state wants to alter or replace the government of a second state, a conflict always exists between the two governments. In addition, the first state may come into conflict with other parties that oppose changing the second state's government. These con-

[16] Owen, John M. The Foreign Imposition of Domestic Institutions. *International Organization* 56 (2). 2002: 375–409.

flicts over governments take many forms, some mild and some severe, some deeply entwined with third parties and some more or less bilateral. Sometimes a state merely exerts subtle influences on another state's elections; at other times, a state supports rebel elements seeking to overthrow the second state's government.

During the Cold War, both superpowers actively promoted changes of government in countries of the global South through covert operations and support of rebel armies. The civil wars in Angola, Afghanistan, and Nicaragua are good examples. Both superpowers poured in weapons, money, military advisers, and so forth—all in hopes of influencing who controlled the country's government.[16]

In 2004–2005, shadows of these old Cold War rivalries fell over Ukraine, as Russia and the West backed opposite sides in a disputed election. The election divided the largely Russian-speaking, Eastern Orthodox part of Ukraine to the east from the Ukrainian-speaking, Catholic, western part of the country. The pro-Russian incumbent carried the eastern region and was declared the winner after an election that international monitors declared unsound. Russian President Putin had personally campaigned with him, and strongly opposed letting Ukraine—a former part of the Soviet Union—come under the influence of the West. Meanwhile the pro-Western candidate was poisoned during the campaign, but survived. His supporters took to the streets in late 2004 demanding new elections, which the top Ukrainian court eventually ordered and which the opposition won. Russia had to accept this setback, though it cut off Ukraine's natural gas for a few days in 2006 in a dispute over gas prices.

Occasionally, one state invades another in order to change its government. The Soviet Union did this in Czechoslovakia in 1968; the United States did so in Iraq in 2003. It is sometimes hard for new governments created in this way to gain legitimacy both domestically and internationally. People generally resent having foreigners choose their government for them—even if they did not like the old government—and the international community frowns on such overt violations of national sovereignty. For instance, the government installed in Afghanistan after the Soviet invasion of 1979 was seen as a Soviet puppet and was finally toppled after a dozen years of rule marked by constant war (a war funded largely by the United States).

Even in Cambodia—where the Khmer Rouge government's atrocities led many people inside and outside the country to welcome the Vietnamese invasion that installed a new Cambodian government in 1979—the new government could not consolidate its international position for more than a decade. It did not gain Cambodia's seat in the UN, and the United States and China sent assistance to rebel groups that fought a long and bloody civil war against the Vietnamese-backed Cambodian government. (In the 1990s, the UN mediated a cease-fire and implemented a peace plan under which the UN basically ran the government while organizing elections.)

International conflicts over the control of governments—along with territorial disputes—are likely to lead to the use of violence. They involve core issues of the status and integrity of states, the stakes tend to be high, and the interests of involved actors are often diametrically opposed. Other types of conflict are both more widespread and less likely to lead to violence. Chief among these is economic conflict among states.

Economic Conflict

Economic competition is the most pervasive form of conflict in international relations because economic transactions are pervasive. Every sale made and every deal reached across international borders entails a resolution of conflicting interests. Costa Rica wants the price of coffee, which it exports, to go up; Canada, which imports coffee, wants the price to go down. Angola wants foreign producers of Angolan oil to receive fewer profits from oil

Economic Conflict

sales; those companies' home states want them to take home more profits. In a global capitalist market, all economic exchanges involve some conflict of interest.

However, such economic transactions also contain a strong element of mutual economic gain in addition to the element of conflicting interests (see Chapters 3 and 8). These mutual gains provide the most useful leverage in bargaining over economic exchanges: states and companies enter into economic transactions because they profit from doing so. The use of violence would for the most part interrupt and diminish such profit by more than could be gained as a result of the use of violence. Thus, economic conflicts do not usually lead to military force and war.

Such restraint has not always been the case. In the sixteenth century, England's Sir Francis Drake intercepted Spanish ships bringing gold and silver from Central America and took the loot in the name of queen and country—a practice known as *privateering*. In the seventeenth century, England fought several naval wars against the Netherlands. An English general, when asked the reason for England's declaration of war in 1652, replied, "What matters this or that reason? What we want is more of the trade the Dutch now have."[17] In 1861, France, Britain, and Spain invaded Mexico when it failed to pay its international debts.

Economic conflict seldom leads to violence today because military forms of leverage are no longer very effective in economic conflicts. With the tight integration of the world economy and the high cost of military actions, the use of force is seldom justified to solve an economic issue. Even if an agreement is not ideal for one side in an economic conflict, rarely is what can be gained by military force worth the cost of war. Thus, most economic conflicts are not issues in international security; they are discussed in Chapters 8 through 13 (international political economy). But economic conflicts do still bear on international security in some ways.

First, many states' foreign policies are influenced by *mercantilism*—a practice of centuries past in which trade and foreign economic policies were manipulated to build up a monetary surplus that could be used to finance war (see "Liberalism and Mercantilism" on pp. 298–300). Because a trade surplus confers an advantage in international security affairs over the long run, trade conflicts have implications for international security relations.

Second, the theory of **lateral pressure** also connects economic competition with security concerns. This theory holds that the economic growth of states leads to geographic expansion as they seek natural resources beyond their borders (by various means, peaceful and violent). As great powers expand their economic activities outward, their competition leads to conflicts and sometimes to war. The theory has been used to help explain both World War I and the expansion of Japan prior to World War II.[18]

Another kind of economic conflict that affects international security concerns *military industry*—the capacity to produce military equipment, especially high-technology weapons such as fighter aircraft or missiles. There is a world trade in such items, but national governments try (not always successfully) to keep control of such production—to try to ensure that national interests take priority over those of manufacturers and that the state is militarily self-sufficient in case of war. Economic competition (over who profits from such sales) is interwoven with security concerns (over who gets access to the weapons). The transfer of knowledge about high-tech weaponry and military technologies to potentially hostile states is a related concern.

---

[17] Howard, Michael. *War in European History*. Oxford, 1976, p. 47.

[18] Choucri, Nazli, and Robert C. North. *Nations in Conflict: National Growth and International Violence*. San Francisco: W. H. Freeman, 1975. Ashley, Richard K. *The Political Economy of War and Peace: The Sino-Soviet-American Triangle and the Modern Security Problematique*. London: Frances Pinter, 1980. Choucri, Nazli, Robert C. North, and Susumu Yamakage. *The Challenge of Japan: Before World War II and After*. NY: Routledge, 1993.

Economic competition also becomes a security issue when it concerns trade in *strategic materials* needed for military purposes, such as special minerals or alloys for aircraft production and uranium for atomic weapons. Few countries are self-sufficient in these materials; the United States imports about half the strategic materials it uses. Thus, economic competition as a source of international conflict has important implications for international security. Nonetheless, military force plays a diminishing role in resolving economic conflicts. In fact, increasing economic reliance between states likely lowers the chances of fighting over economic and political differences.[19]

A different kind of economic conflict revolves around the distribution of wealth within and among states. As discussed in Chapter 12, there are tremendous disparities in wealth in our world, disparities that create a variety of international security problems with the potential for violence—including terrorist attacks on rich countries by groups in poor countries.

Revolutions in poor countries are often fueled by disparities of wealth within the country as well as its poverty relative to other countries. These revolutions in turn frequently draw in other states as supporters of one side or the other in a civil war. If successful, revolutions can abruptly change a state's foreign policy, leading to new alliances and power alignments.

Marxist approaches to international relations, discussed in Chapter 12, treat class struggle between rich and poor people as the basis of interstate relations. According to these approaches, capitalist states adopt foreign policies that serve the interests of the rich owners of companies. Conflicts and wars between the global North and South—rich states versus poor states—are seen as reflections of the domination and exploitation of the poor by the rich—imperialism in direct or indirect form. For example, most Marxists saw the Vietnam War as a U.S. effort to suppress revolution in order to secure continued U.S. access to cheap labor and raw materials in Southeast Asia. Many Marxists portray conflicts among capitalist states as competition over the right to exploit poor areas. Soviet founder V. I. Lenin portrayed World War I as a fight over the imperialists' division of the world.

Events in Haiti, the poorest country in Latin America, illustrate how disparities of wealth can create international security conflicts. For decades, the country was ruled by an absolute dictator, "Papa Doc" Duvalier, backed by a ruthless secret police agency. The dictator and his associates became very rich while the population remained very poor, producing export crops to earn cash for the rich. When the dictator died, his son "Baby Doc" took over. During most of the Cold War, the United States backed the dictatorship because it provided a reliable ally next door to Soviet-allied Cuba (a U.S. enemy after its 1959 revolution). Finally, a popular uprising forced Baby Doc to flee in 1986; a Catholic priest championing the poor, Jean-Bertrand Aristide, was elected president of Haiti. But within a year the military seized power in a coup d'état and began to enrich itself again. This, along with international sanctions against the Haitian economy, led tens of thousands of people to flee on rickety boats heading for the prosperous United States. These boat people were intercepted by the U.S. Navy, and most were sent back to Haiti because they were labeled "economic" refugees (see "Migration and Refugees" on pp. 481–485)—but the issue caused problems in U.S. domestic politics, forcing a response. The United States sent an invasion force, intimidated the military leaders into leaving, and restored Aristide as president. The U.S. military occupation was then converted into a UN peacekeeping operation. In 2004, Aristide was overthrown again and fled to exile in Africa, leading to widespread violence in Haiti. An Aristide ally was elected in 2006, but violence continued. Thus, the disparities of wealth in Haiti had ramifications for global alliances (in

---

[19] Mansfield, Edward D, and Brian M. Pollins. *Economic Interdependence and International Conflict: New Perspectives on an Enduring Debate*. Michigan, 2003.

the Cold War), for regional containment (of Cuba), and for international norms concerning military intervention.

DRUG WARS

Because drug trafficking crosses national borders and involves lots of guns and money, it is a source of interstate conflict. The United States invaded Panama to stop dictator Manuel Noriega's collusion with traffickers shipping illegal drugs to the United States. Here, U.S. forces train in Panama near a billboard advertising the United States's own drug export to Panama (tobacco), 1989.

Drug Trafficking As a form of illegal trade across international borders, drug trafficking is smuggling, which deprives states of revenue and violates states' legal control of their borders. But smuggling in general is an economic issue rather than a security one (see "Illicit Trade" on pp. 319–320). Unlike other smuggled goods, however, drug trafficking supplies illegal products that are treated as a security threat because of their effect on national (and military) morale and efficiency. Drug trafficking also has become linked with security concerns because military forces participate regularly in operations against the heavily armed drug traffickers.[20] Conflicts over drugs generally concern states on one side and nonstate actors on the other. But other states can be drawn in because the activities in question cross national borders and may involve corrupt state officials.

These international ramifications are evident in the efforts of the U.S. government to prevent *cocaine cartels* based in Colombia from supplying cocaine to U.S. cities. Such cocaine derives mostly from coca plants grown by peasants in mountainous areas of Peru, Bolivia, and Colombia itself. Processed in simple laboratories in the jungle, the cocaine moves from Colombia through other countries such as Panama before arriving in the United States. In each of these countries (even the United States), the drug smugglers have bribed some corrupt officials, including military or police officers, to stay clear. But other state officials in each country are working with U.S. law enforcement agencies and the U.S. military to crack down on the cocaine trade. The crackdown inevitably brings some negative side effects. In 2001, Peruvian jets working with U.S. radar trackers shot down a small plane over the Andes that turned out to be carrying U.S. missionaries, not cocaine traffickers.

The truth is that segments of the populations in several of these countries, especially in cocaine-producing regions, benefit substantially from the drug trade. For poor peasants in Bolivia or for residents of the Colombian cocaine cartels' home provinces, the cocaine trade may be their only access to a decent income. This dilemma worsened in 2001–2003 as coffee prices dropped to their lowest level in decades. (Similarly, in 2003 many Ethiopian coffee farmers switched to growing the drug *khat* for export when low coffee prices left them hungry.) In rural Peru and Colombia, leftist guerrillas have funded their operations by controlling peasants' production of coca. In southern Colombia, for example, the Revolutionary Armed Forces (FARC) movement maintained stronger control than military forces of the Colombian government.

[20] Tullis, LaMond. *Unintended Consequences: Illegal Drugs and Drug Policies in Nine Countries*. Boulder, CO: Lynne Rienner, 1995. Toro, Celia. *Mexico's "War" on Drugs: Causes and Consequences*. Boulder, CO: Lynne Rienner, 1995. Kopp, Pierre. *Political Economy of Illegal Drugs*. London: Routledge, 2004.

The cocaine trade thus creates several conflicts between the United States and the states of the region. Most such interstate conflicts are resolved through positive forms of leverage such as U.S. financial or military aid. State officials are also often willing to make common cause with the United States because they are threatened by the drug traffickers, who control great wealth and power, and who, being outlaws, have few incentives against using violence.

Because of the long history of U.S. military intervention in Latin America, state cooperation with U.S. military forces is a sensitive political issue. Governments in the region must respect a delicate balance between the need for U.S. help and the need to uphold national sovereignty. In some countries, governments have faced popular criticism for allowing the "Yankees" to "invade" in the drug war. In one case, the U.S. military literally invaded. In 1989, U.S. forces invaded Panama, arrested its leader, dictator Manuel Noriega, and convicted him in U.S. courts of complicity in drug trafficking through Panama.

The growing world trade in *heroin* created some similar conflicts in the late 1990s. Most of the raw material (opium poppies) comes from two poor and conflict-ridden countries with authoritarian governments—Afghanistan and Burma—where Western governments have little leverage. Afghan production of opium poppies doubled after 1998, making it the supplier of three-quarters of the world total. The Taliban government that controlled most of Afghanistan (see pp. 194–195) then abruptly halted production by early 2001, perhaps in hopes of gaining international aid or perhaps to drive up the price of the Taliban's own large stockpiles. After the U.S. war in Afghanistan and the fall of the Taliban government, opium production reached record levels in 2004, despite the presence of U.S. troops and efforts by the new government. In 2006, despite its pro-Western government, Afghanistan remained the world's main source of opium, enriching local farmers and officials.

Like the other sources of international conflict discussed so far, conflicts over drug trafficking arise from conflicting interests regarding tangible items such as money, territory, or control of governments. More difficult to understand, in some ways, are international conflicts rooted in clashes of ideas. Of course, the two overlap—especially around the material and intangible aspects of nationalism—but conflicts of ideas also require special attention in their own right.

Conflicts of Ideas

If all international conflicts were strictly material in nature, it might be easier to settle them. Given enough positive leverage—a payment in some form—any state would agree to another state's terms on a disputed issue. More difficult are the types of conflict in which intangible elements such as ethnic hatred, religious fervor, or ideology come into play.

Ethnic Conflict and Globalization

Ethnic Conflict

Ethnic conflict is quite possibly the most important source of conflict in the numerous wars now occurring throughout the world.[21] **Ethnic groups** are large groups of people who share ancestral, language, cultural, or religious ties and a common *identity* (individuals

[21] Gurr, Ted Robert. *Peoples Versus States: Minorities at Risk in the New Century*. Washington, DC: U.S. Institute of Peace, 2000. Saideman, Stephen M. *The Ties That Divide*. Columbia, 2001. Horowitz, Donald L. *Ethnic Groups in Conflict*. California, 1985. Rothchild, Donald. *Managing Ethnic Conflict in Africa: Pressures and Incentives for Cooperation*. Washington, DC: Brookings, 1997. Chua, Amy. *World on Fire: How Exporting Free Market Democracy Breeds Ethnic Hatred and Global Instability*. New York: Doubleday, 2003. Williams, Robin M. *The Wars Within: Peoples and States in Conflict*. Cornell, 2003.

DRIVING OUT THE OUT-GROUP

Ethnic conflicts play a role in many international conflicts. Ethnocentrism based on an in-group bias can promote intolerance and ultimately dehumanization of an out-group, as in Bosnian and Rwandan genocide, South African apartheid, the persecution of Jews and other minorities in Nazi Germany, and slavery in the United States. In 2006, the slaughter and expulsion of Black farmers in Darfur, Sudan, by government-sponsored Arab militias continued, even after U.S. officials called it "genocide"—a term that invokes obligations under international law. This Darfur woman returned to what had been her home after fleeing an attack, October 2004.

identify with the group). Although conflicts between ethnic groups often have material aspects—notably over territory and government control—ethnic conflict itself stems from a dislike or hatred that members of one ethnic group systematically feel toward another ethnic group. Ethnic conflict is thus not based on tangible causes (what someone does) but on intangible ones (who someone is).

Ethnic groups often form the basis for *nationalist* sentiments. Not all ethnic groups identify as nations; for instance, within the United States various ethnic groups coexist (sometimes uneasily) with a common *national* identity as Americans. But in locations where millions of members of a single ethnic group live as the majority population in their ancestors' land, they usually think of themselves as a nation. In most such cases they aspire to have their own state with its formal international status and territorial boundaries.[22]

Territorial control is closely tied to the aspirations of ethnic groups for statehood. Any state's borders will deviate to some extent (sometimes substantially) from the actual location of ethnic communities. Members of the ethnic group will be left outside its state's borders, and members of other ethnic groups will be located within the state's borders. The resulting situation can be dangerous, with part of an ethnic group controlling a state and another part living as a minority within another state controlled by a rival ethnic group. Frequently the minority group suffers discrimination in the other state and the "home" state tries to rescue or avenge them.

For example, in 1974, after a pro-Greek coup in Cyprus, Turkish troops took control of the Turkish-populated north of that island, leaving the government in control of only the Greek-populated south. This division along a cease-fire line patrolled by UN peacekeepers has persisted for 30 years—even now that Cyprus has become an EU member and Turkey is beginning EU membership talks. After decades of conflict and years of new negotiations, a UN peace plan was put to both sides in a referendum in 2004. The Turkish side voted in favor but the Greek side rejected it, and the standoff continues as a testament to the persistent power of ethnic conflict.

You Are a Prime Minister

Other ethnic groups lack any home state. Kurds share a culture, and many of them aspire to create a state of Kurdistan. But Kurds reside in four states—Turkey, Iraq, Iran, and Syria—all of which strongly oppose giving up control of part of their own territory to create

[22] Cederman, Lars-Erik. *Emergent Actors in World Politics: How States and Nations Develop and Dissolve*. Princeton, 1997.

FIGURE 5.2 ■ Kurdish Area

Ethnic populations often span international borders. Shaded region shows the approximate area of Kurdish settlements.

a Kurdish state (see Figure 5.2). In the 1990s, rival Kurdish guerrilla armies fought both Iraqi and Turkish military forces and each other. Repeatedly in the late 1990s, Turkey sent large military forces into northern Iraq to attack Kurdish guerrilla bases. Kurds enjoyed autonomy in part of northern Iraq under U.S. protection in the 1990s and maintained a quasi-autonomous status in post-Saddam Iraq. The Kurds' success in the 2006 Iraqi elections gave them a strong position to retain this status.[23]

In ethnic conflicts there are often pressures to redraw borders by force. For example, the former Soviet republic of Moldova is inhabited mostly by ethnic Romanians but also by quite a few ethnic Russians concentrated at the eastern end of Moldova farthest from Romania. When Moldova became independent in 1991 and began asserting its Romanian identity—even considering merging into Romania—the Russians living in the east sought to break away and redraw the international border. Armed conflict ensued, and both Russia and Romania threatened to intervene. Eventually a cease-fire and a peacekeeping arrangement were implemented, with no formal change in borders.

When ethnic populations are minorities in territories controlled by rival ethnic groups, they may even be driven from their land or (in rare cases) systematically exterminated. By driving out the minority ethnic group, a majority group can assemble a more unified, more contiguous, and larger territory for its nation-state, as ethnic Serbs did through "ethnic cleansing" after the breakup of Yugoslavia.

Outside states often worry about the fate of "their people" living as minorities in neighboring states. For instance, Albania is concerned about ethnic Albanians who are the majority population in the Serbian province of Kosovo. But if Kosovo became independent of Serbia (or merged with Albania), then Serbia would worry about the minority of ethnic Serbs living in Kosovo. Similar problems have fueled wars between Armenia and Azerbaijan (in the former Soviet Union) and between India and Pakistan. Before World War II, Adolf Hitler used the fate of ethnic German communities in Poland and Czechoslovakia to justify German territorial expansion into those neighboring states. It appears likely that the dangerous combination of ethnic conflict and territorial disputes will lead to more wars in the future.

In extreme cases, such as Hitler's Germany, governments use genocide—systematic extermination of ethnic or religious groups in whole or in part—to try to destroy scapegoated groups or political rivals. In Rwanda, where the Hutu group is the majority and the Tutsi group the minority, a Hutu-nationalist government in 1994 slaughtered more than half a million Tutsis (and Hutus opposed to the government) in a matter of weeks. The

---

[23] McDowall, David. *A Modern History of the Kurds*. 3rd ed. London: I.B. Tauris, 2004. Barkey, Henri J., and Graham E. Fuller. *Turkey's Kurdish Question*. Lanham, MD: Rowman & Littlefield, 1998.

weak international response to this atrocity reveals how frail are international norms of human rights compared to norms of noninterference in other states' internal affairs—at least when no strategic interests are at stake. The Hutu ultranationalists quickly lost power when Tutsi rebels defeated the government militarily, but the war spread into Democratic Congo where the ultranationalists took refuge.[24]

Iran's President Attacks Israel

In cases both of genocide and of less extreme scapegoating, ethnic hatreds do not merely bubble up naturally, but are provoked and channeled by politicians to strengthen their own power. Arab governments use antisemitism to deflect their populations' anger onto Israel. Similarly, in late 2005 Iran's Islamist president, looking to consolidate his power domestically as the international community pressured Iran over its nuclear program, called the Holocaust a "myth" and said Israel should be "wiped off the map."

Often, in former colonies whose borders were drawn arbitrarily, some ethnic groups span two or more states while others find themselves sharing a state with groups that are traditionally rivals or enemies. For example, Nigeria includes 250 ethnic groups, the largest being two Muslim groups in the north and two Christian groups in the south. Although Nigeria's ethnic populations are slowly developing an overarching national identity as Nigerians, old tensions continue to disrupt politics. After a northern-dominated military government was replaced by an elected president from the south in 1999, as Nigeria democratized, ethnic violence killed hundreds of people.

The Cold War, with its tight system of alliances and authoritarian communist governments, seems to have helped to keep ethnic conflicts in check. In the Soviet Union and Yugoslavia—multinational states—the existence of a single strong state (willing to oppress local communities) kept the lid on ethnic tensions and enforced peace between neighboring communities. The breakup of these states allowed ethnic and regional conflicts to take center stage, sometimes bringing violence and war. These cases may indicate a dilemma in that freedom comes at the expense of order and vice versa. Of course, not all ethnic groups get along so poorly together. After the fall of communism, most of the numerous ethnic rivalries in the former Soviet Union did not lead to warfare, and in Czechoslovakia and elsewhere ethnic relations were relatively peaceful after the fall of communism.

Causes of Ethnic Hostility Why do ethnic groups frequently dislike each other? Often there are long-standing historical conflicts over specific territories or natural resources, or over one ethnic group's economic exploitation or political domination of another. Over time, ethnic conflicts may transcend these concrete historical causes and take on a life of their own. They become driven not by tangible grievances (though these may well persist as irritants) but by the kinds of processes described by social psychology that are set in motion when one group of people has a prolonged conflict with another and experiences violence at the hands of the other group.[25]

The ethnic group is a kind of extended *kinship* group—a group of related individuals sharing some ancestors. Even when kinship relations are not very close, a *group identity* makes a person act as though the other members of the ethnic group were family. For instance, African American men who call each other "brother" express group identity as kinship. Likewise, Jews around the world treat each other as family even though each community has intermarried over time and may have more ancestors in common with local non-Jews than with distant Jews. Perhaps, as technology allows far-flung groups to con-

---

[24] Power, Samantha. *The Problem from Hell: America and the Age of Genocide*. NY: Basic Books, 2002. Barnett, Michael. *Eyewitness to a Genocide: The United Nations and Rwanda*. Cornell, 2003. Gourevitch, Philip. *We Wish to Inform You that Tomorrow We Will Be Killed With Our Families*. NY: Farrar, Straus and Giroux, 1999.
[25] Glad, Betty, ed. *Psychological Dimensions of War*. Newbury Park, CA: Sage, 1990.

POLICY PERSPECTIVES

President of Liberia, Ellen Johnson-Sirleaf

PROBLEM *How to prevent civil war while retaining control of your government.*

BACKGROUND Imagine you are the President of Liberia. Your election in the spring of 2006, as the first woman president in Africa, was hailed as a breakthrough for Liberia. The election ended decades of political violence that devastated your own country as well your neighbors of Ivory Coast and Sierra Leone. Most recently, the violence ended when former Liberian President Charles Taylor went into exile in Nigeria. Tens of thousands of people lost their lives or were subject to human rights abuses, including torture and mutilation, in the wars begun under Taylor's rule.

Recently, however, there is optimism within your country and from the international community. Rebel groups have remained quiet, and Charles Taylor was arrested in 2006 and faces trial in a war crimes tribunal established by the UN for the brutal war in Sierra Leone. Economic aid has begun to stream into your country to assist in development. Your country is resource rich and has the potential to become a middle-income country owing to its vast natural agricultural and mineral resources.

Tremendous challenges, however, lie ahead. Economically, your country is underdeveloped with years of civil war leading to increases in corruption and economic stagnation. Many of the powerful economic actors in your country benefit from the corruption and graft, which you have pledged to end. Unemployment is very high with hundreds of thousands of young men unemployed. You still rely on the United Nations for security and many policing functions within your country. Although you have tried to rebuild an army, the process is slow and the training of the new troops weak.

SCENARIO Now imagine that a group that was involved in the civil war begins to re-open the war. The group had taken refuge in Sierra Leone and now begins to make cross-border raids against your country. You also suspect they are sending weapons and funds to rebels within Liberia. While Sierra Leone does not support the group, its government is experiencing its own political instability and has limited resources to devote to the issue.

One option is to negotiate directly with the group. Negotiations could lead to peace, but might require power sharing in your government that could derail your attempts to lessen corruption.

Another option is to use military force against the rebels. But international donors would disourage you from endangering the fragile peace in Liberia, with the implicit threat of an aid cutoff if you are perceived to be too hard-line. Thus, a military offensive against the rebels would have financial risks. In addition, the re-emergence of a civil war would make your proposed democratic and economic reforms more difficult to implement. Your military is not well trained and you are very uncertain as to the possibility of success against the rebels. A strong military response to the rebels, however, could discourage future aggression and establish that you are a tough leader who is serious about enforcing the peace.

CHOOSE YOUR POLICY How do you handle this new threat from the rebels? Do you adopt a hard-line policy against them in hopes of defeating them? Or do you attempt reconciliation in hopes of minimizing the prospect of further bloodshed, but at the price of bringing your enemies into the government and thus undermining some of your goals?

gregate in cyberspace, there will be less psychological pressure to collect ethnic groups physically in a territorial nation-state.

Ethnocentrism, or *in-group bias*, is the tendency to see one's own group in favorable terms and an *out-group* in unfavorable terms. Some scholars believe that ethnocentrism has roots in a biological propensity to protect closely related individuals, but this idea is quite controversial.[26] More often in-group bias is understood in terms of social psychology.

No *minimum criterion* of similarity or kin relationship is needed to evoke the group identity process, including in-group bias. In psychological experiments, even trivial differentiations can evoke these processes. If people are assigned to groups based on a known but unimportant characteristic (such as preferring, say, circles to triangles), before long the people in each group show in-group bias and find they don't much care for the other group's members.[27]

In-group biases are far stronger when the other group looks different, speaks a different language, or worships in a different way (or all three). All too easily, an out-group can be **dehumanized** and stripped of all human rights. This dehumanization includes the common use of animal names—"pigs," "dogs," and so forth—for members of the out-group. U.S. propaganda in World War II depicted Japanese people as apes. Especially in wartime, when people see members of an out-group killing members of their in-group, dehumanization can be extreme. The restraints on war that have evolved in regular interstate warfare, such as not massacring civilians (see "War Crimes" on pp. 283–286), are easily discarded in interethnic warfare.

In several countries where long internal wars in the 1990s had led to dehumanization and atrocities—notably in South Africa—new governments used *truth commissions* to help the society heal and move forward. The commission's role was to hear honest testimony from the period, to bring to light what really happened during these wars, and in exchange to offer most of the participants asylum from punishment. Sometimes international NGOs helped facilitate the process. However, human rights groups objected to a settlement in Sierra Leone in 1999 that brought into the government a faction that had routinely cut off civilians' fingers as a terror tactic. (Hostilities did end, however, in 2001.) Thus, after brutal ethnic conflicts give way to complex political settlements, most governments try to balance the need for justice and truth with the need to keep all groups on board.

Experience in Western Europe shows that education over time can overcome ethnic animosities between traditionally hostile nations, such as France and Germany. After World War II, governments rewrote the textbooks a new generation would use to learn its peoples' histories. Previously, each state's textbooks had glorified its own past deeds, played down its misdeeds, and portrayed its traditional enemies in unflattering terms. In a continentwide project, new textbooks that gave a more objective and fair rendition were created. This project helped pave the way for European integration in subsequent decades.

The existence of a threat from an out-group promotes the cohesion of an in-group, thereby creating a somewhat self-reinforcing process of ethnic division. However, ethnocentrism also often causes members of a group to view themselves as disunited (because they see their own divisions up close) and the out-group as monolithic (because they see it only from outside). This usually reflects a group's sense of vulnerability. Furthermore, overstating

---

[26] Shaw, Paul, and Yuwa Wong. *Genetic Seeds of Warfare: Evolution, Nationalism, and Patriotism*. Boston: Unwin Hyman, 1989. Groebel, J., and R. A. Hinde, eds. *Aggression and War: Their Biological and Social Bases*. Cambridge, 1989. Somit, Albert. Humans, Chimps, and Bonobos: The Biological Bases of Aggression, War, and Peacemaking [review essay]. *Journal of Conflict Resolution* 34 (3), 1990: 553–82. McGuinness, Diane, ed. *Dominance, Aggression, and War*. NY: Paragon, 1987.

[27] Tajfel, H., and J. C. Turner. The Social Identity Theory of Intergroup Behavior. In Worchel, S. and W. Austin, eds. *Psychology of Intergroup Relations*. 2nd ed. Chicago: Nelson-Hall, 1986, pp. 7–24.

THINKING THEORETICALLY

Explaining Genocide

Ethnic Hutu extremists in the government of Rwanda in 1994 carried out an organized genocide, giving orders throughout the country to kill ethnic Tutsis and those Hutus who had opposed the government. In short order, about 500,000 men, women, and children were massacred, mostly by machete, and their bodies dumped into rivers; thousands at a time washed up on lakeshores in neighboring Uganda. What theories could help explain this event?

Hutu hatred toward Tutsis could reflect concrete interests and experiences of the two groups, especially since the minority Tutsis had earlier held power over the Hutu, and Belgian colonialism had exploited local rivalries. Realists might try to explain how the interests of Hutu extremists were served by their actions in exterminating rivals for power. This explanation is undermined, however, by the outcome in this case: the Hutu extremists lost power as a result of the episode.

We might instead view Hutu-Tutsi hatred as part of a pattern of age-old ethnic hatreds that are cropping up in the post–Cold War era, especially in "backward" areas such as Africa. (This age-old-hatreds theory was often articulated by Western politicians in the Bosnia case, portraying the Balkans, like Africa, as "backward" and conflict-prone.) However, this theory holds up even worse than the realist explanation, since one of the world's most civilized, "advanced" states, Germany, exterminated its Jews even more efficiently than Rwanda did its Tutsis—the difference being simply that the "advanced" society could kill with industrial chemicals instead of at knifepoint.

Social psychology theories would tend to view the Rwandan genocide as pathological—a deviation from both rationality and social norms. In-group biases based on fairly arbitrary group characteristics become amplified by a perceived threat from an out-group, exaggerated by history, myth, and propaganda (including schooling). Such feelings can be whipped up by politicians pursuing their own power. A key threshold is crossed when the out-group is dehumanized; norms of social interaction, such as not slitting children's throats, can then be disregarded.

the threat posed by an enemy is a common way for political leaders to bolster their own position within an in-group. In the Arab-Israeli conflict, Israelis tend to see themselves as fragmented into dozens of political parties and diverse immigrant communities pulling in different directions, while they see Arabs as a monolithic bloc united against them. Meanwhile, Arab Palestinians see themselves as fragmented into factions and weakened by divisions among the Arab states, while Israelis appear monolithic to them.

Ethnic conflicts are hard to resolve because they are not about "who gets what" but about "I don't like you." To cast the conflict in terms of a bargaining situation, each side places value on the other's loss of value (making a zero-sum game; see p. 71). A person inflamed with hatred of an enemy is willing to *lose* value in absolute terms—to lose money, the support of allies, or even life—to deprive the enemy of value as well. Suicide bombers exemplify this fanatical hatred. Almost all the means of leverage used in such conflicts are negative, and bargains are very hard to reach. So ethnic conflicts tend to drag on without resolution for generations.

Ethnic groups are only one point along a spectrum of kinship relations—from nuclear families through extended families, villages, provinces, and nations, up to the entire human race. Loyalties fall at different points along the spectrum. Again there is no minimum criterion for in-group identity. For instance, experts said that of all the African countries, Somalia was surely immune from ethnic conflicts because Somalis were all from the same ethnic group and spoke the same language. Then in 1991–1992 a ruinous civil war erupted between members of different clans (based on extended families), leading to mass starva-

Nations and States

tion and the intervention of foreign military forces (which by 1995 had to withdraw after a humiliating failure to tame the violence).

It is unclear why people identify most strongly at one level of group identity.[28] In Somalia, loyalties are to clans; in Serbia, they are to the ethnic group; in the United States and elsewhere, multiethnic states have managed to gain people's primary loyalty. States reinforce their citizens' identification with the state through flags, anthems, pledges of allegiance, patriotic speeches, and so forth. Perhaps someday people will shift loyalties even further, developing a *global identity* as humans first and members of states and ethnic groups second.

Religious Conflict

Religion and World Order

One reason ethnic conflicts often transcend material grievances is that they find expression as *religious* conflicts. Since religion is the core of a community's value system in much of the world, people whose religious practices differ are easily disdained and treated as unworthy or even inhuman. When overlaid on ethnic and territorial conflicts, religion often surfaces as the central and most visible division between groups. For instance, most Indians are Hindus and most Pakistanis are Muslims. Most people in Azerbaijan are Muslims; Armenians are Christians. Most Croats are Roman Catholic Christians, whereas most Serbs are Orthodox Christians and most Bosnians and Albanians are Muslims. This is a very common pattern in ethnic conflicts.

Nothing inherent in religion mandates conflicts—in many places members of different religious groups coexist peacefully. But religious differences hold the potential for conflict, and for making existing conflicts more intractable, because religions involve core values, which are held as absolute truth.[29] This is increasingly true as *fundamentalist* movements have gained strength in recent decades. (The reasons for fundamentalism are disputed, but it is clearly a global-level phenomenon.) Members of these movements organize their lives and communities around their religious beliefs; many are willing to sacrifice and even die for those beliefs. Fundamentalist movements have become larger and more powerful in recent decades in Christianity, Islam, Judaism, Hinduism, and other religions. Such movements challenge the values and practices of **secular** political organizations—those created apart from religious establishments (the separation of religion and state). For example, an Islamic movement in Turkey and a Christian movement in the United States both seek to change long-standing secular traditions by incorporating religious values into the government.

Among the secular practices threatened by fundamentalist movements are the rules of the international system, whereby states are treated as formally equal and sovereign whether they are "believers" or "infidels." As transnational belief systems, religions often are taken as a higher law than state laws and international treaties. Iranian "revolutionary guards" train and support Islamic fundamentalists in other states such as Algeria, Egypt, Jordan, and Lebanon. Jewish fundamentalists build settlements in Israeli-occupied territories and vow to cling to the land even if their government evacuates it. Christian fundamentalists in the United States convince their government to withdraw from the UN Population Fund because of that organization's views on family planning. All these actions in one way or another run counter to the norms of the international system, and to the assumptions of realism.[30]

---

[28] Krause, Jill, and Neil Renwick, eds. *Identities in International Relations*. NY: St. Martin's, 1996.

[29] Appleby, R. Scott. *The Ambivalence of the Sacred: Religion, Violence, and Reconciliation*. Lanham, MD: Rowman & Littlefield, 2000.

[30] Juergensmeyer, Mark. *The New Cold War? Religious Nationalism Confronts the Secular State*. California, 1993.

Currently, violent conflicts are being prosecuted in the name of all the world's major religions. **Islam,** the religion practiced by **Muslims** (or *Moslems*), has been frequently stereotyped in European and North American political discourse, especially at times of conflict such as the 1973 oil embargo, the 1979 Iranian revolution, the 1991 Gulf War, and the period since the 2001 terrorist attacks on the United States. Islam is no more conflict-prone than other religions, although Christian-Muslim conflicts are taking place in a dozen locations. Islam is in fact broad and diverse. Its divergent populations include Sunni Muslims, Shi'ite Muslims, and many smaller branches and sects. The areas of the world that are predominantly Islamic stretch from Nigeria to Indonesia, centered in the Middle East (see Figure 5.3). Most countries with mainly Muslim populations belong to the Islamic Conference, an IGO. Many international conflicts around this zone involve Muslims on one side and non-Muslims on the other, as a result of geographical and historical circumstances including colonialism and oil. Former Yugoslavia was the historical intersection of predominantly Muslim, Orthodox Christian, and Catholic zones, hundreds of years ago. Politicians in the wartorn 1990s there mobilized populations on all sides by playing to these roots.

In several countries, Islamic fundamentalists reject Western-oriented secular states in favor of governments more explicitly oriented to Islamic values.[31] These movements reflect long-standing *anti-Western* sentiment in these countries—against the old European colonizers who were Christian—and are in some ways *nationalist* movements expressed through religious channels. In some Middle Eastern countries with authoritarian governments, religious institutions (mosques) have been the only available avenue for political opposition. Religion has therefore become a means to express opposition to the status quo in politics and culture. (Political roles have also developed for other religions elsewhere, notably the Falun Gong movement in China in the late 1990s.) These anti-Western feelings in Islamic countries came to a boil in 2006 after a Danish newspaper published offensive cartoons depicting the prophet Mohammed. Across the world, Muslims protested, rioted (with dozens of deaths resulting), and boycotted Danish goods.

FROM FAITH TO FRENZY

Religious intolerance can exacerbate tensions between groups, sometimes crossing the line to violence, with international implications. The bombing of this revered Shi'ite mosque in Samarra in 2006, Iraq set off sectarian violence between Sunnis and Shi'ites that pushed Iraq to the brink of civil war and threatened to undo U.S. efforts to build a new, viable Iraqi state.

In 1979, an Islamic republic was created in Iran. Pakistan and Sudan adopted Islamic laws without a revolution, as did the mostly Muslim northern provinces of Nigeria. In Sudan and Nigeria, however, the adoption of Islamic law in one region heightened tensions with other regions that are not predominantly Muslim-populated.

Islam

[31] Johnson, James Turner, and John Kelsay. *Cross, Crescent, and Sword: The Justification and Limitation of War in Western and Islamic Tradition*. NY: Greenwood, 1990. Piscatori, James. *Islam in a World of Nation-States*. Cambridge, 1984. Binder, Leonard. *Islamic Liberalism: A Critique of Development Ideologies*. Chicago, 1988. Davidson, Lawrence. *Islamic Fundamentalism: An Introduction*. Westport, CT: Greenwood Press, 2003.

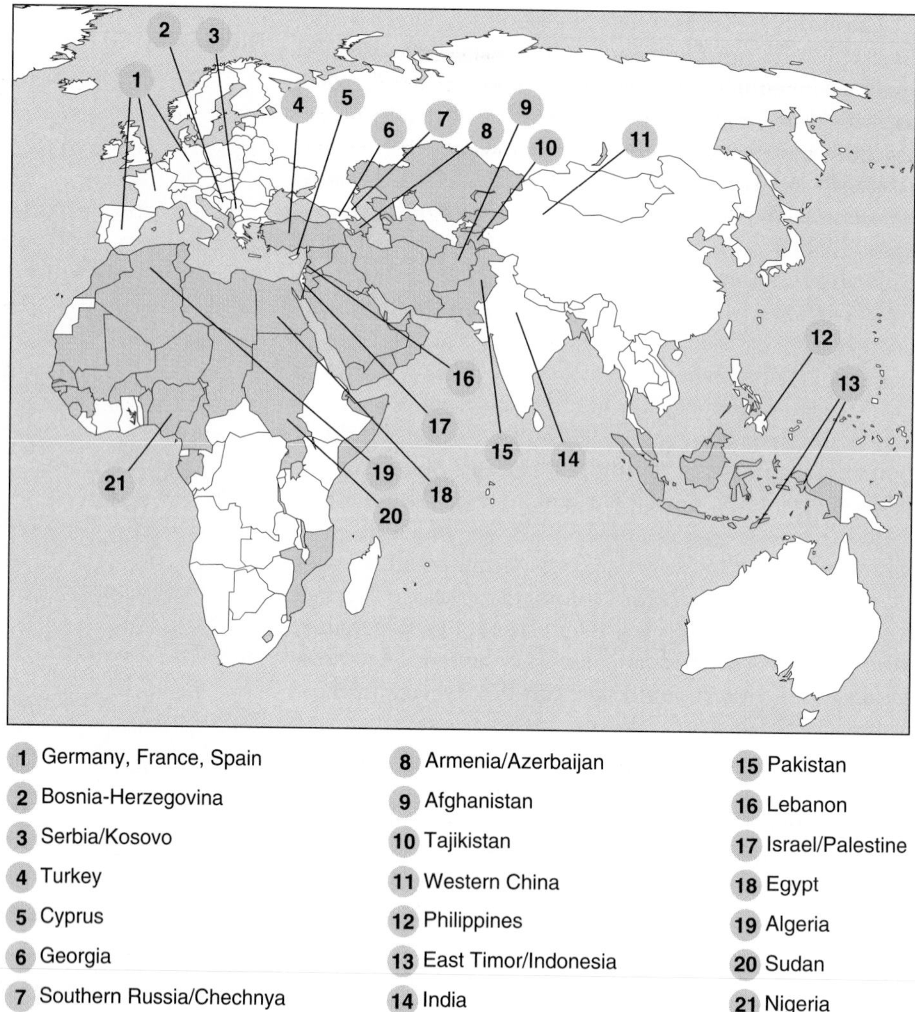

FIGURE 5.3 ■ Members of the Islamic Conference and Areas of Conflict

Shaded countries are members of the conference; numbered regions are areas of conflict between Muslims and non-Muslims or secular authorities.

Sudan's civil war between the mainly Muslim north (including the government) and the mainly Christian and animist south dragged on for two decades and killed millions. A 2005 peace agreement ended the war. The south will have autonomy for six years, followed by a referendum on the region's future, and meanwhile the rebel leaders joined the government. However, Sudan's government recently sponsored brutal attacks in Darfur in the west of the country, by Arabs against fellow Muslims who are Black, demonstrating that religion and ethnicity are equally potent markers of communal identity in civil wars.

An Islamic government was established in Afghanistan in 1992 after a civil war (and following a decade of ill-fated Soviet occupation). Rival Islamic factions then continued the war with even greater intensity for several years. By 1997, a faction called Taliban had taken control of most of Afghanistan and imposed an extreme interpretation of Islamic law. With beatings and executions, the regime forced women to wear head-to-toe coverings, girls to stay out of school, and men to grow beards, among other repressive policies. The Afghanistan war became by the late 1990s the world's most destructive war and threatened to fuel conflicts in Russia, China, and other nearby countries where various forms of Muslim nationalism are at odds with state governments.

The incendiary mixture in Afghanistan in the 1990s—unending war, grinding poverty, Islamic fundamentalism, and an ideologically driven repressive government—allowed Afghanistan to become a base for worldwide terrorist operations, culminating in the 2001 attacks. In response, the United States exerted its power to remove the Taliban from power in Afghanistan and disrupt the al Qaeda terrorist network headquartered there. Despite U.S. successes in the 2001 war, the Taliban still maintains adherents in Afghanistan, who are attempting to destabilize the country.

In Algeria, as many as 100,000 people died in an especially brutal war in the 1990s between the secular military government and an Islamic revolutionary movement. In Jordan, Islamic parties won the largest bloc of seats in Parliament without violence. Similarly, in Palestine the radical Islamist faction Hamas won free Parliamentary elections in 2006, because it was seen as less corrupt than the dominant secular Fatah party. Meanwhile, in the 1990s Islamic parties gained ground in Turkey—a fiercely secular state in which the military has intervened to prevent religious expression in politics—and a former Islamist leader became prime minister in 2003.

In addition to conflicts between religions and between Islamists and secular governments, divisions between the Sunni and Shi'ite wings of Islam have led to violence, especially in and around Iraq—a Shi'ite-majority country ruled by Sunnis under Saddam Hussein. Iraq's war against Shi'ite Iran killed a million people, and Saddam's repression of a Shi'ite uprising after the 1991 Gulf War killed tens of thousands. Under the U.S. occupation of Iraq since 2003, Shi'ite parties have taken power and Shi'ite militias have exacted revenge, while some Sunnis have waged a relentless and brutal insurgency. In 2006, after the bombing of a revered Shi'ite mosque in Iraq, a wave of sectarian killings killed thousands of Iraqis and pushed the country towards civil war.

The more radical Islamic movements not only threaten some existing governments—especially those tied to the West—they also often undermine norms of state sovereignty (for better or worse). They reject Western political conceptions of the state (based on individual autonomy) in favor of a more traditional Islamic orientation based on community. Some aspire to create a single political state encompassing most of the Middle East, as existed in A.D. 600–1200. Such a development would create a profound challenge to the present international system—particularly to its current status quo powers—and would therefore be opposed at every turn by the world's most powerful states. From the perspective of some outsiders, the religious conflicts boiling and simmering at the edges of the Islamic world look like an expansionist threat to be contained. The view from within looks more like being surrounded and repressed from several directions—a view reinforced by massacres of Muslims in Bosnia, Chechnya, and India in the 1990s and by the U.S. invasion of Iraq in 2003.

Overall, Islamic activism (and the opposition to it) is more complex than simply a religious conflict; it concerns power, economic relations, ethnic chauvinism, and historical empires as well.

The same forces contribute to religious fanaticism in non-Muslim countries. In India, Hindu fundamentalists have provoked violent clashes and massacres that have reverberated internationally. In 1992, a Hindu mob destroyed a Muslim mosque at Ayodhya. The incident provoked days of civil violence, mostly directed against Muslims, in which thousands died. In 2002, a similar frenzy of burning, torturing, and raping by Hindu nationalist extremists killed nearly a thousand Muslims in India's Gujarat state, where the Hindu nationalist party controls the state government. In Israel, Jewish fundamentalists have used violence, including the assassination of Israel's own prime minister in 1995, to derail Arab-Jewish peace negotiations.

It has been suggested that international conflicts in the coming years may be generated by a clash of civilizations—based on the differences between the world's major cultural groupings, which overlap quite a bit with religious communities.[32] The idea has been criticized for being overly general, and for assuming that cultural differences naturally create conflict. In fact, although religious and ethnic conflicts receive tremendous attention in the media, *most* ethnic and religious groups living in states do not fight.[33]

Ideological Conflict

To a large extent, ideology is like religion: it symbolizes and intensifies conflicts between groups and states more than it causes them. Ideologies have a somewhat weaker hold on core values and absolute truth than religions do, so they pose somewhat fewer problems for the international system.

For realists, ideological differences among states do not matter much, because all members of the international system pursue their national interests in the context of relatively fluid alliances. For example, during the Cold War there was a global ideological struggle between capitalist democracy and communism. But the alliances and military competitions in that struggle were fairly detached from ideological factors. The two communist giants—the Soviet Union and China—did not stay together very long. India—a democracy and capitalist country—chose not to ally with the Unites States. And even the two great rival superpowers managed to live within the rules of the international system for the most part (such as both remaining UN members).

Over the long run, even countries that experience revolutions based on strong ideologies tend to lose their ideological fervor—be it Iran's Islamic fundamentalism in 1979, China's Maoist communism in 1949, Russia's Leninist communism in 1917, or even U.S. democracy in 1776. In each case, the revolutionaries expected that their assumption of power would dramatically alter their state's foreign policy, because in each case their ideology had profound international implications.

Yet, within a few decades, each of these revolutionary governments turned to the pursuit of national interests above ideological ones. The Soviet Union soon became in many ways just another great power on the European scene—building up its own armed forces, expanding its territory at the expense of Poland, and making alliances with former enemies. Likewise, China's Chairman Mao wanted to spread a "prairie fire" of revolution through the global South to liberate it from U.S. imperialism, but within a few decades Mao was welcoming the very embodiment of U.S. imperialism, President Nixon, to pursue mutual national interests. Iran's Ayatollah Khomeini took power in 1979 determined to revamp foreign policy and struggle against Western, non-Islamic influences—especially the "Great Satan" United States. Twenty-five years later, however, despite the ayatollahs' hold on power, Iran had one of the most pro-American public opinions in the region.

Sometimes even self-proclaimed ideological struggles are not really ideological. In Angola in the 1980s, the United States backed a rebel army called UNITA against a Soviet-aligned government—supposedly a struggle of democracy against Marxism. In truth, the ideological differences were quite arbitrary. The government mouthed Marxist rhetoric to get the Soviet Union to give it aid (a policy that was reversed as soon as Soviet aid dried up). The "democratic" rebels meanwhile adopted democratic rhetoric to get U.S. support but practiced nothing of the sort. In fact, they had earlier received

---

[32] Huntington, Samuel P. *The Clash of Civilizations and the Remaking of World Order*. NY: Simon & Schuster, 1996.

[33] Fearon, James D., and David D. Laitin. Explaining Interethnic Cooperation. *American Political Science Review* 90 (4), 1996: 715–735.

Chinese support and had mouthed Maoist rhetoric. When UN-sponsored elections were won by the government, the "democratic" UNITA refused to accept the results and resumed fighting. This conflict, which finally ended in 2002, really had nothing to do with ideology.

In the short term, revolutions *do* change international relations—they make wars more likely—but not because of ideology. Rather, the sudden change of governments can alter alliances and change the balance of power. With calculations of power being revised by all parties, it is easy to miscalculate or to exaggerate threats on both sides. Saddam Hussein, for example, miscalculated Iran's power after its revolution (see "Estimating Power" on p. 59). But ideology itself plays little role in this postrevolutionary propensity for wars: revolutions are seldom exported to other states.[34]

We should not assume, however, that ideology and political philosophies play no role at all in international politics. Ideologies can help to *mobilize* national populations to support a state in its international dealings, such as war. Fascism (the Nazi ideology) inflamed German nationalism before World War II, legitimizing German aggression by placing it in an ideological framework. And ideology can sharpen and intensify the conflict between two rivals, as happened to the superpowers during the Cold War. In some proxy wars of that era—for instance, in Vietnam in the 1960s and Nicaragua in the 1980s—the rebels and governments had real ideological differences that resonated with the Cold War rivalry.

IDEOLOGICAL SPLIT

Ideology plays only a limited role in most international conflicts. After revolutions, ideologies such as Marxism may affect foreign policy, but over the following decades countries such as China or the Soviet Union typically revert to a foreign policy based more on national interests than ideology. Nonetheless, ideological clashes still occur, as between the United States and Venezuela today, which have a strong trading relationship but suffer from antagonism between the Bush Administration and the leftist Venezuelan president, Hugo Chavez (here, 2006).

If political democracy is an ideology, it may be the exception to the rule that ideology does not affect IR much. Democracy has become a global-level force in world politics, transcending the interests of particular states. A commitment to democracy does not yet outweigh a commitment to national interest in states' foreign policies, and perhaps never will, but global democracy is slowly emerging as a norm that states increasingly are pursuing in their dealings with other states (see "Democracy and Foreign Policy" on pp. 160–163). In fact, some states and IGOs now make the promotion of democracy a centerpiece of their own foreign policy agendas.[35]

Democracies and nondemocracies may increasingly find themselves in conflict with each other if this trend continues. Because democracies almost never fight wars with each other (although they still have conflicts), the spread of democratic ideology may have great implications for future prospects for peace. But recall that the process of becoming a democracy (often referred to as *democratization*) can spur nationalist and ethnic conflicts,

[34] Walt, Stephen M. *Revolution and War*. Cornell, 1996.

[35] Pevehouse, Jon C. *Democracy from Above? Regional Organizations and Democratization*. Cambridge, 2005. Jacoby, Wade. *The Enlargement of the European Union and NATO: Ordering from the Menu in Central Europe*. Cambridge, 2004.

as leaders in new democracies attempt to win elections through fear rather than ideas and policies.[36]

All six types of conflict just discussed can be pursued through peaceful or violent means. We can better understand conflict by examining the types of leverage, violent and otherwise, that come into play in international conflicts.

Means of Leverage

Means of Leverage

Conflicts are settled when some explicit or implicit bargaining process arrives at an outcome acceptable to both parties (see "Bargaining" on pp. 62–63). Acceptable does not mean that both parties are happy or that the outcome is fair—only that neither party thinks it worth the effort to try to change the outcome. Perhaps both parties are satisfied that they have struck a beneficial or fair deal, or one party has been stripped of its leverage (in the extreme case, destroyed altogether) and has no prospect of improving a bad outcome through further bargaining.

War and other violent actions taken in international conflicts are aimed at settling conflicts on favorable terms by inflicting violence as a negative form of leverage. States can also have alternative means of leverage and strategies that often work better than war in resolving conflicts (ending them on mutually acceptable terms).

Types of War

War has been defined in various ways. For present purposes, we may define *war* as sustained intergroup violence (deliberately inflicting death and injury) in which state military forces participate on at least one side—on both sides in the case of *interstate war* and generally on only one side in the case of civil war. Around this definition are gray areas. A military battle that is not sustained over time may or may not be considered a war. The brief Chinese-Soviet border clashes in March and July 1969, for example, entailed several small battles at a few points along the border, in which some hundreds of people were killed. Similarly ambiguous is a long-term violent struggle involving irregular (substate) forces, such as in Northern Ireland. There, uniformed British military forces waged a sustained violent struggle with a nonstate "army," the Irish Republican Army (IRA), until a cease-fire that has held on and off since 1995.

Gang violence in U.S. inner cities is not considered war by most definitions, unlike the gang-type violence in the former Yugoslavia. One difference is scale—"only" hundreds of deaths in the case of U.S. gangs versus hundreds of thousands in Yugoslavia. But the main reason the latter case is generally considered war is the involvement of state military units (and quasi-state military forces created from pieces of state armies that disintegrated).

Thus, many different activities are covered by the general term *war*. Consequently, it is not easy to say how many wars are going on in the world at the moment. Political scientists can count the number of militarized disputes or the number of international conflicts that regularly entail violence. But most lists of wars set some minimum criteria—for instance, a minimum of a thousand battle deaths—to distinguish the large-scale violence implied by war from the more common lower-level violence that occurs in many international conflicts. Criteria that are not often used include formal declarations of war (now largely obsolete) or other legal standards. For example, Japan and the Soviet Union never signed a treaty ending World War II but are not considered to be at war.

---

[36] Mansfield, Edward D. and Jack Snyder. *Electing to Fight: Why Emerging Democracies Go to War*. MIT, 2005.

Figure 5.4 shows the locations of the 15 wars in progress in 2006. Table 5.1 summarizes these wars. Of the 15 wars, none is in North America, Western Europe, Japan/Pacific, or China. All but Chechnya are in the global South—mainly in Africa, South Asia, and the Middle East.

The largest and most active wars in Spring 2006 were in Iraq, Sudan, and Colombia. Most recent wars have been internal (within a state). The first serious interstate war in years was the attack on Iraq in 2003. Wars are sputtering on and off in Israel-Palestine, the Rwanda-Burundi area (including Uganda), Somalia, Tajikistan/Kyrgyzstan, Nepal, Afghanistan, Burma, Indonesia, and the Philippines.

More importantly, a number of intense wars ended in the past decade, including those in Sierra Leone, Angola, East Timor, the former Yugoslavia, Lebanon, Guatemala, and Northern Ireland (following South Africa and Mozambique earlier in the 1990s). Just since 2003, notwithstanding the war in Iraq, settlements ended more of the world's remaining wars of greatest duration and lethality. Liberia, Ivory Coast, and Democratic Congo all established power-sharing governments and brought in international peacekeepers—following in the path of Sierra Leone (which in 2003 held democratic elections). In 2005, the Irish Republican Army finished permanently dismantling its weaponry. India and Pakistan began their first cease-fire in a decade, as did Burma's government and its largest rebel militia. In 2006, Democratic Congo voted for a new constitution, with presidential and parliamentary elections following. In Sri Lanka and Ivory Coast, cease-fires continued despite some lapses, and negotiations inched forward.

In Sudan, the warring sides (largely northern Muslims versus southern Christians) in a decades-long civil war signed a peace agreement in 2003, ending the world's last active war that killed more than a million people. It called for withdrawing government forces from the south of the country, establishing a power-sharing transitional government and army, and holding a referendum in the rebel areas in six years. Unfortunately, following this peace agreement, rebels in the western Darfur region began to protest their exclusion from the peace agreement. In response, the government helped militias raid western villages, committing what the United States and other states have labeled genocide. In late 2004, the government, the Darfur rebels, and the southern rebels reached a tentative peace agreement to be monitored by the African Union and the United Nations, but the war crimes in Darfur continued into 2006 and began to spill over the border into Chad. In 2005, the UN World Food Program had to cut rations to a million Darfur refugees because donor states had given barely half the money needed. The international community's ineffective response to the mass murders in Darfur, like that in Rwanda in 1994, shows the limited reach of international norms in today's state-based international system.

Wars are very diverse. Several types of war tend to arise from different situations and play different sorts of roles in bargaining over conflicts. Starting from the largest wars (which obviously meet the criteria), we may distinguish the following main categories.

Hegemonic war is a war over control of the entire *world order*—the rules of the international system as a whole, including the role of world hegemony (see "Hegemony," p. 82). This class of wars (with variations in definition and conception) is also known as *world war, global war, general war*, or *systemic war*.[37] The last hegemonic war was World War II. Largely because of the power of modern weaponry, this kind of war probably cannot occur any longer without destroying civilization.

Total war is warfare by one state waged to conquer and occupy another. The goal is to reach the capital city and force the surrender of the government, which can then be replaced with one of the victor's choosing (see pp. 180–181). The 2003 Iraq War is a classic case.

[37] Levy, Jack S. Theories of General War. *World Politics* 37 (3), 1985: 344–74. Thompson, William R. *On Global War: Historical-Structural Approaches to World Politics*. South Carolina, 1988.

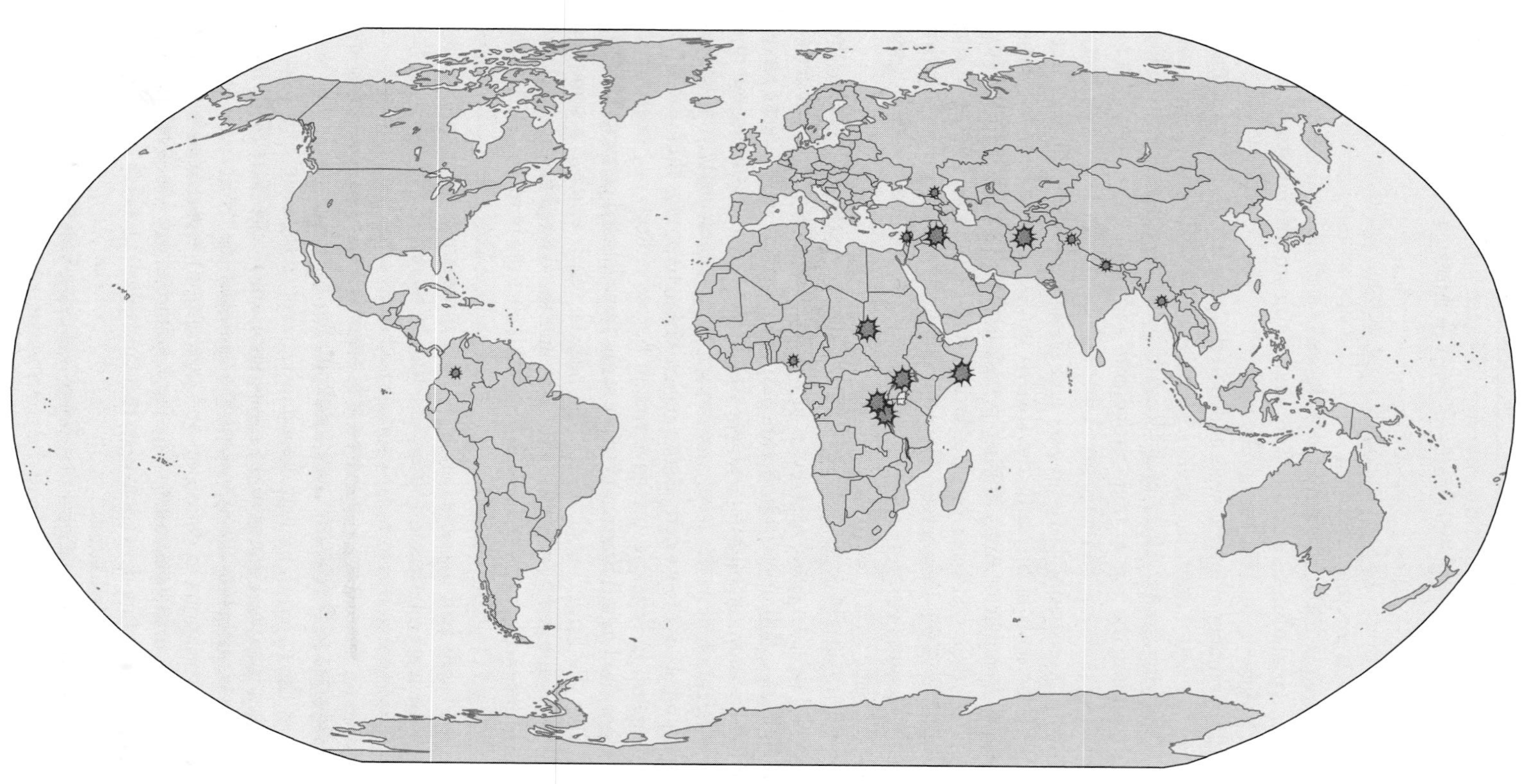

FIGURE 5.4 ■ Wars in Progress, May 2006

TABLE 5.1 ■ Wars by Region

Region	Most Important Wars, May 2006
Africa	**Democratic Congo, Burundi, Uganda, Sudan, Somalia**, Nigeria
South Asia	**Afghanistan**, India, Nepal, Burma
Middle East	**Iraq**, Israel-Palestine
Russia/E. Europe	Russia (Chechnya)
Latin America	Colombia
N. America, W. Europe, Japan/Pacific, China	None

Note: Bold face indicates reported fatalities of more than 100,000.

Total war as we know it began with the massively destructive Napoleonic Wars, which introduced large-scale conscription and geared the entire French national economy toward the war effort. The practice of total war evolved with industrialization, which further integrated all of society and economy into the practice of war. The last total war between great powers was World War II.

In total war, with the entire society mobilized for the struggle, the entire society of the enemy is considered a legitimate target. For instance, in World War II Germany attacked British civilians with V-2 rockets, while British and U.S. strategic bombing killed 600,000 German civilians (and hundreds of thousands more Japanese) in an effort to weaken morale.

Limited war includes military actions carried out to gain some objective short of the surrender and occupation of the enemy. For instance, the U.S.-led war against Iraq in 1991 retook the territory of Kuwait but did not go on to Baghdad to topple Saddam Hussein's government. Many border wars have this character: after occupying the land it wants, a state may stop short and defend its gains.

Raids are limited wars that consist of a single action—a bombing run or a quick incursion by land. In 1981, Israeli warplanes bombed an Iraqi nuclear research facility to stop Iraq from making progress toward the development of nuclear weapons. (Without this raid, Iraq might have had nuclear weapons when it invaded Kuwait in 1990.) The action had a narrow objective—destruction of the facility—and was over within hours. Raids fall into the gray area between wars and nonwars because their destruction is limited and they are over quickly. Raiding that is repeated or fuels a cycle of retaliation usually becomes a limited war or what is sometimes called "low-intensity conflict."

Civil war refers to war between factions within a state trying to create, or prevent, a new government for the entire state or some territorial part of it.[38] (The aim may be to change the entire system of government, to merely replace the people in it, or to split a region off as a new state.) The U.S. Civil War of the 1860s is a good example of a secessionist civil war, as is the war of Eritrea province in Ethiopia (now the internationally recognized state of Eritrea) in the 1980s. The war in El Salvador in the 1980s is an example of a civil war for control of the entire state (not secessionist). Civil wars seem to be often among the most brutal wars. People fighting their fellow citizens act no less cruelly than those fighting people from another state. The 50,000 or more deaths in the civil war in El Salvador, including many from massacres and death squads, were not based on ethnic differences. (Of course, many of today's civil wars do contain ethnic conflicts as well.)

[38] Collier, Paul and Nicholas Sambanis, eds. *Understanding Civil War: Evidence and Analysis. Vol. 1: Africa. Vol 2: Europe, Central Asia, and Other Regions*. Washington, DC: The World Bank, 2005. Walter, Barbara F., and Jack Snyder, eds. *Civil Wars, Insecurity, and Intervention*. Columbia, 1999.

Guerrilla war, which includes certain kinds of civil wars, is warfare without front lines. Irregular forces operate in the midst of, and often hidden or protected by, civilian populations. The purpose is not to directly confront an enemy army but rather to harass and punish it so as to gradually limit its operation and effectively liberate territory from its control. Iraqi paramilitary forces used such methods during the Iraq War in 2003–2005. U.S. military forces in South Vietnam fought against Viet Cong guerrillas in the 1960s and 1970s, with rising frustration. Efforts to combat such a guerrilla army—**counterinsurgency**—often include programs to "win the hearts and minds" of rural populations so that they stop sheltering the guerrillas. In guerrilla war, without a fixed front line, there is much territory that neither side controls; both sides exert military leverage over the same places at the same time. Thus, guerrilla wars are extremely painful for civilians. The situation is doubly painful because conventional armies fighting against guerrillas often cannot distinguish them from civilians and punish both together. In one famous case in South Vietnam, a U.S. officer, who had ordered an entire village burned to deny its use as a sanctuary by the Viet Cong, commented, "We had to destroy the village to save it."

Warfare increasingly is irregular and guerrilla-style; it is less and less often an open conventional clash of large state armies. But conventional wars such as the 1991 Gulf War do still occur. On the whole, state and nonstate actors have a range of political goals that lead them to employ violent forms of leverage, and a range of options for employing force.

Terrorism

Terrorism

Since September 2001, governments and ordinary people have paid much more attention to terrorism than ever before. But terrorism itself is not new. Terrorism is basically just another step along the spectrum of violent leverage, from total war to guerrilla war. Indeed terrorism and guerrilla war often occur together. Yet terrorism differs from other kinds of wars.

Terrorism refers to political violence that targets civilians deliberately and indiscriminately. Beyond this basic definition other criteria can be applied, but the definitions become politically motivated: one person's freedom fighter is another's terrorist. More than guerrilla warfare, terrorism is a shadowy world of faceless enemies and irregular tactics marked by extreme brutality.[39]

Port Security

In the past, most terrorism has occurred in the Middle East, Europe, and South Asia. Although U.S. interests and citizens abroad were repeatedly targeted, little international terrorism took place in the United States itself. The 1993 bombing of the World Trade Center in New York was an exception, but because damage from these attacks was quite limited, the public quickly forgot the terrorist threat.

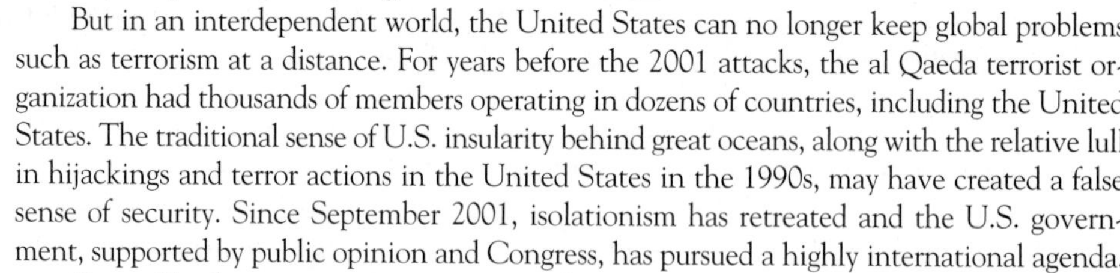

But in an interdependent world, the United States can no longer keep global problems such as terrorism at a distance. For years before the 2001 attacks, the al Qaeda terrorist organization had thousands of members operating in dozens of countries, including the United States. The traditional sense of U.S. insularity behind great oceans, along with the relative lull in hijackings and terror actions in the United States in the 1990s, may have created a false sense of security. Since September 2001, isolationism has retreated and the U.S. government, supported by public opinion and Congress, has pursued a highly international agenda.

Generally, the purpose of terrorism is to demoralize a civilian population in order to use its discontent as leverage on national governments or other parties to a conflict. Related to this is the aim of creating drama in order to gain media attention for a cause. When the IRA planted bombs in London, it hoped to make life miserable enough for Londoners that they

[39] Lutz, James M. *Global Terrorism*. London: Routledge, 2004. Benjamin, Daniel, and Steven Simon. *The Age of Sacred Terror*. NY: Random, 2002. Kushner, Harvey W. *Encyclopedia of Terrorism*. Thousand Oaks, CA: Sage Publications, 2003.

would insist their government settle the Northern Ireland issue. The bombing also sought to keep the issue of Northern Ireland in the news, in the hope that the British government would then be pressured to concede terms more favorable to the IRA than would otherwise be the case. Terrorism is seldom mindless; it is usually a calculated use of violence as leverage. However, motives and means of terrorism vary widely, having in common only that some actor is using violence to send a message to other actors.

The primary effect of terrorism is psychological. In part the effectiveness of terrorism in capturing attention is due to the dramatic nature of the incidents, especially as shown on television news. Terrorism also gains attention because of the randomness of victims. Although only a few dozen people may be injured by a bomb left in a market, millions of people realize "it could have been me," because they, too, shop in markets. Attacks on airplanes augment this fear because many people already fear flying. Terrorism thus amplifies a small amount of power by its psychological effect on large populations; this is why it is usually a tool of the powerless. However, al Qaeda's attacks follow a somewhat different pattern, planned less to create fear than simply to kill as many Americans and their allies as possible—and ultimately to touch off apocalyptic violence that al Qaeda's followers believe will bring about God's intervention. The psychological effect is aimed at Muslim populations worldwide rather than at Americans.

ASYMMETRICAL CONFLICT

Terrorist attacks often reflect the weakness of the perpetrators and their lack of access to other means of leverage. Terror can sometimes amplify a small group's power and affect outcomes. Al Qaeda's September 11, 2001, attacks, staged by a relatively small nonstate actor, ultimately led to the withdrawal of U.S. troops from Saudi Arabia, drew the United States into a counterinsurgency war in Iraq, and brought al Qaeda itself a surge of recruits for new attacks worldwide.

In the shockingly destructive attack on the World Trade Center, tangible damage was far greater than in previous terrorist attacks—reaching into thousands of lives and tens of billions of dollars. The psychological impact was even stronger than the physical damage—changing the U.S. political and cultural landscape instantly. But in contrast to historical instances of terrorism, real costs began to loom large. The same terrorist network was trying to obtain nuclear weapons (see pp. 231–233) with which to kill not thousands but hundreds of thousands of Americans. Similarly, although the mailed anthrax attacks in Fall 2001 killed only a few people, and had far more psychological than physical effect, the door had been opened to a new bioterrorism that could kill tens of thousands.[40]

The classic cases of terrorism—from the 1970s to the 2001 attacks—are those in which a *nonstate* actor uses attacks against *civilians* by secret *nonuniformed* forces, operating *across international borders*, as a leverage against *state* actors. Radical political factions or separatist groups hijack or blow up airplanes, or plant bombs in cafés, clubs, or other crowded places. For example, Chechen radicals seized a school in Beslan, a small city in the Caucasus region in 2004. For three days, nearly 1,200 children, parents, and teachers were held without food or water. When Russian troops stormed the school, they detonated many traps set by the terrorists, setting off explosions. In the end, more than 300 people died, including 172 children. Such tactics create spectacular incidents that draw attention to the terrorists' cause.

Often terrorism is used by radical factions of movements that have not been able to get attention or develop other effective means of leverage. It is often a tactic of desper-

[40] Young, Mitchell, ed. *The War on Terrorism*. Farmington Hills, MI: Greenhaven Press, 2003.

ation, and it almost always reflects weakness in the power position of the attacker. For instance, Palestinian radicals in 1972 had seen Arab states defeated by Israel in war and could not see a way to gain even a hearing for their cause. By capturing media attention worldwide with dramatic incidents of violence—even at the cost of rallying world public opinion against their cause—the radicals hoped to make Palestinian aspirations an issue that Western governments could not ignore when deciding on policies toward the Middle East.

Terrorists are more willing than states are to violate the norms of the international system because, unlike states, they do not have a stake in that system. Conversely, when a political group gains some power or legitimacy, its use of terrorism usually diminishes. This was true of the Palestine Liberation Organization during the peace process in 1993–2000 as well as the Irish Republican Army starting in 1995.

States themselves carry out acts designed to terrorize their own populations or those of other states, but scholars tend to avoid the label "terrorism" for such acts, preferring to call it repression or war. Russia's indiscriminate attacks in Chechnya province in 1995 are an example. (By contrast, the later bombings of Moscow apartment buildings by Chechen radicals were clearly terrorism.) In fact, no violent act taken during a civil or international war—by or toward a warring party—can necessarily fit neatly into the category of terrorism. Of course, because war itself is hard to define, so is terrorism; warring parties often call each other terrorists. In the Central American civil wars of the 1980s, both the states and the guerrillas employed tactics that, if taken in peacetime, would easily qualify as terrorism.

The narrowest definition of terrorism would exclude acts either by or against *uniformed military forces* rather than civilians. This definition would exclude the killing of 243 U.S. Marines by a car bomb in Lebanon in 1983, and the 2001 attack on the Pentagon, because they were directed at military targets. It would also exclude the bombing of German cities in World War II although the purpose was to terrorize civilians. But in today's world of undeclared war, guerrilla war, civil war, and ethnic violence, there is a large gray zone around clear cases of terrorism.[41] Disagreements about whether terrorism included Palestinian attacks on Israel, and Pakistani attacks in Kashmir, scuttled efforts to pass a UN treaty on terrorism in late 2001.

State-sponsored terrorism refers to the use of terrorist groups by states—usually under control of the state's intelligence agency—to achieve political aims. In 1988, a bomb scattered pieces of Pan Am flight 103 over the Scottish countryside. Combing the fields for debris, investigators found fragments of a tape recorder that had contained a sophisticated plastic-explosive bomb. A tiny strand of wire from the triggering device turned out to be a rare variety, through which the investigators traced the origins of the bomb. The U.S. and British governments identified two Libyan intelligence agents who had smuggled the tape recorder onto flight 103 in Frankfurt. In 1992, backed by the UN Security Council, they demanded that Libya turn over the agents for trial. When Libya refused, the UN imposed sanctions including a ban on international flights to or from Libya. In 1999, Libya turned over the suspects for trial—two received life in prison while a third was acquitted—and the UN suspended its sanctions. In 2003, Libya formally took responsibility for the bombing, struck a multibillion-dollar compensation deal with the victims' families, and regained a normal place in the international community.

---

[41] Stern, Jessica. *Terror in the Name of God: Why Religious Militants Kill*. HarperCollins, 2003. Laqueur, Walter. *A History of Terrorism*. Piscataway, NJ: Transaction, 2001. Pilar, Paul R. *Terrorism and U.S. Foreign Policy*. Washington, DC: Brookings, 2001. Pape, Robert A. *Dying to Win: The Strategic Logic of Suicide Terrorism*. NY: Random House, 2005. Bloom, Mia. *Dying to Kill: The Allure of Suicide Terror*. Columbia, 2005. Ross, Jeffrey Ian. *Political Terrorism: An Interdisciplinary Approach*. NY: Peter Lang, 2006.

The United States accuses five states of supporting international terrorism, as of 2006—North Korea, Iran, Syria, Sudan, and Cuba—and has barred U.S. companies from doing business in those states. However, these kinds of unilateral U.S. sanctions are of limited effect. Cuba can do business with Canada, and Iran with Russia. The U.S. position was also undermined when it carved an exception in its rule to allow a U.S. oil company to bid on a lucrative pipeline project in Sudan.

Often, state involvement in terrorism is very difficult to trace. Indeed, had the bomb on flight 103 exploded as scheduled over the Atlantic Ocean, instead of prematurely, the clues would not have been found. Counterterrorism has become a sophisticated operation as well as a big business—a trend that accelerated after September 2001. International agencies, notably the *Interpol* police agency (and in Europe, *Europol*), coordinate the actions of states in tracking and apprehending suspected terrorists (as well as drug traffickers and other criminals). National governments have investigative agencies, such as the FBI and CIA in the United States, to try to break through the wall of secrecy around terrorist operations. Lately, many private companies have expanded the business of providing security services, including antiterrorist equipment and forces, to companies and individuals doing business internationally. These companies are very busy since September 2001, as governments, companies, and individuals worldwide adapt to the new security environment that comes from a global terrorist threat.

Just as there are many possible outcomes of conflict, many types of war, and varied propensities for violence among different states, so too is there great diversity in how force is used if conflict leads to violence. States develop a wide array of military forces, which vary tremendously in their purposes and capabilities—having in common only that they are instruments used to apply violence in some form. It is to these military forces that we now turn.

THINKING CRITICALLY

1. Suppose that you were the mediator in negotiations between two states each claiming the same piece of land. What principles could you follow in developing a mutually acceptable plan for ownership of the territory? What means could you use to convince the two states to accept your plan?
2. How many of the six types of international conflict discussed in this chapter can you connect with the phenomenon of nationalism discussed on pp. 32–33? What are the connections in each case?
3. European textbooks were revised after World War II to reduce ethnic and national stereotypes and to give a fairer portrayal of Europe's various nations. What about the textbooks you used to learn your country's history? Did they give an accurate picture, or did they overstate the virtues of your own ethnic group or nation at the expense of others? How?
4. The rise of fundamentalism among the world's major religions challenges traditional notions of state sovereignty. How might this trend strengthen, or weaken, the United Nations and other attempts to create supranational authority (which also challenge state sovereignty)?
5. Given the definition of war provided on p. 198, name three current international situations that clearly fit the definition of war and three that are ambiguous "quasi-wars" (almost but not quite fitting the definition). Which do you think are more se-

rious, the wars or the quasi-wars? Do they involve different types of actors? Different kinds of conflicts? Different capabilities?

CHAPTER SUMMARY

- War and other forms of international violence are used as leverage to try to improve the terms of settlement of conflicts.
- Many theories have been offered as general explanations about when such forms of leverage come into play—the causes of war. Contradictory theories have been proposed at each level of analysis and, with two exceptions, none has strong empirical support. Thus, political scientists cannot reliably predict the outbreak of war. The two exceptions are: (1) that there are virtually no societies in which war and intergroup violence as means of leverage are unknown, and (2) that democratic states almost never fight wars against other democracies.
- States come into conflict with each other and with nonstate actors for a variety of reasons. Conflicts will always exist among international actors.
- Territorial disputes are among the most serious international conflicts because states place great value on territorial integrity. With a few exceptions, however, almost all the world's borders are now firmly fixed and internationally recognized.
- Conflicts over the control of entire states (through control of governments) are also serious and are relatively likely to lead to the use of force.
- Economic conflicts lead to violence much less often, because positive gains from economic activities are more important inducements than negative threats of violence.
- Some particular kinds of economic conflict, however, have special implications for national security.
- Drug trafficking creates several kinds of conflict that draw in state and nonstate actors alike.
- Ethnic conflicts, especially when linked with territorial disputes, are very difficult to resolve because of psychological biases. It is hard to explain why people's loyalties are sometimes to their ethnic group, sometimes to a multiethnic nation.
- Fundamentalist religious movements pose a broad challenge to the rules of the international system in general and state sovereignty in particular.
- Ideologies do not matter very much in international relations, with the possible exception of democracy as an ideology. State leaders can use ideologies to justify whatever actions are in their interests.
- When violent means are used as leverage in international conflicts, a variety of types of war result. These vary greatly in size and character, from guerrilla wars and raids to hegemonic war for leadership of the international system. Along this spectrum of uses of violence, the exact definition of war is uncertain.
- Like other violent means of leverage, terrorism is used to gain advantage in international bargaining situations. Terrorism is effective if it damages morale in a population and gains media exposure for the cause.
- The September 2001 attacks differed from earlier terrorism both in their scale of destruction and in the long reach of the global al Qaeda terrorist network. The attacks forced dramatic changes in U.S. and worldwide security arrangements, and sparked

U.S. military intervention in Afghanistan to overthrow the Taliban regime and destroy the al Qaeda bases there.

KEY TERMS

conflict 169
settlement 169
cycle theories 172
irredentism 174
ethnic cleansing 176
territorial waters 179
airspace 180
lateral pressure (theory of) 182
ethnic groups 185
ethnocentrism 190
dehumanization 190
secular (state) 192
Islam/Muslims 192
hegemonic war 199
total war 199
limited war 201
civil war 201
guerrilla war 202
counterinsurgency 202
state-sponsored terrorism 204

ONLINE PRACTICE TEST
Take an online practice test at
www.internationalrelations.net

❑ A
❑ B
☑ C
❑ D

LET'S DEBATE THE ISSUE

The West versus Islamism: The New Cold War?

by Mir Zohair Husain

Overview The Western world viewed al Qaeda's September 11, 2001, terrorist attacks as Islamists (Islamic political activists) attacking everything that America and the West represented. Contrary to this belief, Osama bin Laden's al Qaeda (Arabic for "the base") activists are misguided Muslim extremists comprising an infinitesimally small revolutionary fringe group within Islamism

Islamism, a comprehensive religiopolitical ideology, has become a powerful force in world affairs; however, it is not a monolithic religiopolitical ideology with any one leader or power center, such as the Pope and the Vatican in Rome. Three major types of Islamists are: traditionalist, progressive, and revolutionary. Traditionalist Islamists are often apolitical, scholarly, and conservative *ulama* (Islamic clerics). These ulama get involved in politics when they perceive Islam and/or the *ummah* (community of believers) to be in imminent danger. Progressive Islamists are devout Muslims who are rational and analytical, reconcile progressive Islam with modern science. Revolutionary Islamists are characteristically puritanical and committed to establishing an Islamic state based on the rigorous application of the *shariah* (Islamic law). Al Qaeda's extremist and violent strain of revolutionary Islamism is but one tiny aspect of revolutionary Islamism. In fact, most revolutionary Islamists—such as, the Ikhwan al-Muslimun (Muslim Brotherhood) in Egypt or Jama 'at-e-Islami (Islamic Association) in South Asia—most Islamists, and all but a few Muslims, shun this atypical form of revolutionary Islamism. However, it is this virulent strain of Islamism that receives overwhelming mass media coverage with little mention that most Islamists and Muslims repudiate terrorism as inherently irreconcilable with Islam.

In the post-September 11 political climate, Islamophobia (fear of Islamism and Islamists) grew so much that Islamism replaced communism as the alien, monolithic, and dangerous force threatening the West. In the Muslim world, anti-Americanism and anti-Western sentiments provoked scholars, the mass media, and politicians to question whether this incipient clash between the West and Islamism will evolve into a new Cold War.

Argument 1 The Clash Between the West and Islamism Is Inevitable

The West-Islamism confrontation is a "clash of civilizations." Historically, power struggles and international conflict have revolved around states, but a trend is emerging in which the world is dividing along cultural lines. In fact, many scholars have begun using the term "clash of civilizations" interchangeably with conflicts between the West and Islamism.

> In the emerging world, the relations between states and groups from different civilizations will not be close and will often be antagonistic. Yet some . . . are more conflict-prone than others. . . . The dangerous clashes of the future are likely to arise from the interaction of Western arrogance, Islamic intolerance, and Sinic assertiveness.

The West . . . believe[s] that the non-Western peoples should commit themselves to the Western values of democracy, free markets, . . . individualism, [etc.] Minorities in other civilizations embrace and promote these values, but the dominant attitudes toward them . . . range from widespread skepticism to intense opposition. What is universalism to the West is imperialism to the rest. (Samuel Huntington. *The Clash of Civilizations and the Remaking of World Order.* Simon and Schuster, 1996, pp. 183–4.)

Cultural misunderstandings will be devastating. The West and Islamism are strongly grounded in their convictions. The misperceptions imposed on the public of both peoples—specifically the Western mass media, worldwide Wahhabi-sponsored *madrassahs* (Islamic schools) in Muslims communities, and the opportunistic political and religious leaders of both sides—make this clash of the two cultures inevitable.

Given trends, a clash seems inevitable. On the one hand is an arrogance which sees Muslims as violence-prone, backward-looking, inefficient and irrational beings with rituals and customs totally out of place with the modern times—[and] . . . prevents a close look at the root of the problems faced by contemporary human beings. . . . [Moreover,] there is a growing populace which sees the West as the architect of their unhappy existence; . . . there are individuals who are paranoid [of] the growing number of Muslims at home as well as in the Muslim heartlands; [and] a growing militancy which has given up all hope of a peaceful process of reconciliation with the West and has been pushed to take up arms. (Zafar Ishaq Ansari and John L. Esposito. *Muslims and the West: Encounter and Dialogue.* Islamic Research Institute, 2001, pp. 269–70.)

West-Islamism clashes have already begun. The events of September 11 initiated new and recurring conflicts. Although terrorist organizations, such as al Qaeda, are not representative of all Islamists or Muslims, the West's war on terrorism has polarized the West and Muslim worlds. Both sides attempt to gather support for their causes through the demonization of the other. Events such as the Iraqi prisoner abuse scandal (in which-Iraqi prisoners in Abu Ghraib prison were tortured, photographed nude, and forced to engage in degrading acts), offer further proof that a clash of civilizations is already occurring.

"They're disgusting," [said] Senator Dianne Feinstein. "If somebody wanted to plan a clash of civilizations, this is how they'd do it. These pictures play into every stereotype of America that Arabs have: America as debauched. America as hypocrites."

After 9/11, America had the support and sympathy of the world. Now, awash in digital evidence of uncivilized behavior, America has careered into a war of civilizations. The pictures were clearly meant to use the codebook of Muslim anxieties about nudity and sexual and gender humiliation to break down the prisoners. (Maureen Dowd. "Clash of Civilizations." *The New York Times,* May 13, 2004, p. A25.)

Argument 2 West-Islamism Conflict Is Not Inevitable

A clash between civilizations is not responsible for terrorist conflicts with the West. Ironically, the real culprit of Islamic terrorists versus the West is U.S. Cold War strategies, not a clash between civilizations.

In the varied explanations for the 9/11 attacks and the rise in terrorism. . . . one is that Islamic culture itself is to blame, leading to a clash of civilizations . . .

. . . Mahmood Mamdani, a Uganda-born political scientist and cultural anthropologist at Columbia University . . . argues that terrorism does not necessarily have anything to do with Islamic culture: he also insists that the spread of terror as a tactic is largely an outgrowth of American cold war foreign policy.

"In practice," Mr. Mamdani has written. "it translated into a United States decision to harness, or even to cultivate, terrorism in the struggle against regimes it considered pro-Soviet." The real culprit of 9/11, in other words, is not Islam but rather non-state violence in general, during the final stages of the stand-off with the Soviet Union

The best-known C.I.A.-trained terrorist, he notes dryly, is Osama bin Laden. (Hugh Eakin. "When U.S. Aided Insurgents, Did It Breed Future Terrorists?" *The New York Times,* April 10, 2004, p. B7.)

The West and the Muslim world have common interests. A dialogue between these two civilizations could succeed because both share key common interests. For instance, the West wants democracies established in Muslim countries to broker peace and stability. Contrary to Western thought, Muslims also want to have legitimate democracies. Open dialogues would shed light on such misperceptions and provide a better understanding of differences and commonalities.

Bush suggested early on in [America's war on terrorism] that [September 11 was] the result of "people who hate our values," but this analysis was simplistic and self-serving. Most Muslims, . . . want a democratic order, respect for human rights and the ability to get rid of hated regimes.

Most Muslims casually perceive that [the] war against terrorism . . . really is a war against Islam. Nearly all Muslims would subscribe to the belief that Muslim power is a legitimate and worthwhile goal, but most do not believe that it has to be on a collision course with the West. But as long as Western power is seen to dominate the Muslim world, the logic of this argument will strike sympathetic chords. . . .

[Hence,] both sides fail to capture the full reality in front of them, and the [perception] gap must be bridged. . . . the gap of perception is massive—for which there is a price to be paid. (Graham E. Fuller. *The Future of Political Islam.* Palgrave Macmillan, 2003, pp. 86, 151, 162.)

A dialogue between civilizations is possible and desirable. A clash between Western and Islamic civilizations can be avoided. An intercivilizational dialogue is the key to peace and stability. For the West, this means understanding that most Islamists do not condone violence.

> Although some [Islamists] advocate violent revolution, others do not. Islam and most Islamic movements are not necessarily anti-Western. . . . Although they challenge the outdated assumptions of the established order and autocratic regimes, they do not necessarily threaten U.S. interests. Our challenge is to better understand the history and realities of the Muslim world and to recognize the diversity and the many faces of Islam. This approach lessens the risk of creating self-fulfilling prophecies that augur the battle of the West against a radical Islam or a clash of civilizations. (John L. Esposito. *The Islamic Threat: Myth or Reality?* 3rd ed. NY: Oxford, p. 289.)

Questions

1. Is the clash between the West and Islamism inevitable? Why or why not? What can be done to prevent this clash from turning into a new Cold War?
2. What are the major reasons for anti-Americanism in the Muslim world? What are the principal reasons for fear of Islamism in the United States? How can these two negative sentiments be reduced?

The West versus Islamism

Selected Readings

Mir Zohair Husain. *Global Islamic Politics,* 2nd ed. NY: Longman, 2003.

Samuel P. Huntington. *The Clash of Civilizations and the Remaking of World Order.* NY: Simon and Schuster, 1996.

Jobs in Nongovernmental Organizations

SUMMARY

Jobs in NGOs provide personally rewarding experiences for those willing to work hard for a cause, but pay poorly and are hard to obtain.

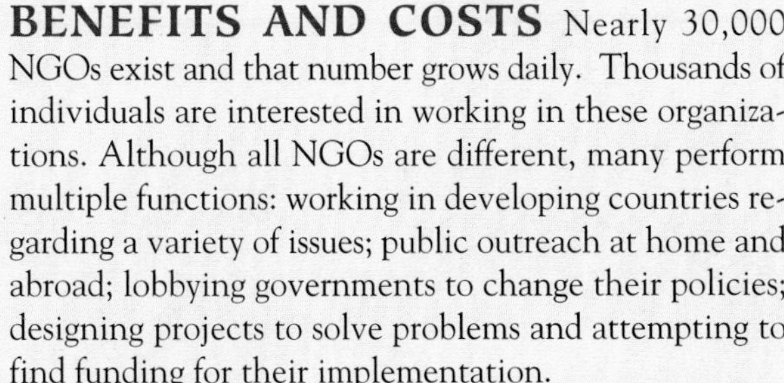

BENEFITS AND COSTS Nearly 30,000 NGOs exist and that number grows daily. Thousands of individuals are interested in working in these organizations. Although all NGOs are different, many perform multiple functions: working in developing countries regarding a variety of issues; public outreach at home and abroad; lobbying governments to change their policies; designing projects to solve problems and attempting to find funding for their implementation.

Working for an NGO has many benefits. Workers often find themselves surrounded by others concerned about the same issues: improving the environment, protecting human rights, advancing economic development, or promoting better health care. The spirit of camaraderie can be exhilarating and rewarding.

While working for an NGO can be extremely rewarding personally, it is rarely rewarding financially. Most NGOs are nonprofit operations that pay workers meagerly for long hours. Moreover, many smaller NGOs engage in a constant fight for funding from governments, think tanks, private foundations or individuals. The process of fundraising can be quite time consuming.

Despite the large number of NGOs, relatively low pay, and long hours, finding a job with an NGO can be difficult. One key is to be specific. Try to narrow down your interests in terms of substantive areas (e.g., human rights, environment) and/or geographic region. Also think about whether you want to work in your own country or abroad. Positions abroad may be more rewarding but are in lower supply and higher demand.

SKILLS TO HONE NGOs are looking for self-starters. Most have little time and few resources for training. Basic office skills (e.g., computer expertise) are essential, but employees also need to cover a range of duties every day. Anything and everything is in your job description. Writing and communication skills are key, especially when fundraising is part of the job. Foreign language skills also matter since many NGOs maintain or work with field offices abroad.

Often, NGOs ask potential employees to volunteer for a period while they train, before being hired. Increasingly, some companies place workers in an NGO or volunteer opportunity for a price. By paying to work, you can gain a probationary period, to develop your skills and familiarize yourself with the operation so as to become efficient before going on the payroll.

Finally, in cities where NGOs cluster (e.g., Washington DC) personal networks play an important role in finding good opportunities. Workers often move from one organization to another. For this reason, many volunteer or accept jobs with NGOs not in their immediate area of interest to gain experience and contacts, which can help future career advancement.

RESOURCES

Sherry Mueller. "Careers in Nonprofit and Educational Organizations" in *Careers in International Affairs*, 7th ed. Washington DC: Georgetown School of Foreign Service, 2003.

Richard M. King. *From Making a Profit to Making a Difference: How To Launch Your New Career In Nonprofits*. River Forest, IL: Planning/Communications, 2000.

www.internships-usa.com

www.idealist.org

www.wango.org/resources/NGO_directory.htm

■ Fighters in Sierra Leone, 2000.

CHAPTER 6

Military Force

The Use of Force

A state leader in a conflict bargaining situation can apply various kinds of leverage to reach a more favorable outcome (see Figure 6.1). One set of levers represents nonviolent means of influencing other states, such as foreign aid, economic sanctions, personal diplomacy, and so forth (less tangible means include use of norms, morality, and other ideas). A second set of levers—the subject of this chapter—represents violent actions. These levers set armies marching or missiles flying. In order to understand the decisions that leaders make about using military force, it is important to know how various military capabilities work, how much they cost, and what effects they have.

Violence as a means of leverage tends to be costly to both the attacker and the attacked. It is therefore not the most effective instrument in most situations: states can generally achieve their objectives in a more cost-effective way by using means of leverage such as economic actions (Chapters 8 and 9), foreign aid (Chapter 13), communication (Chapter 10), or international organizations (Chapter 7). Military force tends to be a last resort. There is also evidence that the utility of military force relative to nonmilitary means is slowly declining over time.

Yet most states still devote vast resources to military capabilities compared to other means of influence. For example, the United States has about 20,000 diplomatic personnel but 2 million soldiers; it spends about $20 billion a year on foreign aid but around $500 billion on military forces (the United States outspends the rest of the world combined on military forces).

The overall utility of military force in IR may be declining, but for the narrow purpose of repelling a military attack there is often no substitute for military means. Because of the security dilemma, states believe they must devote large resources to military capabilities if even only a few other states are doing so. The shocking attacks on the U.S. homeland in 2001 underscored many states' sense of insecurity and their need to maintain capable military forces.

Beyond defending their territories, states develop military capabilities for several other purposes. They often hope to *deter* attack by having the means to retaliate. They may also hope to *compel* other states to behave in certain ways, by threatening an attack if the state does not comply. The sizes and types of military forces make particular threats credible.[1]

States are increasingly using military forces for humanitarian assistance after disasters, surveillance of drug trafficking, and repression of domestic political dissent, among other missions. Peacekeeping operations (see pp. 265–269) are a growing specialization of certain military forces, and a focus of NATO's Partnership for Peace program (see p. 88).

[1] Worley, D. Robert. Shaping U.S. Military Forces: Revolution or Relevance in a Post-Cold War World. Westport, CT: Praeger, 2006.

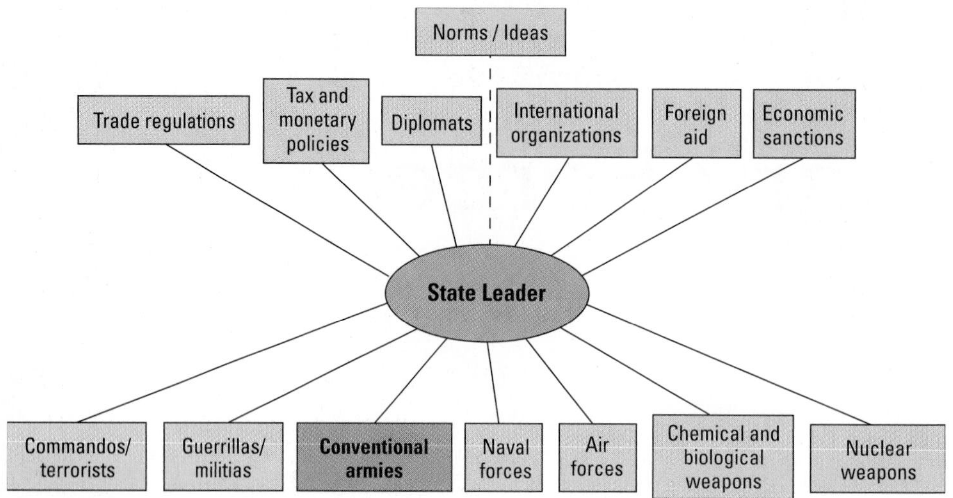

FIGURE 6.1 ■ Military and Nonmilitary Means of Leverage

Conventional armed force is the most commonly used military form of leverage.

Military capabilities are generally divided into two types: conventional forces and weapons of mass destruction (nuclear, chemical, and biological weapons). Almost all of the actual uses of military force to date have involved conventional forces. Weapons of mass destruction nonetheless come into play in international bargaining because even the implicit threat of their use is leverage. Although the superpower nuclear arms race has ended, the spread of weapons of mass destruction to new states and to nonstate actors is a grave concern.

You Are a U.S. President

This chapter discusses the various kinds of military forces used by state leaders. It first considers the major strategic concerns of state leaders in acquiring and maintaining military forces, especially in deciding how much to spend on military budgets. The chapter then considers the civil-military link that allows political leaders to control military forces to be used as leverage in international bargaining. Finally, the chapter sketches the variety of types of military forces that states maintain, including efforts to obtain weapons of mass destruction.[2]

Configuring Forces

Given the range of military capabilities available to states (at various costs), how should state leaders choose which to acquire?

Military Economics

Choices about military forces depend on the connection between a state's military spending and its economic health. Not long ago, it was widely believed in the United States that

[2] Art, Robert J., and Kenneth N. Waltz, eds. *The Use of Force: Military Power and International Politics*, 6th ed. Lanham, MD: Rowman & Littlefield, 2003.

"war is good for the economy" (seemingly, military spending had helped end the Great Depression in the late 1930s). If this were true, state leaders would not face difficult choices in setting military budgets. High military spending would give them both more military capabilities for use in international conflicts *and* more economic growth for domestic needs (buying popular and political support in various ways).

THE WAR IS OVER

U.S. and Russian nuclear forces were greatly reduced in the 1990s. Here, U.S. B-52 bombers are being chopped up, under the eye of Russian satellites, to bring force levels down.

Unfortunately for state leaders, the economics of military spending is not so favorable. In the long run, allocating economic resources for military purposes deprives the rest of the economy and reduces its growth. High-technology military development (using engineers, scientists, and technicians) tends to starve civilian sectors of talent and technology. Fewer jobs are created, per dollar of U.S. government funds, in the military than in education, housing, construction, and similar areas (military spending is more capital-intensive and less labor-intensive). Conversely, reductions in military spending tend to free up economic resources for more productive purposes and strengthen the growth of the economy in the long term. Thus, over the long term, state leaders face a trade-off between increasing their available military leverage and increasing their overall economic health. When the Cold War ended, U.S. leaders cut military spending to reap a peace dividend: more money for cities, education, the environment, and so forth.[3] The savings in the next decade, estimated at more than $100 billion, may not have changed those problems much, but did help reduce the U.S. budget deficit. U.S. citizens and politicians also began to demand that prosperous U.S. allies in Europe and Japan pay more for maintaining U.S. military forces there—a concept known as *burden sharing*. At the same time, Russia and the other former Soviet republics drastically curtailed military spending, which their tattered economies could not support. Russia's cuts in military spending did little to stop its economic free fall, however. There and throughout the former Soviet Union—and somewhat less desperately in the United States and the West—political leaders scrambled to develop plans for **economic conversion**—use of former military facilities and industries for new civilian production.[4]

Both the long- and short-term effects of military spending are magnified by actual warfare. War not only stimulates high military spending, it destroys capital (people, cities, farms, and factories in battle areas) and causes inflation (reducing the supply of various goods while increasing demand for them). Governments must pay for war goods by

[3] Gleditsch, Nils P., ed. *The Peace Dividend*. NY: Elsevier, 1996. Braddon, Derek. *Exploding the Myth?: The Peace Dividend, Regions, and Market Adjustment*. Amsterdam: Harwood, 2000.

[4] Defense Conversion Committee. *Adjusting to the Drawdown: Report of the Defense Conversion Committee*. Collingdale, PA: Diane, 2004. Weber, Rachel N. *Swords into Dow Shares: Governing the Decline of the Military-Industrial Complex*. Boulder, CO: Westview, 2001. Genin, Vlad E., ed. *The Anatomy of Russian Defense Conversion*. Walnut Creek, CA: Vega, 2000.

borrowing money (increasing government debt), by printing more currency (fueling inflation), or by raising taxes (reducing spending and investment). U.S. revolutionary Thomas Paine warned in 1787 that "war . . . has but one thing certain, and that is to increase taxes."[5]

Nonetheless, war and high military spending can have certain economic benefits. The short-term stimulation resulting from a boost in military spending has been mentioned. Another potential benefit is the acquisition of territory (containing resources and capital).[6] Serbian ultranationalists made fortunes off the plunder of Bosnians whom they "ethnically cleansed." Another potential economic benefit of war is to stir up a population's patriotism so that it will work harder for less pay. But overall, the benefits rarely equal the economic costs of war.

The Choice of Capabilities

WEB LINK
Choice of Capabilities

States vary widely in military spending, from Costa Rica, with virtually no military spending at all, to North Korea, which devotes 20 percent or more of all economic activity to military purposes. If military budgets are too low, states may be unprepared to meet a security threat; in the worst case, they may even be overrun and conquered militarily. But if leaders set military budgets too high, they will overburden the national economy in the long run. (So far, Costa Rica has not been attacked despite recent wars in neighboring Nicaragua and Panama, whereas North Korea is virtually bankrupt.)

In recent years, U.S. leaders have been rethinking military capabilities. The primary mission of U.S. armed forces during the Cold War was containing the Soviet Union, especially from attacking Western Europe, while keeping an eye on the Middle East and Southeast Asia. The Gulf War suggested a new type of mission based on the ability to deploy a large armed force to a regional conflict area.

In the 1990s, U.S. strategy called for the ability to fight two regional wars at once. In 2001, this goal was reduced to fighting one war at a time, to make resources available for high-technology weaponry and homeland defense, including ballistic missile defense (see p. 233).[7] Currently, U.S. policymakers envision smaller groups of conventional troops combined with special operations forces stationed around the world, armed with advanced weapons, which could be deployed very quickly in the event of a terrorist threat.

Meanwhile, other states reduced military spending in the 1990s—most dramatically in Russia and the other republics of the former Soviet Union. Although they tried to reduce military spending as quickly as possible, there were no jobs for laid-off soldiers and military-industrial workers and no housing for troops brought home from Eastern Europe. In 2004, however, Russia began stepping up military activities, conducting the largest navy exercise in 20 years and beginning to test new antimissile systems in response to the U.S. withdrawal from the ABM Treaty.

The cutbacks are less dramatic in Western Europe, where NATO members spend several percent of GDP on military forces. In Japan, where military spending was already only 1 percent of GDP, dramatic cutbacks are not in the works. In China, military spending does not affect economic growth greatly because the army is largely self-supporting

---

[5] Paine, Thomas. *The Writings of Thomas Paine*. Vol. 2. NY: Knickerbocker, 1894.

[6] Liberman, Peter. *Does Conquest Pay? The Exploitation of Occupied Industrial Societies*. Princeton, 1996.

[7] O'Hanlon, Michael E. *Defense Policy Choices for the Bush Administration 2001–05*. Washington, DC: Brookings, 2001. Wilson, George C. *This War Really Matters: Inside the Fight for Defense Dollars*. Washington, DC: CQ, 2000.

THINKING THEORETICALLY

The Superpower Arms Race

During the Cold War, the superpowers poured money into military budgets, at rates ranging from 5 to 10 percent of GDP for the United States and perhaps 20 percent for the Soviet Union. What theories can explain the superpowers' military spending levels, as well as the sharp decreases in military spending in the 1990s?

One approach is based on reciprocity (see pp. 66–68). Each superpower responds to the other's military spending by raising or lowering its own military budget in the next time period. From this perspective, the superpower arms race may fit the model of a repeated Prisoner's Dilemma, in which the two players use reciprocity to make sure that the other side's defections do not pay. As in laboratory experiments in which college students play PD repeatedly, both sides eventually learn to get out of the cycle of mutual defection (the spiraling arms race), and lock into stable cooperation. This could explain the recent sharp decrease in military spending.

An alternative model has each superpower's military spending domestically driven. This would follow from ideas such as the organizational process model of foreign policy (see p. 142) and the power of the military-industrial complex (see pp. 154–156). The recent decreases in military spending would probably then be best explained by internal economic problems in both superpowers.

Hundreds of research studies have tried to test these models against the empirical evidence provided by 40 years of military budgets. Typically, they use a mathematical model of the arms race, and then use quantitative data on arms spending to test statistically whether the model explains the data well. The statistical test shows how well, on average, a country's military spending correlates with the other country's previous spending.

So which theory is supported by these tests? The answer is that neither can be evaluated with much confidence because the quantitative data on military spending are unreliable. Not only did both superpowers conceal military spending (and even military activity from which spending levels might be inferred), but comparing the two was problematical. Costs of weapons and salaries were very different in the two countries; the soldiers and equipment were not of comparable quality; rubles were not convertible into dollars; and macroeconomic indicators such as GDP were not compatible across communist and capitalist economies. As a result, no one could say for sure if Soviet military spending was going up or down in a given year, or whether Soviet spending was more or less than U.S. spending. Some research studies found ways around some of these problems, but overall the arms race models have been more useful as purely theoretical models than as testable propositions about the real Cold War arms race.

Thus, military spending can be explained by at least two good theories—good in the sense that they can explain the outcome in terms of a general model with implications for other cases—and neither model can be ruled out by empirical evidence. Note that both the reciprocity model and the domestically driven model have liberal underpinnings, though they operate at different levels of analysis (interstate and domestic). Do conservative or revolutionary world views suggest to you other models that explain military spending levels, beyond these two?

(running its own farms, factories, etc.)—which also makes Chinese military spending hard to calculate. Chinese military forces underwent substantial reduction, along with modernization, in the 1980s and 1990s. Because it lags in technology, China's army remains the weakest of the great-power militaries, but Chinese capabilities are growing quickly.

Great powers continue to dominate the makeup of world military forces. Table 6.1 summarizes the most important forces of the great powers. Together, they account for two-thirds of world military spending, a third of the world's soldiers, about 50 percent of the weapons, 99 percent of nuclear weapons, and 90 percent of arms exports. The table also

TABLE 6.1 ■ Estimated Great-Power Military Capabilities, 2001–2003

			Heavy Weapons[a]				
	Military Expenditures[b] (Billions of US $)	Soldiers[c] (Millions)	Tanks	Carriers/ Warships/ Submarines	Combat Airplanes	Nuclear Weapons[d]	Arms Exported[e] (Billions of US $)
United States	460	1.4	10,000	11 / 112 / 74	3,600	10,000*	14
Russia	10–20*	1.5	20,000*	1 / 40 / 69	1,800	20,000*	4
China	35	2.8	10,000	0 / 29 / 6	2,100*	410	1
France	35	0.3	1,000	0 / 19 / 12	300	350	1
Britain	40	0.2	1,000	0 / 35 / 16	300	185	5
Germany	30	0.2	3,000	0 / 14 / 0	400	0	1
Japan	50	0.2	1,000	0 / 39 / 20	300	0	0
Approximate % of world total	70%	30%	25%	100 / 60 / 50%	40%	99%	85%

Notes: Data are for 2003 unless otherwise noted, and are in 2004 dollars. In the 1990s, the military forces of many of these states—Russia above all—were profoundly restructured. Numbers of weapons or soldiers do not indicate quality (levels of technology) or predict how armed forces would actually perform in combat. Russian forces are disorganized and in disrepair, with rampant desertion, nonoperational equipment, and low morale. Chinese forces are lower-tech than the others. Expenditure data are notoriously unreliable for Russia and China.

Data on soldiers exclude reserves. Tanks include only main battle tanks. Warships are major surface combat ships over 3,000 tons. Nuclear warheads include both strategic and tactical weapons. Arms exports are deliveries, not orders, for 2003.

*Problematic data: Russian military expenditure estimates vary. Many Chinese aircraft and Russian tanks are old and of limited military use. U.S. and Russian nuclear warheads include deployed strategic weapons (6,000 U.S., 6,000 Russian) with the remainder held in reserve or retired (awaiting destruction).

Sources: Author's estimates based on data provided by the Institute for Defense and Disarmament Studies (IDDS). Cambridge, MA. Main sources are:[a] 2001 data from IDDS World Arms Database 2001 (www.idds.org):[b] SIPRI Yearbook 2003. Not adjusted for purchasing power parity.[c] Institute for International and Strategic Studies. *The Military Balance 2001–2002;* 299–304:[d] Carnegie Endowment for International Peace (www.ceip.org).[e] Richard F. Grimmett. *Conventional Arms Transfers to Developing Nations. 1993–2003* (Washington, DC: Congressional Research Service, 2004).

indicates the sizable military forces maintained by Germany and Japan despite their nontraditional roles in international security affairs since World War II.

In the global South, military spending varies greatly across countries, depending in part on the government in power (military or civilian).[8] Spending also depends heavily on available hard currency, from exports of oil or other products to pay for arms purchases.

Arms imports by states of the global South make up more than half of all arms sales. In recent years, about half of the South's arms imports have been in the Middle East, where oil exports create a ready source of funding, but in 2004 India and China took a larger share. Of all international arms exports, a third come from the United States, with Russia and Britain ranked next. Globally, arms sales have declined in the post–Cold War era.[9]

Activists have called attention to the sales of small arms, especially assault rifles, to unstable conflict zones where irregular armies commit brutalities. Of the $4 billion in small arms and ammunition produced in 2000, U.S. exports accounted for $1.2 billion (followed by Germany with $400 million, then Russia and Brazil with $100 million each). In 2001, 140 states agreed to a voluntary pact to curb small-arms sales to conflict zones. The United States blocked proposals to restrict sales of military weapons to rebel movements and to civilians. A follow-up UN conference is planned for 2006.[10]

World military spending decreased by about one-third overall in the 1990s, although it began to increase again after 1998 and jumped back up after 2001. World military spending is about 2 percent of the total goods and services in the world economy—about $800 billion every year, or roughly $1 million every 40 seconds. Most is spent by a few big states, nearly half by the United States alone. World military spending is a vast flow of money that could, if redirected to other purposes, change the world profoundly and improve major world problems.[11] Of course, "the world" does not spend this money or choose how to direct it; states do.

Beyond these considerations about the size of military forces, the configuration of a state's military forces also presents difficult choices. Different missions require different forces. During the Cold War, about half of all military spending in the U.S. budget—and of world military spending—was directed toward the East-West conflict in Europe. Now other missions such as intervention in regional conflicts are more important.[12] And other new missions for military forces include humanitarian assistance, drug interdiction, and aid to other nations in building roads and schools.

Whatever configuration of military forces a state maintains, the leaders of the state face ongoing decisions about when and how to use those forces.

---

[8] Graham, Norman A., ed. *Seeking Security and Development: The Impact of Military Spending and Arms Transfers*. Boulder, CO: Lynne Rienner, 1994. Singh, Ravinder Pal, ed. *Arms Procurement Decision-Making Processes: China, India, Israel, Japan, and South Korea*. NY: Oxford/SIPRI, 1997. Gill, Bates, and J. N. Mak, eds. *Arms Trade, Transparency, and Security in South-East Asia*. NY: Oxford/SIPRI, 1997.

[9] Grimmett, Richard F. *Conventional Arms Transfers to Developing Nations, 1995–2002*. Washington, DC: Congressional Research Service, 2003. Forsberg, Randall, ed. *The Arms Production Dilemma: Contraction and Restraint in the World Combat Aircraft Industry*. MIT, 1994. Keller, William W. *Arm in Arm: The Political Economy of the Global Arms Trade*. NY: Basic Books, 1995.

[10] See http://www.controlarms.org/. Boutwell, Jeffrey, and Michael T. Klare. *Light Weapons and Civil Conflict: Controlling the Tools of Violence*. Lanham, MD: Rowman & Littlefield, 1999.

[11] Forsberg, Randall, Robert Elias, and Matthew Goodman. Peace Issues and Strategies. In *Institute for Defense and Disarmament Studies. Peace Resource Book 1986*. Cambridge, MA: Ballinger, 1985, pp. 5–13.

[12] Hoffman, Peter J. and Thomas G. Weiss. *Sword and Salve: Confronting New Wars and Humanitarian Crises*. Lanham, MD: Rowman & Littlefield, 2006. Feste, Karen A. *Intervention: Shaping the Global Order*. Westport, CT: Praeger, 2003. MacFarlane, S. Neil. *Intervention in Contemporary World Politics*. Oxford, 2002. Haass, Richard N. *Intervention: The Use of American Military Force in the Post–Cold War World*. rev. ed. Washington, DC: Brookings, 1999.

Control of Military Forces

The first issue of concern to a state leader in pulling a lever to exert influence is whether the lever is attached to anything. That is, how are the decisions of leaders translated into actual actions in distant locations that carry out the leaders' plans?

Command

Command

The use of military force generally requires the coordination of the efforts of thousands, sometimes millions, of individuals performing many different functions in many locations. Such coordination is what is meant by *command*. One cannot take for granted the ability of a state leader to make military forces take desired actions. At best, military forces are large and complex institutions, operating in especially difficult conditions during wartime. At worst, military forces have a mind of their own (see pp. 222–224). Sometimes, the state leader appears to exert only incomplete control over the military.

States control military forces through a **chain of command** running from the highest authority through a hierarchy spreading out to the lowest-level soldiers. The highest authority, or commander in chief, is usually the top political leader—the U.S. president, Russian president, and so forth. The military hierarchy consists of levels of officers.

The value of this military hierarchy is illustrated by a story from ancient China in which a king was thinking of hiring Sun Tzu (see pp. 55–56, 68–70) as an adviser. As a test, the king asked Sun Tzu if he could turn his harem of 200 concubines into troops. Sun Tzu divided them into two units, commanded by the king's two favorites. He explained the signals to face forward, backward, right, and left. But when he gave the signals, the women just laughed. Sun Tzu then had the two "officers" executed on the spot and put the next most senior concubines in their places. When he gave the signals again, the women obeyed flawlessly. Sun Tzu declared that "the troops are in good order and may be deployed as the King desires." Thus, military hierarchy and discipline make armed forces function as instruments of state power.

In actual conditions of battle, controlling armed forces is especially difficult because of complex operations, rapid change, and the fog of war created by the gap between battlefield activity and command-level information. Participants are pumped up with adrenaline, deafened by noise, and confused by a mass of activity that—from the middle of it—may seem to make no sense. They are called on to perform actions that may run against basic instincts as well as moral norms—killing people and risking death. It is difficult to coordinate forces effectively in order to carry out overall plans of action.

These factors reduce the effectiveness of military forces as instruments of state power. But military forces have developed several means for counteracting these problems. First is the principle of military discipline. Orders given from higher levels of the hierarchy must be obeyed by the lower levels—whether or not those at the lower level agree. Failure to do so is insubordination, or a mutiny if a whole group is involved. Leaving one's unit is called deserting. These are serious offenses punishable by prison or death.

But discipline depends not only on punishment but also on patriotism and professionalism on the part of soldiers. Officers play to nationalist sentiments, reminding soldiers that they fight for their nation and family. No military force is better than the soldiers and officers that make it up. Combat, logistics, communication, and command all depend on individual performance; motivation matters.

Whatever the motivation of soldiers, they require training in order to function as instruments of state power. Military training includes both technical training and training in the habit of obeying commands—a central purpose of basic training in every military force. Soldiers are deliberately stripped of their individuality—hair styles, clothes, habits, and mannerisms—to become part of a group. This action has both good and bad effects for the individuals, but it works for the purposes of the military. Then in exercises, soldiers practice over and over until certain operations become second nature.

Through a hierarchical chain of command, states control the actions of millions of individual soldiers, creating effective leverage in the hands of state leaders. Here, Chinese women soldiers march in a military parade, Guangzhou, 1991.

To maintain control of forces in battle, military units also rely on soldiers' sense of group solidarity. Soldiers risk their lives because their "buddies" depend on them.[13] Abstractions such as nationalism, patriotism, or religious fervor are important, but loyalty to the immediate group (along with a survival instinct) is a stronger motivator. Recent debates about participation of women and homosexuals in the U.S. armed forces revolve around whether their presence disrupts group solidarity. (Evidence, though sparse, suggests that it need not.)

Troops operating in the field also rely on logistical support in order to function effectively. For states to use military leverage, they must support those armies with large quantities of supplies. Leaders in Prussia (Germany) more than a century ago used well-oiled logistics based on railroads to rapidly defeat both Austria and France.

Homosexuals in the Military

A further difficulty that states must overcome to use military forces effectively is that top officers and political leaders need accurate information about what is going on in the field—intelligence—to make good decisions.[14] They also need extensive communications networks, including the ability to use codes to ensure secrecy. Such functions are known as "command and control" or sometimes C3I—for command, control, communications, and intelligence. This information side of controlling military forces has become ever more important. In the 1991 Gulf War, a top U.S. priority was to target Iraqi communications facilities so as to disable Iraq's command and control. Meanwhile, the U.S. side used computers, satellite reconnaissance, and other information technologies to amplify its effectiveness.

---

[13] Bourke, Joanna. *An Intimate History of Killing: Face-to-Face Killing in Twentieth-Century Warfare*. NY: Basic, 1999. Grossman, Dave. *On Killing: The Psychological Cost of Learning to Kill in War and Society*. Boston: Little Brown, 1995. Holmes, Richard. *Acts of War: The Behavior of Men in Battle*. NY: Free Press, 1985. Kellett, Anthony. The Soldier in Battle: Motivational and Behavioral Aspects of the Combat Experience. In Glad, Betty, ed. *Psychological Dimensions of War*. Newbury Park, CA: Sage, 1990, pp. 215–35. Fussell, Paul. *Wartime: Understanding and Behavior in the Second World War*. Oxford, 1989. Gray, J. Glenn. *The Warriors: Reflections on Men in Battle*. NY: Harper & Row, 1967 [1959].

[14] Lowenthal, Mark M. *Intelligence: From Secrets to Policy*. Washington, DC: CQ, 2000. Richelson, Jeffery T. *A Century of Spies: Intelligence in the Twentieth Century*. Oxford, 1995.

Of course, even the most advanced intelligence systems cannot stop human error. "Friendly fire" incidents account for a substantial fraction of U.S. military fatalities, such as that of football-player-turned-soldier Pat Tillman in Afghanistan in 2004. As another example, in late 2001, U.S. special forces were traveling with Hamid Karzai, arguably the only person who could lead a united, U.S.-allied Afghan government (which indeed he went on to do). As a U.S. soldier called in air strikes on an enemy position, the battery in his GPS unit (see p. 228) needed changing, and its coordinates defaulted to the unit's own position. A U.S. warplane dropped a bomb right on that target, killing three U.S. soldiers, five Afghan allies, and nearly killing Karzai himself. (In late 2004 Karzai was elected president in Afghanistan's first democratic election.)

States and Militaries

Overcoming chaos and complexity is only part of the task for state leaders seeking to control military forces. Sometimes they must overcome their own military officers as well. Although militaries are considered instruments of state power, in many states the military forces themselves control the government. These **military governments** are most common in poor countries, where the military may be the only large modern institution in the country.

Military leaders are able to exercise political control because the same violent forms of leverage that work internationally also work domestically. In fact, domestically there may be little or no counterleverage to the use of military force. Military officers thus have an inherent power advantage over civilian political leaders. Ironically, the disciplined central command of military forces, which makes them effective as tools of state influence, also lets the state lose control of them to military officers. Soldiers are trained to follow the orders of their commanding officers, not to think about politics.

A **coup d'état** (French for "blow against the state") is the seizure of political power by domestic military forces—a change of political power outside the state's constitutional order.[15] Coups are often mounted by ambitious junior officers against the top generals. Officers who thus break the chain of command can take along with them the sections of the military hierarchy below them. Coup leaders move quickly to seize centers of power—official state buildings as well as television stations and transmitters—before other units of the military can put down the coup attempt or unleash a civil war. Civilian politicians in power and uncooperative military officers are arrested or killed. The coup leaders try to create a sense of inevitability around the change in government while claiming their actions will bring long-term stability. For example, after overthrowing Haitian President Aristide, General Raoul Cedras proclaimed, "The Army is steering the ship of state into port."

The outcome of a coup is hard to predict. If most or all of the military go along with the coup, civilian leaders are generally helpless to stop it. But if most of the military officers follow the existing chain of command, the coup is doomed. In the Philippines in the late 1980s, the top general, Fidel Ramos, remained loyal to the civilian president, Corazón Aquino, in seven coup attempts by subordinate officers. In each case, the bulk of the Philippine military forces stayed loyal to Ramos, and the coups failed. In 1992, Ramos himself was elected president with the backing of a grateful Aquino.

---

[15] Feaver, Peter D., and Richard D. Kohn, eds. *Soldiers and Civilians*. MIT, 2001. Choi, Seung-Whan and Patrick James. *Civil-Military Dynamics, Democracy, and International Conflict: A New Quest for International Peace*. NY: Palgrave, 2005. Avant, Deborah. *The Market for Force: The Consequences of Privatizing Security*. Cambridge, 2005. Carlton, Eric. *The State Against the State: The Theory and Practice of the Coup d'etat*. Brookfield, VT: Ashgate, 1997.

Coups may also be put down by an outside military force. A government threatened with a coup may call on foreign friends for military assistance. But because coups are considered largely an internal affair—and because they are over so quickly—direct foreign intervention in them is relatively rare. One exception to this rule occurred in 1996, when Paraguay's larger neighbors—Brazil and Argentina—placed heavy pressure on a general to cease an attempted coup against Paraguay's president.

HIGHLY IRREGULAR

A coup is a change of government carried out by domestic military forces operating outside the state's constitution. The number of military governments is declining, but dozens remain. Pakistan's military government took power in a 1999 coup and became a key U.S. ally in fighting Taliban-ruled Afghanistan in 2001. Here, soldiers deploy to the provincial legislature in Lahore after the coup.

Military governments often have difficulty gaining popular legitimacy for their rule because their power is clearly based on force rather than popular mandate, although the public may support the new regime if the old one was viewed as unstable or incompetent. To stay in power, both military and civilian governments require at least passive acceptance by their people. In relatively new democracies, support from key elite groups such as business leaders and military officers is especially important.

Even in nonmilitary governments, the interaction of civilian with military leaders—called civil-military relations—is an important factor in how states use force. Military leaders may undermine the authority of civilian leaders in carrying out foreign policies, or they may even threaten a coup if certain actions are taken in international conflicts.

NATO forces operate under strong *civilian control*. However, military desires continue to run counter to civilian decisions at times. After the Vietnam War, top U.S. military officers became more reluctant to send U.S. forces into combat. The Pentagon generally supported using military force only when there was a clear goal that could be achieved militarily, when the public supported the action, and when military forces could be used massively for a quick victory. Panama in 1989, Kuwait in 1991, and Afghanistan in 2001 fit these new conditions. The occupation of Iraq generally did not, but U.S. forces are there anyway.

Military officers also want autonomy of decision once force is committed, in order to avoid the problems created in the Vietnam War when President Johnson sat in the White House situation room daily picking targets for bombing raids. In NATO's 1999 bombing of Serbia, specific targets had to be approved by politicians in multiple countries.

Covert operations are the dagger part of the "cloak and dagger" spy business. Several thousand such operations were mounted during the Cold War, when the CIA and its Soviet counterpart, the KGB, waged an ongoing worldwide secret war. CIA covert operations in the 1950s overthrew unfriendly foreign governments—in Iran and Guatemala—by organizing coups against them. The CIA-organized Bay of Pigs invasion in Cuba, in 1961, was its first big failure, followed by other failed efforts against the Castro government (including eight assassination attempts). CIA covert activities were sharply scaled back after congressional hearings in the 1970s revealed scandals. Such covert operations now must be reported to special congressional *oversight* committees through an elaborate set of procedures. After September 2001, the executive branch enjoyed greater authority in conducting covert operations with less congressional scrutiny, although the limits of executive authority remain uncertain.

The traditions of civil-military relations in a state do not necessarily reflect the extent of democracy there. States in which civilians traditionally have trouble controlling the military include some with long histories of democracy, notably in Latin America. And states with strong traditions of civilian control over military forces include some authoritarian states such as the former Soviet Union (where the Communist party controlled the military).

The tradition of civilian (Communist party) control of the military in China is more ambiguous. Regional military leaders coordinate their activities through the Central Military Commission, under direction of the Communist party. But during the Cultural Revolution in the 1960s, and again in the Tiananmen protests in 1989, military forces essentially held power at times of internal splits in the party. Both Mao Zedong and Deng Xiaoping made it a point to control the Military Commission personally.

No matter how firmly state leaders control the military forces at their disposition, those forces are effective only if they are equipped and trained for the purposes the state leaders have in mind.

Conventional Forces

The bargaining power of states depends not only on the overall size of their military forces but on the particular capabilities of those forces in various scenarios. State leaders almost always turn to conventional military forces for actual missions, reserving weapons of mass destruction for making or deterring threats.

If a leader decides that an international conflict could be more favorably settled by applying military force, it matters a great deal whether the application involves bombing another state's capital city, imposing a naval blockade, or seizing disputed territory. Armed forces can apply negative leverage at a distance, but various types of forces have evolved over time for different situations and contexts—on water, on land, or in the air.[16] They match up against each other in particular ways. A tank cannot destroy a submarine, nor vice versa.

Types of Forces

Whatever their ultimate causes and objectives, most wars involve a struggle to *control territory*. Territory holds a central place in warfare because of its importance in the international system, and vice versa. Borders define where a state's own military forces and rival states' military forces are free to move. Military logistics make territoriality all the more important because of the need to control territories connecting military forces with each other. An army's supplies must flow from home territory along *supply lines* to the field. In the 2003 Iraq war, a major challenge for U.S. forces was to secure supply lines hundreds of miles into Iraq. Thus the most fundamental purpose of conventional forces is to take, hold, or defend territory.

[16] Keegan, John. *A History of Warfare*. NY: Random House, 1993. Van Creveld, Martin. *Technology and War: From 2000 B.C. to the Present*. NY: Free Press, 1989. Luttwak, Edward, and Stuart L. Koehl. *The Dictionary of Modern War*. NY: HarperCollins, 1991. Gat, Azar. *A History of Military Thought: From the Enlightenment to the Cold War*. Oxford, 2001.

Armies *Armies* are adapted to this purpose. Infantry soldiers armed with automatic rifles can generally control a local piece of territory. Military forces with such a presence occupy a territory militarily. Although inhabitants may make the soldiers' lives unhappy through violent or nonviolent resistance, generally only another organized, armed military force can displace occupiers.

Foot soldiers are called the **infantry.** They use assault rifles and other light weapons (such as mines and machine guns) as well as heavy artillery of various types. Artillery is extremely destructive and not very discriminating: it usually causes the most damage and casualties in wars. Armor refers to tanks and armored vehicles. In open terrain, such as desert, mechanized ground forces typically combine armor, artillery, and infantry. In close terrain, such as jungles and cities, however, foot soldiers are more important.

For this reason, the armies of industrialized states have a greater advantage over poor armies in open conventional warfare, such as in the Kuwaiti desert. In jungle, mountain, or urban warfare, however—as in Afghan mountains and Iraqi cities—such advantages are eroded, and a cheaper and more lightly armed force of motivated foot soldiers or guerrillas may ultimately prevail over an expensive conventional army. In Afghanistan in 2001, where rugged terrain would have slowed U.S. ground forces, the high-tech U.S. military let low-tech Afghan soldiers on foot and horseback do the fighting on the ground. (However, they failed to capture the al Qaeda leadership.)

INVISIBLE KILLERS

Land mines continue to kill and maim civilians long after wars end. A movement to ban land mines culminated in a 1997 treaty signed by more than 100 countries (not including the United States or China). Britain's Princess Diana, shown here with Angolan mine victims in 1997, was a major supporter of the movement, and her death in 1997 helped galvanize support for the treaty.

Land mines are simple, small, and cheap containers of explosives with a trigger activated by contact or sensor. These mines were a particular focus of public attention in the 1990s because in places such as Angola, Afghanistan, Cambodia, and Bosnia they were used extensively by irregular military forces that never disarmed them. Long after such a war ends, land mines continue to maim and kill civilians who try to reestablish their lives in former war zones. As many as 100 million land mines remain from recent wars; they injure about 25,000 people a year (a third of whom are children); although they are cheap to deploy, it costs about $1,000 per mine to find and disarm them.

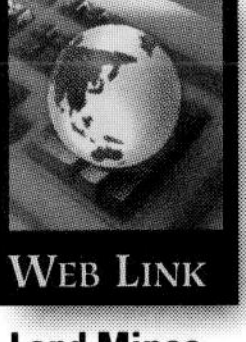

Land Mines

Public opinion and NGOs have pressured governments to restrict the use of land mines. After the death in 1997 of Britain's Princess Diana, who had actively supported the campaign, a treaty to ban land mines was signed by more than 100 countries at a 1997 conference organized by Canada. Russia and Japan signed on shortly afterward, but not China or the United States (which said mines would be needed to slow any North Korean invasion of South Korea). By 2005, 40 million land mines had been destroyed under the treaty, with 69 countries eliminating their stockpiles. A new norm seems to be emerging but its effect on actual military practice is not yet clear.

Navies *Navies* are adapted primarily to control passage through the seas and to attack land near coastlines.[17] Controlling the seas in wartime allows states to move their own goods and military forces by sea while preventing enemies from doing so. In particular, navies protect sealift logistical support. Navies can also blockade enemy ports. For most of the 1990s, Western navies enforced a naval blockade against Iraq.

Aircraft carriers—mobile platforms for attack aircraft—are instruments of **power projection** that can exert negative leverage against virtually any state in the world. Merely sending an aircraft carrier sailing to the vicinity of an international conflict implies a threat to use force—a modern version of what was known in the nineteenth century as "gunboat diplomacy." For example, in 1996 the United States dispatched two carriers to the Taiwan area when Chinese war games there threatened to escalate.

Aircraft carriers are extremely expensive and typically require 20 to 25 supporting ships for protection and supply. Few states can afford even one. Only the United States currently operates large carriers (12 of them, costing more than $5 billion each). Eight other countries (France, India, Russia, Spain, Brazil, Italy, Thailand, and the United Kingdom) maintain smaller carriers that use helicopters or small airplanes.

Surface ships, which account for the majority of warships, rely increasingly on guided missiles and are in turn vulnerable to attack by missiles (fired from ships, planes, submarines, or land). Since the ranges of small missiles now reach from dozens to hundreds of miles, naval warfare emphasizes detection at great distances without being detected oneself—a cat-and-mouse game of radar surveillance and electronic countermeasures.

Marines (part of the navy in the United States, Britain, and Russia) move to battle in ships but fight on land—amphibious warfare. Marines are also useful for great-power intervention in distant conflicts where they can insert themselves quickly and establish local control. In the 1992–1993 intervention in Somalia, U.S. Marines were already waiting offshore while the UN Security Council was debating whether to authorize the use of force.

Air Forces *Air forces* serve several distinct purposes—strategic bombing of land or sea targets; "close air support" (battlefield bombing); interception of other aircraft; reconnaissance; and airlift of supplies, weapons, and troops. Missiles—whether fired from air, land, or sea—are increasingly important. Air forces have developed various means to try to fool such missiles, with mixed results. In the Soviet war in Afghanistan, the U.S.-made portable Stinger missile used by guerrillas took a heavy toll on the Soviet air force. In 2003, the threat from shoulder-fired missiles kept Baghdad airport closed to commercial traffic for more than a year after U.S. forces arrived.

Traditionally, and still to a large extent, aerial bombing resembles artillery shelling in that it causes great destruction with little discrimination. This has changed as smart bombs improve accuracy. For instance, laser-guided bombs follow a sensor pointed at the target from the air or ground. Other bombs use GPS nagivation to hit targets through clouds, smoke, or sandstorms. Most of the bombing in the 1991 Gulf War was high-altitude saturation bombing using large numbers of dumb bombs. In typical wars, such as Russia's 1995 Chechnya War, bombing of cities causes high civilian casualties. But in the 2003 Iraq War, the massive air campaign early in the war entirely used smart bombs, hitting far more targets with fewer bombs. Even so, many thousands of civilians apparently died in U.S. air strikes in Iraq in 2003 and 2004.[18]

---

[17] Keegan, John. *The Price of Admiralty: The Evolution of Naval Warfare*. NY: Viking, 1988.

[18] Roberts, Les et al. Mortality Before and After the 2003 Invasion of Iraq: Cluster Sample Survey. *The Lancet* 364, Nov. 20, 2004: 1857–64.

In cases of low-intensity conflicts and guerrilla wars, especially where forces intermingle with civilians in closed terrain such as Vietnamese jungles or Iraqi cities, bombing is of limited utility—although it was extremely effective in Afghanistan in 2001.

PROJECTING POWER

Different types of military forces are adapted to different purposes. Aircraft carriers are used for power projection in distant regions, such as in the recent Afghanistan and Iraq campaigns.

Even more than ships, aircraft rely heavily on electronics, especially radar. The best-equipped air forces have specialized AWACS (Airborne Warning and Control System) airplanes to survey a large area with radar and coordinate the movements of dozens of aircraft. The increasing sophistication of electronic equipment and high performance requirements of attack aircraft make air forces expensive—totally out of reach for some states. Thus, rich states have huge advantages over poor ones in air warfare. Despite the expense, air superiority is often the key to the success of ground operations, especially in open terrain.

The U.S. bombing of Iraq (1991 and 2003), Serbia (1999), and Afghanistan (2001) demonstrated a new effectiveness of air power, applied not against the morale of enemy populations (as in World War II), but directly targeted from afar at battlefield positions. After enduring weeks of bombing, Iraqi soldiers in 1991 surrendered at the first chance, and Taliban forces crumbled in the face of smaller and weaker opposition armies. The U.S. ability to decimate distant military forces while taking only very light casualties is historically unique. The 2003 Iraq War demonstrated the usefulness of air power, but also its limits. A massive precision bombing raid on Baghdad a few days into the war destroyed hundreds of targets of value to Saddam Hussein's government. It was designed to "shock and awe" enemy commanders into giving up. However, U.S. forces still had to fight it out on the ground to get to Baghdad. Clearly this was one war that could not have been won from the air. As ground soldiers have pointed out, "nobody ever surrendered to an airplane."[19]

Logistics and Intelligence All military operations rely heavily on logistical support such as food, fuel, and ordnance (weapons and ammunition). Military logistics are a huge operation, and in most armed forces the majority of soldiers are not combat troops. Before the Gulf War, the United States moved an army of half a million people and a vast quantity of supplies to Saudi Arabia in a six-month effort that was the largest military logistical operation in such a time frame in history.

[19] Pape, Robert A. The True Worth of Air Power. *Foreign Affairs* 83 (2), 2004: 116–131.

TABLE 6.2 ■ Location of U.S. Military Forces, December 2005

Region	Personnel	Distribution of forces abroad
United States	1,106,000	—
Western Europe	99,500	24%
Japan/Pacific	80,000	19%
Russia/E. Europe	2,500	1%
Middle East	232,700	56%
Latin America	2,000	0%
Africa	1,600	0%
Total abroad	418,000	100%

Note: Totals include personnel afloat in the region.
Data source: U.S. Department of Defense.

Global reach capabilities combine long-distance logistical support with various power projection forces.[20] These capabilities allow a great power to project military power to distant corners of the world and to maintain a military presence in most of the world's regions simultaneously. Only the United States today fully possesses such a capability—with worldwide military alliances, air and naval bases, troops stationed overseas, and aircraft carriers plying the world's oceans (see Table 6.2). Britain and France are in a distant second place, able to mount occasional distant operations of modest size such as the Falkland Islands War. Russia is preoccupied with internal conflicts and its CIS neighbors, and China's military forces are oriented toward regional conflicts and are not global in scope (although they are currently attempting to build a navy capable of better power projection).

Space forces are military forces designed to attack in or from outer space.[21] Ballistic missiles, which travel through space briefly, are not generally included in this category. Only the United States and Russia have substantial military capabilities in space. China put an astronaut in orbit in 2003, but it has fewer space capabilities overall. The development of space weapons has been constrained by the technical challenges and expenses of space operations, and by norms against militarizing space. U.S. policy makers in 2001 announced a plan to begin testing space-based lasers (for intercepting ballistic missiles) in several years.

Satellites are used extensively for military purposes, but these purposes thus far do not include attack. Satellites perform military surveillance and mapping, communications, weather assessment, and early warning of ballistic missile launches (some U.S. satellites are accurate enough to read license plates on cars). Satellites also provide navigational information to military forces—army units, ships, planes, and even guided missiles in flight. Analysts pore over masses of satellite reconnaissance data every day in Washington, DC, and other capitals. Poorer states can buy satellite photos on the commercial market—including high-resolution pictures that Russia sells for hard currency.

Locations are calculated to within about 50 feet by small receivers, which pick up beacons transmitted from a network of 18 U.S. satellites known as a *Global Positioning System* (GPS). Handheld receivers are available commercially, so the military forces of other countries can ride free on these satellite navigation beacons. But, in general, outer space is

[20] Harkavy, Robert E. *Bases Abroad: The Global Foreign Military Presence*. Oxford, 1989.

[21] Preston, Bob, ed. *Space Weapons: Earth Wars*. Santa Monica, CA: Rand, 2002. Jasani, Bhupendra, ed. *Space Weapons and International Security*. Oxford, 1987.

an area in which great powers have great advantages over smaller or poorer states. For instance, U.S. forces in Afghanistan in 2001 took extensive advantage of satellite reconnaissance, communications, and navigation in defeating Taliban and al Qaeda forces.

Intelligence gathering also relies on various other means such as electronic monitoring of telephone lines and other communications, reports from embassies, and information in the open press. Some kinds of information are obtained by sending agents into foreign countries as spies. They use ingenuity (plus money and technology) to penetrate walls of secrecy that foreign governments have constructed around their plans and capabilities. For example, in 1999 a Russian spy taped conversations from a listening device planted in a high-level conference room at the U.S. State Department. The 2001 terrorist attacks showed weakness in U.S. "human intelligence" capabilities. The United States had not penetrated a large terrorist network based in Afghanistan and operating globally.[22]

In 2001, a U.S. reconnaissance airplane that had been eavesdropping along the Chinese coast (from international waters) made an emergency landing in Chinese territory after being bumped by a Chinese fighter jet (which crashed). China held the crew for weeks to protest U.S. surveillance. (And China enjoyed an intelligence bonanza by examining the U.S. plane.)

The largest U.S. military intelligence agency is the National Security Agency (NSA), whose mission is encoding U.S. communications and breaking the codes of foreign communications. The size and complexity of this mission speaks to the increasing importance of information in war (see p. 220). The NSA employs more mathematics Ph.D.s than anyone in the world, is the second largest electricity consumer in the state of Maryland, has a budget larger than the CIA's, and is believed to have the most powerful computer facility in the world. Altogether, the budgets of U.S. intelligence agencies, although officially secret, were revealed in 2005 to be around $44 billion a year. Clearly these operations taken together are very large and are growing in importance as the information revolution proceeds and as the war on terrorism makes their mission more central.

Evolving Technologies

Through the centuries, the lethal power of weapons has increased continuously—from swords to muskets, machine guns to missiles. Technological developments have changed the nature of military force in several ways. First, the resort to force in international conflicts now has more profound costs and consequences than it did at the outset of the international system several centuries ago. Great powers in particular can no longer use force to settle disputes among themselves without risking massive destruction and economic ruin.

A second long-term effect of technological change is that military engagements now occur across greater standoff distances between opposing forces. Missiles of all types are accelerating this trend. Its effect is to undermine the territorial basis of war and of the state itself. The state once had a hard shell of militarily protected borders, but today the protection offered by borders is diminishing.[23] For example, Israel's successful defense of its borders could not stop Iraqi scud missiles from hitting Israeli cities during the Gulf War.

The Revolution in Military Affairs

In recent decades, the technological revolution in electronics has profoundly affected military forces, especially their command and control. **Electronic warfare** (now

[22] Gerdes, Louise I., ed. *Espionage and Intelligence Gathering*. Farmington Hills, MI: Greenhaven Press, 2004. Howard, Russell D., and Reid L. Sawyer, eds. *Terrorism and Counterterrorism: Understanding the New Security Environment*. Guilford, CT: McGraw-Hill/Dushkin, 2003.

[23] Herz, John H. *International Politics in the Atomic Age*. Columbia, 1959.

SMALL BUT DEADLY

The information revolution is making smaller weapons more potent. The U.S.-made Stinger antiaircraft missile—portable and shoulder-launched—helped turn the tide against the Soviet Union in the war in Afghanistan in the 1980s, with far-reaching consequences. Iraqi insurgents like those shown here in late 2003 kept Baghdad airport closed. The missiles pose a threat to commercial aviation worldwide.

broadened to *information warfare*) refers to the uses of the electromagnetic spectrum (radio waves, radar, infrared, etc.) in war—employing electromagnetic signals for one's own benefit while denying their use to an enemy. Electromagnetic signals are used for sensing beyond the normal visual range, through radar, infrared, and imaging equipment to see in darkness, through fog, or at great distances. These and other technologies have illuminated the battlefield so that forces cannot be easily hidden.

Electronic countermeasures are technologies designed to counteract enemy electronic systems such as radar and radio communications. **Stealth technology** uses special radar-absorbent materials and unusual shapes in the design of aircraft, missiles, and ships to scatter enemy radar. However, stealth is extremely expensive (the B-2 stealth bomber costs about $2 billion per plane, or about three times its weight in gold) and is prone to technical problems.

INFOREV

Is Technology an Equalizer?

Electronics are changing the costs and relative capabilities of weapons across the board. Computer chips in guided missiles have made them a formidable weapon on land, sea, and air. The miniaturization of such weaponry is making smaller and cheaper military forces more powerful than ever. An infantry soldier now can use a shoulder-fired missile costing $10,000 to destroy a battle tank costing $1 million. Similarly, a small boat firing an antiship missile costing $250,000 can potentially destroy a major warship costing hundreds of millions of dollars. Technological developments are in some ways increasing the advantages of great powers over less-powerful states, while in other ways undermining those advantages. U.S.-led bombing campaigns against Iraq, Serbia, and Afghanistan in recent years—which used remote sensing and precision-guided munitions extensively—cost far less and caused far fewer civilian casualties than previous air wars had. Yet, "smart" weapons also let guerrillas fire sophisticated anti-aircraft missiles, and new information technologies help China's new radar system detect U.S. "stealth" aircraft.

Strategies for *cyberwar*—disrupting enemy computer networks to degrade command and control, or even hacking into bank accounts electronically—were developed by NATO forces during the 1999 Kosovo war. Though mostly not implemented, they will probably figure in future wars. Some experts fear that terrorist attacks too could target computer networks, including the Internet.[24]

[24] Rattray, Gregory J. *Strategic Warfare in Cyberspace*. MIT, 2001. Hall, Wayne M. *Stray Voltage: War in the Information Age*. Annapolis, MD: Naval Institute Press, 2003.

Weapons of Mass Destruction

Weapons of mass destruction include three general types: nuclear, chemical, and biological weapons. They are distinguished from conventional weapons by their enormous potential lethality, given their small size and modest costs, and by their relative lack of discrimination in whom they kill. Because of these differences, weapons of mass destruction offer state leaders types of leverage that differ from conventional military forces. When deployed on ballistic missiles, they can potentially be fired from the home territory of one state and wreak great destruction on the home territory of another state.[25]

To date this has never happened. But the mere threat of such an action undermines the territorial integrity and security of states in the international system. Thus decision makers and scholars pay special attention to such weapons and the missiles that can deliver them. Of central concern today are the potentials for proliferation—the possession of weapons of mass destruction by more and more states.

Weapons of mass destruction serve different purposes from conventional weapons. With a few exceptions, their purpose is to deter attack (especially by other weapons of mass destruction) by giving state leaders the means to inflict great pain against a would-be conqueror or destroyer. For middle powers, these weapons also provide destructive power more in line with the great powers, serving as symbolic equalizers. For terrorists, potentially, their purpose is to kill a great many people.

Nuclear Weapons

Nuclear weapons are, in sheer power, the world's most destructive weapons. A single weapon the size of a refrigerator can destroy a city. Defending against nuclear weapons is extremely difficult at best.

To understand the potentials for nuclear proliferation, one has to know something about how nuclear weapons work. There are two types. *Fission* weapons (atomic bombs or A-bombs) are simpler and less expensive than *fusion weapons* (also called thermonuclear bombs, hydrogen bombs, or H-bombs).

When a fission weapon explodes, one type of atom (element) is split, or "fissioned," into new types with less total mass. The lost mass is transformed into energy according to Albert Einstein's famous formula, $E = mc^2$, which shows that a little bit of mass is equivalent to a great deal of energy. In fact, the fission bomb that destroyed Nagasaki, Japan, in 1945 converted to energy roughly the amount of mass in a single penny. Two elements can be split in this way, and each has been used to make fission weapons. These elements—known as **fissionable material**—are uranium-235 (or U-235) and plutonium.

Fission weapons work by taking subcritical masses of the fissionable material—amounts not dense enough to start a chain reaction—and compressing them into a critical mass, which explodes. In the simplest design, one piece of uranium is propelled down a tube (by conventional explosives) into another piece of uranium. A more efficient but technically demanding design arranges high explosives precisely around a hollow sphere of plutonium so as to implode the sphere and create a critical mass. Enhanced designs add an outer sphere of neutron-reflecting material to increase the number of speeding neutrons during the explosion.

Although these designs require sophisticated engineering, they are well within the capabilities of many states and some private groups. The obstacle is obtaining fissionable

---

[25] Hutchinson, Robert. *Weapons of Mass Destruction: The No-Nonsense Guide to Nuclear, Chemical and Biological Weapons Today*. NY: Cassell PLC, 2004. Eden, Lynn. *Whole World on Fire: Organizations, Knowledge, and Nuclear Weapons Devastation*. Cornell, 2003.

material. Only 10 to 100 pounds are required for each bomb, but even these small amounts are not easily obtained. U-235, which can be used in the simplest bomb designs, is especially difficult to obtain. Natural uranium (mined in various countries) has less than 1 percent U-235, mixed with nonfissionable uranium. Extracting the fissionable U-235, referred to as enriching the uranium up to weapons grade (or high grade), is slow, expensive, and technically complex—a major obstacle to proliferation. But North Korea, Iran, Iraq, and Libya all built the infrastructure to do so in recent years. North Korea was still actively pursuing this route in 2006. In 2004, Iran agreed to suspend its uranium enrichment, but later broke the deal, resumed enrichment, and was referred to the UN Security Council in 2006. After the U.S. invasion of Iraq, American inspectors discovered that Iraq had shelved its nuclear program years earlier.

How to Make Nuclear Weapons

Plutonium is more easily produced, from low-grade uranium in nuclear power reactors—although extracting the plutonium requires a separation plant. But a plutonium bomb is more difficult to build than a uranium one—another obstacle to proliferation. Plutonium is also used in commercial breeder reactors, which Japan and other countries have built recently—another source of fissionable material. (Thus, if it decided to do so in the future, Japan could build a formidable nuclear arsenal fairly quickly, although this is unlikely.)

Fission weapons were invented 60 years ago by U.S. scientists in a secret World War II science programt known as the *Manhattan Project*. In 1945, one uranium bomb and one plutonium bomb were used to destroy Hiroshima and Nagasaki, killing 100,000 civilians in each city and inducing Japan to surrender unconditionally. By today's standards, those bombs were crude, low-yield weapons. But they are the kind of weapon that might be built by a poor state or a nonstate actor.

Fusion weapons are extremely expensive and technically demanding; they are for only the richest, largest, most technologically capable states. In fusion weapons, two small atoms (variants of hydrogen) fuse together into a larger atom, releasing energy. This reaction occurs only at very high temperatures (the sun "burns" hydrogen through fusion). Weapons designers use fission weapons to create these high energies and trigger an explosive fusion reaction. The explosive power of most fission weapons is between 1 and 200 kilotons (each kiloton is the equivalent of 1,000 tons of conventional explosive). The power of fusion weapons is typically 1 to 20 megatons (a megaton is 1,000 kilotons). In the post–Cold War era fusion weapons have become less important.

The effects of nuclear weapons include not only the blast of the explosion, but also heat and radiation. Heat can potentially create a self-sustaining firestorm in a city. Radiation creates radiation sickness, which at high doses

LIVING WITH NUKES

Nuclear weapons were invented during World War II. Tens of thousands of nuclear weapons have been built; eight or nine countries possess at least a few. Obtaining fissionable materials is the main difficulty in making nuclear weapons. The worldwide nuclear industry—ranging from commercial plants to weapons facilities—is a key security concern since September 2001. Here, a Florida sheriff guards a nuclear power plant, 2001.

kills people in a few days and at low doses creates long-term health problems, especially cancers. Radiation is most intense in the local vicinity of (and downwind from) a nuclear explosion, but some is carried up into the atmosphere and falls in more distant locations as nuclear fallout. Nuclear weapons also create an electromagnetic pulse (EMP) that can disrupt and destroy electronic equipment (some weapons are designed to maximize this effect). Using many nuclear weapons at once (as in a great-power war) would also have substantial effects on global climate—possibly a *nuclear winter* in which years of colder and darker conditions would trigger an environmental catastrophe.

Ballistic Missiles and Other Delivery Systems

Delivery systems for getting nuclear weapons to their targets—much more than the weapons themselves—are the basis of states' nuclear arsenals and strategies (discussed shortly). Inasmuch as nuclear warheads can be made quite small—weighing a few hundred pounds or even less—they are adaptable to a wide variety of delivery systems.

During the Cold War, nuclear delivery systems were divided into two categories. *Strategic* weapons were those that could hit an enemy's homeland, usually at long range (for instance, Moscow from Nebraska). Once carried on long-range bombers, they now are carried mainly on missiles. *Tactical* nuclear weapons were those designed for battlefield use in a theater of military engagement. In the Cold War years, both superpowers integrated tactical nuclear weapons into their conventional air, sea, and land forces using a variety of delivery systems—gravity bombs, artillery shells, short-range missiles, land mines, depth charges, and so forth. However, the tens of thousands of nuclear warheads integrated into superpower conventional forces posed dangers such as theft or accident. Their actual use would have entailed grave risks of escalation to strategic nuclear war, putting home cities at risk. Thus, both superpowers phased out tactical nuclear weapons almost entirely when the Cold War ended. The tactical weapons deployed in the former Soviet republics were shipped back to Russia for storage and eventual disassembly.

The main strategic delivery vehicles are **ballistic missiles;** unlike airplanes, they are extremely difficult to defend against. Ballistic missiles carry a warhead up along a trajectory and let it drop on the target. A trajectory typically rises out of the atmosphere—at least 50 miles high— before descending. A powerful rocket is needed, and a guidance system adjusts the trajectory so that the warhead drops closer to the target. Various ballistic missiles differ in their range, accuracy, and throw weight (how heavy a warhead they can carry). In addition, some missiles fire from fixed sites (silos), whereas others are mobile, firing from railroads or large trailer trucks (making them hard to target). The longest-range missiles are **intercontinental ballistic missiles (ICBMs)** with ranges over 5,000 miles.

Of special interest today are short-range ballistic missiles (SRBMs) with ranges of well under 1,000 miles. The modified scud missiles fired by Iraq at Saudi Arabia and Israel during the Gulf War were (conventionally armed) SRBMs. In regional conflicts, the long range of more powerful missiles may not be necessary. The largest cities of Syria and Israel are only 133 miles from each other; the capital cities of Iraq and Iran are less than 500 miles apart, as are those of India and Pakistan, as shown in Figure 6.2. All these states own ballistic missiles. Short-range and some medium-range ballistic missiles are cheap enough to be obtained and even home-produced by small middle-income states. Table 6.3 lists the capabilities of the 33 states with ballistic missiles.

Many short-range ballistic missiles, including those used by Iraq during the Gulf War, are highly inaccurate but still very difficult to defend against.[26] With conventional

[26] Postol, Theodore A. Lessons of the Gulf War Experience with Patriot. *International Security* 16 (3), 1991/92: 119–71.

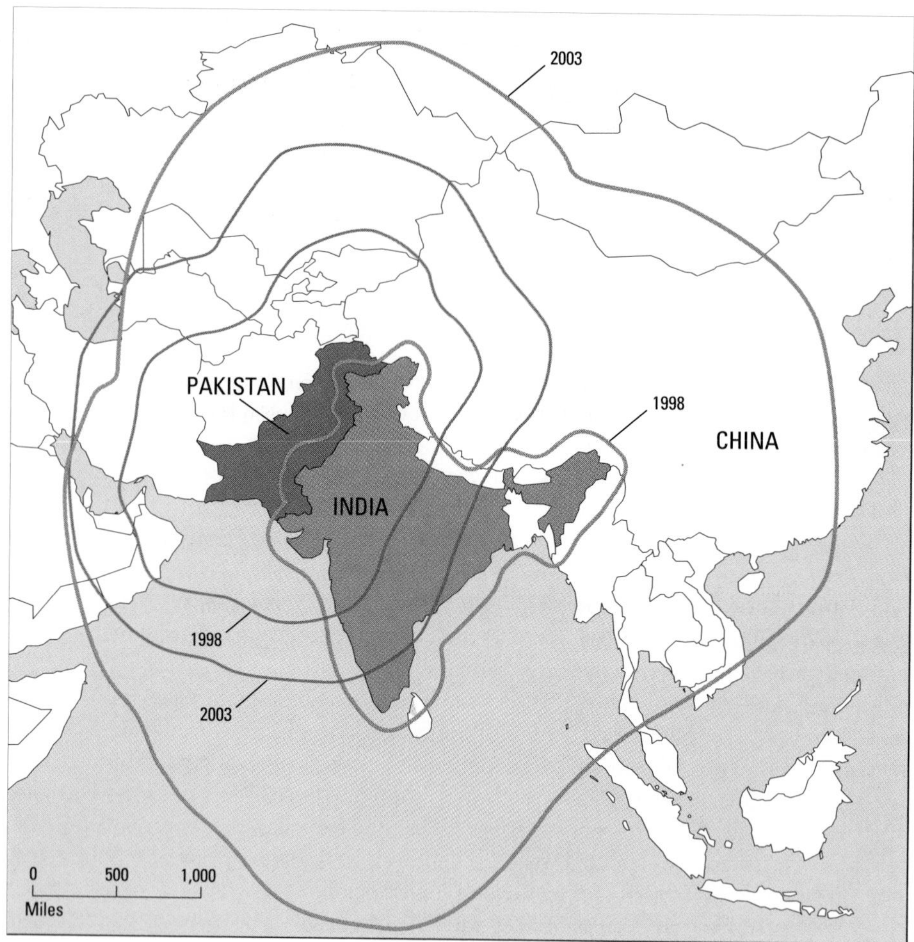

FIGURE 6.2 ■ Expanding Ranges of Indian and Pakistani Missiles, 1998–2003

Source: The Washington Post, May 29, 1999: A32, Table 6.3.

warheads they have more psychological than military utility (demoralizing an enemy population by attacking cities indiscriminately). With nuclear, chemical, or biological warheads, however, these missiles could be deadlier. The accuracy of delivery systems of all ranges improves as one moves to great powers, especially the United States. After traveling thousands of miles, the best U.S. missiles can land within 50 feet of a target half of the time. The trend in the U.S. nuclear arsenal has been toward less-powerful warheads but more accurate missiles, for flexibility.

The **cruise missile** is a small winged missile that can navigate across thousands of miles of previously mapped terrain to reach a target, with the help of satellite guidance. Cruise missiles can be launched from ships, submarines, airplanes, or land. In 1993, President Bill Clinton attacked the Iraqi intelligence headquarters in the first all-cruise-missile attack in history. The United States used cruise missiles extensively against Serbian forces in Bosnia in 1995, against Serbia in 1999, Iraq in 2003, and smaller-scale targets such as terrorist Osama bin Laden's base in Afghanistan in 1998.

TABLE 6.3 ■ Ballistic Missile Capabilities, 2006

Country	Range (Miles)	Potential Targets
United States[a]	13,000	(World)
Russia[a]	13,000	(World)
China[a]	13,000	(World)
Britain[a]	4,600	(World; submarine-launched)
France[a]	3,700 [4,600]	(World; submarine-launched)
North Korea[a]	800 [3,500]	South Korea, Russia, China [All Asia]
Iran[b,c]	900 [3,500]	Iraq, Kuwait, Afghanistan, Israel [Europe to Asia]
Israel[a,c]	900 [3,500]	Syria, Iraq, Saudi Arabia, Egypt [Iran]
India[a,c]	1,500 [2,000]	Pakistan, China, Afghanistan, Iran, Turkey
Pakistan[a]	800 [2,000]	India [Russia, Turkey, Israel]
Saudi Arabia	1,700	Iran, Iraq, Syria, Israel, Turkey, Yemen, Egypt, Libya, Sudan
Syria	300 [400]	Israel, Jordan, Iraq, Turkey
Egypt	400	Libya, Sudan, Israel
Libya	200	Egypt, Tunisia, Algeria
Yemen	200	Saudi Arabia
United Arab Emirates	200	Saudi Arabia, Iran
Afghanistan	200	Pakistan, Tajikistan, Uzbekistan
Kazakhstan	200	Uzbekistan, Tajikistan, Kyrgyzstan, Russia
Turkmenistan	200	Iran, Afghanistan, Uzbekistan, Tajikistan
Armenia	200	Azerbaijan
Belarus	200	Russia, Ukraine, Poland
Ukraine	200	Russia, Belarus, Poland, Hungary, Romania
South Korea	200	North Korea
Vietnam	200	China, Cambodia
Taiwan	80 [200]	China
Greece	100	Turkey
Turkey	100	Greece
Bahrain	100	Saudi Arabia, Qatar
Slovakia	80	Czech Rep., Hungary, Poland
Japan[c]	—	

Number of states with ballistic missiles: 29

[a]States that have nuclear weapons.

[b]States believed to be trying to build nuclear weapons.

[c]States developing space-launch missiles adaptable as long-range ballistic missiles.

Notes: Bracketed range numbers indicate missiles under development. List of potential targets includes both hostile and friendly states, and is suggestive rather than comprehensive. Missile ranges increase with smaller payloads. 200-mile ranges (scud-B) and 300-mile ranges (scud Mod-C) are approximate for a 3/4-ton payload. Saudi range is for a two-ton payload; South Korean range is for a half-ton payload.

Source: Carnegie Endowment for International Peace.

The spread of ballistic missiles has been difficult to control.[27] There is a **Missile Technology Control Regime** through which industrialized states try to limit the flow of missile-relevant technology to states in the global South. One success was the interruption of an Egyptian-Argentinean-Iraqi partnership in the 1980s to develop a medium-range missile. But, in general, the regime has had limited success. Short- and medium-range missiles (ranges up to about 2,000 miles) apparently are being developed by Iran, Israel, Saudi Arabia, Pakistan, India, North Korea, and possibly Argentina and Brazil. Soviet-made short-range ballistic missiles are owned by a number of states. China has also sold its missiles and technology in the global South (bringing lower prices to buyers and hard currency to China)—a sore point in relations with the West.[28]

Small states or terrorists that may acquire nuclear weapons in the future could deliver them through innovative means. Because nuclear weapons are small, one could be smuggled into a target state by car, by speedboat, or in diplomatic pouches.

Since 2001, the United States has begun a container security initiative aimed at preventing weapons of mass destruction from reaching U.S. shores in seaborne shipping containers. But doing so without impeding the prosperity-inducing flow of international trade is a daunting challenge—nearly 8 million shipping containers pass through U.S. ports every year. In 2006, a bipartisan revolt in the U.S. Congress scuttled a deal, approved by the Bush Administration, that would have let a company based in Dubai, an Arab country, control some operations at several U.S. ports (as other foreign companies already do). While the war on terrorism continues, U.S. cities remain at grave risk of destruction by nuclear weapons smuggled into the United States.

Chemical and Biological Weapons

Chemical Weapons

A *chemical weapon* releases chemicals that disable and kill people.[29] A variety of chemicals can be used, from lethal ones such as nerve gas to merely irritating ones such as tear gas. Different chemicals interfere with the nervous system, blood, breathing, or other body functions. Some can be absorbed through the skin; others must be inhaled. Some persist in the target area long after their use; others disperse quickly.

It is possible to defend against most chemical weapons by dressing troops in protective clothing and gas masks and following elaborate procedures to decontaminate equipment. But protective suits are hot, and anti-chemical measures reduce the efficiency of armies. Civilians are much less likely to have protection against chemicals than are military forces (the well-prepared Israeli civilians were an exception). Chemical weapons are by nature indiscriminate about whom they kill. Several times, chemical weapons have been deliberately used against civilians (notably by the Iraqi government against Iraqi Kurds in the 1980s).

Use of chemical weapons in war has been rare. Mustard gas, which produces skin blisters and lung damage, was widely used (in artillery shells) in World War I. After the horrors of that war, the use of chemical weapons was banned in the 1925 Geneva protocol, a treaty that is still in effect. In World War II, both sides were armed with chemical weapons but neither used them, for fear of retaliation. Since then (with possibly a few unclear exceptions) only Iraq has violated the treaty—against Iran in the 1980s.

---

[27] Karp, Aaron. *Ballistic Missile Proliferation: The Politics and Technics*. NY: Oxford/SIPRI, 1996. Mistry, Dinshaw. *Containing Missile Proliferation: Strategic Technology, Security Regimes, and International Cooperation in Arms Control*. Washington, 2003.

[28] Bitzinger, Richard A. Arms to Go: Chinese Arms Sales to the Third World. *International Security* 17 (2), 1992: 84–111.

[29] Price, Richard M. *The Chemical Weapons Taboo*. Cornell, 1997. Adams, Valerie. *Chemical Warfare, Chemical Disarmament*. Indiana, 1990. Spiers, Edward M. *Chemical and Biological Weapons: A Survey of Proliferation*. NY: St. Martin's Press, 1994.

Unfortunately, Iraq's actions not only breached a psychological barrier against using chemical weapons, but showed such weapons to be cheap and effective against human waves of attackers without protective gear. This example stimulated dozens more poor states to begin acquiring chemical weapons. Chemical weapons are a cheap way for states to gain weapons of mass destruction. Chemical weapons can be produced using processes and facilities similar to those for pesticides, pharmaceuticals, and other civilian products. This is a major factor making it difficult to find chemical weapons facilities in suspect countries, or to deny those states access to the needed chemicals and equipment. In 1998, a U.S. cruise missile attack destroyed a suspected weapons facility in Sudan that may have been only a pharmaceutical factory.

VULNERABLE

Civilians are more vulnerable to chemical weapons than soldiers are. A new treaty aims to ban chemical weapons worldwide. Here, Israeli kindergarteners prepare against a chemical warfare threat from Iraqi scud missiles during the Gulf War, 1991.

The 1925 treaty did not ban the production or possession of chemical weapons, and several dozen states built stockpiles of them. The United States and the Soviet Union maintained large arsenals of chemical weapons during the Cold War but have reduced them greatly in the past decade. In 1992, a new **Chemical Weapons Convention** to ban the production and possession of chemical weapons was concluded after years of negotiation; it has been signed by all the great powers and nearly all other states with a few exceptions including Egypt, Syria, and North Korea. The new treaty includes strict verification provisions and the threat of sanctions against violators including (an important extension) those who are nonparticipants in the treaty. The U.S. Senate approved ratification at the last minute in 1997. Several states (including India, China, South Korea, France, and Britain) admitted to having secret chemical weapons programs, which will now be dismantled under international oversight. Russia still faces very costly and long-term work to destroy a 44,000-ton arsenal of chemical weapons built during the Cold War. From 1997 to 2002, the treaty organization oversaw the elimination of about one-sixth of the world's chemical weapons.

Biological weapons resemble chemical ones, except that instead of chemicals they use microorganisms or biologically derived toxins. Some use viruses or bacteria that cause fatal diseases, such as smallpox, bubonic plague, and anthrax. Others cause nonfatal, but incapacitating, diseases or diseases that kill livestock. Theoretically, a single weapon could spark an epidemic in an entire population, but this is considered too dangerous and use of less-contagious microorganisms is preferred. Biological weapons have virtually never been used in war (Japan tried some on a few Chinese villages in World War II). Their potential strikes many political leaders as a Pandora's box that could let loose uncontrollable forces if opened.

For this reason, the development, production, and possession of biological weapons are banned under the 1972 **Biological Weapons Convention,** signed by more than 100 countries including the great powers. The superpowers destroyed their stocks of biological weapons and had to restrict their biological weapons complexes to defensive research rather than the development of weapons. However, because the treaty makes no provision for inspection and because biological weapons programs are, like chemical ones, relatively easy to hide, several states remain under suspicion of having biological weapons. UN inspections of Iraq in the mid-1990s uncovered an active biological weapons program. Evidence surfaced after the collapse of the Soviet Union that a secret biological weapons program was under way there as well. In 2001, the United States pulled out of talks to strengthen the 1972 treaty, declaring the proposed modifications unworkable.

Anthrax spores were one of the main biological weapons produced by the secret Soviet program, and the U.S. military also produced them (to work on defenses). In 2001, soon after the September 11 attacks, someone sent small amounts of anthrax spores through the U.S. mail to high government and media offices, killing several people and massively disrupting mail distribution. The attack was unsolved in early 2006 but showed that deadly biological weapons are a real threat and not a futuristic worry. In 1997, the U.S. military began to vaccinate all 2.4 million U.S. soldiers against anthrax.

Today the United States and perhaps a dozen other countries maintain biological weapons research (not banned by the treaty). Researchers try to ascertain the military implications of advances in biotechnology. Most states doing such research claim that they are doing so only to deter another state from developing biological weapons.[30]

Proliferation

Proliferation

Proliferation is the spread of weapons of mass destruction—nuclear weapons, ballistic missiles, and chemical or biological weapons—into the hands of more actors. The implications of proliferation for international relations are difficult to predict but profound. Ballistic missiles with weapons of mass destruction remove the territorial protection offered by state borders and make each state vulnerable to others. Some realists, who believe in the basic rationality of state actions, are not so upset by this prospect, and some even welcome it. They reason that in a world where the use of military force could lead to mutual annihilation, there would be fewer wars—just as during the arms race of the Cold War the superpowers did not blow each other up. Other IR scholars who put less faith in the rationality of state leaders are much more alarmed by proliferation. They fear that with more and more nuclear (or chemical/biological) actors, miscalculation or accident—or fanatical terrorism—could lead to the use of weapons of mass destruction on a scale unseen since 1945.[31]

The leaders of great powers tend to side with the second group.[32] They have tried to restrict the most destructive weapons to the great powers. Proliferation erodes the great powers' advantage relative to middle powers.

There is also a widespread fear that these weapons may fall into the hands of terrorists or other nonstate actors who would be immune from threats of retaliation (with no terri-

[30] Lederberg, Joshua, ed. *Biological Weapons: Limiting the Threat*. MIT, 1999. Tucker, Jonathan B., ed. *Toxic Terror: Assessing Terrorist Use of Chemical and Biological Weapons*. MIT, 2000. Price-Smith, Andrew T., ed. *Plagues and Politics: Infectious Diseases and International Policy*. NY: Palgrave, 2001. Price-Smith, Andrew T. *The Health of Nations*. MIT, 2001. Dando, Malcom. *The New Biological Weapons: Threat, Proliferation, and Control*. Boulder, CO: Lynne Rienner, 2001.

[31] Paul, T.V., Richard J. Harknett, and James J. Wirtz, eds. *The Absolute Weapon Revisited*. Michigan, 1998. Spector, Leonard S., Gregory P. Webb, and Mark G. McDonough. *Tracking Nuclear Proliferation: A Guide in Maps and Charts, 1998*. Washington, DC: Brookings/Carnegie Endowment for International Peace, 1998. Sagan, Scott D., and Kenneth N. Waltz. *The Spread of Nuclear Weapons: A Debate*. NY: Norton, 1995.

[32] Utgoff, Victor, ed. *The Coming Crisis: Nuclear Proliferation, U.S. Interests, and World Order*. MIT, 1999. Schrafstetter, Susanna, and Stephen Twigge. *Avoiding Armageddon: Europe, the United States, and the Struggle for Nuclear Nonproliferation, 1945–1970*. Westport, CT: Praeger, 2004.

tory or cities to defend). Evidence captured during the 2001 war in Afghanistan showed that the al Qaeda organization was trying to obtain weapons of mass destruction and would be willing to use them. Lax security at the vast, far-flung former Soviet nuclear complex increased fears that fissionable materials could reach terrorists.[33]

However, states that sell technology with proliferation potential can make money doing so. For example, in the mid-1990s the United States pressured both Russia and China to stop selling nuclear technology to Iran (which the United States said was trying to build nuclear weapons). Russia and China did not want to give up hundreds of millions of dollars in sales. This is another international collective goods problem, in which states pursuing their individual interests end up collectively worse off.

Nuclear proliferation could occur simply by a state or nonstate actor's buying (or stealing) one or more nuclear weapons or the components to build one. The means to prevent this range from covert intelligence to tight security measures to safeguards preventing a stolen weapon from being used. But the economic crisis in Russia in the 1990s left vulnerable hundreds of tons of Russian fissionable materials in the control of underpaid civilian workers and military officers at poorly funded facilities with lax security and recurrent corruption. In 2002, the G8 countries pledged $20 billion to address the problem, but in late 2003 a study by 21 research groups (focused on 100 insecure research reactors with weapons-grade uranium in 40 countries) found little of it spent and problems still rampant.

HOT STUFF

The most important hurdle in making nuclear weapons is access to fissionable materials (plutonium and uranium). In 2003, North Korea restarted its plutonium-producing reactor at Yongbyon, shut down since 1994 under an agreement with the United States, and apparently produced a half-dozen bombs from it, becoming the world's ninth nuclear-armed state. This 1996 photo, released in 2003, shows the nuclear fuel rods in a cooling pond at Yongbyon.

A stronger form of nuclear proliferation is the development by states of nuclear complexes to produce their own nuclear weapons on an ongoing basis.[34] Here larger numbers of weapons are involved and there are strong potentials for arms races in regional conflicts and rivalries. The relevant regional conflicts are those between Israel and the Arab states, Iran and its Arab neighbors, India and Pakistan,[35] the two Koreas, and possibly Taiwan and China. India and Pakistan both have exploded nuclear devices underground, and are building arsenals and the missiles to deliver them. In addition, South Africa reported after the fact that it had built several nuclear weapons but then dismantled them in the 1980s (while still under white minority rule).

[33] Finn, Peter. Experts Discuss Chances of Nuclear Terrorism. *Washington Post*, Nov. 3, 2001: A19. Erlanger, Steven. Lax Nuclear Security in Russia Is Cited as Way for bin Laden to Get Arms. *New York Times*, Nov. 12, 2001: B1. Gur, Nadine, and Benjamin Cole. *The New Face of Terrorism: Threats from Weapons of Mass Destruction*. NY: I.B. Tauris, 2000. Falkenrath, Richard A., Robert D. Newman, and Bradley A. Thayer. *America's Achilles' Heel: Nuclear, Biological, and Chemical Terrorism and Covert Attack*. MIT, 1998.

[34] Abraham, Itty. *The Making of the Indian Atomic Bomb: Science, Secrecy, and the Post-Colonial State*. NY: Zed/St. Martin's, 1998. Perkovich, George. *India's Nuclear Bomb: The Impact on Global Proliferation*. California, 1999. Lewis, John Wilson, and Xus Litai. *China Builds the Bomb*. Stanford, 1988.

[35] Albright, David, and Mark Hibbs. India's Silent Bomb. *Bulletin of the Atomic Scientists* 48 (7), 1992: 27–31. Albright, David, and Mark Hibbs. Pakistan's Bomb: Out of the Closet. *Bulletin of the Atomic Scientists* 48 (6), 1992: 38–43.

Israel has never test-exploded nuclear weapons or admitted it has them but is widely believed to have a hundred or more nuclear warheads on combat airplanes and medium-range missiles. Israel wants these capabilities to use as a last resort if it were about to be conquered by its neighbors.[36] Israeli leaders thus hope to convince Arab leaders that a military conquest of Israel is impossible. To prevent Iraq from developing nuclear weapons, Israel carried out a bombing raid on the main facility of the Iraqi nuclear complex in 1981. Without this raid, Iraq probably would have had nuclear weapons by the time of the 1991 Gulf War.

The **Non-Proliferation Treaty (NPT)** of 1968 created a framework for controlling the spread of nuclear materials and expertise.[37] The International Atomic Energy Agency (IAEA), a UN agency based in Vienna, is charged with inspecting the nuclear power industry in member states to prevent secret military diversions of nuclear materials. However, in the 1990s, Pakistan's top nuclear scientist sold bomb kits with low-grade uranium, enrichment centrifuges, and bomb designs to Libya, Iran, and North Korea. A number of potential nuclear states (such as Israel) have not signed the NPT, and even those states that have signed may sneak around its provisions by keeping some facilities secret (as Iraq and Iran did). Under the terms of the Gulf War cease-fire, Iraq's nuclear program was uncovered and dismantled by the IAEA.[38]

Pakistan's Nuclear Sales

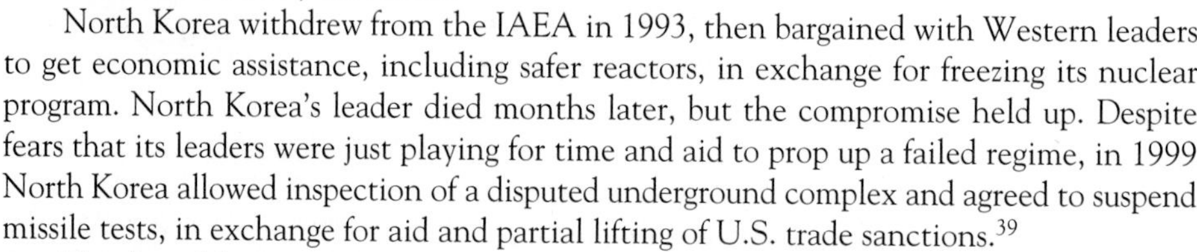

North Korea withdrew from the IAEA in 1993, then bargained with Western leaders to get economic assistance, including safer reactors, in exchange for freezing its nuclear program. North Korea's leader died months later, but the compromise held up. Despite fears that its leaders were just playing for time and aid to prop up a failed regime, in 1999 North Korea allowed inspection of a disputed underground complex and agreed to suspend missile tests, in exchange for aid and partial lifting of U.S. trade sanctions.[39]

This hopeful picture was revealed as false, however, in 2002 when the United States confronted North Korea with evidence of a secret nuclear enrichment program, and the North Koreans admitted it. As relations deteriorated, North Korea pulled out of the agreement and of the IAEA, restarted its nuclear reactor, and threatened to turn existing plutonium into a half dozen bombs within months. U.S. monitoring detected certain molecules indicative of plutonium reprocessing, and North Korea then announced it had finished. Although proof is lacking—unless or until North Korea tests a bomb—there is every reason to believe that North Korea is the world's ninth nuclear weapons power. Since those bombs could plausibly be sold to the highest bidder worldwide, they posed a grave risk to the United States at a time when Iraq preoccupied U.S. leaders. U.S., Chinese, Japanese, and Korean leaders continued to negotiate in 2006 but the outcome remained uncertain.

A number of middle powers and two great powers (Japan and Germany) have the potential to make nuclear weapons but have chosen not to do so. The reasons for deciding against "going nuclear" include norms against using nuclear weapons, fears of retaliation, and practical constraints including cost. At present, undeclared nuclear powers include Israel (with perhaps a hundred warheads) and North Korea (with perhaps a half dozen). Declared nuclear states in addition to the "big five" are India and Pakistan (with dozens each, and growing).

---

[36] Cohen, Avner. *Israel and the Bomb*. Columbia, 1998. Hersh, Seymour M. *The Samson Option: Israel's Nuclear Arsenal and American Foreign Policy*. NY: Random House, 1991. Maoz, Zeev. *Defending the Holy Land: A Critical Analysis of Israel's Security and Foreign Policy*. Michigan, 2006.

[37] Kokoski, Richard. *Technology and the Proliferation of Nuclear Weapons*. NY: Oxford/SIPRI, 1996. Chafetz, Glenn. The Political Psychology of the Nuclear Nonproliferation Regime. *Journal of Politics* 57 (3), 1995: 743–775.

[38] Albright, David, and Mark Hibbs. Iraq's Nuclear Hide-and-Seek. *Bulletin of the Atomic Scientists* 47 (7), 1991: 14–23.

[39] Sigal, Leon V. *Disarming Strangers: Nuclear Diplomacy with North Korea*. Princeton, 1999. Cha, Victor D., and David C. Kang. *Nuclear North Korea: A Debate on Engagement Strategies*. Columbia, 2003.

POLICY PERSPECTIVES

Prime Minister of Israel, Ehud Olmert

PROBLEM *Balancing the tradeoffs in the use of force to confront a potential security threat.*

BACKGROUND Imagine that you are the prime minister of Israel. The Middle East region provides perhaps the clearest illustration of many realist concepts. Military conflicts, security dilemmas, and arms races are endemic to the region. From a military perspective, the key country in the region is Israel. Israel has fought and defeated all of its neighbors several times since its founding in 1948. Despite these victories, Israel still faces threats from outside its borders.

Although they are not neighbors, Iran has repeatedly challenged Israel. Iran has funded Hezbollah, a group operating in Lebanon and considered a terrorist organization by Israel and the United States. Hezbollah raids have killed Israeli troops and civilians in northern Israel. Israel has labeled Iran the predominant threat in the region.

In 2004, Iran admitted that it had developed facilities to produce enriched uranium for use in nuclear power reactors. The enriched uranium, however, can also be used in nuclear weapons. After negotiations with the European Union (EU), Russia, and the UN's International Atomic Energy Agency (IAEA), Iran initially agreed to stop its enrichment of nuclear materials, but in 2005 it resumed enrichment, declaring nuclear technology its inherent right. In the Spring of 2006, the UN Security Council demanded Iran cease this activity, but Iran showed no signs of complying with this demand. Meanwhile Iran has upgraded its missiles, putting Israeli cities within their range.

In 1981, Israel launched a preemptive air strike against Iraq, destroying its nuclear reactor. To conduct such a strike against Iran, however, would be more difficult than the attack on Iraq. While Iraq had one site to attack, Iran has many more (possibly hundreds), requiring a highly coordinated attack.

SCENARIO Now imagine that Iran withdraws from its remaining international agreements and accelerate its enrichment of nuclear material. Once in possession of enough enriched uranium, Iran could easily produce nuclear weapons.

One option is a preemptive military strike on Iran. If successful, such a strike could be the best way to ensure your long-term safety if Iran is developing weapons to attack you. Yet, the strike would be difficult to carry out and could risk a larger war in the region. If the attack fails, it might also bring retaliation by Iran.

You are close allies and have common interests with the United States in keeping Iran from become a nuclear power. The United States has pressured Iran to stop enriching nuclear material. But U.S. armed forces are stretched thin, so the United States may hesitate to carry out such a mission.

You could pressure the IAEA, the EU, or the United States to help stop Iranian nuclear programs, for example by pushing economic sanctions. Clearly, this option is the cheapest in terms of military and human costs, but Iran has rebuffed these organizations in the past.

CHOOSE YOUR POLICY As prime minister of Israel, you must decide the best course of action. How do you balance these options regarding the use of force in trying to secure your state? Do you attempt a preemptive military strike? Do you pressure the United States to launch a preemptive strike? Do you diplomatically pressure the IAEA and the EU? Can you rest your long-term security on the hope that diplomacy works? How do you balance options to use force versus diplomacy to confront this security threat?

Iran denies, but appears to be, working to develop nuclear weapons (as it had begun to do under the shah in the 1970s). Since 2003, Iran first agreed to suspend its uranium enrichment program and allow surprise IAEA inspections, then restarted enrichment, suspended it again, and restarted it again. In 2005, U.S.-backed efforts by Europe to offer Iran economic incentives to dismantle its program, and by Russia to enrich Iran's uranium on Russian soil with safeguards, both broke down. In 2006, the IAEA referred the issue to the UN Security Council, which condemned Iran's actions but could not agree on sanctions. Iran insisted on its sovereign right to enrich uranium for what it called peaceful purposes.

Brazil and Argentina seemed to be headed for a nuclear arms race in the 1980s but then called it off as civilians replaced military governments in both countries.[40] In 2004, after years of resistance, Brazil gave IAEA inspectors access to a controversial uranium enrichment plant (not part of a nuclear weapons program, evidently).

In 1995, the NPT came up for a 25-year review. In that period, the nonnuclear states were supposed to stay nonnuclear; they had largely done so, except for Israel, India, and Pakistan, which had never signed the treaty. The nuclear states were supposed to undertake serious nuclear disarmament; they had largely failed to do so. But a 2005 review conference ended in failure as the United States and other countries disagreed over Iran's program and loopholes in the treaty.

Nuclear Strategy

The term *nuclear strategy* refers to decisions about how many nuclear weapons to deploy, what delivery systems to put them on, and what policies to adopt regarding the circumstances in which they would be used.[41]

The reason for possessing nuclear weapons is almost always to deter another state from a nuclear or conventional attack by threatening ruinous retaliation. This should work if state leaders are rational actors wanting to avoid the huge costs of a nuclear attack. But it will work only if other states believe that a state's threat to use nuclear weapons is credible. The search for a credible deterrent by two or more hostile states tends to lead to an ever-growing arsenal of nuclear weapons. To follow this logic, start with Pakistan's deployment of its first nuclear missile aimed at India (the example also works with the countries reversed). Then India would not attack—that is, unless it could prevent Pakistan from using its missile. India could do this by building offensive forces capable of wiping out the Pakistani missile (probably using nuclear weapons, but that is not the key point here). Then the Pakistani missile, rather than deter India, would merely spur India to destroy the missile before any other attack. An attack intended to destroy—largely or entirely—a state's nuclear weapons before they can be used is called a *first strike*.

Pakistan could make its missile survivable (probably by making it mobile). It could also build more nuclear missiles so that even if some were destroyed in an Indian first strike, some would survive with which to retaliate. Weapons that can take a first strike and still strike back give a state *second-strike* capabilities. A state that deploys the fewest nuclear forces needed for an assured second-strike capability (between tens and hundreds) has a minimum deterrent. Possession of second-strike capabilities by both sides is called **mutually assured**

[40] Leventhal, Paul L., and Sharon Tanzer, eds. *Averting a Latin American Nuclear Arms Race: New Prospects and Challenges for Argentine-Brazil Nuclear Cooperation*. NY: St. Martin's, 1992.

[41] Glaser, Charles L. *Analyzing Strategic Nuclear Policy*. Princeton, 1990. Sagan, Scott D. *Moving Targets: Nuclear Strategy and National Security*. Princeton, 1989. Nye, Joseph S., Graham T. Allison, and Albert Carnesdale, eds. *Fateful Visions: Avoiding Nuclear Catastrophe*. Cambridge, MA: Ballinger, 1988. Rhodes, Edward. *Power and Madness: The Logic of Nuclear Coercion*. Columbia, 1989. Jervis, Robert. *The Meaning of the Nuclear Revolution: Statecraft and the Prospect of Armageddon*. Cornell, 1989. Kull, Steven. *Minds at War*. NY: Basic, 1988. Talbott, Strobe. *The Master of the Game: Paul Nitze and the Nuclear Peace*. NY: Knopf, 1988.

destruction (MAD) because neither side can prevent the other from destroying it. The term implies that the strategy, though reflecting "rationality," is actually insane (mad) because deviations from rationality could destroy both sides.

If India could not assuredly *destroy* Pakistan's missile, it would undoubtedly deploy its own nuclear missile(s) to *deter* Pakistan from using its missile. India, too, could achieve a second-strike capability. Now the question of credibility becomes important. In theory, India could launch a non-nuclear attack on Pakistan, knowing that rational Pakistani leaders would rather lose such a war than use their nuclear weapons and bring on an Indian nuclear response. The nuclear missiles in effect cancel each other out.

During the Cold War, this was the problem faced by U.S. war planners trying to deter a Soviet conventional attack on Western Europe. They could threaten to use nuclear weapons in response, but rational Soviet leaders would know that rational U.S. leaders would never act on such a threat and risk escalation to global nuclear war. Better to lose West Germany, according to this line of thinking, than lose both West Germany and New York. U.S. planners thus tried to convince the Soviets that such an attack would be too risky. They did this by integrating thousands of tactical nuclear weapons into conventional forces so that the escalation to nuclear war might happen more or less automatically in the event of conventional war. This was the equivalent of "throwing away the steering wheel" in a game of Chicken (see p. 73). China currently uses a similar form of "rational irrationality" in its relations with Taiwan, trying to make credible the threat of war (which would be disastrous for China as well as Taiwan) if Taiwan declares independence (see pp. 64–65).

THE RACE IS ON

India and Pakistan are building arsenals of nuclear-tipped missiles that could devastate each other's main cities. Their current arms race follows that of the superpowers during the Cold War. Superpower arms control agreements helped develop norms and expectations about the role of nuclear weapons, but did not stop a buildup of tens of thousands of nuclear weapons. Here, India shows off its new intermediate-range ballistic missile, 2002.

Superpower Arms Race

Defense has played little role in nuclear strategy because no effective defense against missile attack has been devised. However, the United States is spending billions of dollars a year to try to develop defenses that could shoot down incoming ballistic missiles. The program is called the **Strategic Defense Initiative (SDI),** "star wars," or Ballistic Missile Defense (BMD). It originated in President Ronald Reagan's 1983 call for a comprehensive shield that would make nuclear missiles obsolete.[42] However, the mission soon shifted to a (slightly) more realistic one of defending some U.S. missiles in a massive Soviet attack. After the Cold War the mission shifted again, to one of protecting U.S. territory from a very limited missile attack (at most a few missiles), such as might occur in an unauthorized

[42] Lindsay, James M., and Michael O'Hanlon. *Defending America: The Case for Limited National Missile Defense*. Washington, DC: Brookings, 2001. Wirtz, James J., and Jeffrey A. Larsen. *Rocket's Red Glare: Missile Defenses and the Future of World Politics*. Boulder, CO: Westview Press, 2001.

launch, an accident, or an attack by a small state. Japan plans to spend $1 billion a year to build a U.S.-designed missile defense system by 2007, based on land and at sea. North Korea has more than 600 ballistic missiles capable of hitting Japan, however.

Ballistic Missile Defense

In 2004, the United States began deploying both a prototype missile intercept system based in Alaska and a destroyer in the Sea of Japan, off North Korea, that could try to shoot down a North Korean missile in its boost phase. It also moved to put in place—against strong Chinese opposition—a missile-defense collaboration in Asia that would include Japan, Australia, possibly India, and Taiwan. Four Japanese destroyers are to join the U.S. one, and Patriot missiles based in Japan would try to shoot down incoming missiles. Several tests of the U.S. system failed in 2004.

Other technologies are also being tested, including lasers fired from either space or ships to disable ballistic missiles in the boost phase after launch (when their engines make them easy to detect, and warheads and decoys have not yet deployed). Overall, no reliable defense against ballistic missiles exists, and experts disagree on whether such a defense is just a few or many years away.

In addition to the technical challenges of stopping incoming ballistic missile warheads, a true strategic defense would also have to stop cruise missiles (possibly launched from submarines), airplanes, and more innovative delivery systems. If a rogue state or terrorist group struck the United States with a nuclear weapon, it would probably not use an ICBM to do so. Nobody has an answer to this problem. For now, the only real defense against nuclear weapons is a good offense—keeping those weapons out of new hands, and threatening massive retaliation against states that already have them.

Nuclear Arsenals and Arms Control

During the Cold War, the superpowers' nuclear forces grew and technologies developed. These evolving force structures were codified (more than constrained) by a series of arms control agreements. *Arms control* is an effort by two or more states to regulate by formal agreement their acquisition of weapons.[43] Arms control is broader than just nuclear weapons—for instance, after World War I the great powers negotiated limits on sizes of navies—but in recent decades nuclear weapons have been the main focus of arms control. Arms control agreements typically require long formal negotiations with many technical discussions, culminating in a treaty. Some arms control treaties are multilateral, but during the Cold War most were bilateral (U.S.-Soviet). Some stay in effect indefinitely; others have a limited term.

At first, the United States had far superior nuclear forces and relied on a strategy of massive retaliation for any Soviet conventional attack. This threat became less credible as the Soviet Union developed a second-strike capability. In the 1960s, the superpowers turned to nuclear arms control to regulate their relations. They gained confidence from arms control agreements that they could do business with each other and that they would not let the arms race lead them into a nuclear war—fear of which had increased after the Cuban Missile Crisis of 1962. The first agreements banned testing nuclear weapons in the atmosphere or placing nuclear weapons in space. The 1968 Non-Proliferation Treaty (NPT) built on the superpowers' common fears of China and other potential new nuclear states. Other confidence-building measures were directed at the management of potential crises. The hot line agreement connected the U.S. and Soviet heads of state by telephone. Eventually, the superpowers developed centers and systems for the exchange of information in a crisis.

Several treaties in the 1970s locked in the superpowers' basic parity in nuclear capabilities under MAD. The 1972 **Antiballistic Missile (ABM) Treaty** prevented either side

---

[43] Adler, Emanuel, ed. *The International Practice of Arms Control*. Johns Hopkins, 1992.

from using a ballistic missile defense as a shield from which to launch a first strike. However, to allow full-scale testing of missile-defense technologies, the United States withdrew from the ABM Treaty with six months' notice (as provided in the treaty), effective mid-2002. President Bush called the treaty a relic of the Cold War, but critics called U.S. missile defense a costly blunder that could induce China to greatly enlarge its minimal nuclear arsenal (which in turn could accelerate India's nuclear weapons production, and thus Pakistan's as well).

The **Strategic Arms Limitation Treaties (SALT)** in the 1970s put formal ceilings on the growth of both sides' strategic weapons. The U.S. arsenal peaked in the 1960s at more than 30,000 warheads; the Soviet arsenal peaked in the 1980s at more than 40,000.

More recent arms control agreements regulated the substantial reduction of nuclear forces after the end of the Cold War.[44] Under the 2002 U.S.-Russian Strategic Offensive Reductions Treaty, each side is to reduce deployed warheads from about 6,000 to 2,200 within a decade, in addition to the elimination of most tactical nuclear weapons. A **Comprehensive Test Ban Treaty (CTBT)** to halt all nuclear test-explosions was signed in 1996 after decades of stalemate. It aims to impede the development of new types of nuclear weapons. However, the treaty does not take effect until signed and ratified by all 44 states believed capable of building at least a crude nuclear weapon. India did not sign the CTBT, and defied it in 1998 with five nuclear tests. Pakistan followed suit with its own tests. The U.S. Senate voted in 1999 against ratifying the CTBT, and the Bush administration opposes it. Russia ratified it in 2000. No nuclear tests occurred worldwide in 1999–2005.

China, France, and Britain each have several hundred weapons. Britain tends to use U.S.-built nuclear weapons systems; China and France rely on their own efforts. Britain's arsenal includes 185 warheads on long-range submarine-launched missiles and tactical aircraft. France has about 400 warheads on submarine-launched long-range missiles and 50 on aircraft; it dismantled its 18 land-based missiles in 1996. China is thought to have 7 warheads on long-range land missiles, 100 on intermediate-range missiles, 12 on submarines, 150 on long-range bombers, and more than 100 on artillery and rockets.[45]

Efforts to control conventional arms trade through arms control treaties have had no success. After the Gulf War, the five permanent Security Council members tried to negotiate limits on the supply of weapons to the Middle East. The five participants account for most of the weapons sold in the Middle East. But no participant wanted to give up its own lucrative arms sales in the region, which each naturally saw as justified (again, showing the difficulty of overcoming collective action problems).

All the weapons of mass destruction are relatively difficult and expensive to build, yet they provide only specialized capabilities that are rarely if ever actually used. This is why a number of states have decided that such weapons are not worth acquiring, though it would be technically possible to do so. Such cost-benefit thinking also applies more broadly to states' decisions about the acquisition of all kinds of military forces.

States face complex choices regarding the configuration of their military forces in the post–Cold War era. Not only have the immediate contingencies and threats changed drastically, but the nature of threats in the new era is unknown. Perhaps most important, world order itself is evolving even as military technologies do. The next chapter discusses the evolving structures and norms governing international political relations and how they are changing the nature of world order.

---

[44] Larsen, Jeffrey A. *Arms Control: Cooperative Security in a Changing Environment*. Boulder, CO: Lynne Rienner, 2002.

[45] Norris, Robert S., and William M. Arkin. British, French, and Chinese Nuclear Forces. *Bulletin of the Atomic Scientists* 52 (6), 1996: 64–67.

THINKING CRITICALLY

1. If you were the leader of, say, Vietnam, what size and kinds of military forces would you want your country to have? To meet what kinds of threats would you choose each type of capability?
2. Suppose that Libya turned out to have obtained three tactical nuclear warheads from the former Soviet arsenal and was keeping them in unknown locations. What, if anything, should the great powers do about this? What consequences might follow from their actions?
3. Imagine a world in which most of the states, rather than just a few, had nuclear weapons and long-range ballistic missiles. Would it be more peaceful or more war-prone? Why?
4. Most of the great powers are reconfiguring their military forces in the post–Cold War era. What kinds of capabilities do you think your own country needs in this period? Why?
5. World military spending is over $900 billion every year. If you could redirect these funds, how would you use them? Would such uses be better or worse for the states involved? Do you think there is a realistic chance of redirecting military spending in the way you suggest?

CHAPTER SUMMARY

- Military forces provide states with means of leverage beyond the various nonmilitary means of influence widely used in international bargaining.
- Political leaders face difficult choices in configuring military forces and paying for them. Military spending tends to stimulate economic growth in the short term but reduce growth over the long term.
- In the 1990s, military forces and expenditures of the great powers—especially Russia—were reduced and restructured.
- Military forces include a wide variety of capabilities suited to different purposes. Conventional warfare requires different kinds of forces than those needed to threaten the use of nuclear, chemical, or biological weapons.
- Except in time of civil war, state leaders—whether civilian or military—control military forces through a single hierarchical chain of command.
- Military forces can threaten the domestic power of state leaders, who are vulnerable to being overthrown by coups d'état.
- Control of territory is fundamental to state sovereignty and is accomplished primarily with ground forces.
- Air war, using precision-guided bombs against battlefield targets, proved extremely effective in the U.S. campaigns in Iraq in 1991, Serbia in 1999, Afghanistan in 2001, and Iraq in 2003.
- Small missiles and electronic warfare are increasingly important, especially for naval and air forces. The role of satellites is expanding in communications, navigation, and reconnaissance.
- Weapons of mass destruction—nuclear, chemical, and biological—have been used only a handful of times in war.
- The production of nuclear weapons is technically within the means of many states and some nonstate actors, but the necessary fissionable material (uranium-235 or plutonium) is very difficult to obtain.

- Most industrialized states, and many poor ones, have refrained voluntarily from acquiring nuclear weapons. These states include two great powers, Germany and Japan.
- More states are acquiring ballistic missiles capable of striking other states from hundreds of miles away (or farther, depending on the missile's range). But no state has ever attacked another with weapons of mass destruction mounted on ballistic missiles.
- Chemical weapons are cheaper to build than nuclear weapons, they have similar threat value, and their production is harder to detect. More middle powers have chemical weapons than nuclear ones. A new treaty bans the possession and use of chemical weapons.
- Several states conduct research into biological warfare, but by treaty the possession of such weapons is banned.
- Slowing the proliferation of ballistic missiles and weapons of mass destruction in the global South is a central concern of the great powers.
- The United States is testing systems to defend against ballistic missile attack, although none has yet proven feasible, and withdrew from the ABM treaty with Russia to pursue this program.
- The United States and Russia have arsenals of thousands of nuclear weapons; China, Britain, and France have hundreds. Israel, India, and Pakistan each have scores. Weapons deployments are guided by nuclear strategy based on the concept of deterrence.
- Arms control agreements formally define the contours of an arms race or mutual disarmament process. Arms control helped build confidence between the superpowers during the Cold War.

KEY TERMS

economic conversion 215
chain of command 220
military governments 222
coup d'état 222
infantry 225
land mines 225
power projection 226
electronic warfare 229
stealth technology 230
weapons of mass destruction 231
fissionable material 231
ballistic missile 233
intercontinental ballistic missile (ICBM) 233
cruise missile 234
Missile Technology Control Regime 236
Chemical Weapons Convention 237
Biological Weapons Convention 237
proliferation 238
Non-Proliferation Treaty (NPT) 240
mutually assured destruction (MAD) 242
Strategic Defense Initiative (SDI) 243
Antiballistic Missile (ABM) Treaty 244
Strategic Arms Limitation Treaties (SALT) 245
Comprehensive Test Ban Treaty (CTBT) 245

ONLINE PRACTICE TEST

Take an online practice test at
www.internationalrelations.net

❑ A
❑ B
☑ C
❑ D

LET'S DEBATE THE ISSUE

North Korea's Weapons of Mass Destruction: A Threat to World Order?

by Mir Zohair Husain

Overview Weapons of mass destruction (WMD) are one of the greatest threats facing the world. On February 10, 2005, North Korea claimed it had developed nuclear weapons. Additionally, North Korea had serious economic, social, and political concerns: a stagnant economy, economic mismanagement, and a moribund totalitarian communist system. When North Korea—a country that was responsible for the invasion of South Korea and the Korean War (1950–1953)—diverted its limited resources from much needed socioeconomic programs to WMD programs, the world became alarmed.

On the other hand, in June 2000, after 50 years of conflict, North and South Korea seemed to progress toward a permanent peace settlement. Furthermore, North Korea's dire need for foreign assistance (as many as two million North Koreans may have died of starvation and health problems during the late 1990s) makes it more amenable to improving diplomatic and economic relations with the rest of world.

These are the high stakes that the negotiators—China, Russia, Japan, South Korea, and the United States—must consider in deciding whether to pursue constructive engagement (the employment of political and economic relations) with North Korea for positive changes in the regime's objectionable policies, or engage in coercive diplomacy (the use of military, economic, and diplomatic threats) to induce North Korea to discontinue its WMD programs. Therefore, are promises of rewards or threats of punishment more likely to get North Korea to abandon its WMD programs?

Argument 1 Constructive Engagement Should Be the Policy Toward North Korea

North Korea's nuclear weapons development program is its best leverage and deterrence against its enemies. North Korea has reason to fear the United States, which maintains over 30,000 troops in South Korea, has never signed a treaty ending the Korean War, and has referred to North Korea as part of the "axis of evil" (along with Iraq and Iran). Hence, North Korea is using its WMD programs as leverage to diplomatically engage the United States.

> [In 2000, Kim Jong Il was asked why] was North Korea's government spending its scarce resources on ballistic missiles instead of education or other social programs that would directly benefit its starving citizens? [He replied,] "The missiles cannot reach the United States, and if I launch them, the U.S. would fire back thousands of missiles and we would not survive. I know that very well. But I have to let them know I have missiles. I am making them because only then will the United States talk to me." . . .
>
> The disarmament question is even stickier. The [Bush] administration has waged two pre-emptive wars on countries it deemed to be enemies—Afghanistan and Iraq. It does not require Kissingerian smarts to calculate that a member of the axis of evil would be death-wish foolish to relinquish the weapons of mass destruction that may be the only thing, by virtue of the horrible implications of their use, that stands in the way of an American attack. (Peter Maass. "The Last Emperor." *The New York Times,* October 19, 2003.)

North Korea will halt its nuclear weapons development program if the United States gives assurances. North Korea's economy is in shambles, and it can no longer count on Russia or China for economic and humanitarian assistance. To preserve its state, North Korea uses its nuclear weapons development program as leverage to get U.S. aid. Moreover, North Korea would not require such volatile weapons if it had assurances of its safety (similar to those given to Cuba) from the country it has long labeled its "sworn enemy."

> ... most Chinese international security experts insist that the United States holds the two most important keys to resolving the North Korean problem: ending a state of hostility that dates from the earliest days of the cold war and providing tangible assurances to North Korea that Washington does not seek the government's overthrow. Howard W. French. (Doubting U.S., China Is Wary of Korea Role." *The New York Times,* February 19, 2005.)

Constructive engagement provides the best opportunity for disarming North Korea. A peacefully negotiated multilateral settlement would be preferable. As of June 2004, the proposal to North Korea entailed investment in the country and weapons inspections in return for disarmament. However, if a final resolution is not reached, or if North Korea reneges on its commitment to disarm, the United States will likely receive international support to use coercive diplomacy.

> In a proposal whose details are still being refined, [the United States] and four other nations would guarantee not to attack the North in exchange for its commitment to dismantle its nuclear weapons programs.
>
> This proposal makes an eventual peaceful, diplomatic solution to this extremely dangerous problem somewhat more likely. ... If the North does spurn this reasonable offer, [the U.S.] will find it easier to persuade Asian nations to support more coercive steps, like international economic sanctions. ("Trying Diplomacy on North Korea." *The New York Times,* October 21, 2003.)

Argument 2 Coercive Diplomacy Should Be the Policy Toward North Korea

North Korea is a threat to the world. North Korea possesses a potent military establishment, earns foreign exchange from illegal activities, and sells dangerous weapons to developing countries. The best option to ensure that North Korea disarms is to attain unfettered access for UN inspectors to oversee the destruction of all WMD and nuclear weapons development programs. If Kim Jong Il refuses, threats of military force should be employed to pressure North Korea to comply.

> North Korea has the globe's third-largest army, 5,000 tons of sarin nerve gas and (the spooks believe) a secret reserve of the smallpox virus....
>
> North Korea finances its budget partly by peddling drugs, selling weapons to terrorists in places like the Philippines, and counterfeiting American $100 bills. The nightmare scenario would be North Korea raising cash by selling a vial of smallpox to al Qaeda. (Nicholas D. Kristof. "The Greater Danger." *The New York Times,* January 11, 2002.)

Kim Jong Il's regime is untrustworthy. Kim Jong Il cares little about the welfare of his citizens and even less about foreigners. Furthermore, in its desperation for funds, North Korea may secretly retain nuclear weapons to sell later or use them as leverage to get more aid.

> Though friendly with important visitors, Kim is vicious to his own people. An estimated two million of them died during a preventable famine in the 1990s, and several hundred thousand are in prison and labor camps; many have been executed....
>
> Working at the center of the regime, Hwang [Jang Yop] learned what Kim Jong Il wants, what he can do and what he will not do.
>
> Hwang says he does not believe Kim would ever allow foreign aid and investment to benefit the people who need it; Kim has shown no interest in his people's material well-being, and given the choice between regime survival and national prosperity, it's pretty clear which he would prefer....
>
> Hwang says outsiders are naive to believe that Kim is ready to open up his country.
>
> "South Korea is being fooled, and the Chinese, who should know best," he said. "A considerable number of people are being fooled, including the United States." (Peter Maass. "The Last Emperor." *The New York Times,* October 19, 2003.)

Simply paying North Korea not to develop nuclear weapons is a short-term solution. Negotiators must insist that North Korea adopt China's example of economic liberalization as well as fulfill the basic human needs of its people rather than maintain a huge defense establishment.

> Rather than merely buying out North Korea's missile program, the United States and its allies should insist that North Korea accept an arms control regime that would scale back conventional weaponry on the peninsula. If North Korea were willing to begin economic reform, perhaps along a Chinese model, the United States, Japan and South Korea should commit to providing substantial economic assistance—not as bribery, but as genuine aid to help convert the North Korean economy. (Michael O'Hanlon. "Choosing the Right Enemies." *The New York Times,* February 6, 2002.)

North Korea's Weapons of Mass Destruction

Questions

1. Based on the excerpts above, do you think North Korea is a real or perceived threat to world order? Why or why not?
2. Do you foresee problems if the United States takes unilateral steps for the permanent disarmament of North Korea? Explain.

Selected Readings

Michael O'Hanlon and Mike M. Mochizuki. *Crisis on the Korean Peninsula: How to Deal With a Nuclear North Korea.* NY: McGraw-Hill, 2003.

Victor D. Cha and David C. Kang. *Nuclear North Korea: A Debate on Engagement. Strategies.* Irvington, NY: Columbia University Press, 2003.

Greece's foreign minister addresses the UN Security Council, 2006.

World Order
The Evolution of World Order • International Norms and Morality • Roles of International Organizations

The United Nations
The UN System • The Security Council • Peacekeeping Forces • The Secretariat • The General Assembly • UN Programs • Autonomous Agencies

International Law
Sources of International Law • Enforcement of International Law • The World Court • International Cases in National Courts

Law and Sovereignty
Laws of Diplomacy • War Crimes • Just War Doctrine • Human Rights

CHAPTER 7

International Organization and Law

World Order

Most international conflicts are not settled by military force. Despite the anarchic nature of the international system based on state sovereignty, the security dilemma does not usually lead to a breakdown in basic cooperation among states. States generally refrain from taking maximum short-term advantage of each other (such as by invading and conquering). States work *with* other states for mutual gain and take advantage of each other only "at the margin." Unfortunately, the day-to-day cooperative activities of states often are less newsworthy than states' uses of force.

States work together by following rules they develop to govern their interactions. States usually *do* follow the rules. Over time, the rules become more firmly established and institutions grow up around them. States then develop the habit of working through those institutions and within the rules. They do so because of self-interest; given the regulation of international interactions through institutions and rules, they can realize great gains, thereby avoiding the costly outcomes associated with a breakdown of cooperation (see pp. 103–104).

International anarchy thus does not mean a lack of order, structure, and rules. In many ways, actors in international society now work together as cooperatively as actors in domestic society—more so than some domestic societies. Today, most violent conflicts are civil wars, not interstate wars; this change reflects the general success of international norms, organizations, and laws—in addition to the balance of power—in maintaining peace among states.

International anarchy, then, means simply that states surrender sovereignty to no one. Domestic society has government with powers of enforcement; international society does not. When the rules are broken in IR, actors can rely only on the power of individual states (separately or in concert) to restore order.[1]

The Evolution of World Order

Over the centuries, international institutions and rules have grown stronger, more complex, and more important.[2] International order started out based largely on raw power, but

[1] Suganami, Hidemi. *The Domestic Analogy and World Order Proposals*. Cambridge, 1989.

[2] Legalization and World Politics. Special issue of *International Organization* 54 (4), 2000.

it has evolved to be based more on legitimacy and habit. *Domestic law*, too, was once enforced only by the most powerful for the most powerful. The first states and civilizations were largely military dictatorships. Law was what the top ruler decreed. International law and organization likewise began as terms imposed by powerful winners on losers after wars.

The international institutions and rules that operate today took shape especially during periods of hegemony (see "Hegemony" on p. 82), when one state predominated in international power following a hegemonic war among the great powers. The international organizations that today form the institutional framework for international interactions—such as the United Nations, the Organization of American States, and the World Bank—were created after World War II under U.S. leadership.[3]

Rules of international behavior have become established over time as norms and are often codified as international law. This is a more incremental process than the creation of institutions; it goes on between and during periods of war and of hegemony. But still the most powerful states, especially hegemons, have great influence on the rules and values that have become embedded over time in a body of international law.

For example, the principle of free passage on the open seas is now formally established in international law.[4] But at one time warships from one state did not hesitate to seize the ships of other states and make off with their cargoes. This practice was profitable to the state that pulled off such raids, but of course their own shipping could be raided in return. Such behavior made long-distance trade itself more dangerous, less predictable, and less profitable. The trading states could benefit more by getting rid of the practice. So, over time, a norm developed around the concept of freedom of navigation on the high seas. It became one of the first areas of international law developed by the Dutch legal scholar *Hugo Grotius* in the mid-1600s—a time when the Dutch dominated world trade and could benefit most from free navigation.

Dutch power, then, provided the backbone for the international legal concept of freedom of the seas. Later, when Britain was dominant, it enforced the principle of free seas through the cannons of its warships. As the world's main trading state, Britain benefited from a worldwide norm of free shipping and trade. And with the world's most powerful navy, it was in a position to define and enforce the rules for the world's oceans.

Likewise, twentieth-century world order depended heavily on the power of the United States (and, for a few decades, on the division of power between the United States and the Soviet Union). The United States at times came close to adopting the explicit role of "world police force." But in truth the world is too large for any single state—even a hegemon—to police effectively. Rather, the world's states usually go along with the rules established by the most powerful state without constant policing. Meanwhile, they try to influence the rules by working through international institutions (to which the hegemon cedes some of its power). In this way, although states do not yield their sovereignty, they vest some power and authority in international institutions and laws and generally work within that framework.[5]

International Norms and Morality

The rules that govern most interactions in IR are rooted in norms. **International norms** are the expectations held by state leaders about normal international relations. The invasion of

---

[3] Ikenberry, G. John. *After Victory: Institutions, Strategic Restraint, and the Rebuilding of Order after Major Wars*. Princeton, 2001.

[4] Booth, Ken. *Law, Force and Diplomacy at Sea*. Winchester, MA: Allen & Unwin, 1985.

[5] Falk, Richard. *Explorations at the Edge of Time: The Prospects for World Order*. Temple, 1992. Mendes, Errol, and Ozay Mehmet. *Global Governance, Economy and Law: Waiting for Justice*. NY: Routledge, 2003.

Kuwait by Iraq was not only illegal, it was widely viewed as immoral—beyond the acceptable range of behavior of states (that is, beyond the normal amount of cheating that states get away with). Political leaders in the United States and around the world drew on moral norms to generate support for a collective response to Iraq. Thus morality is an element of power (see “Elements of Power” on pp. 59–61).

CRITICAL INTERVENTION

International norms are evolving in such areas as humanitarian intervention versus national sovereignty. These norms help define the roles of international organizations. Here, in 2006, protesters at the UN compound in Ivory Coast object to foreign mediators' decision to dissolve parliament as part of a postwar settlement, which the protesters call an infringement of sovereignty.

Some norms, like sovereignty and respect for treaties, are widely held; they shape expectations about state behavior and set standards that make deviations stand out. Constructivist scholars in IR emphasize the importance of these global norms and standards. The attempt to define universal norms follows a centuries-long philosophical tradition. Philosophers such as Kant argued that it was natural for autonomous individuals (or states) to cooperate for mutual benefit because they could see that pursuing their narrow individual interests would end up hurting all. Thus, sovereign states could work together through structures and organizations (like Kant's proposed world federation) that would respect each member's autonomy and not create a world government over them. In the nineteenth century, such ideas were embodied in practical organizations in which states participated to manage specific issues such as international postal service and control of traffic on European rivers.

International Norms

Agreed norms of behavior, institutionalized through such organizations, become *habitual* over time and gain *legitimacy*. State leaders become used to behaving in a normal way and stop calculating, for each action, whether violating norms would pay off. For example, at the turn of the nineteenth century, U.S. war planners had active war plans for the possibility of a major naval conflict between the United States and Great Britain. Today, such plans would seem ridiculous. Over time, states refrain from behavior not just for cost-benefit reasons (as emphasized by realists and liberals) but for normative reasons having little to do with material calculations (as emphasized by constructivists). Legitimacy and habit explain why international norms can be effective even when they are not codified and enforced.

The power of international norms and standards of morality, however, may vary when different states or world regions hold different expectations of what is normal. To the United States, it was a moral imperative to remove Saddam Hussein from power. But from the perspective of Arab populations, the U.S. invasion was an unjust violation of territorial sovereignty. In cases of diverging norms, morality can be a factor for misunderstanding and conflict rather than a force of stability. Realists point to examples such as these to suggest that international norms do not hold much sway on important matters of IR. Yet, constructivist scholars point out that even if international norms are violated, states (even the United States) go

Consolidating Norms

to tremendous lengths to justify behaviors that violate the norm. This suggests that strong norms do exist and are recognized by even the most powerful states.

The end of the Cold War put basic expectations, such as when U.S. military intervention is warranted, up for grabs. One problem with rapid change is that nobody knows what to expect; norms break down because leaders do not have common expectations. Through a long process of coping with a sequence of cases, international leaders build up new understandings of the rules of the game.

These new norms remain unsettled in 2006. New expectations are emerging in such areas as human rights, UN peacekeeping, humanitarian interventions,[6] Russia's and China's roles as great powers, and the U.S. role as a superpower. The 2001 terrorist attacks on the United States shifted international norms, bringing about greater cooperation among states (including among great powers) and curbing an isolationist streak in U.S. politics. But then the 2003 Iraq war divided the international community, with the majority of countries—big and small, North and South—expressing reservations about the newly assertive U.S. actions. It is unclear how much of this new U.S. posture, caricatured by critics as a "cowboy" foreign policy, is specific to the Bush administration and how much is related to the post-September 11 world order. A major issue in President Bush's second term are U.S. attempts to mend relations with the international community.

Three factors had already combined to shake up international norms—the end of the Cold War, the shifts in economic position of various regions and states (such as China and the United States relative to Japan, Russia, and Africa), and the effects of technological change in creating a "small world." Domestic and local politics now play out on a global stage. In the coming years, international norms may settle down in a new configuration as these trends continue to evolve.

Roles of International Organizations

Especially in times of change, when shared norms and habits may not suffice to solve international dilemmas and achieve mutual cooperation, institutions play a key role. They are concrete, tangible structures with specific functions and missions. These institutions have proliferated rapidly in recent decades, and continue to play an increasing role in international affairs. **International organizations (IOs)** include *intergovernmental organizations (IGOs)* such as the UN, and *nongovernmental organizations (NGOs)* such as the International Committee of the Red Cross.

The number of IOs has grown more than fivefold since 1945, reaching about four hundred independent IGOs and tens of thousands of NGOs (depending somewhat on definitions).[7] Figure 7.1 illustrates this growth. New NGOs are created around the world daily. This weaving together of people across national boundaries through specialized groups reflects interdependence (see pp. 310–313).[8]

---

[6] Weiss, Thomas G. *Military-Civilian Interactions: Humanitarian Crises and the Responsibility to Protect*. 2nd ed. Lanham, MD: Rowman & Littlefield, 2005. Welsh, Jennifer M., ed. *Humanitarian Intervention and International Relations*. Oxford, 2004. Wheeler, Nicholas J. *Saving Strangers: Humanitarian Intervention in International Society*. Oxford, 2001.

[7] Pevehouse, Jon C., Timothy Nordstrom, and Kevin Warnke. The Correlates of War 2 International Governmental Organizations Data Version 2.0. *Conflict Management and Peace Science* 21 (2), 2004: 101–120.

[8] Pease, Kelly-Kate S. *International Organizations: Perspectives on Governance in the Twenty-First Century*. 2nd ed. NY: Prentice Hall, 2002. Barnett, Michael N. and Martha Finnemore. *Rules for the World: International Organizations and Global Politics*. Cornell, 2004. Boli, John, and George M. Thomas, eds. *Constructing World Culture: International Nongovernmental Organizations Since 1875*. Stanford, 1999. Bennett, A. LeRoy, and James K. Oliver. *International Organizations: Principles and Issues*, 7th ed. Upper Saddle River, NJ: Prentice Hall, 2002.

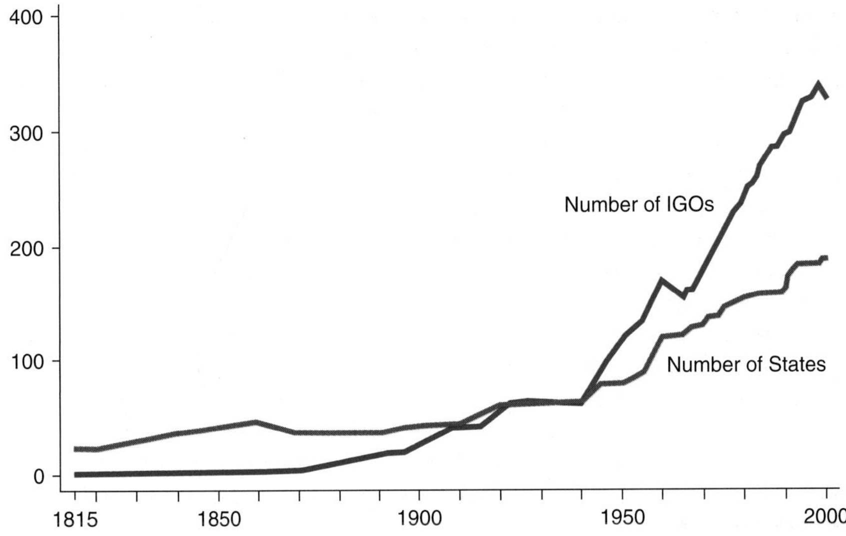

FIGURE 7.1 ■ **States and IGOs in the World, 1815–2000**

Some IGOs are global in scope, others are regional or just bilateral (having only two states as members). Some are general in their purposes, others have specific functional purposes. Overall, the success of these IGOs has been mixed; the regional ones have had more success than the global ones, and those with specific functional or technical purposes have worked better than those with broad purposes (see pp. 377–380). IGOs hold together because they promote the national interests (or enhance the leverage) of their member states—not because of vague ideals.

Among *regional* IGOs, the European Union encompasses some of the most important organizations (see Chapter 10), but it is not the only example. Others include the Association of South East Asian Nations (ASEAN), the Southern Cone Common Market (MERCOSUR), and locust control organizations in Africa (on regional security alliances, see pp. 87–94). The functional roles of IOs are important to their overall effect on international relations, but those roles are taken up in Chapter 10 on international integration. Here, we will rely on the more general theoretical discussion of international institutions begun in Chapter 3.

Global IGOs (aside from the UN) usually have functional purposes involving coordinating actions of some set of states around the world. The IGO called Intelsat, for example, is a consortium of governments and private businesses that operates communications satellites. Members of the Organization of Petroleum Exporting Countries (OPEC) are major oil producers who meet periodically in Vienna to set production quotas for members in an effort to keep world oil prices high and stable. Note that while the key members of IGOs are states, NGOs, businesses, or individuals can have important advisory and consulting roles in IGOs.

NGOs tend to be more specialized in function than IGOs. For instance, someone wanting to meet political scientists from other countries can join the International Political Science Association. Many NGOs have economic or business-related functions. The International Air Transport Association coordinates the work of airline companies. Other NGOs have global political purposes—Amnesty International for human rights or Planned Parenthood for reproductive rights and family planning. Still others have cultural purposes—for example, the International Olympic Committee.

Religious groups are among the largest NGOs—their memberships often span many countries. Both in today's world and historically, sects of Christianity, Islam, Buddhism, Judaism, Hinduism, and other world religions have organized themselves across state borders, often in the face of hostility from one or more national governments. Missionaries have deliberately built and nurtured these transnational links. The Catholic Church historically held a special position in the European international system, especially before the seventeenth century. NGOs with broad purposes and geographical scope often maintain observer status in the UN so that they can participate in UN meetings about issues of concern. For example, Greenpeace attends UN meetings about the global environment.

A web of international organizations of various sizes and types now connects people in all countries. The rapid growth of this network, and the increasingly intense communications and interactions that occur within it, are indicative of rising international interdependence. These organizations in turn provide the institutional mesh to hold together some kind of world order even when leaders and contexts come and go, and even when norms are undermined by sudden changes in power relations. At the center of that web of connection stands the most important international organization today, the United Nations.

The United Nations

The UN and other international organizations have both strengths and weaknesses in the anarchic international system. State sovereignty creates a real need for such organizations on a practical level, because no central world government performs the function of coordinating the actions of states for mutual benefit. However, state sovereignty also severely limits the power of the UN and other IOs, because governments reserve power to themselves and are stingy in delegating it to the UN or anyone else. The UN has had a mixed record with these strengths and weaknesses—in some ways providing remarkable global-level management and in other ways appearing helpless against the sovereignty of even modest-sized states (not to mention great powers).

The UN System

The UN is a relatively new institution, less than 60 years old. Even newer is the more prominent role that the UN has played in international security affairs since the end of the Cold War. Despite this new prominence, the main purposes of the UN are the same now as when it was founded after World War II.[9]

Purposes of the UN The UN is the closest thing to a world government that has ever existed, but it is not a world government. Its members are sovereign states that have not empowered the UN to enforce its will within states' territories except with the consent of those states' governments. Thus, although the UN strengthens world order, its design acknowledges the realities of international anarchy and the unwillingness of states to

[9] Krasno, Jean E. *The United Nations: Confronting the Challenges of a Global Society*. Boulder, CO: Lynne Rienner, 2004. Ziring, Lawrence, et al. *The United Nations: International Organization and World Politics*. 4th ed. Belmont, CA: Wadsworth, 2004. Rittberger, Volker. *Global Governance and the United Nations System*. NY: United Nations University, 2001. Baratta, Joseph Preston. *The Politics of World Federation*. 2 vol. Westfield, CT: Praeger, 2004.

surrender their sovereignty. Within these limits, the basic purpose of the UN is to provide a global institutional structure through which states can sometimes settle conflicts with less reliance on the use of force.

The **UN Charter** is based on the principles that states are *equal* under international law; that states have full *sovereignty* over their own affairs; that states should have full *independence* and *territorial integrity*; and that states should carry out their international *obligations*—such as respecting diplomatic privileges, refraining from committing aggression, and observing the terms of treaties they sign. The Charter also lays out the structure of the UN and the methods by which it operates.

The UN does not exist because it has power to force its will on the world's states; it exists because states have created it to serve their needs. A state's membership in the UN is essentially a form of indirect leverage. States gain leverage by using the UN to seek more beneficial outcomes in conflicts (especially on general multilateral issues where a global forum brings all parties together). The cost of this leverage is modest—UN dues and the expenses of diplomatic representatives, in addition to the agreement to behave in accordance with the Charter (most of the time).

States get several benefits from the UN. Foremost among these is the international stability (especially in security affairs) that the UN tries to safeguard; this allows states to realize gains from trade and other forms of exchange (see Chapter 8). The UN is a *symbol* of international order and even of global identity. It is also a *forum* where states promote their views and bring their disputes. And it is a *mechanism* for *conflict resolution* in international security affairs. The UN also promotes and coordinates development assistance (see Chapter 13) and other programs of *economic* and *social development* in the global South. These programs reflect the belief that economic and social problems—above all, poverty—are an important source of international conflict and war. Finally, the UN is a coordinating system for *information* and planning by hundreds of internal and external agencies and programs, and for the publication of international data.

Despite its heavy tasks, the UN is still a small and fragile institution—a 60-year-old infant. Compare, for instance, what states spend on two types of leverage for settling conflicts: military forces and the UN. Every year, the world spends $800 billion on the military and about $2 billion on the UN. That proportion is about the same in the United States: each U.S. citizen pays (on average) about $1,500 a year for U.S. military forces and about $5 a year for UN dues and assessments. The UN costs about as much as the military budget of a single mid-sized country such as Malaysia or Egypt, or less than what a country such as Thailand or Switzerland spends on military forces.

Sometimes the UN succeeds and sometimes it fails. The UN deals with the issues that are perhaps *the* most difficult in the world. If groups of states could easily solve problems such as ethnic conflicts, human rights, refugees, and world hunger among themselves, they most likely would have done so. Instead, states turn many of these difficult problems over to the UN and hope it can take care of them.

Structure of the UN The UN's structure, shown in Figure 7.2, centers around the **UN General Assembly,** where representatives of all states sit together in a huge room, listen to speeches, and pass resolutions. The General Assembly coordinates a variety of development programs and other autonomous agencies through the *Economic and Social Council (ECOSOC)*. Parallel to the General Assembly is the **UN Security Council,** in which five great powers and ten rotating member states make decisions about international peace and security. The Security Council has responsibility for the dispatch of peacekeeping forces to trouble spots. The administration of the UN takes place through the **UN Secretariat** (executive branch), led by the secretary-general of the UN. The *World Court* (International

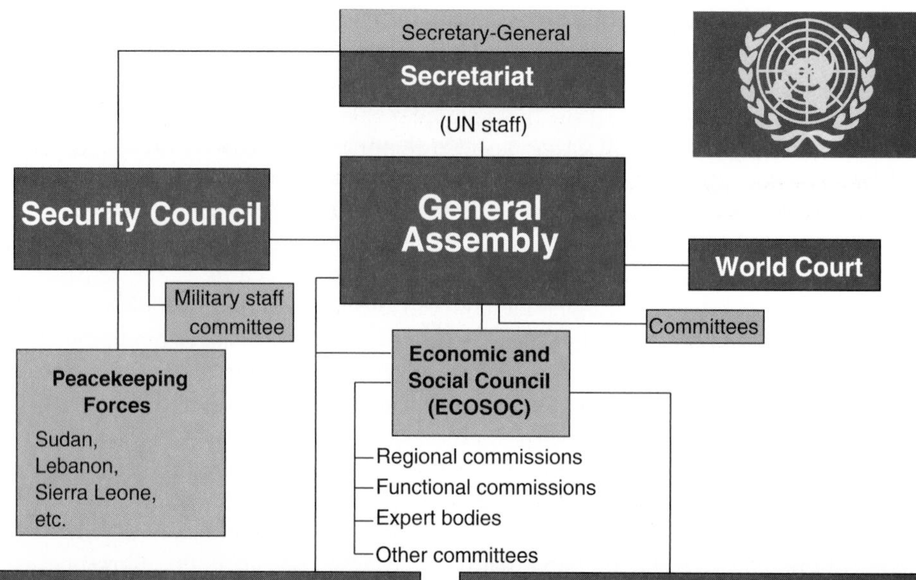

UN Programs

UNEP	UN Environment Program
UNICEF	UN Children's Fund
UNDRO	Office of the UN Disaster Relief Coordinator
UNHCR	Office of the UN High Commissioner for Refugees
UNRWA*	UN Relief Works Agency [for Palestinian Refugees]
UNDP	UN Development Program
UNITAR*	UN Institute for Training and Research
UNIFEM	UN Development Fund for Women
INSTRAW	UN International Research and Training Institute [for women]
UNCTAD	UN Conference on Trade and Development
WFP	World Food Program
WFC	World Food Council
UNCHS	Human Settlements (Habitat)
UNFPA	UN Population Fund
UNU	UN University
UNDCP	Drug Control Program
ITC	International Trade Center

* Does not report to ECOSOC.

Autonomous Agencies

IAEA*	International Atomic Energy Agency (Vienna)
WHO	World Health Organization (Geneva)
FAO	Food and Agriculture Organization (Rome)
IFAD	International Fund for Agricultural Development (Rome)
ILO	International Labor Organization (Geneva)
UNESCO	UN Educational, Scientific, and Cultural Organization (Paris)
UNIDO	UN Industrial Development Organization (Vienna)
ITU	International Telecommunications Union (Geneva)
IPU	International Postal Union (Berne)
ICAO	International Civil Aviation Organization (Montreal)
IMO	International Maritime Organization (London)
WIPO	World Intellectual Property Organization (Geneva)
WMO	World Meteorological Association (Geneva)
MIGA	Multilateral Investment Guarantee Agency
IMF	International Monetary Fund (Washington)
IBRD	International Bank for Reconstruction and Development [World Bank] (Washington)
IDA	International Development Association (Washington)
IFC	International Finance Corporation (Washington)
WTO*	World Trade Organization (Geneva)

* Does not report to ECOSOC.

FIGURE 7.2 ■ The United Nations

Court of Justice), which is discussed later in the chapter, is a judicial arm of the UN. (A *Trusteeship Council* oversaw the transition of a handful of former colonial territories to full independence; with the last trust territory's independence in 1994, the Council suspended operations.)

National delegations to the UN, headed by ambassadors from each member state, work and meet together at UN headquarters in New York City. They have diplomatic status in the United States, which as host country also assumes certain other obligations to facilitate the UN's functioning. For example, the U.S. government has permitted people such as Fidel Castro—normally barred from entry to the United States—to visit New York long enough to address the UN.

ASSEMBLY OF EQUALS

The universal membership of the United Nations is one of its strengths. All member states have a voice and a vote in the General Assembly, where state leaders rotate through each autumn. Here, President Bush takes his turn, 2004.

A major strength of the UN structure is the *universality of its membership*. There were 191 members in 2006. Virtually every territory in the world is either a UN member or formally a province or colony of a UN member. (Switzerland, which traditionally maintains strict neutrality in the international system, joined only in 2003.) Formal agreement on the Charter, even if sometimes breached, commits all states to a set of basic rules governing their relations. The old League of Nations, by contrast, was flawed by the absence of several important actors.

One way the UN induced all the great powers to join was to reassure them that their participation in the UN would not harm their national interests. Recognizing the role of power in world order, the UN Charter gave five great powers each a veto over substantive decisions of the Security Council.

The UN Charter establishes a mechanism for *collective security*—the banding together of the world's states to stop an aggressor. Chapter 7 of the Charter explicitly authorizes the Security Council to use military force against aggression if the nonviolent means called for in Chapter 6 have failed. However, because of the great-power veto, the UN cannot effectively stop aggression by (or supported by) a great power. Thus Chapter 7 was used only once during the Cold War—in the Korean War when the Soviet delegation unwisely boycotted the proceedings (and when China's seat was held by the nationalists on Taiwan). It was under Chapter 7 of the Charter that the UN authorized the use of force to reverse Iraqi aggression against Kuwait in 1990.

History of the UN The UN was founded in 1945 in San Francisco by 51 states. It was the successor to the League of Nations, which had failed to effectively counter aggression in the 1930s—Japan simply quit when the League condemned Japanese aggression against China. Like the League, the UN was founded to increase international order and the rule of law to prevent another world war.

There has long been a certain tension between the UN and the United States as the world's most powerful state. (The United States had not joined the League, and it was partly to assure U.S. interest that the UN headquarters was placed in New York.) The UN in some ways constrains the United States by creating the one coalition that can rival U.S. power—that of all the states. A certain isolationist streak in U.S. foreign policy runs counter to the UN concept. However, the UN *amplifies* U.S. power because the United States leads the global UN coalition. The United States is not rich or strong enough to keep order in the world by itself. And, as a great trading nation, the United States benefits from the stability and order that the UN helps to create.

In the 1950s and 1960s, the UN's membership more than doubled as colonies in Asia and Africa won independence. This expansion changed the character of the General Assembly, where each state has one vote regardless of size. The new members had different concerns from the Western industrialized countries and in many cases resented having been colonized by Westerners. Many states in the global South believed that the United States enjoyed too much power in the UN. They noticed that the UN is usually effective in international security affairs only when the United States leads the effort (which happens when U.S. interests are at stake).

The growth in membership thus affected voting patterns in the UN. During the UN's first two decades, the General Assembly had regularly sided with the United States, and the Soviet Union was the main power to use its veto in the Security Council to counterbalance that tendency. But as newly independent states began to predominate, the United States found itself in the minority on many issues, and by the 1970s and 1980s it had become the main user of the veto.[10]

Until 1971, China's seat on the Security Council (and in the General Assembly) was occupied by the nationalist government on Taiwan island, which had lost power in mainland China in 1949. The exclusion of communist China was an exception to the UN principle of universal membership, and in 1971 the Chinese seat was taken from the nationalists and given to the communist government. Today, the government of Taiwan—which functions autonomously in many international matters despite its formal status as a Chinese province—is not a member of the UN.

Throughout the Cold War, the UN had few successes in international security because the U.S.-Soviet conflict prevented consensus. The UN appeared somewhat irrelevant in a world order structured by two opposing alliance blocs. There were a few notable exceptions, such as defending South Korea during the Korean War and agreements to station peacekeeping forces in the Middle East, but the UN did not play a central role in solving international conflicts. The General Assembly, with its predominantly third-world membership, concentrated on the economic and social problems of poor countries, and these became the main work of the UN.

States in the global South also used the UN as a forum to criticize rich countries in general and the United States in particular. By the 1980s, the U.S. government showed its displeasure with this trend by withholding U.S. dues to the UN (eventually more than $1 billion) and by withdrawing from membership in one UN agency, UNESCO.

After the Cold War, the great powers could finally agree on measures regarding international security. In this context the UN moved to center stage in international security

[10] Gregg, Robert W. *About Face: The United States and the United Nations*. Boulder, CO: Lynne Rienner, 1993. Maynes, Charles W. and Richard S. Williamson. *U.S. Foreign Policy and the United Nations System*. NY: W.W. Norton, 1996.

affairs.[11] The UN had several major successes in the late 1980s in bringing an end to violent regional conflicts (in Central America and the Iran-Iraq War), while introducing peacekeepers to monitor the cease-fires. In Namibia, a UN force oversaw independence from South Africa and the nation's first free elections. By the 1990s, the UN had emerged as the world's most important tool for settling international conflicts. Between 1987 and 1993, Security Council resolutions increased from 15 to 78, peacekeeping missions from 5 to 17, peacekeepers from 12,000 to 78,000, and countries sending troops from 26 to 76.

The new missions ran into serious problems, however. Inadequate funding undermined peacekeeping efforts. In Angola, the UN sent only a few peacekeepers, and when the government won internationally observed elections in 1992, the rebels took to arms and the civil war resumed. Meanwhile in Somalia, the UN sided against one faction leader but could not defeat him and had to pull back. In Cambodia, the Khmer Rouge faction refused to disarm according to the UN-brokered peace plan it had signed; later a coup interrupted Cambodia's transition to democracy.

Such problems were most dramatic in the former Yugoslavia, where the UN in 1993–1995 undertook a large peacekeeping mission with nearly 40,000 foreign troops, costing more than $1 billion annually. The mission was deeply flawed by a mismatch between the types of forces sent (lightly armed, equipped for humanitarian operations) and the situation itself (territorial aggression by heavily armed forces). This unhappy combination was known as "peacekeeping where there is no peace to keep."

In response to these problems (and to the unpaid U.S. dues), the UN scaled back peacekeeping operations in 1995–1997 (from 78,000 to 19,000 troops) and carried out reductions and reforms in the UN Secretariat and UN programs. The changes grew out of a financial crisis in the mid-1990s that saw then Secretary-General Boutros Boutros-Ghali declare at the UN's fiftieth anniversary that "practically, the United Nations is bankrupt." Overseeing reforms and reductions has occupied his successor, Kofi Annan, who took over in 1997. In Annan's first year, CNN founder Ted Turner gave him a boost with a $1 billion private contribution (pledged over ten years), the equivalent of almost a year's UN operating budget (excluding peacekeeping).

For years the United States failed to pay its bills, even though a new secretary-general shrank budgets and jobs as the United States had demanded. However, a vigorous 1999 lobbying campaign by American UN supporters noted that "Great nations pay their bills." Close U.S. allies became outspoken in criticizing U.S. failure to honor its international commitments. Finally, the United States agreed to pay up, but under renegotiated terms for the future. The 2001 terrorist attacks increased U.S. participation in the UN, where a decisive coalition of member states initially supported U.S. positions on terrorism in Afghanistan.

The 2003 Iraq War exposed new and serious divisions among the great powers that sidelined the UN. After reaching consensus to insist on Iraqi disarmament and send back UN weapons inspectors, the Security Council split on whether to authorize force against Iraq—the United States and Britain in favor, France, Russia, and China against. When France threatened to veto a UN resolution authorizing war, a U.S.-British coalition toppled the Iraqi government without explicit UN backing. Annan later called the war "illegal." The UN sent a team to Iraq to help with reconstruction, but suicide truck-bombers destroyed it, killing the chief of the mission and dozens of others. Another bomber destroyed

[11] Weiss, Thomas G., ed. *The United Nations and Civil Wars*. Boulder, CO: Lynne Rienner, 1995. Baehr, Peter R., and Leon Gordenker. *The United Nations at the End of the 1990s*. 3rd ed. NY: St. Martin's, 1999. Price, Richard M. and Mark W. Zacher. *The United Nations and Global Security*. NY: Palgrave Macmillan, 2004. Newman, Edward and Oliver P. Richmond. *The United Nations and Human Security*. NY: Palgrave, 2001.

the Red Cross headquarters in Baghdad. The UN withdrew its staff from Iraq in 2003, and found itself largely sidelined in the world's most prominent international conflict.

United Nations Reform

To further aggravate U.S.-UN tensions, documents recovered during the Iraq war showed that high-ranking UN, French, Chinese, and Russian officials (and American oil companies) illegally profited from the UN's $64 billion oil-for-food program for Iraq, which was supposed to ease the civilian suffering caused by economic sanctions in the 1990s. A Swiss company under investigation for suspected fraud in the Iraq program turned out to be paying Annan's son thousands of dollars a month, creating what Annan admitted was a "perception problem." In 2005, an independent investigation cleared Annan of personal wrongdoing, but found the program corrupt and heavily criticized the UN for mismanagement and poor oversight of the program.

The UN is in some ways just beginning to work as it was originally intended to, through a concert of great powers and universal recognition of the Charter. However, as states turned increasingly to the UN after the Cold War, its modest size and resources became seriously overburdened, leading to contraction of missions and funding. Today, the UN is more important than ever, yet still in danger of failing. In the coming few years the UN must continue to grapple with the challenges of its evolving role in a unipolar world, the limitations of its budget, and the strength of state sovereignty.

MAKING THE CASE

Collective security rests with the UN Security Council, which has authorized such military interventions as the Gulf War and the 2001 campaign in Afghanistan. Military actions not approved by the Council—such as the 1999 bombing of Serbia and the 2003 U.S.-British invasion of Iraq—tend to be controversial. Here, U.S. Secretary of State Colin Powell tries, unsuccessfully, to convince the Security Council to authorize military action against Iraq to eliminate what he claimed were Iraq's weapons of mass destruction, February 2003. Powell holds a vial representing the amount of anthrax spores (a substance Iraq had produced) that could kill thousands of people.

The Security Council

The Security Council is responsible for maintaining international peace and security, and for restoring peace when it breaks down. Its decisions are *binding* on all UN member states. The Security Council has tremendous power to *define* the existence and nature of a security threat, to *structure* the response to such a threat, and to *enforce* its decisions through mandatory directives to UN members (such as to halt trade with an aggressor).

In 57 years, the Council has passed more than 1,500 resolutions, with new ones being added by the week. These resolutions represent the great powers' blueprints for resolving the world's various security disputes, especially in regional conflicts. (Because of the veto system, the Council avoids conflicts among great powers themselves, such as on arms control.) The resolutions reflect what the great powers can all agree upon.

The five *permanent members* of the Council—the United States, Britain, France, Russia, and China—are the most important. The Council also has ten *nonpermanent members* who rotate onto the Council for two-year terms. Nonpermanent members are elected (five each year) by the General Assembly from a list prepared by informal regional caucuses. Usually there is a mix of regions and country sizes, though not by any strict formula. The Council's *chairperson* rotates among the Council members monthly. Sometimes this matters: in 1990, the United States pushed for action against Iraq before the chair passed from the United States to Yemen, which opposed the U.S. position.

UN Security Council

Substantive Security Council resolutions require *nine* votes from among the 15 members. But a "no" vote by any permanent member defeats the resolution—the *veto* power. Many resolutions have been vetoed by the permanent members, and many more have never been proposed because they would have faced certain veto. However, since the mid-1990s the use of the veto has dropped abruptly, to about once a year. Of the nine vetoes cast in 2000–2004, eight were by the United States.

Members can *abstain* on resolutions, an option that some permanent members use to register misgivings about a resolution without vetoing. China abstains with regularity, because it generally reserves its veto for matters directly affecting Chinese security. Its 1997 veto of a resolution on Guatemala (a country with strong ties to Taiwan; see p. 65) was its first veto in nearly 25 years. As a power with more regional than global interests, China avoids alienating other great powers by blocking their actions in distant parts of the world. The United States has abstained several times to register a middle position on resolutions critical of Israel.

The Security Council *meets irregularly* (in the New York UN headquarters) upon request of a UN member—often a state with a grievance regarding another state's actions. When Kuwait was invaded, and when Bosnia was being overrun, the victims called on the Security Council—a kind of 911 phone number for the world (but one without a standing police force). Because international security continues to be troublesome in many regions and because these troubles often drag on for months or years, meetings of the Council are frequent.

The Security Council's *power is limited* in two major ways; both reflect the strength of state sovereignty in the international system. First, the Council's decisions depend entirely on the interests of its member states. The ambassadors who represent those states cannot change a Council resolution without authorization from their governments. Second, although Security Council resolutions in theory bind all UN members, member states in practice often try to evade or soften their effect. For instance, trade sanctions are difficult to enforce because it is tempting and relatively easy to cheat. A Security Council resolution can be enforced in practice only if enough powerful states care about it.

The Security Council has a formal mechanism for coordinating multilateral military action in response to aggression, called the *Military Staff Committee*. It is composed of military officers from the permanent Council members. But the United States opposes placing its forces under non-U.S. commanders, and the committee has never been used.

Instead, military forces responding to aggression under the auspices of Security Council resolutions have remained under national command. For example, neither U.S. forces in the Gulf War charged with enforcing UN resolutions nor U.S. soldiers sent to Somalia in late 1992 to restore humanitarian relief efforts disrupted by civil war displayed UN insignia or flags. Similarly, NATO forces in the former Yugoslavia, the Australian-led force in East Timor, and the British-led force in Afghanistan all operate under their national flags but their missions are authorized by UN resolution. (Peacekeeping operations are different, and are discussed below.)

Even when the Security Council cannot agree on means of enforcement, its resolutions shape the way disputes are seen and ultimately how they are resolved. Security Council Resolution 242 after the Arab-Israeli war of 1967 laid out the principles for a just peace in that conflict—primarily the right of all states in the region to live within secure and well-defined borders and the return by Israel of territories captured in the 1967 war. (The parties are still arguing about whether territories to be returned by Israel means "all" territories.) Reaffirmed in Resolution 338 after the 1973 war, these resolutions helped shape the 1978 Camp David agreement and later formed the basis for peace negotiations between Israel and its Arab neighbors that began in 1991.

After the end of the Cold War, the prestige of the Security Council rose and it became more active than before. The first summit meeting of Council members in 1992 brought together for the first time the leaders of the "big five." However, in the second half of the 1990s, the Council lost influence or was marginalized in such hot spots as Iraq (weapons inspections blocked), Angola (war resumed, UN pulled out), Macedonia (vetoed by China), and the large Ethiopia-Eritrea war (left to the Organization of African Unity). The 1999 NATO bombing campaign against Serbia proceeded without authorization from the Security Council. (Later, the Security Council authorized an international force for Kosovo because Serbia had agreed to it.) Most importantly, when the Security Council deadlocked on how to deal with Iraq's Saddam Hussein in 2003, a U.S.-British coalition withdrew a proposed resolution and went to war without what UN Secretary-General Kofi Annan called the "unique legitimacy" conferred by UN approval.

Proposed Changes The structure of the Security Council is not without problems. Japan and Germany are great powers that contribute substantial UN dues (based on economic size) and make large contributions to UN programs and peacekeeping operations. Yet they have exactly the same formal representation in the UN as tiny states with less than one-hundredth of their populations: one vote in the General Assembly and the chance to rotate onto the Security Council (in practice they rotate on more often than the tiny states). As global trading powers, Japan and Germany have huge stakes in the ground rules for international security affairs and would like seats at the table. In 2003, Japan decided to reduce its UN dues by one-quarter, in part because of unhappiness over the Security Council issue.

But including Japan and Germany as permanent Security Council members would not be simple. If Germany joined, three of the seven permanent members would be European, giving that region unfair weight. The three European seats could be combined into one (a rotating seat or one representing the European Union), but this would water down the power of Britain and France, which can veto any such change in the Charter. Japan's bid for a seat faces Chinese opposition. Also, if Japan or Germany got a seat, then what about India, with 20 percent of the world's population? And what about an Islamic country such as Indonesia? Finally, what about Latin America and Africa? Possible new permanent members could include Germany, Japan, India, Brazil, Egypt, and either Nigeria or South Africa. None of these plans has made much progress. Any overhaul of the Security Council would require a change in the UN Charter, and a change in membership would reduce the power of the current five permanent members, any of which could veto the change, making any change very difficult. In late 2004, an expert panel appointed by Annan recommended expanding the Security Council to 24 members under either of two formulas, neither changing veto powers. These proposals were debated in 2005 but no agreement was reached and the issue was put on hold.

Table 7.1 shows the recent rotations of members onto the Security Council. The system of nomination by regional caucuses has worked to keep the regional balance on the Council fairly constant as individual states come and go. Major regional actors, including those mentioned as candidates for possible new permanent seats (shown in Table 7.1), tend to rotate onto the Council more often than do less important states.

TABLE 7.1 ■ Regional Representation on the UN Security Council

Region	Permanent Members[a]	NONPERMANENT MEMBERS[b] 2006	2005	2004	Possible Contenders for New Permanent Seats[c]
North America	United States				
W. Europe	Britain France	Denmark Greece	Denmark Greece	Germany Spain	Germany
Japan/Pacific		Japan	Japan		Japan
Russia & E. Europe	Russia	Slovakia	Romania	Romania	
China	China				
Middle East		Qatar	Algeria	Algeria	Egypt?
Latin America		Peru Argentina	Brazil Argentina	Brazil Chile	Brazil, Mexico?
South Asia			Philippines	Pakistan Philippines	India, Indonesia?
Africa		Tanzania Ghana Congo Republic	Tanzania Benin	Angola Benin	Nigeria? South Africa?

[a]The five permanent members hold veto power.
[b]Nonpermanent members are elected for two-year terms by the General Assembly, based on nominations by regional caucuses.
[c]Possible new permanent seats might have fewer if any veto powers.

Peacekeeping Forces

Peacekeeping forces are not mentioned in the UN Charter. Secretary-General Dag Hammarskjöld in the 1960s joked that they were allowed under "Chapter Six and a Half"—somewhere between the nonviolent dispute resolution called for in Chapter 6 of the Charter and the authorization of force provided for in Chapter 7. The Charter requires member states to place military forces at the disposal of the UN, but such forces were envisioned as being used in response to aggression (under collective security). In practice, when the UN has authorized force to reverse aggression—as in the Gulf War in 1990—the forces involved have been *national* forces not under UN command.

Peacekeeping Forces

The UN's *own* forces—borrowed from armies of member states but under the flag and command of the UN—have been *peacekeeping* forces to calm regional conflicts, playing a neutral role between warring forces.[12] These forces won the Nobel peace prize in 1988 in

[12] Doyle, Michael W. and Nicholas Sambanis. *Making War and Building Peace:?United Nations Peace Operations*. Princeton, 2006. Whitworth, Sandra. *Men, Militarism and UN Peacekeeping: A Gendered Analysis*. Boulder: Rienner, 2004. Findlay, Trevor. *The Use of Force in UN Peace Operations*. Oxford, 2002. James Mayall, ed. *The New Interventionism, 1991–1994: United Nations Experience in Cambodia, Former Yugoslavia, and Somalia*. Cambridge, 1996. Ratner, Steven R. *The New UN Peacekeeping: Building Peace in Lands of Conflict After the Cold War*. NY: St. Martin's, 1995.

recognition of their growing importance and success. As was learned in Bosnia, however, such neutral forces do not succeed well in a situation where the Security Council has identified one side as the aggressor.

Peacekeeping Missions The secretary-general assembles a peacekeeping force for each mission, usually from a few states totally uninvolved in the conflict, and puts it under a single commander. The soldiers are commonly called **blue helmets.** Peacekeeping forces serve at the invitation of a host government and must leave if that government orders them out often.

Authority for peacekeeping forces is granted by the Security Council, usually for a period of three to six months that may be renewed—in some cases for decades. In one early case, the Suez crisis in 1956, it was the General Assembly that authorized the forces under the "Uniting for Peace" resolution, which allowed the General Assembly to take up security matters when the Security Council was deadlocked. In the Congo in 1960 it was the secretary-general who took the initiative. But today the Security Council controls peacekeeping operations.

Funds must be voted by the General Assembly, and lack of funds is today the single greatest constraint on the use of peacekeeping forces. Special assessments against member states pay for peacekeeping operations. With the expansion of peacekeeping since 1988, the expenses of these forces (nearly $5 billion in 2005) are several times larger than the rest of the UN budget.

TABLE 7.2 ■ UN Peacekeeping Missions as of April 2006

Location	Region	Size	Annual Cost (million $)	Role	Since
Democratic Congo	Africa	17,500	$1,150	Observe cease-fire; protect civilians	1999
Liberia	Africa	17,000	760	Assist transitional govt.	2003
Sudan	Africa	8,800	970	Support agreement; monitor war	2005
Ivory Coast	Africa	8,000	440	Help implement peace agreement	2004
Burundi	Africa	5,000	310	Help implement peace agreement	2004
Ethiopia/Eritrea	Africa	3,500	185	Monitor post-war border	2000
Western Sahara	Africa	350	50	Organize referendum in territory	1991
India/Pakistan	South Asia	80	8	Observe India-Pakistan cease-fire	1949
Kosovo	Russia/E. Eur.	3,100	250	Civil administration; relief	1999
Georgia	Russia/E. Eur.	250	40	Observe cease-fire in civil war	1993
Lebanon	Middle East	2,100	100	Monitor cease-fire on Israeli border	1978
Syria (Golan Heights)	Middle East	1,200	45	Monitor Israel-Syria cease-fire	1974
Cyprus	Middle East	1,000	50	Monitor Greek-Turkish cease-fire	1964
Israel	Middle East	300	30	Observe Arab-Israeli truce	1948
Haiti	Latin America	9,900	540	Assist transitional govt.	2004
Total		77,980	4,928		

Note: Size indicates total international personnel (mostly troops but some civilian administrators and police).

Recent Missions In early 2006, the UN maintained 78,000 troops (including some police) in 15 separate peacekeeping or observing missions, using military personnel from 103 countries, spanning five world regions (see Table 7.2).

The largest peacekeeping mission in early 2006 was in Democratic Congo, where 17,500 peacekeepers monitored a cease-fire and protected civilians after a civil war. In 2005, the Security Council approved a 10,000-troop peacekeeping force for the Darfur region in Sudan at a cost of nearly $1 billion, and after a slow start it is to take over from the African Union's peacekeepers there in 2006. The UN's other largest peacekeeping operations were in Liberia (maintaining a cease-fire after a civil war), Ivory Coast and Burundi (stabilizing peace agreements), and Haiti (trying to maintain stability after a military coup). The largest recent missions reflect the resurgence of UN peacekeeping after the shakeout of the mid-1990s.

UN Aid in Darfur, Sudan

NATO-led forces largely replaced UN peacekeepers in Bosnia in the late 1990s (and, later, took military control of Kosovo). UN operations in these countries focus on civilian governmental functions, leaving security matters largely to UN-authorized but independently commanded international forces.

The same approach was used in East Timor, but with an Australian-led force rather than NATO. In 1999, the UN oversaw elections in which residents of East Timor—a former Portuguese colony occupied by neighboring Indonesia for two decades—voted for independence. In response, the Indonesian army presided over a wave of killing and burning by pro-Indonesian militias, evidently aimed at deterring provinces of Indonesia itself from pursuing separatism. Indonesia then withdrew, and an Australian-commanded international force under a UN mandate took control. The UN itself then began running a transitional administration which led to statehood for East Timor in 2002.

At its peak in the early 1990s, the UN ran several other large peacekeeping operations in addition to those in the former Yugoslavia and in Lebanon. One of the most important was in *Cambodia*. There, 15,000 peacekeepers were coupled with a large force of UN administrators who took over substantial control of the Cambodian government under a fragile pact that ended (for the most part) a long and devastating civil war. Despite difficulty in obtaining the cooperation of the Khmer Rouge faction (which refused to disarm as it had agreed), the UN pressed forward to hold elections in 1993 that chose a Cambodian government (though not a stable one).

The lessons learned in Cambodia helped the UN accomplish a similar mission more easily in *Mozambique*. A peace agreement ended a long and devastating civil war there, setting up mechanisms for disarmament, the integration of military forces, and the holding of internationally supervised elections for a new government. In 1992, the UN had tried to accomplish a similar mission in *Angola* with only 500 personnel. The peace process was on track until the government won the elections; the rebels refused to accept the results and resumed an even more destructive civil war. At the next opportunity, the UN sent a force to Angola ten times larger than before. Results improved, but the war started again and the UN Security Council ended the mission in 1999. These experiences helped the UN respond more effectively after civil wars in Sierra Leone, Ivory Coast, and Liberia in 2002–2003. But problems developed in several locations when UN peacekeepers participated in local prostitution, rape, and even sex trafficking. In 2004, Secretary-General Annan called "shameful" the reported behavior of UN troops from several countries serving in Democratic Congo. Security Council Resolution 1325, passed in 2000, mandates greater inclusion of women and attention to gender in UN peacekeeping and reconstruction.

Observing and Peacekeeping "Peacekeepers" actually perform two different functions—observing and peacekeeping. Observers are unarmed military officers sent to a conflict area in small numbers simply to watch what happens and report back to the UN. With the UN watching, the parties to a conflict are often less likely to break a cease-fire. Observers can monitor various aspects of a country's situation—cease-fires, elections, respect for human rights, and other areas.

The function of *peacekeeping* is carried out by lightly armed soldiers (in armored vehicles with automatic rifles but without artillery, tanks, and other heavy weapons). Such forces play several roles. They can *interpose* themselves physically between warring parties to keep them apart (more accurately, to make them attack the UN forces in order to get to their enemy). UN peacekeepers often try to *negotiate* with military officers on both sides. This channel of communication can bring about tactical actions and understandings that support a cease-fire. But the UN forces in a war zone cannot easily get from one side's positions to those of the other to conduct negotiations.

Peacekeeping is much more difficult if one side sees the UN forces as being *biased* toward the other side. Israel feels this way about UN forces in southern Lebanon, for example. On occasion, Israeli forces have broken through UN lines to attack enemies, and they allegedly have targeted UN outposts on occasion. In Cambodia and the former Yugoslavia in the early 1990s, one party deliberately attacked UN forces many times, causing a number of deaths. In general, when cease-fires break down, UN troops get caught in the middle. More than 1,800 have been killed over the years.

In some conflicts, peacekeepers organized outside the UN framework have been used instead of UN-commanded forces. Currently, African Union forces are attempting to play a peacekeeping role in Sudan, and U.S. forces have acted as peacekeepers in Egypt's Sinai desert since the 1970s. Nearly 5,000 French peacekeepers—not under UN command—serve in Ivory Coast alongside a similar number of UN peacekeepers from other countries, monitoring a 2003 cease-fire between the rebel-held north of the country and the government-held south. When government air strikes killed nine French soldiers in 2004, the French forces retaliated robustly, destroying the government's air force. Peacekeeping forces have generally been unable to make peace, only to keep it. To go into a shooting war and suppress hostilities requires military forces far beyond those of past UN peacekeeping missions. Thus, peacekeepers are usually not sent until a cease-fire has been arranged, has taken effect, and has held up for some time. Often dozens of cease-fires are broken before one sticks. Wars may simmer along for years, taking a terrible toll, before the UN gets its chance.

To address this problem, the secretary-general in 1992 proposed to create UN *peacemaking* (or *peace enforcement*) units that would not only monitor a cease-fire but enforce it if it broke down.[13] The secretary-general called for member states to make available, on a rapid deployment basis, 1,000 soldiers each—specially trained volunteers—to create a standby UN army that could respond quickly to crises. Not only did the member states refuse the request for soldiers, they shot down the idea of peacemaking altogether. Since then the UN has authorized member states to provide real military forces, not peacekeepers, when fighting may be required. In an exception that may or may not indicate a trend, the Security Council broadened the mandate of UN peacekeepers in Democratic Congo to let them protect civilians. In 2005, Pakistani peacekeepers there killed 50 militia fighters after nine peacekeepers from Bangladesh were killed in an ambush.

In the late 1990s, as peacekeeping expanded after several years of reduction, seven countries—Denmark, Norway, Sweden, Poland, the Netherlands, Austria, and Canada—formed a 4,000-troop UN Standby High Readiness Brigade. Headquartered in Denmark

[13] Boutros-Ghali, Boutros. *An Agenda for Peace: Preventive Diplomacy, Peacemaking and Peace-keeping*. NY: United Nations, 1992. Woodhouse, Tom, Robert Bruce, and Malcolm Dando, eds. *Peacekeeping and Peacemaking: Towards Effective Intervention in Post–Cold War Conflicts*. NY: St. Martin's, 1998.

and available to deploy to conflict areas in two to four weeks rather than months as now, the brigade is controlled by the Security Council. It participated in the UN mission to Ethiopia-Eritrea in 2000–2001. In early 2005, the brigade deployed to Sudan to support a peace agreement between northern and southern regions after a long civil war that killed millions. In an effort to provide longer-term support after wars, in late 2005 the UN created a Peacebuilding Commission to coordinate reconstruction, institution-building, and economic recovery efforts in post-war societies after peacekeeping missions end.

The Secretariat

The secretary-general of the UN is the closest thing to a "president of the world" that exists. But the secretary-general represents member states—not the world's six billion people. The past secretary-general, Boutros Boutros-Ghali, was fond of calling himself just the "humble servant" of the member states. Judging from his inability to get the Security Council to follow his lead on peacekeeping, his humility would seem well justified. Where the great powers do not have consensus, it is hard for the secretary-general to make anything happen.

The secretary-general is *nominated* by the Security Council—requiring the consent of all five permanent members—and must be *approved* by the General Assembly. The term of office is five years and may be renewed. Boutros-Ghali in 1996 fought for a second term, with the support of almost every UN member, but the United States opposed him and prevailed. Kofi Annan, the current secretary-general, finally emerged as a consensus choice. He reinvigorated the UN, was reelected in 2001 for five more years, and won the one-hundredth-anniversary Nobel Peace Prize. The Secretariat of the UN is its executive branch, headed by the secretary-general. It is a bureaucracy for administering UN policy and programs, just as the State Department is a bureaucracy for U.S. foreign policy. In security matters, the secretary-general personally works with the Security Council; development programs in poor countries are coordinated by a second-in-command—the director-general for Development and International Economic Co-operation. The Secretariat is divided into functional areas, with undersecretaries-general and assistant secretaries-general.

The *UN staff* in these areas includes administrative personnel as well as technical experts and economic advisers working on various programs and projects. The staff numbers about 15,000 people, and the total number of employees in the UN system (including the World Bank and IMF) is just more than 60,000. There is a concentration of UN-related agency offices in Geneva, Switzerland. Geneva is a frequent site of international negotiations and is seen by some as more neutral than New York. A few development programs are headquartered in cities in the global South.

One purpose of the UN Secretariat is to develop an *international civil service* of diplomats and bureaucrats whose loyalties are at the global level,

WHOLE WORLD IN HIS HANDS

The UN secretary-general has a lofty mission but limited power and resources. Kofi Annan (1997) was the first to rise through the UN bureaucracy to the top position. His term ends in December 2006.

not to their states of origin. The UN Charter sets the secretary-general and staff apart from the authority of national governments and calls on member states to respect the staff's "exclusively international character." The UN has been fairly successful in this regard; the secretary-general is most often seen as an independent diplomat thinking about the whole world's interests, not a pawn of any state. But in the early 1990s the UN bureaucracy came under increasing criticism for both inefficiency and corruption. These criticisms, coming especially from the United States, which saw itself as bearing an unfair share of the costs, led to a reform program. By the late 1990s, UN staff was reduced by one-quarter compared to a decade earlier, and budgets were scaled back year by year. By winter 2002, a strapped UN could not keep its New York headquarters building heated.

The secretary-general is more than a bureaucratic manager. He (it has not yet been a she) is a visible public figure whose personal attention to a regional conflict can move it toward resolution. The Charter allows the secretary-general to use the UN's "good offices" to serve as a neutral mediator in international conflicts—to bring hostile parties together in negotiations. For example, Boutros-Ghali was personally involved in trying to mediate conflicts in Somalia and the former Yugoslavia. Annan tried to talk Iraq into compliance with UN inspections in 1997, unsuccessfully. Annan used his position in 2001 to try to galvanize a stronger (and better funded) international program against AIDS (see p. 446).

The secretary-general also works to bring together the great-power consensus on which Security Council action depends—a much harder job than mere bureaucratic management. The secretary-general has the power under the Charter to bring to the Security Council any matter that might threaten international peace and security, and so to play a major role in setting the UN's agenda in international security affairs. Still, the secretary-general experiences tensions with the Security Council. When the secretary-general asks for authority for a peacekeeping mission for six months, the Security Council is likely to say "three months." If the secretary-general asks for $10 million he might get $5 million. Thus the secretary-general remains, like the entire UN system, constrained by state sovereignty.

Secretary-General Kofi Annan (in office 1997–2006), an American-educated manager who knows the UN bureaucracy well, concentrated on reforming the UN Secretariat's finances and operations and improving relations between the UN and the United States (but faced resistance on both fronts). Annan is the first secretary-general from sub-Saharan Africa (Ghana), and the first to rise through the UN civil service. He was previously undersecretary-general for peacekeeping operations, and gained a reputation for making the best of ill-conceived peacekeeping missions in Somalia and Bosnia in the early 1990s.

Past secretaries-general have come from various regions of the world but never from a great power. They are Trygve Lie (from Norway, 1946–1952), Dag Hammarskjöld (Sweden, 1953–1961), U Thant (Burma, 1961–1971), Kurt Waldheim (Austria, 1972–1982), Javier Perez de Cuellar (Peru, 1982–1992), Boutros Boutros-Ghali (Egypt, 1992–1996), and Kofi Annan (Ghana, 1997–2006).

The General Assembly

The General Assembly

The General Assembly is made up of all 191 member states of the UN, each with one vote.[14] It usually meets every year, from late September through January, in *plenary session*. State leaders or foreign ministers, including the U.S. president, generally come through one by one to address this assemblage. The Assembly sessions, like most UN deliberations, are simultaneously translated into dozens of languages so that delegates from around the

[14] Peterson, M. J. *The United Nations General Assembly*. NY: Routledge, 2005.

world can carry on a single conversation. This global town hall is a unique institution and provides a powerful medium for states to put forward their ideas and arguments. Presiding over it is a president elected by the Assembly—a post without much power.

The Assembly convenes for *special sessions* every few years on general topics such as economic cooperation. The UN special session on disarmament in June 1982 provided the occasion for one of the largest political rallies in U.S. history—a peace demonstration of a million people in New York. The Assembly has met in *emergency session* in the past to deal with an immediate threat to international peace and security, but this has happened only nine times and has now become uncommon.

The General Assembly has the power to accredit national delegations as members of the UN (through its Credentials Committee). For instance, in 1971 the delegation of the People's Republic of China was given China's seat in the UN (including on the Security Council) in place of the nationalists in Taiwan. For decades, neither North nor South Korea became members of the UN (because both claimed the whole of Korea), but they finally took seats as separate delegations in 1991. Some political entities that fall short of state status send *permanent observer missions* to the UN. These missions participate without a vote in the General Assembly. They include the Vatican (Holy See) and the Palestine Liberation Organization (PLO).

The General Assembly's main power lies in its *control of finances* for UN programs and operations, including peacekeeping. It also can *pass resolutions* on various matters, but these are purely advisory and at times have served largely to vent frustrations of the majority of poor countries. The Assembly also *elects members* of certain UN agencies and programs. Finally, the Assembly coordinates UN programs and agencies through its own system of committees, commissions, councils, and so forth.

The Assembly coordinates UN programs and agencies through the Economic and Social Council (ECOSOC), which has 54 member states elected by the General Assembly for three-year terms. ECOSOC manages the overlapping work of a large number of programs and agencies. Its *regional commissions* look at how UN programs work together in a particular region; its *functional commissions* deal with global topics such as population growth, narcotics trafficking, human rights, and the status of women; its *expert bodies* work on technical subjects that cut across various UN programs in areas such as crime prevention and public finances. Outside of ECOSOC, the General Assembly operates many *other specialized committees*. Standing committees ease the work of the Assembly in issue areas such as decolonization, legal matters, or disarmament.

Many of the activities associated with the UN do not take place under tight control of either the General Assembly or the Security Council. They occur in functional agencies and programs having various amounts of autonomy from UN control.

UN Programs

Through the Economic and Social Council, the General Assembly oversees more than a dozen major programs to advance economic development and social stability in poor states of the global South. Through its programs, the UN helps to manage global North-South relations: it organizes a flow of resources and skills from the richer parts of the world to support development in the poorer parts.

The programs are *funded* partly by General Assembly allocations and partly by contributions that the programs raise directly from member states, businesses, or private charitable contributors. The degree of General Assembly funding, and of operational autonomy from the Assembly, varies from one program to another. Each UN program has a staff, a headquarters, and various operations in the field, where it works with host governments in member states.

Several of these programs are of growing importance. The *UN Environment Program (UNEP)* became more prominent in the 1990s as the economic development of the global South and the growing economies of the industrialized world took a toll on the world environment (see Chapter 11). UNEP grapples with global environmental strategies. It provides technical assistance to member states, monitors environmental conditions globally, develops standards, and recommends alternative energy sources.

UNICEF is the UN Children's Fund, which gives technical and financial assistance to poor countries for programs benefiting children. Unfortunately, the needs of children in many countries are still urgent, and UNICEF is kept busy. Financed by voluntary contributions, UNICEF has for decades organized U.S. children in an annual Halloween fund drive on behalf of their counterparts in poorer countries.

The *Office of the UN High Commissioner for Refugees (UNHCR)* is also busy. UNHCR coordinates efforts to protect, assist, and eventually repatriate the many refugees who flee across international borders each year to escape from war and political violence. (The longer-standing problem of Palestinian refugees is handled by a different program, the *UN Relief Works Agency*, or *UNRWA*.)

The *UN Development Program (UNDP)*, funded by voluntary contributions, coordinates all UN efforts related to development in poor countries. With about 5,000 projects operating simultaneously around the world, UNDP is the world's largest international agency for technical development assistance. The UN also runs several development-related agencies for training and for promoting women's role in development.

HELPING WHERE NEEDED

An array of UN programs, operating under the General Assembly, aim to help countries in the global South to overcome social and economic problems. These programs play a crucial role in the massive international assistance effort that followed the December 2004 Indian Ocean tsunami, and in the long-term development of the devastated regions. This helicopter from the UN refugee agency, on loan from the Swiss government, delivers supplies in Indonesia, January 2005.

Many poor countries depend on export revenues to finance economic development, making them vulnerable to fluctuations in commodity prices and other international trade problems. The **UN Conference on Trade and Development (UNCTAD)** seeks to negotiate international trade agreements to stabilize commodity prices and promote development. Because countries of the global South do not have much power in the international economy, however, UNCTAD has little leverage to promote their interests in trade (see p. 524). The World Trade Organization has become the main organization dealing with trade issues.

In 2006, the UN created a new Human Rights Council, replacing a Human Rights Commission notorious for including human rights abusers as member states. The new Council is to have expanded powers and more selective membership.

Other UN programs manage problems such as disaster relief, food aid, housing, and population issues. Throughout the poorer countries, the UN maintains an active presence in economic and social affairs.

Autonomous Agencies

In addition to its own programs, the UN General Assembly maintains formal ties with about 20 autonomous international agencies not under its control. Most are specialized technical organizations through which states pool their efforts to address problems such as health care and labor conditions.

The only such agency in international security affairs is the *International Atomic Energy Agency (IAEA)*, headquartered in Vienna, Austria. It was established under the UN but is formally autonomous. Although the IAEA has an economic role in helping to develop civilian nuclear power plants, it mainly works to prevent nuclear proliferation (see p. 240). The IAEA was responsible for inspections in Iraq in 2002–2003, which found no evidence of a secret nuclear weapons program.

In the area of health care, the Geneva-based **World Health Organization (WHO)** based in Geneva provides technical assistance to improve conditions and conduct major immunization campaigns in poor countries. In the 1960s and 1970s, WHO led one of the great public health victories of all time—the worldwide eradication of smallpox. Today WHO is a leading player in the worldwide fight to control AIDS (see pp. 444–447).

In agriculture, the *Food and Agriculture Organization (FAO)* is the lead agency. In labor standards, it is the *International Labor Organization (ILO)*. *UNESCO*–the *UN Educational, Scientific, and Cultural Organization*—facilitates international communication and scientific collaboration. The *UN Industrial Development Organization (UNIDO)* promotes industrialization in the global South.

The longest-established IOs, with some of the most successful records, are specialized agencies dealing with technical aspects of international coordination such as aviation and postal exchange. For instance, the *International Telecommunications Union (ITU)* allocates radio frequencies. The *Universal Postal Union (UPU)* sets standards for international mail. The *International Civil Aviation Organization (ICAO)* sets binding standards for international air traffic. The *International Maritime Organization (IMO)* facilitates international cooperation on shipping at sea. The *World Intellectual Property Organization (WIPO)* seeks world compliance with copyrights and patents, and promotes development and technology transfer within a legal framework that protects such intellectual property (see pp. 318–319). Finally, the *World Meteorological Organization (WMO)* oversees a world weather watch and promotes the exchange of weather information.

The major coordinating agencies of the world economy (discussed in Chapters 8, 9, and 13) are also UN-affiliated agencies. The World Bank and the International Monetary Fund (IMF) give loans, grants, and technical assistance for economic development (and the IMF manages international balance of payments accounting). The World Trade Organization (WTO) sets rules for international trade.

Overall, the density of connections across national borders, both in the UN system and through other IOs, is increasing year by year. In a less tangible way, people are also becoming connected across international borders through the meshing of ideas, including norms and rules. And gradually the rules are becoming international laws.

International Law

IOs impinge on state sovereignty by creating new structures (both supranational and transnational) for regulating relations across borders. International law and international norms limit state sovereignty in another way. They create principles for governing international relations that compete with the core realist principles of sovereignty and anarchy.

International law, unlike national laws, derives not from actions of a legislative branch or other central authority, but from tradition and agreements signed by states. It also differs in the difficulty of enforcement, which depends not on the power and authority of central government but on reciprocity, collective action, and international norms.[15]

Sources of International Law

Sources of International Law

Laws within states come from central authorities—legislatures or dictators. Because states are sovereign and recognize no central authority, international law rests on a different basis. The declarations of the UN General Assembly are not laws, and most do not bind the members. The Security Council can compel certain actions by states, but these are commands rather than laws: they are specific to a situation. No body of international law has been passed by a national legislative body. Where, then, does international law come from? Four sources of international law are recognized: treaties, custom, general principles of law (such as equity), and legal scholarship (including past judicial decisions).

Treaties and other written conventions signed by states are the most important source.[16] International treaties now fill more than a thousand thick volumes, with tens of thousands of individual agreements. There is a principle in international law that treaties once signed and ratified must be observed (*pacta sunt servanda*). States violate the terms of treaties they have signed only if the matter is very important or the penalties for such a violation seem very small. In the United States, treaties duly ratified by the Senate are considered to be the highest law of the land, equal with acts passed by Congress.

Treaties and other international obligations such as debts are *binding on successor governments* whether the new government takes power through an election, a coup, or a revolution. After the revolutions in Eastern Europe around 1990, newly democratic governments were held responsible for debts incurred by their communist predecessors. Even when the Soviet Union broke up, Russia as the successor state had to guarantee that Soviet debts would be paid and Soviet treaties honored. Although revolution does not free a state from its obligations, some treaties have built-in escape clauses that let states legally withdraw from them, after giving due notice, without violating international law. The United States in 2001 invoked the six-month opt-out provision of the ABM treaty.

Because of the universal commitment for all states to respect certain basic principles of international law, the UN Charter is one of the world's most important treaties. Its implications are broad and far-reaching, in contrast to more specific treaties such as a fishery management agreement. The specialized agreements are usually easier to interpret and more enforceable than broad treaties such as the Charter.

Custom is the second major source of international law. If states behave toward each other in a certain way for long enough, their behavior may become generally accepted practice with the status of law. Western international law (though not Islamic law) tends to be *positivist* in this regard—it draws on actual customs, the practical realities of self-interest, and the need for consent rather than on an abstract concept of divine or natural law.

General principles of law also serve as a source of international law. Actions such as theft and assault recognized in most national legal systems as crimes tend to have the same

---

[15] Shaw, Malcolm N. *International Law*. 4th ed. Cambridge, 1998. D'Amato, Anthony. *International Law: Process and Prospect*. 2nd ed. Ardsley, NY: Transnational, 1995. Franck, Thomas M. *Fairness in International Law and Institutions*. Oxford, 1995. Scott, Shirley V. *International Law in World Politics: An Introduction*. Boulder, CO: Lynne Rienner, 2004. Ku, Charlotte, and Paul F. Diehl. *International Law: Classic and Contemporary Readings*. 2nd ed. Boulder, CO: Lynne Rienner, 2003.

[16] Reuter, Paul. *Introduction to the Law of Treaties*. London: Pinter, 1992. Aust, Anthony. *Modern Treaty Law and Practice*. Cambridge, 2000.

meaning in an international context. Iraq's invasion of Kuwait was illegal under treaties signed by Iraq (including the UN Charter and that of the Arab League) and under the custom Iraq and Kuwait had established of living in peace as sovereign states. Beyond treaty or custom, the invasion violated international law because of the general principle that one state may not overrun its neighbor's territory and annex it by force. (Of course, a state may still think it can get away with such a violation of international law.)

The fourth source of international law, recognized by the World Court as subsidiary to the others, is *legal scholarship*—the written arguments of judges and lawyers around the world on the issues in question. Only the writings of the most highly qualified and respected legal figures can be taken into account, and then only to resolve points not resolved by the first three sources of international law.

Often international law lags behind changes in norms; law is quite tradition-bound. Certain activities such as espionage are technically illegal but are so widely condoned that they cannot be said to violate international norms. Other activities are still legal but have come to be frowned upon and seen as abnormal. For example, China's shooting of student demonstrators in 1989 violated international norms but not international law.

The Place of International Law

Enforcement of International Law

Although these sources of international law distinguish it from national law, an even greater difference exists as to the *enforcement* of the two types of law. International law is much more difficult to enforce. There is no world police force. Enforcement of international law depends on the power of states themselves, individually or collectively, to punish transgressors.

Enforcement of international law depends heavily on reciprocity (see pp. 66–68). States follow international law most of the time because they want other states to do so. The reason neither side in World War II used chemical weapons was not that anyone could *enforce* the treaty banning use of such weapons. It was that the other side would probably respond by using chemical weapons, too, and the costs would be high to both sides. International law recognizes in certain circumstances the legitimacy of *reprisals:* actions that would have been illegal under international law may sometimes be legal if taken in response to the illegal actions of another state.

States also follow international law because of the general or long-term costs that could come from disregarding international law (rather than just immediate retaliation). If a state fails to pay its debts, it will not be able to borrow money on world markets. If it cheats on the terms of treaties it signs, other states will not sign future treaties with it. The resulting isolation could be very costly.

A state that breaks international law may also face a collective response by a group of states, such as the imposition of *sanctions*—agreements among other states to stop trading with the violator, or to stop some particular commodity trade (most often military goods) as punishment for its violation. Over time, a sanctioned state can become a *pariah* in the community of nations, cut off from normal relations with others. This is very costly in today's world, when economic well-being everywhere depends on trade and economic exchange in world markets. Libya suffered for decades from its isolated status in the international community, and decided in late 2003 to make a clean break and regain normal status. Libya admitted responsibility for past terrorism, began to compensate victims, and agreed to disclose and dismantle its nuclear, chemical, and biological weapons programs.

Even the world's superpower constrains its behavior, at least some of the time, to adhere to international law. For example, in late 2002 a North Korean freighter was caught en route to Yemen with a hidden load of 15 Scud missiles. The United States, fighting the war on terrorism, had an evident national interest in preventing such proliferation, and had the power to prevent it. But when U.S. government lawyers determined that the shipment did not violate international law, the United States backed off and let the delivery continue.

International law enforcement through reciprocity and collective response has one great weakness—it depends entirely on national power. Reciprocity works only if the aggrieved state has the power to inflict costs on the violator. Collective response works only if the collective cares enough about an issue to respond. Thus, it is relatively easy to cheat on small issues (or to get away with major violations if one has enough power).

If international law extends only as far as power reaches, what good is it? The answer lies in the uncertainties of power (see Chapter 2). Without common expectations regarding the rules of the game and adherence to those rules most of the time by most actors, power alone would create great instability in the anarchic international system. International law, even without perfect enforcement, creates expectations about what constitutes legal behavior by states. Because violations or divergences from those expectations stand out, it is easier to identify and punish states that deviate from accepted rules. When states agree to the rules by signing treaties (such as the UN Charter), violations become more visible and clearly illegitimate. In most cases, although power continues to reside in states, international law establishes workable rules for those states to follow. The resulting stability is so beneficial that usually the costs of breaking the rules outweigh the short-term benefits that could be gained from such violations.

The World Court

The World Court

As international law has developed, a general world legal framework in which states can pursue grievances against each other has begun to take shape. The rudiments of such a system now exist in the **World Court** (formally called the **International Court of Justice**), although its jurisdiction is limited and its caseload light.[17] The World Court is a branch of the UN.

Only states, not individuals or businesses, can sue or be sued in the World Court. When a state has a grievance against another, it can take the case to the World Court for an impartial hearing. The Security Council or General Assembly may also request advisory Court opinions on matters of international law.

You Are a Judge on the International Court of Justice

The World Court is a panel of 15 judges elected for nine-year terms (five judges every three years) by a majority of both the Security Council and General Assembly. The Court meets in The Hague, Netherlands. It is customary for permanent members of the Security Council to have one of their nationals as a judge at all times. Ad hoc judges may be added to the 15 if a party to a case does not already have one of its nationals as a judge.

The great *weakness* of the World Court is that states have not agreed in a comprehensive way to subject themselves to its jurisdiction or obey its decisions. Almost all states have signed the treaty creating the Court, but only about a third have signed the *optional clause* in the treaty agreeing to give the Court jurisdiction in certain cases—and even many of those signatories have added their own stipulations reserving their rights and limiting the degree to which the Court can infringe on national sovereignty. The United States withdrew from the optional clause when it was sued by Nicaragua in 1986 (over the CIA's mining of Nicaraguan harbors).[18] Similarly, Iran refused to

[17] Meyer, Howard N. *The World Court in Action: Judging Among Nations*. Lanham, MD: Rowman & Littlefield, 2002.

[18] Forsythe, David P. *The Politics of International Law: U.S. Foreign Policy Reconsidered*. Boulder, CO: Lynne Rienner, 1990.

acknowledge the jurisdiction of the Court when sued by the United States in 1979 over its seizure of the U.S. embassy in Iran. In such a case, the Court may hear the case anyway, and usually rules in favor of the participating side—but has no means to enforce the ruling. Justice can also move slowly. In 2006, the Court began hearing Bosnia's case accusing Serbia of genocide, after some 13 years of preliminary maneuvering.

In one of its most notable successes, the World Court in 1992 settled a complex border dispute between El Salvador and Honduras. By mutual agreement, the two states had asked the Court in 1986 to settle territorial disputes along six stretches of border, three islands, and territorial waters. The disputes dated from 1861 and had led to a war in 1969. The World Court drew borders that gave about two-thirds of the total land to Honduras and split the territorial waters among both countries and Nicaragua. Both countries abided by the decision. In 2002, the World Court settled a long-standing and sometimes violent dispute over an oil-rich peninsula on the Cameroon-Nigeria border. It gave ownership to Cameroon, but Nigeria (which is more powerful) had not pulled troops out by early 2006 and negotiations were continuing on implementation of the ruling.

ALL RISE

The World Court hears international disputes but with little power to enforce judgments. Here, in 2004, the judges rule in favor of Mexico's complaint that the U.S. death penalty against Mexican citizens violated a 1963 treaty.

A main use of the World Court now is to arbitrate issues of secondary importance between countries with friendly relations overall. The United States has settled commercial disputes with Canada and with Italy through the Court. Because security interests are not at stake, and because the overall friendly relations are more important than the particular issue, states have been willing to submit to the Court's jurisdiction. In 2004, the court ordered the United States to review death sentences of Mexican nationals to see if their lack of access to Mexican officials had harmed their legal case. Under the 1963 Vienna Convention on Consular Relations, citizens arrested in a foreign country must be advised of their right to meet with their home country's representatives. The United States had often failed to do so, although demanding this right for Americans abroad. The World Court suggested that U.S. courts add relevant language to the Miranda warning for cases when police arrest foreign nationals. There are other international forums for the arbitration of grievances (by mutual consent). Some regional courts, notably in Europe, resemble the World Court in function. Various bodies are capable of conducting arbitration. But for major disputes involving issues of great importance to states, few legal alternatives exist.

Because of the difficulty of winning enforceable agreements on major conflicts through the World Court, states have used the Court infrequently over the years—a dozen or fewer cases per year (about 100 judgments and advisory opinions since 1946).

International Cases in National Courts

Most legal cases concerning international matters—whether brought by governments or by private individuals or companies—remain entirely within the legal systems of one or more states. National courts hear cases brought under national laws and can enforce judgments by collecting damages (in civil suits) or imposing punishments (in criminal ones).

A party with a dispute that crosses national boundaries gains several advantages by pursuing the matter through the national courts of one or more of the relevant states, rather than through international channels. First, judgments are enforceable. The party that wins a lawsuit in a national court can collect from the other party's assets within the state. Second, individuals and companies can pursue legal complaints through national courts (as can subnational governmental bodies), whereas in most areas of international law states must themselves bring suits on behalf of their citizens. (In truth, even national governments pursue most of their legal actions against each other through national courts.)

Third, there is often a choice of more than one state within which a case could legally be heard; one can pick the legal system most favorable to one's case. It is up to each state's court system to decide whether it has *jurisdiction* in a case (the right to hear it), and courts tend to extend their own authority with a broad interpretation. Traditionally, a national court may hear cases concerning any activity on its national territory, any actions of its own citizens anywhere in the world, and actions taken toward its citizens elsewhere in the world. Noncitizens can use the national courts to enforce damages against citizens, because the national court has authority to impose fines and if necessary seize bank accounts and property.

The United States is a favorite jurisdiction within which to bring cases for two reasons. First, U.S. juries have the reputation of awarding bigger settlements in lawsuits than juries elsewhere in the world (if only because the United States is a rich country). Second, because many people and governments do business in the United States, it is often possible to collect damages awarded by a U.S. court. For these reasons, U.S. courts in recent years have ruled on human-rights cases brought by Chinese dissidents over the 1989 Tiananmen massacre, Cuban exiles against the Cuban government, and a Paraguayan doctor suing a Paraguayan police official for torturing the doctor's son. In 2003, U.S. courts ordered large payments by Iraq and Iran to U.S. victims of terrorism and torture. The Alien Tort Claims Act of 1789 gives federal courts jurisdiction over civil lawsuits against foreigners for "violation of the law of nations." Human rights activists have used the law against repressive governments in recent years, as when they sued U.S. oil companies ExxonMobil and Unocal for aiding abusive regimes in Indonesia and Burma, respectively. The rapid extension of U.S. legal jurisdiction may bring a reciprocal response from European (and other) states, which may seek on occasion to extend their national laws to U.S. shores.[19]

Belgium's national courts are a favorite venue to bring international human rights cases, because a 1993 law gives them jurisdiction over any violation of the Geneva convention. In 2001, four people accused of war crimes in Rwanda in 1994 were sent to prison by a Belgian jury. (Rwanda is a former Belgian colony, and ten Belgian soldiers had been killed at the outset of the genocide there.) In 2005, Belgium indicted a former leader of Chad, accused of 40,000 political murders in Chad in the 1980s, and Senegal (where he lived) asked the African Union to rule on whether it should extradite him. The ruling was due in July 2006.

There are important limits to the use of national courts to resolve international disputes, however. Most important is that the authority of national courts stops at the state's

[19] Liptak, Adam. U.S. Courts' Role in Foreign Feuds Comes under Fire. *New York Times*. August 3, 2003: A1.

POLICY PERSPECTIVES

President of Senegal, Abdoulaye Wade

PROBLEM *Balancing respect for international law and national interests.*

BACKGROUND Imagine that you are the president of Senegal. Senegal and Mauritania share a border marked entirely by the Senegal River. On both sides of the river, the land is very fertile due to annual flooding. Much of Mauritania's arable land is near the Senegalese border, making this a very important area for both states. This land was the scene of an ethnic conflict in 1989, which nearly escalated into a war between the two states.

The dominant political group in Mauritania is the Moors, who are of Arab descent, but millions of black Africans (Tukulors and Fulani) also live in Mauritania. Relations between these groups are poor—for example, there are widespread reports that slavery still exists in much of the country. To escape these conditions, many Africans cross the border into Senegal.

Senegal is home to thousands of Moors who are important to the economic activity near the border. During the 1989 dispute, many Moors were deported back to Mauritania, while their businesses were looted and burned. In response, thousands of black Africans fled to Senegal after having their land forcibly taken from them by the Mauritanian government.

When settling the 1989 dispute, both countries agreed to repatriate refugees back to their homes. Both sides also agreed not to escalate their dispute over who has the rights to water from the Senegal River. In the past five years, both states have objected to plans to use more water for irrigation, since projections suggest both states will need additional water in the future to support agriculture.

In Mauritania, several years of drought brought low crop yields. In 2004, a locust plague destroyed up to 40 percent of its crops, leading Mauritania to announce it was on the brink of famine. These food shortages will only exacerbate the political instability in that country. Since 2003, three coups have been attempted.

SCENARIO Now imagine that Mauritania demands access to more river water for irrigation because of the famine. As the president of Senegal, you must decide how to handle these demands. One option is to take the dispute to the International Court of Justice (ICJ)—the World Court. Any ruling would have the force of international law, but the Court has no mechanism for enforcing its judgments. And, of course, there is no guarantee you would actually win the case.

A failure to address Mauritanian demands quickly and peacefully could result in a host of problems. Mauritania has threatened to expel all Africans living near the border. Such a move would create a refugee problem in an area already experiencing food shortages. In addition, increasing tensions along the border would likely lead to more violence between Moors and Africans, which could escalate into a larger conflict between your country and Mauritania.

You could ask the African Union (AU) to mediate the dispute. Although the AU would not have the same legal status as the ICJ, it does receive the support of your regional neighbors, including Mauritania. This makes it more likely that its decision would be respected and enforced. Unfortunately, the AU's predecessor, the Organization of African Unity, failed to effectively mediate your 1989 dispute, leaving the violence to escalate.

CHOOSE YOUR POLICY Do you take this dispute to the ICJ? Do you approach the AU with your dispute? How do you promote your national interests and show respect for international law, while trying to contain violence with your neighbor?

borders, where sovereignty ends. A court in Zambia cannot compel a resident of Thailand to come and testify; it cannot authorize the seizure of a British bank account to pay damages; it cannot arrest a criminal suspect (Zambian or foreigner) except on Zambian soil. To take such actions beyond national borders, states must persuade other states to cooperate.

To bring a person outside a state's territory to trial, the state's government must ask a second government to arrest the person on the second state's territory and hand him or her over for trial. Called *extradition,* this is a matter of international law because it is a legal treaty arrangement *between* states. There are hundreds of such treaties, many dating back hundreds of years. If there is no such treaty, the individual generally remains immune from a state's courts by staying off its territory. Some U.S. allies do not usually extradite suspects who would face the death penalty to the United States. The war on terrorism since 2001, however, has expanded international legal and law-enforcement cooperation.

In one high-profile debate about extradition, the former Chilean military dictator Augusto Pinochet was arrested in England in 1999 on a Spanish warrant, based on crimes committed against Spanish citizens in Chile during Pinochet's rule. His supporters claimed that he should have immunity for acts taken as head of state, but since he was not an accredited diplomat in England (where he had gone for medical treatment), and no longer head of state, the British courts held him on Spain's request to extradite him for trial there. Once on British soil without current diplomatic immunity, Pinochet was subject to British law, including its extradition treaties. However, the British government eventually let him return to Chile, citing his medical condition, and a Chilean court suspended his case on health grounds.

There are gray areas in the jurisdiction of national courts over foreigners. If a government can lure a suspect onto the high seas, it can nab the person without violating another country's territoriality. More troublesome are cases in which a government obtains a foreign citizen from a foreign country for trial without going through extradition procedures. In a famous case in the 1980s, a Mexican doctor was wanted by U.S. authorities for allegedly participating in the torture and murder of a U.S. drug agent in Mexico. The U.S. government paid a group of bounty hunters to kidnap the doctor in Mexico, carry him forcibly across the border, and deliver him to the custody of U.S. courts. The U.S. Supreme Court gave the U.S. courts jurisdiction in the case—showing the tendency to extend state sovereignty wherever possible—although international lawyers and Mexican officials objected strongly. The U.S. government had to reassure the Mexican government that it would not kidnap Mexican citizens for trial in the United States in the future. The doctor himself returned home after the case was thrown out for lack of evidence. In late 2004, Colombia arranged the abduction of a leading Colombian rebel living in Venezuela, provoking Venezuelan protests about the violation of sovereignty.

The principle of territoriality also governs **immigration law.** When people cross a border into a new country, the decision about whether they can remain there, and under what conditions, is up to the new state. The state of origin cannot compel their return. National laws establish conditions for foreigners to travel and visit on a state's territory, to work there, and sometimes to become citizens (*naturalization*). Many other legal issues are raised by people traveling or living outside their own country—passports and visas, babies born in foreign countries, marriages to foreign nationals, bank accounts, businesses, taxes, and so forth. Practices vary from country to country, but the general principle is that *national laws prevail on the territory of a state.*

Despite the continued importance of national court systems in international legal affairs and the lack of enforcement powers of the World Court, it would be wrong to conclude that state sovereignty is supreme and international law impotent. Rather, there is a balance of sovereignty and law in international interactions.

Law and Sovereignty

The remainder of this chapter discusses particular areas of international law, from the most firmly rooted and widely respected, to newer and less-established areas. In each area, the influence of law and norms runs counter to the unimpeded exercise of state sovereignty. This struggle becomes more intense as one moves from long-standing traditions of diplomatic law to recent norms governing human rights.

Laws of Diplomacy

The bedrock of international law is respect for the rights of diplomats. The standards of behavior in this area are spelled out in detail, applied universally, and taken very seriously. The ability to conduct diplomacy is necessary for all other kinds of relations among states, except perhaps all-out war. Since the rise of the international system five centuries ago, it has been considered unjustifiable to harm an emissary sent from another state as a means of influencing the other state. Such a norm has not always existed; it is natural in some ways to kill the messenger who brings an unpleasant message, or to use another state's official as a hostage or bargaining chip. But today this kind of behavior is universally condemned, though it still happens from time to time.

The status of embassies and of an ambassador as an official state representative is explicitly defined in the process of **diplomatic recognition.** Diplomats are *accredited* to each other's governments (they present "credentials"), and thereafter the individuals so defined enjoy certain rights and protections as foreign diplomats in the host country.

Diplomats have the right to occupy an *embassy* in the host country as though it were their own state's territory. On the grounds of the U.S. embassy in Kuwait, for instance, the laws of the United States, and not those of Kuwait, apply. The U.S. armed forces (Marines) occupy the territory, and those of Kuwait may not enter without permission.

A flagrant violation of the sanctity of embassies occurred in Iran after Islamic revolutionaries took power in 1979. Iranian students seized and occupied the U.S. embassy compound, holding the U.S. diplomats hostage for more than a year. The Iranian government did not directly commit this act but did condone it and did refuse to force the students out of the embassy. (Host countries are expected, if necessary, to use force against their own citizens to protect a foreign embassy.)

AGAINST THE LAW

International law prohibits attacks on diplomats. This fundamental principle, like others in international law, can ultimately be enforced only by applying the power of other states (through such leverage as imposing economic sanctions, freezing relations, or threatening military force). Here are U.S. diplomats on their first day as hostages in the U.S. embassy, Tehran, Iran, 1979.

Diplomats enjoy **diplomatic immunity** even when they leave the embassy grounds. The right to travel varies from one country to another; diplomats may be restricted to one city or free to roam about the countryside. Alone among all foreign nationals, diplomats are beyond the jurisdiction of the host country's national courts. If they commit crimes, from jaywalking to murder, they may not be arrested and tried. All the host country can do is to take away a diplomat's accreditation and *expel* the person from the host country. However, strong countries can sometimes pressure weaker ones to lift immunity so that a diplomat may face trial for a crime. This happened twice in 1997, when the United States and France were allowed to prosecute diplomats from Georgia and Zaire, respectively, for reckless driving that killed children.

U.S. commitments as host country to the UN include extending diplomatic immunity to the diplomats accredited to the UN. The UN delegates thus cannot be prosecuted under U.S. law. Given this immunity, delegates simply tear up thousands of parking tickets each year, for example. Occasionally, UN representatives are accused of more serious crimes (murder, in one case in the 1980s), but they cannot be brought to trial in the United States for those crimes.

Because of diplomatic immunity, it is common to conduct espionage activities through the diplomatic corps, out of an embassy. Spies are often posted to low-level positions in embassies, such as cultural attaché, press liaison, or military attaché. If the host country catches them spying, it cannot prosecute them, so it merely expels them. Diplomatic norms (though not law) call for politeness when expelling spies; the standard reason given is "for activities not consistent with his/her diplomatic status." If a spy operates under cover of being a businessperson or tourist, then no immunity applies: the person can be arrested and prosecuted under the host country's laws.

A *diplomatic pouch* is a package sent between an embassy and its home country. As the name implies, it started out historically as a small and occasional shipment, but today there is a large and steady volume of such shipments all over the world. Diplomatic pouches, too, enjoy the status of home country territoriality: they cannot be opened, searched, or confiscated by a host country. Although we do not know how much mischief goes on in diplomatic pouches (because they are secret), it is safe to assume that illicit goods such as guns and drugs regularly find their way across borders in diplomatic pouches.

To *break diplomatic relations* means to withdraw one's diplomats from a state and expel its diplomats from one's own state. This tactic is used to show displeasure with another government; it is a refusal to do business as usual. When a revolutionary government comes into power, some countries may withdraw recognition. Most activity regarding diplomatic recognition today occurs when small states recognize Taiwan diplomatically, are subsequently pressured by China, and occasionally withdraw recognition.

When two countries lack diplomatic relations, they often do business through a third country willing to represent a country's interests formally through its own embassy. This is called an *interests section* in the third country's embassy. Thus, the practical needs of diplomacy can overcome a formal lack of relations between states. For instance, U.S. interests are represented by the Swiss embassy in Cuba, and Cuban interests are represented by the Swiss embassy in the United States. In practice, these interests sections are located in the former U.S. and Cuban embassies and staffed with U.S. and Cuban diplomats.

States register lower levels of displeasure by *recalling their ambassadors* home for some period of time; diplomatic norms call for a trip home "for consultations" even when everyone knows the purpose is to signal annoyance. Milder still is the expression of displeasure by a *formal complaint*. Usually the complaining government does so in its own capital city, to the other's ambassador.

The law of diplomacy is repeatedly violated in one context—terrorism (see pp. 202–205). Because states care so much about the sanctity of diplomats, the diplomats make a tempting target for terrorists, and because terrorist groups do not enjoy the benefits of diplomatic law (as states do), they are willing to break diplomatic norms and laws. An attack on diplomats or embassies is an attack on the territory of the state itself—yet can be carried out far from the state's home territory. Many diplomats have been killed in recent decades. In 1998, al Qaeda terrorists bombed the U.S. embassies in Kenya and Tanzania, killing more than 200 people. In late 2004, al Qaeda forces stormed a U.S. consulate in Saudi Arabia, killing several guards.

IN THE DOCK

War crimes include unnecessary targeting of civilians and mistreatment of prisoners of war (POWs), among others. A Special Court set up by the UN is hearing cases from the war in Sierra Leone, where mutilation, rape, and the use of child soldiers were common. The former president of next-door Liberia, Charles Taylor, was charged with war crimes and crimes against humanity for his role in the war. Arrested in Nigeria where he had been living in exile, Taylor (second from right) here appears before the court in 2006. His trial will likely take place in the Netherlands to avoid a possible destabilizing effect on West Africa.

War Crimes

After the law of diplomacy, international law regarding war is one of the most developed areas of international law. Laws concerning war are divided into two areas—laws in war (*jus in bello*) and laws of war (*jus ad bellum*). Consider these in turn, beginning with laws in wartime, violations of which are considered **war crimes.**[20]

The Roman politician Cicero said: "Laws are silent in time of war."[21] This is no longer true. In wartime, international law is especially difficult to enforce, but there are extensive norms of legal conduct in war that are widely followed. After a war, losers can be punished for violations of the laws of war (war crimes).

In the 1990s, for the first time since World War II, the UN Security Council authorized an international war crimes tribunal, directed against war crimes in the former Yugoslavia. Similar tribunals were later established for genocide in Rwanda and Sierra Leone.[22] The tribunal on the former Yugoslavia, headquartered in The Hague, Netherlands, issued indictments against the top Bosnian Serb leaders and other Serbian and Croatian officers, and in 1999 against Serbian strongman Slobodan Milosevic during the expulsion of Albanians from Kosovo. The tribunal was hampered by lack of funding and by its lack of power to arrest suspects who enjoyed the sanctity of Serbia and Croatia. A new Croatian government that won elections in 1999 began to cooperate with the tribunal, and after Milosevic lost power in Serbia, the new Serbian government turned him

[20] Falk, Richard, Irene Gendzier, and Robert Jay Lifton, eds. *Crimes of War: Iraq*. NY: Nation, 2006. Howard, Michael, George J. Andreopoulos, and Mark R. Shulman, eds. *The Laws of War: Constraints on Warfare in the Western World*. Yale, 1994. Best, Geoffrey. *War and Law Since 1945*. Oxford, 1994. Hartle, Anthony E. *Moral Issues in Military Decision Making*. Kansas, 2004.

[21] Cicero, Pro Milone. In *The Speeches of Cicero*. Edited and translated by N. H. Watts. Harvard, 1931.

[22] Bass, Gary Jonathan. *Stay the Hand of Vengeance: The Politics of War Crimes Tribunals*. Princeton, 2000.

THINKING THEORETICALLY

Paying for a UN War Crimes Tribunal

The UN Security Council established a war crimes tribunal for the former Yugoslavia. Its effectiveness was limited, in its first years, by inadequacy of funding necessary to hire investigators and translators, rent offices and phone lines, and so forth.

The contributions of the great powers to support the tribunal varied, with the United States providing the most support (though still not adequate to the need) and Great Britain providing very little. What theories could help explain why one great power would make a large contribution and its closest ally a small one?

Liberal theorists would quickly recognize a collective goods problem in paying for the tribunal. The world community benefits from the work of the tribunal (inasmuch as it deters future aggression and genocide), but each individual state gains this benefit—however beneficial it ends up being—regardless of its own contribution. By this logic, Britain was being rational to free-ride because the United States and others were willing to pick up enough of the tab to make the tribunal at least minimally effective. The United States for its part exhibited a lingering hegemonic impulse by paying the largest relative share for the tribunal. As the world's most powerful state and a leading global trading country, the United States has the greatest interest in maintaining world order.

Realists might well question this explanation. They might see Britain's lack of support as more straightforward: British leaders may not have wanted the tribunal to succeed because Britain tacitly sided with Serbia (a traditional ally), and Serbia was not cooperating with a tribunal that had indicted the Bosnian Serb leaders as war criminals. Britain saw in Serbia a strong power in the Balkans that could maintain order in a relatively unimportant corner of Europe. The same geopolitical factors that led Britain in the past to side with Serbia (and Russia and France) against Croatia (and Germany, Austria, and Turkey) still operate. War crimes come and go, by this reasoning, but great-power interests remain fairly constant.

Both theories seem to have merit. How could we test whether Britain withheld support because it (1) supported the tribunal but was free-riding on American contributions, or (2) opposed the tribunal and wanted to impede it? Sometimes history provides "experiments" which, even though we do not control them, help sort out competing theoretical explanations. In this case, in 1997 a liberal government headed by Prime Minister Tony Blair replaced the conservative government of John Major. This change did not affect the explanatory "variables" of either theory—the nature of the collective goods problem inherent in the tribunal, and the nature of Britain's strategic and historical interests and alliances in the Balkans. Therefore both theories would predict that Britain would continue to make minimal contributions to the tribunal.

But in fact Blair's government shifted its Bosnia policy dramatically, leading a raid to arrest two war crimes suspects and contributing substantial funds for the tribunal to construct a second courtroom. So both theories are wrong! Can you think of alternative theories that would explain both Britain's initial low contributions and its later change in policy?

over to the tribunal in 2001, and he died in custody in 2006. In late 2004 and early 2005, six suspects from all sides of the conflict surrendered to the Hague tribunal for trial.

Following the civil war in Sierra Leone, the government there runs a war crimes tribunal jointly with the UN. In 2003, it indicted the sitting state leader in next-door Liberia, Charles Taylor, for his role in the war's extreme brutality. He fled to Nigeria shortly afterwards but was captured there and turned over to the tribunal for trial in 2006.

Following up on the UN tribunals for former Yugoslavia and Rwanda, in 1998 most of the world's states signed a treaty to create a permanent **International Criminal Court (ICC).** It would hear cases of genocide, war crimes, and crimes against humanity from anywhere in the world. By the deadline date in December 2000, the United States and 138 other states had signed the treaty, and by 2002 the 60 needed to make the court operational—but not the

United States—had ratified it. The ICC opened for business in 2003 in the Hague, with 18 judges sworn in from around the world (but not the United States, a nonparticipant). In 2002, the UN Security Council gave U.S. peacekeeping soldiers a year's exemption from the court, but U.S. objections remained and the exemption was not renewed. The ICC issued its first arrest warrants, arising from the long civil war in Uganda, in 2005. War crimes in Darfur, Sudan—which a UN commission found grave but short of "genocide"—have also been referred to the ICC after the United States dropped its objections in 2005 (when exemptions for U.S. soldiers were restored).

War Crimes in Sudan

As with most international law, the enforcement of laws of war occurs mostly through practical reciprocity and group response, reinforced by habit and legitimacy. A state that violates laws of war can find itself isolated without allies and subject to reprisals.

The most important principle in the laws of war is the effort to limit warfare to the combatants and to protect civilians when possible. It is illegal to target civilians in a war unless there is a compelling military utility in doing so. Even then the amount of force used must be *proportional* to the military gain, and only the *necessary* amount of force can be used.

To help separate combatants from civilians, soldiers must wear uniforms and insignia; for example, U.S. armed forces typically have a shoulder patch with a U.S. flag. This provision is frequently violated in guerrilla warfare, making that form of warfare particularly brutal and destructive of civilian life. If one cannot tell the difference between a bystander and a combatant, one is likely to kill both when in doubt. By contrast, in a large-scale conventional war such as the Gulf War, it is much easier to distinguish civilians from soldiers, although the effort is never completely successful.[23] When U.S. special forces in Afghanistan made friends with local fighters by operating out of uniform and with bushy beards, humanitarian aid agencies complained and the Pentagon ordered the soldiers back into uniform. In the Iraq War since 2003, the insurgents repeatedly targeted civilians, attacked in civilian clothes, from hospitals and schools, and after feigning surrender—all against the laws of war.

Soldiers have the right under the laws of war to surrender, which is to abandon their status as combatants and become **prisoners of war (POWs).** They give up their weapons and their right to fight, and earn instead the right (like civilians) not to be targeted. POWs may not be killed, mistreated, or forced to disclose information beyond their name, rank, and serial number. The law of POWs is enforced through practical reciprocity. Once, late in World War II, German forces executed 80 POWs from the French partisan forces (whom Germany did not recognize as legitimate belligerents). The partisans responded by executing 80 German POWs.

The laws of war reserve a special role for the **International Committee of the Red Cross (ICRC).** The ICRC provides practical support—such as medical care, food, and letters from home—to civilians caught in wars and to POWs. Exchanges of POWs are usually negotiated through the ICRC. Armed forces must respect the neutrality of the Red Cross, and usually do so (again, guerrilla war is problematical). In the current war on terrorism, the United States does not consider the "enemy combatants" it detains to be POWs, but has granted the ICRC access to most (though not all) of them. More controversial is the U.S. policy called "extraordinary rendition"which lets terrorist suspects captured overseas be transferred to other countries, including some that use torture, for questioning.

The laws of warfare impose moral responsibility on individuals in wartime, as well as on states. The Nuremberg Tribunal after World War II established that participants can be held accountable for war crimes they commit. German officers defended their actions as "just following orders," but this was rejected; the officers were punished, and some executed, for their war crimes.

Nuremberg

[23] Fotion, Nicholas G. The Gulf War: Cleanly Fought. *Bulletin of the Atomic Scientists* 47 (7), 1991: 24–29. Lopez, George A. The Gulf War: Not So Clean. *Bulletin of the Atomic Scientists* 47 (7), 1991: 30–35. Sterba, James P., ed. *Terrorism and International Justice*. Oxford 2003.

Not all Nuremberg defendants were found guilty, however. For example, laws of war limit the use of force against civilians to what is necessary and proportional to military objectives. In World War II, the German army besieged the Russian city of Leningrad (St. Petersburg) for two years, and civilians in the city were starving. Sieges of this kind are permitted under international law if an army cannot easily capture a city.

Changing Context The laws of warfare have been undermined by the changing nature of war. Conventional wars by defined armed forces on defined battlegrounds are giving way to irregular and "low-intensity" wars fought by guerrillas and death squads in cities or jungles. The lines between civilians and soldiers blur in these situations, and war crimes become more commonplace. In the Vietnam War, one of the largest problems faced by the United States was an enemy that seemed to be everywhere and nowhere. This led frustrated U.S. forces into attacking civilian villages seen as supporting the guerrillas. In one infamous case, a U.S. officer was court-martialed for ordering his soldiers to massacre hundreds of unarmed civilians in the village of My Lai in 1968 (he was convicted but given a light sentence). In today's irregular warfare, frequently inflamed by ethnic and religious conflicts, the laws of war are increasingly difficult to uphold.

Another factor undermining laws of war is that states rarely issue a *declaration of war* setting out whom they are warring against and the cause of their action. Ironically, such declarations are historically the exception, not the rule. This trend continues today since declarations of war bring little benefit to the state declaring war and incur obligations under international law. In many cases, such as revolutionary and counterrevolutionary civil wars, a declaration would not even be appropriate, because wars are declared only against states, not internal groups. In undeclared wars the distinctions between participants and nonparticipants are undermined (along with the protection of the latter). The Bush administration called the 2001 terrorist attacks acts of war, and the response a war on terrorism, but Congress did not formally declare war (just as it had not during the Korean and Vietnam wars).

Just War Doctrine

In addition to the laws about how wars are fought (war crimes), international law distinguishes **just wars** (which are legal) from wars of aggression (which are illegal). This area of law grows out of centuries-old religious writings about just wars (which once could be enforced by threats to excommunicate individuals from the church). Today, the legality of war is defined by the UN Charter, which outlaws aggression. Above and beyond the legal standing of just war doctrine, it has become a strong international norm, not one that all states follow but an important part of the modern intellectual tradition governing matters of war and peace that evolved in Europe.[24]

The idea of aggression, around which the doctrine of just war evolved, is based on a violation of the sovereignty and territorial integrity of states. Aggression refers to a state's use of force, or an imminent threat to do so, against another state's territory or sovereignty—unless the use of force is in response to aggression. Tanks swarming across the border constitute aggression, but so do tanks massing at the border if their state has threatened to invade. The lines are somewhat fuzzy. But for a threat to constitute aggression (and justify the use of force in response) it must be a clear threat of using force, not just a hostile policy or general rivalry.

---

[24] Walzer, Michael. *Arguing About War*. Yale, 2004. Walzer, Michael. *Just and Unjust Wars: A Moral Argument with Historical Illustrations*. 2nd ed. NY: Basic, 1992. Twenty Years of Just and Unjust Wars [symposium with articles by Michael Joseph Smith, David C. Hendrickson, Theodore J. Koontz, and Joseph Boyle]. *Ethics & International Affairs* 11, 1997: 3–104.

States have the right to respond to aggression in the only manner thought to be reliable—military force. Just war doctrine is not based on nonviolence. Responses can include both the *repelling* of the attack itself and the *punishment* of the aggressor. Responses can be taken by the victim of aggression or by other states not directly affected—as a way of maintaining the norm of nonaggression in the international system. The collective actions of UN members against Iraq after its invasion of Kuwait are a classic case of such response.

Response to aggression is the only allowable use of military force according to just war doctrine. The just war approach thus explicitly rules out war as an instrument to change another state's government or policies, or in ethnic and religious conflicts. In fact, the UN Charter makes no provision for "war" but rather for "international police actions" against aggressors. The analogy is with law and order in a national society, enforced by police when necessary. Because only aggression justifies military force, if all states obeyed the law against aggression there would be no international war.

For a war to be *morally* just, it must be more than a response to aggression; it must be waged for the *purpose* of responding to aggression. The *intent* must be just. A state may not take advantage of another's aggression to wage a war that is essentially aggressive. Although the U.S.-led war effort to oust Iraq from Kuwait in 1991 was certainly a response to aggression, critics found the justness of the war to be compromised by the U.S. interest in obtaining cheap oil from the Middle East—not an allowable reason for waging war.

Just war doctrine has been undermined, even more seriously than have laws of war crimes, by the changing nature of warfare.[25] In civil wars and low-intensity conflicts, the belligerents range from poorly organized militias to national armies, and the battleground is often a patchwork of enclaves and positions with no clear front lines (much less borders). It is harder to identify an aggressor in such situations, and harder to balance the relative merits of peace and justice.

Human Rights

One of the newest and least developed areas of international law concerns **human rights**—the universal rights of human beings against certain abuses of their *own* governments.[26] The very idea of human rights flies in the face of the sovereignty and territorial integrity of states. Efforts to promote human rights are routinely criticized by governments with poor human rights records (including China and Russia) as "interference in our internal affairs." This charge puts human rights law on shaky ground.

Yet norms and even laws concerning human rights continue to develop, if only because what happens within one state can so easily spill over national borders. A prime example occurred when Iraq cracked down brutally on a Kurdish uprising in northern Iraq. The norm of noninterference in Iraq's internal affairs would dictate that the slaughter was Iraq's business alone. But when the Kurds fled in huge numbers to the Turkish border, they threatened to overwhelm Turkey's resources and perhaps inflame a Kurdish uprising in Turkey. The anti-Iraqi alliance therefore declared the matter an international concern and

---

[25] Johnson, James Turner. *Can Modern War Be Just?* Yale, 1984.

[26] Falk, Richard A. *Human Rights Horizons*. NY: Routledge, 2000. Thomas, Daniel. *The Helsinki Effect: International Norms, Human Rights, and the Demise of Communism*. Princeton, 2001. Risse, Thomas, Stephen C. Ropp, and Kathryn Sikkink, eds. *The Power of Human Rights: International Norms and Domestic Change*. Cambridge, 1999. Cohen, Cynthia Price, ed. *Human Rights of Indigenous Peoples*. Ardsley, NY: Transnational, 1998. Steiner, Henry J., and Philip Alston. *International Human Rights in Context: Law, Politics, Morals*. Oxford: Clarendon, 1996. Cronin, Bruce. *Institutions for the Common Good: International Protection Regimes in International Society*. Cambridge, 2003.

WE WANT OUR RIGHTS

International norms concerning human rights conflict with state sovereignty, causing friction in relationships such as Burma's with Japan. Here, Burmese residents in Japan, holding pictures of their leader Aung San Suu Kyi, protest Burma's military government for its human rights abuses.

imposed its own armed forces within northern Iraq to provide security and coax the Kurds back home. Eventually the Kurdish groups gained virtual autonomy under foreign military cover, compromising Iraq's sovereignty. Because of Iraq's lack of military reach into the area, Turkey was able to invade several times in 1995–1998 to attack bases of the Kurdish guerrillas operating in Turkey.

Even in cases that do not so directly spill over national borders, the world is more interconnected and interdependent than ever. A government's abuses of its citizens can inflame ethnic conflicts, undermine moral norms of decency, and in other ways threaten the peace and stability of the international community. At least this is the rationale for treating human rights as a question of international law and norms.

Laws concerning human rights date back to the Nuremberg trials. Beyond the war crimes committed by German officers were their acts of *genocide* (attempts to exterminate a whole people) in which about ten million civilians had been killed in death camps. Clearly this ranked among the most terrible crimes ever committed, yet it did not violate either international law or German law. The solution was to create a new category of legal offenses—**crimes against humanity**—under which those responsible were punished. The category was not applied again until 1994–1995, when the tribunal for the former Yugoslavia handed down indictments for genocide.

WEB LINK
Universal Declaration of Human Rights

Soon after the experience of World War II, in 1948, the UN General Assembly adopted the *Universal Declaration of Human Rights*. It does not have the force of international law, but it sets forth (hoped-for) international norms regarding behavior by governments toward their own citizens and foreigners alike. The declaration roots itself in the principle that violations of human rights upset international order (causing outrage, sparking rebellion, etc.) and in the fact that the UN Charter commits states to respect fundamental freedoms. The declaration proclaims that "all human beings are born free and equal" without regard to race, sex, language, religion, political affiliation, or the status of the territory on which they were born. It goes on to promote norms in a wide variety of areas, from banning torture to guaranteeing religious and political freedom to the right of economic well-being.

Clearly this is a broad conception of human rights, and one far from today's realities. No state has a perfect record on human rights, and states differ as to which areas they respect or violate. When the United States criticizes China for prohibiting free speech, using prison labor, and torturing political dissidents, China notes that the United States has 40 million poor people, the highest ratio of prison inmates in the world, and a history of racism and violence.[27] Overall, despite the poor record of the world's states on some

[27] People's Republic of China, State Council. America's "Abominable" Human Rights Conditions. *Washington Post*, February 16, 1997: C3.

points, progress has been made on others. For example, slavery—once considered normal worldwide—has been largely abandoned in the past 150 years.

Today, human rights efforts center on winning basic political rights in authoritarian countries—beginning with a halt to the torture, execution, and imprisonment of those expressing political or religious beliefs. The leading organization pressing this struggle is **Amnesty International,** an NGO that operates globally to monitor and try to rectify glaring abuses of human rights.[28] Amnesty International has a reputation for impartiality and has criticized abuses in many countries, including the United States. Other groups, such as Human Rights Watch, work in a similar way but often with a more regional or national focus. The UN also operates a Commission on Human Rights with a global focus. In 1993, the General Assembly after 40 years of debate created the position of High Commissioner for Human Rights (whose powers do not, of course, include making states do anything, but do include publicizing their abuses).

Enforcement of norms of human rights is difficult, because it involves interference in a state's internal affairs. Cutting off trade or contact with a government that violates human rights tends to hurt the citizens whose rights are being violated by further isolating them (as with sanctions on Iraq and Taliban-ruled Afghanistan in recent years). The most effective method yet discovered is a combination of *publicity* and *pressure*. Publicity entails digging up information about human rights abuses, as Amnesty International does. The pressure of other governments, as well as private individuals and businesses, consists of threats to punish the offender in some way through nonviolent means. For instance, one faction in the U.S. Congress repeatedly sought in the early 1990s to link the terms of U.S.-Chinese trade to China's human rights record. But inasmuch as most governments seek to maintain normal relations with each other most of the time, this kind of intrusive punishment by one government of another's human rights violations is rare—and not reliably successful. Governments in a number of states have cracked down on NGOs promoting human rights. Zimbabwe passed a law effectively banning NGOs from operating there, as the authoritarian government prepared for an election in 2005.

The U.S. State Department has actively pursued human rights since the late 1970s, when President Jimmy Carter made human rights a major goal of U.S. foreign policy. An annual U.S. government report assesses human rights in states around the world. In states where abuses are severe or becoming worse, U.S. foreign aid has been withheld from these states or their armed forces. (But in other cases, CIA funding supported the abusers.)[29]

Currently, human rights is one of the two main areas of conflict (along with Taiwan) in China's relationship with the United States. Several practices draw criticism; these include imprisoning political opponents of the government, the use of prison labor, and a criminal justice system prone to abuses. According to Amnesty International, China executes more people than the rest of the world combined—thousands each year—sometimes within days of the crime and sometimes for relatively minor crimes.[30]

A variety of covenants and conventions on human rights have been drawn up as legally binding (though not easily enforceable) treaties. These include a major covenant on civil and political rights (ratified by the United States) and on economic, social, and

[28] Amnesty International. *Amnesty International Report*. London, annual. Clark, Ann Marie. *Diplomacy of Conscience: Amnesty International and Changing Human Rights Norms*. Princeton, 2000.

[29] Liang-Fenton, Debra, ed. *Implementing U.S. Human Rights Policy: Agendas, Policies, and Practices*. Herndon, VA: United States Institute of Peace Press, 2004.

[30] Amnesty International. *Executed "According to Law"? The Death Penalty in China*. March 17, 2004. Amnesty International.

cultural rights (not U.S.-ratified). More specific conventions cover genocide, racial discrimination, women's rights, torture, and the rights of the child. The treaties have been ratified by various groups of the world's states. Some states (including both the United States and China) have general concerns about the loss of sovereignty implicit in such treaties. China signed the Covenant on Economic, Social, and Cultural Rights in 1997, just before the first U.S.-Chinese summit meeting in a decade (and ratified it in 2001). The United States has not signed it. In 1998, China signed the Covenant on Civil and Political Rights (which the United States ratified in 1992). All but two UN members—the United States and Somalia—have ratified the 1990 Convention on the Rights of the Child.

Despite many limitations, concern about human rights is a force to be reckoned with in international relations. There are now widely held norms about how governments *should* behave, and someday governments may actually adhere to those norms as they have already begun to do in select areas such as the abolition of legal slavery. With the downfall of many authoritarian and military governments in the former Soviet Union, Eastern Europe, Latin America, and Africa, a growing emphasis on human rights seems likely.

The concern of states for the human rights of individuals living in other states is a far cry from the realist concerns that have dominated the theory and practice of IR in the past. Indeed, the entire area of international law and organization runs counter to the fundamental assertions about international anarchy made by realists. Whether liberal theories or constructivist approaches better describe this area is still an open question, however. The remaining chapters of this book move away from two other aspects of realism—its emphasis on military force above other forms of leverage, and its pessimism about the potentials for international cooperation as an outcome of bargaining.

THINKING CRITICALLY

1. Suppose you were asked to recommend changes in the structure of the UN Security Council (especially in permanent membership and the veto). What changes would you recommend, if any? Based on what logic?
2. The former UN secretary-general Boutros-Ghali proposed (without success) the creation of a standby army of peacemaking forces loaned by member states (see p. 268). This would reduce state sovereignty a bit and increase supranational authority. Discuss this plan's merits and drawbacks.
3. Collective security against aggression depends on states' willingness to bear the costs of fighting wars to repel and punish aggressors. Sometimes great powers have been willing to bear such costs; at other times they have not. What considerations do you think should guide such decisions? Give examples of situations (actual or potential) that would and would not merit the intervention of great powers to reverse aggression.
4. Given the difficulty of enforcing international law, how might the role of the World Court be strengthened in future years? What obstacles might such plans encounter? How would they change the Court's role if they succeeded?
5. Although international norms concerning human rights are becoming stronger, China and many other states continue to consider human rights an internal affair over which the state has sovereignty within its territory. Do you think human rights are a legitimate subject for one state to raise with another? If so, how do you reconcile the tensions between state autonomy and universal rights? What practical steps could be taken to get sovereign states to acknowledge universal human rights?

CHAPTER SUMMARY

- International anarchy is balanced by world order—rules and institutions through which states cooperate for mutual benefit.
- World order has always been grounded in power, but order mediates raw power by establishing norms and habits that govern interactions among states.
- States follow the rules—both moral norms and formal international laws—much more often than not.
- International rules operate through institutions (IOs), with the UN at the center of the institutional network.
- The UN embodies a tension between state sovereignty and supranational authority. In its Charter and history, the UN has made sovereignty the more important principle. This has limited the UN's power.
- The UN particularly defers to the sovereignty of great powers, five of whom as permanent Security Council members can each block any security-related resolution binding on UN member states.
- In part because of its deference to state sovereignty, the UN has attracted virtually universal membership of the world's states, including all the great powers.
- Each of the 191 UN member states has one vote in the General Assembly, which serves mainly as a world forum and an umbrella organization for social and economic development efforts.
- The Security Council has ten rotating member states and five permanent members: the United States, Russia, China, Britain, and France.
- The UN is administered by international civil servants in the Secretariat, headed by the secretary-general.
- The regular UN budget plus all peacekeeping missions together amount to far less than 1 percent of what the world spends on military forces.
- Voting patterns and coalitions in the UN have changed over the years with the expanding membership and changing conditions. Currently U.S.-UN relations are tense because of conflicts over Iraq.
- UN peacekeeping forces are deployed in regional conflicts in five world regions. Their main role is to monitor compliance with agreements such as cease-fires, disarmament plans, and fair election rules. They were scaled back dramatically in 1995–1997, then grew rapidly again in 1998–2001.
- UN peacekeepers operate under UN command and flag. Sometimes national troops operate under their own flag and command to carry out UN resolutions.
- IOs include UN programs (mostly on economic and social issues), autonomous UN agencies, and organizations with no formal tie to the UN. This institutional network helps to strengthen and stabilize the rules of IR.
- International law, the formal body of rules for state relations, derives from treaties (most importantly), custom, general principles, and legal scholarship—not from legislation passed by any government.
- International law is difficult to enforce and is enforced in practice by national power, international coalitions, and the practice of reciprocity.
- The World Court hears grievances of one state against another but cannot infringe on state sovereignty in most cases. It is an increasingly useful avenue for arbitrating relatively minor conflicts.
- Most cases involving international relations are tried in national courts, where a state can enforce judgments within its own territory.

- A permanent International Criminal Court (ICC) began operations in 2003. Taking over from two UN tribunals, it will hear cases of genocide, war crimes, and crimes against humanity, starting with war crimes in Sudan.
- In international law, the rights of diplomats have long had special status. Embassies are considered to be the territory of their home country.
- Laws of war are also long-standing and well established. They distinguish combatants from civilians, giving each certain rights and responsibilities. Guerrilla wars and ethnic conflicts have blurred these distinctions.
- Wars of aggression violate norms of just war—one waged only to repel or punish aggression. It is sometimes (but not always) difficult to identify the aggressor in a violent international conflict.
- International norms concerning human rights are becoming stronger and more widely accepted. However, human rights law is problematical because it entails interference by one state in another's internal affairs.

KEY TERMS

international norms 252
international organizations (IOs) 254
UN Charter 257
UN General Assembly 257
UN Security Council 257
UN Secretariat 257
blue helmets 266
UN Conference on Trade and Development (UNCTAD) 272
World Health Organization (WHO) 273
World Court (International Court of Justice) 276
immigration law 280
diplomatic recognition 281
diplomatic immunity 282
war crimes 283
International Criminal Court (ICC) 284
prisoners of war (POWs) 285
International Committee of the Red Cross (ICRC) 285
just wars 286
human rights 287
crimes against humanity 288
Amnesty International 289

ONLINE PRACTICE TEST

Take an online practice test at *www.internationalrelations.net*

☐ A
☐ B
☑ C
☐ D

LET'S DEBATE THE ISSUE

The United Nations–United States Relationship: A Marriage of Convenience?

by Mir Zohair Husain

Overview In 1945 when the United Nations was established, the United States promoted it as the best means for engineering collective security and maintaining peace, enhancing human rights, and promoting socioeconomic development. With 40 percent of the UN's funding contributed by American taxpayers at the time, U.S. leaders believed that a veto power in the UN Security Council would protect America's national interests.

Today, however, times have changed. The United States frequently questions the UN's ability to engender global peace and order. Since the mid-1990s, collective security has increasingly been implemented by other intergovernmental actors including the Economic Community of West African States (ECOWAS) in Liberia and the Ivory Coast; NATO in Bosnia, Kosovo, and Afghanistan; the European Union in the Democratic Republic of the Congo.[a]

Today, international organizations and international law play a prominent role in world affairs. The UN is the most prominent, universal, and influential international organization in world history. Furthermore, following America's failure to gain the UN Security Council's approval for regime change in Iraq, the relationship between the UN and the United States came under fierce criticism at home and abroad. In fact, UN supporters argue that the United States hypocritically uses the UN to promote its national interests, but vetoes UN resolutions when America's national interests could be undermined.

These events have led many to ask several questions: Can the UN further U.S. national interests? Is U.S. participation key to the UN's success? Is the UN undermined by the United States withholding dues and disregarding UN resolutions?

Argument 1 The United Nations and the United States Share Mutual Interests

The United States needs the UN. U.S. unilateralism is creating an anti-American backlash in the world. Engaging in diplomacy within the UN would legitimize and strengthen America's foreign policy initiatives. Despite U.S. military and economic power, there is always greater strength in numbers; no number is greater than the 191 member-states of the United Nations.

> "In the cold war you could argue that American unilateralism had no cost," [one expert said]. "But as we're finding out with regard to Iraq, Iran and North Korea, we need the Europeans and we need institutions like the UN. The fact is that the United States can't run the world by itself, and the problem is, we've done a lot of damage in our relations with allies, and people are not terribly enthusiastic about helping us now." (Richard Bernstein. "Foreign Views of U.S. Darken Since Sept. 11." *The New York Times,* September 11, 2003.)

The UN needs active U.S. support. In a recent meeting with UN Secretary General Kofi Annan, following a horrible public relations year for the UN in which its oil-for-food program in Iraq faced charges of corruption and its sovereign states. Therefore, the UN cannot be expected to

[a]"Hot Spots and UN-Managed Forces." *The New York Times,* August 28, 2003.

adapt to this new terrorist threat when its member-states have failed to learn how to cope with this problem. It is not the UN, but its individual member-states, that are not adapting to the changed global environment.

> . . . after World War II, the main form of troublemaking was cross-border aggression. (The first President Bush's response to Iraq's invasion of Kuwait—a multilateral attack sanctioned by the Security Council—was a textbook use of the United Nations' power.) Still, the United Nations Charter, in charging the Security Council with preserving "international peace and security," is broad enough to also address post-9/11 threats, like weapons of mass destruction and terrorism. (Robert Wright. "George Bush, Multilateralist?" *The New York Times,* February 4, 2003.)

Argument 2 The United Nations Is Not Necessary to the United States

The UN is unable to manage new global problems. Many continuing problems, such as illegal drugs and arms trade, as well as new threats, such as terrorist cells and failed states, remain beyond the UN's capability. Moreover, the UN was in large part sidelined during the crises in Bosnia, Kosovo, Liberia, Afghanistan, and Iraq, leaving the United States, NATO, and ECOWAS to do the "heavy lifting." Therefore, it is difficult for any nation, even the United States, to rely solely on the UN to provide for its collective security.

> Clearly, the world has changed. Developments in technology have given small groups of people the kind of destructive power once available only to national governments. . . .
>
> . . . The principal mechanisms the world has devised to deal with [security threats]—foreign aid, nongovernmental institutions, the World Bank, the United Nations—have not succeeded in dealing with the most troublesome and difficult cases. (Alexander Stille. "What Is America's Place in the World Now?" *The New York Times,* January 12, 2002.)

Foreign nations use the UN to undermine U.S. national interests. Even though the UN's main objective is to provide its member-states with collective security, recent UN collective security measures have failed. Additionally, the UN has not helped U.S. security while permitting smaller and weaker countries to gain undue leverage over U.S. policies in international relations.

> . . . if lesser powers contrive to turn the council into a forum for counterbalancing American power with votes, words and public appeals, they will further erode its legitimacy and credibility. . . .
>
> The United Nations, sadly, has drifted far from its founding vision. . . . It was a wartime document of a military alliance, not a universal peace platform. Pleas for reform of the Security Council, however, stress equity and representation—not effectiveness and responsibility. (Edward C. Luck. "Making the World Safe for Hypocrisy." *The New York Times,* March 22, 2003.)

The UN is becoming irrelevant. In an "anarchic" global system, decisions made by the UN lack the binding authority of policies made by states. While the UN excels in many socioeconomic fields, collective security is not its strong suit. Therefore, the UN will need to rely on NATO and the EU to assist with collective security.

> Since the United Nations no longer tries to organize or oversee the use of force itself, this has been left largely to the discretion of member states. Even Secretary-General Kofi Annan has acknowledged that unilateral military action is sometimes necessary. . . .
>
> Unless both the enforcement and legal pillars of the Charter are reinforced, what is left will indeed look a lot like the ill-fated League of Nations. (Edward C. Luck. "Making the World Safe for Hypocrisy." *The New York Times,* March 22, 2003.)

Questions

1. Is the continuing allocation of American resources to the UN a good investment? Explain.
2. Do you think that the world would be a better or a worse place without a United Nations? Why? How should the UN be strengthened to meet future challenges?

WEB LINK

UN-U.S. Relationship

Selected Readings

John English. *Enhancing Global Governance: Towards a New Diplomacy.* NY: United Nations University Press, 2002.

Frederick H. Fleitz. *Peacekeeping Fiascoes of the 1990s: Causes, Solutions, and U.S. Interests.* Westport, CT: Greenwood Publishing Group, Inc., 2002.

Jobs in Government and Diplomacy

SUMMARY

Jobs in government and diplomacy offer team players the chance to affect policy, but require patience with large bureaucracies.

BENEFITS AND COSTS Both governments and intergovernmental organizations (IGOs) play key roles in international relations and employ millions of people with interests and training in IR.

Despite differences between careers in IGOs and governments, there are numerous similarities. Both are hierarchical organizations, with competitive and highly regulated working environments. Whether in the U.S. State Department or the UN, entrance into and promotion in these organizations is regulated by exams, performance evaluations, and tenure with the organization.

Another similarity lies in the challenges of being pulled in many directions concerning policies. Governments face competing pressures of public opinion, constituencies, and interests groups – each with distinct policy opinions. IGOs also deal with interest groups (such as NGOs), but the IGO's constituents are states, which in many cases disagree among themselves.

Many employees of IGOs or governments thrive on making decisions that influence policies. Both work environments also attract coworkers with deep interests in international affairs, and the resulting networks of contacts can bring professional and intellectual rewards. Finally, jobs in governments or IGOs may involve travel or living abroad, which many enjoy.

However, promotion can be slow and frustrating. Usually, only individuals with advanced degrees or technical specializations achieve non-entry level positions. It can take years to climb within the organization and the process may involve working in departments far from your original interests. In addition, both IGOs and governments are bureaucracies with formal rules and procedures, requiring great patience. Employees often express frustration that initiative and "thinking outside the box" are not rewarded.

SKILLS TO HONE The key to working in IGOs or government is to get your foot in the door. Be flexible and willing to take entry positions that are not exactly in your area of interest. For example, the State Department is only one of many parts of the U.S. government that deal with IR. Do not assume that to work in foreign affairs, one must be a diplomat.

Foreign language training is also important, especially for work in large IGOs with many field offices. The ability to work well in groups and to network within and across organizations is an important asset. People who can strengthen lines of communication can gain support from many places in an organization.

Finally, strong analytical and writing abilities are extremely important. Both IOs and governments deal with massive amounts of information daily. The ability to analyze information (even including mathematical or computational analysis) and to write clear, concise interpretations will make one invaluable.

RESOURCES

Shawn Dorman. 2003. *Inside a U.S. Embassy: How the Foreign Service Works for America.* 2nd ed. Washington, DC: American Foreign Service Assoc.

Linda Fasulo. 2005. *An Insider's Guide to the UN.* New Haven: Yale University Press.

http://jobs.un.org

http://www.state.gov/p/io/empl/

http://www.usajobs.opm.gov/EI10.asp

■ Port in Valparaiso, Chile, 2005.

From Security to Political Economy
Liberalism and Mercantilism • Globalization

Markets
Global Patterns of Trade • Comparative Advantage • Prices and Markets • Centrally Planned Economies • Politics of Markets • Balance of Trade • Interdependence

Trade Strategies
Autarky • Protectionism • Industries and Interest Groups • Cooperation in Trade

Trade Regimes
The World Trade Organization • Resistance to Trade • Bilateral and Regional Agreements • Cartels

Trade

From Security to Political Economy

Scholars of *international political economy (IPE)* study the politics of international economic activities.[1] The most frequently studied of these activities are trade, monetary relations, and multinational corporations (see this chapter and Chapter 9). Two topics of special interest in recent years are the economic integration of Europe and other regions (Chapter 10) and the international politics of the global environment (Chapter 11). Most scholars of IPE focus on the industrialized regions of the world, where most of the world's economic activity occurs. However, the global South has received growing attention, especially because economic relations and conditions there may be a more frequent source of international conflict and war in the post–Cold War era. We shall return to North-South aspects of these third world issues in Chapters 12 and 13. Although all of these issues overlap (to varying degrees) with international security matters, they all deal primarily with political bargaining over economic issues and thus fit within IPE broadly defined.

The conceptual framework used to study international security affairs applies to IPE as well. The core concepts of power and bargaining developed initially in Chapter 2 apply to IPE, as does the emphasis on states as the most important actors (though not the only important actors) and the idea that states tend to act in their own interests. As Brazil's foreign minister explained in 2001, his country shared with the United States the same guiding principle in negotiating a hemisphere-wide free trade area: "What's in it for us?"[2]

The collective goods problem is important throughout IPE (see Chapter 3). For example, although all states would be better off if there were few tariffs on trade, one state placing high tariffs could create a significant source of income for itself. Thus, all states face an incentive to raise their own tariffs while free riding on other nations' low tariffs.

---

[1] Oatley, Thomas H. *International Political Economy: Interests and Institutions in the Global Economy*. NY: Longman, 2003. Frieden, Jeffry A., and David A. Lake. *International Political Economy: Perspectives on Global Power and Wealth*. 4th ed. NY: St. Martin's, 2000. Lipson, Charles, and Benjamin J. Cohen, eds. *Theory and Structure in International Political Economy*. MIT, 1999. Peterson, V. Spike. *A Critical Rewriting of Global Political Economy: Integrating Reproductive, Productive, and Virtual Economies*. NY: Routledge, 2003. Chase-Dunn, Christopher, ed. *The Historical Evolution of the International Political Economy*. Brookfield, VT: Edward Elgar, 1995. Murphy, Craig N. *International Organization and Industrial Change, Global Governance since 1850*. Cambridge, UK: Polity, 1994. Yarbrough, Beth V. and Robert M. Yarbrough. *The World Economy: Trade and Finance*. 7th ed. Belmont, CA: South-Western, 2006.

[2] Rohter, Larry, with Jennifer L. Rich. Brazil Takes a Trade Stance and Offers a Warning to U.S. *The New York Times*, Dec. 19, 2001: W1.

Liberalism and Mercantilism

Mercantilism

On a key assumption of realism—international anarchy—two major approaches within IPE differ.[3] One approach, called **mercantilism,** generally shares with realism the belief that each state must protect its own interests at the expense of others—not relying on international organizations to create a framework for mutual gains. Mercantilists therefore emphasize relative power (as do realists): what matters is not so much a state's absolute amount of well-being as its position relative to rival states.[4]

In addition, mercantilism (like realism) holds that the importance of economic transactions lies in their implications for the military. States worry about relative wealth and trade because these can be translated directly into military power. Thus, while military power may not necessarily be an effective source of leverage in economic negotiations, mercantilists believe the outcome of economic negotiations matter for military power.

Liberalism, an alternative approach, generally shares the assumption of anarchy but does not see this condition as precluding extensive cooperation to realize common gains.[5] It holds that by building international organizations, institutions, and norms, states can mutually benefit from economic exchanges. It matters little to liberals whether one state gains more or less than another—just whether the state's wealth is increasing in *absolute* terms. This concept parallels the idea that IOs allow states to relax their narrow, short-term pursuit of self-interest in order to realize longer-term mutual interests (see p. 100 and pp. 251–252).

Liberalism and mercantilism are *theories* of economics and also *ideologies* that shape state policies. Liberalism is the dominant approach in Western economics, though more so in *microeconomics* (the study of firms and households) than in *macroeconomics* (the study of national economies). Marxism is often treated as a third theoretical/ideological approach to IPE, along with mercantilism and liberalism. Marxist approaches are attuned to economic exploitation as a force shaping political relations. We will explore Marxist theories in depth in Chapter 12 as they find their greatest explanatory power in North-South relations.

In IPE, contrary to international security, liberalism is the dominant tradition of scholarship and mercantilism is secondary. Thus, IR has a split personality. In matters of military force and security, scholars focus on anarchy and inherently conflicting interests. In matters of international political economy, however, they focus on international regimes and institutions that allow states to achieve mutual interests.

In truth, most international economic exchanges (as well as security relationships) contain some element of mutual interests—joint gains that can be realized through cooperation—and some element of conflicting interests. Game theorists call this a "mixed interest" game. For example, in the game of Chicken (see p. 73), the two drivers share an interest in avoiding a head-on collision, yet their interests diverge in that one can be a hero only if the other is a chicken. In international trade, even when two states both benefit

---

[3] Crane, George T., and Abla M. Amawi, eds. *The Theoretical Evolution of International Political Economy: A Reader*. 2nd ed. Oxford, 1997.

[4] Gilpin, Robert. *Global Political Economy: Understanding the International Economic Order*. Princeton, 2001. Grieco, Joseph, and John Ikenberry. *State Power and World Markets: The International Political Economy*. NY: Norton, 2002. Conybeare, John A. *Trade Wars: The Theory and Practice of International Commercial Rivalry*. Columbia, 1987. Keshk, Omar M. G., Brian M. Pollins, Rafael Reuveny. Trade Still Follows the Flag: The Primacy of Politics in a Simultaneous Model of Interdependence and Armed Conflict. *Journal of Politics* 66 (4), 2004: 1155–79.

[5] Neff, Stephen C. *Friends but No Allies: Economic Liberalism and the Law of Nations*. Columbia, 1990. Ward, Benjamin. *The Ideal Worlds of Economics: Liberal, Radical, and Conservative Economic World Views*. NY: Basic, 1979.

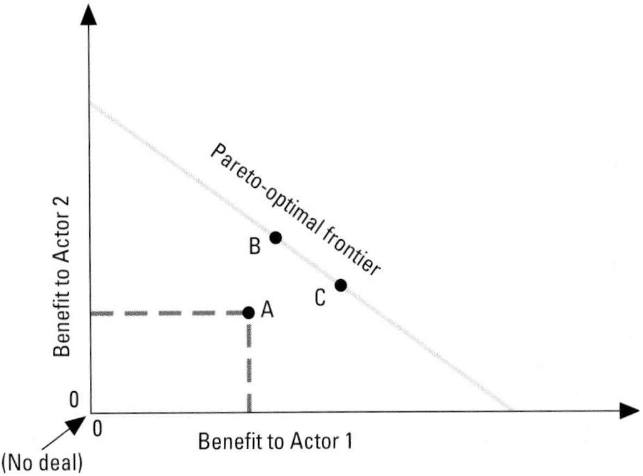

FIGURE 8.1 ■ Joint and Individual Benefits

Any deal struck, such as at point A, yields certain benefits to each actor (dotted lines). Joint benefits are maximized at the Pareto-optimal frontier, but the distribution of those benefits, as between points B and C (both of which are better than A for both actors), is a matter for bargaining. Liberalism is more concerned with joint benefits, mercantilism more with the relative distribution.

from a trade (a shared interest), one or the other will benefit more depending on the price of the transaction (a conflicting interest).

Liberalism places emphasis on the shared interests in economic exchanges, whereas mercantilism emphasizes the conflicting interests. Liberals see the most important goal of economic policy as the maximum creation of total wealth through achieving optimal *efficiency* (maximizing output, minimizing waste). Mercantilists see the most important goal as the creation of the most favorable possible *distribution* of wealth.

The main reason for the dominance of liberalism in IPE is that great gains have been realized from free trade. In any economic exchange that is not coerced by negative leverage, both parties gain. Both can gain because they place different values on the items being exchanged. For instance, when a supermarket sells a head of cabbage, the consumer values the cabbage more than the cash paid for it, and the supermarket values the cash more than the cabbage. This simple principle is the basis for economic exchange.

Even though both parties gain in an exchange, they may not gain equally: the distribution of benefits from trade may not be divided equally among participating states. One party may benefit greatly from an exchange, whereas the other party benefits only slightly. Liberal economists are interested in maximizing the overall (joint) benefits from exchange—a condition called *Pareto-optimal* (after economist Wilfred Pareto). They have little to say about how total benefits are distributed among the parties (see Figure 8.1).

Rather, the distribution of benefits is a matter for implicit or explicit bargaining, and hence a matter for politics and the use of leverage to influence the outcomes.[6] States as participants in the international economy try to realize the greatest overall gains for all states while simultaneously bargaining to maximize their own share of those gains. Power does matter in such bargaining, but the most relevant forms of leverage are positive (the prospect of

[6] Grieco, Joseph M. *Cooperation Among Nations: Europe, America, and Non-Tariff Barriers to Trade*. Cornell, 1990. Gowa, Joanne. *Allies, Adversaries, and International Trade*. Princeton, 1993. Hirschman, Albert O. *National Power and the Structure of Foreign Trade*. California, 1945.

gains by striking a deal) rather than negative. Because the exchange process creates much wealth, there is much room for bargaining over the distribution of that wealth.

Liberalism sees individual households and firms as the key actors in the economy and views government's most useful role as one of noninterference in economics except to regulate markets in order to help them function efficiently (and to create infrastructure such as roads that also help the economy function efficiently). Politics, in this view, should serve the interests of economic efficiency. With the hand of government removed from markets, the "invisible hand" of supply and demand can work out the most efficient patterns of production, exchange, and consumption (through the mechanism of prices). Because of the benefits of free trade, liberals disdain realists' obsession with international borders, because borders constrain the maximum efficiency of exchange.

For mercantilists, by contrast, economics should serve politics: the creation of wealth underlies state power. Because power is relative, trade is desirable only when the distribution of benefits favors one's own state over rivals. The terms of exchange shape the relative rates at which states accumulate power and thus shape the way power distributions in the international system change over time. As Japan and Germany, for instance, have achieved great prosperity, mercantilists saw them potentially threatening to overtake the United States. Liberals, by contrast, thought Japanese and German wealth boosted the entire world economy and ultimately benefited the United States—for example, by expanding markets for American goods.

Mercantilism achieved prominence several hundred years ago, and Britain used trade to rise in relative power in the international system around the eighteenth century. At that time mercantilism meant specifically the creation of a trade surplus (see "Balance of Trade" later in this chapter) in order to stockpile money in the form of precious metal (gold and silver), which could then be used to buy military capabilities (mercenary armies and weapons) in time of war.

Mercantilism declined in the nineteenth century as Britain decided it had more to gain from free trade than from protectionism. It returned as a major approach in the period between World Wars I and II, when liberal global trading relations broke down. Again in recent years, with the weakening of the liberal international economic order created after World War II, mercantilism has begun to become more prominent.[7]

The distinction between liberalism and mercantilism is reflected in the difference between hegemony and empire. Under hegemony (see p. 82), a dominant state creates an international order that facilitates free trade, but does not try to control economic transactions by itself. An empire, by contrast, controls economic transactions in its area. Historically, empires have a poor record of economic performance whereas hegemony has been much more successful in achieving economic growth and prosperity.[8] Of course, under hegemony, rival states also share (with the hegemon) in the overall growth and prosperity, which can ultimately erode the hegemon's relative power and end its hegemony.

Globalization

The ascendence of liberal over mercantilist economics in recent decades forms one strand of a complex mosaic of changes in the world political economy—changes that together are called **globalization.** This term refers to the increasing importance of the global level of analysis in economics, as the scope of economic activities expands worldwide.

[7] Jayasuriya, Kanishka. Embedded Mercantilism and Open Regionalism: The Crisis of a Regional Political Project. *Third World Quarterly* 24 (2), 2003: 339–56.

[8] Rosencrance, Richard. *The Rise of the Virtual State: Wealth and Power in the Coming Century*. NY: Basic, 2000.

Globalization encompasses many trends, including expanded international trade, telecommunications, monetary coordination, multinational corporations, technical and scientific cooperation, cultural exchanges of new types and scales, migration and refugee flows, and relations between the world's rich and poor countries. The coming chapters address this broad range of topics, each affected by globalization.[9]

However, although globalization clearly is very important, it is also rather vaguely defined and not well explained by any one theory. One popular conception of globalization is as "the widening, deepening and speeding up of worldwide interconnectedness in all aspects of contemporary social life . . . "[10] At least three competing conceptions of this process exist, however.

THINK GLOBALLY

As the world economy becomes more integrated, markets and production are becoming global in scope. This volunteer in London in 2004 offers fair trade coffee, which guarantees a decent price to producers in the global South.

One view sees globalization as the fruition of liberal economic principles. A global marketplace has brought growth and prosperity (not to all countries but to those most integrated with the global market). This economic process has made traditional states obsolete as economic units. States are thus losing authority to supranational institutions such as the IMF and EU, and to transnational actors such as MNCs and NGOs. The values of technocrats and elite educated citizens in liberal democracies are becoming global values, reflecting an emerging global civilization. The old North-South division is seen as less important, since the global South is moving in divergent directions depending on countries' and regions' integration with world markets.

A second perspective is skeptical of these claims about globalization. These skeptics note that the world's major economies are no more integrated today than before World War I (when British hegemony provided a common set of expectations and institutions). The skeptics also doubt that regional and geographic distinctions such as the North-South divide are disappearing in favor of a single global market. Rather, they see the North-South gap as increasing with globalization. Also, the economic integration of states may be leading not to a single world free trade zone, but to distinct and rival regional blocs in America, Europe, and Asia. The supposed emerging world civilization is disproved by the fragmenting of larger units (such as the Soviet Union) into smaller ones along lines of language, religion, and other such cultural factors.

---

[9] Held, David, Anthony McGrew, David Goldblatt, and Jonathan Perraton. *Global Transformations: Politics, Economics and Culture*. Stanford, 1999. Cusimano, Maryann K. *Beyond Sovereignty: Issues for a Global Agenda*. NY: Palgrave, 1999. Kapstein, Ethan. *Sharing the Wealth: Workers and the World Economy*. NY: Norton, 2001. Kirton, John J., Joseph P. Daniels, and Andreas Freytag, eds. *Guiding Global Order: G8 Governance in the Twenty-first Century*. Burlington, VT: Ashgate, 2001. Friedman, Thomas L. *The Lexus and the Olive Tree*. NY: Farrar, Straus and Giroux, 1999. Steger, Manfred B., ed. *Rethinking Globalism*. NY: Rowman & Littlefield, 2004. Stiglitz, Joseph E. *Globalization and its Discontents*. NY: W. W. Norton, 2002. Snow, Donald M. *National Security for a New Era: Globalization and Geopolitics*. NY: Longman, 2004. Baldwin, Robert E. and L. Alan Winters. *Challenges to Globalization: Analyzing the Economics*. Chicago, 2004.

[10] Held et al. (see footnote 9 above): 2.

A third school of thought sees globalization as more profound than the skeptics believe, yet more uncertain than the view of supporters of liberal economics. These "transformationalists" see state sovereignty as being eroded by the EU, WTO, and other new institutions, so that sovereignty is no longer an absolute but just one of a spectrum of bargaining leverages held by states. The bargaining itself increasingly involves nonstate actors. Thus globalization diffuses authority. State power is not so much strengthened or weakened by globalization, but transformed to operate in new contexts with new tools.

Exporting U.S. Professional Jobs

While scholars debate these conceptions of globalization, popular debates focus on the growing power of large corporations operating globally, the disruptive costs associated with joining world markets (for example, job loss and environmental impacts), the perception of growing disparities between the rich and the poor, and the collusion of national governments in these wrongs through their participation in IOs such as the WTO and IMF.[11]

Policies to expand free trade are a central focus of anti-globalization protesters (see "Resistance to Trade," pp. 325–326). Street protests have turned host cities into besieged fortresses in Seattle (1999), Washington, DC (2000 IMF and World Bank meetings), Quebec (2001 summit working toward a Free Trade Area of the Americas), and Genoa, Italy (2001 G8 summit), where some protesters engaged police in battles that killed one person. The key 2001 WTO meeting to launch a new trade round was held in Qatar where protesters had little access. At the 2003 WTO meeting in Cancun, Mexico, thousands of protesters marched against the talks and the economic elites conducting them, but were kept away from the WTO conference center. At the 2005 Hong Kong WTO meeting, protesters blocked nearby roads and some even tried to swim across Hong Kong harbor to disrupt the meeting.

Just as scholars disagree on conceptions of globalization, so do protesters disagree on their goals and tactics. Union members from the global North want to stop globalization from shipping their jobs south. But workers in impoverished countries in the global South may desperately want those jobs as a first step toward decent wages and working conditions (relative to other options in their countries). Window-smashing anarchists meanwhile steal media attention from environmentalists seeking to amend the trade agenda. Thus, neither globalization nor the backlash to it are simple. However one feels about the positive and negative effects of globalization, it is important to understand the interrelated processes that make up today's world political economy—trade, money, business, integration, communication, environmental management, and the economic development of poor countries. Trade is central to this list.

Markets

International exchanges of goods and services now occur in *global markets*. Liberalism supports the use of market processes, relatively unhindered by political elements; mercantilism favors greater political control over markets and exchanges. The stakes in this debate are high because of the growing volume and importance of international trade.

[11] Broad, Robin. *Citizen Backlash to Economic Globalization*. Lanham, MD: Rowman & Littlefield, 2002. Milani, Brian. *Designing the Green Economy: The Post-Industrial Alternative to Corporate Globalization*. Lanham, MD: Rowman & Littlefield, 2000. Drainville, André C. *Contesting Globalization: Space and Place in the World Economy*. NY: Routledge, 2004.

Global Patterns of Trade

Global Patterns of Trade

International trade amounts to a sixth of the total economic activity in the world. About $10 trillion worth of trade crosses international borders each year.[12] This is a very large number, about ten times the world's military spending, for example. The great volume of international trade reflects the fact that trade is profitable.

The role of trade in the economy varies somewhat from one nation to another, but overall, it is at least as important in the global South as in the industrialized North. Although the global South accounts for a relatively small part of all trade in the world economy, this is because its economic activity itself is only 40 percent of the world total (see p. 24). This creates an asymmetric dependence in North-South trade (see Chapters 12 and 13).

Overall, most political activity related to trade is concentrated in the industrialized West (North America, Western Europe, and Japan/Pacific), which accounts for about two-thirds of all international trade. Trade between these areas and the global South, although less important in volume, is also a topic of interest to IPE scholars (see Chapter 13).[13]

Two contradictory trends are at work in global trading patterns today. One trend is toward the integration of the industrialized regions with each other in a truly global market. The World Trade Organization (discussed later in this chapter) is especially important to this global integration process. The second trend is the emerging potential division of the industrialized West into three competing trading blocs, each internally integrated but not very open to the other two blocs. Regional free trade areas in Europe and North America, and perhaps in Asia in the future, raise the possibility of trading zones practicing liberalism inwardly and mercantilism outwardly. However, as information technologies link the world across space, the integrating trend seems to have the upper hand and the more global vision of free trade is shaping the agenda.

Comparative Advantage

The overall success of liberal economics is due to the substantial gains that can be realized through trade.[14] These gains result from the **comparative advantage** that different states enjoy in producing different goods (a concept pioneered by economists Adam Smith and David Ricardo 200 years ago). States differ in their abilities to produce certain goods because of differences in natural resources, labor force characteristics, technology, and other such factors. In order to maximize the overall creation of wealth, each state should specialize in producing the goods for which it has a comparative advantage and then trade for goods that another state is better at producing. Of course, the costs of transportation and of processing the information in the trade (called *transaction costs*) must be included in the costs of producing an item. But frequently both of these are low relative to the differences in the cost of producing items in different locations.

Decentralizing Markets

Two commodities of great importance in the world are oil and cars. It is much cheaper to produce oil (or another energy source) in Saudi Arabia than in Japan, and much

[12] Data in this chapter are calculated from World Trade Organization. *International Trade Statistics 2005*. Geneva: WTO.

[13] McKeown, Timothy J. A Liberal Trade Order? The Long-Run Pattern of Imports to the Advanced Capitalist States. *International Studies Quarterly* 35 (2), 1991: 151–72.

[14] Lake, David A., ed. *The International Political Economy of Trade*. Brookfield, VT: Edward Elgar, 1993. Odell, John S., and Thomas D. Willett, eds. *International Trade Policies: Gains from Exchange Between Economics and Political Science*. Michigan, 1990. Cohen, Benjamin J. The Political Economy of International Trade [review article]. *International Organization* 44 (2), 1990: 261–78.

THINKING THEORETICALLY

Trade Negotiations as "Chicken"

In 2001, when the WTO ministers' meeting in Qatar extended the adjournment deadline to snatch an agreement from the jaws of defeat, it was only the latest instance of the last-minute heroics in trade conflicts. Earlier in 2001, a U.S.-European dispute over bananas threatened to escalate to a trade war, as the U.S. side prepared to impose tariffs on EU goods to compensate for EU preferences given to bananas grown in certain former European colonies. Europe threatened counterretaliation, but again at the last minute an agreement was reached. The same thing happened with several U.S.-European and U.S.-Chinese trade disputes in the 1990s. And agreement on the Uruguay Round of the GATT came at the last moment before a real deadline. Why do these economic agreements so often come at the last moment?

Game theorists might look to the game of Chicken as an explanatory model. In most trade disputes, each state would rather get to a deal, even on terms that somewhat favor the other state if need be. But each would like if possible to get a deal on its own terms. Similarly, in a game of Chicken each player wants to avoid the head-on collision, and being a hero or a chicken is a secondary consideration. In trade negotiations, both states hold out for their own terms (not swerving) for as long as possible, then come to agreement only when faced with an imminent collision—the expiration of a deadline past which there will be no deal at all.

A different theoretical explanation would be that decision makers in trading states hold out for their best terms, but always avert a trade war in the end because their ideas and belief systems have been shaped by historical experiences. The failure of the Smoot-Hawley tariffs and the trade wars that followed, in the 1930s, led to the acceptance by foreign policy elites (in the United States and elsewhere) of the idea that trade wars are disastrous and must be avoided. The power of that idea, rather than rational calculations of national interest per se by the decision makers of the moment, would explain why trade wars keep being averted.

What kind of "experiment" could help test these theories against each other? In Chicken, there is no incentive to give ground before the last minute. But strongly held norms and historical analogies should influence leaders to compromise and narrow the bargaining gap more steadily throughout the negotiating process. We could follow the progress of the Doha WTO negotiating round that is supposed to conclude in 2006. Will the negotiations rack up steady progress over the next few years, or make little headway until a sudden round of big compromises at the end?

cheaper to produce cars in Japan than in Saudi Arabia. Japan needs oil to run its industry (including its car industry), and Saudi Arabia needs cars to travel its vast territory (including reaching its remote oil wells). Even with shipping and transaction costs, it saves a huge amount of money to ship Japanese cars to Saudi Arabia and Saudi oil to Japan, compared to the costs if each were self-sufficient.

A state need not have an absolute advantage (that is, be the most efficient producer in the world) in producing one kind of good in order to make specialization pay. It need only specialize in producing goods that are lower in cost than other goods relative to world market prices. Imagine that Japan discovered a way to produce synthetic oil using the same mix of labor and capital that it now uses to produce cars, and that this synthetic oil could be produced a bit more cheaply than what it cost Saudi Arabia to produce oil, but that Japan could still produce cars *much* more cheaply than could Saudi Arabia. From a strictly economic point of view, Japan should keep producing cars (its comparative advantage) and not divert capital and labor to make synthetic oil (where it had only a slight advantage).

The extra profits Japan would make from exporting more cars would more than compensate for the slightly higher price it would pay to import oil.

Thus, international trade generally expands the Pareto-optimal frontier by increasing the overall efficiency of production. Free trade allocates global resources to states that have the greatest comparative advantage in producing each kind of commodity. As a result, prices are both lower overall and more consistent worldwide. Increasingly, production is oriented to the world market.

Trade is not without drawbacks, however, when seen from a political rather than purely economic vantage point. One drawback is familiar from the preceding discussions of international security—long-term benefits may incur short-term costs. When a state begins to import goods that it had been producing domestically, there may be disruptions to its economy: workers may need to retrain and find new jobs, and capital may not be easy to convert to new uses. Thus, state leaders may feel political pressure to become involved in economic policy (see "Resistance to Trade" at the end of this chapter).

Another problem is that the benefits and costs of trade tend not to be evenly distributed *within* a state. Some industries or communities may benefit at the expense of others. For example, if a U.S. manufacturing company moves its factory to Mexico to take advantage of cheaper labor there, and exports its goods back to the United States, the workers at the old U.S. factory lose their jobs, but U.S. consumers enjoy cheaper goods. The costs of such a move fall heavily on a few workers, but the benefits are spread thinly across many consumers.

By the same logic, protectionist measures benefit a few people greatly, and cost many people a bit. By one estimate, a 20 percent steel tariff enacted by the Bush administration in 2002–2003 cost consumers $7 billion and saved 7,300 U.S. jobs—a pricey $326,000 per job.[15] Yet, those 7,300 workers (and their unions and companies) benefit greatly, whereas the roughly $20 cost per U.S. citizen goes unnoticed. This kind of unequal distribution of costs and benefits often creates political problems for free trade even when the *overall* economic benefits outweigh the costs. One is far more likely to find worker or industry interest groups (see pp. 316–318) forming to complain about the concentrated costs (losing jobs) rather than consumer groups forming to complain about the loss of diffuse benefits (such as a $20 increase in the cost of a steel good such as a car).

Trade versus Security

Between states (as well as within each state) the distribution of benefits from trade can also be unequal. The new wealth created by international trade can be divided in any manner between the participants. For instance, it would be worthwhile for Saudi Arabia to import cars even at a price much higher than what it cost Japan to produce them, as long as the price was less than what it would cost Saudi Arabia to produce cars itself (or to buy them elsewhere). Similarly, Saudi Arabia would profit from selling oil even at a price just a bit above what the oil costs to produce (or what it can sell the oil for elsewhere). With so much added value from the exchange process, there is a great deal of room for bargaining over the distribution of benefits.

If there were only two states in the world, the bargaining over prices (that is, over the distribution of benefits from trade) would essentially be a political process entailing the use of leverage, possibly including military force. But in a world of many states (and even more substate economic actors such as companies and households), this is less true. Prices are set instead by market competition. If Japan's cars are too expensive, Saudi Arabia can buy German cars; if Saudi oil is too expensive, Japan can buy Alaskan oil.

---

[15] Kahn, Joseph. U.S. Trade Panel Backs Putting Hefty Duties on Imported Steel. *The New York Times*, Dec. 8, 2001: C1, C3.

Prices and Markets

The *terms* of an exchange are defined by the price at which goods are traded. Often the *bargaining space*—defined by the difference between the lowest price a seller would accept and the highest price a buyer would pay—is quite large. For example, Saudi Arabia would be willing to sell a barrel of oil (if it had no better option) for as little as, say, $10 a barrel, and industrialized countries are willing to pay at least $70 a barrel for the oil. (In practice, oil prices have fluctuated in this broad range in recent decades.) How are prices determined within this range? That is, how do the participants decide on the distribution of benefits from the exchange?

When there are multiple buyers and sellers of a good (or equivalent goods that can be substituted for it), prices are determined by market competition.[16] In terms of the above bargaining framework, sellers bargain for a high price, using as leverage the threat to sell to another buyer. Meanwhile buyers bargain for a low price, with the leverage being a threat to buy from another seller. In practice, free markets are supposed to (and sometimes do) produce stable patterns of buying and selling at a fairly uniform price. At this *market price*, sellers know that an effort to raise the price would drive the buyer to seek another seller, and buyers know that an effort to lower the price would drive the seller to seek another buyer. Because of this stability, the process of bargaining is greatly simplified and most economic exchanges take place in a fairly routine manner.

Buyers vary in the value they place on an item (like a barrel of oil); if the price rises, fewer people are willing to buy it, and if the price drops, more people are willing to buy it. This is called the *demand curve* for the item. Sellers also vary in the value they place on the item. If the price rises, more sellers are willing to supply the item to buyers; if the price drops, fewer sellers are willing to supply the item. This is called the *supply curve*.

In a free market, the price at which the supply and demand curves cross is the *equilibrium price*. At this price sellers are willing to supply the same number of units that buyers are willing to purchase. (In practice, prices reflect *expectations* about supply and demand in the near future.) In a trade of Saudi oil for Japanese cars, for example, the prices would be determined by the world demand for, and supply of, oil and cars.

Thus, in liberal economics, *bilateral* relations between states are less important than they are in security affairs. The existence of world markets reduces the leverage that one state can exert over another in economic affairs (because the second state can simply find other partners). For example, U.S. sanctions on Iran, a major oil exporter, invited European companies to fill the void in recent years. In IPE, then, power is more diffuse and involves more actors at once than in international security.

Centrally Planned Economies

One major alternative to a market economy is a **centrally planned** (or *command*) **economy,** in which political authorities set prices and decide on quotas for production and consumption of each commodity according to a long-term plan. This type of economy was for decades the standard in the communist states of the former Soviet Union, Eastern Europe, China, and several smaller countries—it is still in place in Cuba and North Korea. Within the Soviet economic bloc (which included Eastern Europe and Mongolia), international trade also took place at government-controlled prices.

The proponents of central planning claimed it would make economies both more rational and more just. By controlling the economy, governments could guarantee the basic needs of citizens (as in China's "iron rice bowl" policy under Chairman Mao) and could

[16] Lindblom, Charles E. *The Market System: What It Is, How it Works, and What to Make of It*. Yale, 2001.

mobilize the state fully for war if necessary (as the Soviet Union did in World War II under Stalin). Proponents of central planning also hoped that government's long-term view of resources and needs would smooth out the "boom and bust" fluctuations of capitalist economies.

Instead, communist economics has in recent years been discredited as hopelessly inefficient and discarded in whole or in part by virtually all of its former followers. The economies of Russia and Eastern Europe stagnated over the Cold War decades while environmental damage and military spending both took an increasing economic toll. Now the former Soviet republics and Eastern Europe are almost all **transitional economies,** trying to make the change to a market-based economy connected to the world capitalist economy.[17] This transition has proven very difficult. In the first half of the 1990s, the total GDP of the region *shrank* by about 35 percent—a depression worse than the Great Depression the United States experienced in the early 1930s (see p. 356). Living standards dropped dramatically for most citizens, and remained low for the rest of the decade. A program of *shock therapy*—a radical, sudden shift over to market principles—seemed to work in Poland despite short-term dislocation. But a similar program in Russia stalled after being effectively blocked by old-time communist officials. Through the final years of Boris Yeltsin's administration (1991–1999), Russia's economy remained dysfunctional, owing to depression, corruption, tax delinquency, and the vast differences between the old communist and new capitalist models. President Vladimir Putin (2000–present) brought new energy to economic reform, and progress in some areas, but his centralization of power could choke off capitalist growth, and the overall path of Russia's transition remains difficult.[18]

DUSTBIN OF HISTORY

The unreliable, polluting East German Trabant car reflected the inefficiency of production in the centrally planned economies of the communist countries during the Cold War era. All those countries are now making transitions—by various routes and with various degrees of success—toward market-based economies. This Trabant in East Berlin was discarded as Germany unified, 1990.

China, whose government continues to follow a Marxist *political* line (central control by the Communist party), has shifted substantially toward a market *economy*.[19] This transition dramatically increased China's economic growth ever since the 1980s, reaching a sustained annual rate of about 10 percent throughout the 1990s, and nearly as fast in recent years (see "The Chinese Experience" on pp. 502–505).

[17] Gustafson, Thane. *Capitalism Russian-Style*. Cambridge, 1999. Aslund, Anders. *How Russia Became a Market Economy*. Washington, DC: Brookings, 1995. Frye, Timothy. *Brokers and Bureaucrats: Building Market Institutions in Russia*. Michigan, 2000.

[18] Chazan, Guy and Gregory L. White. Russian Economy Feels a Chill. *Wall Street Journal*. December 13, 2004: A14.

[19] Gore, Lance L. P. *Market Communism: The Institutional Foundation of China's Post-Mao Hyper-Growth*. Oxford, 1999.

Today, the world's economic activity follows the principles of free markets more than central planning but often falls somewhere between the extremes. Many governments control domestic prices on some goods (for instance, subsidizing certain goods to win political support). Many states *own* (all or part of) industries thought to be vital for the national economy—**state-owned industries** such as oil production companies or national airlines. For some types of goods, such as electricity service, it has traditionally been considered inefficient for competing suppliers to operate (each with its own transmission lines running along the street); in such cases governments sometimes supply the service themselves. Also, the government sector of the economy (military spending, road building, Social Security, and so on) makes up a substantial fraction of the industrialized countries' economies. Because they contain both some government control and some private ownership, the economies of the industrialized West are called **mixed economies.**[20]

Politics of Markets

A free and efficient market requires a fairly large number of buyers looking for the same item and a large number of sellers supplying it. It also requires that participants have fairly complete information about the other participants and transactions in the market. Also, the willingness of participants to deal with each other should not be distorted by personal (or political) preferences but should be governed only by price and quality considerations. Failures to meet these various conditions are called *market imperfections:* they reduce efficiency (to the dismay of liberal economists). Most political intrusions into economic transactions are market imperfections.

International trade occurs more often at world market prices than does *domestic* economic exchange. No world government owns industries, provides subsidies, or regulates prices. Nonetheless, world markets are often affected by politics. When states are the principal actors in international economic affairs, the number of participants is often small. When there is just one supplier of an item—a *monopoly*—the supplier can set the price quite high. For example, the South African company De Beers produces half the world supply and controls two-thirds of the world market for uncut diamonds. An *oligopoly* is a monopoly shared by just a few large sellers—often allowing for tacit or explicit coordination to force the price up. For example, OPEC members agree to limit oil production to keep prices up. To the extent that companies band together along national lines, monopolies and oligopolies are more likely.

Governments can use antitrust policies to break up monopolies and keep markets competitive. But home governments often *benefit* from the ability of their companies to distort international markets and gain revenue (whether they are state-owned or just taxed by the state). *Foreign* governments have little power to break up such monopolies.

Another common market imperfection in international trade is *corruption;* individuals may receive payoffs to trade at nonmarket prices. The government or company involved may lose some of the benefits being distributed, but the individual government official or company negotiator gets increased benefits (see pp. 513–514).

One difficulty in transitioning from centrally planned to market economies is market imperfections, which can cause (and can be caused by) political corruption. For example, to become competitive internationally, states sell their state-owned industries to private citizens, who allow markets to determine prices of their goods on international markets (which are higher than were set under the old system). These industries, however, continue to receive supplies domestically at fixed prices (set under the old system). The result

---

20 Meso-Lago, Carmelo. *Market, Socialist, and Mixed Economies: Comparative Policy and Performance—Chile, Cuba and Costa Rica.* Johns Hopkins, 2000.

is that the private citizens make high profits turning subsidized raw materials into highly priced goods for the international market. This partial reform brings some short-term gains, but concentrates abnormally excess profits into the hands of a powerful few.[21] In Russia, President Putin jailed a leading oil tycoon who became politically outspoken, a move widely interpreted as a warning to Russia's new capitalist elite.

PLAY BALL

Economic sanctions, such as the U.S. restrictions on trade with Cuba, are among the most obvious ways that politics interferes in markets. But sanctions are hard to enforce, especially when not all countries participate, because doing business is profitable. The U.S. government first tried to exclude Cuba from the World Baseball Classic in 2006 but backed down after strong complaints from other countries that do not apply sanctions to Cuba. Here, Japan's Ichiro Suzuki and Cuban players celebrate after Japan beat Cuba in the championship game in San Diego.

Politics provides a *legal framework* for markets—assuring that participants keep their commitments, that contracts are binding, buyers pay for goods they purchase, counterfeit money is not used, and so forth. In the international economy, lacking a central government authority, rules are less easily enforced. As in security affairs, such rules can be codified in international treaties, but enforcement depends on practical reciprocity (see pp. 275–276).

Taxation is another political influence on markets. Taxes are used both to generate revenue for the government and to regulate economic activity by incentives. For instance, a government may keep taxes low on foreign companies in hopes of attracting them to locate and invest in the country. Taxes applied to international trade itself, called *tariffs*, are a frequent source of international conflict (see "Protectionism," p. 314).

Political interference in free markets is most explicit when governments apply *sanctions* against economic interactions of certain kinds or between certain actors. Political power then prohibits an economic exchange that would otherwise have been mutually beneficial. A 1998 report counted U.S. trade restrictions on 22 states in response to those states' political actions, such as human rights violations, a number that has since shrunk somewhat.[22]

Enforcing sanctions is always a difficult task, because there is a financial incentive to break the sanctions through black markets or other means.[23] For instance, despite UN sanctions against trading with Serbia in the early 1990s, many people and companies took risks to smuggle goods across Serbia's borders, because doing so was profitable. Without

[21] Hellman, Joel S. Winners Take All: The Politics of Partial Reform in Postcommunist Transitions. *World Politics* 50 (2), 1998: 203–34.

[22] Institute for International Economics data. In *The Washington Post*, July 12, 1998: C4.

[23] Drezner, Daniel W. *The Sanctions Paradox: Economic Statecraft and International Relations*. Cambridge, 1999. Haass, Richard N., and Meghan L. O'Sullivan, eds. *Honey and Vinegar: Incentives, Sanctions, and Foreign Policy*. Washington, DC: Brookings, 2000. Lopez, George A., and David Cortwright. *Smart Sanctions: Targeting Economic Statecraft*. Lanham, MD: Rowman & Littlefield, 2002. Martin, Lisa L. *Coercive Cooperation: Explaining Multilateral Economic Sanctions*. Princeton, 1992.

broad multilateral support for international sanctions, they generally fail. When the United States tried to punish the Soviet Union in the 1970s by applying trade sanctions against a Soviet oil pipeline to Western Europe, it did not stop the pipeline. It just took profitable business away from a U.S. company (Caterpillar) and allowed European companies to profit instead (because European states did not join in the sanctions).

The difficulty of applying sanctions reflects a more general point made earlier—that power in IPE is more diffused among states than it is in security affairs. If one state tries to use economic means of leverage to influence another, other states can profitably take over. Refusing to participate in mutually profitable economic trade often harms oneself more than the target of one's actions, unless nearly all other states follow suit (note that sanctions enforcement is a form of the collective goods problem).

Balance of Trade

Mercantilists favor political control of trade so that trade relations serve a state's political interests—even at the cost of some lost wealth that free markets might have created. Their preferred means of accomplishing this end is to create a favorable balance of trade. The **balance of trade** is the value of a state's imports relative to its exports.

A state that exports more than it imports has a *positive balance of trade*, or *trade surplus*. Japan has run a trade surplus in recent years: it gets more money for cars and other goods it exports than it pays for oil and other imported goods. A state that imports more than it exports has a *negative balance of trade* (*trade deficit*). A trade deficit is different from a budget deficit in government spending. In the late 1990s, the U.S. budget deficit became a surplus (until September 2001), but the U.S. trade deficit kept growing, reaching hundreds of billions of dollars per year with the majority accounted for by Japan, China, and Taiwan. (In January of 2006 alone, the U.S. trade deficit totaled nearly $70 billion.)

The balance of trade must ultimately be reconciled, one way or another. It is tracked financially through the system of national accounts (see pp. 352–353). In the short term, a state can trade for a few years at a deficit and then a few years at a surplus. The imbalances are carried on the national accounts as a kind of loan. But a trade deficit that persists for years becomes a problem for the state. Japan in recent years has run a trade surplus overall (and in U.S.-Japanese bilateral trade), while the United States has run a deficit. To balance trade, the United States then "exports" currency (dollars) to Japan, which can use the dollars to buy such things as shares of U.S. companies, U.S. Treasury bills, or U.S. real estate. In essence (oversimplifying a bit), a state with a chronic trade deficit must export part of its standing wealth (real estate, companies, bank accounts, etc.) by giving ownership of such wealth to foreigners.

This is one reason mercantilists favor national economic policies to create a trade surplus. Then the state can "own" parts of other states, providing a potential source of economic and political leverage. Rather than being unable to find the money it might need to cope with a crisis or fight a war, the state sits on a pile of money representing potential power. Historically, mercantilism literally meant stockpiling gold (gained from running a trade surplus) as a fungible form of power (see Figure 8.2). Such a strategy is attuned to realism's emphasis on relative power. For one state to have a trade surplus, another must have a deficit.

There is a price for mercantilist-derived power. Often a trade surplus lowers the short-term standard of living. For instance, if the Japanese people cashed in their trade surplus each year for imported goods, they could enjoy those goods now instead of piling up money for the future. Mercantilists are willing to pay such short-term costs because they are more concerned with power than with standards of living.

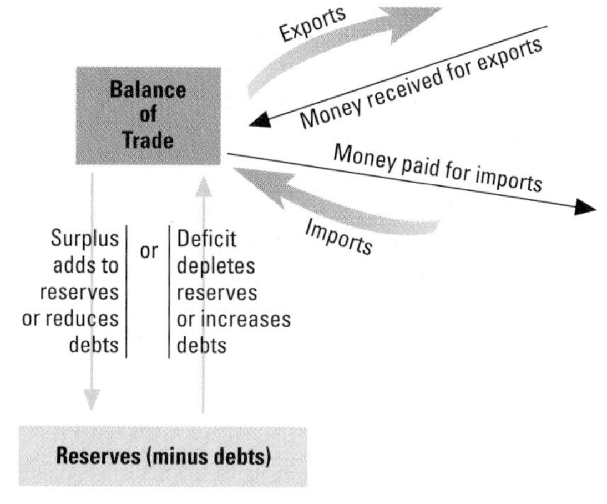

FIGURE 8.2 ■ Balance of Trade

Interdependence

When the well-being of a state depends on the cooperation of a second state, the first state is *dependent* on the second. When two or more states are simultaneously dependent on each other, they are *interdependent*. **Interdependence** is a political and not just an economic phenomenon. States that trade become mutually dependent on each other's *political* cooperation in order to realize economic gains through trade. In IPE, interdependence refers less often to a *bilateral* mutual dependence than to a *multilateral* dependence in which each state depends on the political cooperation of most or all of the others to keep world markets operating efficiently. Most states depend on the world market, not on specific trading partners (though for large industrialized states each bilateral trade relationship is important as well).

The mutual dependence of two or more states does not mean that their degree of dependence is equal or symmetrical. Often one is more dependent than another. This is especially true because world markets vary in their openness and efficiency from one commodity and region to another. Saudi Arabia, for instance, has more power over the price of oil than Japan has over the price of cars.

The degree of a state's *short-term* dependence on another may differ from its *long-term* dependence. The short-term dislocation that is caused by disrupting exchange with another country is the *sensitivity* of supply. When oil prices rose sharply in the early 1970s, Japan and other industrialized states did not have policies to cope with the increases: they were *sensitive* to the disruption, and long lines formed at gas stations. Over the longer term, states may be able to change their policies to take advantage of alternatives that could substitute for disrupted trade. Japan then expanded nuclear power in response to oil price increases—a long-term strategy. A state that *cannot* adjust its policies to cope with disrupted trade, even over the long run, suffers from *vulnerability* of supply.[24]

Over time, as the world economy develops and technology advances, states are becoming *increasingly interdependent*. Some IR scholars point out that this is not entirely new. The great powers were very interdependent before World War I; for instance,

[24] Keohane, Robert O., and Joseph S. Nye. *Power and Interdependence*. 3rd ed. NY: Longman, 2001.

UNSETTLING CHANGES

Growing trade makes states more interdependent. This may make them more peaceful, but can also introduce new insecurities and sources of conflict. Free trade creates both winners and losers. Backlash against free trade agreements led to a spectacular failure at the WTO summit meeting in Seattle, 1999. As environmentalists and labor unions led protests in the streets, the assembled states could not agree on an agenda for a new round of trade talks.

international trade was about the same percentage of GDP then as now. But several other dimensions of interdependence show dramatic change. One is the extent to which individual *firms*, which used to be nationally based, now are international in their holdings and interests (becoming MNCs), and thus dependent on the well-being of other states in addition to their home state (making them tend to favor free trade).[25]

Another key aspect of interdependence is the tight integration of world markets through the ever-expanding flow of *information* and communication worldwide (see pp. 394–398). This facilitates the free competition of goods and services in global markets as well as the expanding volume of money (capital) that moves around the world every day. Yet another dimension of change is the expansion of *scope* in the global economy, from one based in Europe to a more diffuse network encompassing the world. Asian economic expansion, and the integration of Russia and Eastern Europe into the world market economy, are accelerating this trend.

Whether based on a specific bilateral trading relationship, an integrated global (or regional) market, or the international nature of corporate holdings, interdependence arises from comparative advantage—that is, from the greater absolute wealth that two or more states can produce by collaborating. This wealth depends on international political cooperation, which is therefore in the interests of all participants. Furthermore, violence is usually not an effective leverage in bringing about such cooperation. Thus, many IR scholars argue that *interdependence inherently promotes peace*.[26] It alters the cost-benefit calculations of national leaders so as to make military leverage less attractive. (Some IR scholars saw similar trends in international interdependence just before World War I, but war occurred anyway.)

Trade and Conflict

Despite the added wealth that states enjoy as a result of trade and the power that such wealth creates, interdependence does have drawbacks. The more a state gains from trade cooperation, the more its own well-being depends on other states, which therefore have power over it. In situations of asymmetrical interdependence, in particular, the economic benefits of cooperation may come with inherent vulnerabilities. For example, it is cheaper for Japan to import energy than to produce it domestically, but dependence on energy imports has historically put Japan at a disadvantage in power. In the 1930s, the United States cut off its oil exports to Japan to protest Japanese militarism. Of course, exports as well as imports can create dependence (on those who buy the product). Interdependence thus ties the well-being of a state's population and society to policies and conditions in

[25] Milner, Helen V. *Resisting Protectionism: Global Industries and the Politics of International Trade*. Princeton, 1988.

[26] Mansfield, Edward D., ed. *International Conflict and the Global Economy*. Brookfield, VT: Edward Elgar, 2004.

other states, outside its control. The price of trade-generated wealth (and the power it brings) is a loss of state autonomy and sovereignty.

As states become more interdependent, power (although not necessarily military power) is becoming more, not less, important in IR. The intensification of linkages among states multiplies the number of issues affecting the relations of states and the avenues of influence by which outcomes are shaped. It is true that because power operates on multiple complex dimensions in a highly interdependent world, the importance of one dimension—military power—is gradually diminishing relative to other means of influence (diplomatic, economic, cultural, etc.). But the overall importance of international power on all dimensions combined is increasing as the world becomes more interdependent.

Trade Strategies

To manage the trade-offs of gains and losses in power and wealth, states develop economic strategies—trade strategies in particular—in order to maximize their own wealth while minimizing their vulnerability and dependence on others. Some strategies can be implemented by single states; most involve participation in some broader framework.

Autarky

One obvious way to avoid becoming dependent on other states, especially for a weak state whose trading partners would tend to be more powerful, is to avoid trading and instead to try to produce everything it needs by itself. Such a strategy is called *self-reliance* or **autarky.** As the theory of comparative advantage suggests, such a policy has proven ineffective. A self-reliant state pays a very high cost to produce goods for which it does not have a comparative advantage. As other states cooperate among themselves to maximize their joint creation of wealth, the relative power of the autarkic state in the international system tends to fall.

In practice, when states have relied on a policy of autarky they have indeed lagged behind others. A classic case in recent decades was the small state of Albania, next to Yugoslavia. A communist state that split from both the Soviet Union and China, Albania for decades did not participate in world markets but relied on a centrally planned economy designed for self-sufficiency. Few foreigners were allowed to visit, little trade took place, and Albania pursued autarky to prevent outsiders from gaining power over it. When this curtain of isolation finally fell in 1991, Albania was as poor as decades earlier. Little additional wealth had been generated; little economic development had taken place. This contributed to Albania's political instability, which affected conflicts in Kosovo and Macedonia that precipitated NATO military intervention.

China's experience also illustrates the problems with autarky. China's economic isolation in the 1950s and 1960s, resulting from an economic embargo imposed by the United States and its allies, was deepened during its own Cultural Revolution in the late 1960s when it broke ties with the Soviet Union as well. In that period, all things foreign were rejected. When China opened up to the world economy in the 1980s, the pattern was reversed. The rapid expansion of trade, along with some market-oriented reforms in its domestic economy, resulted in rapid economic growth, which continued into the new century.

By contrast, North Korea has maintained a policy of self-reliance and isolation even after the Cold War. This policy (along with high military spending and other problems) led to mass starvation in the 1990s.

Protectionism

Although few states pursue strategies of autarky, many states try to manipulate international trade in such a manner so as to strengthen one or more domestic industries and shelter them from world markets. Such policies are broadly known as **protectionism**—protection of domestic industries from international competition. Although this term encompasses a variety of trade policies arising from various motivations, all are contrary to liberalism in that they seek to distort free markets to gain an advantage for the state (or for substate actors within it), generally by discouraging imports of competing goods or services.[27]

Government policies discouraging imports can help domestic industries or communities avoid the costs inherent in full participation in world markets. Recall that these costs often fall disproportionately on a small part of the population and lead that group to pressure the government for protection. The benefits, by contrast, are spread more broadly across the population and do not create such domestic pressures.

A state's *motivation* to protect domestic industry can arise from several sources. Often governments simply cater to the political demands of important domestic industries and interests, regardless of the overall national interest. An industry may lobby or give campaign contributions in order to win special tax breaks, subsidies, or restrictions on competing imports (see "Industries and Interest Groups" later in this chapter).

States often attempt to protect an *infant industry* as it starts up in the state for the first time, until it can compete on world markets. For instance, when South Korea first developed an automobile industry, it was not yet competitive with imports, so the government gave consumers incentives to buy Korean cars. Eventually the industry developed and could compete with foreign producers and even export cars profitably. In a number of poor states, the *textile* trade has been a favored infant industry (adding value without heavy capital requirements) that governments have protected.[28] Protection of infant industry is considered a relatively legitimate reason for (temporary) protectionism.

Another motivation for protection is to give a domestic industry breathing room when market conditions shift or new competitors arrive on the scene. Sometimes domestic industry requires time to adapt and can emerge a few years later in a healthy condition. When gas prices jumped in the 1970s, U.S. auto producers were slow to shift to smaller cars, and smaller Japanese cars gained a great advantage in the U.S. market. The U.S. government used a variety of measures, including import quotas and loan guarantees, to help the U.S. industry through this transition.

Yet another motivation is the protection of industry considered vital to national security. In the 1980s, U.S. officials sought to protect the U.S. electronics and computer industries against being driven out of business by Japanese competitors, because those industries were considered crucial to military production. A government-sponsored consortium of U.S. computer chip companies called Sematech was formed to promote the U.S. capability to produce chips cheaply (ordinarily the government would discourage such a consortium as an antitrust violation). Autarky may not pay in most economic activities, but for military goods states are often willing to sacrifice some economic efficiency for the sake of self-sufficiency. Then, in the event of war the state will be less vulnerable.

Finally, protection may be motivated by a defensive effort to ward off predatory practices by foreign companies or states. *Predatory* generally refers to efforts to unfairly capture a large share of world markets, or even a near-monopoly, so that eventually the predator can raise prices without fearing competition. Most often these efforts entail

---

[27] Salvatore, Dominick, ed. *Protectionism and World Welfare*. Cambridge, 1993. Goldstein, Judith. The Political Economy of Trade: Institutions of Protection. *American Political Science Review* 80 (1), 1986: 161–84.

[28] Aggarwal, Vinod K. *Liberal Protectionism: The International Politics of Organized Textile Trade*. California, 1985.

dumping products in foreign markets at prices below the minimum level necessary to make a profit. In 1992, Japan was accused of dumping minivans on the U.S. market, and in 2001 foreign countries were accused of dumping steel. How can a company make money selling its products below cost, and why would the importing state complain about such a good deal? Cheaper minivans are indeed a good deal for U.S. consumers in the short term, but they weaken the competing U.S. automobile industry in the longer term. The reason a state would want its companies to dump products in foreign markets is that money lost in the short term could lead to dominance of a market, which eventually lets the state's companies raise prices enough to recoup their losses and to profit more.

Within a domestic economy, the government can use antitrust laws to break up an impending monopoly, but because no such mechanism exists in IR, governments try to restrict imports in such situations to protect their state's industries. Such restrictions are recognized as legitimate, although there are great disagreements about whether a given price level is predatory or merely competitive. These conflicts now generally are resolved through the WTO (see pp. 322–325).

WE CAN'T COMPETE

Protectionism uses various means to keep foreign imports from competing with domestic products. U.S. tariffs on imported steel, imposed in 2002 to please steel industry and labor union constituents, were removed after being ruled illegal by the WTO. Here, Russian steel is loaded for export to the United States, 2002.

Just as there are several motivations for protectionism, so too governments use several tools to implement this policy. The simplest is a **tariff** or *duty*—a tax imposed on certain types of imported goods (usually as a percentage of their value) as they enter the country. Tariffs not only restrict imports but also can be an important source of state revenues. If a state is going to engage in protectionism, international norms favor tariffs as the preferred method of protection because they are straightforward and not hidden (see pp. 322–325). Most states maintain a long and complex schedule of tariffs, based on thousands of categories and subcategories of goods organized by industry.

Other means to discourage imports are **nontariff barriers** to trade. Imports can be limited by a *quota*. Quotas are ceilings on how many goods of a certain kind can be imported; they are imposed to restrict the growth of such imports. The extreme version is a flat prohibition against importing a certain type of good (or goods from a certain country). The U.S. government used quotas to restrict the number of Japanese-made cars that could enter the United States in the 1980s, when the U.S. automobile industry was losing ground rapidly to Japanese imports. Most of those quotas were *voluntary* in that Japan and the United States negotiated a level that both could live with.

A third way to protect domestic industry is *subsidies* to a domestic industry, which allow it to lower its prices without losing money. Such subsidies are extensive in, but not limited to, state-owned industries. Subsidies can be funneled to industries in a variety of ways. A state can give *tax breaks* to an industry struggling to get established or facing

Subsidies

strong foreign competition. It can make *loans* (or guarantee private loans) on favorable terms to companies in a threatened industry. Sometimes governments buy goods from domestic producers at high *guaranteed prices* and resell them on world markets at lower prices; the European Community does this with agricultural products, to the dismay of U.S. farmers, as does the United States, to the dismay of European farmers.

Fourth, imports can be restricted by *restrictions* and *regulations* that make it hard to distribute and market a product even when it can be imported. In marketing U.S. products in Japan, U.S. manufacturers often complain of complex bureaucratic regulations and a tight system of corporate alliances funneling the supply of parts from Japanese suppliers to Japanese manufacturers. Environmental and labor regulations can function as nontariff barriers as well. This is a significant source of controversy in the WTO (see pp. 322–325). Finally, when a state nationalizes an entire industry, such as oil production or banking, foreign competition is shut out.

Dubai Ports Deal Fallout

Sometimes a country's culture, rather than state action, discourages imports. Citizens may (with or without government encouragement) follow a philosophy of *economic nationalism*—use of economics to influence international power and relative standing in the international system (a form of mercantilism). Many U.S. citizens ignore the advice of liberal economists to buy the best car they can find at the best price, regardless of where it is produced—to participate freely in an international marketplace. They prefer instead to "buy American" even if it means paying a bit more for an equivalent product. Although such a bias reduces the overall efficiency of world production, it does result in distribution of more benefits to U.S. workers. In Japan, consumers have shown a preference for Japanese-made products even when their government has urged them to buy more imported goods (to reduce U.S.-Japanese trade frictions).

Protectionism has both positive and negative effects on an economy, most often helping producers but hurting consumers. For instance, although U.S. automobile manufacturers were aided somewhat by the restrictions imposed on Japanese imports in the 1980s, U.S. automobile consumers paid more for cars as a result (several hundred dollars more per car by some estimates). Another problem with protectionism is that domestic industry may use protection to avoid needed improvements and may therefore remain inefficient and uncompetitive—especially if protection continues over many years.

Although it violates liberal principles, temporary protectionism can have a stabilizing effect under certain conditions. When U.S. motorcycle manufacturer Harley-Davidson lost half its U.S. market share in just four years, the U.S. government imposed tariffs on imported Japanese motorcycles. The tariffs started at 45 percent in 1983; they were to decline each year for five years and then be eliminated. With the clock running, Harley scrambled to improve efficiency and raise quality. As a result, Harley regained its market share and the tariffs were lifted a year early. In the late 1980s, a reinvigorated Harley raised its market share even more and began exporting Harleys to Japan. Protectionism worked in this case because it was short-term and straightforward. Most protectionist policies are longer term, more complex, and more likely to backfire.

Industries and Interest Groups

Industries and other domestic political actors often seek to influence a state's foreign economic policies (see "Interest Groups," pp. 152–154).[29] These pressures do not always

[29] Rothgeb, John M., Jr. *U.S. Trade Policy: Balancing Economic Dreams and Political Realities*. Washington, DC: CQ Press, 2001. Dester, I. M., and Peter J. Balint. *The New Politics of American Trade: Trade, Labor, and the Environment*. Washington, DC: Institute for International Economics, 1999. Verdier, Daniel. *Democracy and International Trade: Britain, France, and the United States, 1860–1990*. Princeton, 1994.

favor protectionism. Industries that are advanced and competitive in world markets often try to influence their governments to adopt free trade policies. This strategy promotes a global free trade system in which such industries can prosper. By contrast, industries that lag behind their global competitors tend to seek government restrictions on imports or other forms of protection.

Interest Groups

Means to influence foreign economic policy include lobbying, forming interest groups, paying bribes, even encouraging coups. Actors include industry-sponsored groups, companies, labor unions, and individuals. Within an industry, such efforts usually work in a common direction because, despite competition among companies and between management and labor, all share common interests regarding the trade policies. However, a different industry may be pushing in a different direction. For instance, some U.S. industries supported the North American Free Trade Agreement (NAFTA); others opposed it.

A good example of how competing domestic interests can pull in opposite directions on state trade policy is U.S. tobacco exports. U.S. companies have a comparative advantage globally in producing cigarettes. As the U.S. market for cigarettes shrank in the 1980s (because of education about the dangers of smoking), manufacturers more aggressively marketed U.S. cigarettes overseas. They challenged regulations in foreign countries restricting cigarette advertising, claiming that these regulations were protectionist measures aimed at excluding a U.S. product from lucrative markets. In the late 1980s, the U.S. government sided with the U.S. tobacco companies and pressed foreign states to open their markets to U.S. cigarettes, threatening retaliatory trade measures if they refused. In 2002, Turkey met a U.S.-backed IMF demand to privatize the state tobacco monopoly, allowing foreign companies such as Philip Morris to greatly expand their market in Turkey.

Health groups such as the American Cancer Society opposed such U.S. policies, which they saw as unethical. But with the U.S. government's help, the tobacco companies racked up high profits from rapidly growing sales in new foreign markets. The U.S. government was also criticized for putting up obstacles to negotiations for an international tobacco-control agreement in 2001–2003.

In many countries, government not only responds to industry influence, but works actively with industries to promote their growth and tailor trade policy to their needs.[30] Such **industrial policy** is especially common in states where one or two industries are crucial to the entire economy (and of course where states own industries directly). But it is becoming a major issue in economic relations among great powers as well.[31] In Japan, the government coordinates industrial policy through the powerful Ministry of International Trade and Industry (MITI), which plans an overall strategy to take best advantage of Japan's strengths by directing capital and technology into promising areas.

Interest groups not organized along industry lines also have particular interests in state trade policies. U.S. environmentalists, for example, do not want U.S. companies to use NAFTA to avoid pollution controls by relocating to Mexico (where environmental laws are less strict). U.S. labor unions do not want companies to use NAFTA to avoid paying high wages. However, Mexican American citizens' groups in the United States tend to support NAFTA because it strengthens ties to relatives in Mexico.

---

[30] Strange, Susan. *States and Markets: An Introduction to International Political Economy*. 2nd ed. NY: St. Martin's, 1994.

[31] Skalnes, Lars S. *Politics, Markets, and Grand Strategy: Foreign Economic Policies as Strategic Instruments*. Michigan, 2000. Busch, Marc L. *Trade Warriors: States, Firms, and Strategic Policy in High Technology Competition*. Cambridge, 1999. Tyson, Laura D'Andrea. *Who's Bashing Whom? Trade Conflict in High Technology Industries*. Washington, DC: Institute for International Economics, 1992. Krugman, Paul R. *Pop Internationalism*. MIT, 1996. Hart, Jeffrey A. *Technology, Television, and Competition: The Politics of Digital TV*. Cambridge, 2004.

Cambodian Textiles after Quotas

Several industries are particularly important in trade negotiations currently. Atop the list is the textile and garment sector. As of 2005, textile quotas worldwide were dropped as a part of previously negotiated WTO deals. At the same time, China began dominating world clothing exports, with whole cities specializing in one type of garment produced for mass export to giant retailers.[32] With vast pools of cheap and disciplined labor, China threatened to drive U.S. textile and clothing producers out of business and give stiff new competition to exporters such as Pakistan and Bangladesh where textiles make up 70 percent of exports. Later in 2005, the European Union and the United States each reached bilateral agreements with China to reimpose textile quotas for a few years.

A second key issue in negotiation in 2006 was agriculture, which traditionally has been protected from foreign competition on grounds that self-sufficiency in food reduces national vulnerability (especially in time of war). Although such security concerns have now faded somewhat, farmers are well-organized and powerful domestic political actors in Europe, the United States, Japan, and other countries. In Japan, farmers are a key constituency in the Liberal Democratic Party (LDP), which governed for decades. The farmers argue that Japan's rice-centered culture demands self-sufficiency in rice production. In France, farmers enjoy wide political support and have a huge stake in the trade policies of the European Union. Subsidies to farmers in France (and elsewhere in Europe) protect them against competition from U.S. farmers. In the Doha Round of WTO negotiations that began in 2001, agricultural subsidies are a key sticking point. The talks collapsed in 2003 in Cancun, Mexico, over the subsidies, but were revived the next year by U.S. promises to cut farm subsidies 20 percent. At the 2005 Hong Kong talks, wealthy countries agreed to end all farm export subsidies by 2013.

Intellectual property rights are a third contentious area of trade negotiations. Intellectual property rights are the rights of creators of books, films, computer software, and similar products to receive royalties when their products are sold. The United States has a major conflict with some states over piracy of computer software, music, films, and other creative works—products in which the United States has a strong comparative advantage globally. It is technically easy and cheap to copy such works and sell them in violation of the copyright, patent, or trademark. Because U.S. laws cannot be enforced in foreign countries, the U.S. government wants foreign governments to prevent and punish such violations. Countries that reportedly pirate large amounts of computer software and music and entertainment products include China, Taiwan, India, Thailand, Brazil, and the former Soviet republics. The Russian government estimated in 2002 that more than 80 percent of films sold in Russia on video and DVD were produced illegally. The worldwide piracy rate was estimated at 40 percent in 2001. Infringement of intellectual property rights is widespread in many third world countries, on products ranging from videotaped movies to prescription drugs.

In response, the international community has developed an extensive IGO with 181 member states, the World Intellectual Property Organization (WIPO), which tries to regularize patent and copyright law across borders. Most states have signed an important 1994 patent treaty and a 1996 copyright treaty. The 2001 WTO meeting raised serious disputes about drug patents—especially expensive AIDS medications produced under patent in the West but available from India and Brazil in cheap generic versions (ignoring the patent). This dispute slowed the effective distribution of medicines to millions of Africans with AIDS for several years, though progress picked up after 2004.

Companies trying to protect intellectual property in an international context cannot rely on enforcement of rules in the way they can in domestic contexts. They need to bring their own state's government to bear, as well as using their own resources. Because of

[32] Barboza, David. In Roaring China, Sweaters Are West of Socks City. *The New York Times*, Dec. 24, 2004: A1.

state sovereignty in legal matters, private international economic conflicts easily become government-to-government issues.[33]

A fourth key trade issue is the openness of countries to trade in the **service sector** of the economy. This sector includes many services, especially those concerning information, but the key focus in international trade negotiations is on banking, insurance, and related financial services. U.S. companies, and some in Asia, enjoy a comparative advantage in these areas because of their information-processing technologies and experience in financial management. The North American Free Trade Agreement (NAFTA) allows U.S. banks and insurance companies to operate in Mexico. In general, as telecommunications become cheaper and more pervasive, services offered by companies in one country can be efficiently used by consumers in other countries. U.S. consumers phoning customer service at U.S. companies and connecting to India or another English-speaking developing country engage in a long-distance trade in services.

Another especially important industry in international trade is the arms trade, which operates largely outside of the framework of normal commercial transactions because of its national security implications. Governments in industrialized countries want to protect their domestic arms industries rather than rely on imports to meet their weapons needs. And those domestic arms industries become stronger and more economically viable by exporting their products (as well as supplying their own governments). Governments usually participate actively in the military-industrial sector of the economy, even in countries such as the United States that lack industrial policy in other economic sectors. For example, fighter jets are a product for which the United States enjoys a global comparative advantage (see pp. 154–155). In the 1990s, the U.S. arms industry, like the tobacco industry, looked overseas for new customers to offset declining demand at home (in 2004, U.S. arms sales totaled nearly $19 billion). The Middle East has been the leading arms-importing region of the global South., with India and China increasing recently.

CRUSHING PIRACY

Intellectual property rights have been an important focus of recent trade negotiations. In many countries, pirated copies of videos, music, and software sell on the street with no royalty payments. Occasionally governments collect and destroy pirated copies, as here in Brazil in 2003, but without putting much of a dent in the problem.

Illicit Trade A different problem is presented by the "industry" of illicit trade, or *smuggling*. No matter what restrictions governments put on trading certain goods, someone is usually willing to risk punishment to make a profit in such trade. Smuggling exists because it is profitable to sell fake Taiwanese copies of MS-DOS in Germany, or

[33] Marlin-Bennett, Renée. *Knowledge Power: Intellectual Property, Information, and Privacy*. Boulder: Rienner, 2004.

Colombian cocaine in the United States, even though these products are illegal in those countries. Even with legal goods, profits can be increased by evading tariffs (by moving goods secretly, mislabeling them, or bribing customs officials), as for example by smuggling U.S. cigarettes into Canada.

Illegal goods, and legal goods imported illegally, often are sold in black markets—unofficial, sometimes secret markets. Black markets are widespread, and flourish particularly in economies heavily regulated by government, such as centrally planned economies. In many third world countries, and in most of the transitional economies such as Russia, black markets are a substantial though hard-to-measure fraction of the total economic activity and deprive the government of significant revenue. Black markets also exist for foreign currency exchange (see Chapter 9).

The extent of illicit trade varies from one country and industry to another, depending on profitability and enforcement. Drugs and weapons are most profitable, and worldwide illegal trade networks exist for both. International black markets for weapons trade, beyond government controls, are notorious. A state with enough money can buy—although at premium prices—most kinds of weapons.

Different states have different interests in enforcing political control over illicit trade. In illegal arms exports, the exporting state may gain economically from the trade and the importing state gains access to the weapons; the losers are the other exporters that neither got the export revenue nor kept the weapons out of the hands of the importer. Thus, illicit trade often creates conflicts of interest among states and leads to complex political bargaining among governments, each looking after its own interests.

THE MEDIUM IS THE MESSAGE

Agriculture and trade in services are two issues high on the agenda of international trade negotiations. This British farmer combines a little of each: when an outbreak of mad cow disease halted exports of British beef in 1996, the farmer decided to use his location near a busy freeway to sell advertising space to a U.S. company—in effect, an export of services.

Cooperation in Trade

Successful trade strategies are those that achieve mutual gains from cooperation with other states. A global system of free trade is a collective good. Given the lack of world government, the benefits of trade depend on international cooperation—to enforce contracts, prevent monopolies, and discourage protectionism. A single state can profitably subsidize its own state-owned industries, create its own monopolies, or erect barriers to competitive imports as long as not too many other states do so. If other states also break the rules of free trade, the benefits of free exchange slip away from all parties involved.

As with international law generally, economic agreements between states depend strongly on reciprocity for enforcement (see pp. 66–68, 275). If one state protects its industries, or puts tariffs on the goods of other states, or violates the copyright on works produced in other countries, the main resort that other states have is to apply similar measures against the offending state. The use of reciprocity to enforce equal terms of exchange is especially important in international trade, where states often negotiate complex agreements—commodity by commodity, industry by industry—based on reciprocity.[34]

Enforcement of equal terms of trade is complicated by differing interpretations of what is "fair." States generally decide which practices of other states they consider unfair (often prodded by affected domestic industries) and then take (or threaten) retaliatory actions to punish those practices. A U.S. law, the Super 301 provision, mandates retaliation against states that restrict access of U.S. goods to their markets. However, if the other state does not agree that its practices were unfair, the retaliatory actions may themselves seem unfair and call for counterretaliation. One disadvantage of reciprocity is that it can lead to a downward spiral of noncooperation, popularly called a trade war (the economic equivalent of the arms races discussed on p. 68). To prevent this, states often negotiate agreements regarding what practices they consider unfair. In some cases, third-party arbitration can also be used to resolve trade disputes. Currently, the World Trade Organization (see pp. 322–325) hears complaints and sets levels of acceptable retaliation. In some cases, regional trade agreements have authority to hear and resolve complaints as well.

Retaliation for unfair trade practices usually is based on an attempt to match the violation in type and extent. Under WTO rules, a state may impose retaliatory tariffs equivalent to the losses caused by another state's unfair trade practices (as determined by WTO hearings). In 2001, the European Union threatened the United States with sanctions on an unprecedented $4 billion of goods in response to U.S. tax credits to exporters such as Microsoft and Boeing (which the WTO had ruled unfair). Usually, at the last minute, negotiators reach agreements to avert large-scale retaliatory sanctions or trade wars, but in 2004 Europe imposed the retaliatory tariffs and lifted them in January 2005 only after the U.S. Congress repealed the tax breaks (disputed details remain).

In cases of dumping, retaliation is aimed at offsetting the advantage enjoyed by goods imported at prices below the world market. Retaliatory tariffs raise the price back to market levels. In 2001, the weakened U.S. steel industry pleaded for U.S. government protection from cheap foreign steel, under an antidumping rationale. The Bush administration, although usually favoring free trade, agreed to offer relief (scoring points with labor unions and swing voters in Pennsylvania and West Virginia).

International Trade Commission

Before such tariffs are imposed, a U.S. government agency, the International Trade Commission (ITC), decides whether the low-priced imports have actually hurt the U.S. industry.[35] The ITC ruled that U.S. steelmakers had indeed been hurt, and suggested tariffs of 5 to 40 percent. President Bush imposed 30 percent tariffs in 2002, and other countries challenged them in the WTO, which ruled against the United States in 2003. The WTO gave other countries the right to impose $2 billion in retaliatory tariffs against the United States. As Europeans drew up their list of tariffs, targeting maximum damage to swing electoral states in 2004, President Bush backed down and abolished the steel tariffs (declaring them successful and no longer needed). By making the cost of tariffs higher than the benefits, the WTO effectively changed U.S. policy—an indication of the WTO's growing power.[36]

Trade disputes and retaliatory measures are common. States keep close track of the exact terms of trade. Large bureaucracies monitor international economic transactions (prices

---

[34] Bayard, Thomas O., Kimberly Ann Elliott, Amelia Porges, and Charles Iceland. *Reciprocity and Retaliation in U.S. Trade Policy*. Washington, DC: Institute for International Economics, 1994. Bhagwati, Jagdish, ed. *Going Alone: The Case for Relaxed Reciprocity in Freeing Trade*. MIT, 2002.

[35] Hansen, Wendy L. The International Trade Commission and the Politics of Protectionism. *American Political Science Review* 84 (1), 1990: 21–46.

[36] Sanger, David E. A Blink from the Bush Administration: Backing Down on Tariffs, U.S. Strengthens Trade Organization. *The New York Times*, Dec. 5, 2003: A25.

relative to world market levels, tariffs, etc.) and develop detailed policies to reciprocate any other state's deviations from cooperation.[37]

Trade cooperation is easier to achieve under hegemony (see "Hegemony" on p. 82, and "Hegemonic Stability" on pp. 105–106). The efficient operation of markets depends on a stable political framework such as hegemony can provide. Political power can protect economic exchange from the distorting influences of violent leverage, of unfair or fraudulent trade practices, and of uncertainties of international currency rates. A hegemon can provide a world currency in which value can be universally calculated. It can punish the use of violence and can enforce norms of fair trade. Because its economy is so large and dominating, the hegemon has a potent leverage in the threat to break off trade ties, even without resort to military force. For example, to be denied access to U.S. markets today would be a serious punishment for export industries in many states.

U.S. hegemony helped create the major norms and institutions of international trade in the post-1945 era. Now that U.S. hegemony seems to be giving way to a more multipolar world—especially in economic affairs among the great powers—institutions are even more important for the success of the world trading system. The role and operation of the major trade regimes and institutions occupy the remainder of this chapter.

Trade Regimes

Trade regimes are the common expectations governments have about the rules for international trade. A variety of partially overlapping regimes concerned with international trade have developed, mostly since World War II. The most central of these is the World Trade Organization.

The World Trade Organization

The **World Trade Organization (WTO)** is a global, multilateral IGO that promotes, monitors, and adjudicates international trade. Together with the regional and bilateral arrangements described shortly, the WTO is central to the overall expectations and practices of states with regard to international trade.[38] The WTO is the successor organization to the **General Agreement on Tariffs and Trade (GATT),** which was created in 1947 to facilitate freer trade on a multilateral basis. The GATT was more of a negotiating framework than an administrative institution. It did not actually regulate trade. Before the GATT, proposals for a stronger institutional agency had been rejected because of U.S. fears that overregulation would stifle free trade. Although the GATT was a regime with little institutional infrastructure until the mid-1990s, it did have a small secretariat with headquarters in Geneva, Switzerland. In addition to its main role as a negotiating forum, the GATT helped to arbitrate trade disputes (as in the European agricultural subsidy case), clarifying the rules and helping states observe them.

In 1995, the GATT became the WTO. The GATT agreements on manufactured goods were subsumed into the WTO framework and then extended to include trade in services and intellectual property. The WTO has some powers of enforcement and an international bureaucracy (more than 600 people), which monitors trade policies and practices in each member state and adjudicates disputes among members. The WTO wields

[37] U.S. Trade Representative. *2001 National Trade Estimate Report on Foreign Trade Barriers*. March 30, 2001.

[38] Hoekman, Bernard, and Michel Kostecki. *The Political Economy of the World Trading System: From GATT to WTO*. 2nd ed. Oxford, 1999.

some power over states, but as with most international institutions, this power is limited. A growing public backlash against free trade (see below) reflects uneasiness about the potential power of a foreign and secretive organization to force changes in democratically enacted national laws. But the WTO is the central international institution governing trade and therefore one that almost all countries want to participate in and develop.

Over time, the membership of the WTO has grown, including some states from the former Soviet bloc. By 2006, 149 countries—almost all the world's major trading states except Russia—had joined the WTO. A breakthrough 1999 U.S.-China trade agreement, after 13 years of negotiations, led to China's admission in 2001. The United States and other countries demand, as a condition of membership, liberalization of the trading practices of would-be members. These new practices may have major effects on China's economic and political future (see pp. 502–505). The most notable remaining nonmember is Russia. It is among 30 states seeking admission.

The WTO framework is based on the principles of reciprocity—that one state's lowering of trade barriers to another should be matched in return—and of nondiscrimination. The latter principle is embodied in the **most-favored nation (MFN)** concept, which says that trade restrictions imposed by a WTO member on its most-favored trading partner must be applied equally to all WTO members. If Australia applies a 20 percent tariff on auto parts imported from France, it is not supposed to apply a 40 percent tariff on auto parts imported from the United States. Thus, the WTO does not get rid of barriers to trade altogether but equalizes them in a global framework to create a level playing field for all member states. States are not prevented from protecting their own industries but cannot play favorites among their trading partners. States may also extend MFN status to others that are not WTO members, as the United States did with China before it joined the WTO.

An exception to the MFN system is the **Generalized System of Preferences (GSP),** dating from the 1970s, by which industrialized states give trade concessions to third world states to help the latter's economic development. Preferences amount to a promise by rich states to allow imports from poor ones under lower tariffs than those imposed under MFN.[39]

The WTO continues the GATT's role as a negotiating forum for multilateral trade agreements that lower trade barriers on a fair and reciprocal basis. These detailed and complex agreements specify the commitments of various states and regions to lower certain trade barriers by certain amounts on fixed schedules. Almost every commitment entails domestic political costs, because domestic industries lose protection against foreign competition. Even when other states agree to make similar commitments in other areas, lowering of trade barriers is often hard for national governments.

As a result, negotiations on these multilateral agreements are long and difficult. Typically they stretch on for several years or more in a *round of negotiations;* after it is completed the members begin on a new round. Among the five rounds of GATT negotiations from 1947 to 1995, the Kennedy Round in the 1960s—so called because it started during the Kennedy administration—paid special attention to the growing role of the (increasingly integrated) European Economic Community (EEC), which the United States found somewhat threatening. The Tokyo Round (begun in Tokyo) in the 1970s had to adjust rules to new conditions of world interdependence as, for instance, OPEC raised oil prices and Japan began to dominate the automobile export business.

The **Uruguay Round** started in 1986 (in Uruguay). Although the rough outlines of a new GATT agreement emerged after a few years, closure eluded five successive G7 summit

---

[39] Hirata, Akira, and Ippei Yamazawa, eds. *Trade Policies Towards Developing Countries*. NY: St. Martin's, 1993. Glover, David J., and Diana Tussie, eds. *The Developing Countries in World Trade: Policies and Bargaining Strategies*. Boulder, CO: Lynne Rienner, 1993. Finlayson, Jock A., and Mark W. Zacher. *Managing International Markets: Developing Countries and the Commodity Trade Regime*. Columbia, 1988.

meetings in 1990–1994. As the round dragged on year after year, participants said the GATT should be renamed the "general agreement to talk and talk." A successful conclusion to the round would add more than $100 billion to the world economy annually. But that money was a collective good, to be enjoyed both by states that made concessions in the final negotiations and by states that did not. Agreement was finally reached in late 1994. The United States had pressured Europe to reduce agricultural subsidies and third world states to protect intellectual property rights. In the end, the United States got some, but not all, of what it wanted. France held out adamantly and won the right to protect its film industry against U.S. films.

From 1947, the GATT tried to encourage states to use import tariffs rather than other means of protecting industries and to lower them over time. The GATT concentrated on manufactured goods and succeeded in substantially reducing the average tariffs, from 40 percent of the goods' value decades ago to 3 percent by 2002 (under the Uruguay Round agreement). Tariff rates in the global South are much higher, around 30 percent (reflecting the greater protection that third world industry sees itself as needing).

Agricultural trade is politically more sensitive than trade in manufactured goods and was seriously addressed only in the Uruguay Round.[40] Trade in services, such as banking and insurance, is another current major focus of the WTO. Such trade approached one-quarter of the total value of world trade in the 1990s. Trade in telecommunications is a related area of interest. In 1997, 70 states (negotiating through the WTO) agreed on a treaty to allow telecommunications companies to enter each other's markets.

The problems in expanding into these and other sensitive areas became obvious in 1999. First, a North-South divide in the WTO emerged when the WTO could not agree on a new leader and split the five-year term between a New Zealander supported mostly by the North and a Thai politician supported mainly by the South (especially Asia).

Then, the 1999 Seattle WTO conference, where trade ministers had hoped to launch a new round of trade negotiations, turned into a fiasco. Most industrialized countries wanted to include provisions on the negotiating agenda for the round, in areas such as environmental protection and labor laws, that poorer countries considered an attack on their sovereignty and a way for the North to maintain its advantage in trade. (The North's main advantage is technology whereas the South's is cheap labor and natural resources.) Representatives of poor countries argued that they needed trade to raise incomes, and could not meet the standards of industrialized countries (which had allowed low wages, harsh working conditions, and environmental destruction when *they* began industrializing). Environmental and labor activists, joined by window-smashing anarchists, staged street protests that delayed the conference opening by a day. The trade ministers could not agree on a new agenda for trade talks, and the meeting ended in failure.

Recovering from Seattle, in 2001 trade ministers meeting in Doha, Qatar, agreed to launch a new round of trade negotiations, the **Doha Round**. The issues under negotiation include agriculture, services, industrial products, intellectual property, WTO rules (including how to handle antidumping cases), dispute settlement, and some trade and environmental questions. At the 2003 meeting, in Cancun, Mexico, states from the global South walked out after the industrialized countries would not agree to lift their agricultural subsidies, which were shutting out poor countries' agricultural exports. At the 2005 Hong Kong meeting, wealthy states agreed to end the export subsidies, but tough negotiations continue over tariffs on manufactured goods, protection of intellectual property, and opening financial sectors. WTO members face much work to conclude

---

[40] Avery, William P., ed. *World Agriculture and the GATT*. Boulder, CO: Lynne Rienner, 1992. Marlin-Bennett, Renee Elizabeth. *Food Fights: International Regimes and the Politics of Agricultural Trade Disputes*. NY: Gordon and Breach, 1993.

the Doha Round before President Bush's Congressional "fast-track" authorization (which commits Congress to vote on trade deals in full without amending them) expires in July 2007.

In general, states continue to participate in the WTO because the benefits, in terms of global wealth creation, outweigh the costs, in terms of harm to domestic industries or painful adjustments in national economies. States try to change the rules in their favor during the rounds of negotiations (never with complete success), and between rounds they try to evade the rules in minor ways. But the overall benefits are too great to jeopardize by nonparticipation or by allowing frequent trade wars to occur.

MAKING MAGIC

Rounds of trade negotiations, such as the current Doha Round begun in 2001, last for years as members negotiate complex deals that must be approved by consensus of all 149 member states. A conference of trade ministers in December 2005 tried to regain momentum for the stalled Doha Round, with mixed success. Here, WTO head Pascal Lamy opens the conference with the tool he hopes will bring success—a magic wand.

Resistance to Trade

The globalization of the world economy, which includes growing trade and other aspects (see Chapters 9–13), has created a backlash in many parts of the world, including the United States. Global-level integration has fueled a countercurrent of growing nationalism in several world regions where people believe their identities and communities to be threatened by the penetration of foreign influences (see Chapter 5). Even more fundamental to the backlash against trade are the material dislocations caused by globalization, which directly affect the self-interests of certain segments of a population.

Resistance to Trade

Workers in industrialized countries, in those industries—from steel and automobiles to electronics and clothing—that face increasing competition from low-wage countries in the global South, are among the most adversely affected by free trade. Inevitably, the competition from low-wage countries holds down wages in those industries in the industrialized countries. It also creates pressures to relax standards of labor regulation, such as those protecting worker safety, and it can lead to job losses if manufacturers close down plants in high-wage countries and move operations to the global South. Not surprisingly, labor unions have been among the strongest political opponents of unfettered trade expansion. (Although the United States stands at the center of these debates, other industrialized countries face similar issues.)

Human rights NGOs have joined labor unions in pushing for trade agreements to include requirements for improving working conditions in low-wage countries; these could include laws regarding a minimum wage, child labor, and worker safety. The U.S. Congress in 1997 banned U.S. imports of goods (mostly rugs) manufactured by South Asia's 15 million indentured (slave) child laborers. Clothing manufacturers such as Nike and Reebok, meanwhile, stung by criticism of "sweatshop" conditions in their Asian factories, adopted a voluntary program to end the worst abuses; critics claimed it would make little difference, however. About 250 million children under age 14 are working in the global South, according to the UN-affiliated International Labor Organization—about 20 percent of 10- to

CHEAP LABOR

Labor, environmental, and human rights organizations have all criticized unrestricted free trade. They argue that free trade agreements encourage MNCs to produce goods under unfair and unhealthy conditions, including the use of child labor. This boy in India makes soccer balls, 2002.

14-year-olds in Latin America and Asia and 40 percent in Africa. In Ivory Coast, the world's largest exporter of cocoa (for chocolate consumed in the global North), tens of thousands of children work for low wages, or even as slaves, on cocoa plantations.

Environmental groups also have actively opposed the unrestricted expansion of trade, which they see as undermining environmental laws in industrialized countries and promoting environmentally harmful practices worldwide (see pp. 421–422). For example, U.S. regulations require commercial shrimp boats to use devices that prevent endangered species of sea turtles from drowning in shrimp nets. Indonesia, Malaysia, Thailand, and Pakistan, whose shrimp exports to the United States were blocked because they do not require use of such devices, filed a complaint with the World Trade Organization, arguing that the U.S. regulation unfairly discriminated against them. In 1998, the United States lost the WTO ruling and appeal. Sea turtles became a symbol of environmentalist opposition to the WTO. (In 2001, the WTO ruled the U.S. law acceptable after changes had made application of the law more even-handed.) In 1996, Brazil and Venezuela took the United States to the WTO and forced a change in U.S. environmental rules regarding imported gasoline, claiming regulations under the Clean Air Act were functioning as nontariff barriers.

In general, unrestricted trade tends to force countries to equalize their regulations in a variety of areas not limited to labor and environmental rules. For example, the WTO ruled in 1997 that Europeans' fears about the use of growth hormones in beef were not scientifically warranted, and therefore EU regulations could not be used to exclude U.S. beef containing hormones. When the European Union persisted, the United States was allowed to retaliate by imposing high tariffs on a list of EU exports such as French cheeses. Similarly, in 2006 the WTO ruled that European restrictions on imports of genetically modified food from the United States violated trade rules. Meanwhile, U.S. consumers harbored fears about pesticide-laced produce grown in Mexico.

These examples illustrate the variety of sources of backlash against free trade agreements. Labor, environmental, and consumer groups all portray the WTO as a secretive bureaucracy outside democratic control that serves the interests of big corporations at the expense of ordinary people in both the global North and South. The WTO's critics object to its holding all major deliberations behind closed doors. More fundamentally, these critics distrust the corporate-driven "globalization" (see pp. 300–302) of which the WTO is just one aspect. Street protests have become a regular feature of any major international meeting concerning economic policies.

The benefits of free trade, as was noted earlier, are much more diffuse than the costs. U.S. consumers enjoy lower prices on goods imported from low-wage countries, such as toys from China. The consumers may spend more money on other products and services, eventually employing more U.S. workers. Cheap imports also help keep inflation low, which benefits citizens and politicians.

Bilateral and Regional Agreements

Although the WTO provides an overall framework for multilateral trade in a worldwide market, most international trade is governed by more specific international political agreements. These are of two general types: bilateral trade agreements and regional free trade areas.

Bilateral Agreements Bilateral treaties covering trade are reciprocal arrangements to lower barriers to trade between two states. Usually they are fairly specific. For instance, one country may reduce its prohibition on imports on product X (which the second country exports at competitive prices) while the second country lowers its tariff on product Y (which the first country exports).

Part of the idea behind the GATT/WTO was to strip away the maze of bilateral agreements on trade and simplify the system of tariffs and preferences. This effort has only partially succeeded. Bilateral trade agreements continue to play an important role. They have the advantages of reducing the collective goods problem inherent in multilateral negotiations and facilitating reciprocity as a means to achieve cooperation.[41] When WTO negotiations bog down, bilateral agreements can keep trade momentum going. Since most states have only a few most-important trading partners, a few bilateral agreements can go a long way in structuring a state's trade relations. In 2006, the United States and South Korea pushed to complete a bilateral free trade agreement by April 2007.

Free Trade Areas Regional free trade areas are also important in the structure of world trade. In such areas, groups of neighboring states agree to remove the entire structure of trade barriers (or most of it) within their area. Beyond free trade areas, states may decide to reduce trade barriers *and* adopt a common tariff toward states that are not members of the agreement. This type of an arrangement is known as a *customs union*. If members of a customs union decide to coordinate other policies such as monetary exchange, the customs union becomes a *common market*. The creation of a regional trade agreement (of any type) allows a group of states to cooperate in increasing their wealth without waiting for the rest of the world. In fact, from an economic nationalist perspective, a free trade area can enhance a region's power at the expense of other areas of the world.

The most important free trade area is in Europe; it is connected with the European Union but with a somewhat larger membership. Because Europe contains a number of small industrialized states living close together, the creation of a single integrated market allows these states to gain the economic advantages that come inherently to a large state such as the United States. The European free trade experiment has been a great success overall, contributing to Europe's accumulation of wealth since World War II (see Chapter 10).

The United States, Canada, and Mexico signed the **North American Free Trade Agreement (NAFTA)** in 1994, following a U.S.-Canadian free trade agreement in 1988.[42] In NAFTA's first decade, U.S. imports from both Mexico and Canada more than doubled, then fell back somewhat (after 1999). Canada and Mexico were the largest and third-largest U.S. trading partners, respectively (Japan was second). Initially, Mexico's currency dropped drastically relative to the dollar in 1994–1995. But, over the long run, neither the great benefits predicted by NAFTA supporters nor the disasters predicted by opponents materialized.

---

[41] Oye, Kenneth A. *Economic Discrimination and Political Exchange: World Political Economy in the 1930s and 1980s*. Princeton, 1992.

[42] Hakim, Peter and Robert E. Litan, eds. *The Future of North American Integration: Beyond NAFTA*. Washington DC: Brookings, 2002. Andreas, Peter and Thomas J. Biersteker, eds. *The Rebordering of North America: Integration and Exclusion in a New Security Conflict*. NY: Routledge, 2003. Hufbauer, Gary Clyde, and Jeffrey J. Schott. *NAFTA: An Assessment*. Washington, DC: Institute for International Economics, 1993.

U.S. opponents of NAFTA, including various U.S. labor unions and environmental groups, criticized the low wages and poor labor laws in Mexico, which they feared would drag down U.S. labor standards. Environmentalists similarly criticized Mexico's lax environmental laws (relative to the United States) and saw NAFTA as giving U.S. corporations license to pollute by moving south of the border (see pp. 420–421). For seven years until 2003, the U.S. government delayed letting Mexican trucks operate in the United States. (The Teamsters Union argued that Mexican trucks did not meet safety standards.)

You Are a Political Leader

Politicians in North and South America have long spoken of creating a single free trade area in the Western hemisphere, from Alaska to Argentina—the *Free Trade Area of the Americas (FTAA)*. To empower him to do so, President Clinton asked Congress in 1997 to reinstate fast-track legislation (see p.325). But Democrats in Congress defeated the measure, demanding that free trade agreements include requirements for labor and environmental standards for other countries—points on which they found NAFTA's record wanting. President Bush had more success, winning fast-track authority from Congress.

FTAA negotiations began in 2003 with a target date of 2005. But by then several factors had created pressures against the FTAA. The 2001 recession and post-September 11 security measures reduced trade; China provided U.S. companies with a better source of cheap labor; and left-leaning governments, wary of liberal economic advice, came to power in several main Latin American countries. The latter cared most about tariff-free trade, while the U.S. position emphasized a range of other issues such as services, intellectual property, and financial openness. In late 2005, trade talks failed at a summit meeting in Argentina where one participant, Venezuelan president Hugo Chavez, led a 25,000-person anti-American rally in the streets. In early 2006 the FTAA talks remained in near-hibernation, and the weight of trade negotiations fell to the WTO negotiations. Meanwhile, however, a bilateral U.S.-Chile free trade agreement was reached in 2002, and a U.S. agreement with five Central American countries in 2004.

Efforts to create a free trade area, or even a semi-free trade area, in Asia began in the late 1980s but moved slowly. Unlike the European and North American arrangements, an Asian bloc would include very different kinds of states—rich ones such as Japan, poor ones such as the Philippines; democracies, dictatorships, and communist states. It is unclear how well such a diverse collection could coordinate their common interests, especially because their existing trade patterns are not focused on each other but are spread out among other states including the United States (again in contrast to trade patterns existing before the creation of the European and North American free trade areas). But despite these problems, China and the ASEAN states are negotiating to remove most tariffs by 2010.

During the Cold War, the Soviet bloc maintained its own trading bloc, the Council for Mutual Economic Assistance (CMEA), also known as COMECON. After the Soviet Union collapsed, the members scrambled to join up with the world economy, from which they had been largely cut off. The Commonwealth of Independent States (CIS), formed by 12 former Soviet republics, remains economically integrated. It was previously a free trade zone by virtue of being part of a single state using transportation, communication, and other infrastructure links.

Other efforts to create free trade areas have had mixed results. The Southern Cone Common Market (Mercosur) began in the early 1990s with Brazil, Argentina, Uruguay, and Paraguay, and Venezuela was in the process of joining in 2006. Chile and Bolivia have joined as associate members. Still, Mercosur members trade more with the United States as they do with each other. In 2002, the countries agreed to allow their 250 million citizens free movement and residency across countries. A Caribbean common market (CARICOM) was created in 1973, but the area is neither large nor rich enough to make regional free trade a very important accelerator of economic growth. Eleven countries created a

POLICY PERSPECTIVES

President of Brazil, Luiz Inacio Lula da Silva

PROBLEM *How to balance the demands of key trading partners with domestic economic needs.*

BACKGROUND Imagine that you are the president of Brazil. You are popular and riding a good economy, which is the seventeenth largest in the world. Growth in 2005 was 2.4 percent, up from –0.5 percent in 2003. Your country's export-led growth strategy is an important piece of this economic picture. Exports to industrialized countries are at an all-time high and in 2005 you ran a current account surplus for the first time since 1992. Domestically, you are being pressured to ensure continued market access for your industrial and agricultural products in international markets.

The United States, Argentina, China, the Netherlands, and Germany are your key export partners. The United States alone accounts for 23 percent of your exports and 20 percent of your imports. EU states combine to account for more than 26 percent of your exports, but far less of your imports.

You have been pressured extensively by the United States to join a Free Trade Area of the Americas (FTAA), but have refused to do so. In fact, along with India and China, your objections to new World Trade Organization rules effectively stalled trade talks in 2003. Your goal for the WTO and the FTAA is that developed countries lower their agricultural subsidies and increase their quotas for Brazilian farm products. To date, America has largely turned down your demands in the agricultural realm. Given U.S. bargaining power, this may be a difficult concession to extract in future negotiations.

Trade relations with your neighbors are relatively good. You are the largest state in the Southern Cone Common Market (Mercosur). You recently pushed to bring several other Latin American states (such as Mexico and Peru) into Mercosur as associate members to hedge your bets against a collapse in the FTAA negotiations. Unfortunately, you cannot rely on your Merocosur partners alone to absorb your export production. For example, your three full partners in Mercosur (Argentina, Paraguay, and Uruguay) have a combined total GDP smaller than Canada's.

SCENARIO Now imagine that the EU offers a free trade agreement with better terms (especially concerning agricultural goods) than a potential FTAA agreement. Because several EU states are key trading partners, this is an attractive offer. In order for your exports to continue to grow, your market opportunities must expand. This would provide such an opportunity while satisfying those export-oriented industries.

But accepting the EU offer would likely anger the United States. If the United States then completed an FTAA without you, this would be costly to your economy because any similar goods produced by your neighbors would have preferential access to U.S. markets, making them more attractive than Brazilian goods to U.S. businesses and consumers.

CHOOSE YOUR POLICY Do you accept the EU offer? Do you attempt to bargain more with the United States in hopes of achieving a breakthrough? How do you balance the demands of competing (and important) trade partners, while trying to achieve the best outcome for your public?

Latin American Free Trade Association (LAFTA) in 1960 (changed in 1980 to the Latin American Integration Association), but the effort was held back by the different levels of poverty and wealth among the members and their existing patterns of trade (as in the Asian efforts just mentioned). Venezuela, Colombia, Ecuador, Peru, and Bolivia created the Andean Common Market in 1969; it had modest successes but not dramatic results, because trade within the bloc was not important enough (compared with, say, Venezuelan oil exports to the United States).

If regional free trade areas such as now exist in Europe and in North America gain strength and new ones arise, the WTO may be weakened. The more that states are able to meet the political requirements of economic growth through bilateral and regional agreements, the less they may depend on the worldwide agreements developed through the WTO. The overlap of WTO rules and regional agreements can create confusion, as in 2006 when a WTO panel upheld U.S. duties on Canadian softwood lumber while a NAFTA panel overturned the duties and ordered refunds to Canada.

Cartels

A **cartel** is an association of producers or consumers, or both, of a certain product—formed to manipulate its price on the world market. It is an unusual but interesting form of trade regime. Most often it is producers and not consumers that form cartels, because there are usually fewer producers than consumers, and it seems possible for them to coordinate their actions so as to keep prices high. Cartels can use a variety of means to affect prices; the most effective is to coordinate limits on production by each member so as to lower the supply, relative to demand, of the good.

WEB LINK

Organization of Petroleum Exporting Countries

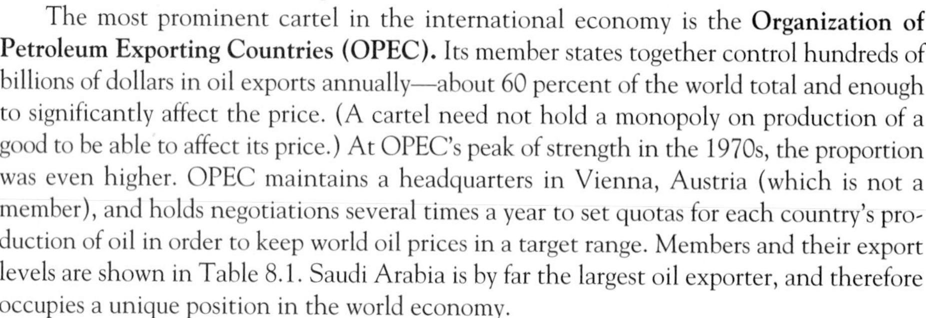

The most prominent cartel in the international economy is the **Organization of Petroleum Exporting Countries (OPEC).** Its member states together control hundreds of billions of dollars in oil exports annually—about 60 percent of the world total and enough to significantly affect the price. (A cartel need not hold a monopoly on production of a good to be able to affect its price.) At OPEC's peak of strength in the 1970s, the proportion was even higher. OPEC maintains a headquarters in Vienna, Austria (which is not a member), and holds negotiations several times a year to set quotas for each country's production of oil in order to keep world oil prices in a target range. Members and their export levels are shown in Table 8.1. Saudi Arabia is by far the largest oil exporter, and therefore occupies a unique position in the world economy.

OPEC illustrates the potential that a cartel creates for serious collective goods problems. Individual members of OPEC can (and do) cheat a bit by exceeding their production quotas while still enjoying the collective good of high oil prices. The collective good breaks down when too many members exceed their quotas, as has happened repeatedly to OPEC. Then world oil prices drop. (Iraq's accusations that fellow OPEC member Kuwait was exceeding production quotas and driving oil prices down was one factor in Iraq's invasion of Kuwait in 1990.)

OPEC may work as well as it does only because one member, Saudi Arabia, has enough oil to unilaterally manipulate supply enough to drive prices up or down—a form of hegemonic stability within the cartel. Saudi Arabia can take up the slack from some cheating in OPEC (cutting back its own production) and keep prices up. Or if too many OPEC members are cheating on their quotas, it can punish them by flooding the market with oil and driving prices down until the other OPEC members collectively come to their senses.

Consumers usually do not form cartels. However, in response to OPEC, the major oil-importing states formed their own organization, the *International Energy Agency (IEA)*, which has some of the functions of a cartel. The IEA coordinates the energy policies of major industrialized states—such as the maintenance of oil stockpiles in case of a shortage on

TABLE 8.1 ■ OPEC Members and Oil Production, March 2006

Member State	Millions of Barrels/Day
Saudi Arabia	9.4
Iran	3.9
Kuwait	2.6
Venezuela	2.5
United Arab Emirates	2.5
Nigeria	2.2
Iraq	1.7
Libya	1.7
Algeria	1.4
Indonesia	1.0
Qatar	0.8
Total OPEC	29.6
Percent of World	40%

Note: Major oil exporters not in OPEC include Russia, Kazakhstan, Mexico, China, Britain, and Norway. Ecuador and Gabon, minor exporters, left OPEC in 1992 and 1995, respectively. The United States, until several decades ago a major oil exporter, is now a major importer.

Source: Data adapted from United States Department of Energy, Energy Information Administration.

world markets—in order to keep world oil prices low and stable. The largest importers of oil are the members of the G8 (large industrialized states). Considering the importance of oil to the world economy, and the existence of both producer and consumer cartels, the price of oil has been surprisingly unstable, with prices fluctuating over the years from barely above $10 per barrel to near $70. High oil prices in 2000 contributed to a world recession in 2001, which brought oil prices back down temporarily. But by early 2006, with China driving up demand and continued instability in the Middle East, world oil prices surpassed $70 per barrel.

For a few commodities that are subject to large price fluctuations on world markets—detrimental to both producers and consumers—joint producer-consumer cartels have been formed. In order to keep prices stable, producing and consuming states use the cartel to coordinate the overall supply and demand globally. Such cartels exist for coffee, several minerals, and some other products. In the coffee cartel, Colombia argued in the late 1980s for a higher target price for coffee, so that Colombian peasants would have an incentive to switch from growing coca (for cocaine production) to coffee. But the United States, as the major coffee-consuming state, would not agree to the proposal for higher prices.[43] Coffee prices hit a 100-year low by 2002, forcing many coffee growers to switch to coca (or, in Africa, khat), before recovering modestly. NGOs introduced Fair Trade Certified coffee, guaranteeing farmers a price above their production costs through the price booms and busts. By 2006, 400 companies sold Fair Trade Certified products through 33,000 outlets.

Fair Trade on Campus

In general, the idea of cartels runs counter to liberal economics because cartels are deliberate efforts to distort free markets. However, in occasional cases where free markets create large fluctuations in price, the creation of a cartel can bring some order to chaos and result in greater efficiency. Cartels usually are not as powerful as market forces in determining overall world price levels: too many producers and suppliers exist, and too many substitute

[43] Bates, Robert H. *Open-Economy Politics: The Political Economy of the World Coffee Trade*. Princeton, 1997.

goods can replace ones that become too expensive, for a cartel to corner the market. The exceptions, such as OPEC in the 1970s, are rare.

States have found it worthwhile to expand trade steadily, using a variety of regimes and institutions to do so—the WTO, free trade areas, bilateral agreements, and cartels. Overall, despite a loss of state sovereignty as a result of growing interdependence, these efforts have benefited participating states. Stable political rules governing trade allow states to realize the great economic gains that can result from international exchange. Such political stability is equally important in international monetary and business relations, which are the subject of Chapter 9.

THINKING CRITICALLY

1. Suppose your state had a chance to reach a major trade agreement by making substantial concessions. The agreement would produce $5 billion in new wealth for your state, as well as $10 billion for each of the other states involved (which are political allies but economic rivals). What advice would a mercantilist give your state's leader about making such a deal? What arguments would support the advice? How would liberal advice and arguments differ?
2. China seems to be making a successful transition to market economics and is growing rapidly. It is emerging as the world's second-largest economy. Do you think this is a good thing or a bad thing for your state? Does your reasoning reflect mercantilist or liberal assumptions?
3. Given the theory of hegemonic stability, what effects might a resurgence of U.S. power in the post–Cold War era have on the world trading system? How might those effects show up in concrete ways?
4. Before reading this chapter, to what extent did you have a preference for buying products made in your own country? Has reading this chapter changed your views on that subject? How?
5. NAFTA, the free trade agreement between Canada, Mexico, and the United States, is a decade old. Given that wages in Mexico are lower and technology is less developed than in the United States, which U.S. industries do you think have gained from NAFTA? Specifically, do you think labor-intensive industries or high-technology industries were winners or losers? Why?

CHAPTER SUMMARY

- Mercantilism emphasizes the use of economic policy to increase state power relative to other states. It is related to realism.
- Liberalism emphasizes international cooperation—especially through worldwide free trade—to increase the total creation of wealth (regardless of its distribution among states). Liberalism is conceptually related to idealism.
- Most international exchanges entail some conflicting interests and some mutual interests on the part of the states involved. Deals can be made because both sides benefit, but conflict over specific outcomes necessitates bargaining.
- Globalization is conceived differently by various scholars, but generally refers to the growing scope, speed, and intensity of connectedness worldwide. The process may be

weakening, strengthening, or transforming the power of states. Antiglobalization activists oppose growing corporate power but disagree on goals and tactics.

- The volume of world trade is very large—about one-sixth of global economic activity—and is concentrated heavily in the states of the industrialized West (Western Europe, North America, and Japan/Pacific).
- Trade creates wealth by allowing states to specialize in producing goods and services for which they have a comparative advantage (and importing other needed goods).
- The distribution of benefits from an exchange is determined by the price of the goods exchanged. With many buyers and sellers, prices are generally determined by market equilibrium (supply and demand).
- Communist states during the Cold War operated centrally planned economies in which national governments set prices and allocated resources. Almost all these states are now in transition toward market-based economies, which seem to be more efficient in generating wealth. The transition has been very painful in Russia and Eastern Europe, less so in China.
- Politics intrudes into international markets in many ways, including the use of economic sanctions as political leverage on a target state. However, sanctions are difficult to enforce unless all major economic actors agree to abide by them.
- Mercantilists favor trade policies that produce a trade surplus for their own state. Such a positive trade balance generates money that can be used to enhance state power.
- States are becoming more and more interdependent, in that the well-being of states depends on each other's cooperation. Some scholars have long argued that rising interdependence makes military force a less useful form of leverage in international bargaining.
- States that have reduced their dependence on others, by pursuing self-sufficient autarky, have failed to generate new wealth to increase their well-being. Self-reliance, like central planning, has been largely discredited as a viable economic strategy.
- Through protectionist policies, many states try to protect certain domestic industries from international competition. Such policies tend to slow down the global creation of wealth but do help the particular industry in question.
- Protectionism can be pursued through various means, including import tariffs (the favored method), quotas, subsidies, and other nontariff barriers.
- Industries often lobby their own governments for protection. Governments in many states develop industrial policies to guide their efforts to strengthen domestic industries in the context of global markets.
- Certain products—especially food, intellectual property, services, and military goods—tend to deviate more than others from market principles. Political conflicts among states concerning trade in these products are frequent.
- A world market based on free trade is a collective good (available to all members regardless of their individual contribution) inasmuch as states benefit from access to foreign markets whether or not they have opened their own markets to foreign products.
- Because there is no world government to enforce rules of trade, such enforcement depends on reciprocity and state power. In particular, states reciprocate each other's cooperation in opening markets (or punish each other's refusal to let in foreign products). Although it leads to trade wars on occasion, reciprocity has achieved substantial cooperation in trade.
- Over time, the rules embodied in trade regimes (and other issue areas in IR) become the basis for permanent institutions, whose administrative functions provide yet further stability and efficiency in global trade.
- The World Trade Organization (WTO), formerly the GATT, is the most important multilateral global trade agreement. The GATT was institutionalized in 1995 with the

creation of the WTO, which expanded the focus on manufactured goods to consider agriculture and services. Intellectual property is another recent focus.

- In successive rounds of GATT negotiations over 50 years, states have lowered overall tariff rates (especially on manufactured goods). The Uruguay Round of the GATT, completed in 1994, added hundreds of billions of dollars to the global creation of wealth. The Doha Round began in 2003 and might conclude by 2006. Meanwhile textile tariffs were dropped worldwide in January 2005.
- Although the WTO provides a global framework, states continue to operate under thousands of bilateral trade agreements specifying the rules for trade in specific products between specific countries.
- Regional free trade areas (with few if any tariffs or nontariff barriers) have been created in Europe, North America, and several other less important instances. NAFTA includes Canada, Mexico, and the United States.
- International cartels are occasionally used by leading producers (sometimes in conjunction with leading consumers) to control and stabilize prices for a commodity on world markets. The most visible example in recent decades has been the oil producers' cartel, OPEC, whose members control more than half the world's exports of a vital commodity, oil.
- Free trade agreements have led to a backlash from politically active interest groups adversely affected by globalization; these include labor unions, environmental and human rights NGOs, and certain consumers.

KEY TERMS

mercantilism 298
liberalism 298
globalization 300
comparative advantage 303
centrally planned economy 306
transitional economies 307
state-owned industries 308
mixed economies 308
balance of trade 310
interdependence 311
autarky 313
protectionism 314
dumping 315
tariff 315
nontariff barriers 315
industrial policy 317
intellectual property rights 318
service sector 319
World Trade Organization (WTO) 322
General Agreement on Tariffs and Trade (GATT) 322
most-favored nation (MFN) 323
Generalized System of Preferences (GSP) 323
Uruguay Round 323
Doha Round 324
North American Free Trade Agreement (NAFTA) 327
cartel 330
Organization of Petroleum Exporting Countries (OPEC) 330

ONLINE PRACTICE TEST

Take an online practice test at *www.internationalrelations.net*

❑ A
❑ B
☑ C
❑ D

LET'S DEBATE THE ISSUE

America's Commitment to Free Trade: A Hollow Promise?

by Mir Zohair Husain

Overview After World War II, the United States played a leadership role in free trade, establishing the General Agreements on Tariffs and Trade (GATT) in 1947—renamed the World Trade Organization (WTO) in 1995—and the North American Free Trade Agreement (NAFTA) in 1993. In the early 1990s, the United States promoted a Free Trade Area of the Americas (North and South America). In fact, the United States consistently championed free trade as the best way for countries to use their comparative advantages for producing and exporting goods.

However, other countries question America's commitment to free trade, asserting that the United States aggressively advocates free trade, but only to open up foreign markets for U.S. goods and services while protecting its domestic businesses and farms. Moreover, critics say, the United States uses its enormous economic power to negotiate trade agreements that are in its favor, then disregards any clauses in those agreements that adversely affect America.

America's supporters counter that free trade remains the centerpiece of U.S. trade policies. After all, the international system underwent a dramatic economic transformation from the birth of the modern free-trade era in the mid-1940s. The evolution of globalization forced changes in free trade. No longer can countries—especially in Asia, Africa, and Latin America—compete economically without some degree of protectionism. Furthermore, the United States essentially plays by the same rules of free trade as other countries. In February 2004, the United States removed its steel tariff in immediate compliance with a WTO ruling that upheld the European Union's 2002 complaint that the United States was protecting its domestic steel industry.

Are critics correct that the United States only pays lip service to free trade? Or are such expectations unrealistic of the U.S. free trade policy in today's international political economy?

Argument 1 The United States Is Insincere About Free Trade

The U.S. sometimes fails to fulfill its free trade commitments because of domestic lobbyists. After September 11, 2001, despite Pakistan's support in America's war against terrorism, the Bush administration failed to fulfill its pledge to lower U.S. tariffs on Pakistani textiles.

> Two months after the September 11 terrorist attacks, the United States pledged $600 million in economic assistance to Pakistan. . . . Last February, the United States gave Pakistan a three-year package of trade bonuses, including the relaxation of quotas on certain textile imports. But many of the breaks affected products that Pakistan did not produce in substantial volume. Three weeks ago, Pakistan's commerce minister, Humayun Akhtar Khan, said that only about $20 million out of $143 million in potential benefits actually appeared in the first year. (Daniel Altman. "Trade Pact With Pakistan Reflects Politics, Not Economics, Critics Say." *The New York Times,* July 2, 2003.)

The United States promotes free trade only when it is in its national interests. Repeatedly, the United States urges other states to open up their domestic markets and practice free trade. However, Vietnam's catfish industry illustrates that the United States is not above later arbitrarily changing those trade rules in its favor.

> The United States government has just added a final flourish of hypocrisy to its efforts to crush the Vietnamese catfish industry under a mountain of protectionism. The Vietnamese . . . have been declared trade violators deserving permanent, prohibitive tariffs by the United States International Trade Commission.
>
> The case against the Vietnamese was brutally rigged by American fishing and political interests. . . . No convincing evidence was presented that Vietnam is dumping its fish on

the American market at prices below cost. To the contrary, a competitive edge was clearly won by hundreds of thousands of Vietnamese fishermen who were encouraged by the United States itself to set aside old wartime enmities and enter the emerging world market. . . . [As a result]. . . . fillets imported from Vietnam [of] genuine, obvious catfish . . . can be called only "basa" or "tra" in this country [by order of Congress]. And they will also be saddled with punitive tariffs. ("The 'Free Trade' Fix Is In." *The New York Times,* July 25, 2003.)

Hypocritical trade policies harm the United States as well as other countries. By protecting its farmers and other businesses, the United States has provoked other countries—especially developing ones—to protect their markets and buy less from U.S. service industries.

> . . . the dominance of American manufacturing and agriculture has been eclipsed by the service industries. Such exports from banking to travel and tourism typically make up 25 percent to 30 percent of our annual exports. They are also one of the few bright spots in our trade balance: the service sector ended last year with a $49 billion trade surplus, preventing America's $435 billion trade deficit from being even larger. . . . [However,] out of frustration over the way America and Europe protect their farmers, textile producers and others, developing countries like Brazil are refusing to further open their markets to service imports. . . . [Hence,] maintaining our agricultural subsidies not only hurts the developing world, it also puts millions of American service jobs at risk. (Rick Lazio. "Some Trade Barriers Won't Fall." *The New York Times,* August 9, 2003.)

Argument 2 Claims of U.S. Trade Hypocrisy Are False

Today's commercial markets demand some protectionism in free trade. In an interdependent global system, even free traders such as the United States must employ some protectionist policies to remain competitive.

> . . . a seismic shift in the world economy [is being] brought on by three major developments. First, new political stability is allowing capital and technology to flow far more freely around the world. Second, strong educational systems are producing tens of millions of intelligent, motivated workers in the developing world, particularly in India and China, who are as capable as the most highly educated workers in the developed world but available to work at a tiny fraction of the cost. Last, inexpensive, high-bandwidth communications make it feasible for large work forces to be located and effectively managed anywhere. . . . these new developments call into question some of the key assumptions supporting the doctrine of free trade. (Charles Schumer and Paul Craig Roberts. "Second Thoughts on Free Trade." *The New York Times,* January 6, 2004.)

The principle of comparative advantage is outdated. A primary argument for free trade is that each country can be an economic winner if it concentrates on producing what it does best. However, multinational corporations have changed the very concept of comparative advantage.

> The case for free trade is based on the British economist David Ricardo's principle of "comparative advantage," the idea that each nation should specialize in what it does best and trade with others for other needs. . . .
>
> However, when Ricardo said that free trade would produce shared gains for all nations, he assumed that the resources used to produce goods, what he called the "factors of production," would not be easily moved over international borders. Comparative advantage is undermined if the factors of production can relocate to wherever they are most productive: in today's case, to a relatively few countries with abundant cheap labor. In this situation, there are no longer shared gains, some countries win and others lose. (Charles Schumer and Paul Craig Roberts. "Second Thoughts on Free Trade." *The New York Times,* January 6, 2004.)

The United States is making significant progress in pushing freer trade. The United States leads Europe and Japan in lowering subsidies to farmers and tariffs for agricultural imports as demanded by developing countries.

> Despite the billions of dollars in farm subsidies agreed to by the Bush administration under pressure from farm-state lawmakers, Washington has been a strong and constructive voice in pushing the wealthy countries toward a fairer agricultural policy. . . .
>
> Washington has rightly advocated that tariffs be capped at reasonably low levels, while Japan and the European Union prefer an "across the board" cut that would leave excessively high barriers in place. Of what use is a one-third reduction of Japan's 500 percent tax on imported rice? ("Inching Toward Trade Fairness." *The New York Times.* August 15, 2003.)

Questions

1. Give five examples illustrating how the United States has been a champion of free trade, and five examples illustrating how the United States uses its economic power to engage in protectionism.
2. Is it difficult for a country to be a free trader in today's competitive, globally interconnected system? Why or why not?

WEB LINK

America's Commitment to Free Trade

Selected Readings

Michael Lusztig. *The Limits of Protectionism: Building Coalitions for Free Trade.* Pittsburgh: University of Pittsburgh Press, 2004.

Mehdi Shafeddin. *Trade Policy at the Crossroads.* NY: Palgrave Macmillan, 2005.

Jobs in International Business

SUMMARY

Jobs in international business offer high pay, interesting work, and demanding hours for those with language and cultural skills .

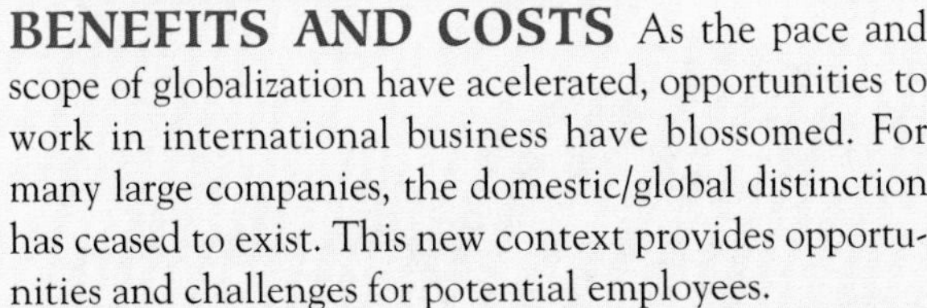

BENEFITS AND COSTS As the pace and scope of globalization have acelerated, opportunities to work in international business have blossomed. For many large companies, the domestic/global distinction has ceased to exist. This new context provides opportunities and challenges for potential employees.

Careers in international business offer many advantages. Business jobs can pay substantially more than those in governments or NGOs and can open opportunities to travel extensively and network globally. Foreign-based jobs mean relocation to another country to work and immerse oneself in another culture.

However, such a career choice also has potential costs. Many jobs require extensive hours, grueling travel, and frequent relocation. As with any job, promotion and advancement may fall victim to external circumstances such as global business cycles. And these jobs can be especially hard on families.

International opportunities arise in many business sectors. Banking, marketing (public relations), sales, and computing/telecommunications have seen tremendous growth in recent years. These jobs fall into three broad categories: (1) those located domestically, yet involving significant interactions with firms abroad; (2) domestic jobs working for foreign-based companies; and (3) those based abroad, for foreign or domestic firms.

SKILLS TO HONE One key to landing in the international business world is to develop to families of skills: those related to international relations and those related to business operations. Traditional MBA (Masters in Business Administration) and business school programs will be helpful for all three types of job, yet for jobs based abroad, employers often also look for a broader set of skills taught in economics, political science, and communications. Thus, not only traditional business skills, but language and cultural skills, are essential. Employers look for those who have knowledge of a country's human and economic geography as well as culture. Experience with study abroad, especially including working abroad, can help show an ability to adapt and function well in other cultures. Strong analytical and especially writing abilities also matter greatly to employers.

Research also helps in landing a job. Employers often look for knowledge of a particular industry or company, in order to make best use of an employee's language and cultural skills. Of course, while experience in non-international business never hurts, be mindful that the practices, customs, and models of business in one country may not apply well abroad. Cross-cultural skills combined with substantive business knowledge in order to translate the operational needs of companies from the business world to the global realm are highly valued.

RESOURCES

Edward J. Halloran, *Careers in International Business*, 2nd ed. NY: McGraw-Hill, 2003.

Deborah Penrith, ed., *The Directory of Jobs and Careers Abroad*, 12th ed. Oxford, UK: Vacation Work Publications, 2005.

http://www.rileyguide.com/internat.html
http://www.jobsabroad.com/search.cfm
http://www.transitionsabroad.com/listings/work/careers/index.shtml

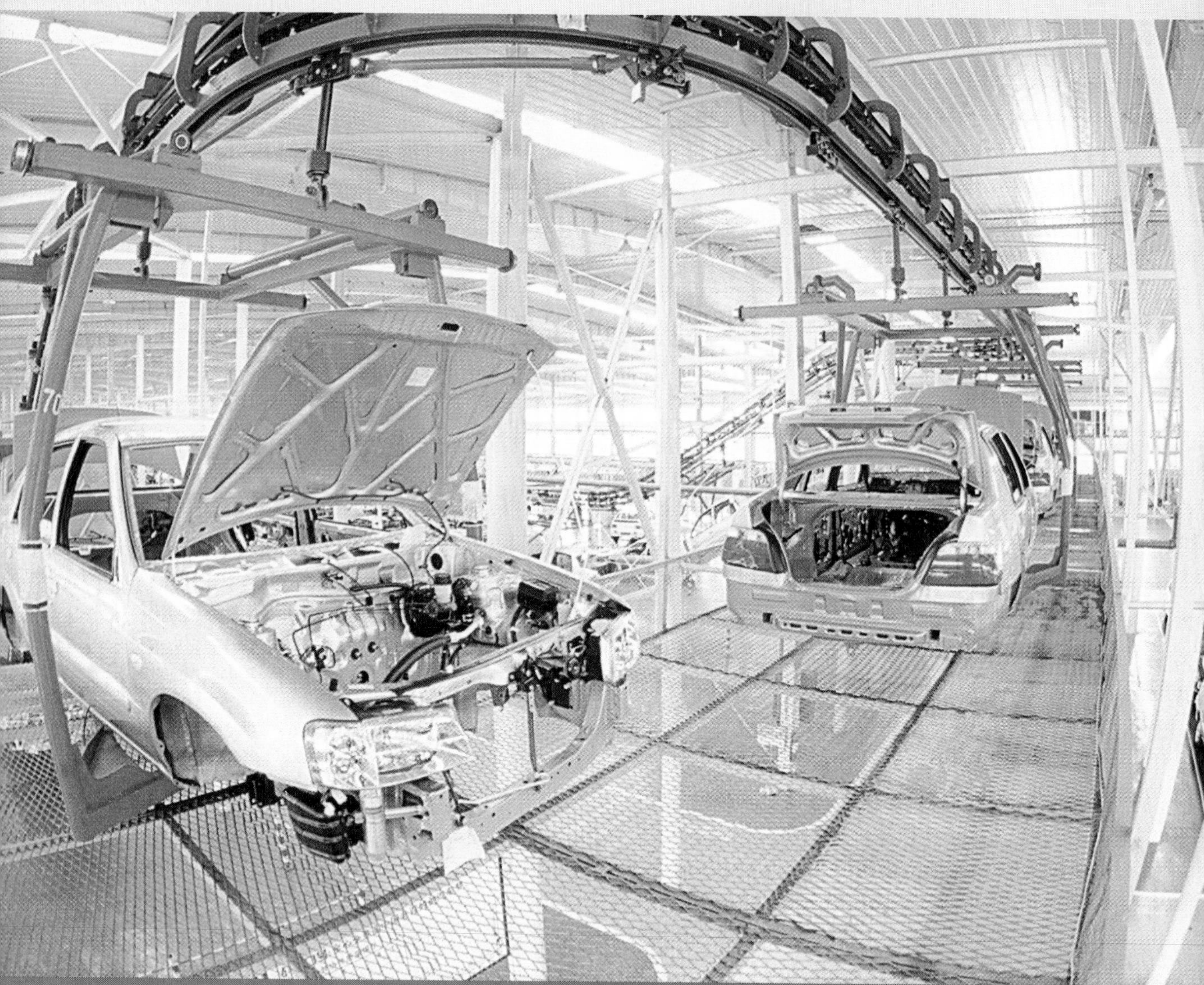

Chinese auto factory, 2003.

About Money

The Currency System

International Currency Exchange • Why Currencies Rise or Fall • Central Banks • The World Bank and the IMF

State Financial Positions

National Accounts • International Debt • The Position of the United States • The Position of Russia and Eastern Europe • The Position of Asia

Multinational Business

Multinational Corporations • Foreign Direct Investment • Host and Home Government Relations • Business Environments

CHAPTER 9

Money and Business

About Money

This chapter summarizes the politics of the world monetary system and then discusses the role of private companies as nonstate actors in the world economy. The monetary system is just one aspect of the political environment governments create, an environment that shapes the rules for international business and the context for the actions of multinational corporations (MNCs).

Imagine a world *without* money. In order to conduct an economic exchange, the goods being exchanged would have to be brought together in one place and traded in quantities reflecting the relative values the parties placed on them. This kind of trade, involving no money, is called *barter*. It still occurs sometimes when monetary systems do not operate well. For example, during the Angolan civil war in the 1990s, when the government's currency dropped to one-billionth its value, transactions were commonly expressed in terms of cans of beer.

The unit of currency used in an economy is arbitrary, but it must have roughly the same value for different people. With money, goods can move directly from sellers to buyers without having to meet in a central place. In a world economy, goods can flow freely among many states—the exchange of money keeps track of who owes whom for what. Money provides a single medium against which all goods can be valued. Different buyers and sellers place different values on goods, but all buyers and sellers place about the same value on money, so it serves as a standard against which other values can be measured.

Money itself has little or no inherent value. What gives it value is the widespread belief that it has value—that it can be exchanged for goods. Because it depends on the willingness of people to honor and use it, money's value rests on trust. Governments have the job of creating money and of maintaining public confidence in its value. For money to have stable value, the political environment must be stable. Political instability erodes public confidence that money today will be exchangeable for needed goods tomorrow. The result is inflation (discussed later in this chapter).

Due to the nature of state sovereignty, the international economy is based on national currencies, not a world currency. One of the main powers of a national government is to create its own currency as the sole legal currency in the territory it controls. The national currencies are of no inherent value in another country, but can be exchanged one for another.[1] How can the value of goods or currencies be judged in a world lacking a central government and a world unit of money?

Traditionally, for centuries, the European state system used *precious metals* as a global currency, valued in all countries. *Gold* was most important, and *silver* second. These metals had inherent value because they looked pretty and were easily molded into jewelry or similar objects. They were relatively rare, and the mining of new gold and silver was relatively slow. These metals lasted a long time, and they were difficult to dilute or counterfeit.

Over time, gold and silver became valuable *because* they were a world currency—because other people around the world trusted that the metals could be exchanged for future goods—and this overshadowed any inherent functional value of gold or silver. Bars of gold and silver were held by states as a kind of bank account denominated in an international currency. These piles of gold (literal and figurative) were the object of mercantilist trade policies in past centuries (see Chapters 2 and 8). Gold has long been a key power resource with which states could buy armies or other means of leverage.

In recent years the world has not used such a **gold standard** but has developed an international monetary system divorced from any tangible medium such as precious metals. Even today, some private investors buy stocks of gold or silver at times of political instability, as a haven that would reliably have future value. But gold and silver have now become basically like other commodities, with unpredictable fluctuations in price. The change in the world economy away from bars of gold to purely abstract money makes international economics more efficient; the only drawback is that without tangible backing in gold, currencies may seem less worthy of people's confidence.

The Currency System

Exchange Rates

Today, national currencies are valued against each other, not against gold or silver. Each state's currency can be exchanged for a different state's currency according to an **exchange rate**—defining, for instance, how many Canadian dollars are equivalent to one U.S. dollar. These exchange rates are important because they affect almost every international economic transaction—trade, investment, tourism, and so forth.[2] We will consider first the mechanics by which exchange rates are set and adjusted, then the factors influencing the longer-term movements of exchange rates, and finally the banking institutions that manage these issues.

International Currency Exchange

Most exchange rates are expressed in terms of the world's most important currencies—the U.S. dollar, the Japanese yen, and the EU's euro. Thus, the rate for exchanging Danish kroner for Brazilian reals depends on the value of each relative to these world currencies. Exchange rates that most affect the world economy are those *within* the G7 states—U.S. dollars, euros, yen, British pounds, and Canadian dollars. China has held its currency at a fixed rate to the U.S. dollar in recent years.

---

[1] Solomon, Robert. *Money on the Move: The Revolution in International Finance Since 1980*. Princeton, 1999. Blecker, Robert A. *Taming Global Finance: A Better Architecture for Growth and Equity*. Washington, DC: Economic Policy Institute, 1999. Cohen, Benjamin J., *The Future of Money*. Princeton, 2004. Eichengreen, Barry. *International Monetary Arrangements for the 21st Century*. Washington, DC: Brookings, 1995.
[2] Aliber, Robert Z. *The New International Money Game*. Chicago, 2002.

The relative values of currencies at a given point in time are arbitrary; only the *changes* in values over time are meaningful. For instance, the euro happens to be fairly close to the U.S. dollar in value, whereas the Japanese yen is denominated in units closer to the U.S. penny. In itself this disparity says nothing about the desirability of these currencies or the financial positions of their states. However, when the value of the euro rises (or falls) *relative* to the dollar, because euros are considered more (or less) valuable than before, the euro is said to be strong (or weak).

Some states do not have **convertible currencies.** The holder of such money has no guarantee of being able to trade it for another currency. Such is the case in states cut off from the world capitalist economy, such as the former Soviet Union. Few such states remain, but a lingering challenge is to make the Russian ruble a fully convertible currency (see "The Position of Russia and Eastern Europe" later in this chapter). In practice, even nonconvertible currency can often be sold, in black markets or by dealing directly with the government issuing the currency, but the price may be extremely low.

Some currencies are practically nonconvertible because they are inflating so rapidly that holding them for even a short period means losing money (this was the biggest problem with the Russian ruble in the 1990s). Nobody wants to hold currency that is rapidly inflating—losing value relative to goods and services. So inflation reduces a currency's value relative to more stable (more slowly inflating) currencies.

IT'S JUST MONEY

Money has value only because people trust its worth. Inflation erodes a currency's value if governments print too much money or if political instability erodes public confidence in the government. Brazil initially survived the loss of confidence in emerging markets that resulted from the 1997 Asian financial crisis. The next year, however, Brazil had to devalue its currency. This trader reacts to a stock market crash in 1998, after domestic politics threatened a $41 billion IMF agreement and shook investors' confidence in Brazil's economy.

The industrialized West has kept inflation relatively low—mostly below 5 percent annually—since 1980. (The 1970s saw inflation of more than 10 percent per year in many industrialized economies, including the United States.) Inflation in the global South is lower than a decade ago (see Table 9.1). Latin America brought inflation from 750 percent to below 15 percent, while China and South Asia got inflation rates below 5 percent. Most dramatically, in Russia and other former Soviet republics, inflation rates of more than 1,000 percent came down to less than 10 percent.

Extremely high, uncontrolled inflation—more than 50 percent per month, or 13,000 percent per year—is called **hyperinflation.** The 10-billion-dinar notes printed by Serbia in 1993 were worth only pennies after hyperinflation reached 100 trillion percent per year. Even at less extreme levels, currencies can lose 95 percent of their value in a year. In such conditions, money loses 5 percent of its value every week, and it becomes hard to conduct business domestically, let alone internationally.

In contrast with nonconvertible currency, **hard currency** is money that can be readily converted to leading world currencies (which now have relatively low inflation). For example, a Russian oil producer can export oil and receive payment in euros or another hard currency, which can then be used to pay for imported goods from outside Russia. But a

TABLE 9.1 ■ Inflation Rates by Region, 1993–2005

Region	Inflation Rate (percent per year) 1993	1996	2005[a]
Industrialized West	3	2	2
Russia and Eastern Europe	1,400	48	11
China	15	8	4
Middle East	27	34	4
Latin America	750	19	6
South Asia	6	6	7
Africa	112	37	10

[a]Data are estimates based on partial data for 2005.

Note: Regions are not identical to those used elsewhere in this book.

Source: Adapted from United Nations. *World Economic Situation and Prospects 2006.* New York: United Nations, 2006, pp. 133–4.

Russian sausage producer selling products within Russia would be paid in rubles, which could not be used outside the country.

States maintain **reserves** of hard currency. These are the equivalent of the stockpiles of gold in centuries past. National currencies are now backed by hard-currency reserves, not gold. Some states continue to maintain gold reserves as well. The industrialized countries have financial reserves roughly in proportion to the size of their economies.

One form of currency exchange uses **fixed exchange rates.** Here governments decide, individually or jointly, to establish official rates of exchange for their currencies. For example, the Canadian and U.S. dollars were for many years equal in value; a fixed rate of 1-to-1 was maintained (this is no longer true). States have various means for trying to maintain, or modify, such fixed rates in the face of changing economic conditions (see "Why Currencies Rise or Fall" later in this chapter).

Floating exchange rates are now more commonly used for the world's major currencies. Rates are determined by global currency markets in which private investors and governments alike buy and sell currencies. There is a supply and demand for each state's currency, with prices constantly adjusting in response to market conditions. Just as investors might buy shares of General Motors stock if they expected its value to rise, so they would buy a pile of Japanese yen if they expected that currency's value to rise in the future. Through short-term speculative trading in international currencies, exchange rates adjust to changes in the longer-term supply and demand for currencies.

There are major international currency markets in a handful of cities—the most important being New York, London, Zurich (Switzerland), Tokyo, and Hong Kong—linked together by instantaneous computerized communications. These markets are driven in the short term by one question: What will a state's currency be worth in the future relative to what it is worth today? These international currency markets involve huge amounts of money—a trillion and a half dollars every day—moving around the world (actually only the computerized information moves). They are private markets, not as strongly regulated by governments as are stock markets.[3]

[3] O'Brien, Richard. Who Rules the World's Financial Markets? [review article]. *Harvard Business Review* 73 (2), 1995: 144–51.

National governments periodically *intervene* in financial markets, buying and selling currencies in order to manipulate their value. (These interventions may also involve changing interest rates paid by the government; see pp. 348–349.) Such government intervention to manage the otherwise free-floating currency rates is called a **managed float** system. The leading industrialized states often, but not always, work together in such interventions. If the price of the U.S. dollar, for instance, goes down too much relative to other important currencies (a political judgment), governments will step into the currency markets, side by side with private investors, and buy dollars. With this higher demand for dollars, the price may then stabilize and perhaps rise again. (If the price got too high, governments would step in to sell dollars, increasing supply and driving the price down.) Such interventions usually happen quickly, in one day, but may be repeated several times within a few weeks in order to have the desired effect.[4] Note that monetary intervention requires costly multilateral cooperation among states. Liberals point to such cooperation as evidence that states recognize their long-term interest in a mutually beneficial international economy.

In their interventions in international currency markets, governments are at a disadvantage because even acting together they control only a small fraction of the money moving on such markets; most of it is privately owned. Governments do have one advantage in that they can work together to have enough impact on the market to make at least modest changes in price. Governments can also operate in secret, keeping private investors in the dark regarding how much currency governments may eventually buy or sell, and at what price. Only *after* a coordinated multinational intervention into markets does the public find out about it. (If speculators knew in advance they could make money at the government's expense.)

A successful intervention can make money for the governments at the expense of private speculators. If, for example, the G7 governments step in to raise the price of U.S. dollars by buying them around the world (selling other hard currencies), and if they succeed, the governments can then sell again and pocket a profit. However, if the intervention fails and the price of dollars keeps falling, the governments will *lose* money and may have to keep buying and buying in order to stop the slide. In fact, if investors become aware of such moves, they may interpret this action as a signal that the currency being bought is weak, which could depress the price even further. In extreme cases, the governments might run out of their stockpiles of hard currencies before then and have to absorb a huge loss. Thus governments have to be realistic about the limited effects they can have on currency prices.

These limits were well illustrated in the *European currency crisis* of September 1992. The European Union (EU) tried to maintain the equivalent of a fixed exchange rate among the various European currencies while letting the European currencies as a whole float freely relative to the rest of the world (see "The Single European Act" on p. 385). For 1992, the British pound was pegged at 2.95 German marks, and if it slipped from that rate, European governments were supposed to take various actions to bring it back into line. This was called the **Exchange Rate Mechanism (ERM),** and it was a step toward establishing the euro (see "Monetary Union" on pp. 387–389).

In September 1992, Germans feared inflation due to the costs of reunifying their country and wanted to restrict money supply to prevent this. Britons were worried about recession and unemployment, and so wanted to loosen the money supply. Given these economic forces, currency speculators began to gamble that Britain would not be able to maintain the value of the British pound relative to the German mark.

---

[4] Kirshner, Jonathan. *Currency and Coercion: The Political Economy of International Monetary Power*. Princeton, 1997. Henning, C. Randall. *Currencies and Politics in the United States, Germany, and Japan*. Washington, DC: Institute for International Economics, 1994. Dominguez, Kathryn M., and Jeffrey A. Frankel. *Does Foreign Exchange Intervention Work?* Washington, DC: Institute for International Economics, 1993.

As the pound began to fall, the British government intervened to buy pounds and drive the price back up. But speculators, who controlled far more money than the European governments, kept selling pounds. The speculators were convinced that the British government would be unable to prop up the pound's value, and they proved correct. With no way to stop the decline, Britain pulled out of the ERM and allowed the pound to float freely; it quickly fell in value. All the pounds that the British government had bought during its intervention were then worth less—a loss of billions of dollars. The government's loss was the private speculators' gain. One financial fund manager, George Soros, made a billion dollars for his clients in a few weeks. Although such large profits are rare—and although Soros later lost half a billion dollars in a week—the episode illustrates the problem governments have in controlling exchange rates when most money is privately owned.

The problems of the 1992 European currency crisis recurred spectacularly in the 2001 Argentine financial collapse. Argentina in the 1990s had pegged the value of its currency at a fixed rate to the U.S. dollar—a wonderfully effective way to stop runaway inflation that had recently wreaked devastation on Argentina's economy. A dollar peg seemed to have worked well for Hong Kong (see pp. 360–361).

Tying the peso to the dollar, however, represented a loss of sovereignty over monetary policy, one of the key levers to control an economy. Just as Germany and Britain had different needs in 1992, so did Argentina and the United States in the late 1990s. As a historic U.S. expansion brought unprecedented prosperity (allowing interest rates to be kept relatively high), Argentina suffered four years of recession, but could not lower interest rates to stimulate growth. Argentina accumulated $132 billion in foreign loans, and could not service its debts. IMF assistance in restructuring debt was contingent on a tight financial policy of tax increases and spending cuts—a mistake during a major multiyear recession, according to critics. In 2001, as the United States and IMF stood by, Argentina's economy collapsed, two presidents resigned in short order, and a populist took power, defaulted on foreign debts, and devalued the peso to create jobs—an embarrassing chapter for the IMF and a painful one for Argentina. In 2003, Argentina defaulted on a $3 billion payment to the IMF, the largest default in IMF history.

PARTING OF THE WAYS?

Private investors, not central banks, control most of the money traded internationally—more than $1.5 trillion every day. Governments' attempts to maintain fixed rates of exchange typically run into trouble when countries' economies diverge, as happened to Argentina in 2001. China's currency (shown here in 2004) has been pegged at a fixed rate to the U.S. dollar in recent years, but China's growth and U.S. deficits put pressure on China in 2005 to let its currency increase in value relative to the dollar.

Now pressures are building in a vastly more important case—China's currency. Like in Europe in 1992 and Argentina in 2001, the current policy of "pegging" China's currency to the dollar does not adjust to different

POLICY PERSPECTIVES

President of China, Hu Jintao

PROBLEM *Balancing international political pressures with domestic economic concerns.*

BACKGROUND Imagine that you are the president of China. The Chinese economy has grown rapidly in the past decade. Growth rates have risen to near 10 percent as of 2005, exceeding nearly all countries in the developing world. In particular, China's exports have boomed during this period. In 2005, exports rose by 25 percent to nearly $750 billion. China's trade surplus exceeded $100 billion in 2005.

This economic growth is important for your country. Given the country's large population, increases in jobs are important to keep unemployment low. Higher wages help to ensure low birthrates (through the demographic transition; see pp. 440–441). Exports are a key part of this picture, contributing heavily to your economic growth. Exports generate hard currency for your economy and create jobs.

Your position in the international economy is unique, because China's currency, the yuan, has been pegged to the U.S. dollar for nearly a decade (and to a basket of currencies, with just small adjustments, starting in mid-2005). Thus, even though the demand for the yuan may rise and fall, China's exchange rate does not change much.

Many feel your pegged currency is one explanation for the tremendous economic growth and trade surplus. The demand for the yuan is high (to pay for your exports), but because its value cannot rise relative to the dollar, the peg keeps the yuan low. The result is that Chinese exports are much cheaper on the world market, making your goods very attractive.

Recently, however, two dangers have appeared on the horizon. The first is economic. Some economists believe your growth rates have been too high for too long, risking inflation. High inflation erodes the buying power of increased wages and could lead investors to pull their money out of your country. The second danger is political. Both Europe and the United States have complained bitterly about your pegged exchange rate and your trade surplus. The United States recently blamed the yuan-dollar peg for costing America 1.5 million jobs, further exacerbating political tensions.

SCENARIO Now imagine that the advanced economy countries approach you with possible membership into the G7. Their condition is that you allow the yuan to float freely on international currency markets. Such a move would be very popular in international political circles and would lessen the chances that your own economy will "overheat" and become inflationary. In the long run, such a move will ensure your further integration into the international economy. In addition, a closer link to G7 states would provide significant prestige to your government.

Of course, there are also dangers in this course of action. If the yuan rises rapidly in value, your exports will be less competitive internationally, risking a stall in a key engine of your economy. You also become more vulnerable to international currency shocks, such as the 1997 Asian economic crisis, which you avoided in large part due to your pegged exchange rate.

CHOOSE YOUR POLICY Do you remove the yuan-dollar peg? If yes, how do you make sure your economy stays on a moderate growth rate and your exports stay competitive? If no, how do you deal with the political pressure arising from your fixed exchange rate? Can you also run the risk your economy will grow too fast, risking inflation and domestic discontent?

economic conditions in China and the United States. In recent years, China has continued a monumental and sustained boom of rapid growth, while the United States suffered an economic slowdown and jobless recovery. China runs a big trade surplus while the United States runs a big trade deficit—more than $200 billion with China alone in 2005 and several times higher in total. Because of underlying U.S. economic problems, the value of the U.S. dollar dropped by about one-quarter against the European currency in 2001–2004. The same underlying trends would have pushed the dollar lower against the Chinese yuan, too, if rates floated freely. Instead, the dollar-yuan ratio was held artificially high, which makes China's exports to the United States cheaper and contributes to the trade imbalance and the loss of U.S. manufacturing jobs—an issue in U.S. domestic politics.

The Falling Dollar

In Lesotho, a poor country in southern Africa, the fall of the U.S. dollar and the Chinese dollar peg combined to inflict economic pain in 2005. Lesotho depends on textile exports to the United States, and garments account for 90 percent of the country's manufacturing industry. With less income received for each garment sold in U.S. markets, and more competition from Chinese textiles in 2005 (see p. 318), Lesotho saw large-scale layoffs and factory closings. Note that currency policies directly affect trade issues, but are not governed by the WTO regime.

Why Currencies Rise or Fall

In the short term, exchange rates depend on speculation about the future value of currencies. But over the long term, the value of a state's currency tends to rise or fall relative to others because of changes in the long-term supply and demand for the currency. *Supply* is determined by the amount of money a government prints. Printing money is a quick way to generate revenue for the government, but the more money printed, the lower its price. Domestically, printing too much money creates inflation because the amount of goods in the economy is unchanged but more money is circulating to buy them with. *Demand* for a currency depends on the state's economic health and political stability. People do not want to own the currency of an unstable country, because political instability leads to the breakdown of economic efficiency and of trust in the currency. Conversely, political stability boosts a currency's value. In 2001, when a new Indonesian president took office after a period of political and economic turmoil, the Indonesian currency jumped 13 percent in two days on expectations of greater stability.

A *strong* currency is one that increases its value relative to other currencies—not just in day-to-day fluctuations on currency markets, but in a longer-term perspective. A weak currency is the opposite. The strength of a state's currency tends to reflect that state's monetary policy and economic growth rate. Investors seek a currency that will not be watered down by inflation and that can be profitably invested in a growing economy.

To some extent, states have *common* interests—opposed to those of private investors—in maintaining stable currency exchange rates. This is hard to achieve. In 1995, when the U.S. dollar suddenly dropped from 110 Japanese yen to 80, U.S. goods in Japan became cheaper and Japanese goods imported into the United States became more expensive. The U.S. trade deficit with Japan shrank a bit. The next year, when the dollar strengthened to 110 yen again, the trade deficit widened again. By 1998, the dollar jumped to 140 yen, then down to 110 in 2000, then up over 130 in 2001, and back down to 105 in 2004.

This kind of instability in exchange rates disrupts business in trade-oriented sectors since companies face sudden and unpredictable changes in their plans for income and expenses (for example, how much will computer chips from Japan cost which are needed to manufacture computers in Taiwan). States also have a shared interest in currency stability because instability tends to be profitable for speculators at the expense of central banks—as it was for Britain in 1992. States also share an interest in the integrity of their currencies against counterfeiting, but "rogue" states may feel otherwise. In 2006, the Unites States accused North Korea of passing off tens of millions of dollars in extremely realistic counterfeit $100 bills—a direct gain for the North Korean regime at the expense of the U.S. Treasury.

Despite these shared interests in currency stability, states also experience *conflicts* over currency exchange. States often prefer a *low* value for their own currency relative to others, because a low value promotes exports and helps turn trade deficits into surpluses—as mercantilists especially favor (see "Balance of Trade" on p. 310).

PRICES SUBJECT TO CHANGE

Changes in the dollar-yen exchange rate—reflecting underlying trends in the two national economies as well as the two governments' monetary policies—directly affect the prices of imported goods like these U.S.-made Apple computers for sale in Japan, 1992.

To some extent, exchange rates and trade surpluses or deficits tend to adjust automatically toward equilibrium (the preferred outcome for liberals). An *overvalued* currency is one whose exchange rate is too high, resulting in a chronic trade deficit. The deficit can be covered by printing more money, which waters down the currency's value and brings down the exchange rate (assuming it is allowed to float freely).

Because they see adjustments as harmless, liberals are not bothered by exchange rate changes such as the fall of the dollar relative to the euro. These are viewed as mechanisms for allowing the world economy to work out inefficiencies and maximize overall growth.

A unilateral move to reduce the value of one's own currency by changing a fixed or official exchange rate is called a **devaluation.** Generally, devaluation is a quick fix for financial problems in the short term, but it can create new problems. It causes losses to foreigners who hold one's currency (which is suddenly worthless). Such losses reduce the trust people place in the currency. As a result, demand for the currency drops, even at the new lower rate. Investors become wary of future devaluations, and indeed such devaluations often follow one after another in unstable economies. A currency may be devalued by allowing it to float freely, often bringing a single sharp drop in values. This is what Britain did in the European currency crisis in 1992.

The weakening of a currency, while encouraging exports, carries dangers. For example, the Mexican peso dropped 20 percent in one day (50 percent over several months) when allowed to float freely in 1994. With imported goods shooting up in price, inflation jumped to a 45 percent annualized rate and standards of living fell. Mexico's dollar-denominated loans suddenly becoming more expensive to service since more pesos were needed to pay back each dollar of the loan. This led corporate profits to drop and the Bank of Mexico had to offer 50 percent interest rates to attract capital. The resulting economic dislocations set back Mexico's economic growth and development, although Mexico eventually stabilized and paid back its loans in 1997. In general, any sharp or artificial change in exchange rates tends to disrupt smooth international trade and interfere with the creation of wealth.

Central Banks

Central Banks

Governments control the printing of money. In some states, the politicians or generals who control the government directly control the amounts of money printed. It is not surprising that inflation tends to be high in those states, because political problems can often be solved by printing more money to use for various purposes. But in most industrialized countries, politicians know they cannot trust themselves with day-to-day decisions about printing money. To enforce self-discipline and enhance public trust in the value of money, these decisions are turned over to a **central bank.**[5]

The economists and technical experts who run the central bank seek to maintain the value of the state's currency by limiting the amount of money printed and not allowing high inflation. Politicians appoint the people who run the bank, but generally for long terms that do not coincide with those of the politicians. Thus, central bank managers try to run the bank in the national interest, a step removed from partisan politics. If a state leader orders a military intervention the generals obey, but if the leader orders an intervention in currency markets the central bank does not have to comply. In practice, the autonomy of central banks varies; the head of Thailand's central bank was fired by the prime minister in a dispute over interest rates in 2001.

In the United States, the central bank is the *Federal Reserve*, or the Fed. The "reserve" is the government's stockpile of hard currency. The Fed can affect the economy by releasing or hoarding its money. Internationally, it does this by intervening in currency markets (as described earlier). Multilateral interventions are usually coordinated by the heads of central banks and treasury (finance) ministries in the leading countries. The long-term, relatively nonpartisan perspective of central bankers makes it easier for states to achieve the collective good of a stable world monetary system.

Domestically, the Fed exercises its power mainly by setting the **discount rate**—the interest rate the government charges when it loans money to private banks. (Central banks have only private banks, not individuals and corporations, as their customers.) In effect, this rate controls how fast money is injected into the economy. If the Fed sets too low a discount rate, too much money will come into circulation and inflation will result. If the rate is set too high, too little money will circulate and consumers and businesses will find it hard to borrow as much or as cheaply from private banks; economic growth will be depressed. Again, a state leader cannot order the central bank to lower the discount rate and inject more money into the economy but can only ask for such action. The central bankers will inject the money only if they are convinced that it will not be too inflationary.

Central bank decisions about the discount rate have important international consequences. If interest rates are higher in one state than another, foreign capital tends to be attracted to the state with the higher rate. And if economic growth is high in a foreign country, more goods can be exported to it. So states care about other states' monetary policies. The resulting international conflicts can be resolved only politically (such as at G7 meetings), not technically, because each central bank, although removed from domestic politics, still looks out for its own state's interests. For example, in the unfolding global recession of 2001, the U.S. Fed worried more about slow economic growth than about inflation, so it lowered interest rates repeatedly. The European Central Bank, which controlled the new euro currency, was more worried about inflation than about slow growth. Therefore the Europeans waited longer to lower their lending rates.

Low U.S. interest rates helped pull the world economy out of the 2001 recession. But they also lowered the dollar's value (as did a wave of U.S. deficit spending), making imports

[5] Blinder, Alan S. *The Quiet Revolution: Central Banking Goes Modern*. Yale, 2004. Sinclair, Peter, and Juliette Healey, eds. *Financial Stability and Central Banks*. NY: Routledge, 2003.

more expensive. In 2001–2004, the dollar lost more than a quarter of its value against the euro. The Fed could prop up the dollar by raising interest rates (in effect choking off money and raising its value), but this would risk slowing economic growth and triggering a new recession.

Although central banks control sizable reserves of currency, they are constrained by the limited share of world money they own. Most wealth is controlled by private banks and corporations. As economic actors, states do not drive the direction of the world economy; in many ways they follow it, at least over the long run. However, states still have key advantages as actors in the international economy. Most important, states control the monopoly on the legal use of force (violent leverage) against which even a large amount of wealth usually cannot stand—leaders can jail corporate executives who do not follow the state's rules. Ultimately, then, political power is the state's trump card as an economic actor.

IT'S ALL RELATIVE

Gold historically served as a world currency but has now been largely replaced by the World Bank's SDRs ("paper gold"). Thus currencies are valued only against each other, not an external standard like gold. Here, currency trading in São Paulo, Brazil, 2006.

The World Bank and the IMF

Because of the importance of international cooperation for a stable world monetary system and because of the need to overcome collective goods problems, international regimes and institutions have developed around norms of behavior in monetary relations. Just as the UN institutionally supports regimes based on norms of behavior in international security affairs (see Chapter 7), the same is true in the world monetary regime.

As in security affairs, the main international economic institutions were created near the end of World War II. The **Bretton Woods system** was adopted at a conference of the winning states in 1944 (at Bretton Woods, New Hampshire). It established the *International Bank for Reconstruction and Development (IBRD)*, more commonly called the **World Bank,** as a source of loans to reconstruct the Western European economies after the war and to help states through future financial difficulties. (Later, the main borrowers were third world countries and, in the 1990s, Eastern European ones.) Closely linked with the World Bank was the **International Monetary Fund (IMF).** The IMF coordinates international currency exchange, the balance of international payments, and national accounts (discussed shortly). The World Bank and the IMF continue to be the pillars of the international financial system. (The roles of the World Bank and the IMF in third world development are taken up in Chapter 13.)[6]

World Bank

Bretton Woods set a regime of stable monetary exchange, based on the U.S. dollar and backed by gold, which lasted from 1944 to 1971.[7] During this period, the dollar had a fixed

[6] Fischer, Stanley. *IMF Essays from a Time of Crisis: The International Financial System, Stabilization, and Development*. MIT, 2004.

[7] Eichengreen, Barry. *Globalizing Capital: A History of the International Monetary System*. Princeton, 1996. Andrews, David M., C. Randall Henning, and Louis W. Pauly, eds. *Governing the World's Money*. Cornell, 2002.

THINKING THEORETICALLY

Stability of Exchange Rates

This and the next two "Thinking Theoretically" boxes will take up the collective goods problem (see pp. 103–104) in several areas of international political economy. Relatively stable exchange rates for international currency can be seen as a collective good, in that all members of the international economy benefit from a stable framework for making investments and sales, yet an individual country can benefit from devaluing its own currency. (Whether such benefits are actually economic, or merely political benefits tied to perceptions of national interest, does not matter here, as long as state leaders perceive that defection from existing exchange rates can benefit their countries.)

According to the theory of collective goods, international exchange rate stability should be more readily achieved in two circumstances—under hegemony and under a small-group arrangement. Hegemonic stability, in this theory, includes providing backing for world currency stability, using the hegemon's own economic clout and its influence over other great powers. Lacking a hegemon, collective goods are thought to be easiest to assure if controlled by a small group rather than one with many members. In the small-group setting, defectors stand out and mutual cooperation is more readily enforced.

Hegemonic stability theory would seem to predict more and more stable currency exchange rates over the past decade as U.S. hegemony has increased. Especially stable periods should have been those of greatest U.S. strength and engagement in world affairs—after the 1991 Gulf War (and the Soviet collapse), at the height of U.S. economic prosperity in the late 1990s, and in the aftermath of the September 2001 terrorist attacks. In fact, exchange rates have been fairly volatile over that decade of unprecedented U.S. hegemony.

Followers of the small-group theory (which is not incompatible with the hegemonic approach) would be interested in the 1999 expansion of the G7 to a "Group of 20" for purposes of stabilizing global markets in future financial crises. Realizing that, even acting together, they cannot control global financial turmoil, the G7 members held a G20 meeting with Russia, China, India, Indonesia, Brazil, Mexico, Argentina, Turkey, South Korea, South Africa, Saudi Arabia, Australia, and the European Union. At that time, control of international monetary coordination also was shifting slightly away from the G7 and toward the IMF's governing committee, which has 24 state members. Collective goods theory would predict that such expansions would weaken exchange rate stability. This may help to explain recent volatility in exchange rates. Eventually, a new core group with fewer members might have to be formed to restore stability.

value equal to 1/35 of an ounce of gold, and the U.S. government guaranteed to buy dollars for gold at this rate (from a Fort Knox, Kentucky, stockpile). Other states' currencies were exchanged at fixed rates relative to the dollar. These fixed exchange rates were set by the IMF based on the long-term equilibrium level that could be sustained for each currency (rather than short-term political considerations). The international currency markets operated within a narrow range around the fixed rate. If a country's currency fell more than 1 percent from the fixed rate, the country had to use its hard-currency reserves to buy its own currency back and thus shore up the price. (Or, if the price rose more than 1 percent, it had to sell its currency to drive the price down.)

The gold standard was abandoned in 1971—an event sometimes called the "collapse of Bretton Woods." The term is not quite appropriate: the institutions survived, and even the monetary regime underwent more of an adjustment than a collapse. The U.S. economy no longer held the overwhelming dominance it had in 1944—mostly because of European and Japanese recovery from World War II, but also because of U.S. overspending on the

Vietnam War and the outflow of U.S. dollars to buy oil. Throughout the 1950s and 1960s, the United States had spent dollars abroad to stimulate world economic growth and fight the Cold War, but these had begun to far exceed the diminishing stocks of gold held by the Federal Reserve. So successful were the efforts to reinvigorate the economies of Japan and Europe that the United States suffered a relative decline in its trade position.

As a result, the dollar became seriously overvalued. By 1971, the dollar was no longer worth 1/35 of an ounce of gold, and the United States had to abandon its fixed exchange rate—much as Britain did in its 1992 crisis. President Nixon unilaterally dumped the dollar-gold system, and the dollar was allowed to float freely; soon it had fallen to a fraction of its former value relative to gold.

The abandonment of the gold standard was good for the United States and bad for Japan and Europe, where leaders expressed shock at the unilateral U.S. actions. The interdependence of the world capitalist economy, which had produced record economic growth for all the Western countries after World War II, had also created the conditions for new international conflicts.

To replace gold as a world standard, the IMF created a new world currency, the **Special Drawing Right (SDR).** The SDR has been called "paper gold" because it is created in limited amounts by the IMF, is held as a hard-currency reserve by states' central banks, and can be exchanged for various international currencies. The SDR is today the closest thing to a world currency that exists, but it cannot buy goods—only currencies. And it is owned only by states (central banks), not by individuals or companies.

The value of the U.S. dollar was pegged to the SDR rather than to gold, at a fixed exchange rate (but one that the IMF periodically adjusted to reflect the dollar's strength or weakness). SDRs are linked in value to a basket of several key international currencies. When one currency rises a bit and another falls, the SDR does not change value much; but if all currencies rise (worldwide inflation), the SDR rises with them.

Since the early 1970s, the major national currencies have been governed by the managed float system. Transition from the dollar-gold regime to the managed float regime was difficult. The United States was no longer dominant enough to single-handedly provide stability to the world monetary system. States had to bargain politically over the targets for currency exchange rates in the meetings now known as G7 summits. (In 1997, Russia joined the G7 summits, making it the G8, but Russia usually does not participate in meetings on economic affairs, so the group still often meets as the G7.)

The technical mechanisms of the IMF are based on each member state's depositing financial reserves with the IMF. Upon joining the IMF, a state is assigned a *quota* for such deposits, partly of hard currency and partly of the state's own currency (this quota is not related to the concept of trade quotas, which are import restrictions). The quota is based on the size and strength of a state's economy. A state can then borrow against its quota (even exceeding it somewhat) to stabilize its economy in difficult times, and repay the IMF in subsequent years.

The International Monetary Fund

Unlike the UN General Assembly, the IMF and the World Bank use a *weighted voting* system—each state has a vote equal to its quota. Thus the G7 states control the IMF, although nearly all the world's states are members. The United States has the single largest vote, and its capital city is headquarters for both the IMF and the World Bank.

Since 1944, the IMF and the World Bank have tried to accomplish three major missions. First they sought to provide stability and access to capital for states ravaged by World War II, especially Japan and the states of Western Europe. This mission was a great success, leading to growth and prosperity in those states. Second, especially in the 1970s and 1980s but still continuing today, the World Bank and the IMF have tried to promote economic development in poor countries. That mission was far less successful—

as seen in the lingering (and even deepening) poverty in much of the global South (see Chapter 12). The third mission, in the 1990s, was the integration of Eastern Europe and Russia into the world capitalist economy. This effort posted a mixed record and the long-term outlook remains promising but uncertain.

State Financial Positions

As currency rates change and state economies grow, the overall positions of states relative to each other shift.

National Accounts

The IMF maintains a system of *national accounts* statistics to keep track of the overall monetary position of each state. A state's **balance of payments** is like the financial statement of a company: it summarizes all the flows of money in and out of the country. The system itself is technical and not political in nature. Essentially, three types of international transactions go into the balance of payments: the current account, flows of capital, and changes in reserves.

The *current account* is basically the balance of trade discussed in Chapter 8. Money flows out of a state to pay for imports and flows into the state to pay for exports. The goods imported or exported include both merchandise and services. For instance, money spent by a British tourist in Florida is equivalent to money spent by a British consumer buying Florida oranges in a London market; in both cases money flows into the U.S. current account. The current account includes two other items. *Government transactions* are military and foreign aid grants, as well as salaries and pensions paid to government employees abroad. *Remittances* are funds sent home by companies or individuals outside a country. For example, a Ford Motor Company subsidiary in Britain may send profits back to Ford in Detroit. Conversely, a British citizen working in New York may send money to her parents in London.

The second category in the accounts is *capital flows*, which are foreign investments in, and by, a country.[8] Capital flows are measured in *net* terms—the total investments and loans foreigners make *in* a country minus the investments and loans that country's companies, citizens, and government invest in *other* countries. Most of such investment is private, although some is by (or in) government agencies and state-owned industries. Capital flows are divided into **foreign direct investment** (or *direct foreign investment*)—such as building a factory, owning a company, or buying real estate in a foreign country—and indirect *portfolio investment*, such as buying stocks and bonds or making loans to a foreign company. These various kinds of capital flows have somewhat different political consequences (see "International Debt" and "Foreign Direct Investment" later in this chapter), but they are basically equivalent in the overall national accounts picture.

The third category, *changes in foreign exchange reserves*, makes the national accounts balance. Any difference between the inflows and outflows of money (in the current account and capital flows combined) is made up by an equal but opposite change in reserves. These changes in reserves consist of the state's purchases and sales of SDRs, gold, and hard currencies other than its own, and changes in its deposits with the IMF. If a state has more money flowing out than in, it gets that money from its reserves. If it has more money flowing in than out, it puts the money in its reserves.

[8] Kindleberger, Charles P. *International Capital Movements*. Cambridge, 1987.

Thus, national accounts always balance in the end. At least, they almost balance; there is a residual category—errors and omissions—because even the most efficient and honest government (many governments are neither) cannot keep track of every bit of money crossing its borders.

International Debt

In one sense, an economy is constantly in motion, as money moves through the processes of production, trade, and consumption. But economies also contain *standing wealth*. The hard-currency reserves owned by governments are one form of standing wealth, but not the most important. Most standing wealth is in the form of homes and cars, farms and factories, ports and railroads. In particular, *capital* goods (such as factories) are products that can be used as inputs for further production. Nothing lasts forever, but standing wealth lasts for enough years to be treated differently from goods that are quickly consumed. The main difference is that capital can be used to create more wealth: factories produce goods, railroads support commerce, and so forth. Standing wealth creates new wealth, so the economy tends to grow over time. As it grows, more standing wealth is created. In a capitalist economy, money makes more money.

Interest rates reflect this inherent growth dynamic. *Real* interest rates are the rates for borrowing money above and beyond the rate of inflation (for instance, if money is loaned at an annual interest rate of 8 percent but inflation is 3 percent, the real interest rate is 5 percent). Businesses and households borrow money because they think they can use it to create new wealth faster than the rate of interest on the loan.

Borrowing and lending are like any other economic exchange; both parties must see them as beneficial. The borrower values the money now more than the promise of more money in the future, whereas the lender values the promise of more money in the future more than the money now. The distribution of benefits from the exchange is, as usual, subject to bargaining. Imagine that a profitable business can use a loan to generate 10 percent annual profit (above the inflation rate). At one extreme, the business could pay 1 percent real interest and keep 9 percent of the profit for itself; at the other, it could pay 9 percent interest and keep 1 percent.

The actual split, reflected in interest rates, is determined by the market for money. Lenders seek out businesses profitable enough to pay high interest; businesses seek out lenders with enough idle cash to lend it at low interest rates. In an imperfect but workable way, the supply and demand for money determine interest rates.

Imagine now that the business borrowing the money is an entire state—the government, companies, and households. If the state's economy is healthy, it can borrow money from foreign governments, banks, or companies and create enough new wealth to repay the debts a few years later. But states, like businesses, sometimes operate at a loss; then their debts mount up. In a vicious circle, more and more of the income they generate goes to paying interest, and more money must be borrowed to keep the state in operation. If its fortunes reverse, a state or business can create wealth again and over time pay back the principal on its debts to climb out of the hole. If not, it will have to begin selling off part of its standing wealth (buildings, airplanes, factories, and the like). The *net worth* of the state or business (all its assets minus all its liabilities) will decrease.

When a state's debts accumulate, the standing wealth of the state is diminished as assets are sold off to pay the debts. Yet failure to repay debts makes it hard to borrow in the future, a huge impediment to economic growth. In the 1970s and 1980s, debts accumulated in some third world countries to the point of virtual national bankruptcy. The debts became unpayable, and the lenders (banks and governments) had to write them off the books or settle them at a fraction of their official value.[9] In 2001, Argentina collapsed under more than $100 billion of debt accumulated over the prior decade, and creditors had to accept less than one-third of their money in a 2005 restructuring deal.

The industrialized states, by contrast, have enough standing wealth that even in their most indebted times they have substantial net worth. Still, rising debts are encumbrances against the future creation of wealth, and foreign lenders come to own a greater share of the state's total standing wealth. Naturally, such a situation horrifies mercantilists. National debt to them represents a loss of power. It is the opposite of the pile of reserves that mercantilists would like to be sitting on.[10]

Why do states go into debt? One major reason is a trade deficit. In the balance of payments, a trade deficit must somehow be made up. It is common to borrow money to pay for a trade deficit. A second reason is the income and consumption pattern among households and businesses. If people and firms spend more than they take in, they must borrow to pay their bills. The credit card they use may be from a local bank, but that bank may be getting the money it lends to them from foreign lenders.

A third reason for national debt is government spending relative to taxation. Under the principles of **Keynesian economics** (named for economist John Maynard Keynes), governments sometimes spend more on programs than they take in tax revenue—*deficit spending*—to stimulate economic growth. If this strategy works, increased economic growth eventually generates higher tax revenues to make up the deficit. The government lends money to the nation and recovers it later from a healthier economy. Where does the government get this money? It could print more money, but this step would be inflationary so central banks try to prevent it. So the government often borrows the money, from both domestic and foreign sources.

Government decisions about spending and taxation are called **fiscal policy;** decisions about printing and circulating money are called **monetary policy.**[11] These are the two main tools available for government to manage an economy. There is no free lunch: high taxation chokes off economic growth, printing excess money causes inflation, and borrowing to cover a deficit places a mortgage on the state's standing wealth. Thus, for all the complexities of governmental economic policies and international economic transactions, a state's wealth and power ultimately depend more than anything on the underlying health of its economy—the education and training of its labor force, the amount and modernity of its capital goods, the morale of its population, and the skill of its managers. In the long run, international debt reflects these underlying realities.

Shifts in financial fortune among the great powers often accompany changing power relations. Consider how the past decade has changed the financial positions of the United States, of Russia and Eastern Europe, and of Asia. (The position of Europe, including the new European currency, is discussed in Chapter 10.)

The Position of the United States

The United States is an extraordinarily wealthy and powerful state. Its most *unique* strengths may be in the area of international security—as the world's only superpower—but its economic strengths are also striking. It is not only the world's largest economy but

---

[9] Cline, William R. *International Debt Reexamined*. Washington, DC: Institute for International Economics, 1994.

[10] Kapstein, Ethan B. *Governing the Global Economy: International Finance and the State*. Harvard, 1994. Helleiner, Eric. *States and the Reemergence of Global Finance: From Bretton Woods to the 1990s*. Cornell, 1994.

[11] Kirshner, Jonathan, ed. *Monetary Orders: Ambiguous Economics, Ubiquitous Politics*. Cornell, 2003.

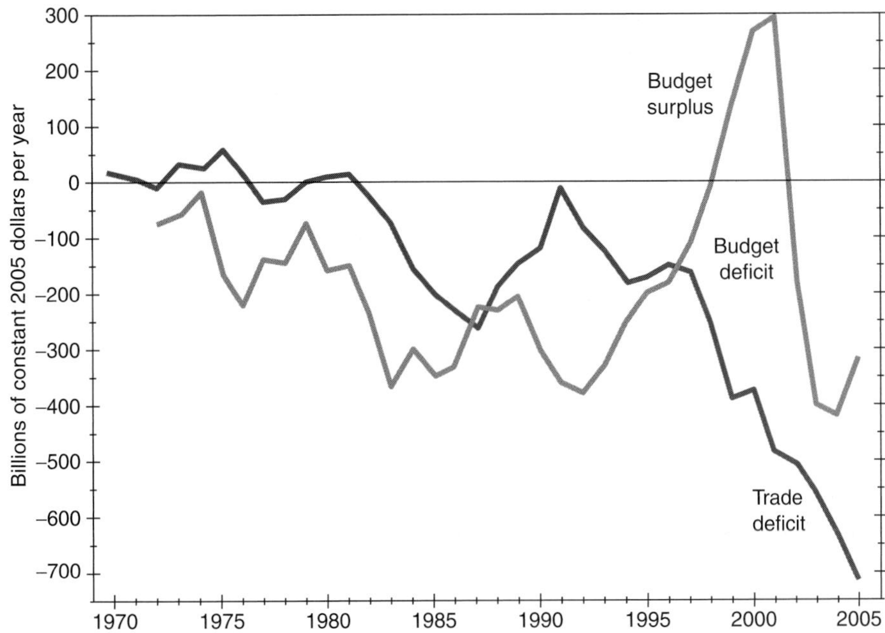

FIGURE 9.1 ■ U.S. Financial Position, 1970–2005

For decades the United States has imported more than it exported (the current account balance or trade deficit), and its government has spent more than its income (the budget deficit). The budget deficit leaves behind a large national debt.

Note: Trade deficit refers to current account balance.

Source: Based on data from World Bank and IMF.

also the most technologically advanced one in such growth sectors as computers, telecommunications, aviation and aerospace, and biotechnology. The U.S. position in scientific research and higher education is unparalleled in the world.

Trade Deficit

The U.S. position in the international economy, however, has shifted over the decades. U.S. hegemony peaked after World War II, then gradually eroded as competitors gained relative ground (especially in Western Europe and Asia). In the early 1950s, the U.S. economy (GDP) was about twice the size of the next six advanced industrial states *combined*. By the 1980s, its relative share of world GDP had dropped almost by half. In 1950, the United States held half of the world's financial reserves; by 1980, it held less than 10 percent. This long-term decline after the extraordinary post–1945 U.S. hegemony was a natural and probably unavoidable one. The shifting U.S. financial position since the 1980s is illustrated in Figure 9.1. In the early 1980s, the trade deficit (exports minus imports) grew from near zero to $200 billion in just a few years. The trade deficit shrank back, but then grew to over $500 billion a year by 2004. The budget deficit meanwhile jumped to $300 billion per year in the early 1980s, then closed in the 1990s and briefly became a large surplus, only to hit a deficit of $500 billion by 2004 as a result of war spending, tax cuts, and recession. These trends have caused alarm regarding U.S. international economic leadership.[12]

[12] Dam, Kenneth W. *The Rules of the Global Game: A New Look at U.S. International Economic Policy Making*. Chicago, 2001.

The U.S. economy showed strength in the mid- to late-1990s, as those of other industrialized countries (notably Japan) stumbled. Technological change and restructuring created strong growth of productivity, especially as computer networks took on more of the work. The United States ended the 1990s with all-time low unemployment, low inflation, robust growth, stock market gains, and a budget surplus. Despite these successes, the U.S. expansion eventually ran out of steam, the bubble of Internet investment burst, and the United States was again in recession by 2001—this time joined by all the world's major economies, and hammered painfully home by the economic disruptions that followed the September 2001 terrorist attacks.

While growth has resumed, the accumulated debt from 20 years of deficit spending remains. The U.S. government's **national debt** grew from about $1 trillion at the beginning of the 1980s to $3 trillion by the end of that decade, to $8 trillion today. The interest payments are equivalent to what would otherwise be a healthy rate of economic growth. Not long ago, the United States was the world's leading lender state; now it is the world's leading debtor state.

These U.S. financial trends have profound implications for the entire world political economy. They first undermined (in the 1980s), then reconstructed (in the 1990s), and then undermined again (since 2000) the leading U.S. role in stabilizing international trade and monetary relations, in assuring the provision of collective goods, and in providing capital for the economic development of other world regions. In a more decentralized, more privatized world economy with an uncertain U.S. role, collective goods problems would be harder to solve and free trade harder to achieve.

The Position of Russia and Eastern Europe

The United States has provided limited capital (investments, loans, and grants) to help get the Russian and Eastern European region on its feet again after the Cold War. The United States has not repeated in Russia and Eastern Europe the aid program that stimulated new growth in Western Europe and Japan after World War II.

Instead, states in this region face daunting challenges as they try to convert from centrally planned to capitalist economies and to join the world capitalist economy. These challenges include integration into the world trading system (membership in the WTO, bilateral trade agreements, and so forth) and attracting foreign investment. Among the most difficult tasks are the attempts of states in this region to join the international monetary system. These matter greatly because having a stable and convertible currency is a key element in attracting foreign business and expanding international trade.

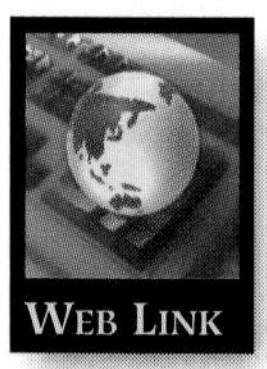

The IMF in Russia

Most of the states of the former Soviet bloc became members of the IMF and were assigned quotas. But the IMF and the World Bank would not make loans available freely to these states until their governments took strong action to curb inflation, balance government budgets, and assure economic stability. Such stability would have been easier to achieve with the foreign loans, however, creating a chicken-and-egg problem.

All the economies of the region experienced a deep depression (shrinking GDP) in 1989–1991. By 1992, only Poland had resumed economic growth—a 1 to 4 percent annual growth of GDP following a 20 percent shrinkage in 1990–1991. The rest of Eastern Europe (except Bulgaria and Slovakia) stopped shrinking by 1994. But the states of the former Soviet Union continued downward, until by 1996 the total economic activity of those states had been cut by half over seven years (see Table 9.2).

In general, the Eastern European countries have turned around their economies more effectively than have the former Soviet republics. Among the latter, Russia was better off than some others; it had inherited much of the Soviet Union's economic infrastructure and natural resources and was large enough to gain the attention of the West. But internal power

TABLE 9.2 ■ Economic Collapse in Russia and Eastern Europe

Country	Cumulative (10-Year) Change in GDP, 1990–1999
Former Soviet Republics[a]	–50%
Former Yugoslavia	–35%
Estonia, Latvia, and Lithuania	–29%
Bulgaria	–29%
Romania	–28%
Albania	–12%
Czech Republic	–11%
Slovakia	–1%
Hungary	–1%
Poland	+21%

[a] Russia, Ukraine, and 10 other CIS members.

Source: Authors' estimates based on United Nations, *World Economic and Social Survey 1999.* New York: United Nations, 1999, p. 263.

struggles created political instability in Russia, discouraging foreign investment. The costs of wars in Chechnya made matters worse. Russia was not a WTO member as of 2006. Inflation reached 1,500 percent in 1992 but was brought down to around 10 percent by 2005. Growth returned—over 6 percent a year in 2000–2005—and a new flat tax on income boosted tax collections but Russia's future remains uncertain.

Ukraine had even more severe economic woes (as did some other former Soviet republics). Ukraine's 1992 inflation rate of 2,700 percent was tamed eventually, but political zigzags slowed economic reform and Ukraine suffered eight straight years of negative GDP growth. Political instability over a disputed presidential election in 2004 placed further strain on Ukraine's economy. In next-door Belarus, democratic reforms evaporated and the transition from a centrally planned economy stalled. Thus, the states of Eastern Europe had varying experiences, ranging from Poland's relative speed in making the transition away from communism to Belarus's slowness. Russia was somewhere in between—itself a mix of successes and failures.

The region's financial problems were similar to those facing third world countries trying to stabilize their economies (see Chapter 13), but they were compounded by special problems resulting from the breakup of the Soviet Union. Some states printed their own currency while others kept using the Russian ruble (through the framework of the CIS). In other former Soviet republics—Azerbaijan, Armenia, Georgia, and Tajikistan—devastating wars wrecked economies and further fueled inflation.

The soaring inflation and general economic collapse throughout the region made it much harder to resolve all these problems and arrive at a stable political and economic environment in which IMF and World Bank assistance would be useful and not just wasted. In any case, the amounts of money available for such assistance were limited because of the economic recession of the early 1990s in the world's leading economies. Nonetheless, the former Soviet republics joined the IMF after negotiating reform plans. In 1996, creditor states renegotiated (to a longer-term basis) $40 billion in previous Russian debts; this reduced interest payments but did not address the underlying causes of the debts.

Several billion dollars were collected from the major economic powers in the early 1990s to create a "ruble-convertibility fund" that could be used to intervene in currency

BITTER FRUITS

Inflation and unemployment in Russia and other former Soviet republics in the 1990s have cut the GDP about in half and created political turmoil. These women in Moscow try to make ends meet by selling pickled vegetables grown in their yards, 1999.

markets to shore up the value of the Russian ruble if necessary. This fund, combined with other forms of economic assistance (mostly loans rather than grants), made about $20 billion available for the task of helping the region through its transition. Such a sum, however, was inadequate for such a massive, historic, and unprecedented transition of an entire economic system. By way of comparison, international bailouts of much smaller countries with less severe financial problems, such as Mexico and South Korea in the 1990s, each required tens of billions of dollars.

To get access to these assistance funds, Russia had to take steps to control inflation and government spending, sell off state-owned industry, and institute a market system throughout its economy. The attempt to implement such measures turned out to be even more painful than expected. Russian President Boris Yeltsin found himself challenged by a coalition of former communists and industry leaders, who demanded continuing state subsidies of major industries. To stop the subsidies risked alienating those political forces, deepening the shrinkage of GDP, and throwing more people out of work. But continuing the subsidies risked widening the budget deficit and triggering high inflation.

Organized crime emerged as a major problem in the 1990s; for example, in 1996 a U.S. entrepreneur was killed gangland-style in Moscow (this did not encourage foreign investment), and the chairman of Russia's central bank had his apartment windows shot out. "Plutocrats" seized formerly state-owned companies and drained their wealth into private bank accounts. The chaos of transition also provided fertile ground for corruption among government officials. In 2004, Russia's largest oil company (Yukos) was shut down by President Vladimir Putin due to nonpayment of a $10 billion tax bill, only to have its assets purchased by a state-owned business. While officials claim this move will lower corruption in the Russian oil market, critics denounced the move as politically motivated (Yukos's owner was an opponent of Putin).

The economic and financial problems of the region have been compounded by security problems—ethnic and national conflicts along the southern rim of the former Soviet Union—which disrupted trade and monetary relations. For example, rail traffic from Russia was disrupted by separatists in Georgia, and Azerbaijan cut off energy supplies to Armenia. The main oil pipeline from Azerbaijan went right through the bombed-out capital of Chechnya, and was shut down for years.

It appears that for some years to come, Russia will struggle to find the economic and political stability to integrate into the world capitalist economy. Until then, Russia and its neighbors remain largely cut off from the potential benefits that could result from stable convertible currencies, expanded trade, and increased foreign investment.

The Position of Asia

Financial positions in the leading economies of Asia in some ways were reversed from the U.S. path since the 1980s. Whereas the U.S. position deteriorated in the 1980s and early 1990s but strengthened in the late 1990s, the main Asian economies enjoyed a tremendous boom in the 1980s and early 1990s but suffered financial setbacks in the late 1990s (except in China). Only in the 2001 recession did Asia and North America find synchrony, along with Europe.

Japan led Asia up and down. Following decades of robust growth since the devastation of World War II, Japan by the 1980s seemed to be emerging as a possible rival to the United States as the world's leading industrial power. Japanese auto manufacturers gained ground on U.S. rivals when smaller cars became popular after the oil-price shocks of the 1970s. In electronics and other fields, Japanese products began to dominate world markets, and Japanese capital became a major economic force in nearby developing economies (such as China and Thailand) and even in the United States where Japanese creditors financed much of the growing U.S. national debt.

These successes masked serious problems. The economic growth of the 1980s drove prices of stocks and real estate to unrealistic levels based on speculation rather than inherent value. When these collapsed at the end of the 1980s, many banks were left with bad loans backed by deflated stocks and real estate. These losses were covered up, and the underlying problems—lax banking regulation, political cronyism, and outright corruption—persisted through the 1990s. A reform-oriented prime minister (Junichiro Koizumi) took office in 2001, but Japan faced a worldwide recession that depressed exports.

Despite the example of Japan's financial system, these mistakes were repeated almost exactly in the 1990s by the newly industrializing countries (NICs, see pp. 499–501) of East and Southeast Asia. Real estate and stocks became overvalued as rapid economic growth led to speculation and ever-rising expectations. Banks made massive bad loans based on the overvalued assets and got away with it because of political corruption and cronyism. In 1997, these economies suffered a serious financial crisis, which jumped across international borders and sent shock waves around the globe that reverberated for two years.

The *1997 Asian financial crisis* began when currency speculators began selling off the currencies of Southeast Asian countries. Thailand, the Philippines, Malaysia, and Indonesia were forced to let their currencies be devalued. Such pressure on currencies creates pressure on prospects for economic growth—because governments will have to cut back money supplies (raise interest rates) in response. The reduced prospects for economic growth in turn put pressure on stock prices, since companies will be less profitable. Also, currency devaluation reduces foreign investment (because investors lose confidence) and makes foreign loans harder to repay (since more local currency is needed to repay each unit of foreign currency). Thus, the currency problems of Asian countries led to stock market crashes in several of them. Other so-called *emerging markets* around the world—notably Brazil—suffered as investors generalized the problems in Asia.

The Philippines addressed the problem in the manner that international agencies and foreign investors preferred. After losing $1 billion unsuccessfully defending its currency's value, the Philippines let its currency float and then asked the IMF for a $1 billion stabilization loan, which the IMF approved in a week. In return for the IMF loan, the Philippines' government agreed to keep interest rates high and budget deficits low (to reduce inflation), to pass a tax reform law, and to tighten control of banks that had made bad real estate loans. These kinds of tough measures create political problems, especially when banks are politically connected or when governments are corrupt. The Philippines, by addressing such problems, won international approval.

Thailand promised, in return for a $16 billion IMF bailout, to close dozens of indebted banks, raise taxes, cut government deficits, and lower economic growth rates by more than half. The government of Thailand, a shaky coalition based on political patronage, soon collapsed as street protests vented anger at the economic downturn. A reform-minded prime minister was appointed and the situation stabilized.

Other Asian countries did not act decisively. In Malaysia, the prime minister annoyed foreign investors by accusing currency speculators, including George Soros (see p. 344), of political motives in undermining Asian economies, because of racism and differences regarding human rights. He said that currency speculation should be illegal. (Soros in fact has used his wealth to support programs in transitional countries to foster an "open society." But there is no reason to doubt that the speculators' motive in Malaysia was making money.) Malaysian controls on capital and currency had some success in this case.

The currency speculators, meanwhile, moved on to attack Indonesia, which had to let its currency fall, raise interest rates, and let its stock market drop. Within months, Indonesia too sought tens of billions of dollars in IMF loans, with the usual conditions attached. Indonesia resisted implementing the promised reforms, however, and its economy continued to slide (as did its political stability) in 1998. Conflict over the status of East Timor brought international criticism, which further decreased political stability. Riots and student protests eventually forced Indonesia's President Suharto to resign after 30 years of dictatorship. Megawati Sukarnoputri, the daughter of Suharto's archrival, became president in 2001 (until 2004).

Overall, in Thailand, Malaysia, and Indonesia, stock markets lost about half their value and currencies about a quarter of their value in the first nine months of 1997. Observers declared the "Asian economic miracle" to be at an end. However, many of these economies have seen a healthy resurgence since 1997.

China escaped harm from the 1997 crisis, for several reasons: Its economic growth had been less speculative (although rapid), its currency was not freely convertible, it held massive reserves of hard currency, and its government had shown the discipline necessary to bring inflation under control. Lowering the economic growth rate from 14 to 10 percent annually, the government reduced inflation from 20 percent to less than 4 percent in 1995–1997. The engineer of this tight-money policy, Zhu Rongji, became the Chinese prime minister in 1998, just as successful inflation-fighters became presidents of Brazil and Argentina in the 1990s. China then rode out the Asian crisis without devaluing its currency, by further lowering growth to 7 percent by 1999, still a very strong pace.

Hong Kong, like China, did not devalue in 1997. Just months after coming under Chinese control, Hong Kong became the central target of currency speculators. To maintain the Hong Kong dollar, which was (and still is) pegged at a fixed rate per U.S. dollar, the Hong Kong government had to raise interest rates drastically and watch the stock market lose a third of its value in weeks. The Hong Kong stock crash triggered a huge global sell-off, but the Hong Kong government remained firm in maintaining its currency's value—which it saw as critical to foreign investors' long-term confidence—despite the costs of financial collapse and economic slowdown. In the first test of China's "one country, two systems" formula, the Chinese government allowed the Hong Kong administration to manage the crisis.

When South Korea caught the "Asian flu," however, the stakes increased. South Korea is the largest of the NICs, an economic power in the region ranking behind only Japan and China. Yet by the end of 1997, South Korea's currency was down 20 percent, its stock markets were collapsing, and its banks were saddled with $50 billion in bad loans based on cronyism. The IMF stepped in with a $60 billion international bailout—the largest ever—and the Korean government adopted stringent austerity measures. Some nationalist South Koreans called the IMF agreement a Day of National Humiliation, but

Koreans elected a new reformist president, Kim Dae Jong—a former political prisoner. He convinced South Koreans that foreign investment was positive; they accepted the IMF and even started using it as a face-saving way to reduce the costs of extravagant status-oriented weddings and funerals.[13] Thus in South Korea, as in Thailand and Indonesia, the financial crisis brought about reform as well as pain.

The IMF—Playing Favorites?

The Asian crisis suddenly dried up huge sums of capital that had poured into Southeast Asia, doubling every two years and reaching nearly $100 billion annually. In 1997 and 1998, about $10 billion annually moved *out* of Southeast Asia. The capital flight also hit other so-called emerging markets in other regions. Brazil was the recurrent target of currency speculators, because Brazil found it hard to pass legislation to stem a $50 billion government deficit. Every time the Brazilian political system stumbled in making promised reforms, Brazil's stock market fell and its currency came under attack. It devalued in 1999.

Liquid Capital

In theory, the instant free flow of capital around the world—a result of global communications technologies—should stabilize economies. Investors can shift money quickly, and thus incrementally, as conditions indicate shifting strength and weakness of different currencies and economies. Instead of waiting for governments to devalue or revalue currencies when problems are far along, markets can gradually adjust values day by day. In practice, however, the global liquidity of capital has also shown a destabilizing tendency, as small events can be amplified and reverberate in distant locations. Thus the problems of Thailand became an Asian crisis and then an emerging-markets crisis, as liquid capital fled for cover at the speed of light.

The Asian financial crisis of 1997 illustrates the importance of currency exchange rates in overall economic stability and growth. Governments face a dilemma in that politically desirable policies—from stimulating growth and keeping taxes low to supporting banks and businesses owned by friends and relatives—tend to undermine currency stability. If allowed to continue, such policies may lead to an economic collapse and the loss of foreign investment, but tough policies to maintain currency stability may cause a government to lose power.

Overall, troubling signs of economic instability have shadowed the past decade—in the turbulent, recession-plagued years that followed the end of the Cold War, in the financial collapses in Asia and Russia in the late 1990s, in Japan's decade-long stagnation, in the U.S. technology sector's bursting stock bubble, and in the synchronized global recession of 2001–2002.

In all the regions just discussed—North America, Asia, and especially Russia and Eastern Europe—the role of private businesses is expanding relative to that of the state. Throughout the remainder of the world, private business plays a role in the economy that exceeds that of the state. The remainder of this chapter considers the international political issues related to the operation of private businesses across state borders.

Multinational Business

Although states are the main rule makers for currency exchange and other international economic transactions, those transactions are carried out mainly by private firms and individuals, not governments. Most important among these private actors are MNCs.

---

[13] Sugawara, Sandra. A "Xenophobic" Nation Is Sold on Aid from Foreigners. *The Washington Post*, Feb. 24, 1998: A15.

DOING BUSINESS WORLDWIDE

Multinational corporations play important roles in international relations and are powerful actors with considerable resources in negotiating with governments. Here, Coca-Cola sells its product in Indonesia, 1998.

Multinational Corporations

Multinational corporations (MNCs) are companies based in one state with affiliated branches or subsidiaries operating in other states. There is no exact definition, but the clearest case of an MNC is a large corporation that operates on a worldwide basis in many countries simultaneously, with fixed facilities and employees in each. With no exact definition, there is also no exact count of the total number of MNCs, but most estimates are in the tens of thousands worldwide.

Most important are *industrial corporations*, which make goods in factories in various countries and sell them to businesses and consumers in various countries. The automobile, oil, and electronics industries have the largest MNCs. Almost all of the largest MNCs are based in G7 states.[14]

Financial corporations (the most important being banks) also operate multinationally—although often with more restrictions than industrial MNCs. Among the largest commercial banks worldwide, the United States does not hold a leading position—reflecting the traditional U.S. antitrust policy that limits banks' geographic expansion. The growing international integration of financial markets was spectacularly illustrated in 1995, when a single 28-year-old trader in Singapore lost $1 billion speculating on Japanese stock and bond markets and bankrupted his employer, a 200-year-old British investment bank. The 1997 stock market crash in Hong Kong created a wave of sell-offs across international time zones as markets opened in Europe and then North America. Money moves across borders at the rate of $1.5 trillion per day. In this context, financial corporations are becoming more internationalized.

Multinational Corporations

Some MNCs sell *services*.[15] McDonald's fast-food chain and American Telephone and Telegraph (AT&T) are good examples. So are the international airlines, which sell tickets in dozens of states (and currencies) for travel all over the world. More down-to-earth service businesses such as retail grocery stores can also become MNCs. During the Gulf War, U.S. personnel could shop at Safeway supermarkets in Saudi Arabia. The United States predominates in service MNCs as it does in industrial ones (though service companies are generally somewhat smaller and less internationalized).

The role of MNCs in international political relations is complex and in some dispute.[16] Some scholars see MNCs as virtually being agents of their home national gov-

[14] United Nations. *World Investment Report 1994: Transnational Corporations, Employment and the Workplace*. NY: United Nations, 1994.

[15] Aronson, Jonathan D. The Service Industries: Growth, Trade, and Development Prospects. In John W. Sewell and Stuart K. Tucker, eds. *Growth, Exports and Jobs in a Changing World Economy: Agenda 1988*. New Brunswick, NJ: Transaction [for the Overseas Development Council], 1988.

ernments. This view resonates with mercantilism, in which economic activity ultimately serves political authorities; thus MNCs have clear national identities and act as members of their national society under state authority. A variant of this theme (from a more revolutionary world view) considers national governments as being agents of their MNCs; state interventions (economic and military) serve private, monied interests.

Others see MNCs as citizens of the world beholden to no government. The head of Dow Chemical once said he dreamed of buying an island beyond any state's territory and putting Dow's world headquarters there. In such a view, MNCs act globally in the interests of their (international) stockholders and owe loyalty to no state. In any case, MNCs are motivated by the need to maximize profits, and managers who fail to do so are likely to be fired. Only in the case of state-owned MNCs—an important exception but a small minority of the total companies worldwide—do MNC actions reflect state interests. Even then, managers of state-owned MNCs have won greater autonomy to pursue profit in recent years (as part of the economic reforms instituted in many countries), and in many cases state-owned enterprises are being sold off (privatized).

As independent actors in the international arena, MNCs are increasingly powerful. Dozens of industrial MNCs have annual sales of tens of billions of dollars each (hundreds of billions of dollars for the top corporations such as ExxonMobil, Wal-Mart, and GM). Only about 35 states have more economic activity per year (GDP) than does the largest MNC in 2005, Exxon Mobil. A more apt comparison might be between MNCs and IOs as nonstate actors operating in the international arena. MNCs more than match most such organizations in size and financial resources. The largest IGO (the UN) has about $6 billion a year in revenue, compared to more than $300 billion for the largest MNC. However, the largest *government* (the United States) has government revenues of $2 trillion—about eight times larger than Exxon Mobil. Thus the power of MNCs does not rival that of the largest states but exceeds that of many poorer states and many IOs; this affects MNC operations in the global South (see pp. 514–516).

Giant MNCs contribute to global interdependence. They are so deeply entwined in so many states that they have a profound interest in the stable operation of the international system—in security affairs as well as in trade and monetary relations. MNCs prosper in a stable international atmosphere that permits freedom of trade, of movement, and of capital flows (investments)—all governed by market forces with minimal government interference. Thus MNCs are, overall, a strong force for liberalism in the world economy, despite the fact that particular MNCs in particular industries do push for certain mercantilist policies to protect their own interests.

Most MNCs have a world management system based on *subsidiaries* in each state in which they operate. The operations within a given state are subject to the legal authority of that state's government. But the foreign subsidiaries are owned (in whole or in substantial part) by the parent MNC in the home country. The parent MNC hires and fires the top managers of its foreign subsidiaries.The business infrastructure is a key aspect of *transnational relations*—linkages among people and groups across national borders.

In addition to the direct connections among members of a single MNC, the operations of MNCs support a global business infrastructure connecting a transnational community of

---

[16] Doremus, Paul N., William W. Keller, Louis W. Pauly, and Simon Reich. *The Myth of the Global Corporation*. Princeton, 1998. Saari, David J. *Global Corporations and Sovereign Nations: Collision or Cooperation?* Westport, CT: Quorum/Greenwood, 1999. Gilpin, Robert. *U.S. Power and the Multinational Corporation*. NY: Basic, 1975. Haley, Usha C. V. *Multinational Corporations in Political Environments: Ethics, Values and Strategies*. River Edge, NJ: World Scientific Publishing Company, Inc., 2001.

businesspeople. A U.S. manager arriving in Seoul, South Korea, for instance, does not find a bewildering scene of unfamiliar languages, locations, and customs. Rather, he or she moves through a familiar sequence of airport lounges, telephone calls and faxes, international hotels, business conference rooms, and CNN broadcasts—most likely hearing English spoken in all.

Foreign Direct Investment

Foreign Direct Investment

MNCs do not just operate in foreign countries, they also own capital (standing wealth) there—buildings, factories, cars, and so forth. For instance, U.S. and German MNCs own some of the capital located in Japan, and Japanese MNCs own capital located in the United States and Germany. *Investment* means exchanging money for ownership of capital (for the purpose of producing a stream of income that will, over time, more than compensate for the money invested). Investments in foreign countries are among the most important, and politically sensitive, activities of MNCs.

Unlike portfolio investment (on paper), *foreign direct investment* involves tangible goods such as factories and office buildings (including ownership of a sizable fraction of a company's total stock, as opposed to a portfolio with little bits of many companies). Paper can be traded on a global market relatively freely, but direct investments cannot be freely moved from one state to another when conditions change. Direct investment is long term, and it is more visible than portfolio investment. Investments in the manufacturing sector usually entail the greatest investment in fixed facilities, which are difficult to move, and in training workers and managers. Investments in the service sector tend to be less expensive and easier to walk away from if conditions change.[17]

Mercantilists tend to view foreign investments in their own country suspiciously. In third world countries, foreign direct investment often evokes concerns about a loss of sovereignty, because governments may be less powerful (and possibly less wealthy) than the MNCs that invest in their country. These fears also reflect the historical fact that most foreign investment in the global South used to come from colonizers. Furthermore, although such investments create jobs, they also bring dislocations of traditional ways of life and cultures. For example, in 2001, villagers in Thailand tried to block a planned $500 million gas pipeline in their area, fearful that it would destroy their way of life and attract problems ranging from industrial pollution to AIDS.[18]

But because many poor and transitional states also desperately need capital from any source to stimulate economic growth, foreign direct investment is generally welcomed and encouraged despite the fears of economic nationalists (North-South investment is discussed further in Chapter 13, pp. 514–516).[19] Most foreign direct investment (like most portfolio investment) is not in the global South, however, but in industrialized countries.

Economic nationalists in industrialized countries also worry about losing power and sovereignty due to foreign investment. In Canada, for instance, mercantilists are alarmed that U.S. firms own more than half of Canada's manufacturing industry and more than two-thirds of Canada's oil and gas industry. Canada is much smaller than the United

---

[17] Moosa, Imad A. *Foreign Direct Investment: Theory, Evidence and Practice*. NY: Palgrave Macmillan, 2002. Phelps, Nicholas A., and Jeremy Alden, eds. *Foreign Direct Investment and the Global Economy: Corporate and Institutional Dynamics of Global-Localisation*. NY: Routledge, 2002.

[18] Arnold, Wayne. A Gas Pipeline to World Outside. *The New York Times*, Oct. 26, 2001: C1.

[19] Gomes-Casseres, Ben, and David B. Yoffie, eds. *The International Political Economy of Direct Foreign Investment*. Brookfield, VT: Edward Elgar, 1993.

States, yet it depends heavily on U.S. trade. In this asymmetrical situation, some Canadians worry that they are being turned into an annex of the United States—economically, culturally, and ultimately politically—losing their own national culture and control of their economy.

Meanwhile, U.S. economic nationalists have similar concerns over foreign direct investment in the United States. Partly this reflects alarm over the accumulation of U.S. debts. Mercantilists see a loss of power when foreign investors buy up companies and real estate in a debtor country. Such concerns seem to be stronger when a foreign MNC buys an existing company or building than when it builds a new factory or other facility. For example, in 2005, an outcry in the United States forced a Chinese oil company to withdraw its bid to buy the U.S. company Unocal, which ended up selling itself for a lower price to a U.S. company. (Chinese business and government leaders resented what they saw as a U.S. double standard.) But when Honda builds a new car factory in Ohio, adding jobs and facilities to the U.S. economy, Americans perceive no such loss.

Liberalism does not condone such arguments. Liberal economists emphasize that global efficiency and the increased generation of wealth result from the ability of MNCs to invest freely across international borders. Investment decisions should be made solely on economic grounds, not nationalistic ones. Liberals also point out a glaring inconsistency in the U.S. public's preoccupation with Japanese investment in the United States in the late 1980s: more than half of all foreign investment in the United States was from Western Europe, and only a third as much was from Japan. Yet there was little outcry about a loss of U.S. sovereignty to Europe. Presumably this disparity reflects either racism or a lingering shadow of World War II in the U.S. public's perceptions. The tables were turned in the late 1990s when financial crises in Japan made Americans worry that Japanese investors would pull out of the United States, not that more would come in.

In the view of liberal economists, foreign investments in the United States help, rather than hurt, the U.S. economy. Many of the benefits of a profitable Japanese factory in the United States accrue to U.S. workers at the plant and U.S. consumers of its products, even if some profits go back to Japan (and even those profits may be reinvested in the United States). Since U.S. MNCs have more than $1 trillion of foreign direct investment outside the United States, the picture is by no means one-sided.

Host and Home Government Relations

A state in which a foreign MNC operates is called the **host country;** the state where the MNC has its headquarters is called its **home country.** MNC operations create a variety of problems and opportunities for both the host and home countries' governments. Conflicts between the host government and the MNC may spill over to become an interstate conflict between the host government and home government. For example, if a host government takes an MNC's property without compensation or arrests its executives, the home government may step in to help the MNC.[20]

You Are the CEO of an MNC

Because host governments can regulate activities on their own territories, in general an MNC cannot operate in a state against the wishes of its government. Conversely, because MNCs have many states to choose from, a host government cannot generally force an MNC to do business in the country against the MNC's wishes. At least in theory,

[20] Rodman, Kenneth A. *Sanctity Versus Sovereignty: U.S. Policy Toward the Nationalization of Natural Resource Investments in the Third World.* Columbia, 1988. Andersson, Thomas. *Multinational Investment in Developing Countries: A Study in Taxation and Nationalization.* NY: Routledge, 1991.

IT'S A JOB

Foreign direct investment is often sought by host governments because it stimulates employment and economic growth, though at wages that home countries would not tolerate. Here, Muslim women in Indonesia assemble Barbies at a Mattel factory. Note that along with investment, a host country imports certain cultural trappings of the MNC's activity—such as Mattel's rendition of femininity in its doll. (This is a literal case of what postmodern feminists call the social construction of gender roles.)

MNCs operate in host countries only when it is in the interests of both the MNC and the host government. Common interests result from the creation of wealth in the host country by the MNC. Both the MNC and the host government benefit—the MNC from profits, the government directly by taxation and indirectly through economic growth (generating future taxes and political support).

However, there are also conflicts in the relationship. One obvious conflict concerns the distribution of new wealth between the MNC and host government. This distribution depends on the rate at which MNC activities or profits are taxed, as well as on the ground rules for MNC operations. Before an MNC invests or opens a subsidiary in a host country, it sits down with the government to negotiate these issues. Threats of violent leverage are largely irrelevant. Rather, the government's main leverage is to promise a favorable climate for doing business and making money; the MNC's main leverage is to threaten to take its capital elsewhere.

Governments can offer a variety of incentives to MNCs to invest. Special terms of taxation and of regulation are common. In cases of resource extraction, negotiations may revolve around the rates the government will charge to lease land and mineral rights to the MNC. National and local governments may offer to provide business infrastructure—such as roads, airports, or phone lines—at the government's expense. (An MNC could also offer to build such infrastructure if allowed to operate on favorable terms in the country.) Over time, certain locations may develop a strong business infrastructure and gain a comparative advantage in luring MNCs to locate there.

These issues all concern the distribution of the new wealth that will be created by MNC operations. MNCs seek host governments that will let the MNC keep more of that wealth; governments seek MNCs that will let the government keep more. With many MNCs and quite a few governments involved in such negotiations, there is a market process at work in the worldwide investment decisions of MNCs.

In addition to these relatively straightforward questions of distribution, MNC relations with host governments contain several other sources of potential conflict. One is the potential for governments to break their agreements with MNCs and change the terms of taxes, regulations, or other conditions. The extreme case is nationalization, in which a host government takes ownership of MNC facilities and assets in the host country (with or without compensation). Once an MNC has invested in fixed facilities, it loses much of its leverage over the government because it cannot move to another country without incurring huge expenses. However, governments hesitate to break their word with MNCs because then other MNCs may not invest in the future. Nationalization of foreign assets is rare now.

Another source of conflict is the trade policies of the host government. Government restrictions on trade seldom help foreign MNCs; more often they help the host country's own industries—which often directly compete with foreign MNCs. Ironically, although they favor global free trade, MNCs may funnel direct investment to states that restrict imports, because MNCs can avoid the import restrictions by producing goods in the host country (rather than exporting from the home country). Trade restrictions are thus another form of leverage that states have in luring foreign direct investment. In fact, regional economic arrangements (see pp. 327–330) can be helpful in combining the power of several states to regulate trade policy, giving them increased leverage over MNCs which may have operations in several states in the region.

Trade regulations often seek to create as many jobs and as much taxable income as possible within the host country. If Toyota assembles cars at a factory in the United States (perhaps to avoid U.S. import restrictions), the U.S. government tends to pressure Toyota to use more U.S. parts in building the cars (such "domestic content" rules were part of the 1992 North American Free Trade Agreement). MNCs generally want the freedom to assemble goods anywhere from parts made anywhere; governments by contrast want to maximize the amount of wealth created on their own territories. With parts and supplies now routinely converging from many countries to go into a product completed in one country, it is very difficult to say exactly where the product was made. The question is a complex one that entails long negotiations between MNCs and host governments.

Monetary policy also leads to conflicts between MNCs and host governments. When a state's currency is devalued, imports suddenly become more expensive. A foreign MNC selling an imported product (or a product assembled from imported parts) in the host country can be devastated by such a change. For example, if the dollar falls relative to the yen, Toyota-U.S.A. may have to charge more U.S. dollars for its cars in order to pay for the parts it brings in from Japan. Therefore, an MNC making a long-term investment in a host country wants the country's currency to be reasonably stable.

Finally, MNCs may conflict with host governments on issues of international security as well as domestic political stability. When an MNC invests in a country, it assumes that its facilities there operate profitably over a number of years. If a war or revolution takes away the MNC's facility, the company loses not just income but capital—the standing wealth embodied in that facility. In 2001, ExxonMobil suspended operations at gas fields in Aceh province of Indonesia for three months until the Indonesian government—which earns $1 billion a year from the operation—brought in military forces to suppress armed separatists who had been attacking ExxonMobil. In 2003, Chevron Texaco, Shell, and TotalFinaElf had to shut down oil production in Nigeria for weeks owing to ethnic violence.

Chinese Investments in Africa

In negotiating over these various sources of conflict, MNCs use a variety of means to influence host governments. These generally follow the same patterns as those used by domestic corporations (see "Interest Groups" on pp. 152–154, and "Industries and Interest Groups" on pp. 316–319). MNCs hire lobbyists, use advertisements to influence public opinion, and offer incentives to host-country politicians (such as locating facilities in their districts). Such activities are politically sensitive because host-country citizens and politicians may resent foreigners' trying to influence them.

Corruption is another means of influence over host governments that cannot be overlooked. Nobody knows the full extent to which MNCs use payoffs, kickbacks, gifts, and similar methods to win the approval of individual government officials for policies favorable to the MNC. Certainly this occurs frequently with host governments in the global South (where government officials may be more desperate for income), but corruption also occurs regularly in rich industrialized countries. For example, in the early 1990s the Bank of Commerce and Credit International (BCCI) was found to have operated a vast illegal worldwide network of money laundering, fraud, and corruption.[21]

MNCs have a range of conflicts with their home governments (where their headquarters are located), just as they do with their host states.[22] Because MNCs are not foreigners but citizens in their home states, they have somewhat more freedom of action in influencing their home governments than they do in influencing host governments. For instance, U.S. MNCs routinely contribute to U.S. politicians' campaigns in hopes that those politicians will support policies favorable to the MNCs' global operations.

Some MNC conflicts with home governments resemble the conflicts with host governments. Taxation is an important one. Trade policies are another. A recurrent complaint of MNCs against home governments is that policies adopted to punish political adversaries—economic sanctions and less extreme restrictions—end up harming the home-country MNCs more than the intended target. Usually, a competing MNC from another country is able to step into the gap when a government restricts its own MNCs. Unless ordered to do so, MNCs tend to go on doing business wherever it is profitable, with little regard for the political preferences of their governments. True to the wealth-maximizing principles of liberalism, MNCs generally prefer to keep politics from interfering with business.

For example, the U.S.-based oil company Unocal described as "positive" the 1996 capture of Afghanistan's capital by the fundamentalist Taliban faction, whose treatment of women Secretary of State Madeline Albright called "despicable." The oil company hoped that if any faction, of whatever political or religious beliefs, could capture all of Afghanistan and end a civil war, then a multibillion dollar natural gas pipeline crossing Afghanistan could be built.

Sometimes governments do prevail, since MNCs often need the support of their home governments. The U.S.-based Conoco oil company agreed to a billion-dollar oil development project in Iran, just when the U.S. government was trying to isolate Iran as a rogue state. Under pressure from the U.S. government, Conoco quickly decided to back out of the deal. This move saved Conoco a fight with its home government, but cost Conoco a lucrative contract that went instead to a European company.

The location of an MNC's headquarters determines its home nationality. The shareholders and top executives of an MNC are mostly from its home country. But as the world economy becomes more integrated, this is becoming less true. Just as MNCs are increasingly doing business all over the world and assembling products from parts made in many countries, so are shareholders and managers becoming more international in composition.

Business Environments

All business activity takes place within an environment shaped by politics.[23] In some places, states allow private businesses to compete freely with little interference from government; elsewhere, states own and operate their own businesses and forbid competition altogether. In some places, goods flow freely from producers to consumers; elsewhere, the same goods may be taxed, restricted, or even stolen on their way to the consumer. In

---

[21] Adams, James Ring, and Douglas Frantz. *A Full Service Bank: How BCCI Stole Billions Around the World*. NY: Pocket, 1992.

[22] Pauly, Louis W. *Who Elected the Bankers? Surveillance and Control in the World Economy*. Cornell, 1997. Smith, Roy C. and Ingo Walter. *Global Banking*, 2nd ed. Oxford, 2003.

[23] Bernhard, William T. and David Leblang. *Democratic Processes and Financial Markets: Pricing Politics*. Cambridge, 2006. Braithwaite, John, and Peter Drahos. *Global Business Regulation*. Cambridge, 2000. Preston, Lee E., and Duane Windsor. *The Rules of the Game in the Global Economy: Policy Regimes for International Business*, 2nd ed. Hingham, MA: Kluwer Academic, 1997.

some places, markets are dominated by oligopolies; elsewhere, large companies are forcibly broken up into smaller ones.

The international business environment most conducive to the creation of wealth by MNCs is one of stable international security. It is difficult and risky to make money in a situation of international conflict, especially one that threatens to degenerate into violence and war. War destroys wealth, reduces the supply of labor, and distorts markets in many ways. Certainly some businesses profit from international instability and the threat of war—such as arms merchants and smugglers—but these are the exceptions.

In part, the MNCs' great interest in stability derives from the nature of investment, which pays back a stream of income over time. Money invested today may not be recovered for many years into the future. Any disruption of the economic framework in which MNCs expect to do business may mean the loss of investments. Large corporations, especially banks, put much effort into political **risk assessment** before making international investments. They want to determine the probability that political conditions in future years (during which the investments will be paid back) will change so radically that the flow of income will be disrupted. These future political conditions include not only wars but also international exchange rates, taxation policies, and trade policies. However, international security risks are among the most threatening to business.

WHICH WAY OUT?

International business prospers in stable political environments in host countries, but the relationship of a host country with an investing MNC can be complex. Foreign investors are wary of putting money into business environments marked by inflation, crime, corruption, and especially armed violence that could hit their facilities and employees. Oil companies have had trouble finding politically stable countries through which to export Caspian Sea oil. This pipeline under construction in 2003 runs from Azerbaijan to Georgia to Turkey, bypassing Chechnya.

In favoring stable international security, MNCs illustrate the fundamental connection between peace and prosperity in the liberal view of IPE. The world in which realists and mercantilists think we are doomed to live is, from a liberal perspective, an impoverished world. According to liberalism, the growing interdependence and growing prosperity of our world go hand in hand and create the conditions for stable peace. MNCs are merely the leading edge of a strong trend in IR: actors would rather make money than make war, and making war is not an effective way to make money.

Beyond these international security concerns, MNCs favor political stability in the broader rules of the game governing international business. When an MNC decides to do business in a new country, it hopes to know at the outset what to expect in terms of trade regulations, monetary policies, tax rates, and even public sentiments toward foreign companies. In a way, the actual policies of states regarding tax rates, exchange rates, tariffs, and so forth matter less than the stability of those policies. Businesses can easily adapt to a variety of conditions, but they adapt to rapid changes in those conditions less easily.

In monetary policy, international business benefits from the stability of rates that the managed float system tries to achieve. In trade policy, business benefits from the stability of tariff levels in the slowly shifting WTO framework. In norms of international law, business benefits from the traditions holding governments responsible for their predecessors' debts and requiring compensation for foreign assets nationalized.

MNCs also depend on national governments to provide security domestically for business operations. If Toyota builds a factory in Italy, it wants the Italian government to apprehend criminals who kidnap Toyota executives or steal Toyota payrolls, not to mention terrorists who might plant bombs to protest Toyota's presence. Many corporations have their own security personnel, and independent companies provide security services to businesses. But such capabilities do not compare with those of the armed forces maintained by states, so MNCs ultimately rely on host and home governments to provide a secure environment for business.

Occasionally, MNCs can get their home governments to provide security when host governments fail to do so. During the colonial era, home governments directly ran foreign colonies where home businesses operated. Many of these businesses continued to operate profitably after those colonies gained independence. In the postcolonial era, military interventions by industrialized countries in the global South continue to occur, and some IR scholars see those interventions as efforts to impose on smaller states the political arrangements for profitable MNC operations. This is an area of controversy, however. IR scholars continue to study the relationships between the international economic activities of MNCs and the international security activities of their home governments.[24]

MNCs themselves influence the evolving international security environment. Just as states form alliances to augment their capabilities, so do companies ally with other companies to enhance their pursuit of wealth. Corporate alliances involving MNCs often have international implications. When business alliances in an industry that has international markets occur within a single state, the alliances may in effect promote economic nationalism. Increasingly, however, corporate alliances are forming across national borders. Such alliances tend to promote liberalism rather than economic nationalism. For example, inter-MNC alliances, and even transnational mergers such as Chrysler with Daimler-Benz, have made the auto industry and others more international than ever.

These international business alliances undermine both economic nationalism and the concept of a world splitting into rival trading blocs based in Europe, North America, and East Asia. In fact, international business alliances create interdependence among their home states. National interests become more intertwined and interstate conflicts tend to be reduced. By operating in multiple countries at once, all MNCs have these effects to some degree. But because they are based in one home country, MNCs are foreigners in other countries. International alliances of MNCs, however, are at home in several countries at once.

We do not yet live in a world without national borders—by a long shot—but the international activities of MNCs are moving us in that direction. Chapter 10 explores some of the ways in which people, companies, and ideas are becoming globally integrated across states.

THINKING CRITICALLY

1. Find a recent newspaper article about a change in currency exchange rates (usually located in the business section). Analyze the various influences that may have been at work in the change of currency values—monetary policies, the underlying

---

[24] Krasner, Stephen D. *Defending the National Interest: Raw Materials Investments and U.S. Foreign Policy*. Princeton, 1978. Gibbs, David N. *The Political Economy of Third World Intervention: Mines, Money, and U.S. Policy in the Congo Crisis*. Chicago, 1991. Lipson, Charles. *Standing Guard: Protecting Foreign Capital in the Nineteenth and Twentieth Centuries*. California, 1985.

state of national economies, the actions of central banks (separately or in coordination), and factors such as political uncertainty that affect investors' confidence in a currency.

2. In the late 1990s, serious financial problems emerged in Asian economies such as Japan, South Korea, and Indonesia. Meanwhile, the U.S. economic position was strengthening. Given both competition and interdependence in U.S.-Asian trade, was the 1997 Asian financial crisis good or bad for the United States? Why?
3. Many scholars and politicians alike think private international investment is the best hope for the economies of Russia and Eastern Europe. Given the current economic and political disarray in that region, what kinds of investors from the industrialized West might be willing to invest there? What actions could the governments of Western states take to encourage such investment? What pitfalls would the governments and investors have to watch out for?
4. If you were representing an MNC such as Toyota in negotiations over building an automobile factory in a foreign country, what kinds of concessions would you ask the host government for? What would you offer as incentives? In your report to Toyota's top management regarding the deal, what points would you emphasize as most important? If instead you were representing the host state in the negotiations and reporting to top state leaders, what would be your negotiating goals and the focus of your report?
5. Suppose that the head of Dow Chemical had his way and established Dow's world headquarters on an island outside all state territory. How do you think such a location would change Dow's strategies or business operations? What problems might it create for Dow?

CHAPTER SUMMARY

- Each state uses its own currency. These currencies have no inherent value but depend on people's belief that they can be traded for future goods and services.
- Gold and silver were once used as world currencies that had value in different countries. Today's system is more abstract: national currencies are valued against each other through exchange rates.
- The most important currencies—against which most other states' currencies are compared—are the U.S. dollar, euro, and Japanese yen.
- Inflation, most often resulting from the printing of currency faster than the creation of new goods and services, causes the value of a currency to fall relative to other currencies. Inflation rates vary widely but are generally much higher in the global South and former Soviet bloc than in the industrialized West.
- States maintain reserves of hard currency and gold. These reserves back a national currency and cover short-term imbalances in international financial flows.
- Fixed exchange rates can be used to set the relative value of currencies, but more often states use floating exchange rates driven by supply and demand on world currency markets.
- Governments cooperate to manage the fluctuations of (floating) exchange rates but are limited in this effort by the fact that most money traded on world markets is privately owned.
- Over the long term, the relative values of national currencies are determined by the underlying health of the national economies and by the monetary policies of governments (how much money they print).

- Governments often prefer a low (weak) value for their own currency, as this promotes exports, discourages imports, and hence improves the state's balance of trade. However, a sudden unilateral devaluation of the currency is a risky strategy because it undermines confidence in the currency.
- To ensure discipline in printing money—and to avoid inflation—industrialized states turn monetary policy over to semiautonomous central banks such as the U.S. Federal Reserve. By adjusting interest rates on government money loaned to private banks, a central bank can control the supply of money in a national economy.
- The World Bank and the International Monetary Fund (IMF) work with states' central banks to maintain stable international monetary relations. From 1945 to 1971, this was done by pegging state currencies to the U.S. dollar and the dollar in turn to gold (backed by gold reserves held by the U.S. government). Since then the system has used Special Drawing Rights (SDRs)—a kind of world currency controlled by the IMF—in place of gold.
- The IMF operates a system of national accounts to keep track of the flow of money into and out of states. The balance of trade (exports minus imports) must be balanced by capital flows (investments and loans) and changes in reserves.
- International debt results from a protracted imbalance in capital flows—a state borrowing more than it lends—in order to cover a chronic trade deficit or government budget deficit. The result is that the net worth of the debtor state is reduced and wealth generated is diverted to pay interest (with the creditor state's wealth increasing accordingly).
- The U.S. financial position declined naturally from an extraordinary predominance immediately after World War II. The fall of the dollar-gold standard in 1971 reflects this decline.
- In the 1980s, the U.S. position worsened dramatically. A chronic budget deficit and trade deficit expanded the country's debt burden. Economic growth in the mid-1990s helped bring the budget deficit down temporarily, but it exploded again after 2001.
- The positions of Russia and the other states of the former Soviet bloc have declined drastically in the past decade as they have tried to make the difficult transition from communism to capitalism. Though the uncontrolled inflation of the early 1990s has subsided, the economies of the former Soviet republics are about half their former size. Western states have not extended massive economic assistance to Russia and Eastern Europe.
- Multinational corporations (MNCs) do business in more than one state simultaneously. The largest are based in the leading industrialized states, and most are privately owned. MNCs are increasingly powerful in international economic affairs.
- MNCs contribute to international interdependence in various ways. States depend on MNCs to create new wealth, and MNCs depend on states to maintain international stability conducive to doing business globally.
- MNCs try to negotiate favorable terms and look for states with stable currencies and political environments in which to make direct investments. Governments seek such foreign investments on their territories so as to benefit from the future stream of income.
- MNCs try to influence the international political policies of both their headquarters state and the other states in which they operate. Generally MNCs promote policies favorable to business—low taxes, light regulation, stable currencies, and free trade. They also support stable international security relations, because war generally disrupts business.

- Increasingly, MNCs headquartered in different states are forming international alliances with each other. These inter-MNC alliances, even more than other MNC operations across national borders, are creating international interdependence and promoting liberal international cooperation.
- MNCs sometimes promote economic nationalism over liberalism, however, especially in the case of state-owned MNCs or alliances of MNCs based in a single country.

KEY TERMS

gold standard 340
exchange rate 340
convertible currency 341
hyperinflation 341
hard currency 341
reserves 342
fixed exchange rates 342
floating exchange rates 342
managed float 343
Exchange Rate Mechanism (ERM) 343
devaluation 347
central bank 348
discount rate 348
Bretton Woods system 349
World Bank 349
International Monetary Fund (IMF) 349
Special Drawing Right (SDR) 351
balance of payments 352
foreign direct investment 352
Keynesian economics 354
fiscal policy 354
monetary policy 354
national debt 356
multinational corporations (MNCs) 362
host country 365
home country 365
risk assessment 369

ONLINE PRACTICE TEST

Take an online practice test at *www.internationalrelations.net*

❑ A
❑ B
☑ C
❑ D

LET'S DEBATE THE ISSUE

Multinational Corporations: Engines of Modernization or Agents of Imperialism?

by Mir Zohair Husain

Overview Globalization has become the dominant idea in international relations and a large contributor to the emergence of liberalism as the prevailing theory in international political economy (IPE). Likewise, liberalism has also facilitated globalization. A key reason for this dynamic process has been the emergence of transnational actors, such as multinational corporations (MNCs), which are major economic forces in globalization. MNCs are large, integrated, and diversified business enterprises operating in two or more countries. An MNC is headquartered in a home country, while a country allowing an MNC to conduct business within its borders is a host country. Other MNC traits include multinational management, stock ownership, and labor force; worldwide access to capital; economic dependence on international sources; substantial revenues and assets derived from outside the home country; and management with a global perspective.

MNCs are powerful global economic forces. In 2003, MNCs accounted for half of the top 100 economic entities in the world and had revenues rivaling the gross domestic product (GDP) of 50 countries.[a] Moreover, as of 2002, 65,000 of these MNCs have 850,000 affiliates in foreign countries and account for 10 percent of the world's GDP and 33 percent of all world exports.[b]

Multinational corporations have been criticized for using their wealth and influence to control high-level government officials, allowing MNCs to exploit developing countries. So, are these MNCs engines of economic growth and modernization, or are they agents of imperialism exploiting their host countries?

Argument 1 MNCs Are Engines for Positive Global Change

MNCs significantly contribute to a host country's economic modernization. China, the fastest growing country over the past three decades, illustrates the benefits associated with MNCs. Continuing at this pace, China could be a superpower in the next two decades.

> . . . [China] has begun to rival Japan as the pivotal player in Asia's economy. It has become the largest export market for both South Korea and Taiwan, for example, and has elbowed out Japan to become Asia's biggest exporter to the United States. . . .
>
> This year, it appears set to attract a record $50 billion in foreign investment, multiples more than the amount received by any other developing country and perhaps more than the United States. . . .
>
> Fierce competition and falling prices have forced multinational corporations to move production lines to China, which can make goods for less than its Asian neighbors can. So, its growth has come partly at the expense of the region. Still, about half of its exports, or about $275 billion last year, consists of products made in China by foreign companies or joint ventures of Chinese and foreign companies. (Joseph Kahn. "China's Hot, at Least for Now." *The New York Times,* December 16, 2002.)

MNCs accelerate economic growth in India and foster peace in South Asia. MNCs require a stable and predictable environment to conduct business. Countries such as India, which benefit from MNCs, make every effort to provide a stable socioeconomic and political environment. In this way, MNCs contribute to a country's economic growth and to global peace and security.

> [In June of 2002,] India and Pakistan appeared headed for a nuclear war. Colin Powell, the U.S. secretary of state and a for-

[a]"World's Largest Corporations," *Fortune,* July 26, 2004; "World Development Indicators Database." World Bank, September 2004.
[b]Currier, Nuchhi," Slow Economic Recovery Forecast," *UN Chronicle,* June–August 2003.

mer general, played a key role in talking the two parties back from the brink. But here in India, I've discovered that there was another new, and fascinating, set of pressures that restrained the Indian government and made nuclear war, from its side, unthinkable. Quite simply, India's huge software and information technology industry, which has emerged over the last decade and made India the back-room and research hub of many of the world's largest corporations, essentially told the nationalist Indian government to cool it. And the government here got the message and has sought to de-escalate ever since. That's right—in the crunch, it was the influence of General Electric, not General Powell, that did the trick. (Thomas L. Friedman. "India, Pakistan and G.E." *The New York Times,* August 11, 2002.)

MNCs are forces of global integration. MNCs impart invaluable skills essential to successful business transactions in a globalized economy, create needed jobs in the host countries, and raise the standard of living of millions.

> Sierra Atlantic, a midsize software services company whose clients include the Oracle Corporation of Redwood City, Calif., says that one-fourth of its 400 employees, all but a handful of them Indian and most of them working out of the Hyderabad offices, are constantly interacting with foreigners....
>
> Such companies already provide services for some multinationals, primarily those based in the United States, including General Electric, American Express and Nike. They are expected to gross an estimated $12 billion in export revenues this year, up from $9.5 billion last year.... And that means more contact with customers and clients abroad—and more often as full professional partners....
>
> Across the world, Global Savvy, a consulting company in Palo Alto, Calif., trains high-tech employees to work together in projects around the world. "The training in American culture is not to make Indian software professionals less Indian," said Lu Ellen Schafer, the executive director. "It is to make them more globally competent." (Saritha Rai. "Indian Companies Are Adding Western Flavor." *The New York Times,* August 19, 2003.)

Argument 2 MNCs Are Agents of Exploitation and Neoimperialism

Economic development is achieved through domestic businesses. Countries that have successfully attained self-sustaining economic development have protected and nurtured their domestic businesses, not foreign ones.

> Examples of companies on the road to becoming global, with thousands of small local suppliers that have been taught modern business techniques, include Embraer in Brazil (aerospace), Vitro in Mexico (glass), Legend in China (computers), Wipro in India (software), Giant in Taiwan (bicycles), the Siam group in Thailand (cement) and Samsung in Korea (electronics).
>
> What enabled those successful companies to grow and flourish? In their countries, business and government worked closely together to strengthen domestic industry. Foreign enterprises were discouraged, by deliberate red tape, from entering certain industries, so that national companies could get a head start. State-owned banks lent money at subsidized rates to help local firms acquire the technologies and capital equipment they needed.... In much of manufacturing, subsidies were allocated by professional bureaucracies according to relatively transparent procedures. (Alice H. Amsden. "Why Are Globalizers So Provincial?" *The New York Times,* January 31, 2002.)

MNCs benefit their home country far more than the host country. While MNCs provide jobs in host countries, the higher skilled and better-paying jobs remain with the executives from the home countries. Moreover, most MNC profits are sent back to the headquarters based in the MNC's home country.

> Globalization's locomotive, the multinational firm, has similar limits. Its novel technologies and famous brand names conquer the planet's consumers, but the top management and advanced scientific researchers of most multinationals remain headquartered in roughly a dozen high-income countries. (Alice H. Amsden. "Why Are Globalizers So Provincial?" *The New York Times,* January 31, 2002.)

MNCs pollute and degrade the environment of host countries. MNCs facing stiff environmental standards in their home countries find that they can pollute the host countries without penalties for their company's environmental pollution.

> [Two huge power plants] will generate billions of watts for millions of Californians, a handful of jobs for Mexicans and pollution on both sides of the border.
>
> ... [One] California congressman calls placing the plants in Mexico a form of environmental imperialism.
>
> ... One is being built by InterGen, owned by Shell Oil and the Bechtel Corporation. The company concedes that the plant does not meet California's pollution standards and would not be licensed across the border.
>
> [However], Mexico's environmental law enforcement is weaker, its government less transparent, its desire for foreign capital bottomless. California's energy demand is enormous—as big as its citizens' resistance to huge power plants. (Tim Weiner. "U.S. Will Get Power, and Pollution, From Mexico." *The New York Times,* September 17, 2002.)

WEB LINK

Multinational Corporations

Questions

1. What is the role of multinational corporations in international relations?
2. Describe, analyze, and explain the positive and negative effects of MNCs for host countries in the developing world (South).

Selected Readings

Alfred D. Chandler and Bruce Mazlish, eds. *Leviathans: Multinational Corporations and the New Global History.* NY: Cambridge University Press, 2005.

David C. Korten. *When Corporations Rule the World.* Bloomfield, CT: Kumarian Press, Incorporated, 2001.

■ Blogger in Bahrain, 2005.

Supranationalism

Integration Theory

The European Union

The Vision of a United Europe • The Treaty of Rome • Structure of the European Union • The Single European Act • The Maastricht Treaty • Monetary Union • Expanding the European Union

The Power of Information

Wiring the World • Information as a Tool of Governments • Information as a Tool Against Governments

International Culture

Telecommunications and Global Culture • Transnational Communities

CHAPTER 10

Integration

Supranationalism

This chapter and the next continue to develop a theme from the discussion of MNCs—that of nonstate actors in interaction with state actors. Although MNCs are *substate* actors in the formation of state foreign policy (see pp. 150–160), they are also *transnational* actors bridging national borders and creating new avenues of interdependence among states.[1] This chapter discusses transnational and international nonstate actors whose roles and influences are **supranational**—they subsume a number of states and their functions within a larger whole.

The UN, as we have seen, has some supranational aspects, though they are limited by the UN Charter, which is based on state sovereignty. On a regional level, the European Union (EU) is a somewhat more supranational entity than the UN; other regional organizations have tried to follow Europe's path as well, but with only limited success. These IOs all contain a struggle between the contradictory forces of *nationalism* and *supranationalism*—between state sovereignty and the higher authority (in level but not yet in power or legitimacy) of supranational structures.

Formal IGOs such as the UN and EU are not the only way that supranationalism is developing. Even more far-reaching in many ways are the effects of information technologies that operate globally and regionally across state boundaries without formal political structures. Here, too, supranational influences compete for influence with the sovereign state. This chapter considers these various supranational influences on international politics, from the formal structures of the EU to the globalizing effects of information.

Integration Theory

The theory of international integration can help to explain these developments, which challenge once again the foundations of realism (state sovereignty and territorial integrity). **International integration** refers to the process by which supranational institutions replace national ones—the gradual shifting upward of sovereignty from state to regional or global structures. The ultimate expression of integration would be the merger of several (or many) states into a single state—or ultimately into a single world government. Such a shift in sovereignty to the supranational level would probably entail some version of federalism, in which states or other political units recognize the sovereignty of a central government

[1] Nye, Joseph S., Jr., and Robert O. Keohane, eds. *Transnational Relations and World Politics*. Harvard, 1972. Rissen-Kappen, Thomas, ed. *Bringing Transnational Relations Back In: Non-state Actors, Domestic Structures, and International Relations*. Cambridge, 1995.

TEAR DOWN THE WALLS

Integration processes in Europe and elsewhere are making state borders more permeable to people, goods, and ideas—increasing interdependence. The European Union is deepening economic integration while expanding eastward. Here, the opening of the Berlin Wall makes integration very tangible, 1989.

while retaining certain powers for themselves. This is the form of government adopted (after some debate) in the U.S. Constitution.

Today one hears some calls for a "United States of Europe"—or even of the world—but in practice the process of integration has never gone beyond a partial and uneasy sharing of power between state and supranational levels. States have been unwilling to give up their exclusive claim to sovereignty and have severely limited the power and authority of supranational institutions. The UN certainly falls far short of a federal model (see Chapter 7). It represents only a step in the direction of international integration. Other modest examples of the integration process have been encountered in previous chapters—for example, NAFTA and the WTO. But these arrangements hardly challenge states' territorial integrity and usually challenge political sovereignty on a handful of issues (such as trade).

The most successful example of the process of integration by far—though even that success is only partial—is the European Union. Although we can observe aspects of international integration at work elsewhere in the world, these processes have gone much further in Europe than anywhere else. The regional coordination now occurring in Western Europe is a new historical phenomenon achieved only since World War II.[2]

Until 50 years ago, the European continent was the embodiment of national sovereignty, state rivalry, and war. For 500 years, until 1945, the states of Europe were locked in chronic intermittent warfare; in the twentieth century alone two world wars left the continent in ruins. The European states have historical and present-day religious, ethnic, and cultural differences. The 25 members of the EU in 2006 spoke 21 different official languages. If ever there were a candidate for the failure of integration, Europe would appear to be it. Even more surprising, European integration began with the cooperation of Europe's two bitterest enemies over the previous 100 years, enemies in three major wars since 1870—France and Germany (references to "Germany" refer to West Germany from 1944 to 1990, and unified Germany since).

United States of Europe

That Western European states began forming supranational institutions and creating an economic community to promote free trade and coordinate economic policies caught the attention of IR scholars, who used the term *integration* to describe what they observed. Seemingly, integration challenged the assumption of realism that states were strictly autonomous and would never yield power or sovereignty.

[2] Moravcsik, Andrew. *The Choice for Europe: Social Purpose and State Power from Messina to Maastricht*. Cornell, 1998. Dinan, Desmond. *Europe Recast: A History of the European Union*. Boulder, CO: Lynne Rienner, 2004. Kahler, Miles. *International Institutions and the Political Economy of Integration*. Washington, DC: Brookings, 1995.

These scholars proposed that European moves toward integration could be explained by *functionalism*—growth of specialized technical organizations that cross national borders.[3] According to functionalists, technological and economic development lead to more and more supranational structures as states seek practical means to fulfill necessary *functions* such as delivering mail from one country to another or coordinating the use of rivers that cross borders. As these connections became denser and the flows faster, functionalism predicted that states would be drawn together into stronger international economic structures.

The European experience, however, went beyond the creation of specialized agencies to include the development of more general, more political supranational bodies, such as the European Parliament. **Neofunctionalism** is a modification of functional theory by IR scholars to explain these developments. Neofunctionalists argue that economic integration (functionalism) generates a *political* dynamic that drives integration further. Closer economic ties require more political coordination in order to operate effectively and eventually lead to political integration as well—a process called *spillover*.

Some scholars focused on the less-tangible *sense of community* ("we" feeling) that began to develop among Europeans, running contrary to nationalist feelings that still existed as well. The low expectation of violence among the states of Western Europe created a **security community** in which such feelings could grow.[4]

Elsewhere in the world, economies were becoming more interdependent at both the regional and global levels. In Asia, the Association of South East Asian Nations (ASEAN), founded in 1967, chalked up some successes in promoting regional economic coordination over several decades. The Andean Common Market, begun in 1969, promoted a limited degree of regional integration in the member states of Venezuela, Colombia, Ecuador, Peru, and Bolivia. Other South American countries (Argentina, Brazil, Paraguay, and Uruguay) founded Mercosur in 1991 to increase economic trade and integration. Most recently, the countries of Africa in 2002 formed the African Union, an ambitious plan to coordinate economic and foreign policies, elect an African parliament, and create a stronger infrastructure than the predecessor Organization of African Unity (OAU). Funding for the African Union is a problem, however.[5]

Interest in integration theory among IR scholars has waxed and waned with the uneven pace of European integration. In the 1960s and 1970s, European integration seemed to slow down; regional efforts elsewhere in the world also failed to develop as hoped. For most of the Cold War decades, integration took a secondary position among IR scholars (and policy makers) to the concerns of East-West conflict, nuclear weapons, and related security issues. Then, in the 1980s, Europe accelerated its progress toward integration again, the Cold War ended, and the North American Free Trade Agreement took form; the scholarly interest in integration expanded again.

---

[3] Mitrany, David. *The Functional Theory of Politics*. London: The London School of Economics/M. Robertson, 1975. Haas, Ernst B. *Beyond the Nation-State: Functionalism and International Organization*. Stanford, 1964. Haas, Ernst B. *When Knowledge Is Power: Three Models of Change in International Organizations*. California, 1989. Skolnikoff, Eugene B. *The Elusive Transformation: Science, Technology, and the Evolution of International Politics*. Princeton, 1994.

[4] Adler, Emanuel, and Michael Barnett, eds. *Security Communities*. Cambridge, 1998. Deutsch, Karl W., et al. *Political Community and the North Atlantic Area: International Organization in the Light of Historical Experience*. Princeton, 1957. Ullman, Richard H. *Securing Europe*. Princeton, 1991.

[5] Mattli, Walter. *The Logic of Regional Integration: Europe and Beyond*. Cambridge, 1999. Thomas, Kenneth P., and Mary Ann Tétreault, eds. *Racing to Regionalize: Democracy, Capitalism, and Regional Political Economy*. Boulder, CO: Lynne Rienner, 1999. Gleditsch, Kristian S. *All International Politics is Local: The Diffusion of Conflict, Integration, and Democracy*. Michigan, 2002.

Costs of Integration The new wave of integration in Europe and elsewhere encountered limits and setbacks. Integration reduces states' ability to shield themselves and their citizens from the world's many problems and conflicts. For example, in the early 1990s Venezuela found that its open border with Colombia brought in large trans-shipments of cocaine bound for the United States. Moreover, as states increasingly fear transnational terrorism, the prospects of open borders can give state leaders pause.

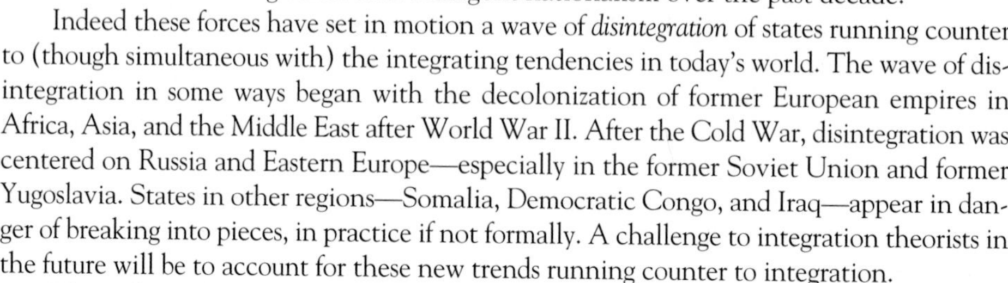

Integration can mean greater centralization at a time when individuals, local groups, and national populations demand more say over their own affairs. The centralization of political authority, information, and culture as a result of integration can threaten both individual and group freedom. Ethnic groups want to safeguard their own cultures, languages, and institutions against the bland homogeneity that a global or regional melting pot would create. As a result, many states and citizens, in Europe and elsewhere, responded to the new wave of integration with resurgent nationalism over the past decade.

SIMULATION

You Are an Ambassador to the UN

Indeed these forces have set in motion a wave of *disintegration* of states running counter to (though simultaneous with) the integrating tendencies in today's world. The wave of disintegration in some ways began with the decolonization of former European empires in Africa, Asia, and the Middle East after World War II. After the Cold War, disintegration was centered on Russia and Eastern Europe—especially in the former Soviet Union and former Yugoslavia. States in other regions—Somalia, Democratic Congo, and Iraq—appear in danger of breaking into pieces, in practice if not formally. A challenge to integration theorists in the future will be to account for these new trends running counter to integration.

Throughout the successful and unsuccessful efforts at integration runs a common thread—the tension between nationalism and supranational loyalties (regionalism or globalism). In the less-successful integration attempts, nationalism stands virtually unchallenged, and even in the most successful cases nationalism remains a potent force locked in continual struggle with supranationalism. This struggle is a central theme even in the most successful case of integration—the European Union.

The European Union

Like the UN, the **European Union (EU)** was created after World War II and has developed since. But whereas the UN structure has changed little since its Charter was adopted, the EU has gone through several waves of expansion in its scope, membership, and mission over the past 50 years.[6]

The Vision of a United Europe

Europe in 1945 was decimated by war. Most of the next decade was spent recovering with help from the United States through the Marshall Plan. But already two French leaders, Jean Monnet and Robert Schuman, were developing a plan to implement the idea of functionalism in Europe—that future wars could be prevented by creating economic linkages that would eventually bind states together politically.

[6] Sidjanski, Dusan. *The Federal Future of Europe: From the European Community to the European Union*. Michigan, 2000. Caporaso, James A. *The European Union: Dilemmas of Regional Integration*. Boulder: Westview, 2000. Hancock, Donald M., et.al. *Politics in Europe*. 3rd ed. NY: Seven Bridges Press, 2003. Frankland, Gene E. *Global Studies: Europe*. 7th ed. Guilford, CT: McGraw-Hill/Dushkin, 2002. Nelsen, Brent F., and Alexander Stubb. *European Union: Readings on the Theory and Practice of European Integration*. Boulder, CO: Lynne Rienner, 2003.

In 1950, Schuman as French foreign minister proposed a first modest step—the merger of the French and German steel (iron) and coal industries into a single framework that could most efficiently use the two states' coal resources and steel mills. Coal and steel were key to European recovery and growth. The Schuman plan gave birth in 1952 to the *European Coal and Steel Community (ECSC)*, in which France and Germany were joined by Italy (the third large industrial country of continental Europe) and by three smaller countries—Belgium, Netherlands, and Luxembourg (together called the Benelux countries). These six states worked through the ECSC to reduce trade barriers in coal and steel and to coordinate their coal and steel policies. The ECSC also established a High Authority that to some extent could bypass governments and deal directly with companies, labor unions, and individuals. Britain did not join, however.

Jean Monnet

If coal and steel sound like fairly boring topics, that was exactly the idea of functionalists. The issues involved were matters for engineers and technical experts, and did not threaten politicians. Since 1952, technical experts have served as the leaders of the integration process in other aspects of European life and outside Europe. (Of course, coal and steel were not chosen by accident, since both were essential to make war.) As mentioned in Chapter 7, technical IOs such as the Universal Postal Union came before political ones such as the UN.

International scientific communities deserve special mention in this regard. If German and French steel experts had more in common than German and French politicians, this is even truer of scientists. Today the European scientific community is one of the most internationally integrated areas of society. For example, the EU operates the European Space Agency and the European Molecular Biology Laboratory.

Although technical cooperation succeeded in 1952, political and military cooperation proved much more difficult. In line with the vision of a united Europe, the six ECSC states signed a second treaty in 1952 to create a European Defense Community to work toward integrating Europe's military forces under one budget and command. But the French Parliament failed to ratify the treaty, and Britain refused to join such a force. The ECSC states also discussed formation of a European Political Community in 1953, but could not agree on its terms. Thus, in economic cooperation the supranational institutions succeeded but in political and military affairs state sovereignty prevailed.

The Treaty of Rome

In the **Treaty of Rome** in 1957, the same six states (France, Germany, Italy, Belgium, Netherlands, Luxembourg) created two new organizations. One extended the coal-and-steel idea into a new realm, atomic energy. **Euratom,** the European Atomic Energy Community, was formed to coordinate nuclear power development by pooling research, investment, and management. It continues in operation today with an expanded membership. The second organization was the *European Economic Community (EEC)*, later renamed the *European Community (EC)*. After its founding in 1957, the EEC was often called simply the *Common Market*. Actually a common market was not immediately created but was established as a goal, which has since been largely realized.

As discussed briefly in Chapter 8, there are important differences between *free trade areas, customs unions*, and *common markets*. Creating a **free trade area** meant lifting tariffs and restrictions on the movement of goods across (EEC) borders, as was done shortly after 1957. Today the *European Free Trade Association (EFTA)* is an extended free trade area associated with the European Union; its members are Norway, Iceland, Liechtenstein, and Switzerland. (All but Switzerland became, with the EU, the European Economic Area, participating in the "Europe 1992" single market described below.)

POLITICS AND MARKETS

Under the free trade area first created by the 1957 Treaty of Rome, goods can move freely across European borders to reach consumers in any member country. In agriculture, creating an integrated free market in Europe has not been easy; the EC adopted a Common Agricultural Policy in the 1960s to address the problem. Prices in this French marketplace are affected by subsidies to French farmers, 1991.

A **customs union** means that participating states adopt a unified set of tariffs with regard to goods coming in from outside the free trade area. Without this, each type of good could be imported into the state with the lowest tariff and then reexported (tariff-free) to the other states in the free trade area; this would be inefficient. The Treaty of Rome committed the six states to creating a customs union by 1969. A customs union creates free and open trade within its member states, bringing great economic benefits. Thus, the customs union remains the heart of the EU and the one aspect widely copied elsewhere in the world.

A **common market** means that in addition to the customs union, member states allow labor and capital (as well as goods) to flow freely across borders. For instance, a Belgian financier can invest in Germany on the same terms as a German investor. Although the Treaty of Rome adopted the goal of a common market, even today it has been only partially achieved.

One key aspect of a common market was achieved, at least in theory, in the 1960s when the EU (then the EC) adopted a **Common Agricultural Policy (CAP).** In practice, the CAP has led to recurrent conflicts among member states and tensions between nationalism and regionalism. Recall that agriculture has been one of the most difficult sectors of the world economy in which to achieve free trade (see pp. 316–320). To promote national self-sufficiency in food, many governments give subsidies to farmers. The CAP was based on the principle that a subsidy extended to farmers in any member state should be extended to farmers in all EU countries. That way, no member government was forced to alienate politically powerful farmers by removing subsidies, yet the overall policy would be equalized throughout the community in line with the common market principle. As a result, subsidies to farmers today absorb about 40 percent of the total EU budget, with France as the main beneficiary, and are the single greatest source of trade friction between Europe and the United States (see pp. 320–322).

The fourth step in the plan for European integration (after a free trade area, customs union, and common market) was an *economic and monetary union (EMU)* in which the overall economic policies of the member states would be coordinated for greatest efficiency and stability. In this step, a single currency would replace the separate national currencies now in use (see "Monetary Union," below). A future fifth step would be the supranational coordination of economic policies such as budgets and taxes.

To reduce state leaders' fears of losing sovereignty, the Treaty of Rome provides that changes in its provisions must be approved by all member states. For example, France vetoed Britain's application for membership in the EEC in 1963 and 1967. However, in 1973 Britain did finally join, along with Ireland and Denmark. This action expanded the organization's membership to nine, including the largest and richest countries in the region.

In 1981, Greece was admitted, and in 1986 Portugal and Spain joined. Inclusion of these poorer countries with less industry and lower standards of living created difficulties in effectively integrating Europe's economies (difficulties that persist today). Richer European states give substantial aid to the poorer ones in hopes of strengthening the weak links. Greece, Portugal, Spain, and Ireland were called the *"poor four"* within the EU, but have grown more prosperous, and new "poor" members have now joined from Eastern Europe.

Structure of the European Union

The structure of the EU reflects its roots in technical and economic cooperation. The coal and steel experts have been joined by experts on trade, agriculture, and finance at the heart of the community. The EU headquarters and staff have the reputation of colorless bureaucrats—sometimes called *Eurocrats*—who care more about technical problem solving than about politics. These supranational bureaucrats are balanced in the EU structure by provisions that uphold the power of states and state leaders.

Although the rule of Eurocrats follows the functionalist plan, it has created problems as the EU has progressed. Politicians in member states have qualms about losing power to the Eurocrats. Citizens in those states have become more uncomfortable in recent years with the growing power of faceless Eurocrats over their lives. Citizens can throw their own political leaders out of office in national elections, but the Eurocrats seem less accountable.

The EU's structure is illustrated in Figure 10.1. The Eurocrats consist of a staff of 24,000, organized under the **European Commission** at EU headquarters in Brussels, Belgium. The Commission has 25 individual members—one from each member state—who are chosen for four-year renewable terms. Their role is to identify problems and propose solutions to the Council of Ministers. They select one of their members as the commission president. These individuals are supposed to represent the interests of Europe as

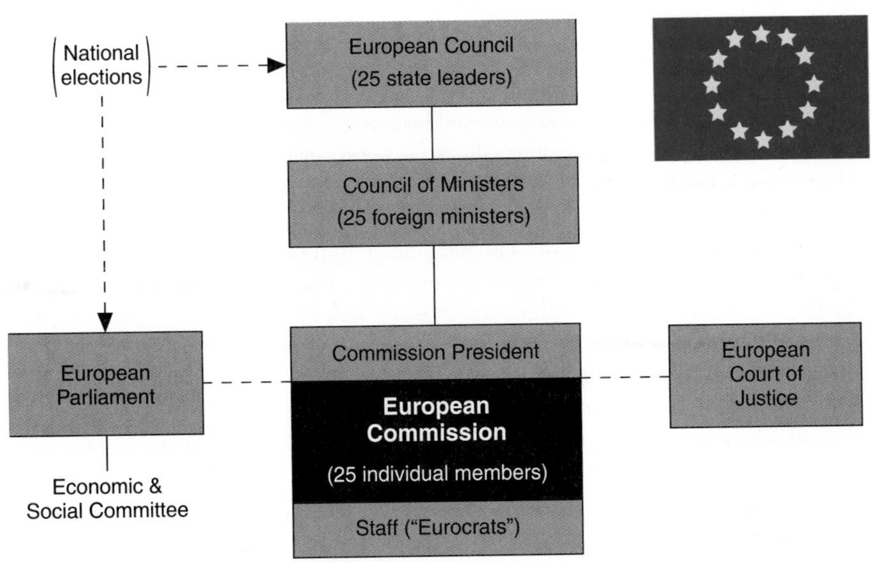

FIGURE 10.1 ■ Structure of the European Union (EU)

a whole (supranational interests), not their own states, but this goal has been only imperfectly met.

The European Commission lacks formal autonomous power except for day-to-day EU operations. Formally, the Commission reports to, and implements policies of, the **Council of Ministers.** The Council is a meeting of the relevant ministers (foreign, economic, agriculture, finance, etc.) of each member state—politicians who control the bureaucrats (or who try to). This formal structure reflects states' resistance to yielding sovereignty. It also means that the individuals making up the Council of Ministers vary from one meeting to the next, and that technical issues receive priority over political ones. The arrangement thus gives some advantage back to the Commission staff. Recall the similar tension between politicians and career bureaucrats in national foreign policy making (see "Bureaucracies" on pp. 150–152).

The Council of Ministers in theory has a weighted voting system based on each state's population, but in practice it operates by consensus on major policy issues (all members must agree). On other issues, decisions can be made by qualified majorities, overriding national sovereignty. The Council has a rotating presidency (with limited power). The Council of Ministers must approve the policies of the European Commission and give it general directions.[7]

In the 1970s, state leaders (prime ministers or presidents) created a special place for themselves in the EC, to oversee the direction of the community; this structure again shows the resistance of state leaders to being governed by any supranational body. This *European Council* of the 25 state leaders meets with the European Commission president twice a year. They are the ones with the power to get things done in their respective national governments (which still control most of the money and power in Europe).

European Parliament

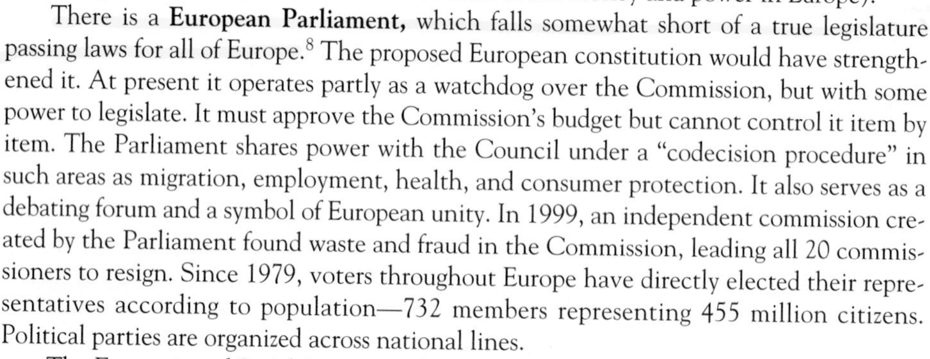

There is a **European Parliament,** which falls somewhat short of a true legislature passing laws for all of Europe.[8] The proposed European constitution would have strengthened it. At present it operates partly as a watchdog over the Commission, but with some power to legislate. It must approve the Commission's budget but cannot control it item by item. The Parliament shares power with the Council under a "codecision procedure" in such areas as migration, employment, health, and consumer protection. It also serves as a debating forum and a symbol of European unity. In 1999, an independent commission created by the Parliament found waste and fraud in the Commission, leading all 20 commissioners to resign. Since 1979, voters throughout Europe have directly elected their representatives according to population—732 members representing 455 million citizens. Political parties are organized across national lines.

The *Economic and Social Committee* discusses continentwide issues that affect particular industries or constituencies. This committee is purely advisory; it lobbies the European Commission on matters it deems important. It is designed as a forum in which companies, labor unions, and interest groups can bargain transnationally.

The **European Court of Justice** in Luxembourg adjudicates disputes on matters covered by the Treaty of Rome—which covers many issues. Unlike the World Court (see pp. 276–277), the European Court has actively established its jurisdiction and does not merely serve as a mechanism of international mediation. The European Court can overrule national law when it is in conflict with EU law—giving it unique powers among international courts. It hears cases brought by individuals, not just governments. In hundreds of

[7] Kirchner, Emil Joseph. *Decision Making in the European Community: The Council Presidency and European Integration*. Manchester, 1992. Pollack, Mark A. *The Engines of Integration: Delegation, Agency, and Agenda Setting in the European Union*. Oxford, 2003.

[8] Judge, David, and David Earnshaw. *The European Parliament*. NY: Palgrave, 2003. Nugent, Neill. *The Government and Politics of the European Union*. 5th ed. Duke, 2003.

cases, the Court has ruled on matters ranging from discrimination in the workplace to the pensions of Commission staff members.

The Single European Act

European integration has proceeded in a step-by-step process that produces tangible successes, reduces politicians' fears of losing sovereignty, and creates pressures to continue the process. Often major steps forward are followed by periods of stagnation or even reversals in integration. The first major revision of the Treaty of Rome—the 1985 **Single European Act**—began a new phase of accelerated integration. The EU set a target date of the end of 1992 for the creation of a true common market in Europe.[9] This comprehensive set of changes was nicknamed *Europe 1992*.

The 1992 process centered on about 300 directives from the European Commission, aimed at eliminating nontariff barriers to free trade in goods, services, labor, and capital within the EC. The issues tended to be complex and technical. For instance, professionals licensed in one state should be free to practice in another; but Spain's licensing requirements for, say, physical therapists, may have differed from those of Britain. The Commission bureaucrats worked to smooth out such inconsistencies and create a uniform set of standards. Each national government had to pass laws to implement these measures.

For example, a dispute raged for decades over the definition of chocolate. Belgium—famous for its chocolates—requires the exclusive use of cocoa butter for a product to be called chocolate; Britain and other countries use a cheaper process that partially substitutes other vegetable oils. With deepening integration and seamless trade, Belgium worried that it would lose its competitive advantage in the $30 billion worldwide chocolate market (half of which came from Europe). Britain and six other EU countries that joined the EU since 1973 won an exemption from the all-cocoa butter rule that applies to the other eight EU members. Under the pressure of integration, however, the EU is moving to unify standards such as food regulations. The chocolate wars illustrate that the seemingly simple concept of economic integration sets in motion forces of change that reach into every corner of society and affect the daily lives of millions of people.

The Single European Act also gave a new push to the creation of a European Central Bank (in Frankfurt, Germany), and a single currency and monetary system—long-standing goals that have since been accomplished. As long as the economies of the EU members were tied to separate states (with separate central banks), efforts to maintain fixed exchange rates were difficult. For example, British politicians in 1992 were reluctant to deepen a recession in order to save German politicians from inflation (the source of the controversial British devaluation discussed in Chapter 9).

The 1992 process moved economic integration into more political and controversial areas, eroding sovereignty more visibly than before. It also deepened a trend toward the EU's dealing directly with provinces rather than the states they belong to—thus beginning to "hollow out" the state from below (stronger provincial governments) as well as from above (stronger Europewide government). However, Europe 1992 continued to put aside for the future the difficult problems of political and military integration.

The Maastricht Treaty

The **Maastricht Treaty,** signed in the Dutch city of Maastricht in 1992, renamed the EC as the EU and committed it to further progress in three main areas. The first was monetary

[9] Moravcsik, Andrew. Negotiating the Single European Act: National Interests and Conventional Statecraft in the European Community. *International Organization* 45 (1), 1991: 19–56.

INTEGRATION MARCHES ON

The Maastricht Treaty called for a monetary union with a common currency. In 2002, the euro currency came into effect smoothly in 12 countries and, after a year of weakness, gained strength and emerged as a world currency that rivals the U.S. dollar. This Italian chef celebrated the new currency by making a pizza decorated with a euro symbol (€).

union (discussed shortly), in which the existing national currencies were abolished and replaced by a single European currency. A second set of changes, regarding justice and home affairs, created a European police agency and responded to the new reality that borders were opening to immigrants, criminals, sex traffickers, and contraband alike. It also expanded the idea of citizenship, so that, for example, a French citizen living in Germany can vote in local elections there. A third goal of Maastricht—political and military integration was even more controversial. The treaty commits European states to work toward a common foreign policy with a goal of eventually establishing a joint military force.

The Maastricht Treaty encountered problems soon after its signing. One problem was the fractious response of EU members to the war in the former Yugoslavia—next door on the European continent. Efforts by the EU to mediate the conflict failed repeatedly, as the war spread and a humanitarian and refugee crisis deepened. In 1992, French President Mitterrand secretly flew straight from an EU summit meeting to the embattled Bosnian capital, Sarajevo; this unilateral initiative reflected the EU's inability to act in unison. Over time, the EU's response became more unified, but the policy still was very ineffective until the United States began leading the effort in 1995 (see p. 44).

Maastricht Treaty

Closer to home, some citizens of Europe began to react strongly against the loss of national identity and sovereignty implicit in Maastricht.[10] Through the years of European integration, public opinion has been largely supportive. In recent years, polls have shown a strong majority of European citizens in favor of greater political and military integration, and of expanding the powers of the European Parliament—although support for political union is weak in Denmark and Britain. Perhaps the Eurocrats took public support too much for granted, for a substantial and growing minority was having second thoughts.

As an amendment to the Treaty of Rome, Maastricht had to be ratified by all (then 12) members. The ratification process stirred up strong public feelings against closer European union in several countries. British politicians had already gotten assurances that allowed Britain to stay outside a monetary union and a unified European social policy, if it so chose. In other EU states, however, political leaders and citizens had not fully anticipated the public reactions to Maastricht before signing it. Suddenly, citizens and leaders in several countries seemed to realize that the faceless Eurocrats in Brussels were stripping away their national sovereignty!

---

[10] Cowles, Maria Green, James Caporaso, and Thomas Risse, eds. *Transforming Europe: Europeanization and Domestic Change*. Cornell, 2001. Gstohl, Sieglende. *Reluctant Europeans: Norway, Sweden, and Switzerland and the Process of Integration*. Boulder: Rienner, 2002. Cafruny, Alan W., and Carl Lankowski, eds. *Europe's Ambiguous Unity: Conflict and Consensus in the post-Maastricht Era*. Boulder: Rienner, 1997.

The EU implemented the Maastricht Treaty, although more slowly and with fewer participating countries than originally hoped. Economic and technical integration, including the new monetary union among 12 members, maintained momentum.

Europe's economic integration has begun to reshape political economy at a global level. The EU now sets the rules for access to one of the world's largest markets, for a vast production and technology network, and for the world's strongest currency. Europe's new power is illustrated in its environmental initiatives. The U.S. chemical industry has operated under U.S. regulations that exempt 80 percent of chemicals (those introduced before 1979). The EU is adopting stricter chemical regulations, requiring tests of health effects of all chemicals used in products, and mandating efforts to substitute for toxic chemicals in everyday products. The U.S. government and U.S. companies alike lobbied heavily against the program with European states and the EU, but approval was widely expected in 2005. (Companies accustomed to lobbying and negotiating with individual governments have had to learn their way around Brussels, the EU headquarters.) Similarly, several major U.S. cosmetics companies are reformulating their products to comply with new EU cosmetics regulations calling for removal of unhealthy substances. And Japanese car manufacturers are adapting production processes to meet the EU's requirement that new cars consist of 85 percent recyclable components by 2006 (and 95 percent by 2015).[11] Political and military integration have been much more problematical. The EU decided in 1999 to create a 60,000-troop military force (see p. 88), but NATO will continue to be more important and may even subsume the new force in practice.[12] The struggle between nationalism and supranationalism seems precariously balanced between the two; the transition to supranationalism has not yet been accomplished as to questions of sovereignty and foreign and military policy. Even after 50 years of preparation, spillover from economic to political issues is elusive.

Monetary Union

A European currency, the **euro,** has replaced national currencies in 12 of the 15 EU members, as mandated in the Maastricht process. After several years as an abstract unit like the IMF's SDR (see p. 351), used by national governments and for international exchange, the euro came into full circulation in 2002 and the national currencies ceased to exist. The European Central Bank took over the functions of states' central banks.[13]

Monetary union is difficult for both economic and political reasons. In participating states, fundamental economic and financial conditions must be equalized. One state cannot stimulate its economy with low interest rates (for example, because of a recession) while another cools inflation with high interest rates (because of high economic growth). For example, in 2005 the unemployment rate was 18 percent in Poland but 5 percent in the Netherlands. In an integrated economy that is also politically centralized, the central government can reallocate resources, as the United States might do if Texas were booming and Massachusetts were in recession. But the EU does not have centralized powers of taxation or control of national budgets. This split of fiscal and monetary policy is unusual.

---

[11] Schapiro, Mark. New Power for "Old Europe." *The Nation*, Dec. 27, 2004.

[12] Duke, Simon. *The Elusive Quest for European Security: From EDC to CFSP*. NY: St. Martin's, 2000. Salmon, Trevor C., and Alistair J. K. Shepherd. *Toward a European Army: A Military Power in the Making?* Boulder, CO: Lynne Rienner, 2003.

[13] De Grauwe, Paul. *The Economics of Monetary Union*. 5th ed. Oxford, 2004. Henning, C. Randall, and Pier Carlo Padon. *Transatlantic Perspectives on the Euro*. Washington, DC: Brookings, 2000. Eichengreen, Barry and Jeffry Frieden. *The Political Economy of European Monetary Unification*. Boulder: Westview, 2000. Pentecost, Eric J., and Andre Van Poeck, eds. *European Monetary Integration: Past, Present, and Future*. Northampton, MA: Edward Elgar, 2001.

One solution is to work toward equalizing Europe's economies. For example, to reduce the disparity between rich and poor EU states, the Maastricht Treaty increased the EU budget by $25 billion annually to provide economic assistance to the poorer members. But the richer EU members pay the cost for this aid—in effect carrying the poor countries as free riders on the collective good of EU integration. Partly for this reason, $25 billion annually is far too small to truly equalize the rich and poor countries.

The main solution adopted at Maastricht was to restrict membership in the monetary union, at least in the first round, to only those countries with enough financial stability not to jeopardize the union. To join the unified currency, a state had to achieve certain benchmarks: a budget deficit less than 3 percent of GDP, a national debt less than 60 percent of GDP, an inflation rate no more than 1.5 percentage points above the average of the three lowest-inflation EU members, and stable interest rates and national currency values.

These targets proved difficult to meet for many EU members. There was talk of loosening the standards for admission, but EU leaders believed this to be a dangerous course that could undermine the ultimate stability of the euro. Instead, the leaders of states wanting to participate agreed to buckle down and try to meet the standards. This meant hard choices by governments in France, Spain, Italy, and other countries, to cut budgets and benefits and to take other politically unpopular moves. French workers responded with massive strikes on several occasions. Governments fell to opposition parties in several countries, but the new leaders generally kept to the same course. As a result of their newfound fiscal discipline, all 12 EU members that wanted to participate in the euro ultimately qualified. Britain, Denmark, and Sweden opted to retain their national currencies, though Britain may join soon. In a 2003 referendum, a strong majority of Swedes opposed adopting the euro.

Germany's participation was central because its currency, the mark, was the strongest European currency. In a sense, the euro replaced the mark and the other countries tagged along. (This is why the European Central Bank is in Frankfurt where the German central bank was located.) Proponents of monetary union hope that Germany's sacrifice of its own respected currency will help reassure Europe that German reunification (see p. 43) does not threaten other European countries.

Money is more political than steel tariffs or chocolate ingredients. A monetary union infringes on a core prerogative of states—the right to print currency. Because citizens use money every day, a European currency along these lines could deepen citizens' sense of identification with Europe—a victory for supranationalism over nationalism. When the euro went into circulation in 2002, people for the first time could "put Europe in their pocket." However, precisely for this reason some state leaders and citizens resisted the idea of giving up the symbolic value of their national currencies. These problems were reflected in the task of designing euro banknotes and coins. How could any country's leaders or monuments become Europewide symbols? The solution was to put generic architectural elements (not identifiable by country) on the front of the banknotes and a map of Europe on the back. Coins come in various member-state designs (all valid throughout the euro zone).

The EU met its timetable to launch the euro in 2002. Production of euro banknotes and coins began in 1998. Currency exchange rates were frozen in 1999, and a transition to European Central Bank control began. International currency markets began trading the euro instead of the national currencies. Cash registers across Europe were reprogrammed, and prices were displayed in both euros and national currencies for the transition years. The circulation of euros as legal tender, and the cancellation of national currencies, came in 2002. On E-day, January 1, 2002, 300 million Europeans met $600 billion in freshly printed money in a surprisingly smooth process.

But in 2003 and 2004, Germany and France ran budget deficits higher than allowed under euro rules, raising conflicts within the euro zone. In 2004, the European Commission sued the EU member states for voting to let France and Germany break the euro rules, but after the European Court of Justice told both sides to work harder at resolving the dispute, the Commission suspended its threats (although it continued to apply serious pressure on Germany in 2006). Meanwhile, Greece admitted it had falsified its economic data in order to be admitted. And Latvia's government lost power within six months of the country's joining the EU, under pressure of unpopular budget cuts needed to meet the euro rules within four years.

The EU faces uncharted waters in actually making a monetary union work over the long term without political unification. Before the euro even went into circulation, its value slumped (from $1.17 to $0.88) as investor confidence in the experiment initially proved shaky. Having survived its birth, however, the euro gained back its value, standing at $1.21 as of April 2006. The creation of a European currency is arguably the largest financial overhaul ever attempted in history, and in its first four years it was largely successful.

Expanding the European Union

Despite the resistance encountered in the Maastricht process, the EU has been successful enough to attract neighboring states that want to join. In fact, the larger and more integrated the EU becomes, the less attractive is the prospect of remaining outside it for any state in the vicinity of Europe. The EU expanded from 15 members to 25 in 2004, with potentially far-reaching changes in how the community operates.

Spain and Portugal, admitted in 1986 as the eleventh and twelfth members, filled out the western side of Europe. In 1995, Austria, Sweden, and Finland joined the EU. They are located on the immediate fringe of the present EU area, and as relatively rich countries they did not disrupt the EU economy. Norway applied to join and was accepted, but its citizens voted down the idea in a referendum in 1994, leaving the EU with 15 members after 1995—all but two of the main states of Western Europe. (Switzerland's plans to join were, like Norway's, halted by a popular referendum in the early 1990s.)

WE'RE IN!

The European Union added ten members, mostly from Eastern Europe, in 2004. Here, Latvia's president and prime minister sign the treaty of accession, 2003.

The EU's current expansion is guided by the 2000 Treaty of Nice, which came into effect in 2003 after Irish voters reversed an earlier vote and approved it (the last country to ratify it). Ten new members joined in 2004: Poland, Czech Republic, Slovakia, Hungary, Slovenia, Estonia, Latvia, Lithuania, Malta, and Cyprus. The European Commission expanded to 25 members, without the five largest having two seats, and with new voting rules that move away from a requirement for consensus. The expanded EU has 450

THINKING THEORETICALLY

More Members in the EU Club

Over the years, the membership of the European Union has expanded, from 6 members to 25. According to collective goods theory (see pp. 103–104), the expanding membership should make it easier to free-ride on the community's larger, richer members without being so visible and without disrupting the overall provision of collective goods by the community. This approach could help to explain the difficulties the EU faced in the decade after the 1992 Maastricht Treaty—popular resistance and razor-thin referendum margins, disunity over foreign affairs such as in Bosnia, Britain's shunning of the euro, and squabbles over future expansion.

However, other theories could explain these outcomes as well. A realist could simply point to differences in national interests as creating a natural barrier to integration beyond a certain point. In this view, it was the gradual infringement of national sovereignty (hitting some natural limit) rather than the expansion of membership that explains the problems of EU integration in the 1990s.

We can judge these theories in part by how well they predict the effects of EU expansion into Eastern Europe in 2004. The number-of-actors theory would predict increasing difficulties in holding the EU together as the number of actors keeps growing. Institutional structures and rules would have to change as a result. In particular, the unanimity rule, giving each member state a veto, would have to be much more narrowly restricted. Eventually, a smaller core group might emerge—perhaps even a German-French duopoly or German hegemony—to dictate policy and enforce cooperation in order to overcome collective goods problems.

By contrast, the second theory should predict little effect of the expansion in membership, since the problem is the level of infringement on sovereignty (which does not change when more members are added). Indeed, by one logic, the expansion of membership is slowing down the deepening of ties among today's EU members. In that case, expansion would actually smooth out the EU's problems by slowing the assault on national sovereignty. Power would shift to Brussels (the EU headquarters) rather than Berlin and Paris.

In the first year after the 2004 expansion, evidence supported the second, more realist theory. Despite continuing differences on unrelated issues such as the war in Iraq, EU members and structures took the expansion from 15 to 25 members in stride. Collective goods problems such as absorbing poorer members and allocating agricultural subsidies did not provoke major crises, and power continued to shift to Brussels. Theories play different roles, but one important feature of a theory is the ability to improve projections of future possibilities. By watching the ongoing effects of EU expansion in the coming years, we can see which theory best explains the outcome.

million citizens and nearly equals the U.S. economy in GDP. Romania and Bulgaria may join in 2007, and Turkey continues to seek membership. Although it rebuffed Turkey in 2002, the EU later agreed to begin formal entry negotiations with Turkey in October 2005—the start of a years-long process. Turkey has made major economic and political changes, including abolishing the death penalty and improving human rights, to try to win EU membership. A major sticking point for Turkey now is Cyprus, which Turkey and Greece have fought wars over to protect their respective ethnic populations there.

As these states joined the EU in 2004, the ability of the EU to reach decisions by consensus became more complicated. The working time required to make decisions in the Council of Ministers expanded with potential conflicts and alliances on a particular issue among 25 rather than 15 members.

POLICY PERSPECTIVES

Chancellor of Germany, Angela Merkel

PROBLEM *Maintaining a domestic coalition while following European Union regulations.*

BACKGROUND Imagine that you are the Chancellor of Germany. Your party, the Christian Democratic Union (CDU), won a narrow victory in German elections in late 2005. Your party did not gain a majority of seats in the legislature, however, so you have entered into a coalition with your rival party, the Social Democrats (SPD). It is a tense coalition that experts say could easily fall apart, given the longstanding rivalry between the two parties.

One of the key issues confronting your coalition is the economy. While Germany is the largest economy in Europe, it has been struggling lately. Growth rates have fallen to below one percent and unemployment is quite high, hovering above 11 percent last year. Your weak economy has led to ballooning budget deficits over the past four years owing to lower tax revenue and increased spending on social welfare programs.

While this would never be good news for any leader, your situation in Europe makes it particularly troublesome. Because Germany is one of the countries that has adopted the euro, it has agreed to keep its budget deficit to less than 3 percent of your GDP. For the last four years, it has failed to do so. Your fellow Eurozone states (all countries who have adopted the euro) have threatened to fine Germany if you do not bring the deficits under control.

You have attempted to bring the deficit under control by raising taxes, lowering the retirement age to encourage less pension collection, and making large cuts in the budget. Yet, these moves will likely be politically unpopular, especially with your coalition partners in the SPD. If a public backlash against these policies were to develop, your coalition government (and thus your position as Chancellor) could end. The silver lining, however, is that economists now predict that your country's growth rate will increase in 2007, helping your economy to recover.

SCENARIO Now suppose that projections of economic recovery in your country are mistaken. Rather than realizing an increase in economic growth (and therefore tax income), your economy suffers further contraction. The increase in taxes and changes in pension policies do not help reverse your growing budget deficit, and for a fifth year in a row, your budget deficit exceeds the limit of 3 percent of GDP.

The EU is now deciding whether to lodge heavy fines to punish you for ignoring the deficit ceiling that is required for the euro. The SPD is demanding that you do not take further cuts from welfare or other spending programs. Do you bow to the SPD and risk punishment from the EU? While the short-term punishment from the EU may not be costly, the long-term effects of high budget deficits could undermine international confidence in the euro and weaken German leadership within the EU. Or do you chance losing the support of the SPD and propose major cutbacks in spending to balance the budget? Such cuts would help to comply with the EU but risk a domestic backlash at home.

CHOOSE YOUR POLICY How do you balance the needs of your domestic economy, the demands of your government coalition partners, and the requirements of the EU? Do you continue to turn your back on the EU to please domestic constituents or do you comply with the directives of your partners in supranationalism?

Expanding the European Union

Furthermore, by Western European standards, the new members are relatively poor. Existing EU members are wary of being dragged down by these economies, most of which are still embroiled in the painful transition from socialism to capitalism and sometimes lack stable currencies. Their prospects for joining a European monetary union appear some years in the future at best. The tensions between nationalism and supranationalism might intensify, with more states pulling in more directions at once.

Perhaps as a result of these pressures, the EU in the last decade shows signs of dividing into "inner" and "outer" layers—those states such as France and Germany joining a currency union and deepening their integration, and those such as Britain and perhaps the new members operating at the edges of the EU with more autonomy. This division of the EU was illustrated in 1995 when seven countries from Portugal to Germany abolished border controls and the need for passports but in turn tightened border controls between themselves and the eight other EU members that did not join the free-movement zone. Suddenly, Germans who crossed into Denmark (a nonparticipant) on Sunday mornings to buy bread (because German bakeries were closed on Sunday) began to need identification at the border; formerly they had just waved their bags of bread at the border guards as they crossed back into Germany.

Immigration and Islam in Europe

Netherlands Votes on the EU Constitution

To grapple with the implications of an expanding EU, the 25 leaders signed an EU constitution in late 2004 and the European Parliament gave it a strong vote of support in 2005. To take effect, it was to be ratified by all 25 states, including several requiring referendums. The constitution was to establish a stronger president of the EU, and a foreign minister, to represent Europe as a global superpower in world affairs. It was to replace the requirement for consensus in EU decision making with majority voting in more cases. And it was to guarantee fundamental rights to all EU citizens. (After long debate, the document did not refer to Christianity as a core European value.) But voters in France and the Netherlands rejected the constitution and the process halted, with EU leaders entering a period of self-described "reflection" on Europe's future. Despite the rejection of the constitution, however, the EU continues to function as well as ever under the existing rules.

Beyond the EU itself, Europe is a patchwork of overlapping structures with varying memberships (see Figure 10.2). Despite the Single European Act, there are still many Europes. Within the EU are the "inner six," the "poor four," and the possible new joiners, each with its own concerns. Around the edges are the EFTA states participating in the European Economic Area. NATO membership overlaps partly with the EU. Russia and even the United States are European actors in some respects but not others.[14]

One truly universal intergovernmental organization exists in Europe—the *Organization for Security and Cooperation in Europe (OSCE)*. Operating by consensus, with a large and universal membership of 55 states, the OSCE has little power except to act as a forum for discussions of security issues. In the late 1990s, the OSCE shifted into new tasks such as running elections, helping political parties in Bosnia and Kosovo, and providing various forms of monitoring and assistance in a half dozen Eastern European countries.

Thus, international integration is not a matter of a single group or organization but more a mosaic of structures tying states together. These various structures of the European political system, centered on the EU, are IGOs composed of states as members. But a less-tangible aspect of integration is the sense of identity that develops over time as economic (and other functional) ties bring people closer together across borders. Supranational identity, culture, and communication are also aspects of international integration. The remainder of this chapter considers how information technologies are bypassing states and bringing about this kind of integration globally.

---

[14] Croft, Stuart, John Redmond, G. Wyn Rees, and Mark Webber. *The Englargement of Europe*. Manchester, 1999.

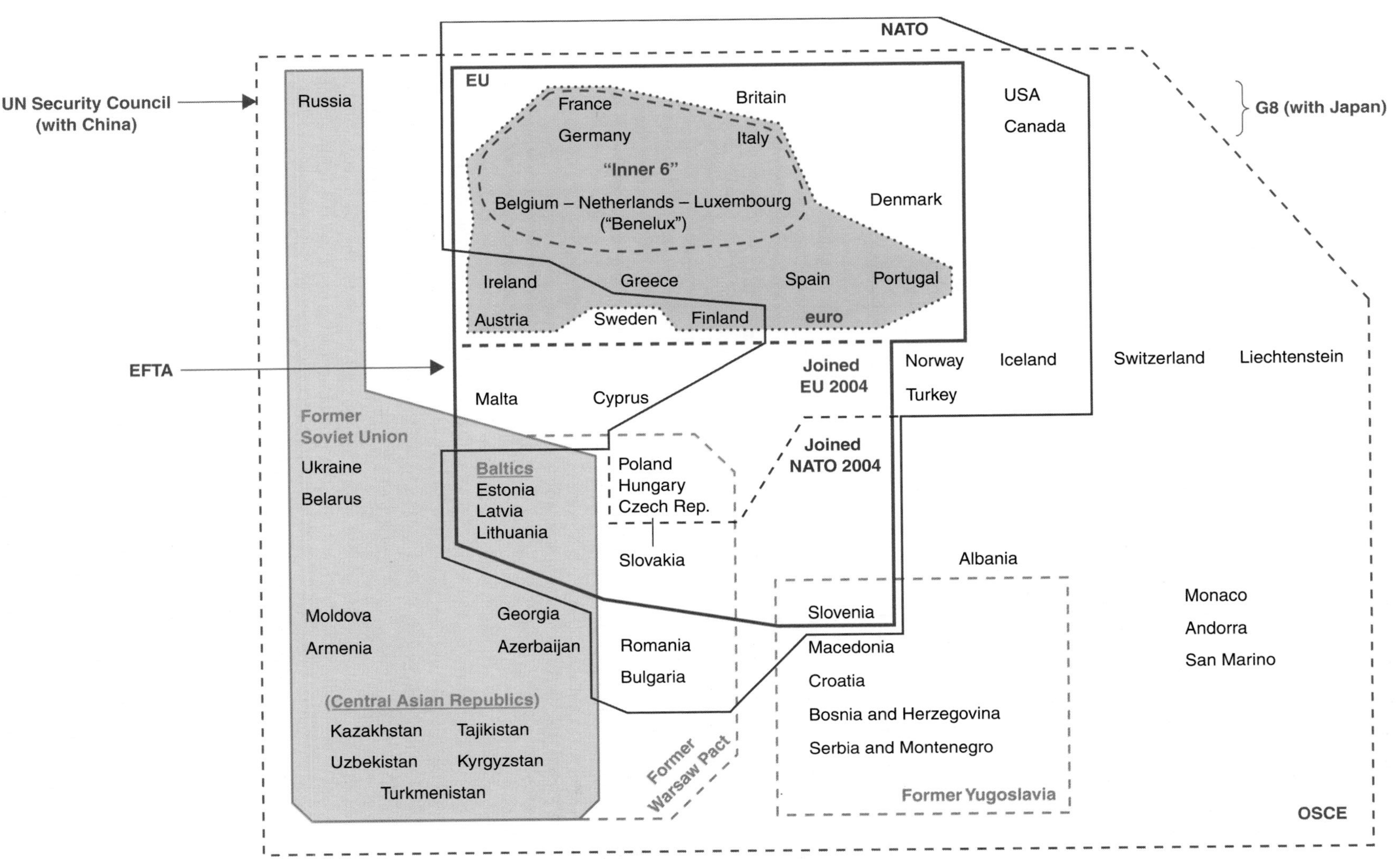

FIGURE 10.2 ■ Overlapping Memberships of European States

The Power of Information

Global telecommunications are profoundly changing how information and culture function in international relations.[15] Information is now a vital tool of national governments in their interactions with each other. Yet technology is at the same time undermining and disempowering those governments and shifting power to substate actors and individuals. Those newly empowered individuals and groups have begun to create new transnational networks worldwide, bypassing states.

Wiring the World

Wiring the World

New international political possibilities arise from technological developments.[16] Just a hundred years ago, the idea of instant global communication was incomprehensible. It would have seemed unthinkable that anyone could push a dozen buttons on a handheld instrument and be able to talk with any of billions of people anywhere in the economically developed areas of the world (and many of the poorer areas). Equally ridiculous was the idea that you could look at a box no bigger than a suitcase and see in it moving pictures of things happening at that moment in distant lands. For most of the history of the international system, until about 150 years ago, the fastest way to send information was to write it down and bring it to the recipient by horse or sailing ship.

The media over which information travels—telephones, television, films, magazines, and so forth—shape the way ideas take form and spread from one place to another. The media with the strongest political impact are radio and (especially) television. There are about one and a half billion TV sets and two and a half billion radio receivers in the world (roughly one-third are in North America, one-third in Western and Eastern Europe and Russia, and the rest in the global South and Japan/Pacific).[17] The power of these media is to take a single source of information (a moving picture or a voice) and reproduce it in many copies in many locations.

Radio, and increasingly TV, reaches the poorest rural areas of the global South. Peasants who cannot read can understand radio. Shortwave radio—typically stations such as Voice of America (VOA), the British Broadcasting Corporation (BBC), and Radio Moscow—is popular in remote locations.

TV is especially powerful. The combination of pictures and sounds affects viewers emotionally and intellectually. Viewers can experience distant events more fully. Traditionally this participation has been passive. But as technology has developed in recent decades, the passive nature of TV is changing. More and more channels of information on TV give viewers power over what they watch—from the local city council meeting, to simultaneous translation of the Russian evening news (in the United States), to MTV music videos (in Russia). Less and less frequently are millions of TV viewers all forced to march to the beat of the same drummer; rather, the global TV audience is being fragmented into many small pieces, often not along national lines. In recent years, independent TV news channels have attracted large audiences in India, Pakistan, and Nepal.

---

[15] Comor, Edward A., ed. *The Global Political Economy of Communication: Hegemony, Telecommunication and the Information Economy*. NY: St. Martin's, 1994. Frederick, Howard H. *Global Communication and International Relations*. Belmont, CA: Wadsworth, 1993. Tehranian, Majid. *Global Communication and World Politics: Domination, Development, and Discourse*. Boulder, CO: Lynne Rienner, 1999.

[16] Pool, Ithiel de Sola. *Technologies Without Boundaries: On Telecommunications in a Global Age*. Edited by Eli M. Noam. Harvard, 1990. Treverton, Gregory F. *Reshaping National Intelligence in an Age of Information*. Cambridge, 2001. Allison, Juliann E, ed. *Technology, Development, and Democracy: International Conflict and Cooperation in the Information Age*. SUNY, 2002.

[17] UNESCO. *UNESCO Yearbook*. NY: United Nations (annual).

Ordinary over-the-air TV and radio signals are radio waves carried on specific frequencies. Frequencies are a limited resource in high demand, which governments regulate and allocate to users. Because radio waves do not respect national borders, the allocation of frequencies is a subject of interstate bargaining. International regimes have grown up around the regulation of international communications technologies.[18]

Cable TV does not use the airwaves of the radio spectrum and can carry hundreds of signals at once. Cable also has the potential to carry signals *from* viewers. Satellite transmissions also bypass the normal over-the-air radio spectrum and transmit signals over a huge area to dish-shaped antennas.

The Qatar-based all-news satellite TV network, al Jazeera, begun in 1996, has become a force in Middle East politics. It reaches an influential audience across the region and world. (Reportedly only 10 to 15 percent of Arabs have satellite dishes, but that fraction still amounts to millions of viewers.) It is considered one of the few media that does not stick narrowly with a government line, and it has influenced Arabs' views of the Palestinian conflict. Criticized by Western governments for airing Osama bin Laden videos and anti-American propaganda generally, al Jazeera also occasionally broadcasts interviews with top U.S. officials. The only foreign network allowed to report regularly from Taliban-ruled Afghanistan during the 2001 U.S. bombing, its office there was destroyed by a U.S. missile.

LET'S TALK

Global communication, a very new capability on the time scale of the international system, is changing the rules of IR and empowering nonstate transnational actors. Telecommunications could change the path of development in poor countries, possibly bypassing traditional infrastructure like phone lines and leapfrogging to a wireless networked economy. Cheap phones and prepaid calling cards are putting cell phones in reach of a growing segment of the population in the global South. This shop does a brisk business in Abidjan, Ivory Coast, 2001.

Images and sounds are being recorded, reproduced, and viewed in new ways through audiotapes and videotapes. Videocassette recorders (VCRs) have proliferated in many countries in recent years. Audio- and videotapes can be played repeatedly and passed from person to person, again giving the listener and viewer more control. Video cameras are empowering ordinary citizens to create their own visual records, such as videos of political demonstrations in one country that end up on the TV news in another country.

Even more empowering of ordinary citizens is the telephone. Unlike TV and radio, phones are a two-way medium through which users interact without any centralized information source. In Africa, cheap cell phones with cheap prepaid calling cards have let millions of relatively poor individuals bypass the lack of infrastructure previously needed to communicate. (Sub-Saharan Africa in total has fewer phone lines than Manhattan alone.)

[18] Franda, Marcus. *Governing the Internet: The Emergence of an International Regime*. Boulder, CO: Lynne Rienner, 2001. Krasner, Stephen D. Global Communications and National Power: Life on the Pareto Frontier. *World Politics* 43 (3), 1991: 336–66. Braman, Sandra, ed. *The Emergent Global Information Policy Regime*. NY: Palgrave, 2004.

From 1999 to 2004, African subscribers increased from fewer than 8 million to nearly 80 million. Worldwide, about one billion people have cell phones. Telephones, perhaps more than any other technology, make individuals international actors. The increased flows of information from state to state reflect the growing interdependence of today's world.

Information technologies have security implications. Capabilities such as fiber-optic cables or satellite communications serve governments in conducting their foreign and military policies (see "Evolving Technologies" on pp. 229–230). Nonstate actors such as terrorist organizations have also harbored the power of cellular phones and the Internet to recruit operatives, raise money, and coordinate attacks.

In a subtle but pervasive way, communication technologies may be diffusing power away from governments and toward ordinary people and other nonstate actors.[19] Recall that new "smart weapons" technologies are empowering the foot soldier relative to large-weapons systems (see p. 230). New communications technologies may be doing the same for ordinary citizens relative to governments and political parties.

Information as a Tool of Governments

Not all aspects of the information revolution work against governments. With more information traveling around the world than ever before, information has become an important instrument of governments' power (domestic and interstate).[20] Above all, governments want *access to information*. In 1992, U.S. Secretary of State James Baker made his first visit to the newly independent Asian republics of the former Soviet Union (the poorest and most remote CIS members). At each stop, one of the first questions Baker was asked by the state leader was, "How do I get CNN?"[21] CNN, state leaders hoped, would tie them directly to the Western world and symbolize their independence from Russia. Access to CNN was also considered a status symbol.

CNN

U.S. military leaders recognized the importance of playing to a global audience when, during the bombing of Bosnian Serb forces in 1995, they designated an ammunition dump close to Sarajevo the "CNN site" because they knew the explosion would make good footage for Sarajevo-based TV cameras. During the 1991 Gulf War, the U.S. military fed TV networks pictures of precision weapons striking their targets, to help "sanitize" the bombing campaign (which mostly used unguided bombs).

With today's information technologies, it is easier for governments to gather, organize, and store huge amounts of information. In this respect, the information revolution empowers governments more than ever. In the past, a wanted criminal, druglord, or terrorist could slip over the border and take refuge in a foreign country. The terrorists who attacked the United States in 2001 demonstrated how easy this was. Today, however, it is more likely that a routine traffic ticket in the foreign country could trigger an instant directive to arrest the person. Information technologies give repressive governments more power to keep tabs on citizens, spy on dissidents, and manipulate public opinion. Those technologies are now also being mobilized in force to strengthen international counterterrorism.

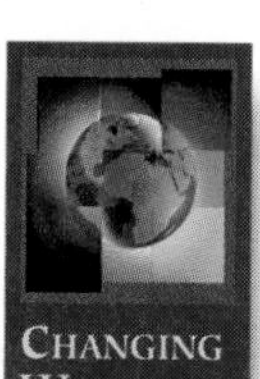

Big Brother Is Watching

Just as citizens and terrorists find it harder to hide from governments, so are state governments finding it harder to hide information from each other. The military importance

[19] Rosenau, James N. *Turbulence in World Politics: A Theory of Change and Continuity*. Princeton, 1990. Rosenau, James N., and Ernst-Otto Czempiel, eds. *Governance Without Government: Order and Change in World Politics*. Cambridge, 1992.

[20] Deutsch, Karl W. *The Nerves of Government: Models of Political Communication and Control*. NY: Free Press, 1969.

[21] *The New York Times*, February 2, 1992: A10.

of satellite reconnaissance has been cited (see p. 228). A powerful state such as the United States can increase its power through information technologies. It can and does monitor the phone calls, faxes, data transmissions, and radio conversations in foreign countries.

As the cost of information technology decreases, it comes into reach of more states. The great powers have always been able to maintain a worldwide presence and gather information globally. Now small states can gain some of the same capabilities electronically—if only by monitoring world affairs on CNN. Even sophisticated information is more available and cheaper—high-resolution satellite photos are now available commercially within the price range of most states. These images can be used for both military purposes and natural-resource management—knowing which states (including one's own) have such resources as minerals, forests, and farmland, and the rate at which they are being used.

HOT OFF THE PRESS

Information, which easily crosses state borders, is a major factor in both international and domestic politics and may even be laying technological foundations for a global identity. Governments and their opponents struggle over control of information. Here a staff member of Kenya's daily newspaper surveys the damage after police—responding to unfavorable coverage of the president—stormed its offices and burned tens of thousands of copies, 2006.

The very nature of interstate interactions is affected by changes in information technology. The risks of surprise in IR are reduced by the information revolution. The security dilemma is less severe as a result (states do not need to arm against unknown potential threats since they know what the real threats are). Similarly, the ability to monitor performance of agreements makes collective goods problems easier to resolve since cheaters and free riders can be identified (see pp. 103–104). Moreover, the ability of governments to bargain effectively with each other and to reach mutually beneficial outcomes is enhanced by the availability of instant communications channels.

In addition to gaining access to information, governments use information as a power capability by disseminating it internationally and domestically. In today's information-intensive world, TV transmitters may be more powerful than tanks. Even in war itself, propaganda plays a key role. For instance, in the 2003 War in Iraq pamphlets and loudspeakers were used to appeal to Iraqi soldiers and citizens, asking them to not take up arms against U.S. forces.

The information disseminated by a government often crosses international borders, intentionally and otherwise. The government of Jordan, for example, is well aware that its Arabic programs are received by Arab citizens of Israel and that its English programs are watched by Israeli Jews. When Jordanian TV broadcasts, say, a U.S. documentary about the U.S. civil rights movement (with Arabic subtitles), the message influences Israeli-Palestinian relations across the border.

Most governments create explicit channels of information dissemination to influence domestic and international audiences. Stations such as Radio Moscow broadcast radio programs in dozens of languages aimed at all the world's regions. The United States operates the VOA shortwave radio network, which is picked up in many third world regions where it may be one of the few outside information sources. The United States also beams specialized programming into Cuba (TV/Radio Marti) and China (Radio Free Asia, which includes programs in the minority Tibetan and Uighur languages), among others. During the 2001 U.S.-Chinese crisis regarding a U.S. reconnaissance plane that crash-landed in China, the Chinese government heavily jammed broadcasts into China of VOA and Radio Free Asia.

Governments spread false as well as true information as a means of international influence. This is called *disinformation*. In the 1930s, the Nazis discovered that the "big lie," if repeated enough times, would be accepted as truth by most people. It is harder to fool international audiences these days, but domestic ones can still respond to propagandistic misinformation. Anyone who follows international events should remember that even stories reported in the Western news as fact are sometimes disinformation.

America's Arabic TV Channel

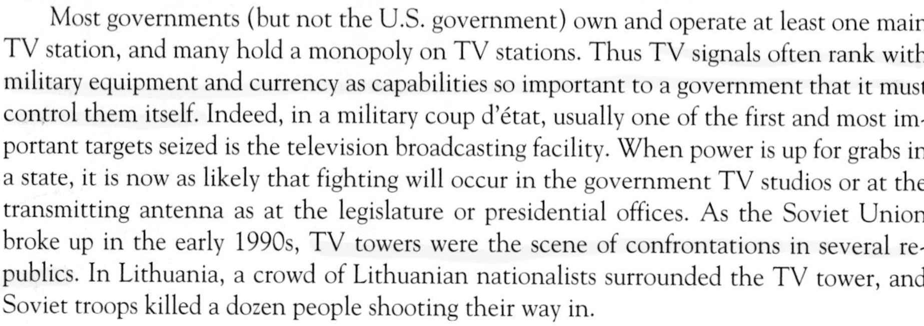

Most governments (but not the U.S. government) own and operate at least one main TV station, and many hold a monopoly on TV stations. Thus TV signals often rank with military equipment and currency as capabilities so important to a government that it must control them itself. Indeed, in a military coup d'état, usually one of the first and most important targets seized is the television broadcasting facility. When power is up for grabs in a state, it is now as likely that fighting will occur in the government TV studios or at the transmitting antenna as at the legislature or presidential offices. As the Soviet Union broke up in the early 1990s, TV towers were the scene of confrontations in several republics. In Lithuania, a crowd of Lithuanian nationalists surrounded the TV tower, and Soviet troops killed a dozen people shooting their way in.

Information as a Tool Against Governments

Information can be used against governments as well, by foreign governments or by domestic political opponents.[22] Governments, especially repressive ones, fear the free flow of information, for good reason. When they are allowed to circulate among a population, ideas become a powerful force that can sweep aside governments, as when the idea of democracy swept away the white-rule system of apartheid in South Africa in the early 1990s. New information technologies have become powerful tools of domestic opposition movements and their allies in foreign governments. Television coverage fed popular discontent regarding the U.S. war in Vietnam in the 1960s and 1970s, and the Russian war in Chechnya in 1995.

In Iran, the government was brought down in part by audiotapes containing speeches and sermons by Ayatollah Khomeini, who spoke against the inequalities and harsh repression of the pro-Western government of the Shah of Iran. In today's Iran, millions of people use the Internet, uncensored, to talk about taboo topics such as sex, fashion, and politics. Stores sell prepaid Internet cards good for ten hours of access. Similarly, in China today, people just call in to a service provider from any modem to access the Internet, without a subscription, and get the bill for 36 cents an hour added to their phone bill. More than a hundred million Chinese use the Internet. Both Iran and China want the economic benefits of information on the Internet, despite their governments' usual impulse to control access to information.

In Thailand in 1992, military leaders lost power in what some Thais called "the cellular phone revolution." Students protesting against the military government were joined by newly affluent Thais with access to cellular phones and fax machines. When the government shot the demonstrators in the streets, arrested them, and cut off their phone

[22] Jones, Adam. Wired World: Communications Technology, Governance, and the Democratic Uprising. In Edward A. Comor, see footnote. 15.

lines, the protesters stayed organized by using mobile phones and fax machines. In the Philippines in 2001, huge protests that swept a president from office were organized through text messages on cell phones (sent to entire lists at a time). The phones are used by 2 million Filipinos including some homeless people. The harsh military government in Burma (Myanmar) faced the power of shortwave radio broadcasts by the opposition movement, made using a transmitter owned by the government of Norway. In Ghana, very popular talk-shows on private FM radio programs—allowed after 1995—gave voice to ordinary people who then threw out the ruling party in 2000. The global peace demonstrations preceding the 2003 Iraq War carried the power of information technologies to new levels. Reacting quickly to developments, organizers were able to turn out millions of people in dozens of countries on short notice. One U.S. group (moveon.org) used a Web site to schedule protesters' phone calls to their Congressional representatives every minute of one day, the kind of coordinated action that would have required a large staff and budget in the past (moveon.org had a staff of four at the time).[23]

To counteract such uses of information, governments throughout the world try to limit the flow of unfavorable information—especially information from foreign sources. For example, China and several other developing countries have channeled all access to the Internet (and the World Wide Web) through a few state-controlled service providers. This system lets the government monitor and control who can have access to the mass of information available through the Internet. During and after the 1989 Tiananmen protests, before the Internet was a factor, the Chinese government tried desperately to suppress the flow of information into and out of China. It stationed police at every fax machine in the country to screen incoming faxes. In 2004, the Chinese government began filtering the hundreds of billions of instant text messages exchanged annually among 300 million Chinese cell phone subscribers. The U.S. company Google, complying with Chinese law but angering U.S. critics, blocks politically sensitive words from its Chinese search engine.

THE WHOLE WORLD IS WATCHING

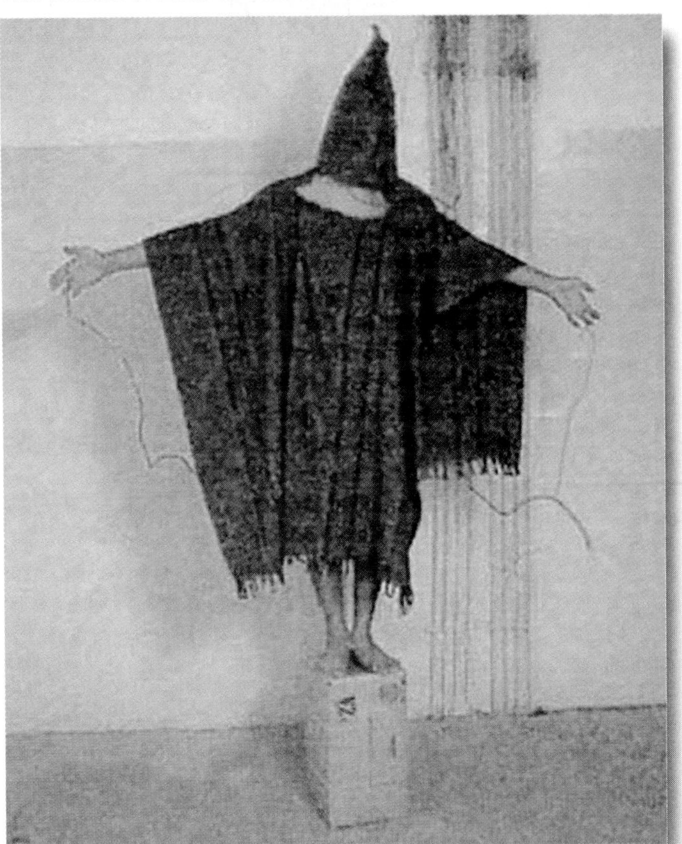

States do not control the global flow of information, which has become a potent force in world politics. State leaders are becoming just another set of players in a worldwide competition to reach audiences and markets and to "spin" stories a certain way. For example, U.S. actions in Iraq since 2003 play out regionally and globally in the media, making the Iraq issue a high priority even for citizens of Arab countries not materially affected by the conflict. This photo and others showing Iraqi prisoners being abused and humiliated by U.S. soldiers were reprinted widely throughout the Arab world and elsewhere in 2004, deepening anti-American sentiment and setting back U.S. efforts to win allies and support for its foreign policy goals.

[23] Fathi, Nazila, and Erik Eckholm. Taboo Surfing: Click Here for Iran . . . And Click Here for China. *The New York Times*, Aug. 4, 2002. Shenon, Philip. Mobile Phones Primed, Affluent Thais Join Fray. *The New York Times*, May 20, 1992: A10. Schmetzer, Uli. Cellphones Spurred Filipinos' Coup. *The Chicago Tribune*, Jan. 22, 2001. Crossette, Barbara. Burmese Opposition Gets Oslo Radio Service. *The New York Times*, July 19, 1992: A11. Friedman, Thomas L. Low-Tech Democracy. *The New York Times*, May 1, 2001: A27.

In an extreme case, the Soviet Union during the Cold War prohibited all but a few photocopy machines. Dissidents' writings were passed from hand to hand and recopied on typewriters. In 1987, the Soviet Union had only 16 international long-distance circuits in and out of the country, all routed through Moscow. This helped the government to reduce the influence of foreign ideas and to closely monitor foreigners—but at a huge cost in economic efficiency. When the Soviet Union broke up there were only 91 circuits. A decade later Russia had 50,000.[24]

Efforts by one government to project power through media broadcasts often bring counterefforts by other governments to block such broadcasts. The VOA, the BBC, and other foreign media were routinely jammed by the Soviet Union and other closed societies during the Cold War. But Soviet efforts to control information did not prevent the collapse of that government. To the contrary, the effort to run a modern economy without photocopy machines, international phone lines, computers, and other information technologies clearly contributed to the economic stagnation of the country.

All in all, the tide of technology seems to be running against governments (though not all scholars would agree with this assessment). Information gets through, and no political power seems capable of holding it back for long. As more and more communication channels carry more information to more places, governments become just another player in a crowded field.

As the information revolution continues to unfold, it will further increase international interdependence, making actions in one state reverberate in other states more strongly than in the past. Information is thus slowly undermining the assumptions of state sovereignty and territorial integrity held dear by realists. At the same time, by empowering substate and transnational actors, information technology is undermining the centrality of states themselves in world affairs.

International Culture

As the information revolution increases the power and importance of transnational actors, it puts into motion two contradictory forces. One we have just discussed—the empowering of substate actors. This force was a factor in the disintegration of the Soviet Union and Yugoslavia, and the proliferation of civil wars since the end of the Cold War. As substate groups gain power, they demand their own national rights of sovereignty and autonomy. Nationalism reasserts itself in smaller but more numerous units.

The second force, however, is the forging of transnational communities and supranational identities—a process alluded to earlier with reference to the EU. Here regionalism or globalism asserts itself as an internationalized culture resting on communication links among people in different states. This second force, perhaps more than the first, challenges the realist emphasis on national borders and territorial integrity.

Telecommunications and Global Culture

Global Culture

Not only can people in one part of the world communicate with those elsewhere, they can also now find common interests to talk about. Riding the telecommunications revolution, a **global culture** is beginning to develop, notwithstanding the great divisions remaining in culture and perspective (especially between the rich and poor regions of the world; see Chapter 12). In the global village, distance and borders matter less and less. Across dozens

[24] Ramirez, Anthony. Dial Direct to Moscow and Beyond. *The New York Times*, May 20, 1992: D1. United States. *CIA World Factbook*, 2001.

of countries, people are tuned in to the same news, the same music, the same sports events. Along with international politics, these activities now take place on a world stage with a world audience. The process might be seen as a form of cultural integration, similar to economic and technical integration.

Cultures, languages, and locations interact more quickly as the unfinished process of cultural integration proceeds. For example, in a rural town in Massachusetts, the local cable TV channel on weekends carries live news broadcasts from around the world (without translation), downloaded from a satellite consortium. One weekend, the Brazilian TV news on this broadcast included an ad for a U.S. film set in the Brazilian rain forest, dubbed in Portuguese. Information is bouncing around the world—Brazilian rain forest to Hollywood movie production to Brazilian movie theaters to Massachusetts cable TV. Such trends clearly undermine assumptions of state autonomy.

Ultimately, transnational cultural integration might lead to the emergence of supranational identities, including a global identity. If citizens in EU states can begin to think as Europeans, will citizens in UN member states someday begin to think as human beings and residents of Planet Earth? The answer is unclear. As we have seen, group identity is an important source of conflict between in-groups and out-groups (see "Ethnic Conflict" on pp. 185–192). Nationalism has tapped into the psychological dynamics of group identity in a powerful way that has legitimized the state as the ultimate embodiment of its people's aspirations and identity. Now the information revolution may aid the development of supranational identity. So far, nationalism continues to hold the upper hand. Global identity has not yet come to rival national identity in any state.

For a fleeting moment at the turn of the millennium such a global identity seemed almost possible. The feared "Y2K" computer bug, which would cause old software to think time had jumped back 100 years, was fixed in a massive technology upgrade that "leveraged the resources of the whole planet," in the words of an IBM executive. On December 31, 1999, as each time zone passed midnight, people around the world watched to see whether fears of computer failures, terrorist attacks, or riots would materialize. UN Secretary-General Annan said that "each city seemed to be rooting for cities in the next time zone to get through Y2K without any problems. It was like, 'O.K., Tokyo is through, now how about Beijing?' And then, 'Moscow is through, how about New York?' For one brief moment there was a pulling together all over the planet."[25] As the feared problems did not materialize, the world was left with a 24-hour moment of good feeling broadcast live on CNN and the Internet.

Cultural Imperialism Like international integration generally, global culture has its down side. The emerging global culture is primarily the culture of white Europeans and their descendants in rich areas of the world (mixed slightly with cultural elements of Japan and local third world elites). For many people, especially in the global South, the information revolution carrying global culture into their midst is, despite its empowering potential, an invasive force in practice. Because cultures are being subsumed, half of the world's nearly 7,000 languages risk extinction this century, according to UNESCO.

Above all, the emerging global culture is dominated by the world's superpower, the United States; this dominance has been referred to as **cultural imperialism.**[26] U.S. cultural influence is at least as strong as U.S. military influence. If there is a world language, it is English.

[25] Friedman, Thomas L. The Spirit of Y2K. *The New York Times*, Jan. 7, 2000.

[26] Maxwell, Richard. *Culture Works: The Political Economy of Culture*. Minnesota, 2001. Wilkins, Karin Gwinn. *Redeveloping Communication for Social Change: Theory, Practice, Power*. Lanham, MD: Rowman & Littlefield, 2000. Friedman, Thomas L. *The Lexus and the Olive Tree*. NY: Farrar, Straus and Giroux, 1999. Barber, Benjamin R. *Jihad vs. McWorld*. NY: Times Books, 1995. Tomlinson, John. *Cultural Imperialism: A Critical Introduction*. Johns Hopkins, 1991.

U.S. films and TV shows dominate world markets. For instance, U.S. movies predominate in countries from Europe to Asia to Latin America (although top music titles, and most top TV shows, tend to be national, not American).[27] Culture may be just another economic product, to be produced in the place of greatest comparative advantage, but culture also is central to national identity and politics. France held up the GATT agreement in 1994 until it could protect its film industry from U.S. competition. The prospect of cultural imperialism thus opens another front in the conflict of liberalism and mercantilism.

Industrialized countries have responded in various ways to U.S. cultural dominance. Canada has allowed U.S. cultural influence to become fairly pervasive, with some resentment but few severe frictions. France has been especially wary of U.S. influence; commissions periodically try to weed English expressions out of the French language (not an easy task). However, Japan seemingly incorporated whole segments of U.S. culture after World War II, from baseball to hamburgers, yet remained Japanese.

Global culture and cultural imperialism shape the news that is reported by the TV, radio, and print media. In the United States alone, 50 million viewers watch network news nightly.[28] To an increasing extent, everyone in the world follows the same story line of world news from day to day. To some extent, there is now a single drama unfolding at the global level, and the day's top international story on CNN very likely will also be reported by the other U.S. television networks, the national TV news in France, Japan, Russia, and most other states, and the world's radio and print media. The fact that everyone is following the same story reflects the globalizing influence of world communications. Cultural imperialism is reflected in the fact that the story often revolves around U.S. actions, reflects U.S. values, or is reported by U.S. reporters and news organizations. The attack on Iraq in 1991 illustrates in the extreme how the whole world watches one story—a story shaped by U.S. perspectives. When the bombing of Baghdad began, Saddam Hussein reportedly sat in his bunker watching the war unfold on CNN.

Transnational Communities

Although a global culture is still only nascent and the most powerful identity is still at the national level, people have begun to participate in specific communities that bridge national boundaries. International journalists, for example, are members of such a community. They work with colleagues from various countries and travel from state to state with each other. Though a journalist's identity *as* a journalist rarely takes precedence over his or her national identity, the existence of the transnational community of journalists creates a new form of international interdependence.

Like journalists, scientists and church members work in communities spanning national borders. So do members of transnational movements, such as those linking women from various countries, or environmentalists, or human rights activists. The effect once again is to undermine the state's role as the primary actor in international affairs. More important, the links forged in such transnational communities may create a new functionalism that could encourage international integration on a global scale.

International sports competition is one of the broadest-based transnational communities, especially strong at the regional level. Millions of fans watch their teams compete with teams from other countries. Of course, international sports competition can stir up animosities between neighbors, as when British soccer hooligans rampage through another

---

[27] Shenon, Philip. Indonesian Films Squeezed Out by U.S. Giant. *The New York Times*, Oct 29, 1992: A17. The Media Business: What Is Playing in the Global Village? *The New York Times*, May 26, 1997: D4–D5.
[28] Jordan, Donald L., and Benjamin I. Page. Shaping Foreign Policy Opinions: The Role of TV News. *Journal of Conflict Resolution* 36 (2), 1992: 227–41.

European country after their team loses a game. But sports also create a sense of participation in a supranational community. This is especially true of world-level sports events in which a global athletic community participates. The Olympic Games (sponsored by the International Olympic Committee, an NGO) are a global event broadcast to a worldwide audience.[29]

Some people see sports as a force for peace. Sports events bring people from different countries together in shared activities. Citizens of different states share their admiration of sports stars, who become international celebrities. The U.S.-Chinese rapprochement of 1971 was so delicate that political cooperation was impossible until the way had first been paved by sports—the U.S. table tennis team that made the first official U.S. visit to China.

Most communication over the world's broadcasting networks is neither news nor sports, but drama—soap operas, films, situation comedies, documentaries, and so forth. Here U.S. cultural imperialism is strong, because so many films and TV shows watched around the world originate in Hollywood. The entertainment industry is a strong export sector of the U.S. economy. Large third world countries such as Brazil and India have concentrated their TV production efforts in an area where local contexts can gain viewers' interest and where production costs are modest—soap operas. They are immensely popular in these and other third world countries.

The popularity of Brazilian soap operas notwithstanding, many international viewers see less of their own experiences than of dramas set in the United States. These dramas, of course, give a distorted view of U.S. life, such as the impression that all Americans are rich. Recall that "deconstruction" of such TV shows, according to postmodernists, reveals hidden political subtexts (see pp. 122–123).

MAC ATTACK

Some call it "global community" others, "cultural imperialism." The power of information, opening up a wave of globalization in international business, is bringing together cultures in sometimes incongruous ways. Chinese leaders seemed unsure for years about whether McDonald's brought Western-style prosperity or spiritual pollution—maybe a bit of each.

The power of such messages was demonstrated in 1991, when Albania's communist government was crumbling along with its economy. Desperately poor Albanians rode overloaded ferries to nearby Italy (where authorities eventually sent them back home). As it turned out, Albanians had an exaggerated view of Italian prosperity (though Italy was indeed more prosperous than Albania). Albanians had seen Italian TV commercials in which cats were fed their dinners on silver platters. Having been cut off from contact with the West for decades, many Albanians took such commercials literally—even the cats in Italy were rich!

Both live performances and recordings of music have become increasingly internationalized. In the world of classical music, a great conductor or violinist can roam the world

[29] Hill, Christopher R. *Olympic Politics*, 2nd ed. Manchester, 1996. Allison, Lincoln. *The Changing Politics of Sports*. NY: St. Martin's, 1993. Bale, John, and Joseph McGuire, eds. *The Global Sports Arena: Athletic Talent Migration in an Interdependent World*. Ilford, UK: Frank Cass, 1994. Dauncey, Hugh, and Geoff Hare, eds. *France and the 1998 World Cup: The National Impact of a World Sporting Event*. Ilford, UK: Frank Cass, 1999.

in search of great orchestras and appreciative audiences, with almost complete disregard for national borders. International tours are a central element in rock music and jazz as well. Some genres of music are essentially more international than national, spanning several continents and explicitly global in outlook. Even highly specialized national music forms—such as Bulgarian chants or Mongolian throat singing—are gaining worldwide audiences. It is significant that people who cannot understand each other's languages can understand each other's music.

Advertising is crucial to the emerging international culture. Advertising links the transnational products and services of MNCs with the transnational performances and works of actors, athletes, and artists. Most global broadcasts and performances—from the Olympic Games to reruns of *Baywatch*—are paid for by advertising. As with the Italian commercial just mentioned, advertising often carries subtle (or not so subtle) messages about culture, race, gender roles, and other themes. In Europe and Japan, international advertising may contain a subtext of U.S. superiority. In Eastern Europe and Russia, the advertising of products from Europe, Japan, and the United States may imply the superiority of the West over the East, whereas in the global South advertising may promote the values of the industrialized world over local and native cultures. For example, ads for cosmetics may portray stereotypical images of white Euro-American women as the ideal of beauty, even on billboards or TV shows in Asia or Latin America. Despite the cultural frictions that advertising can cause, it seems evident that without advertising the emerging global culture would lack the money needed to broadcast the Olympic Games or launch new communication satellites.

Finally, tourism also builds transnational communities.[30] International tourists cross borders 500 million times a year. Tourism ranks among the top export industries worldwide. People who travel to other countries often develop both a deeper understanding and a deeper appreciation for them. Person-to-person contacts and friendships maintained across borders make it harder for nationalism to succeed in promoting either war or protectionism. For example, a U.S. citizen who has visited Japan may be more likely to favor expanded U.S.-Japanese trade; a Greek who has visited Turkey and made friends there may be more likely to oppose a Greek-Turkish military confrontation (a hope shared by the neofunctionalists).

Added to these contacts are exchange students and those who attend college in a foreign country. These students learn about their host countries, teach friends there about their home countries, and meet other foreign students from other countries. These kinds of person-to-person international contacts are amplified by the electronic media.

The Internet now allows transnational dialogues to take place at a global level. The World Wide Web allows people to move seamlessly from site to site around the world. Significantly, the Web creates organizing structures and communities that can be almost totally divorced from physical location, bringing together people with common cultural or economic interest from anywhere in the world. In the 1990s, the Web quickly gained acceptance as a key infrastructure for business, and increasingly for governments (which control country-coded domain names).

The transnational connections forged by various communities—sports, music, tourism, and so forth—deepen the international interdependence that links the well-being of one state to that of other states. This may promote peace, because a person who knows more about a foreign country and has developed empathy for its culture is likely to reject political conflict with that country and support positive cooperation with it. But sometimes cultural contact increases awareness of differences, creating distrust.

---

[30] Goldstone, Patricia. *Making the World Safe for Tourism*. Yale, 2001. Leheny, David R. *The Rules of Play: National Identity and the Shaping of Japanese Leisure*. Cornell, 2003.

Furthermore, as the Internet wires parts of the world into a tight network centered on the United States, other regions are largely left out. Poor countries and poor people cannot afford computers—the equivalent of eight years' wages for a typical Bangladeshi, for example. Users of the World Wide Web in 2006 made up nearly 70 percent of the population in the United States, 16 percent in Russia, and 2 percent in South Asia, the Middle East, and Africa. More than 90 percent of users in the world community of Web users live in North America, Western Europe, and East Asia. English is the language of a majority of Web sites worldwide, even though non-English speakers now make up a majority of Web users. Just from 1999 to 2005, Internet users increased from 150 million to more than 1 billion worldwide, with China going from 7 million to 110 million. But this explosive growth is occurring mainly among the richest strata of the world's people.[31]

Poor Countries and the Internet

Even the architecture of cyberspace assumes the United States as the default in such domain names as .gov (U.S. government) and .mil (U.S. military). At the UN-sponsored World Summit on the Information Society in 2005, Europe and developing countries tried unsuccessfully to break the monopoly held by a U.S. consortium over registering domain names, including country-code domains such as ".uk" (Britain) and ".cn" (China) that states want to control as a matter of national sovereignty.

Some activists hope that the Internet can transform poor villages in the global South, partly by letting them produce traditional goods locally and market them globally. The UN ECOSOC (see p. 257) hopes to place an Internet computer within a mile of most of the world's villages, to be funded by $1 billion in hoped-for contributions (which seem unlikely to materialize in full). In one successful experiment in India in recent years, a businessman placed computer screens with pointing and clicking devices and high-speed Internet access in walls and kiosks in very poor slums. In each location, neighborhood kids quickly gathered, taught themselves to browse the Internet, and even invented their own terminology to describe the unfamiliar cursor and icons on the screen. This small-scale "hole in the wall experiment" shows that simple methods can go far to break down the digital divide between the world's rich and poor.

A model project in Cambodia in 2001 helped revive a village silk-weaving industry by marketing locally made scarves on a village Web site. However, critics noted that the project was feasible only because a satellite company owned by the Thai prime minister donated $18,000 per year of link time. A U.S. aid organization provided the computers, training, Web site design, and credit card processing required to sell scarves from the village. The reality is that most poor villages cannot afford the Internet, cannot read the language of most Web sites, and cannot maintain computers and Web sites without extensive training.[32]

The Internet in many ways empowers small fringe groups relative to states, and leaves states vulnerable in new ways. Hackers have taken over control of U.S. government computers and have unleashed costly viruses against businesses and people worldwide.

World Wide Web

These cyberattacks by small-scale actors may target foreign countries. Thousands of Israeli teenagers attacked Web sites in the Arab world, and Arab hackers knocked out Israeli sites in return, during the violent "Intifada II" of Fall 2000. During the U.S.-China spy plane standoff in 2001, nationalistic Chinese hackers claimed to have put pro-Chinese graffiti on 1,000 U.S. Web sites, and U.S. hackers returned the favor. An Ohio school district found that its site now played China's national anthem. The Chinese communist party criticized "Web terrorism" and the crisis eased.[33] After September 11, 2001, however, the U.S. government worried that real terrorists could use the Internet to cause massive

[31] United Nations Development Program. *Human Development Report 1999*. NY: UN, 1999.

[32] Chandrasekaran, Rajiv. Cambodian Village Wired to Future. *The Washington Post*, May 13, 2001: A1.

[33] Hockstader, Lee. Pings and E-Arrows Fly in Mideast Cyber-War. *The Washington Post*, Oct. 27, 2000: A1. Cha, Ariana Eunjung. Chinese Suspected of Hacking U.S. Sites. *The Washington Post*, April 13, 2001: A13.

disruptions in U.S. economic life. The al Qaeda network had already used the Internet extensively to help coordinate its worldwide operations.

These supranational cultural influences are still in their infancy. Over the coming years and decades their shape will become clearer, and scholars will be able to determine more accurately how they are influencing world politics and state sovereignty. We need not wait as long to see the effects of a different kind of supranational influence, however. Environmental problems, which rarely recognize national borders, have forced states into ever-closer cooperation as political leaders find that the only effective responses are at a supranational level. These issues occupy Chapter 11.

THINKING CRITICALLY

1. Functional economic ties among European states have contributed to the emergence of a supranational political structure, the EU, which has considerable though not unlimited power. Do you think the same thing could happen in North America? Could the U.S.-Canadian-Mexican NAFTA develop into a future North American Union like the EU? What problems would it be likely to face, given the experience of the EU?
2. Suppose you happened to be chatting with the president of the European Commission, who is complaining about the public reaction in European states against the growing power of the Commission's Eurocrats. What advice would you give? What steps could the Commission take to calm such fears without reversing the process of integration? How would your suggestions address the resentments that many European citizens or governments feel against Brussels?
3. Suppose the government of Turkey hired you as a consultant to help it develop a presentation to the EU about why Turkey should be admitted as a member. What arguments would you propose using? What kinds of rebuttals might you expect from the present EU members? How would you recommend responding?
4. Information technologies are strengthening transnational and supranational communications and identity. However, they are also providing states with new instruments of power and control. Which aspect do you find predominant now? Are these new capabilities helpful or harmful to state governments? Why? Do you expect your answer will change in the future, as technology continues to develop?
5. What are the good and bad effects, in your opinion, of the emergence of global communications and culture? Should we be cheering or lamenting the possibility of one world culture? Does the answer depend on where one lives in the world? Give concrete examples of the effects you discuss.

CHAPTER SUMMARY

- Supranational processes bring states together in larger structures and identities. These processes generally lead to an ongoing struggle between nationalism and supranationalism.
- International integration—the partial shifting of sovereignty from the state toward supranational institutions—is considered an outgrowth of international cooperation in functional (technical and economic) issue areas.
- Integration theorists thought that functional cooperation would spill over into political integration in foreign policy and military issue areas. Instead, powerful forces of disintegration are tearing apart previously existing states in some regions (especially in the former Soviet Union and Yugoslavia).
- The European Union (EU) is the most advanced case of integration. Its 25 member states have given considerable power to the EU in economic decision making and 12 have adopted a common currency, the euro. However, national power still outweighs supranational power even in the EU.
- Since the founding of the European Coal and Steel Community (ECSC) in 1952, the mission and membership of what is now the EU have expanded continually.
- The most important and most successful element in the EU is its customs union (and the associated free trade area). Goods can cross borders of member states freely, and the members adopt unified tariffs with regard to goods entering from outside the EU.
- Under the EU's Common Agricultural Policy (CAP), subsidies to farmers are made uniform within the community. Carrying out the CAP consumes 40 percent of the EU's budget. EU agricultural subsidies are a major source of trade conflict with the United States.
- The EU has a new monetary union with a single European currency (the euro) in 12 of the 25 EU states. It is the biggest experiment with money in history and had great success in its first years. Such a union requires roughly comparable inflation rates and financial stability in participating states.
- In structure, the EU revolves around the permanent staff of Eurocrats under the European Commission. The Commission's president, individual members, and staff all serve Europe as a whole—a supranational role. However, the Council of Ministers representing member states (in national roles) has power over the Commission.
- The European Parliament has members directly elected by citizens in EU states, but it has few powers and cannot legislate the rules for the community. The European Court of Justice also has limited powers, but has extended its jurisdiction more successfully than any other international court, and can overrule national laws.
- The Single European Act, or "Europe 1992," created a common market throughout the EU, with uniform standards, open borders, and freedom of goods, services, labor, and capital within the EU.
- The 1991 Maastricht Treaty on closer European integration (monetary union and political-military coordination) provoked a public backlash in several countries. Some citizens began to resent the power of EU bureaucrats over national culture and daily life. The treaty was ratified despite these difficulties, however.
- The EU took in three new members in 1995—Austria, Finland, and Sweden—but Norwegians voted not to join. Ten new members, mostly Eastern European, joined the EU in 2004. The EU's structures and procedures are being adapted as it moves from 15 to 25 members. The EU faces challenges in deciding how far to expand its membership, particularly regarding Turkey. To some extent, the broadening of membership conflicts with the deepening of ties among the existing members.

- In addition to the EU and the associated European Free Trade Association (EFTA), a variety of overlapping groupings, formal and informal, reflect the process of integration in Europe.
- A different type of international integration can be seen in the growing role of communication and information operating across national borders. Supranational relationships and identities are being fostered by new information technologies—especially mass media such as TV, radio, and the Internet—although such a process is still in an early stage.
- Greater access to information increases government power both domestically and internationally. Governments also use the dissemination of information across borders as a means of influencing other states. Thus information technologies can serve national and not just supranational purposes.
- Government access to information increases the stability of international relationships. The security dilemma and other collective goods problems are made less difficult in a transparent world where governments have information about each others' actions.
- The greater and freer flow of information around the world can undermine the authority and power of governments as well. It is now extremely difficult for authoritarian governments to limit the flow of information in and out of their states. Information technologies can empower ordinary citizens and contribute to transnational and supranational structures that bypass the state.
- Telecommunications are contributing to the development of global cultural integration. This process may hold the potential for the development of a single world culture. However, some politicians and citizens worry about cultural imperialism—that such a culture would be too strongly dominated by the United States.
- Transnational communities are developing in areas such as sports, music, and tourism. Such communities may foster supranational identities that could compete with the state for the loyalty of citizens someday.

KEY TERMS

supranationalism 377
international integration 377
neofunctionalism 379
security community 379
European Union (EU) 380
Treaty of Rome 381
Euratom 381
free trade area 381
customs union 382
common market 382
Common Agricultural Policy (CAP) 382
European Commission 383
Council of Ministers 384
European Parliament 384
European Court of Justice 384
Single European Act 385
Maastricht Treaty 385
euro 387
global culture 400
cultural imperialism 401

ONLINE PRACTICE TEST

Take an online practice test at
www.internationalrelations.net

❑ A
❑ B
☑ C
❑ D

LET'S DEBATE THE ISSUE

European Union–United States Relations: Will Divergent Interests Replace Old Ties?

by Mir Zohair Husain

Overview Ties between the European powers and the United States date back to the colonial period, but the bond that developed in the wake of the two world wars is more significant. Moreover, the purpose of the North Atlantic Treaty Organization (NATO), whose purpose in 1949 was to deter the Soviet Union, contain the spread of the Soviet communism, and maintain peace and order in Western Europe, formalized the U.S.-European alliance. That alliance remained strong beyond the Cold War (1947–1989). However, as the EU underwent a major transformation—including an expansion from 15 to 25 member states in May 2004 and greater independence from America—relations between the transatlantic allies also have begun to change.

In fact, the U.S. bypassing of the United Nations Security Council to take unilateral military action in Iraq caused a deep rift between the transatlantic allies and strengthened European concerns about America's ability, as the world's sole superpower, to act without a counterweight.

The United States also is reassessing its relations with the EU. After all, the greatest challenge to American hegemony may come from an economically and militarily stronger EU, and not from foreign terrorists. German and French opposition to America's military action against Iraq in 2003 demonstrated the EU's increasing ability to challenge the dominance of the United States. Since George W. Bush's reelection in November 2004, the U.S. and the EU have engaged in dialogue to bridge their differences.

Will these transatlantic allies decide to work out their differences? Or have their relations been irrevocably damaged?

Argument 1 EU–U.S. Ties Are Diminishing

The European Union and the United States have divergent views of the international system. In addition to specific grievances, the EU and the United States have a major philosophical difference in defining how the international system should operate. As a result, a more liberal EU emphasized a multilateral UN approach to Iraq, while a more realist and unilateralist United States took a more militaristic approach because it had less faith in the UN.

> At the heart of the divergence [is] a fundamentally different vision of global organizations. The Europeans . . . have always placed a greater premium on international organizations.
>
> In the United States, international organizations like the United Nations have always been viewed with suspicion. . . . The emergence of the United States as the sole military, economic, and cultural superpower has only deepened the resistance . . . to any potential international restraints on American powers. (Serge Schmemann. "U.S. vs. UN Court: Two Worldviews." *The New York Times,* July 2, 2002.)

Divergent interests will replace old ties. Supporters of the EU–U.S. relationship point to the historical bonds between these two entities. Now, however, both sides are defined differently. Europe's new era began in 1989 with the fall of the Berlin Wall, ushering in peace and unity, while the U.S.'s began in 2001 following terrorist attacks on its homeland, resulting in a more defensive mentality.

> Many of the difficulties predated Sept. 11, of course. [One expert lists]: "Economic disputes relating to steel and farm subsidies; limits on legal cooperation because of the death penalty in the United States; repeated charges of U.S. 'unilateralism' over actions in Afghanistan; and the U.S. decisions on the ABM Treaty, the Kyoto Protocol, the International Criminal Court and the Biological Weapons Protocol."
>
> . . . [T]he divergence will not be a temporary phenomenon but permanent. (Richard Bernstein. "Foreign Views of U.S. Darken Since Sept. 11." *The New York Times,* September 11, 2003.)

Divergent interests would benefit the international system. Many in the world worry that the United States has become a global hegemon with too much power. The best way to counteract America's global hegemony is the EU.

> The 25-nation European Union weighs in with $11 trillion in economic output, roughly on par with the United States, and a currency so strong that the euro may one day replace the dollar as the principal means of exchange. And as a whole, the most turbulent Arab societies, including the Palestinians, trust the European Union's emissaries to look after their interests more than they trust President Bush. . . . This new Europe is not always in tune with American goals. (Steven R. Weisman. "Europe United Is Good, Isn't It?." *The New York Times,* February 20, 2005.)

Argument 2 EU–U.S. Relations Are Evolving, Not Ending

Strained EU–U.S. relations are only temporary. The mass media has exaggerated the differences between the European Union and the United States. In the long run, their relationship will endure despite present disagreements.

> The [Iraq] war has estranged the United States from the antiwar group led by France and Germany. . . .
>
> "I am not worried that the differences cannot be overcome because we are friends and allies and that will not change," [France Foreign Minister Dominique de Villepin] said. "Our relationship with the United States is irreplaceable." (Elaine Sciolino. "Europe Assesses Damage to Western Relationships and Takes Steps to Rebuild." *The New York Times,* April 2, 2003.)

The European Union and United States still have strong common interests. The EU shares U.S. interests in the stability of the Middle East, especially since Europe is geographically closer to that region. But, even if the EU developed a divergent military and political agenda, economic interdependence will still provide strong incentives to maintain friendly relations.

> Germany exported $56 billion worth of cars and other goods to the United States last year, making it the fifth largest exporter, after China. While Poland . . . imported about $620 million worth of American goods, Germany imported more than $24 billion.
>
> With a gross domestic product of more than $1.3 trillion, France's economy is larger than the combined economies of Spain, Portugal, Poland, Hungary, Slovakia, and the Czech Republic. The German economy, the world's third largest, is twice the size of all those countries together. (Mark Landler. "Old Trading Partners Are Concerned About Effects of the Split Over War." *The New York Times,* February 14, 2003.)

The EU and U.S. need each other. The EU and the United States are both powerful global actors. However, when they unite, the probability of success in their common endeavors increases exponentially.

> The case for the overriding importance of a united Europe to Mr. Bush's goals is in many ways obvious. Although the United States proved it could win the Iraq war by itself, it has found it cannot win the peace unless the world—and Europe in particular—blesses Iraq's transition to democracy.
>
> Nor can it hope to lead Israel to the peace table without the Europeans leading the Palestinians there, too. Cooperation between the world's two biggest economic blocs, on everything from terrorism to natural disasters, is clearly critical for progress.
>
> Simply put, if a united Europe can agree with the United States, the two acting together are much more likely to succeed. (Steven R. Weisman. "Europe United Is Good, Isn't It?" *The New York Times,* February 20, 2005.)

European Union-United States Relations

Questions

1. Will EU–U.S. relations strengthen or weaken? Why?
2. Is the world better off with EU–U.S. competition or cooperation? Explain.

Selected Readings

Robert Kagan. *Of Paradise and Power: America and Europe in the New World Order.* NY: Knopf Publishing Group, 2003.

Charles A. Kupchan. *End of the American Era: U.S. Foreign Policy and the Geopolitics of the Twenty-First Century.* NY: Knopf Publishing Group, 2003.

Windmill and nuclear power plant, Britain, mid-1980s.

Interdependence and the Environment
Sustainable Economic Development • Rethinking Interdependence

Managing the Environment
The Atmosphere • Biodiversity • Forests and Oceans • Pollution

Natural Resources
World Energy • Minerals, Land, Water • International Security and the Environment

Population
World Population Trends • The Demographic Transition • Population Policies • Mortality and AIDS • Population and International Conflict

CHAPTER 11

Environment and Population

Interdependence and the Environment

As we have seen, world industrialization and technological development have increased international interdependence through functional economic integration and transnational communication. Industrialization has also intensified international interdependence in another, less direct way, through its impact on the world's natural environment. Actions taken by one state now routinely affect other states' access to natural resources and to the benefits of a healthy environment. The global threats to the natural environment are thus a major new source of interdependence.

Because environmental effects tend to be diffuse and long term and because such effects easily spread from one location to another, international environmental politics creates difficult collective goods problems (see pp. 103–104). A sustainable natural environment is a collective good, and states bargain over how to distribute the costs of providing that good. The technical, scientific, and ethical aspects of managing the environment are complex, but the basic nature of states' interests is not. The collective goods problem arises in each issue area concerning the environment, natural resources, and population.

For example, the world's major fisheries in international waters are not owned by any state; they are a collective good. The various fishing states must cooperate (partly by regulating nonstate actors such as MNCs) to avoid depleting the stocks of fish. If too many states fail to cooperate, the fish populations are diminished and everyone's catch is much reduced. In fact, this has already happened in many of the world's largest fisheries—fish catches worldwide dropped sharply in the early 1990s. The fishing industry worldwide started losing more than $50 billion a year, and relied increasingly on government subsidies. Cod in North American waters were wiped out in the early 1990s, with the North Sea cod likely to follow. The EU cut quotas for cod fishing by 80 percent in 1998–2003, after long political negotiations, but scientists do not expect stock to recover short of a total ban. Worldwide, according to a 2003 study, the oceans' population of large fish including cod has dropped by 90 percent in the past 50 years.[1]

This depletion occurred because each additional fishing boat—and the MNC that owns it as well as its state of origin—gains by catching an additional fish. The benefits of that fish go entirely to the one catching it, whereas the eventual costs of depleted stocks will be shared by all who fish there. But what is a state's fair quota of fish? There is no

---

[1] Myers, Ransom A., and Boris Worm. Rapid Worldwide Depletion of Predatory Fish Communities. *Nature* 423, May 15, 2003: 280–283.

TOO MANY COOKS

Management of environmental issues is complicated by the large numbers of actors involved, which make collective goods problems hard to resolve (individuals may be more tempted to free-ride). The 1992 Earth Summit (UN Conference on Environment and Development) in Rio de Janeiro, Brazil was the largest gathering of state leaders in history.

world government to decide such a question, so states must enter into multilateral negotiations, agreements, and regimes. Such efforts create new avenues for functionalism and international integration, but also new potentials for conflict and "prisoner's dilemmas."

States negotiate complex agreements to try to manage the fisheries dilemma. In 1999, a UN-sponsored agreement among all the world's major fishing states set goals to reduce fleet overcapacity. (There are 4 million fishing boats worldwide, of which 40,000 are ships larger than 100 tons.) Participating nations are capping the size of fishing fleets and then scaling them back gradually, while reducing subsidies. The pain of unemployment and economic adjustment would thus be shared. However, the agreement is voluntary, its implementation delayed, and its effect on collapsing fisheries probably too little, too late.

This type of collective goods dilemma has been called the **tragedy of the commons.**[2] Centuries ago, the commons was shared grazing land in Britain. As with fisheries, if too many people kept too many sheep, the commons would be overgrazed. Yet adding one more sheep was profitable to that sheep's owner. Britain solved the problem (although creating other problems) by **enclosure** of the commons—splitting it into privately owned pieces on each of which a single owner would have an incentive to manage resources responsibly. The world's states are gradually taking a similar approach to fisheries by extending territorial waters to put more fish under the control of single states (see "Minerals, Land, Water" later in this chapter). The *global commons* refers to the shared parts of the earth, such as the oceans and outer space.

As in other areas of IPE, the solution of environmental collective goods problems is based on achieving shared benefits that depend on overcoming conflicting interests.[3] *Regimes* are an important part of the solution, providing rules to govern bargaining over who gets the benefits and bears the costs of environmental protection. So are functional IOs that specialize in technical and management aspects of the environment.[4]

[2] Hardin, Garrett. The Tragedy of the Commons. *Science* 162, December 16, 1968: 1243–48. Keohane, Robert O., and Elinor Ostrom, eds. *Local Commons and Global Interdependence: Heterogeneity in Two Domains*. Thousand Oaks, CA: Sage, 1995.

[3] Kütting, Gabriela. *Globalization and the Environment: Greening Global Political Economy*. SUNY, 2004. Stevis, Dimitris, and Valerie J. Assetto, eds. *The International Political Economy of the Environment: Critical Perspectives*. Boulder: Rienner, 2001. Garner, Robert. *The International Politics of the Environment*. NY: St. Martin's Press, 2000. Schreurs, Miranda A., and Elizabeth Economy, eds. *The Internationalization of Environmental Protection*. Cambridge, 1997.

[4] Young, Oran R., ed. *The Effectiveness of International Environmental Regimes: Casual Connections and Behavioral Mechanisms*. MIT, 1999. Peterson, M. J. *International Regimes for the Final Frontier*. SUNY, 2005.

Increasingly, these IOs overlap with broader communities of experts from various states that structure the way states manage environmental issues; these have been called **epistemic communities** (knowledge-based communities). For example, the transnational community of experts and policy makers concerned with pollution in the Mediterranean is an epistemic community.[5]

In global environmental politics, it is hard to manage collective goods problems because of the large number of actors. Collective goods are easier to provide in small groups, where individual actions have more impact on the total picture and where cheating is more noticeable. The opposite is true with the environment. The actions of nearly 200 states (albeit some more than others) aggregate to cause indirect but serious consequences throughout the world. This large number of actors was seen in the 1992 *UN Conference on Environment and Development* (the "*Earth Summit*") in Rio de Janeiro, Brazil; it was the largest summit meeting of state leaders ever, more than a hundred in all.[6]

Earth Summit

With a few exceptions, only in the last two decades has the global environment become a major subject of international negotiation and of IR scholarship.[7] Interest in the environment has grown rapidly since the first Earth Day was held by environmental activists in 1970. The energy crises of the 1970s seemed to underline the issue in industrialized regions. Oil spills, urban air pollution, pesticide residues, and difficulties at nuclear power plants elevated the environment on the international agenda.

The first UN conference on the international environment took place in Stockholm, Sweden, in 1972. It adopted general principles—that one state's actions should not cause environmental damage to another, for instance—and raised awareness about international aspects of environmental damage. A second conference was held, with less publicity, in 1982 in Nairobi, Kenya (headquarters of the UN Environment Program). The larger and more ambitious 1992 Earth Summit was the third conference. The fourth took place in Johannesburg, South Africa, in 2002.

Sustainable Economic Development

At the 1992 Earth Summit, the major theme was *sustainable* economic development. This refers to economic growth that does not deplete resources and destroy ecosystems so quickly that the basis of that economic growth is itself undermined. The concept applies to both the industrialized regions and the global South.[8]

In the past, the growth of population, industry, energy use, and the extraction of natural resources on the planet has been exponential—growing faster and faster over time. Such exponential growth cannot continue indefinitely, almost by definition. Several possibilities emerge. First, new technologies may allow *unabated economic growth*, but will shift the basis of that growth away from the ever-increasing use of energy and other

---

[5] Haas, Peter M. Introduction: Epistemic Communities and International Policy Coordination [special issue]. *International Organization* 46 (1), 1992: 1–36. Haas, Peter M. *Saving the Mediterranean: The Politics of International Environmental Cooperation*. Columbia, 1990.

[6] Maniates, Michael, ed. *Encountering Global Environmental Politics: Teaching, Learning, and Empowering Knowledge*. Lanham, MD: Rowman & Littlefield, 2002.

[7] DeSombre, Elizabeth R. *Domestic Sources of International Environmental Policy*. MIT, 2000. Bernstein, Steven F. *The Compromise of Liberal Environmentalism*. Columbia, 2001. Sprout, Harold, and Margaret Sprout. *The Ecological Perspective on Human Affairs, with Special Reference to International Politics*. Princeton, 1965.

[8] Harrison, Paul. *The Third World Revolution: Population, Environment, and a Sustainable World*. NY: Penguin USA, 1994. Brown, Lester R., et al. *State of the World* (annual). NY: Norton/Worldwatch Institute. Cooper, Richard N. *Environment and Resource Policies for the World Economy*. Washington, DC: Brookings, 1995.

NOT SUSTAINABLE

Pollution from industrialization caused great environmental damage in the Soviet Union, contributing to the stagnation and collapse of the Soviet economy—an unsustainable path. Many environmental problems remain in post-Soviet states, such as this heavily polluting nickel plant in Siberia. Today's poor countries will have to industrialize along cleaner lines to realize sustainable development.

resources. This is what optimists with faith in technology expect. Goods and services would continue to multiply, raising the global standard of living, but would do so more efficiently to reduce strains on the environment.

A second possibility is a *collapse* of population and living standards in the world, as excessive growth leads to ecological disaster. Pessimists worry that the present course will overshoot the **carrying capacity** of the planetary ecosystem and cause ecosystems to break down because of long-term environmental problems such as species depletion and global warming. By the time such problems produced severe short-term effects, it would be too late to correct them. In effect, what has happened to the world's largest fisheries would happen on a global scale—overuse and collapse.

During the past 30 years scholars have produced computer models of the world—population, economic activity, pollution, and other key variables—that show that a finite earth cannot sustain infinite growth and that we are already reaching the "limits to growth."[9] These models are controversial, however. A variety of computer simulations have been developed to try to analyze the carrying capacity of the planet, given available resources and the demands of industrialization and population growth. Some of these models explicitly consider international politics as a factor.[10]

A third possibility is that the past curve of exponential growth will flatten out to form an *S-curve*. The curve rises from a fairly flat slope to an exponential growth curve and then levels off back to a flat slope (at a higher level). Instead of overshooting the planet's limits of human population and energy (triggering collapse), human beings would adapt to those limits in time to achieve a *steady-state* economy in which population, food production, energy use, and other key processes are stable from year to year. It has been argued that our generation is the "hinge of history," just past the middle point of the S-curve. If so, we are experiencing the most rapid change of any generation in the past *or* the future.[11] In this

---

[9] Meadows, Donella H., et al. *The Limits to Growth: A Report for the Club of Rome's Project on the Predicament of Mankind*. NY: Universe, 1972. Meadows, Donella, John Richardson, and Gerhart Bruckmann. *Groping in the Dark: The First Decade of Global Modelling*. NY: Wiley, 1982.

[10] Bremer, Stuart A., and Barry B. Hughes. *Disarmament and Development: A Design for the Future?* Englewood Cliffs, NJ: Prentice Hall, 1990. Bremer, Stuart A., ed. *The GLOBUS Model: Computer Simulation of Worldwide Political and Economic Developments*. Boulder, CO: Westview, 1987.

[11] Platt, John R. The Step to Man. *Science* 149, August 6, 1965: 607–13.

scenario, the key task of our generation would be to adapt our economics and our politics, including IR, to level out into a sustainable long-term relationship with the environment.

The Earth Summit produced an overall plan, called *Agenda 21*, whereby large third world states promise to industrialize along cleaner lines (at a certain cost to economic growth) and industrialized states promise to funnel aid and technology to them to assist in that process.[12]

The Earth Summit established the **Commission on Sustainable Development,** which monitors states' compliance with the promises they made at the Earth Summit and hears evidence from environmental NGOs such as Greenpeace. But it lacks powers of enforcement over national governments—again reflecting the preeminence of state sovereignty over supranational authority (see pp. 377–379). Of the 53 Commission members, as of 2006, 19 were from the global North, 11 from Africa, 10 from Latin America, and 13 from the Middle East, South Asia, and China combined. It was hoped that the Commission's ability to monitor and publicize state actions would discourage states from cheating on the Earth Summit plan.[13] But the Commission's first meeting, two years after the Earth Summit, found the states of the global North providing only half of the level of financial support pledged for sustainable development in the South. Funding for sustainable development in the global South—a collective good—continued to lag throughout the 1990s.

China and other developing countries in Asia stood at the center of the debate over sustainable development. In the drive for rapid economic growth, these countries have cut corners environmentally, resulting in the world's worst air pollution and other serious problems. China is building the Three Gorges Dam, which will be the world's largest hydroelectric station; it provides a clean source of energy in a coal-burning country, but environmentalists fear it will damage a large river ecosystem. Because of China's size, any success in developing its economy along Western industrialized lines (for example, with widespread ownership of automobiles) could create massive shocks to the global environment. Yet no practical alternative has been taken seriously. By 2004 China was also scouring the planet for raw materials—such as imports of 200 million tons of iron a year—to fuel its extraordinary growth. China has begun to switch away from dirty coal, helping ease air pollution, but its thirst for imported oil and gas drove up world oil prices in 2003–2006.

Rethinking Interdependence

We have thus far treated international environmental issues as problems of interstate bargaining, an approach that reflects a liberal theoretical orientation. This approach has been challenged in recent years by an emerging theoretical framework that is more revolutionary in orientation, seeking more fundamental change in the nature of the international community's approach to environmental problems. This approach is well reflected in the grassroots activism of Greenpeace and other environment-related NGOs. Environmentalists object to free trade provisions that weaken environmental standards by empowering international bureaucrats who care more about wealth generation than eco-preservation (see p. 424). Similarly, environmental groups have objected to management of economic development in the global South by international institutions, in particular the World Bank.

---

[12] O'Riordan, Tim, and Heather Voisey, eds. *Sustainable Development in Europe: Coming to Terms with Agenda 21*. Ilford, UK: Frank Cass, 1997. Miller, Marian A. L. *The Third World in Global Environmental Politics*. Boulder, CO: Lynne Rienner, 1995. Litfin, Karen T. *The Greening of Sovereignty in World Politics*. MIT, 1998.

[13] Lewis, Paul. UN Implementing the Earth Summit. *The New York Times*, Dec. 1, 1992: A16.

Thus the more revolutionary theoretical perspective rejects the liberal goal of maximizing wealth (see pp. 298–300). Although liberal concepts of rationality are longer-term than conservative ones (see p. 100), environmentalists take an even broader and longer-term view. From this perspective, the collective goods problem among states is not the problem; it is the growth of industrial civilization out of balance with the planetary ecosystem that must ultimately support it. True rationality, for environmentalists, must include very long-term calculations about how the self-interest of humanity itself is undermined by a greedy drive to exploit nature—that is, interdependence and the collective goods problem are broadened to include humanity versus nature, not just state versus state.[14]

The remainder of this chapter will focus primarily on interstate bargaining processes concerning the environment, but will include the broader forces of concern to environmentalists. As these forces shape the contexts for interstate bargaining, they must be of concern even to liberals and conservatives.

Managing the Environment

In discussing the issue areas in which states are bargaining over environmental problems, we begin with the most global problems—those that are collective goods for all states and people in the world. Later sections consider more localized conflicts over pollution and natural resources.

The Atmosphere

Preserving the health of the earth's atmosphere is a benefit that affects people throughout the world without regard for their own state's contribution to the problem or its solution. Two problems of the atmosphere have become major international issues—global warming and depletion of the ozone layer.

Global Warming

Global Warming Global climate change, or **global warming,** is a slow, long-term rise in the average world temperature. Scientists are not certain that such a rise is occurring, or if so how fast, but there is growing evidence that global warming is a real problem, that it is caused by the emission of carbon dioxide and other gases, and that it will get worse in the future. Many scientists believe it prudent to address the problem soon, because once the symptoms become obvious it will be too late to prevent disaster. The time frame is unclear: 1998 and 2001 were the two warmest years on record, but this may or may not indicate a rapid onset of serious global warming.

It is not easy to guess who will be harmed and how soon. But over the next few decades, according to most estimates, global temperatures may rise by between two and nine degrees Fahrenheit if nothing is done. The high end of this temperature range corresponds with the difference between today's climate and that of the last ice age; it is a major climate change. Possibly within a few decades the polar ice caps would begin to melt and cause the sea level to rise by as much as a few feet. Such a rise could flood many coastal cities and devastate low-lying areas such as the heavily populated coastal areas of Bangladesh and China. Urgent calls for action to avert global warming come from island states in the Pacific that could disappear this century.

---

[14] Pirages, Dennis Clark, and Theresa Manley DeGeest. *Ecological Security: An Evolutionary Perspective on Globalization*. Lanham, MD: Rowman & Littlefield, 2003.

Global climate change could also alter weather patterns in many regions, causing droughts, floods, and widespread disruption of natural ecosystems. It is also possible that climate changes (at least mild ones) could *benefit* some regions and make agriculture more productive. Melting of polar ice may open new shipping routes north of Canada and Russia that could potentially cut weeks off the transit time from northern Europe or America to Asia. But sudden environmental changes are usually much more destructive than helpful.

It is costly to reduce the emissions of gases—mainly carbon dioxide—that cause global warming. These gases result from the broad spectrum of activities that drive an industrial economy. They are a by-product of burning **fossil fuels**—oil, coal, and natural gas—to run cars, tractors, furnaces, factories, and so forth. These activities create **greenhouse gases**—so named because when concentrated in the atmosphere these gases act like the glass in a greenhouse: they let energy in as short-wavelength solar radiation but reflect it back when it tries to exit again as longer-wavelength heat waves. The greenhouse gases are *carbon dioxide* (responsible for two-thirds of the effect), *methane gas*, *chlorofluorocarbons* (CFCs), and *nitrous oxide*. The concentration of these gases in the global atmosphere is slowly increasing, though the rates and processes involved are complicated (carbon is exchanged among the atmosphere, oceans, and trees).

MELTING AWAY

International treaties have been much more successful at addressing ozone depletion than global warming, mostly because the costs of the latter are much higher and the benefits further in the future. A 1997 conference in Kyoto, Japan, set goals for industrialized countries to reduce their output of carbon dioxide and related gases modestly over the next decade, but the goals are not being met. If global warming melts polar ice caps in the coming decades, sea levels could rise and devastate many cities. This crack in the Antarctic ice shelf in 1997, and mounting evidence since, shows that this process is already underway.

Thus the costs of reducing the greenhouse effect are high, because the solutions entail curbing economic growth or shifting it onto entirely new technological paths.[15] The political costs of such actions—which would likely increase unemployment, reduce corporate profits, and lower personal incomes—could be severe. For example, as the U.S. government headed to global warming negotiations in 1997, it faced lobbying against the proposed treaty by a powerful coalition of big business, labor unions, and agriculture. As with trade policy, changes bring concentrated costs such as job losses, but the benefits are diffuse. For example, public opinion polls showed U.S. public opinion to support action against global warming, but this sentiment was abstract, was not tied to concrete costs, and was not politically mobilized in the way that industry groups and labor unions were.

Silicon versus Fossil Fuels?

For individual states, the costs of reducing greenhouse emissions are almost unrelated to the benefits of a solution. If one state reduces its industrial production or makes expensive investments in new technologies, this will have little effect on the long-term outcome unless other states do likewise. And if most states took such steps, a free rider that did not go along would save money and still benefit from the solution.

[15] Luterbacher, Urs, and Detlef F. Sprinz. *International Relations and Global Climate Change*. MIT, 2001. Fisher, Dana R. *National Governance and the Global Climate Change Regime*. Lanham, MD: Rowman and Littlefield, 2004.

Global warming thus presents states with a triple dilemma. First, there is the dilemma of short-term (and predictable) costs to gain long-term (and less predictable) benefits. Second, specific constituencies such as oil companies and industrial workers pay the costs, whereas the benefits are distributed more generally across domestic society and internationally. Third, there is the collective goods dilemma among states: benefits are shared globally but costs must be extracted from each state individually.

This third dilemma is complicated by the North-South divide. How can the industrialization of today's poor countries (China and India in particular) take place without pushing greenhouse emissions to unacceptable levels? Greenhouse gases are produced by each state roughly in proportion to its industrial activity. Eighty percent of greenhouse gases now come from the industrialized countries—25 percent from the United States alone. U.S. carbon dioxide emissions amount to 20 tons per person annually, about twice the European rate and eight times China's. Yet the most severe impacts of global warming are likely to be felt in the global South.

All of these elements make for a difficult multilateral bargaining situation, one not yet resolved. The *Framework Convention on Climate Change* adopted at the 1992 Earth Summit set a nonbinding goal, to limit greenhouse emissions to 1990 levels by the year 2000; that goal was not met. The treaty did not commit the signatory states to meet target levels of greenhouse emissions by a particular date, owing to U.S. objections to such a commitment. Western Europe and Japan have been more willing to regulate greenhouse emissions than is the United States (which burns more fossil fuel per person). The 1997 *Kyoto Protocol* adopted a complex formula for reducing greenhouse emissions to 1990 levels in the global North over about a decade.[16] Countries in the global South received preferential treatment since their levels (per capita) were much lower. Yet China in the 1990s was the world's second-largest producer of carbon dioxide (after the United States) and its fast-growing, coal-burning economy is projected to be a major factor in the coming years. India was the sixth largest (after Russia, Japan, and Germany). Objecting to this free ride, the U.S. Congress promptly declared that it would not ratify the treaty. President George W. Bush then dropped out of follow-up negotiations to Kyoto, declaring the treaty "dead." China meanwhile began lowering its carbon emissions, independently of the treaty, as it began switching away from its predominant fuel, coal.

Moving forward without U.S. support, 160 countries in 2001 agreed to implement the Kyoto Protocol. The agreement calls for 40 industrialized countries to reduce emissions to 5 percent below 1990 levels, by 2012, with binding penalties for failure. The EU pledged $400 million per year to help the global South reduce its emissions. The needed ratifications to put the treaty into effect (from states totaling 55 percent of world emissions) came when Russia finally ratified it in late 2004, and the treaty entered into effect in February 2005. (By 2006, 162 states with 62 percent of emissions had ratified.) The European Union began operation of markets to trade carbon emission credits among 12,000 industrial facilities across Europe. And internationally the treaty created trading in carbon credits, using free market principles to make reduction in carbon emissions more efficient. For example, a venture in Brazil earned carbon credits by burning methane gas from a garbage dump (to generate electricity) instead of venting it as a strong greenhouse gas. European investors bought the credits and could then sell them to, say, a polluting factory in Eastern Europe where reducing carbon might be especially expensive.[17]

---

[16] Victor, David G. *The Collapse of the Kyoto Protocol and the Struggle to Slow Global Warming*. Princeton, 2001. Grubb, Michael, and Duncan Brack, eds. *The Kyoto Protocol: A Guide and Assessment*. London: Royal Institute of International Affairs, 1999.

[17] Stowell, Deborah. *Climate Trading: Development of Greenhouse Gas Markets*. Basingstoke, UK: Palgrave, 2005.

Mandatory carbon cuts under the Kyoto Protocol are to begin in 2008 and expire in 2012. In the long run, it is unclear how effective the treaty can be without U.S. participation. In 2004 and 2005, evidence mounted that global warming is occurring much more quickly than expected, and weather damage cost insurance companies a lot, especially in Hurricane Katrina which devastated New Orleans. But in December 2005 the U.S. delegation walked out of climate talks, and plans for after 2012 remain unsettled. Meanwhile, about half the states of the United States (notably California), and a number of cities, began taking their own steps to limit greenhouse emissions. This shows how environmental issues span multiple levels of analysis. More broadly, the dilemma of global warming remains fundamentally unsolved, and with weak enforcement mechanisms even the states that signed the Kyoto Protocol may not meet their targets on schedule, if ever.

U.S. Resistance on Climate Change

Technology may help to make the bargaining a bit easier in the future. Many technical experts now argue that dramatic gains can be made through energy efficiency measures and other solutions that do not reduce the amount of economic activity but do make it cleaner and more efficient. Although costly, such investments would ultimately pay for themselves through greater economic efficiency. If this approach succeeds, international conflicts over global warming will be reduced.

Japanese leaders think their country can profit by gaining a comparative advantage in environmental technologies. The government- and industry-funded *Research Institute of Innovative Technology for the Earth (RITE)*, with 200 employees in 2003, is developing methods to filter carbon dioxide out of industrial exhausts.[18] RITE is part of a government campaign called *New Earth 21*, to coordinate a movement of Japanese industry into environmental technologies.

The **UN Environment Program (UNEP),** whose main function is to monitor environmental conditions, works with the World Meteorological Organization to measure changes in global climate from year to year. Since 1989 the UN-sponsored *Intergovernmental Panel on Climate Change* has served as a negotiating forum for this issue.[19]

Ozone Depletion A second major atmospheric problem being negotiated by the world's governments is the depletion of the world's **ozone layer.**[20] Ozone high in the atmosphere screens out harmful ultraviolet rays from the sun. Certain chemicals expelled by industrial economies float up to the top of the atmosphere and interact with ozone in a way that breaks it down. The chief culprits are CFCs, widely used in refrigeration and in aerosol sprays. (Unfortunately, ozone produced by burning fossil fuels does not replace the high-level ozone but only pollutes the lower atmosphere.)

Intergovernmental Panel on Climate Change

As the ozone layer thins, more ultraviolet radiation is reaching the earth's surface. Over Antarctica, where the ozone is thinnest, a hole in the ozone appears to be growing larger and lasting longer year by year. Depleted ozone levels over North America were detected in the early 1990s, and people have been warned to limit exposure to the sun to lower the risk of skin cancer. Eventually, the increased radiation could begin to kill off vegetation, reduce agricultural yields, and disrupt ecosystems.

Clearly, this is another collective goods problem in that one state benefits from allowing the use of CFCs in its economy, provided that most other states prohibit their use. But the costs of replacing CFCs are much lower than the costs of addressing global warming: CFCs can be replaced with other chemicals at relatively modest costs. Furthermore,

[18] Japan Bids for Global Leadership in Clean Industry. *Science* 256, May 22, 1992: 1144.
[19] United Nations Environment Program. *Global Environment Outlook (2002)*. Oxford, 2002.
[20] Litfin, Karen. *Ozone Discourses: Science and Politics in Global Environmental Cooperation*. Columbia, 1993. Rowlands, Ian H. *The Politics of Global Atmospheric Change*. NY: St. Martin's Press, 1995.

the consequences of ozone depletion are both better understood and more immediate than those of global warming.

Therefore, states have had more success in negotiating agreements and developing regimes to manage the ozone problem. In the 1987 **Montreal Protocol,** 22 states agreed to reduce CFCs by 50 percent by 1998. In 1990, the timetable was accelerated and the signatories expanded: 81 states agreed to eliminate all CFCs by 2000. In 1992, as evidence of ozone depletion mounted, the schedule was again accelerated, with major industrial states phasing out CFCs by 1995. The signatories agreed in principle to establish a fund (of unspecified size and source) to help third world states pay for alternative refrigeration technologies not based on CFCs. Without such an effort, the states of the global South would be tempted to free-ride and could ultimately undermine the effort. These countries were also given until 2010 to phase out production. Rich countries stopped making CFCs in 1996, and poor countries began to reduce emissions—helped somewhat by the global North's contribution of more than $1 billion during the 1990s to 110 countries in the South. However, even the reduced levels of global CFC emissions further damage the ozone layer (since they take decades to break down). The ozone hole continues to grow larger. With payments by rich countries lagging, and a black market in cheap CFCs, it is unclear whether countries in the global South will succeed in eliminating CFCs by 2010 as agreed.

The Montreal Protocol on CFCs is the most important success yet achieved in international negotiations to preserve the global environment. It showed that states can agree to take action on urgent environmental threats, can agree on targets and measures to counter such threats, and can allocate the costs of such measures in a mutually acceptable way. Recent measurements of CFCs in the atmosphere show a decrease of several percent since the 1990s. But the international cooperation on the ozone problem has not been widely repeated on other environmental issues.

Biodiversity

Biodiversity refers to the tremendous diversity of plant and animal species making up the earth's (global, regional, and local) ecosystems.[21] Biologists believe that the 1.4 million species they have identified and named are only a small fraction of the total number of species in existence (most of which are microorganisms). Some species, such as humans, are distributed broadly around the world, whereas others live in just one locale.

Because of humans' destruction of ecosystems, large numbers of species are already *extinct* and others are in danger of becoming so. Extinct species cannot return. The causes of their extinction include overhunting, overfishing, and introducing nonnative species that crowd out previous inhabitants. But the most important cause is *loss of habitat*—the destruction of rain forests, pollution of lakes and streams, and loss of agricultural lands to urban sprawl. Because ecosystems are based on complex interrelationships among species, the extinction of a few species can cause deeper changes in the environment. For example, the loss of native microorganisms can lead to chronic pollution of rivers or to the transformation of arable land into deserts.

Because ecosystems are so complex, it is usually impossible to predict the consequences of a species' extinction or of the loss of a habitat or ecosystem. Generally the activities that lead to habitat loss are economically profitable, so there are real costs associated with limiting such activities. For example, logging in the northwest United

[21] Swanson, Timothy M., ed. *The Economics and Ecology of Biodiversity Decline: The Forces Driving Global Change*. Cambridge, 1998.

States has been restricted to save the northern spotted owl from extinction. Nobody can be sure what effect the owl's extinction would have, but the costs to loggers are clear and immediate.

Species preservation is thus a collective good resembling global warming; the costs are immediate and substantial but the benefits are long term and ill defined. As to biodiversity, the effects of policies tend to be more local than those of global warming, so the problem to some degree can be enclosed within the purview of states. But to a surprising extent the biodiversity in one state affects the quality of the environment in other states. Topsoil blown away in Africa is deposited in South America; monarch butterflies that failed to breed in Mexico in 1991 did not appear in New England in 1992.

Species Preservation

It has been difficult to reach international agreement on sharing the costs of preserving biodiversity. A UN convention on trade in endangered species has reduced but not eliminated such trade. At the 1992 Earth Summit, a treaty on biodiversity was adopted that committed signatories to preserving habitats, and got rich states to pay poor ones for the rights to use commercially profitable biological products extracted from rare species in protected habitats (such as medicines from rain forest trees). However, because of fears that it could limit U.S. patent rights in biotechnology, the United States did not sign the treaty. It signed in 1993, with stipulations, but did not ratify the treaty. As of 2001, parties to the biodiversity treaty include all UN member states except the United States and nine small countries. The United States does participate in other biological treaties, such as a 1971 wetlands convention and the 1973 Convention on International Trade in Endangered Species (CITES).

Many environmentalists have a special concern for whales and dolphins, which like humans are large-brained mammals. In the past 20 years, environmental activists have persuaded states to agree to international regimes to protect whales and dolphins. The **International Whaling Commission** (an IGO) sets quotas for hunting certain whale species; participation is voluntary, and Norway dropped out in 1992 when it decided unilaterally that it could increase its catch without endangering the species. The *Inter-American Tropical Tuna Commission* (another IGO) regulates methods used to fish for tuna, aiming to minimize dolphin losses.

The United States, which consumes half the world's tuna catch, has gone further and unilaterally requires—in the Marine Mammal Protection Act—that dolphin-safe methods be used for tuna sold in U.S. territory. Under this law, the United States in 1990 banned imports of tuna from Mexico and Venezuela. These countries, which could not comply with the U.S. law as easily as the U.S. tuna industry could, took their case to the GATT (see pp. 322–324) and won. But the United States did not comply with the GATT ruling, despite appeals from the EC and dozens of other states. Venezuela's tuna fleet was reduced to less than a third of its former size.[22]

Such conflicts portend future battles between environmentalists and free trade advocates.[23] Free traders argue that states must not use domestic legislation to seek global environmental goals. Environmentalists do not want to give up national laws that they worked for decades to enact, over the opposition of industrial corporations. For example, the U.S. Clean Air Act has successfully reduced air pollution in U.S. cities, but the regulations had to be revised in 1997, on order of the WTO, to allow gasoline refined in

[22] Brooke, James. America—Environmental Dictator? *The New York Times*, May 3, 1992: F7.

[23] Chambers, W. Bradnee, ed. *Inter-Linkages: The Kyoto Protocol and the International Trade and Investment Regimes*. Washington, DC: Brookings, 2001. Rodrik, Dani. *Has Globalization Gone Too Far?* Washington, DC: Institute for International Economics, 1997. Esty, Daniel C. *Greening the GATT: Trade, Environment and the Future*. Washington, DC: Institute for International Economics, 1994. Copeland, Brian R., and M. Scott Taylor. *Trade and the Environment: Theory and Evidence*. Princeton 2003.

Venezuela and Brazil to compete in U.S. markets. Environmentalists adopted the sea turtle as a symbol of their opposition to the WTO after the WTO overturned U.S. regulations that required shrimp to be caught in nets from which sea turtles (an endangered species) can escape. The WTO's actions in cases such as the gasoline or shrimp disputes are based on unfair *application* of environmental rules to domestic versus foreign companies. In practical terms, however, the effect is negative from environmentalists' perspective.

In recent years, most spectacularly at the WTO's failed 1999 Seattle summit, a coalition of U.S. environmental groups campaigned against the "faceless bureaucrats" at the WTO who override national laws such as the tuna act; these bureaucrats are portrayed as agents of the MNCs, out to increase profits with no regard for the environment. Recent conflicts have arisen over U.S. laws restricting imports of foods with pesticide residues, and over European laws on imports of genetically engineered agricultural and pharmaceutical products, which the United States wants to export worldwide.

Thus, unilateral approaches to biodiversity issues are problematical because they disrupt free trade; multilateral approaches are problematical because of the collective goods problem. It is not surprising that the international response to species extinction has been fairly ineffective to date.

DEVELOPMENT OR DESTRUCTION?

Some environmentalists criticize the World Bank and other international institutions promoting economic development in poor countries for interfering destructively in local ecosystems such as rain forests. The green revolution increased yields but shifted patterns of agriculture in complex ways, such as by increasing pesticide and fertilizer runoff. Now genetically engineered crops promise further increases in agricultural productivity—more food on the table—but with environmental consequences that are not fully understood. This corporate president holds a genetically modified seedling, 2001.

Forests and Oceans

Two types of habitat—tropical rain forests and oceans—are especially important to biodiversity *and* the atmosphere. Both are also reservoirs of commercially profitable resources such as fish and wood. They differ in that forests are located almost entirely within state territory, but oceans are largely beyond any state territory, in the global commons.

Rain Forests As many as half the world's total species live in *rain forests*, which replenish oxygen and reduce carbon dioxide in the atmosphere—slowing down global warming. Rain forests thus benefit all the world's states; they are collective goods.

International bargaining on the preservation of rain forests has made considerable progress, probably because most rain forests belong to a few states. These few states have the power to speed up or slow down the destruction of forests—and international bargaining amounts to agreements to shift costs from those few states onto the broader group of states benefiting from the rain forests. This collective goods problem is simpler and has fewer actors than the global warming problem.

Although some rich states (including the United States) have large forests, most of the largest rain forests are in poor states such as Brazil, Indonesia, Malaysia, and Madagascar. Such states can benefit

POLICY PERSPECTIVES

President of Ireland, Mary McAleese

PROBLEM *Balancing environmental and economic concerns.*

BACKGROUND Imagine that you are the president of Ireland. Genetically modified organisms (GMOs) are highly controversial in Europe and this certainly includes your country. In 1997, for example, Ireland reluctantly approved a permit for the global MNC Monsanto to grow sugar beets near Dublin. After several legal attempts to halt the planting of the crop failed, activists destroyed the crop in the ground before it could be harvested.

You have quietly supported several Irish biotechnology firms in the past with joint ventures in research. These have produced a variety of advances that give Ireland a significant advantage in this field over other European states. Several MNCs stand to benefit from this research, providing you with investment and tax income.

Unfortunately, your "positive but precautionary" approach is unpopular with the public. Some worry that Ireland's reputation as "the Green Island" will suffer, possibly posing a threat to tourism—a major source of income for your country. Others join the chorus of European opposition to GMOs based on concerns over the possible environmental effects of these products. A recent Eurobarometer poll found that 54% of European consumers consider GMO foods "dangerous."

In the spring of 2004, the European Union (EU) approved an end to the moratorium on GMO product sales (with your country voting in the majority), partially under a threat from the United States to bring a WTO complaint against EU states. The United States is your largest single trade partner, but other EU states combined are your most significant export market.

SCENARIO Imagine that the balance of power in the EU shifts against GMOs with the admission of new Central European states. Now, the EU will not approve the sale of GMO products within Europe. Thus, although it would still be legal to grow GMO crops, it would not be legal to export them to EU countries.

GMO crops could provide economic benefits to your country. Given your comparative technological advantage in this area, your economy stands to profit from expanding GMO use through increased agricultural output and increased business activity from MNCs. The United States has no regulations concerning the importation of GMO products and would be open to exports of these crops.

GMOs carry possible dangers as well. Some environmentalists warn that GMOs could have negative effects on ecology, wildlife, and human health. Many of your EU partners will shun your GMO products, robbing you of a large export market for these goods. Domestically, expanding the production of GMOs will be controversial.

CHOOSE YOUR POLICY Do you continue to quietly encourage the advance of GMO crops? Do you follow the new EU members in opposing GMOs, out of respect for the long-term environmental concerns raised by these products? Do you work with MNCs to use your comparative advantage for economic gain? How do you balance economic prosperity with a concern for the environment?

economically from exploiting the forests—freely cutting lumber, clearing land for agriculture, and mining.[24] Until recently (and still to an extent), leaders of rich states have been most interested in encouraging maximum economic growth in poor states so that foreign debts could be paid—with little regard for environmental damage. The World Bank, for example, has been criticized by environmentalists for providing technical assistance and investment to build large dams in environmentally sensitive third world areas.

Now that rich states have an interest in protecting rain forests, they are using money and development assistance as leverage to induce poorer states to protect their forests rather than exploiting them. Under international agreements of the early 1990s, rich countries are contributing hundreds of millions of dollars in foreign aid for this purpose. In some third world countries burdened by large foreign debts, environmentalists and bankers from rich countries have worked out "debt-for-nature swaps" in which a debt is canceled in exchange for the state's agreement to preserve forests.

You Are the Brazilian President

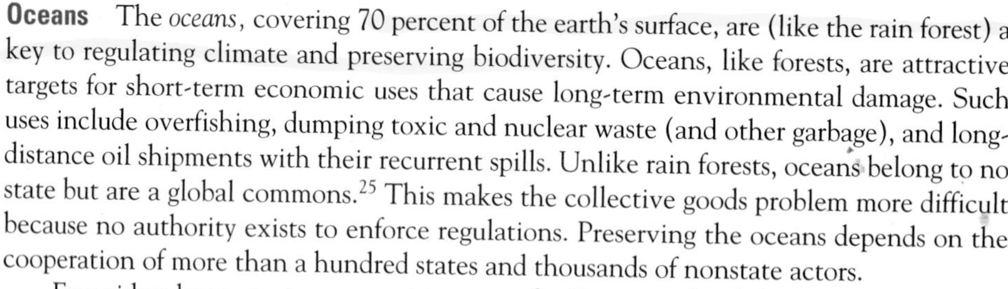

Brazil in particular has responded to these agreements with significant steps. A major government-sponsored drive to settle and exploit the Amazon basin had begun in the 1960s. In the early 1990s, the government adopted sweeping new policies to balance economic exploitation of the Amazon basin with the needs of environmental preservation and the rights of indigenous peoples. In 2005, Brazil announced that deforestation had fallen 50 percent since 2003, though environmentalists find the figure overly optimistic.

Oceans The *oceans*, covering 70 percent of the earth's surface, are (like the rain forest) a key to regulating climate and preserving biodiversity. Oceans, like forests, are attractive targets for short-term economic uses that cause long-term environmental damage. Such uses include overfishing, dumping toxic and nuclear waste (and other garbage), and long-distance oil shipments with their recurrent spills. Unlike rain forests, oceans belong to no state but are a global commons.[25] This makes the collective goods problem more difficult because no authority exists to enforce regulations. Preserving the oceans depends on the cooperation of more than a hundred states and thousands of nonstate actors.

Free riders have great opportunities to profit. For example, *drift nets* are huge fishing nets, miles long, that scoop up everything in their path. They are very profitable but destructive of a sustainable ocean environment. Most states have now banned their use (under pressure from the environmental movement). However, no state has the authority to go onto the **high seas** (nonterritorial waters) and stop illegal use of these nets.

One solution that states have pursued involves "enclosing" more of the ocean. Territorial waters have expanded to hundreds of miles off the coast (and around islands), so that state sovereignty encloses substantial resources (fisheries and offshore oil and mineral deposits). This solution has been pursued in the context of larger multilateral negotiations on ocean management.

The **UN Convention on the Law of the Sea (UNCLOS),** negotiated from 1973 to 1982, governs the uses of the oceans. After more than a decade's delay and renegotiation of some of the deep-sea mining aspects, the United States signed UNCLOS in 1994. The UNCLOS treaty established rules on territorial waters (see Figure 11.1)—12 miles for shipping and a 200-mile exclusive economic zone (EEZ) for economic activities, such as

---

[24] Dauvergne, Peter. *Loggers and Degradation in the Asia-Pacific: Corporations and Environmental Management*. Cambridge, 2001. Guimãraes, Roberto P. *The Ecopolitics of Development in the Third World: Politics and Environment in Brazil*. Boulder, CO: Lynne Rienner, 1991.

[25] Borgese, Elisabeth Mann. *The Oceanic Circle: Governing the Seas as a Global Resource*. NY: UN University Press, 1999. Pontecorvo, Giulio, ed. *The New Order of the Oceans*. Columbia, 1986.

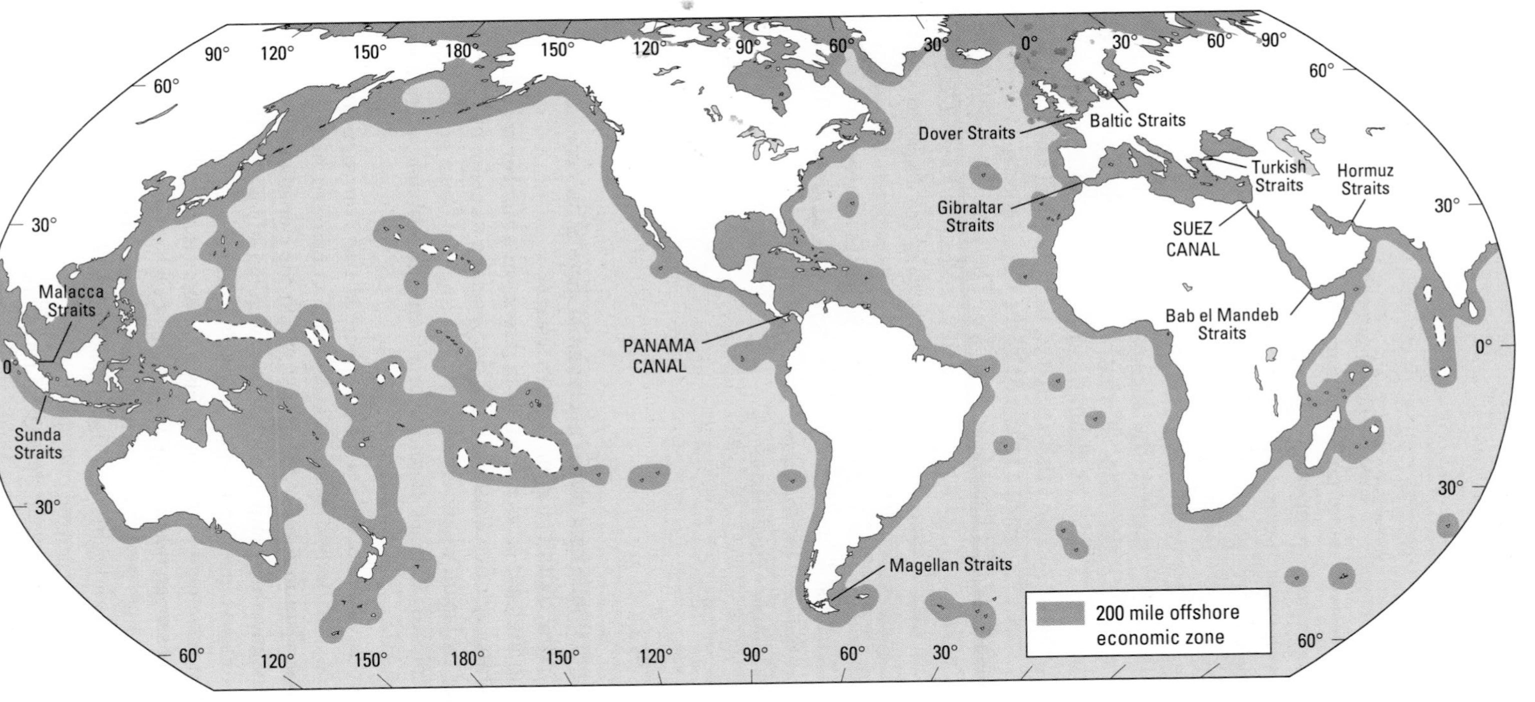

FIGURE 11.1 ■ State-Controlled Waters

Overfishing and similar problems of managing the "commons" of world oceans have been addressed by enclosing the most important ocean areas under the exclusive control of states. Shaded areas are within the 200-mile economic zones controlled by states under terms of the UNCLOS treaty.

Source: Adapted from Andrew Boyd, *An Atlas of World Affairs,* 9th ed. New York: Routledge, 1992.

THINKING THEORETICALLY

Fighting over Fish

In 1995, Canada began unilaterally enforcing fishing rules just outside its 200-mile exclusive economic zone, using military force several times to threaten Spanish fishing ships, once even seizing one. The actions seemed to set the stage for a nasty confrontation between allies (Canada and the European Union). Instead, an agreement was reached that limited fishing methods and catches in the area, as Canada had wanted. How might we explain this episode in theoretical terms?

Realism would note the effectiveness of Canada's resort to military leverage, which drove the cost of European resistance way up and made it worthwhile for the EU to come to terms with Canadian demands. Since treaties such as UNCLOS are viewed with some skepticism by realists, they would attribute Canada's success to its proximity—the greater ease with which its navy could deploy to the disputed area—and its stronger will to prevail (reflecting the fact that the issue affected Canada's national interests much more than those of the EU).

Liberals could note, however, that the EU is far more powerful than Canada overall, so sheer power politics does not provide a very good starting point for explaining the outcome. Rather, liberals might emphasize the collective goods problem involved in overfishing, and note that Canada's willingness to unilaterally take on the enforcement costs effectively resolved the dilemma. It remained only to negotiate the terms of what was being enforced (the specific rules for fishing), and there the conflicts of interest were small compared to the overall range of mutual benefits produced by the close economic cooperation of Canada and the EU. The idea that unilateral enforcement could resolve collective goods dilemmas is supported by the comments of the chairman of a UN conference working on an international fishing treaty. He noted that the Canadian-EU agreement "will help our discussions here because it establishes the principle that there can be boarding and monitoring on the high seas."

fishing and mining. The 200-mile limit placed a substantial share of the economically profitable ocean resources in the control of about a dozen states.

Varying interpretations leave economic rights in dispute in a number of locations. In the East China Sea, China sent five warships in 2005 to back up its claim to an undersea gas field partly claimed by Japan, where China began drilling and Japan granted drilling rights to a Japanese company. China's claim under a Continental Shelf treaty conflicts with Japan's claim of an EEZ.

Another conflict developed over a small piece of the continental shelf off Newfoundland that was just beyond the 200-mile range controlled by Canada. The Canadian Navy harassed Spanish fishing ships there, which the Canadians claimed were overfishing and thus endangering fish populations that were mostly within the 200-mile limit. Although the European Union accused Canada of "piracy" on the high seas, the two sides in 1995 reached an agreement on fishing levels and practices. In 1994, Russian warships drove away dozens of foreign fishing ships in the Sea of Okhotsk (where the 200-mile limit leaves a small hole of high seas in the center). Similar conflicts could develop near Norway, West Africa, the South Pacific, and the Indian Ocean.

UNCLOS also developed the general principle that the oceans are a common heritage of humankind. A mechanism was created, through an International Sea-Bed Authority, for sharing some of the wealth that rich states might gain from extracting minerals on the ocean floor (beyond 200 miles).

Private environmental groups have been active players on oceans, as in rain forests—pressuring governments and MNCs to change policies and activities. Tactics include direct action (such as Greenpeace ships shadowing garbage barges), lobbying, lawsuits, and public education. These tactics have effectively used global communications (see Chapter 10, pp. 396–398)—a dramatic event videotaped in a remote location on the high seas can be seen on millions of TV sets.

Antarctica Like the oceans, *Antarctica* belongs to no state.[26] The continent's strategic and commercial value are limited, however, and not many states care about it. Thus, states have been successful in reaching agreements on Antarctica because the costs were low and the players few. The **Antarctic Treaty of 1959**—one of the first multilateral treaties concerning the environment—forbids military activity as well as the presence of nuclear weapons or the dumping of nuclear waste. It sets aside territorial claims on the continent for future resolution and establishes a regime under which various states conduct scientific research in Antarctica. The treaty was signed by all states with interests in the area, including both superpowers. By 1991, Greenpeace had convinced the treaty signatories to turn the continent into a "world park." Antarctica is largely a success story in international environmental politics.

Pollution

Pollution generally creates a collective goods problem, but one that is not often global in scale. Pollution is more often a regional or bilateral issue. With some exceptions—such as dumping at sea—the effects of pollution are limited to the state where it occurs and its close neighbors—U.S. industrial smokestack emissions affect acid rain in Canada but do not directly affect distant states. China's terrible air pollution kills nearly half a million Chinese a year, but few foreigners. Even when pollution crosses state borders, it often has its strongest effects closest to the source. This localized effect makes for a somewhat less intractable collective goods problem, because a polluting state can seldom get an entirely free ride, and there are a limited number of actors. The effects of pollution also are more tangible than global warming or the ozone hole.

In several regions—notably Western and Eastern Europe and the Middle East—states are closely packed in the same air, river, or sea basins. In such situations, pollution controls must often be negotiated multilaterally. In Europe during the Cold War, the international pollution problem was exacerbated by the inability of Western European states to impose any limits on Eastern ones, whose pollution was notorious. These problems are only now being addressed.

Several regional agreements seek to limit **acid rain,** caused by air pollution. Acid rain often crosses borders. European states—whose forests have been heavily damaged—have agreed to limit air pollution and acid rain for their mutual benefit. In 1988, 24 European states signed a treaty to limit nitrogen oxide emissions to 1988 levels by 1995. After long negotiations, the United States and Canada have signed bilateral agreements to limit such pollution as well. These regional agreements have worked fairly well.

Even when air pollution itself does not cross borders, it can create international conflicts. For example, Indonesian villagers complained that mercury vapor released into the air from a gold mining operation that began in 1996 made them sick. It would have been a local issue between the villagers, the company, and the Indonesian government except that the company was the world's largest gold mining firm, based in the United States. An internal company report in 2001 had warned that efforts to increase gold output (and

[26] Stokke, Olav Schram, and Davor Vidas, eds. *Governing the Antarctic: The Effectiveness and Legitimacy of the Antarctic Treaty System*. Cambridge, 1997. Osherenko, Gail, and Oran R. Young. *The Age of the Arctic: Hot Conflicts and Cold Realities*. Cambridge, 1989.

POISONED WATERS

Pollution easily crosses national borders. For example, here industrial waste and sewage in the New River crosses from Mexico into California, 2003.

hence profits) were bypassing pollution controls and putting dangerous amounts of mercury into the air. By 2004, with the gold all extracted, the mine closed. In 2005, Indonesian officials filed criminal charges against American executives, who denied wrongdoing.[27]

Water pollution often crosses borders as well, especially because industrial pollution, human sewage, and agricultural fertilizers and pesticides all tend to run into rivers and seas. For instance, in 2005, a huge chemical spill in northeast China polluted a river that flows into Russia. Long-standing regional agencies that regulate shipping on heavily used European rivers now also deal with pollution. The Mediterranean basin is severely polluted, and difficult to manage because so many states border it.[28] The Great Lakes on the U.S.-Canadian border had become heavily polluted by the 1970s. But because the issue affected only two countries, it was easier to address, and the situation has improved in recent years.

Toxic and *nuclear wastes* are a special problem because of their long-term dangers. States occasionally try to ship such wastes out of the country. International agreements now ban the dumping of toxic and nuclear wastes at sea (an obvious collective goods problem). But such wastes have been sent to third world countries for disposal, for a fee. For instance, toxic ash from Pennsylvania became material for bricks in Guinea, and Italian nuclear waste was shipped to Nigeria.

Norms have developed in recent years against exporting toxic wastes—a practice seen as exploitive of the receiving country. In 1989, 100 states signed a treaty under UN auspices to regulate shipments of toxic and nuclear wastes and prevent their secret movements under corrupt deals. Forty more countries, in Africa, did not sign the treaty but called for a complete halt to toxic waste shipments to Africa. In one famous case in the 1980s, a ship carrying 14,000 tons of toxic waste from Philadelphia's trash incinerator spent three years traveling from continent to continent in search of a state that would take its cargo, which eventually was illegally dumped at sea and on a beach in Haiti, where it remains. The ship's owners were jailed for perjury.

In the 1950s, atmospheric nuclear tests created radioactive fallout that traveled thousands of miles before falling back to the ground. After milk drunk by U.S. schoolchildren was found to contain radioactive iodine, alarm over fallout led to the 1963 limited test ban, which stopped nuclear tests above ground.

---

[27] Perlez, Jane. Mining Giant Told It Put Toxic Vapors into Indonesia's Air. *The New York Times*, Dec. 22, 2004: A1.

[28] Haas, Peter M. *Saving the Mediterranean* (see footnote 5 in this chapter).

Chernobyl

In 1986, a meltdown at the Soviet nuclear power plant at **Chernobyl,** in Ukraine, created airborne radioactivity that spread over much of Europe, from Italy to Sweden. The accident exemplified the new reality—that economic and technical decisions taken in one state can have grave environmental consequences for other countries. Soviet leaders made matters worse by failing to notify neighbors promptly of the accident.

On the various issues of water and air pollution, both unilateral state actions and international agreements have often been feasible and effective. In recent decades, river water quality has improved in most industrialized regions. Market economies have begun to deal with pollution as just another cost of production that should be charged to the polluter instead of to society at large. Some governments have begun to allocate "pollution rights" that companies can buy and sell on a free market.

In the former Soviet bloc, decades of centrally planned industrialization have created more severe environmental problems, which may prove more intractable.[29] With staggering environmental damage and human health effects, the economically strapped former Soviet republics now must bargain over limiting pollution and repairing the damage. For example, the severely polluted Aral Sea, formerly contained within one state, the Soviet Union, is now shared by two, Kazakhstan and Uzbekistan. Once the world's fourth largest inland sea, it shrank in half, its huge fisheries destroyed, after a Soviet-era mega-irrigation project to grow cotton in the desert diverted the Aral Sea's inlet rivers and polluted them with pesticides. Former fishing towns found themselves dozens of miles away from the shoreline. In the 1990s, environmentalists gave up efforts to save the Aral Sea, after local and international political leaders failed to implement plans to address the problem. Local populations suffered from widespread health effects of the disaster.

Natural Resources

The natural environment is not only a delicate ecosystem requiring protection; it is also a repository of natural resources. Because the extraction of resources brings states wealth (and hence power), these resources regularly become a source of international conflicts.[30] Because they are mostly located within individual states, they do not present a collective goods problem. Rather, states bargain (with leverage) as to these vital resources.

Three aspects of natural resources shape their role in international conflict. First, they are required for the operation of an industrial economy (sometimes even an agrarian one). Second, their sources—mineral deposits, rivers, and so forth—are associated with particular territories over which states may fight for control. Third, natural resources tend to be unevenly distributed, with plentiful supplies in some states and an absence in others. These aspects mean that trade in natural resources is extremely profitable; much additional wealth is created by such trade. They also mean that trade in resources is fairly politicized—creating market imperfections such as monopoly, oligopoly, and price manipulation, sometimes by cartels (see "Politics of Markets" on pp. 308–310).

---

[29] Feshbach, Murray. *Ecological Disaster: Cleaning Up the Hidden Legacy of the Soviet Regime*. Washington, DC: Brookings, 1995. Schleicher, Klaus, ed. *Pollution Knows No Frontiers: A Reader*. NY: Paragon, 1992. Weinthal, Erika. *State Making and Environment Cooperation: Linking Domestic and International Politics in Central Asia*. MIT, 2002.

[30] Zacher, Mark W., ed. *The International Political Economy of Natural Resources*. Brookfield, VT: Edward Elgar, 1993. Lipschutz, Ronnie D. *When Nations Clash: Raw Materials, Ideology, and Foreign Policy*. NY: Ballinger, 1989. Bannon, Ian, and Paul Collier, eds. *Natural Resources and Violent Conflict: Options and Actions*. Washington: World Bank, 2003.

World Energy

Of the various natural resources required by states, energy resources (fuels) are central. The commercial fuels that power the world's industrial economies are oil (about 40 percent of world energy consumption), coal (30 percent), natural gas (25 percent), and hydroelectric and nuclear power (5 percent). The fossil fuels (coal, oil, gas) thus account for 95 percent of world energy consumption. Some energy consumed as electricity comes from hydroelectric dams or nuclear power plants, but most of it comes from burning fossil fuels in electric-generating plants.

Imagine a pile of coal weighing 26,000 pounds (12 metric tons, about the weight of nine automobiles). The energy released by burning that much coal is equivalent to the amount of energy North Americans use per person each year. Wealthier people, of course, consume more energy per person than do poorer people, but 12 tons is the average.

Table 11.1 shows energy consumption per person in the nine world regions. The four industrialized regions of the North use much more energy per person than those of the South. Because Asia and Africa have little industry, North America uses 25 times as much as Asia or Africa. Among industrialized countries there are differences in the *efficiency* of energy use—GDP produced per unit of energy consumed. The least efficient are Russia and Eastern Europe (even before that region's current economic depression); North America is also rather inefficient; Europe and Japan are the most energy efficient.

International trade in energy plays a vital role in the world economy. As Table 11.1 shows, the regions of the industrialized West are all net importers of energy. Together they import from the rest of the world, each year, energy equivalent to more than a billion tons of coal. The other six world regions are net exporters of energy.

Although all forms of energy are traded internationally, the most important by far is oil, the cheapest to transport over long distances. Russia and Eastern Europe receive vital hard currency earnings from exporting oil. Venezuela and Mexico (in Latin America) and Nigeria and Angola (in Africa) are major oil exporters. But by far the largest source

TABLE 11.1 ■ Per Capita Energy Consumption and Net Energy Trade, 2003

	Per Capita Consumption (million BTU)	Total Net Energy Exports[a] (quadrillion BTU)
North America	380	−25
Western Europe	150	−30
Japan/Pacific	170	−21
Russia & Eastern Europe	140	+16
China	35	−5
Middle East	100	+38
Latin America	55	+7
South Asia	20	−2
Africa	15	+17
World as a whole	70	

[a]Net exports refers to production minus consumption. Net exports worldwide do not equal net imports for technical reasons.

Source: Calculated from data in U.S. Department of Energy. Energy Information Administration. See www.eia.doe.gov/iea/.

of oil exports is the Middle East—especially the countries around the Persian Gulf (Saudi Arabia, Kuwait, Iraq, Iran, and the small sheikdoms of United Arab Emirates, Qatar, Bahrain, and Oman). Saudi Arabia is the largest oil exporter and sits atop the largest oil reserves (see Table 8.1 on p. 331). The politics of world energy revolve around Middle East oil shipped to Western Europe, Japan/Pacific, and North America.

Oil and International Relations

The importance of oil in the industrialized economies helps to explain the political importance of the Middle East in world politics.[31] Iraq's 1990 invasion of Kuwait (and the mere possibility that Iraq's army could move into Saudi Arabia) threatened the West's access to stable, inexpensive supplies of oil. World oil prices immediately more than doubled. But Saudi Arabia could increase its own rate of oil exports massively enough to compensate for both Kuwaiti and Iraqi exports cut off by the invasion and the UN sanctions against Iraq. When it became clear that Saudi exports would not be disrupted, the price of oil dropped again on world markets. Thus, not only is energy a crucial economic sector (on which all industrial activity depends), but it is also one of the most politically sensitive (because of the dependence of the West on energy imported from the Middle East and other third world regions).

To secure a supply of oil in the Middle East, Britain and other European countries colonized the area early in the twentieth century, carving up territory into protectorates in which European power kept local monarchs on their thrones. (Iraq, for instance, argued that Kuwait was part of Iraq, that it was cut off and made into a separate state by the British.) The United States did not claim colonies or protectorates, but U.S. MNCs were heavily involved in the development of oil resources in the area from the 1920s through the 1960s—often wielding vast power. Local rulers depended on the expertise and capital investment of U.S. and European oil companies. The "seven sisters"—a cartel of Western oil companies—kept the price paid to local states low and their own profits high.

After World War II the British gave up colonial claims in the Middle East, but the Western oil companies kept producing cheap oil there for Western consumption. Then in 1973, during an Arab-Israeli war, the oil-producing Arab states of the region decided to punish the United States for supporting Israel. They cut off their oil exports to the United States and curtailed their overall exports. This supply disruption sent world oil prices skyrocketing. OPEC realized its potential power and the high price the world was willing to pay for oil. After the war ended, OPEC agreed to limit production to keep oil prices high.

This 1973 **oil shock** had a profound effect on the world economy and on world politics. Huge amounts of hard currency accumulated in the treasuries of the Middle East oil-exporting countries, which in turn invested them around the world (these were called *petrodollars*). High inflation plagued the United States and Europe for years afterward. The economic instability and sense of U.S. helplessness—coming on top of the Vietnam debacle—seemed to mark a decline in American power and perhaps the rise of the third world.

In 1979, the revolution in Iran led to another major increase in oil prices. This second oil shock further weakened the industrialized economies. But these economies were already adjusting to the new realities of world energy. Higher oil prices led to the expansion of oil production in new locations outside of OPEC—in the North Sea (Britain and Norway), Alaska, Angola, Russia, and elsewhere. By the mid-1980s, the Middle East was rapidly losing its market share of world trade in oil. At the same time, industrialized economies

[31] Kapstein, Ethan B. *The Insecure Alliance: Energy Crises and Western Politics Since 1944*. Oxford, 1990. Parra, Francisco R. *Oil Politics: A Modern History of Petroleum*. London: I. B. Tauris, 2004. Yergin, Daniel. *The Prize: The Epic Quest for Oil, Money, and Power*. NY: Simon & Schuster, 1991. Goldstein, Joshua S., Xiaoming Huang, and Burcu Akan. Energy in the World Economy, 1950–1992. *International Studies Quarterly* 41 (2), 1997: 241–66.

learned to be more *energy efficient*. With supply up and demand down, oil prices dropped in the late 1980s to historic lows below $20/barrel. Because of the market adjustments that followed high oil prices, the industrialized West became somewhat less dependent on Middle East oil and the power of OPEC has been greatly reduced. Still, energy continues to be a crucial issue in which the Middle East plays a key role.

In the late 1990s, the Caspian Sea region beckoned as a new and largely untapped oil source (see Figure 11.2). However, international politics and geography hampered the development of this zone. The oil must travel overland by pipeline to reach world markets (the Caspian is an inland sea). But the main pipeline from oil-producing Azerbaijan to the Black Sea (where tanker ships could load) traveled through war-torn Chechnya in southern Russia. Russia built a bypass route around Chechnya that carries a large and growing amount of Caspian oil for export through the Black Sea.

FIGURE 11.2 ■ Dividing the Caspian Sea

The Caspian Sea is the world's largest inland body of water. It could be defined under international law as either a lake or a sea. The middle of a *lake* (beyond territorial waters) is a joint area (see left panel), which can be exploited only if the countries agree on terms. In a *sea* less than 400 miles wide, the bordering countries' Exclusive Economic Zones (EEZs) split up the whole sea (right panel).

After a 1912 treaty, the Soviet Union and Iran treated the Caspian as a lake and made agreements on fishing. Later, substantial oil deposits were found offshore. When the Soviet Union broke up, the Caspian was suddenly bordered by five countries instead of two, with most of the oil and gas in or near Azerbaijan and Turkmenistan, not Russia. Under the "lake" interpretation, however, Russia could share in revenues from some of the offshore oil. In the 1990s, more oil and gas was discovered, including some potentially big fields near Russia. This made Russia more inclined to accept a "sea" interpretation and begin drilling, without waiting to negotiate a complex deal with contentious neighbors.[a] Iran sent a warship in 2001 to drive away an Azerbaijan-based oil exploration ship (owned by British Petroleum) from disputed waters. In 2003, Russia and Kazakhstan finalized an agreement to share the northern seabed, a bilateral approach that Iran rejected. Five-party talks continued.

[a]Sciolino, Elaine. "It's a Sea! It's a Lake! No. It's a Pool of Oil!" *The New York Times*, June 21, 1998.

But Western powers sought other pipeline routes that did not cross Russia, while Turkey sought to control a larger market share and reduce environmental damage to the Bosporus waterway (through which Russian tankers must travel). After long negotiations, in 2002–2004, states and oil companies built a large-capacity pipeline costing billions of dollars, through Azerbaijan and Georgia to Turkey's Mediterranean coast. Violent conflicts in the region make pipeline routes particularly complex. All three countries on the new pipeline route were at war in the past decade. A dozen other existing and proposed oil pipelines for Caspian Sea oil are no easier. Across the Caspian Sea, Turkmenistan wants to export natural gas to Pakistan, and from there to Asia, but a pipeline has to cross war-torn Afghanistan. Meanwhile in 2005 Russia had to decide whether a new pipeline to carry Siberian oil would run to China or Japan (it chose both). Thus, although borders and geography may be less and less important in communications and business, they still matter greatly in such international economic transactions as oil pipelines.

The West has diversified its oil supplies, supplementing the Middle East with African, Asian, Russian, and Latin American sources. In 2003, a new $4 billion pipeline began carrying oil from Chad through Cameroon for export, promising to help both countries alleviate poverty.

High Oil Prices

Despite this diversification, oil prices have been relatively high since 2000, reaching $75 a barrel in 2006 and pushing U.S. gas prices above $3 a gallon. High oil prices hurt the industrialized economies, but they have two major benefits. First, burning oil contributes to global warming, and high prices make it profitable to burn less oil and be more energy efficient. Second, high oil prices increase the export earnings of oil-producing countries. Countries such as Venezuela and Mexico count on oil revenues in their economic development plans and to repay foreign debts. These countries eased their debt problems as a result of higher prices. High oil prices in recent years have played a crucial part in the economic recovery of Russia, an oil exporter.

Minerals, Land, Water

To build the infrastructure and other manufactured goods that create wealth in a national economy, states need other raw materials in addition to energy. These include metals, other minerals, and related materials extracted through mining.

The political economy of minerals—iron, copper, platinum, and so forth—differs from that of world energy. The value of international trade in oil is many times greater than that of any mineral. Mineral production is distributed more evenly than is oil production—supply is not so concentrated in one region of the world. Industrialized countries have also reduced their vulnerability by stockpiling strategic minerals (easier to do with minerals than with energy because of smaller quantities and values).

Nonetheless, industrialized countries do have certain vulnerabilities with regard to mineral supply, and these do affect international politics. Among the industrialized regions, Japan and Europe are most dependent on mineral imports; the United States is more self-sufficient. The former Soviet Union was a leading exporter of key minerals—a role that Russia may continue in the future. Despite its economic problems, one great strength of the Russian economy is being self-sufficient in both energy and mineral resources.

Another major exporter of key minerals is South Africa. For a few strategic minerals, notably manganese and chromium, South Africa controls three-quarters or more of the world's reserves. Western leaders worried that political instability in South Africa (where the black majority struggled for years under white minority rule) could disrupt the supply of these minerals. This is one reason why the industrialized countries were reluctant to impose trade sanctions on South Africa over human rights issues. South Africa's leading position in supplying diamonds, gold, and platinum to world markets gave South Africa a valuable

WATER, WATER EVERYWHERE

As population growth and economic development increase the demand for water, more international conflicts arise over water rights. Many important rivers pass through multiple states, and many states share access to seas and lakes. The Aral Sea, once part of the Soviet Union but now shared between Kazakhstan and Uzbekistan, was among the world's largest lakes until it was decimated by the diversion of its water sources to irrigate cotton. This scene shows the former seabed, now 70 miles from shore, in 1997.

source of income, but in the end the West did apply economic sanctions that hurt the South African economy and helped end apartheid.

Most important to industrialized economies are the minerals that go into making industrial equipment. Traditionally most important is iron, from which steel is made. The leading producers of steel are the former Soviet Union, Japan, the United States, China, and Germany, followed by Brazil, Italy, South Korea, France, and Britain. Thus, major industrialized countries produce their own steel (Germany and Japan are the leading exporters worldwide). To preserve self-sufficiency in steel production, the United States and others have used trade policies to protect domestic steel industries (such as the Bush administration's steel tariffs, see p. 321).

Some industrialized countries, notably Japan, depend heavily on importing iron ore for their steel industry. Iron ore is not concentrated in one location but is exported from developing and industrialized countries around the world. There is an *Association of Iron Ore Exporting Countries (AIOEC)*, but it is limited to consultation, and the United States, Canada, and the former Soviet Union are exporters that are not among the 12 members.

For other important industrial minerals such as copper, nickel, and zinc, the pattern of supply and trade is much more diffuse than for oil, and the industrialized countries are largely self-sufficient. Even when third world states are the main suppliers, as with tin and bauxite, they have not gained the power of OPEC. There is a producer cartel in some cases (copper), a producer-consumer cartel in some (tin), and separate producer and consumer cartels in others (bauxite).

Certain agricultural products have spawned producer cartels such as the Union of Banana Exporting Countries (UBEC) and the African Groundnut Council. Like minerals, some export crops come mainly from just a few countries. These include sugar (Cuba), cocoa (Ivory Coast, Ghana, Nigeria), tea (India, Sri Lanka, China), and coffee (Brazil, Colombia). Despite the concentrations, producer cartels have not been very successful in boosting prices of these products, which are less essential than energy.

Water Disputes In addition to energy and minerals, states need water. Need of water increases as a society industrializes, as it intensifies agriculture, and as its population grows. World water use is 35 times higher than just a few centuries ago, and grew twice as fast as population in the twentieth century. Yet water supplies are relatively unchanging, and are becoming depleted in many places. One-fifth of the world's population lacks safe drinking water, and 80 countries suffer water shortages. Water supplies—rivers and water tables—often cross international boundaries; thus access to water is increasingly a source of international conflict. Sometimes—as when several states share access to a single water table—these conflicts are collective goods problems.

Water problems are especially important in the Middle East. For instance, the Euphrates River runs from Turkey through Syria to Iraq before reaching the Persian Gulf. Iraq objects to Syrian diversion of water from the river, and both Iraq and Syria object to Turkey's diversion.

The Jordan River originates in Syria and Lebanon and runs through Israel to Jordan. In the 1950s, Israel began building a canal to take water from the Jordan River to "make the desert bloom." Jordan and its Arab neighbors complained to the UN Security Council, but it failed in efforts to mediate the dispute, and each state went ahead with its own water plans (Israel and Jordan agreeing, however, to stay within UN-proposed allocations). In 1964, Syria and Lebanon tried to build dams and divert water before it reached Israel, rendering Israel's new water system worthless. Israeli air and artillery attacks on the construction site forced Syria to abandon its diversion project, and Israel's 1967 capture of the Golan Heights precluded Syria from renewing such efforts.[32]

Water also contains other resources such as fish and offshore oil deposits. The UNCLOS treaty enclosed more of these resources within states' territory—but this enclosure creates new problems. Norms regarding territorial waters are not firmly entrenched; some states disagree on who owns what. Also, control of small islands now implies rights to surrounding oceans with their fish, offshore oil, and minerals. A potentially serious international dispute has been brewing in the Spratly Islands, where some tiny islands are claimed by China, Vietnam, and other nearby countries (see pp. 178–179). With the islands come nearby oil drilling rights and fisheries. China has invited a U.S. company to explore for oil there, promising protection by the Chinese Navy. For similar reasons, Iran and the United Arab Emirates dispute control of several small islands in the Persian Gulf.

A common theme runs through the conflicts over fuels, minerals, agricultural products, and territorial waters. They are produced in fixed locations but traded to distant places. Control of these locations gives a state both greater self-sufficiency (valued by mercantilists) and market commodities generating wealth (valued by liberals).

International Security and the Environment

IR scholars have expanded their studies of environmental politics to systematically study the relationship of military and security affairs with the environment.[33] One side of this relationship is the role of the environment as a source of international conflict. We have seen how environmental degradation can lead to collective goods problems among large numbers of states, and how competition for territory and resources can create conflicts among smaller groups of states. Environmental damage from the oil industry in the very poor river delta region of Nigeria has inflamed a local insurgency which attacked oil installations and kidnapped foreign oil workers in 2006.

The other side of the environment-security relationship concerns the effect of activities in the international security realm on the environment. Military activities—especially warfare—are important contributors to environmental degradation, above and beyond the degradation caused by economic activities such as mining and manufacturing.

---

[32] Conca, Ken. *Governing Water: Contentious Transnational Politics and Global Institution Building*. MIT, 2005. Selby, Jan. *Water, Power, and Politics in the Middle East*. London: I. B. Tauris, 2003.

[33] Kahl, Colin H. *States, Scarcity, and Civil Strife in the Developing World*. Princeton, 2006. Dalby, Simon. *Environmental Security*. Minnesota, 2002. Lowi, Miriam R. and Brian R. Shaw. *Environment and Security: Discourses and Practices*. Basingstoke, UK: Palgrave, 2000. Homer-Dixon, Thomas F. *Environment, Scarcity, and Violence*. Princeton, 1999.

WAR IS NOT GREEN

Wars often bring environmental destruction, sometimes deliberately and sometimes as a by-product. Military operations in peacetime also contribute to environmental problems. Here, U.S. forces pass a sabotaged oil pipeline near Fallujah, Iraq, in November 2004.

During the 1991 Gulf War, Iraqi forces spilled large amounts of Kuwaiti oil into the Persian Gulf and then, before retreating from Kuwait, blew up hundreds of Kuwaiti oil wells, leaving them burning uncontrollably and covering Iraq and Iran with thick black smoke. Iraq's environment also suffered tremendous damage from the massive bombing campaign. After the war, Iraq built a giant canal to drain marshes used for refuge by rebels—another environmental disaster. Since 2003, oil wells and pipelines have become a favorite target of insurgents, but restoration of the marshes has begun.

Armies sometimes adopt a "scorched earth policy" to deny sustenance to their adversaries. Fields are burned and villages leveled. In World War II, the Soviets left a scorched earth behind as they retreated before the Nazi invasion. Japan used incendiary devices carried in high-altitude balloons to start forest fires in the U.S. Northwest. The United States sprayed defoliants massively in Vietnam to destroy jungles in an attempt to expose guerrilla forces. The Vietnamese countryside still shows effects from these herbicides, as do U.S. veterans who suffer lingering health effects due to contact with chemicals such as *Agent Orange*.

Military activity short of war also tends to damage the environment. Military industries pollute. Military forces use energy less efficiently than civilians do. Military aircraft and missiles contribute to ozone depletion. Military bases contain many toxic waste dumps.

The greatest *potential* environmental disaster imaginable would be a large nuclear war. Ecosystems would be severely damaged throughout the world by secondary effects of nuclear weapons—radioactive fallout and the breakdown of social order and technology. Some scientists also think that global climate changes, leading to famine and environmental collapse, could result—"nuclear winter" (see p. 233).

Population

WEB LINK
Population

The international system is having to cope with increasing conflict and complexity in managing the global environment. The problem is increasing over time because human demands on the environment keep growing but the environment tends to remain static. The growing demands have two causes—economic growth (higher GDP per person) and a growing number of people.

We have so far focused on the first cause—world industrialization as a source of demands. This cause is the more important one in the industrialized regions. But in the global South, with less industry and more people, population pressures are more important. The rest of this chapter, which focuses on population issues, thus also serves to lead into Chapters 12 and 13 on North-South relations.

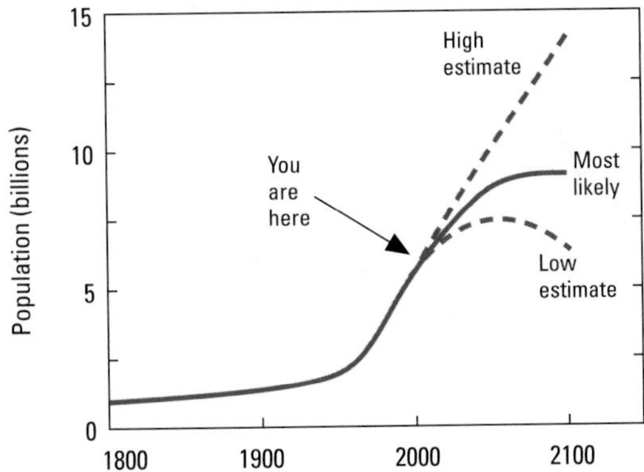

FIGURE 11.3 ■ World Population Trends and Projections

Source: Based on data from the UN Population Office.

World Population Trends

Global population reached a record high today, as it does every day. World population, 6.5 billion in 2005, is growing by 75 million each year—200,000 additional people per day.

Forecasting future population is easy in some respects. Barring a nuclear war or an environmental catastrophe, today's children will grow up and have children of their own. For the coming 20 to 30 years, world population growth will be driven, rather mechanistically, by the large number of children in today's third world populations. The projected world population in 25 years will be 7 to 8 billion people, and there is little anyone can do to change that projection.

Of the increase in population in that period, 96 percent will be in the global South. Currently, half the world's population growth occurs in just six countries: India, China, Pakistan, Nigeria, Bangladesh, and Indonesia. Among the world's poorest countries, population is expected to triple in the next 50 years, whereas many rich countries will see population shrinkage in that period.[34]

Forecasting beyond 25 years is difficult. When today's children grow up, the number of children they bear will be affected by their incomes (because of the "demographic transition," discussed shortly). To the extent that third world countries accumulate wealth—a subject taken up in Chapter 13—their populations will grow more slowly. A second factor affecting the rate of population growth will be government policies regarding women's rights and birth control.

Because of these two uncertainties, projections beyond a few decades have a range of uncertainty (see Figure 11.3). By 2050, world population could be 8 or 9 billion, with a final leveling out around 9 to 10 billion in the next 200 years. In the 1980s, the decline in birthrates stalled in a number of countries and economic growth in the global South fell below expectations, pushing population projections up. However, successes in third world regions outside Africa—in raising incomes and lowering birthrates in the 1990s—brought projections downward. New data in 2002 showed that higher women's status and literacy are reducing population growth more than expected in large, poor countries.[35] The actions of states and IOs *now* will determine the earth's population in 200 years.

[34] UNFPA data. See United Nations. *State of World Population Report 2004*. NY: UN, 2004.

[35] Horiuchi, Shiro. Stagnation in the Decline of the World Population Growth Rate During the 1980s. *Science* 257, Aug. 7, 1992: 761–65. Crossette, Barbara. Population Estimates Fall as Women Assert Control. *The New York Times*, March 10, 2002.

Two hundred years ago, British writer *Thomas Malthus* warned that population tends to increase faster than food supply and predicted that population growth would limit itself through famine and disease. Today, experts and officials who warn against world overpopulation are sometimes called *Malthusian*. Critics point out that technology has kept pace with population in the past, allowing more food and other resources to be extracted from the environment even as population keeps growing.

However, leaders of most third world states now recognize that unrestrained population growth drags down per capita income. But actions taken to slow population growth tend to have short-term costs and long-term benefits. Doing nothing is the cheapest and often most politically acceptable course in the short run—and the most expensive in the long run.

The Demographic Transition

Population growth results from a difference between rates of birth (per 1,000 people) and rates of death. In agrarian (preindustrial) societies, both birthrates and death rates are high. Population growth is thus slow—even negative at times when death rates exceed birthrates (during a famine or plague, for instance).

The process of economic development—of industrialization and the accumulation of wealth on a per capita basis—brings about a change in birth and death rates that follows a fairly universal pattern called the **demographic transition** (see Figure 11.4). First, death rates fall as food supplies increase and access to health care expands. Later, birthrates fall as people become educated, more secure, and more urbanized, and as the status of women in society rises. At the end of the transition, as at the beginning, birthrates and death rates are fairly close to each other, and population growth is limited. But during the transition, when death rates have fallen more than birthrates, population grows rapidly.

One reason poor people tend to have many children is that under harsh poverty a child's survival is not assured. Disease, malnutrition, or violence may claim the lives of many children, leaving parents with no one to look after them in their old age. Having many children helps ensure that some survive. (The collective goods problem appears again, because each family wants more children but when all pursue this strategy the economic development of the whole community or state is held back.)

As a state makes the demographic transition, the structure of its population changes dramatically. At the beginning and middle of the process, most of the population is young. Families have many children, and adults do not have a long life expectancy. Because children are not very productive economically, the large number of children in poor countries tends to slow down the accumulation of wealth. But by the end of the demographic transition, because adults live longer and families have fewer children, the average age of the population is much older. Eventually a substantial section of the population is elderly—a different nonproductive population that the economy must support.

The industrialized countries have been through the demographic transition and now have slow population growth. In Europe and Japan populations are actually shrinking. Most third world countries are in the middle of the transition and have rapid population growth.

The dilemma of the demographic transition is this: rapid population growth and a child-heavy population are powerful forces lowering per capita income. Yet the best way to slow population growth is to raise per capita income.

Population growth thus contributes to a vicious cycle in many poor states. Where population rises at the same rate as overall wealth, the average person is no better off over

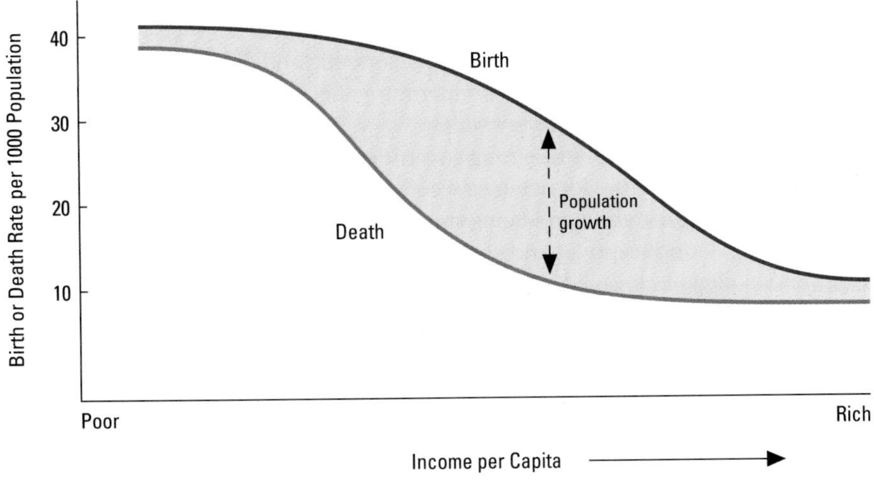

FIGURE 11.4 ■ The Demographic Transition

As income rises, first death rates and then birthrates fall. The gap between the two is the population growth rate. Early in the transition, the population contains a large proportion of children; later it contains a large proportion of elderly people.

time. Even when the economy grows faster than population, so that the *average* income rises, the total *number* of poor people may increase. From 1987 to 1998, according to the World Bank, the *proportion* of people living in dire poverty (under a dollar per day) dropped from 29 to 24 percent worldwide. But the actual *number* of people living in poverty increased from just below to just above 1.2 billion.

The demographic transition tends to widen international disparities of wealth. States that manage to raise incomes a bit enter an upward spiral—as population growth slows, income levels per capita rise more, which further slows population growth, and so forth. Meanwhile, states that do not raise incomes have unabated population growth; per capita incomes stay low, which fuels more population growth—a downward spiral.

Globally, this disparity contributes to the gap in wealth between the North and South (see Chapter 12). Within the South disparities are also sharpened, as a few countries manage to slow population growth and raise incomes while others fail to do so. Even within a single country, the demographic transition sharpens disparities. Cities, richer classes, richer ethnic groups, and richer provinces tend to have low birthrates compared to the countryside and the poorer classes, ethnic groups, and provinces. In countries such as France, Israel, and the United States, wealthier ethnic groups (often white) have much slower population growth than poorer ethnic groups (often nonwhite).

In recent decades, the global South seems to be splitting into two groups of states. The first group, including China and India, entered the phase of the demographic transition marked by falling birthrates in the 1970s. But in nearly 70 other poor states, death rates kept falling faster than birthrates, leading to accelerating population growth. These population trends contributed to disparities within the global South that emerged in the 1990s, notably between Africa and Asia.

Although the demographic transition is universal in its outlines, particular changes in birthrates and death rates vary depending on local conditions and government policies.

Population Policies

The policies that governments adopt—not just economic and demographic conditions—influence the birthrate. Among the most important policies are those regarding birth control (contraception). State policies vary widely.

At one extreme, China uses its strong government control to try to enforce a limit of one child per couple. Penalties for having a second child include being charged for services that were free for the first child and being stigmatized at work. Beyond two children, the penalties escalate. Contraceptives and abortions are free, and citizens are educated about them. China's policy has lowered growth rates considerably in the cities but less so in the countryside, where 80 percent of the people live. Still, in a single decade (the 1970s) China's fertility rate fell from 6 children per woman to about 2.5, a dramatic change. (It now stands at 1.7.)

But the Chinese policy has drawbacks. It limits individual freedom in favor of government control. Forced or coerced abortions have been reported. In traditional Chinese society (as in some other countries), sons are valued more than daughters. Couples who have a daughter may keep trying until they have a son. In some cases, Chinese peasants have reportedly killed newborn daughters so they could try for a son. Simply bribing or paying fines became more common routes around the one-child policy in the 1990s. Most often, parents in China (and some places in India) are using information technology—ultrasound scans—to determine their fetus's gender and abort it if female. China's 2000 census showed the percent of female births at 0.85 per boy, rather than the normal .95, a difference that amounts to a million "missing" girls per year. In the countryside, the sex differential is twice as high as in the cities, reaching 140 men per 100 women in some areas where the one-child policy is strictly enforced. In recent years, hundreds of thousands of young women there have been kidnapped and sold as brides.[36]

India's policies are less extreme but have been slower. The birthrate fell from just under 6 per woman to about 4.7 in the 1970s to 2.7 in 2006. India's government, strongly committed to birth control, has tried to make information and means widely available, but as a democracy it does not have China's extreme government control over society.

Countries with somewhat higher incomes than India or China can succeed more easily. Mexico's strong but noncoercive family-planning program, adopted in 1974, cut birthrates in half over 15 years, to 2.7 per woman (and to 2.4 in 2006).[37]

At the other extreme from China are governments that encourage or force childbearing, and outlaw or limit access to contraception. Such a policy is called **pronatalist** (pro-birth). Traditionally, many governments have adopted such policies because population was seen as an element of national power. More babies today meant more soldiers later. Recall (from p. 59) that the major difference in potential power between Iraq and Iran was population—Iran's being three times larger. On the battlefield, this power played out as "human wave" assaults of Iranian men and boys (who were slaughtered by the tens of thousands), which ultimately wore the Iraqis down.

Today, only a few third world governments have strongly pronatalist policies, but many do not make birth control or sex education available to poor women. In some such states, population is not considered a problem (and may even be seen as an asset); in other states, the government simply cannot afford effective measures to lower birthrates. (Again, birth control has short-term costs and long-term benefits.) According to the

[36] Dugger, Celia W. Modern Asia's Anomaly: The Girls Who Don't Get Born. *The New York Times*, May 6, 2001: Week in Review. Rosenthal, Elisabeth. Harsh Chinese Reality Feeds a Black Market in Women. *The New York Times*, June 25, 2001: A1. Hudson, Valerie M. and Andrea M. Den Boer. *Bare Branches: The Security Implications of Asia's Surplus Male Population*. MIT, 2004.

[37] Anderson, John Ward. Six Billion and Counting—But Slower. *The Washington Post*, Oct. 12, 1999: A1.

United Nations Population Fund (UNFPA), 300 million women do not have access to effective contraception.

Industrialized states have provided financial assistance for family planning programs in poor countries. One reason the drop in birthrates slowed in the 1980s is that international financial assistance slowed dramatically. The U.S. government, providing more than a quarter of the voluntary contributions that finance the UNFPA's annual budget of $225 million, terminated contributions in 1976 after U.S. anti-abortion activists protested that some UNFPA funds were financing abortions. Some U.S. funding of the UNFPA was restored in the 1990s.

Women's Status Perhaps most important, birthrates are influenced by the status of women in society. In cultures that traditionally see women as valuable only in producing babies, great pressures exist against women who stop doing so. Many women do not use birth control because their husbands will not allow them to. These husbands may think that having many children is proof of their manliness. As women's status improves and they can work in various occupations, own property, and vote, women gain the power as well as the education and money necessary to limit the size of their families.

According to the UNFPA, improving the status of women is one of the most important means of controlling world population growth. Government policies about women's status vary from one state to another. International programs and agencies, such as the UN commission on the status of women, are working to address the issue on a global scale. International economic aid programs have been criticized for paying insufficient attention to the status of women, focusing on economic development in isolation from population growth (see "Women in Development" on pp. 480–481).

Mortality and AIDS

Population growth is determined by the death rate as well as the birthrate. In a way, the death rate is more complicated than the birthrate: births have only one source (sex involving women of childbearing age), whereas people die from many different causes at different ages. In poor countries, people tend to die younger, often from infectious diseases; in richer countries, people live longer and die more often from cancer and heart disease. The proportion of babies who die within their first year is the **infant mortality rate.** This rate is an excellent indicator of overall health, since it reflects a population's access to nutrition, water, shelter, and health care. Infant mortality is 5 percent worldwide, 1 percent or less in rich countries but over 10 percent in the poorest countries and even higher in local pockets of extreme poverty (especially in Africa and in war zones such as Sierra Leone and Afghanistan, with the world's highest infant mortality rate at 16 percent).

Although death rates vary greatly from one state or region to another, the overall trends are stable from decade to decade. Wars, droughts, epidemics, and disasters have an effect locally but hardly matter globally. In the poorest countries, which are just beginning the demographic transition, the death rate declined from nearly 30 deaths per thousand population in 1950 to less than 15 since 1990. In the *industrialized countries*, the death rate bottomed out around 10 per thousand by 1960, and now stands around 7 in the West. However, Russia's death rate *rose* from 11 in 1980 to 15 in 1995 (and rates are high elsewhere in Eastern Europe and central Asia). In the *midtransition* countries (including China and India), the death rate fell from 25 in 1950 to 10 in 1980 and has equaled the rich countries since then. (Between 1980 and 1995, China's death rate went from 6 to 7; India's fell from 13 to 9.) In this middle group of developing countries, infant mortality is generally much lower than in the poorest countries.

These stable trends in mortality mean that the death rate is not a means by which governments or international agencies can affect population growth—worsening poverty

BE CAREFUL OUT THERE

AIDS is spreading rapidly in Southeast Asia and Africa. The worldwide effort to slow AIDS, coordinated by the World Health Organization (WHO), illustrates how global-level problems such as AIDS are making IOs such as WHO more important. Here is an AIDS poster in Nigeria, 2001.

may cause famine and a rising death rate, but this is not a realistic way to control population growth. It would mean moving backward through the demographic transition, which would wreck any chance of lowering birthrates. Nor can wars kill enough people to reduce population growth (short of global nuclear war). Even a major famine or war, one killing a million people, hardly alters world population trends because every year about 75 million people die—200,000 every day. In short, most of the world is already at or near the end of the transition in *death* rates; the key question is how long birthrates take to complete the transition.[38]

Three mortality factors, however—AIDS, other infectious diseases, and smoking—deserve special attention because they have begun to exact very high costs even if they do not much affect global population trends. In these cases, actions taken in the short term have long-term and often international consequences, and once again there are short-term costs and long-term benefits.

AIDS In the worldwide AIDS epidemic, one state's success or failure in limiting the spread of HIV (human immunodeficiency virus) affects infections in other states as well. There is a delay of five to ten years after infection by the virus before symptoms appear, and during this period an infected individual can infect others (through sex or blood). AIDS spreads internationally—through business, tourism, migration, and military operations—reflecting the interdependence of states.

By 2006, an estimated 40 million people were infected with HIV worldwide, two-thirds of them in Africa and half of the rest in South Asia (see Table 11.2). In addition, the epidemic had killed more than 30 million people and left 15 million orphans. Of the 40 million currently infected, only a small fraction had yet developed AIDS (most did not even know they were infected), so the main costs of the epidemic—human, economic, and political—are yet to be felt. Each year, 5 million people are newly infected with HIV, and 3 million die from AIDS, including half a million children. About 85 percent of people with AIDS are in the global South.

AIDS in the Developing World

In Africa, already the world's poorest and most war-torn region, AIDS has emerged as one of several powerful forces driving the region backward into deeper poverty. About 8 percent of adults are infected with HIV, more than half of them women. In the most affected African countries in southern Africa, one in six adults has HIV (one in three for Botswana, the worst case). Infection is also rampant in African armies, with direct implications for international security. In Angola, it was the *end* of a long civil war that opened borders and increased traffic with neighboring states that had high HIV infection rates. As Angola's infection rate began to climb, military officers took the initiative to set up education programs and comprehensive HIV testing within the army. In contrast to other African states with high military infection rates, Angola's aggressive program kept the rate as low as in the general population, below 10 percent.

[38] Soubbotina, Tatyana P., and Katherine Sheram. *Beyond Economic Growth: Meeting the Challenges of Global Development*. Washington: World Bank, 2000.

TABLE 11.2 ■ Population and AIDS by World Region, 2005

Region[a]	Population (millions)	Population Growth Rate 1991–2004	HIV Infections (millions)
World	6,200	1.3%	40
Global North	1,300	0.3	2
Global South	4,900	1.6	37
of which:			
China/East Asia	1,300	1.0	1
Middle East	400	2.3	1
Latin America	500	1.6	2
South Asia	2,100	1.9	7
Africa (sub-Saharan)	600	2.6	26

[a]Regions do not exactly match those used elsewhere in this book.

Source: Calculated from World Bank.. *World Development Indicators.* World Bank, 2005. UNAIDS. *AIDS Epidemic Update.* UN, December 2005.

In North America and other industrialized regions, new drug therapies (which could keep the virus in check for years) dramatically lowered the death rate from AIDS in the late 1990s. But these treatments were too expensive to help much in Africa and other poor regions. India and Brazil began to export cheap generic versions of these drugs, violating patent rights of western drug companies. The U.S. government threatened to punish South Africa and other countries if they allowed import of these drugs without compensating U.S. corporations holding patents. It filed a complaint against Brazil with the WTO. In response, AIDS activists demonstrated loudly and mobilized public opinion to get the policies changed. The United States withdrew its complaint against Brazil in 2001. Meanwhile, drug companies began offering lower prices to poor countries, but delivery of the drugs to millions of poor people remains painfully slow. In 2004, the international community finally began gearing up for large-scale delivery of antiviral drugs to AIDS patients in poor countries, but the drugs will reach only a small minority of those in need.[39]

In 2001, during a special UN session on AIDS, Kofi Annan proposed a $7 to $10 billion per year global budget to combat AIDS (a fivefold increase in funding). The G8 states responded with pledges of $1.2 billion—"laudable" but "not enough" in Annan's view—and the large funding increase became more even difficult to reach as the global recession unfolded and the war on terrorism absorbed attention and resources.[40] In 2003, President Bush pledged $15 billion over five years to help slow AIDS in Africa. But overall, of worldwide spending on AIDS, less than 10 percent has been in third world countries where more than 80 percent of infected people live. Thus, AIDS has deepened the global North-South division. The 2001 UN session also revealed sharp differences between Western, secular states and a number of Islamic states that objected to any reference to gay people. Catholic authorities worldwide, furthermore, objected to programs that encourage

[39] UNAIDS. *AIDS Epidemic Update: December 2004*. Geneva: UNAIDS/WHO, 2004.

[40] Annan, Kofi A. We Can Beat AIDS. *The New York Times*, June 25, 2001: A21. Sanger, David E. Rich Nations Offer a Hand, but the Poor Hope for More. *The New York Times*, July 21, 2001: A6.

condom use. But the most effective prevention measures are public education and the distribution of condoms (especially to prostitutes) and clean needles to drug users—none of which can make individuals act responsibly—and all of these are culturally and politically sensitive issues.

States cannot readily protect themselves from infection from the outside—a particular concern in countries with current low infection rates, such as China. Even if they could seal themselves off from contact with foreigners or monitor foreigners on their territory, they would lose the benefits of economic exchange discussed in Chapter 8. Thus they must cooperate with other states worldwide to try to bring the epidemic under control.

These international efforts are coordinated primarily by WHO and funded mainly by the industrialized countries. But WHO depends on national governments to provide information and carry out policies, and governments have been slow to respond. Governments falsify statistics to underreport the number of cases (lest tourists be driven away), and many governments are reluctant to condone or sponsor sex education and distribution of condoms because of religious or cultural taboos. In January 2005, Nelson Mandela was praised internationally when he declared publicly that his eldest son recently had died of AIDS.

In recent years, HIV has spread rapidly in South Asia, China, and Russia/Eastern Europe, where prostitution and drug use are growing. Thailand was especially vulnerable because of its huge prostitution industry, acceptance of male promiscuity, and large tourism industry. "Sex tours" attract thousands of foreign men each year to visit brothels in Thailand and other Southeast Asian countries. In addition, hundreds of thousands of young women are trafficked across international borders in the growing sex slave trade. However, Thailand was one of the first developing countries to develop an effective anti-AIDS program, which focuses on public education. Condom use among prostitutes went from 20 percent to 90 percent in four years (1988–1992), and cases of sexually transmitted diseases among men (an indicator of HIV spread) dropped by 80 percent. Thailand still faces serious problems with AIDS, but it dramatically lowered the infection rate in the 1990s.[41]

In China, the government has been slow to act, and a stigma still prevents effective identification or treatment of the rapidly growing HIV-positive population. Unscrupulous cash-for-blood businesses, especially in one rural region, caused massive HIV infection. In rural China, medical practice relies heavily on shots—often with poorly sterilized needles—when other forms of treatment would be as effective. As a result, 60 percent of China's population has had hepatitis B, compared with 1 percent in the United States and Japan—a danger sign for the future growth of HIV in China.[42] There were an estimated 1 million infected people in China in 2005, with projections of 10 million or more by 2010.

Overall, worldwide, the AIDS epidemic is on track to kill more people in this decade than died in both world wars together—about 100 million people. The international response to the AIDS epidemic is crucial in determining its ultimate course. AIDS illustrates the transnational linkages that make international borders less meaningful than in the past. Effective international cooperation could save millions of lives and significantly enhance the prospects for economic development in the poorest countries in the coming

[41] Shenon, Philip. Brash and Unabashed, Mr. Condom Takes on Sex Death in Thailand. *The New York Times*, Dec. 20, 1992. Altman, Lawrence K. AIDS Surge Is Forecast for China, India, and Eastern Europe. *The New York Times*, Nov. 4, 1997.

[42] Rosenthal, Elisabeth. Doctors' Dirty Needles Spreading Disease in China. *The New York Times*, Aug. 20, 2001: A1.

decades. But there is once again a collective goods problem regarding the allocation of costs and benefits from such efforts. A dollar spent by WHO has the same effect regardless of which country contributed it.

PANDEMIC PREVENTION

In 2006, avian influenza (bird flu) spread rapidly across much of the world, outpacing the small and poorly funded international institutions devoted to global health, such as the World Health Organization. If bird flu mutates to spread easily from person to person, it could cause a pandemic that kills millions. Here, in a scene repeated in dozens of countries with millions of domestic birds, health workers in India dispose of infected chickens, 2006.

Other Infectious Diseases AIDS is the most severe epidemic of infectious disease in the world, but not the only concern. Tuberculosis (TB), malaria, hepatitis, dengue fever, and cholera have all reemerged or spread in recent decades, often mutating into drug-resistant forms that are increasingly difficult to treat. TB now kills 1.5 million people per year (in addition to AIDS patients who also contract TB). Meanwhile, new and poorly understood diseases have emerged, among them HIV, Ebola virus, hantavirus, and hepatitis C. Pneumonia, influenza, diarrhea-causing diseases, and measles all continue to be major problems but are not growing or spreading to the same extent. Vaccination programs have reduced the incidence of both polio and measles in recent years. Epidemics among animals have major economic effects. Since the late 1990s, Britain lost billions of dollars during an outbreak of mad cow disease and bird flu shut down poultry exports from several Asian countries. Currently, scientists fear that bird flu could mutate and spread person-to-person, sparking a global pandemic that could potentially kill millions.[43]

The Next Flu Epidemic

Smoking In the case of smoking, which kills four million people a year, states that fail to curb the spread of nicotine addiction face high future costs in health care—costs that are just beginning to come due in many poor countries. The costs are largely limited to the state itself; its own citizens and economy pay the price. Nonetheless, the tobacco trade makes smoking an international issue. Worldwide, more than a billion people smoke, five-sixths of them in developing countries, and five million people a year die from tobacco-related disease. Tobacco companies' new marketing campaigns targeting third world women could produce a huge increase in smokers in that group, according to the World Health Organization. In 2001, tobacco companies with some U.S. support sought to weaken a new proposed treaty, the Framework Convention on Tobacco Control, but in 2003 the United States dropped its objections and WHO member states adopted the treaty. After ratification by 40

The Return of Smallpox

[43] U.S. Central Intelligence Agency. *The Global Infectious Disease Threat and Its Implications for the United States* [National Intelligence Estimate 99-17D]. Washington, DC: CIA, January 2000. Garrett, Laurie. *The Coming Plague: Newly Emerging Diseases in a World Out of Balance*. NY: Farrar, Straus & Giroux, 1994. See also footnote 35 in this chapter.

signatories, the treaty entered into force in 2005. Parties to the treaty will ban tobacco advertising within five years and will be encouraged to raise taxes on tobacco 5 percent a year above the inflation rate. U.S. ratification is still uncertain.

Population and International Conflict

Population issues are sometimes portrayed as simply too many people using up too little food and natural resources. This is too simplified a picture. In particular, the idea that overpopulation is the cause of hunger in today's world is not really accurate. Poverty and politics more than population are the causes of malnutrition and hunger today (see "World Hunger" on pp. 477–478). There is enough food in the world to feed all the world's people. There is also enough water, enough petroleum, enough land, and so forth—but these are unequally distributed.

Nonetheless, growing populations do put more strain on resources, regionally and globally. Though resources do not usually run out, it costs more to extract them as the quantity needed increases. New agricultural land is less productive than existing plots; new oil or water supplies must come from greater depths; and so on. For example, food production grew more slowly than population in two-thirds of the developing countries in the 1980s. In the 1960s and 1970s, the "green revolution" increased yields enough to stay ahead of population growth (see "Technology Transfer" on pp. 516–520). But local environmental damage—such as soil erosion and water table depletion—has begun to reduce agricultural productivity in some areas. The faster populations grow, the more pressing will be world food problems.

Growing populations exacerbate all the international conflicts over natural resources discussed earlier. Conflicts over water, which are very serious in several regions, become worse as populations grow. So do a range of issues such as overfishing, deforestation, and the loss of agricultural land to urban sprawl. Although it does not cause these problems, population growth affects how severe they become and how quickly they develop.

There is not a simple linear relationship between the number of people in a state and its need for resources. Rather, as an economy develops, population growth slows but the demand for resources continues to rise. The resources are then needed for raising incomes (industrialization) rather than just feeding more mouths. The type of resources needed also changes—less food and more petroleum—as the state's technological style evolves. But overall, while more states moving through the demographic transition more quickly will slow population growth, it will not decrease the quantity of resources they use or the environmental damage they cause. More likely the opposite is true.

If population growth can be limited at lower income levels—shifting the demographic curve by using government policies to encourage lower birthrates—strains on the environment will be less. A country would then not only increase its per capita income sooner and faster but would do so at lower total population levels. This outcome would reduce the load on the environment and resources as compared with industrializing at a higher level of population. Presumably, international conflicts would also be reduced. Another source of international conflict connected with demographics is migration from poor states with high population growth to rich states with low population growth. For example, illegal immigration from Mexico to the United States is an irritant in U.S.-Mexican relations. Refugees are a recurrent source of interstate conflict as well. Migration and refugees are population issues, but discussion of them is reserved for Chapter 12 (pp. 481–485) in the context of North-South relations.

Demographics can exacerbate ethnic conflicts (which in turn often fuel international conflicts due to ethnic ties with foreign states). Often one ethnic group is richer than another, and usually the poorer group has a higher rate of population growth (because of the demographic transition). In Lebanon, Muslims have a higher birthrate than Christians. At the time of Lebanese independence in 1944, a power-sharing arrangement was devised between Christian and Muslim political groups. By the 1970s, the size of the two populations had changed but the political structure had remained frozen in place. This was a factor in the Lebanese civil war of the late 1970s and 1980s. That civil war, in turn, pulled in outside states including Syria, Israel, and the United States.

Thus, population pressures are not a simple explanation for the world's problems but contribute in various ways to international conflicts. Demographic and environmental factors are playing a larger role and receiving more attention from IR scholars.

As we have seen, the implications of population issues differ greatly in the world's North and South. Strains on the environment and on natural resources are global in scope, yet in the North they arise from industrialization (growing GDP per capita), whereas in the South they are more affected by growing populations.

These differences in environmental impacts are by no means the only such North-South difference. In many ways the world seems to be splitting in two, with different realities in the rich and poor regions—a trend running contrary to the integration theme of the last few chapters. The next two chapters turn to that global North-South divide.

THINKING CRITICALLY

1. Given the collective goods problem in managing environmental issues—heightened by the participation of large numbers of actors—what new international organizations or agreements could be created in the coming years to help solve this problem? Are there ways to reduce the number of actors participating in the management of global problems like ozone depletion? What problems might your proposals run into regarding issues such as state sovereignty?
2. Few effective international agreements have been reached to solve the problem of global warming. Given the several difficulties associated with managing this problem, what creative international solutions can you think of? What would be the strengths and weaknesses of your solutions in the short term and in the long term?
3. Does the record of the international community on environmental management reflect the views of mercantilists, of liberals, or of both? In what ways?
4. Some politicians call for the Western industrialized countries, including the United States, to be more self-sufficient in energy resources in order to reduce dependence on oil imports from the Middle East. In light of the overall world energy picture and the economics of international trade, what are the pros and cons of such a proposal?
5. Dozens of poor states appear to be stuck midway through the demographic transition: death rates have fallen, birthrates remain high, and per capita incomes are not increasing. How do you think these states, with or without foreign assistance, can best get unstuck and complete the demographic transition?

CHAPTER SUMMARY

- Environmental problems are an example of international interdependence and often create collective goods problems for the states involved. The large numbers of actors involved in global environmental problems make them more difficult to solve.
- To resolve such collective goods problems, states have used international regimes and IOs, and have in some cases extended state sovereignty (notably over territorial waters) to make management a national rather than an international matter.
- International efforts to solve environmental problems aim to bring about sustainable economic development. This was the theme of the 1992 UN Earth Summit.
- Global warming results from burning fossil fuels—the basis of industrial economies today. The industrialized states are much more responsible for the problem than are third world states. Solutions are difficult to reach because costs are substantial and dangers are somewhat distant and uncertain.
- Damage to the earth's ozone layer results from the use of specific chemicals, which are now being phased out under international agreements. Unlike global warming, the costs of solutions are much lower and the problem is better understood.
- Many species are threatened with extinction due to loss of habitats such as rain forests. An international treaty on biodiversity and an agreement on forests aim to reduce the destruction of local ecosystems, with costs spread among states.
- The UN Convention on the Law of the Sea (UNCLOS) establishes an ocean regime that puts most commercial fisheries and offshore oil under control of states as territorial waters. The United States signed the treaty after a decade's delay.
- Pollution—including acid rain, water and air pollution, and toxic and nuclear waste—tends to be more localized than global and has been addressed mainly through unilateral, bilateral, and regional measures rather than global ones.
- The economies of the industrialized West depend on fossil fuels. Overall, these economies import energy resources, mostly oil, whereas the other world regions export them. Oil prices rose dramatically in the 1970s but declined in the 1980s as the world economy adjusted by increasing supply and reducing demand. Prices spiked again around 1991 and have been high since 2000. Such fluctuations undermine world economic stability.
- The most important source of oil traded worldwide is the Persian Gulf area of the Middle East. Consequently, this area has long been a focal point of international political conflict, including the 1991 Gulf War.
- States need other raw materials such as minerals, but no such materials have assumed the importance or political status of oil. Water resources are a growing source of local international conflicts, however.
- War and other military activities cause considerable environmental damage—sometimes deliberately inflicted as part of a war strategy.
- World population—now at 6.4 billion—will reach 7 to 8 billion within 25 years and may eventually level out around 9 to 10 billion. Virtually all of the increase will come in the global South.
- Future world population growth will be largely driven by the demographic transition. Death rates have fallen throughout the world, but birthrates will fall proportionally only as per capita incomes go up. The faster the economies of poor states develop, the sooner their populations will level out.
- The demographic transition sharpens disparities of wealth globally and locally. High per capita incomes and low population growth make rich states or groups richer, whereas low incomes and high population growth reinforce each other to keep poor states and groups poor.

- Within the overall shape of the demographic transition, government policies can reduce birthrates somewhat at a given level of per capita income. Effective policies are those that improve access to birth control and raise the status of women in society. Actual policies vary, from China's very strict rules on childbearing to pronatalist governments that encourage maximum birthrates and outlaw birth control.
- Death rates are stable and little affected in the large picture by wars, famines, and other disasters. Raising the death rate is not a feasible way to limit population growth.
- Although the global AIDS epidemic may not greatly slow world population growth, it will impose huge costs on many poor states in the coming years. Currently 40 million people are infected with HIV, and 30 million more have died. Most are in Africa, and new infections are growing rapidly in Asia and Russia.
- AIDS demonstrates that growing international interdependence—the shrinking world—has costs and not just benefits. Because states cannot wall themselves off from the outside world, international cooperation in addition to unilateral state actions will be necessary to contain AIDS.
- Population pressures do not cause, but do contribute to, a variety of international conflicts including ethnic conflicts, economic competition, and territorial disputes.

KEY TERMS

ONLINE PRACTICE TEST

Take an online practice test at
www.internationalrelations.net

❑ A
❑ B
☑ C
❑ D

LET'S DEBATE THE ISSUE

Overpopulation in the South: The Underestimated Priority?

by Mir Zohair Husain

Overview British economist Thomas Malthus (1766–1834) hypothesized two centuries ago that population increases geometrically (2, 4, 8, 16, etc.), while food supplies grow arithmetically (2, 4, 6, 8, etc.). As a result, he predicted that population will grow faster than the food supply until it is significantly reduced by war, disease, famine, and death. Today, this population debate continues unabated.

In 1804, the population of the entire world reached one billion. In 1927, the figure doubled. In 1960, there were three billion, and then four billion in 1973. By 1999, the world population was six billion, a sure sign that these already high numbers will continue increasing at an alarming rate.[a] In the past, experts predicted that the world's largest developing countries, comprised of large extended families whose members number in the hundreds of millions, would push the global population to a precarious 10 billion people by 2100 A.D.[b] In fact, in the time it took to read these two paragraphs, "245 people were born and 106 died, for a net increase of 139."[c]

The contemporary neo-Malthusians, who concur with gloomy Malthusian predictions, believe that the population explosion inhibits economic growth in developing countries and places enormous pressure on limited government funds used to provide basic human needs (food, clothing, shelter, clean water, hygiene and sanitation, education, and health care). Conversely, the optimists believe that scientific innovations will increase the production of sufficient resources to accommodate a much larger population.

So, is overpopulation a serious threat to developing countries and global order? Or are the claims of the neo-Malthusians exaggerated?

Argument 1 Overpopulation Threatens World Order

The population in developing countries will continue to increase. While population growth rates are decreasing in developed countries, they continue to increase in developing countries. In addition, massive migration from rural to urban areas contributes to inflation, malnutrition, unemployment, and high crime rates as well as inadequate housing, education, health care, and transportation.

. . . The population of the world will grow from the current 6.1 billion to 7.2 billion by 2015. Ninety-five percent of that growth is expected to occur in the developing world, and nearly all of it in rapidly expanding urban areas.

"Megacities" of more than 10 million people will continue to grow, straining or even crippling roads, bridges and sewerage and electrical systems. The population of Jakarta will more than double, from 9.5 million to 21.2 million; Lagos will double from 12.2 million to 24.4 million. (Elaine Sciolino. "2015 Outlook: Enough Food, Scarce Water, Porous Borders." *The New York Times,* December 18, 2000.)

Overpopulation will generate conflicts over scarce resources, such as fresh water. Even with scientific advances such as miracle seeds and genetically modified foods, the world has a chronic overpopulation.

Water is a vital resource for sustaining human life, growing crops and running many industrial activities. . . . in many areas

---

[a]*World Population Estimates and Projections, 1998 Revision.* United Nations Family Planning Association, 1999.

[b]Barbara Crossette. "Population Estimates Fall as Poor Women Assert Control." *The New York Times,* March 10, 2002.

[c]Sam Roberts. "The Years Ahead: Population Signs of Aging in the Global Head Count." *The New York Times,* December 28, 2003.

of the world the demand for fresh water is rising faster than the supply, leaving about a billion people without access to clean drinking water. Regional water shortages have raised the specter of armed conflict, forced relatively affluent societies to finance huge water projects and left some of the world's most impoverished nations in deepening misery. . . . Only a little more than half the world's available fresh water is used each year. But by 2015, according to UN estimates, at least 40 percent of the world's population will live in countries where it is difficult or impossible to get enough water to satisfy basic needs. ("Water for a Thirsty World." *The New York Times,* August 29, 2002.)

Developing countries still suffer problems even if population growth decreases. Even India, which has significantly curtailed its population growth in the last two decades and experienced an economic resurgence, still faces the challenges of all developing countries in resolving its chronic population-related socioeconomic and political problems.

> India's experience highlights the link between population growth and economic advancement in poor countries. . . . Fertility rates in India's southern states have dropped markedly, but the northern states' rates—around five children for each woman—have stayed stubbornly high. . . . the growing population dilutes resources for education and saps funds for the delivery of basic services like electricity. Even family planning programs, which can help to solve the underlying problem, cannot keep up. (Daniel Altman. "Bracing for Economic Changes, When the Population Grows No More." *The New York Times.* August 20, 2002.)

Argument 2 Overpopulation Does Not Threaten World Order

Population growth is decreasing globally, especially in several heavily populated countries. While population increases in some countries, the global population growth rate has markedly declined in recent years.

> Remember the population bomb, the fertility explosion set to devour the world's food and suck up or pollute all its air and water? Its fuse has by no means been plucked. But over the last three decades, much of its Malthusian detonation power has leaked out.
>
> Birthrates in developed countries from Italy to Korea have sunk below the levels needed for their populations to replace themselves; the typical age of marriage and pregnancy has risen, and the use of birth control has soared. . . .
>
> The threat is now more regional than global, explosive only in places like India and Pakistan. Ever since 1968, when the United Nations Population Division predicted that the world population, now 6.3 billion, would grow to at least 12 billion by 2050, the agency has regularly revised its estimates downward. Now it expects population to plateau at nine billion. (Donald G. McNeil Jr. "Demographic 'Bomb' May Only Go 'Pop!'" *The New York Times,* August 29, 2004.)

Declining birth rates demonstrate that overpopulation can be managed. Demographers have long advocated educating women and providing access to birth control in order to better manage the size of families, as well as to better promote hygiene and access to medicine.

> . . . AIDS and abortion are drops in the demographic bucket. The real missing billions are the babies who were simply never conceived. They weren't conceived because their would-be elder brothers and sisters survived, or because women's lives improved.
>
> Beyond that, simple public health measures like dams for clean water, vitamins for pregnant women, hand-washing for midwives, oral rehydration salts for babies, vaccines for youngsters and antibiotics for all helped double world life expectancy in the 20th century, to 60 years from 30.
>
> More surviving children means less incentive to give birth as often. As late as 1970, the world's median fertility level was 5.4 births per woman; in 2000, it was 2.9. Barring war, famine, epidemic or disaster, a country needs a birthrate of 2.1 children per woman to hold steady. (Donald G. McNeil Jr. "Demographic 'Bomb' May Only Go 'Pop!'" *The New York Times,* August 29, 2004.)

Substantial increases in population will not be a problem. Science will enable the world to adapt to population growth. Even in Africa, where malnutrition and famine are commonplace, scientific advancements will prevail.

> The key to economic development in Africa is agriculture. . . . Fortunately, we have the economic and technological means to bring about an agricultural revolution. Using proven agricultural techniques, Africa could easily double or triple the yields of most of its crops. It has the potential not only to feed itself but even to become a dynamic agricultural exporter within a few decades.
>
> African farmers face three main problems: depleted soil, a scarcity of water and distorted economics caused in large part by primitive transportation systems. None of these problems is beyond our capacity to solve. (Norman E. Borlaug. "The Next Green Revolution." *The New York Times,* July 11, 2003.)

Questions

Overpopulation in the South

1. Do you think population growth is one of the greatest problems that the world faces? Why or why not? Will population growth become a serious threat to global order? Explain.
2. If overpopulation becomes a serious threat to global order, what actions should governments and international organizations take to curtail the problem of overpopulation? Do you think they will implement such actions? Why or why not?

Selected Readings

Rob Bowden. *Overcrowded World? Our Impact on the Planet.* Austin, TX: Raintree Publishers, 2002.

Klaus M. Leisinger et al. *Six Billion and Counting: Population Growth and Food Security in the 21st Century.* Washington, DC: International Food Policy Research Institute, 2002.

Ethiopian refugees, 2000.

Poverty

Theories of Accumulation

Economic Accumulation • Capitalism • Socialism • Economic Classes

Imperialism

The Globalization of Class • The World-System • European Colonialism • Anti-Imperialism • Postcolonial Dependency

The State of the South

Basic Human Needs • World Hunger • Rural and Urban Populations • Women in Development • Migration and Refugees

Revolution

Revolutionary Movements • Islamic Revolutions • Postrevolutionary Governments

CHAPTER 12

The North-South Gap

Poverty

This and the following chapter concern the world's poor regions—the global South—where most people live. States in these regions are called by various names, used interchangeably: third world countries, **less-developed countries** (LDCs), *underdeveloped countries* (UDCs), or **developing countries.**[1] This chapter discusses the gap in wealth between the industrialized regions (the North) and the rest of the world (the South). Chapter 13 discusses international aspects of economic development in the South.

Third world poverty can be viewed from several theoretical perspectives. IR scholars do not all agree on the causes or implications of such poverty, nor on solutions (if any) to the problem. Thus, they also disagree about the nature of relations between rich and poor states (North-South relations).[2] Everyone agrees, however, that much of the global South is extremely poor.[3]

Such poverty is difficult for North Americans to grasp. It is abject poverty—far worse than the poverty of U.S. ghettos. The extreme case is starvation. As conveyed in pictures from places such as Somalia and Sudan, starvation is dramatic and horrible. But it is not the most important aspect of poverty, because it affects few of the world's poor people. Starvation is generally caused by war or extreme drought or both. In most places, people who die from poverty do not starve but succumb to diseases after being weakened by malnutrition. A lack of adequate quality of nutrition kills many more people than outright starvation does—but less dramatically because people die in many locations day in and day out rather than all at once in one place. Hunger and malnutrition are sometimes caused by war but more often by other factors that displace people from farmable land to cities where many are unable to find other income (see "World Hunger" later in this chapter).

---

[1] Swatuk, Larry A., and Timothy M. Shaw, eds. *The South at the End of the Twentieth Century: Rethinking the Political Economy of Foreign Policy in Africa, Asia, the Caribbean and Latin America*. NY: St. Martin's, 1994. Dorraj, Manochehr, ed. *The Changing Political Economy of the Third World*. Boulder, CO: Lynne Rienner, 1995.

[2] Owen, Sarah, and Paris Yeros, eds. *Poverty in World Politics: Whose Global Era?* NY: St. Martin's, 1999. Haggard, Stephan, ed. *The International Political Economy and the Developing Countries*. Brookfield, VT: Edward Elgar, 1994. Davidian, Zaven N. *Economic Disparities Among Nations: A Threat to Survival in a Globalized World*. Oxford, 1994. Seligson, Mitchell A., and John T. Passe-Smith, eds. *Development and Underdevelopment: The Political Economy of Inequality*. 3rd ed. Boulder, CO: Lynne Rienner, 2003. Thomas-Slayter, Barbara P. *Southern Exposure: International Development and the Global South in the Twenty-first Century*. Bloomfield, CT: Kumarian Press, 2003.

[3] UN Development Program. *Human Development Report* (annual). Oxford. World Bank. *World Development Report* (annual). Oxford.

DIRT POOR

Nearly a billion people in the global South—most of them in Africa and South Asia—live in abject poverty. The majority lack such basic needs as safe water, housing, food, and the ability to read. Natural disasters, droughts, wars, or other events that displace subsistence farmers from their land can quickly put large numbers at risk for their lives. These earthquake survivors isolated in the mountains of Pakistan try to get through the winter in makeshift shelters and tents, 2006.

People who die from malnutrition do not die because of a lack of food in the world, or usually even a lack of food in their own state, but because they cannot *afford* to buy food. Likewise, people lack water, shelter, health care, and other necessities because they cannot afford them. The widespread, grinding poverty of people who cannot afford necessities is more important than the dramatic examples of starvation triggered by war or drought, because chronic poverty affects many more people.

Of all the world's people, about half are without adequate supplies of safe drinking water. About half live in substandard housing or are homeless altogether. About a third are malnourished, and one in seven is chronically undernourished (unable to maintain body weight). Nearly half are illiterate, and 99 percent do not have a college education. Multiplied by six billion people, these percentages add up to a staggering number of extremely poor people.

Globalization since the 1990s has increased the gap between the world's richest and poorest countries. The number of people living on less than $1 per day—about one billion—has grown since the mid-1980s. The greatest setbacks have been in Africa, where 29 of the 34 lowest-ranked countries are located, and where the AIDS epidemic is worsening a bad situation (see pp. 444–445). Dozens of countries are worse off than 20 years ago, even while other countries in the South rise gradually out of poverty.[4] Environmental disasters linked to deforestation, climate change, and urbanization have also contributed to the dire situation of the poorest countries in recent years, driving 25 million people from their homes in 1998, for example. The El Niño weather shift triggered drought in Indonesia, ultimately leading to both massive forest fires and food riots.[5]

Globalization has sharpened inequality within both the North and the South, as well as between the North and the South. As North America and Western Europe enjoy unprecedented prosperity, incomes in Russia and Eastern Europe have shrunk by about half. As China and parts of Southeast Asia, along with much of Latin America, climb gradually out of poverty, much of Africa slips further into it. In the global South as a whole, some trends such as environmental degradation are alarming, while others such as reduced warfare and slow reductions in hunger are encouraging. Clearly, globalization creates both winners and losers, with the world's poorest billion people mostly among the losers.

---

[4] United Nations Development Program. *Human Development Report 1999*. NY: United Nations, 1999. Lewis, Paul. World Bank Says Poverty Is Increasing. *The New York Times*, June 3, 1999: C7.

[5] International Committee of the Red Cross. *World Disasters Report 1999*. Geneva: Red Cross, 1999.

In all, about a billion people live in utter, abject poverty, without access to basic nutrition or health care. They are concentrated in the densely populated states of South Asia and in Africa.[6] The average income per person in South Asia—home to nearly two billion people—is only $2,800 per year, and in Africa $1,800 (even after adjusting for the lower costs of living in these regions compared to richer ones). In fact, nearly half of all people globally have incomes of less than $2 a day.[7]

If these statistics are difficult to digest, consider the bottom line. Every six seconds, somewhere in the world, a child dies as a result of malnutrition. That is 600 every hour, 14,000 every day, 5 million every year. The world produces enough food to nourish these children and enough income to afford to nourish them, but their own families or states do not have enough income. They die, ultimately, from poverty. Consider that in the same six seconds in which another child dies this way, the world spends $180,000 on military forces. A thousandth of that amount could save the child's life. This reality shadows the moral and political debates about North-South relations.

Children in Poverty

Theories of Accumulation

How do we explain the enormous gap between income levels in the world's industrialized regions and those in the global South? What are the implications of that gap for international politics? There are several very different approaches to these questions; we will concentrate on two contrasting theories of wealth accumulation, based on more liberal and more revolutionary world views.

Economic Accumulation

A view of the problem from the perspective of capitalism is based on liberal economics—stressing overall efficiency in maximizing *economic growth*. This view sees the global South as merely lagging behind the industrialized North. More wealth creation in the North is a good thing, as is wealth creation in the South—the two are not in conflict.

A more revolutionary view of things, from the perspective of socialism, is concerned with the distribution of wealth as much as the absolute creation of wealth. It sees the North-South divide as more of a zero-sum game in which the creation of wealth in the North most often comes at the expense of the South. It also gives politics (the state) more of a role in redistributing wealth and managing the economy than does capitalism. Socialism thus parallels mercantilism in some ways. But socialists see economic classes rather than states as the main actors in the political bargaining over the distribution of the world's wealth. And mercantilism promotes the idea of concentrating wealth (as a power element), whereas socialism promotes the broader distribution of wealth.

For socialists, international exchange is shaped by capitalists' exploitation of cheap labor and cheap resources—using states to help create the political conditions for this exploitation. (Some socialists focus on workers in poor third world countries, some on workers in richer industrialized countries, and some on both.) Thus, whereas mercantilists see political interests (of the state) as driving economic policies, socialists see economic interests (of capitalists and of workers) as driving political policies.

---

[6] Callaghy, Thomas M., and John Ravenhill, eds. *Hemmed In: Responses to Africa's Economic Decline*. Columbia, 1993. Belshaw, Deryke, and Ian Livingstone. *Renewing Development in Sub-Saharan Africa: Policy, Performance and Prospects*. NY: Routledge, 2002.

[7] World Bank. *World Development Indicators*. Washington: World Bank, 2004.

LOW-TECH

Production in the global South uses relatively little capital and much labor (at low wages), reflecting an early stage of industrialization. To develop economically, poor countries must generate self-sustaining capital accumulation. Agriculture, energy, and textiles are classic export products from the global South, relatively low-capital and labor-intensive. Here, a weaver in Bangladesh, where textiles make up three-quarters of exports, dries cotton in the sun, 2004.

Capitalist and socialist approaches are rather incompatible in their language and assumptions about the problem of third world poverty and its international implications. This chapter somewhat favors socialist approaches, focusing on the past history of imperialism as a central cause of the North-South divide, and on revolutionary strategies and massive redistribution of wealth as solutions to it. Chapter 13, in turn, leans toward capitalist approaches.

Economic development is based on **capital accumulation**—the creation of standing wealth (capital) such as buildings, roads, factories, and so forth. In order for human populations and their capital to grow, they must produce an **economic surplus** by using capital to produce more capital. This is done by investing money in productive capital rather than using it for consumption. The more surplus an economy produces, the more resources are available for investment above the minimum level of consumption needed to sustain human life.

Early human societies had a very simple stock of capital—mostly clothes and hand tools—and produced little surplus. Then came the discovery of agriculture about 10,000 years ago. A group of people could produce a surplus—more grain than they could eat—decade after decade. The extra grain could feed specialists who made tools from metals, built houses, and constructed irrigation works. Ever since, the human species has been on an uninterrupted growth cycle based on economic surplus. More and more wealth has accumulated, and the human population has grown larger and larger.

China's Coal Mines

The Industrial Revolution of several centuries ago greatly accelerated the process of world accumulation, drawing on large amounts of energy from fossil fuels. But industrialization has occurred very unevenly across the world regions. The North has accumulated vast capital. Though the South produces spurts of wealth and has pockets of accumulation, in most areas it remains a preindustrial economy—the reason why the North consumes nearly ten times as much commercial energy per person as the South does (see Table 11.1 on p. 432).

Information technology now is making a fuel-burning infrastructure relatively less important, in the advanced economies. The countries of the global South may need to pass through a phase of heavy industrialization, as countries in the North did, or perhaps they can develop economically along different paths, using new technology from the start. The problem is that, just as industrial infrastructure is located mostly in the North, so is the world's information infrastructure (see pp. 396–398). While a generation of students in industrialized countries go online, poorer countries still struggle to extend literacy to rural populations.

Nonetheless, neither the absolute size of GDP nor its size relative to other countries indicates whether a national economy is growing or shrinking. Accumulation, or profit, in a national economy corresponds with the *economic growth rate*. States that operate profitably grow from year to year; those that operate at a loss shrink. (GDP and related concepts refer here to real values after adjusting for inflation.)

A state's economic growth rate does not indicate how much wealth it has accumulated in the past. In recent years the United States has grown only slowly—even shrinking a bit at times of recession (see "The Position of the United States" on pp. 354–356). But it starts from a large amount of standing wealth amassed over the previous 200 years. By contrast, Mexico may have stronger economic growth (rate of accumulation), but because it starts from a much poorer position it still lags far behind in total wealth. On a global scale, the South will continue to lag behind the North in GDP (income), even if its economic growth rate continues to be higher than the North's, as it has been in the last few years. The concentration of surplus in the world economy—in the North—tends to be self-reinforcing for two reasons. First, concentrating wealth allows it to be invested more efficiently, which generates more wealth. Second, the more wealth is concentrated, the more power its owners gain. With 60 percent of the world's wealth, the North dominates world politics. Because socialists see a conflict of interest between rich and poor, they see the North's political power as oppressive to the South.

Sharpening Disparities?

Ultimately, the distribution of the benefits of world accumulation is an issue for international bargaining, just as the distribution of benefits from trade is (see Chapter 8, pp. 298–300). In the bargaining between rich and poor regions over the process of world accumulation, the two sides have very unequal power.[8]

Capitalism

Earlier chapters referred to capital in a general way as standing wealth. More precisely, *capital* is the set of goods that are used in producing other goods. Thus, a warehouse full of refined tin is capital, as is a tin can or a canning factory—all these goods go into producing further goods. But a stamp collection, a set of Lego toys, and a pleasure boat are not capital in this sense, even though they have value; they are **consumption goods.** Their consumption does not contribute directly to the production of other goods and services.

A cycle of accumulation depends on capital goods more than consumption goods. Mines, factories, oil refineries, railroads, and similar goods contribute directly to the cycle of surplus production by which more factories and oil refineries are produced.

Investment competes with consumption. Foregoing consumption for investment is another case where short-term costs produce long-term benefits (as in aspects of trade, environmental, and population policies).

Capitalism is a system of *private ownership of capital* that relies on market forces to govern distribution of goods. Under capitalism, the cycle of accumulation is largely controlled by private individuals and companies. When a surplus is produced, it is profit for the owners of the capital that produced the surplus (after taxes). Private ownership encourages reinvestment of surplus because private individuals and companies seek to maximize their wealth. The concentration of capital ownership in few hands also allows investment to be shifted easily from less productive sectors and technologies to more productive ones. Capitalism concentrates wealth, promoting efficient and rapid accumulation; it does not seek an equitable distribution of benefits.

---

[8] Lake, David A. Power and the Third World: Toward a Realist Political Economy of North-South Relations [review article]. *International Studies Quarterly* 31 (2), 1987: 217–34.

In reality, no state is purely capitalistic. Almost all have some form of mixed economy that includes both private and state ownership.[9] Also, in most capitalist countries the government balances the inhuman side of capitalism by redistributing some wealth downward (and regulating capitalists). A "welfare state" provides education, certain health benefits, welfare for the poor, and so forth. Over the past century, capitalism has become more responsive to the need to balance efficiency with equity.

The principles of capitalism underlie the global economy with its great disparities of wealth. The concentration of capital in the global North furthers the development of global trade, of technology, and of reinvestment for maximum profit (overall growth). The private ownership of companies and of currency makes international markets operate more efficiently. Capital can be moved around from less productive to more productive countries and economic sectors. If wealth were distributed equally across world regions, these efficiencies might be lost and world economic growth might be slower.

Socialism

Socialism

Socialism—the idea that workers should have political power—favors the *redistribution of wealth* toward the workers who produce that wealth. Because such redistribution does not happen naturally under capitalism, socialism generally endorses the use of the state for this purpose. It favors *governmental planning* to manage a national economy rather than leaving such management entirely to market forces. Often, socialists advocate *state ownership* of capital, rather than private ownership, so that the accumulation of wealth is controlled by the state, which can distribute it equitably.

Socialism includes many political movements, parties, and ideologies, both historical and present-day. No socialist party has been influential in U.S. politics since the 1930s, but elsewhere in the global North socialist or social-democratic parties held important roles in recent years as governing parties (Britain, France), parts of governing coalitions (Germany, Japan), or main opposition parties (Russia). In the global South, where great poverty and disparities of wealth make the idea of redistributing wealth popular, most revolutionaries and many reformers consider themselves socialists of some sort.

Communist governments, including in China (and the former Soviet Union), base their political philosophy on socialism as well. In practice, however, they tend to extract wealth toward the center and have thus been called a form of state capitalism. For example, in the Soviet Union under Stalin in the 1930s there was a tremendous concentration of capital, which allowed rapid industrialization but starved millions of people. This took place under dictatorial political control rather than workers' control.

Marxism is a branch of socialism that includes both communism and other approaches. (Not all socialists are Marxist.) In the mid-nineteenth century, *Karl Marx* emphasized labor as the source of economic surplus. At that time, the Industrial Revolution was accompanied by particular hardship among industrial workers (including children) in Europe. Marxists still believe that the surplus created by labor should be recaptured by workers through political struggle. Today, Marxism is most influential in third world countries where capital is scarce and labor conditions are wretched.

Like capitalism, socialism does not exist anywhere in a pure form. There is an element of socialism in mixed economies. China now calls its economic system "market socialism"—a combination of continuing state ownership of many large industries, capitalism at the local level, and openness to international investment and trade.

---

[9] Freeman, John R. *Democracy and Markets: The Politics of Mixed Economies*. Cornell, 1989.

Some socialist theories argue that state ownership of industry increases efficiency by avoiding problems that arise from the fragmentation of decision making under capitalism. In theory, central planners are supposed to use resources in a rational way that maximizes overall efficiency. But after decades of experimentation, it is clear that whatever its benefits in equity, state ownership is not very efficient. State planners who set quotas for production at each factory cannot adjust to economic conditions as efficiently as market-based prices can. State ownership is still promoted in many countries in order to redistribute wealth, to coordinate development of key industries, or to maintain self-sufficiency in military production—but not because it is more efficient in general.

Russia and Eastern European states are now in a difficult transition to market economies because of the failure of centrally planned economies. Many third world countries are also moving to sell off large state-owned industries—*privatization*—in hopes of increasing growth. Phone companies, oil companies, railroads—all are going on the auction block.

Privatization took place quickly in several Eastern European and former Soviet republics, where the state owned virtually the whole economy during decades of communism. Before Czechoslovakia split in two, citizens received coupons representing a small bit of stock in state-owned companies. They could sell the coupons for cash or invest them in any of several new mutual funds established by entrepreneurs. The mutual fund managers pooled the coupons and bought up state-owned companies they thought would be profitable. Lured by promises of large profits, most Czechoslovak citizens as new capitalists invested in this way. But when a similar scheme was tried in Russia, citizens weary from economic depression did not put much value in the coupons. Many Russians invested in a leading mutual fund that promised high profits but then went bankrupt.

Thus, in the region of Russia and Eastern Europe, communism had collapsed under the weight of inefficiency, but the beginning stages of capitalism were even more inefficient, leading to a reduction of economic activity by roughly half over several years. Some countries, including Russia, slowed the pace of reforms in response, while reformists argued that what was needed was a speedup to get through the transition. Some countries democratically threw out the reformers and brought back the old communist leaders. In coming years, it is likely that the various experiments being tried by the different countries of Eastern Europe and the former Soviet Union will sort themselves out, making clearer the best routes of transition for former communist economies.

In any event, the collapse of Soviet communism has closed the books on a historic experiment in one type of socialism that failed—old-style **Stalinism** as articulated and practiced by *Joseph Stalin*, which was marked by totalitarian state control under the Communist party. But the failures of state-owned enterprises do not mean that socialism is dead. Rather, other types of socialism are now more salient. And new mixes of socialism and capitalism are being created.

Economic Classes

Socialists argue that IR and domestic politics alike are structured by unequal relationships between **economic classes.** (This emphasis on classes denies the realist dichotomy between domestic and international politics.) The more powerful classes oppress and exploit the less powerful by denying them their fair share of the surplus they create. The oppressed classes try to gain power, in order to seize more of the wealth for themselves. This process, called **class struggle,** is one way of looking at the political relationships between richer and poorer people, and between richer and poorer world regions.

Marx used a particular language to describe the different classes in an industrial economy; Marxists still use those terms. The **bourgeoisie** is the class of owners of capital—

RICH AND POOR

Disparity of wealth is a central aspect of global North-South relations. Marxists see international relations and domestic politics alike as being shaped by a class struggle between the rich and the poor. In Sao Paulo, Brazil, rich and poor neighborhoods sit side by side.

people who make money from their investments rather than from their labor. Under capitalism they are also the ruling class (sometimes in concert with politicians, military officers, or other powerful allies). The *petty bourgeoisie* are small-time owners of capital, such as shopkeepers. They tend to think like owners and to identify with the bourgeoisie. *Intellectuals* (including college professors and students) are treated ambiguously in most Marxist analyses; they often see the world from the perspective of the rich, yet they sometimes are radicalized and side with the oppressed.

The **proletariat**—industrial factory workers—are considered potentially the most powerful class because their labor is necessary for the production of surplus. They are supposed to lead the revolution against the bourgeoisie. But factories have changed since the time of Marx: they are more capital-intensive, and workers in them are better paid. Various Marxist theories try to come to terms with these changes, none very successfully. Marxists also do not agree on how to categorize increasingly important classes such as technical workers and managers. The class of economically unproductive people at the bottom of society is the *lumpenproletariat*—prisoners, criminals, drug addicts, and so forth. They are so down-and-out that they seldom become effective political revolutionaries.

WEB LINK
Proletariat

One very important class in revolutions during the past century (contrary to Marxist expectations) has been *peasants*.[10] Marxists traditionally consider peasants backward, ignorant, individualistic, and politically passive as compared to the well-educated and class-conscious proletariat. But, in practice, the successful third world revolutions have been peasant rebellions (often led by Marxists talking about the proletariat). The largest was the Chinese revolution in the 1930s and 1940s.

According to Marxism, capitalism is just one stage of social evolution, preceded by feudalism and followed by socialism (when workers seize the state and use it to redistribute wealth) and eventually by communism (when everyone would be equal and the state would wither away). Each stage has its own forms of politics and culture, which make up society's **superstructure.** This superstructure is shaped by the **economic base** of society—its mode of production, such as slavery, feudalism, or capitalism.

In their particulars, Marxist analyses have been more often wrong than right in their predictions about the stages of social development, about class alliances, and about the

[10] Moore, Barrington. *Social Origins of Dictatorship and Democracy: Lord and Peasant in the Making of the Modern World*. Boston: Beacon, 1993 [1966]. Scott, James C. *Weapons of the Weak: Everyday Forms of Peasant Resistance*. Yale, 1986.

results of revolutions. But Marxist revolutions have occurred in many third world states, and Marxism (along with other forms of socialism) remains a force in third world development and North-South relations.

Imperialism

Marx's theories of class struggle were oriented toward *domestic* society in the industrializing countries of his time, not toward poor countries or international relations. Traditional Marxists looked to the advanced industrialized countries for revolution and socialism, which would grow out of capitalism. In their view, the third world would have to develop through its own stages of accumulation from feudalism to capitalism before taking the revolutionary step to socialism. What actually happened was the opposite. Proletarian workers in industrialized countries enjoyed rising standards of living and did not make revolutions. Meanwhile, in the backward third world countries, oppressed workers and peasants have staged a series of revolutions, successful and failed, over the past 70 years.

The Globalization of Class

Why did revolutions occur in backward rather than advanced countries? The answer largely shapes how one sees North-South relations today.[11] Marxists have mostly (but not exclusively) followed a line of argument developed by *V. I. Lenin*, founder of the Soviet Union, before the Russian Revolution of 1917.[12] Russia was then a relatively backward state, as the global South is today, and most Marxists considered a revolution there unlikely (looking instead to Germany).

Lenin's theory of **imperialism** argued that European capitalists were investing in colonies where they could earn big profits and then using part of these to *buy off* the working class at home. The only limit Lenin saw was that after the scramble for colonies in the 1890s, few areas of the world were left to be colonized. Imperialist expansion could occur only at the expense of other imperialist states, leading to interimperialist competition and wars such as World War I. Seizing on Russia's weakness during that war, Lenin led the first successful communist revolution there in 1917.

Lenin's general idea still shapes a major approach to North-South relations—the idea that industrialized states exploit poor countries (through both formal and informal colonization) and buy off their own working classes with the profits. Through this *globalization of class relations*, world accumulation concentrates surplus toward the rich parts of the world and away from the poor ones. Revolutions, then, would be expected in poor regions.

Many third world revolutionaries sought to break loose from exploitation by the European colonizers. After European colonization ended, the United States as the world's richest country (with large investments in the global South and a global military presence) became the target of revolutionaries agitating against exploitation in poor countries. In a number of countries, imperialists were thrown out (often violently, sometimes not) and revolutionary nationalists took power.

One of the most important such revolutions was in China, where Mao Zedong's communists took power in 1949 on a Leninist platform adapted to the largely peasant-based

[11] Brewer, Anthony. *Marxist Theories of Imperialism: A Critical Survey*. 2nd ed. NY: Routledge, 1990. Kubálková, Vendulka, and Albert Cruickshank. *Marxism and International Relations*. Oxford: Clarendon, 1985.

[12] Lenin, V. I. Imperialism the Highest Stage of Capitalism [1916]. In *Essential Works of Lenin*. NY: Bantam, 1966, pp. 177–270.

movement they led. Mao declared that "China has stood up"—on its own feet, throwing off foreign domination and foreign exploitation. In India at the same time, the movement led by Gandhi used a different means (nonviolence) to achieve similar ends—national independence from colonialism. Indonesia threw out the Dutch. Lebanon threw out the French. Cuba threw out the Americans. This pattern was repeated, with variations, in dozens of countries.

According to the revolutionaries in these countries, exploitation of third world countries by rich countries takes away the economic surplus of the global South and concentrates the accumulation of wealth toward the rich parts of the world. By breaking free of such exploitation, third world states can then retain their own surplus and begin to accumulate their own wealth. Eventually they can generate their own self-sustaining cycles of accumulation and lift themselves out of poverty.[13]

In reality such an approach has not worked well. A policy of autarky does not foster growth (see p. 313). And within a single poor country, trade-offs arise between concentrating or distributing wealth. For former colonies, the realities of economic development after independence have been complex.

Not all Marxist approaches favor a policy of self-reliance after revolution. *Leon Trotsky*, a Russian revolutionary, believed that after the 1917 revolution Russia would never be able to build socialism alone and should make its top priority the spreading of revolution to other countries to build a worldwide alliance. Trotsky's archrival Stalin wanted to build "*socialism in one country*" and he prevailed (and had Trotsky killed).[14] Most third world revolutions since then, including China's, have had a strongly nationalist flavor.

The World-System

The global system of regional class divisions has been seen by some IR scholars as a **world-system** or a *capitalist world economy*.[15] This view is Marxist in orientation (focusing on economic classes) and relies on a global level of analysis. In the world-system, class divisions are regionalized. Third world regions mostly extract raw materials (including agriculture)—work that uses much labor and little capital, and pays low wages. Industrialized regions mostly manufacture goods—work that uses more capital, requires more skilled labor, and pays workers higher wages. The manufacturing regions are called the **core** (or *center*) of the world-system; the extraction regions are called the **periphery.**

The most important class struggle today, in this view, is that between the core and the periphery of the world-system.[16] The core uses its power (derived from its wealth) to concentrate surplus from the periphery, as it has done for about 500 years. Conflicts among great powers, including the two world wars and the Cold War, basically result from competition among core states over the right to exploit the periphery.

The core and periphery are not sharply delineated. Within the periphery, there are also centers and peripheries (for instance, the city of Rio de Janeiro compared to the

---

[13] Tickner, J. Ann. *Self-Reliance Versus Power Politics*. Columbia, 1987. Amin, Samir. Self-Reliance and the New International Economic Order. *Monthly Review* 29 (3), 1977: 1–21.

[14] Mandel, Ernest. *From Stalinism to Eurocommunism: The Bitter Fruits of "Socialism in One Country."* Translated by Jon Rothschild. London: N. L. B., 1978. Howe, Irving. *Leon Trotsky*. NY: Viking, 1978.

[15] Wallerstein, Immanuel. *The Modern World-System*. 3 vols. NY: Academic, 1974, 1980, 1989. Amin, Samir, Giovanni Arrighi, André Gunder Frank, and Immanuel Wallerstein. *Dynamics of Global Crisis*. NY: Monthly Review Press, 1982. Frank, André Gunder. *World Accumulation, 1492–1789*. NY: Monthly Review Press, 1978. Chew, Sing C., and Robert A. Denemark, eds. *The Underdevelopment of Development: Essays in Honor of André Gunder Frank*. Thousand Oaks, CA: Sage, 1996.

[16] Boswell, Terry, ed. *Revolution in the World-System*. NY: Greenwood, 1989.

Amazon rain forest) as there are within the core (such as New York City compared to the Mississippi Delta). The whole global structure is one of overlapping hierarchies. The concentration of capital and the scale of wages each form a continuum rather than a sharp division into two categories.[17]

In world-system theory, the **semiperiphery** is an area in which some manufacturing occurs and some capital concentrates, but not to the extent of the most advanced areas in the core. Eastern Europe and Russia are commonly considered to be semiperipheral, as are some of the newly industrializing countries (see pp. 499–501) such as Taiwan and Singapore. The semiperiphery acts as a kind of political buffer between the core and periphery because poor states can aspire to join the semiperiphery instead of aspiring to rebel against domination by the core.

Over time, membership in the core, the semiperiphery, and the periphery changes somewhat, but the overall global system of class relations remains.[18] Areas that once were beyond the reach of Europeans, such as the interior of Latin America, become incorporated as periphery. Areas of the periphery can become semiperiphery and even join the core, as North America did. And core states can slip into the semiperiphery if they fall behind in accumulation, as Spain did in the late sixteenth to early seventeenth centuries. Because world-system theory provides only general concepts but not firm definitions of what constitutes the core, semiperiphery, and periphery, it is hard to say exactly which states belong to each category.[19]

The actual patterns of world trade support world-system theory to some extent. Table 12.1 shows the net exports (exports minus imports) of each world region for several types of goods. As the circled numbers indicate, different regions specialize in exporting different kinds of goods. In 1997, the industrialized West fit the profile of the core, exporting $300 billion more than it imported in machinery, chemicals, and similar heavy manufactured goods. All the other regions imported more than they exported in such goods. But by 2002, as the table shows, the West's net exports in this category dropped to $121 billion. Manufacturing shifted to Asia—here including China, Taiwan, Hong Kong, and South Korea (but not Japan)—which had been a net importer of heavy manufactured goods in 1997 but by 2002 had net exports of $105 billion. Asia also still has a niche in light manufacturing including textile production; it exports $119 billion more of these goods than it imports. Such a pattern fits the semiperiphery category. The industrialized West is net importer of $123 billion of these light manufactures. The shift of export-oriented manufacturing from the industrialized countries to Asia reflects globalization.

The industrialized West's net imports of energy in 2002 reached $235 billion—an enormously important type of trade and another indication of globalization. The Middle East (including North Africa) specializes in exporting oil—$136 billion of net energy exports. Russia, Latin America, and Africa all export energy on balance as well ($125 billion altogether). This is an extraction role typical of the periphery. Latin America has net exports of $10 billion in food, agricultural products, and minerals—also typical of the periphery. These regions' patterns of specialization must be kept in perspective, however. All

---

17 Boswell, Terry, and Christopher Chase-Dunn. *The Spiral of Capitalism and Socialism: Toward Global Democracy*. Boulder, CO: Lynne Rienner, 2000. Chase-Dunn, Christopher. *Global Formation: Structures of the World-Economy*. Cambridge, MA: Basil Blackwell, 1989.

18 Friedman, Edward, ed. *Ascent and Decline in the World-System*. Beverly Hills, CA: Sage, 1982. Goldgeier, James M., and Michael McFaul. A Tale of Two Worlds: Core and Periphery in the Post–Cold War Era. *International Organization* 46 (2), 1992: 467–92.

19 Thompson, William R., ed. *Contending Approaches to World System Analysis*. Beverly Hills, CA: Sage, 1983. Hopkins, Terence K., and Immanuel Wallerstein. *The Age of Transition: Trajectory of the World-System, 1945–2025*. London: Zed, 1996.

TABLE 12.1 ■ Commodity Structure of World Trade by Region
Net Exports (Exports Minus Imports) for 2002, in Billions of 2004 Dollars

	Manufactured Goods		Raw Materials	
Region[a]	Machinery/ Chemicals[b]	Textiles	Agriculture and Minerals	Energy
North America/Western Europe/Japan	121	–123	–4	–235
Russia and Eastern Europe	–19	0	3	35
Middle East	–73	3	–4	136
Latin America	–20	6	10	33
Asia[c]	105	119	–6	–25
Africa	–45	1	1	57

[a]Regions do not exactly match those used elsewhere in this book. World total imports do not equal exports owing to discrepancies in data from national government.

[b]Machinery, metal manufactures, and chemicals.

[c]China, Taiwan, Hong Kong, and South Korea are here included in Asia.

Source: Calculated from data in United Nations. *World Economic and Social Survey 2004.* NY: United Nations, 2004, pp. 156–9.

regions both import and export all these types of goods, and the net exports listed in the table amount to only a small part of the world's $6 trillion in trade.

European Colonialism

Colonialism

For most states in the global South, the history of having been colonized by Europeans is central to their national identity, foreign policy, and place in the world. For these states—and especially for those within them who favor socialist perspectives—international relations revolves around their asymmetrical power relationships with industrialized states. (Capitalists tend to pay less attention to history and to focus on present-day problems in the South such as unbalanced economies, unskilled work forces, and corrupt governments.) The North plays a central role in creating, maintaining, and perhaps someday solving poverty in the South.

Today's global disparities did not exist until a few centuries ago. Eight hundred years ago there were a variety of relatively autonomous, independent civilizations in the world, none of which held power over each other—the Sung dynasty in China, the Arab empire in the Middle East, the Aztecs and Incas in Central America, the African kingdoms near present-day Nigeria, the shoguns in Japan, Genghis Khan's society in Siberia, and the feudal society of Europe (see pp. 24–27).

Europe between the twelfth and fifteenth centuries saw the rise of capitalism, a merchant class, science, and stronger states. Technological improvements in agriculture, industry, and the military gave Europe an edge over other world civilizations for the first time. European states conquered and colonized different world regions at different times (see "Imperialism, 1500–2000" on pp. 31–32). Decolonization in some regions (such as the United States in 1776) overlapped with new colonizing in other regions.[20] But most of the world's territory was colonized by Europe at one time or another (see Figure 12.1).

[20] Strang, David. Global Patterns of Decolonization, 1500–1987. *International Studies Quarterly* 35 (4), 1991: 429–54.

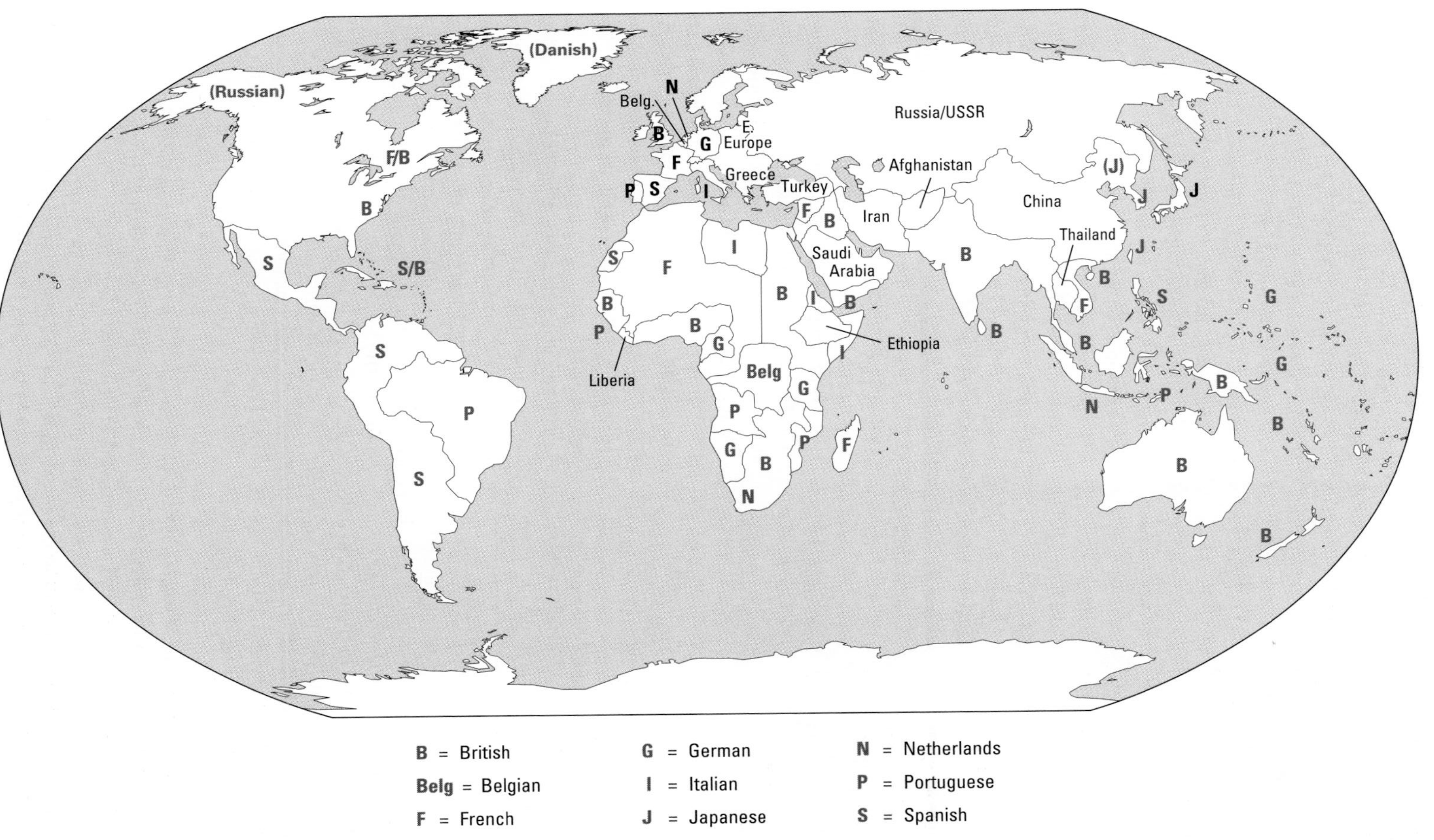

FIGURE 12.1 ■ Conquest of the World

Former colonial territories of European states.

FASHION STATEMENT

European colonialism worldwide promoted values and norms implying that the colonizer's culture was superior to the indigenous culture. Lingering effects remain in postcolonial societies. Evo Morales, Bolivia's first president to come from an indigenous rather than Spanish ancestry, makes a point of wearing a Bolivian alpaca sweater rather than Western-style suit and tie. Here Morales meets with Spain's prime minister, 2006. Almost all the countries of South America have recently elected leftist presidents committed to anticolonial values.

Decolonization occurred only 25 to 50 years ago in most of Asia, Africa, and the Middle East. In Asia, the most important British colony was India (which included today's Pakistan and Bangladesh). Hong Kong was until 1997 a British colony. British possessions also included Malaysia, Singapore, Papua New Guinea, Australia, New Zealand, and others. Almost all the Asian colonies became independent around the time of World War II and the two decades afterward.

In Africa, European colonizers included Portugal, the Netherlands, Britain, France, Belgium, Germany, and Italy. In the late nineteenth century, European states rushed to grab colonies there (France and Britain gaining the most territory). Africa then became a patchwork collection of colonies without coherent ethnic or geographic foundations. The Middle East came under European influence as the Ottoman Empire disintegrated in the late nineteenth and early twentieth centuries—and as oil became a key fuel. Britain and France were most prominent there as well. Present-day Israel and Jordan were British-run until 1948. Syria and Lebanon were French. Iraq's claims on Kuwait in 1990 stemmed from Britain's creation of Kuwait as an independent territory.

Being colonized has a devastating effect on a people and culture. Foreigners overrun a territory with force and take it over. They install their own government, staffed by their own nationals. The inhabitants are forced to speak the language of the colonizers, to adopt their cultural practices, and to be educated at schools run under their guidance. The inhabitants are told that they are racially inferior to the foreigners.

White Europeans in third world colonies in Africa and Asia were greatly outnumbered by native inhabitants but maintained power by a combination of force and (more important) psychological conditioning. After generations under colonialism, most native inhabitants either saw white domination as normal or believed that nothing could be done about it. The whites often lived in a bubble world separated from the lives of the local inhabitants.

Colonialism also had certain negative *economic* implications. The most easily accessible minerals were dug up and shipped away. The best farmland was planted in export crops rather than subsistence crops, and was sometimes overworked and eroded. The infrastructure that was built served the purposes of imperialism rather than the local population—for instance, railroads going straight from mining areas to ports. The education and skills needed to run the economy were largely limited to whites. As a result, when colonies attained independence and many of the whites departed, what remained was an undereducated population with a distorted economic structure and valuable natural resources depleted.

The economic effects were not all negative, however. Colonialism often fostered local economic accumulation (although controlled by whites). Cities grew. Mines were dug and farms established. It was in the colonial administration's interest to foster local cycles of capital accumulation. Much of the infrastructure that exists today in many third world countries was created by colonizers. In some cases (though not all), colonization combined disparate communities into a cohesive political unit with a common religion, language, and culture, thus creating more opportunities for economic accumulation. In some cases, the local political cultures replaced by colonialism were themselves oppressive to the majority of the people.

Anti-Imperialism

Wherever there were colonizers, there were anticolonial movements. Independence movements throughout Africa and Asia gained momentum during and after World War II, when the European powers were weakened. Through the 1960s, a wave of successful independence movements swept from one country to the next, as people stopped accepting imperialism as normal or inevitable (see Figure 12.2).

Although many third world countries gained independence around the same time, the methods by which they did so varied. In India, the most important colony of the largest empire (Britain), Gandhi led a movement based on nonviolent resistance to British rule (see "Nonviolence" on pp. 132–133). However, nonviolence broke down in the subsequent Hindu-Muslim civil war, which split India into two states—India mostly with Hindus, and Pakistan (including what is now Bangladesh) mostly with Muslims.

Some colonies—for example, Algeria and Vietnam—won independence through warfare to oust their European masters; others won it peacefully by negotiating a transfer of power with weary Europeans. In Algeria, France abandoned its colonial claims in 1962 only after fighting a bitter guerrilla war. Some colonial liberation movements fought guerrilla wars based on communist ideology. The Viet Minh, for instance, defeated the French occupiers in 1954 and established communist rule in all of Vietnam by 1975. The Soviet Union supported such movements, and the United States opposed them. But in most cases the appeal of liberation movements was the general theme of anticolonialism rather than any ideology.

Colonialism and Vietnam

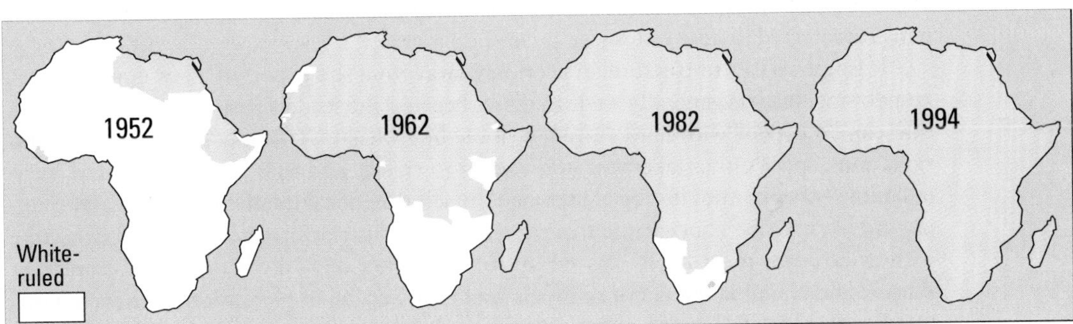

FIGURE 12.2 ■ Areas of White Minority Rule in Africa, 1952–1994

Formal colonialism was swept away over 40 years. However, postcolonial dependency lingers on in many former colonies.

Source: Adapted from Andrew Boyd. *An Atlas of World Affairs.* 9th ed. NY: Routledge, 1992, p. 91.

Across the various methods and ideologies of liberation movements in the global South, one common feature was reliance on nationalism for strong popular support. Nationalism was only one idea that these movements took from Europe and used to undermine European control; others included democracy, freedom, progress, and Marxism. Leaders of liberation movements often had gone to European universities. Under European control many states also developed infrastructures, educational and religious institutions, health care, and military forces on the European model. Europe's conquest of the global South thus contributed tools to undo their conquest.[21]

Postcolonial Dependency

If imperialism concentrated the accumulation of wealth in the core and drained economic surplus from the periphery, one might expect that accumulation in the global South would take off once colonialism was overthrown. Generally this has not been the case. A few states, such as Singapore, have accumulated capital successfully since becoming independent. But others, including many African states, seem to be going backward, with little new capital accumulating to replace the old colonial infrastructure. Most former colonies are making only slow progress in accumulation. Political independence has not been a cure-all for poor countries.

One reason for these problems is that under colonialism the training and experience needed to manage the economy were often limited to white Europeans. A few native inhabitants went to Europe for university training, but most factory managers, doctors, bankers, and so forth were whites. Often the white Europeans fled the country at the time of independence, leaving a huge gap in technical and administrative skills.

Another problem faced by newly independent states was that, as colonies, their economies had been narrowly developed to serve the needs of the European home country. Many of these economies rested on the export of one or two products. For Zambia, it was copper ore; for El Salvador, coffee; for Botswana, diamonds; and so forth.

Such a narrow export economy would seem well suited to use the state's comparative advantage to specialize in one niche of the world economy. But it leaves the state vulnerable to price fluctuations on world markets. Given North-South disparity in power, the raw materials exported by third world countries do not tend to receive high prices (oil, from the mid-1970s to the mid-1980s, was an exception). The liberal free trade regime based around the WTO corrected only partially for the North's superior bargaining position in North-South trade. And the GATT/WTO has allowed agriculture (exported by the periphery) to remain protected in core states (see p. 325).

It is not easy to restructure an economy away from the export of a few commodities. Nor do state leaders generally want to do so, because the leaders benefit from the imports that can be bought with hard currency (including weapons). In any case, coffee plantations and copper mines take time and capital to create, and they represent capital accumulation—they cannot just be abandoned. In addition, local inhabitants' skills and training are likely to be concentrated in the existing industries. Furthermore, infrastructure such as railroads most likely was set up to serve the export economy. For instance, in Angola and Namibia the major railroads lead from mining or plantation districts to ports (see Figure 12.3). Political borders also may follow lines dictated by colonial economies. For example, an Angolan enclave (surrounded by Democratic Congo) contains the area's most profitable oil wells. A South African enclave, surrounded by Namibia, controls the best port in the area.

[21] Barraclough, Geoffrey. *An Introduction to Contemporary History*. Chap. 6. NY: Penguin, 1964.

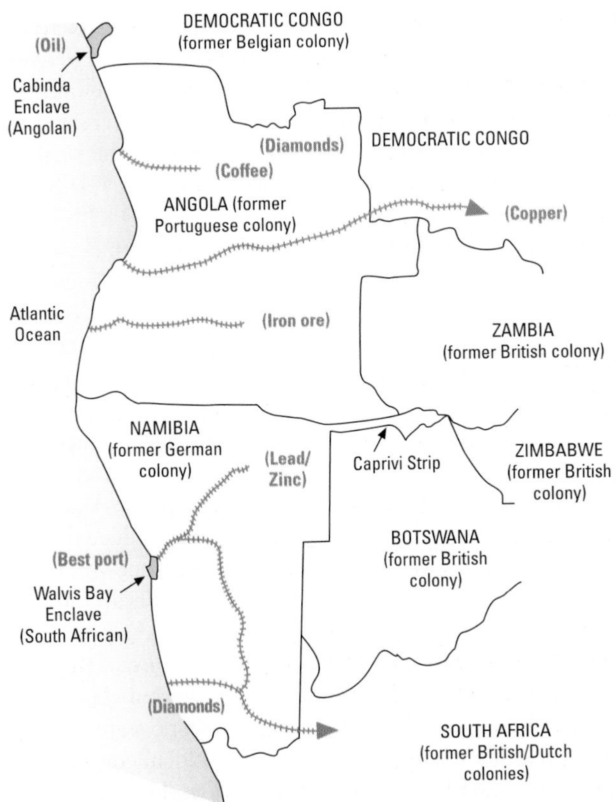

FIGURE 12.3 ■ Borders, Railroads, and Resources in Angola and Namibia

Despite the independence of Angola and Namibia, colonial times shaped the borders and infrastructure in the region.

The newly independent states inherited borders that were drawn in European capitals by foreign officers looking at maps. As a result, especially in Africa, the internal rivalries of ethnic groups and regions made it very difficult for the new states to implement coherent economic plans. In a number of cases, ethnic conflicts within third world states contributed to civil wars, which halted or reversed capital accumulation.

In quite a few cases, the newly independent countries of Africa were little more than puppet governments serving their former colonizers. According to a recent memoir by a French official, France in the 1960s punished and even helped assassinate African leaders who opposed French policies. Those supporting France gave France open-ended permission for military intervention. French officials auditioned a potential president of Gabon before allowing him to take office, and the self-declared emperor of the Central African Republic (later accused of cannibalism) called President de Gaulle of France "Papa."[22]

Finally, governments of many postcolonial states did not function very effectively, creating another obstacle to accumulation. In some cases, corruption became much worse after independence (see "Corruption" on pp. 513–514). In other cases, governments tried to impose central control and planning on their national economy, based on nationalism, mercantilism, or socialism.

[22] French, Howard W. French Held the Strings in Africa. *The New York Times*, Feb. 28, 1995: A14.

In sum, liberation from colonial control did not change underlying economic realities. The main trading partners of newly independent countries were usually their former colonial masters. The main products were usually those developed under colonialism. The administrative units and territorial borders were those created by Europeans. The state continued to occupy the same peripheral position in the world-system after independence as it had before. And in some cases it continued to rely on its former colonizer for security.

For these reasons, the period after independence is sometimes called **neocolonialism**—the continuation of colonial exploitation without formal political control (see p. 31). This concept also covers the relationship of the global South with the United States, which (with a few exceptions) was not a formal colonizer. And it covers the North-South international relations of Latin American states, independent for almost two centuries.

Dependency Marxist IR scholars have developed **dependency theory** to explain the lack of accumulation in the third world.[23] These scholars define dependency as a situation where accumulation of capital cannot sustain itself internally. A dependent country must borrow capital to produce goods; their debt payments then reduce the accumulation of surplus. (Dependency is a form of international interdependence—rich regions need to loan out their money just as poor ones need to borrow it—but it is an interdependence with an extreme power imbalance.)

Dependency theorists focus not on the overall structure of the world-system (center and periphery) but on how a peripheral state's own internal class relationships play out. The development (or lack of development) of a third world state depends on its local conditions and history, though it is affected by the same global conditions as other countries located in the periphery. Recall that within the third world there are local centers and local peripheries. There are capitalists and a national government within the state in addition to the external forces such as MNCs and governments of industrialized countries. These various forces can take on different configurations.

One historically important configuration of dependency is the **enclave economy,** in which foreign capital is invested in a third world country to extract a particular raw material in a particular place—usually a mine, oil well, or plantation. Here the cycle of capital accumulation is primed by foreign capital, is fueled by local resources, and completes itself with the sale of products on foreign markets. Such an arrangement leaves the country's economy largely untouched except to give employment to a few local workers in the enclave and to provide taxes to the state (or line the pockets of some state officials). Over time, it leaves the state's natural resources depleted.

Angola's Cabinda province, located up the coast from the rest of Angola, is a classic enclave economy. Chevron pumps oil from a large field of offshore wells, with the money going to Angolan government officials who spend some on weapons for the civil war there and pocket large sums in flagrant acts of corruption. The people of Cabinda, aside from a tiny number who work for Chevron, live in poverty with crumbling infrastructure, few government services, few jobs, and recurrent banditry by unpaid soldiers. Inside the Chevron compound, however, U.S. workers drive on paved roads, eat American food, and enjoy an 18-hole golf course. They spend 28 days there, working 12-hour days, then fly back to the United States for 28 days of rest. Traveling the 12 miles

[23] Cardoso, Fernando Henrique, and Enzo Faletto. *Dependency and Development in Latin America*. Translated by Marjory Mattingly Urquidi. California, 1979. Packenham, Robert A. *The Dependency Movement: Scholarship and Politics in Dependency Studies*. Harvard, 1992. Painter, James. *Bolivia and Coca: A Study in Dependency*. Boulder, CO: Lynne Rienner, 1994. Evans, Peter. *Dependent Development: The Alliance of Multinational, State, and Local Capital in Brazil*. Princeton, 1979.

THINKING THEORETICALLY

Lingering Effects of Imperialism

Let us return to the example of genocide in Rwanda in 1994. We have discussed the theory that ethnic groups develop in-group biases that can lead to dehumanization of a rival group. Conservative realists might even say that violence of this type between ethnic groups is inevitable and natural, if deplorable. Since these conflicts are driven by "ancient ethnic hatreds," there is little the international community can do about them. Similar arguments were used, as we saw earlier, to justify the international community's feeble response in Bosnia as well.

Socialist approaches provide different perspectives on the violence in Rwanda, pointing us to different kinds of explanations and evidence. For starters, the position of a peripheral country such as Rwanda in the world-system can help explain violence and social upheaval there. Rwanda is one of the world's poorest countries, with a dense, fast-growing, and extremely poor population, more than 90 percent rural. Typically for a peripheral state, Rwanda's main exports are coffee and tin; it imports machinery, fuel, and other manufactured goods. But income from its exports pays less than half the costs of its imports. Before its recent troubles, the annual GDP was only $1,000 per person, and the land is depleted. Naturally such poverty drives a desperate struggle to survive, in which human life is cheapened.

Furthermore, dependency theories point to specific colonial histories as sources of explanation for the current problems of former colonies. Rwanda was colonized by Germany in the scramble for colonies by European powers at the end of the nineteenth century, and then grabbed by Belgium as Germany lost World War I. Although the minority Tutsi group (about 10 percent of the population) had ruled the majority Hutu group for several centuries before colonialism, it was under Belgian rule that large-scale Hutu violence against Tutsis first erupted.

It might be hypothesized that Belgium's interest would be to undermine the strongest political powers in a colony and support rival political forces that would be dependent on Belgium. Ultimately, among other things, keeping Rwanda down in this way could keep coffee prices low for Belgian consumers (who would then, according to Lenin's theory, live more comfortable lives and not make trouble for their bosses and politicians). In 1959, the Tutsi king and hundreds of thousands of Tutsis were driven into exile (from where they fought back for 35 years). Rwanda under Hutu rule was then granted independence from Belgium in 1962. In the following decade, the government repeatedly used massacres of Tutsis to respond to efforts of the Tutsi rebels in exile to return to power. As late as 1990, when Tutsi rebels advanced back into Rwanda, it was the Belgian army that showed up to save the Rwandan government—demonstrating the lasting nature of colonial ties. Ultimately, the government of Hutu extremists that perpetrated genocide against the Tutsis in 1994 must be understood in the context of Rwanda's colonial history. (This telling is of course highly simplified, but the point is that the colonial element, while not necessarily determinative of outcomes, must be a part of any useful explanation.)

to the airport by helicopter, the Americans rarely leave the fenced compound, which Chevron is believed to have surrounded with land mines.

A different historical pattern is that of nationally controlled production, in which a local capitalist class controls a cycle of accumulation based on producing export products. The cycle still depends on foreign markets, but the profits accrue to the local capitalists, building up a powerful class of rich owners within the country. This class—the local bourgeoisie—tends to behave in a manner consistent with the interests of rich industrialized countries (on whose markets the class depends). They are not unpatriotic, but their interests tend to converge with those of foreign capitalists. For instance, they want to keep local wages as low as possible, to produce cheap goods for consumers in the rich countries.

The local capitalists, in alliance with political authorities, enforce a system of domination that ultimately serves the foreign capitalists. This is another form of dependency.

MNCs in the Third World

After World War II, a third form of dependency became more common—penetration of national economies by MNCs. Here the capital is provided externally (as with enclaves), but production is for local markets. For instance, a GM factory in Brazil would produce cars mostly for sale within Brazil. To create local markets for such manufactured goods, income must be concentrated enough to create a middle class that can afford such goods. This sharpens disparities of income within the country (most people remain poor). The cycle of accumulation depends on local labor and local markets, but because MNCs provide the foreign capital they take out much of the surplus as profit.

According to dependency theory, the particular constellation of forces within a country determines which coalitions form among the state, the military, big landowners, local capitalists, foreign capitalists (MNCs), foreign governments, and middle classes such as professionals and skilled industrial workers. On the other side, peasants, workers, and sometimes students and the church, form alliances to work for more equal distribution of income, human and political rights, and local control of the economy. These class alliances and the resulting social relationships are not determined by any general rule but by concrete conditions and historical developments in each country. Like other Marxist theories, dependency theory pays special attention to class struggle as a source of social change.

Some people think that under conditions of dependency, economic development is almost impossible. Others think that development is possible under dependency, despite certain difficulties. We will return to these possibilities in Chapter 13.

The State of the South

In the postcolonial era, some third world states have made progress toward accumulation; some have not. Some (though not all) are caught in a cycle of abject poverty. Until incomes rise, the population will not move through the demographic transition (see pp. 440–441); population growth will remain high and incomes low.[24]

Basic Human Needs

In order to put accumulation on a firm foundation, and to move through the demographic transition, the **basic human needs** of most of the population must be met.[25] People need food, shelter, and other necessities of daily life in order to feel secure. Furthermore, as long as people in the global South blame imperialism for a lack of basic needs, extreme poverty fuels revolution, terrorism, and anti-Western sentiments.

Primary Education in Kenya

Children are central to meeting a population's basic needs. In particular, education allows a new generation to meet other basic needs and move through the demographic transition.[26] Literacy—which UNESCO defines as the ability to read and write a simple sentence—is the key component of education. A person who can read and write can obtain a wealth of information about farming, health care, birth control, and so forth. Some poor countries have raised literacy rates substantially; others lag behind. Nearly half the adults in South Asia, Africa, and the Middle East are illiterate, compared with fewer than

[24] World Bank. *World Development Report 2004*. Oxford, 2004.

[25] Goldstein, Joshua S. Basic Human Needs: The Plateau Curve. *World Development* 13, 1985: 595–609. Moon, Bruce E. *The Political Economy of Basic Human Needs*. Cornell, 1991.

[26] Noor, Abdun. *Education and Basic Human Needs*. Washington: World Bank, 1981.

10 percent in some middle-income countries, and fewer than 5 percent in the industrialized West.

There is also great variation in schooling. Primary school attendance is fairly high in most poor states, which bodes well for future literacy. Secondary education—middle and high school—is another matter. In the North, about 90 percent are enrolled, but in most of the global South, fewer than half are enrolled. College is available to only a small fraction of the population. Relative to population size, the United States has more than 30 times more college students than Africa.

In 2004, in the global South, according to UNICEF, one in six children suffers severe hunger, one in seven lacks access to health care, and one in five has no safe drinking water. The AIDS epidemic now threatens to undo progress made over decades in reducing child mortality and increasing education. In all, half of the world's children, more than a billion kids, live in extreme deprivation.[27]

DO THE MATH

Children are a main focus of efforts to provide basic human needs in the global South. Education is critical to both economic development and the demographic transition. Girls worldwide receive less education than boys, and in Afghanistan under the Taliban, they were banned from schools altogether. This math class in Kandahar, Afghanistan, in 2002 followed the Taliban's fall.

Effective health care in poor countries is not expensive—just $4 per person per year for primary care. For instance, UNICEF has promoted four inexpensive methods that together are credited with saving the lives of millions of children each year. One method is growth monitoring. It is estimated that regular weighing and advice could prevent half of all cases of malnutrition. A second method is oral rehydration therapy (ORT), which stops diarrhea in children before they die from dehydration. A facility that produced 300 packets per day of the simple sugar-salt remedy, at a cost of 1.5 cents each, was built in Guatemala for just $550. Child deaths from diarrhea were cut in half in one year. The third method is immunization against six common deadly diseases: measles, polio, tuberculosis, tetanus, whooping cough, and diphtheria. In recent decades, the number of children immunized in third world countries has risen from 5 percent to more than 50 percent.

The fourth method is the promotion of breast feeding rather than the use of infant formula. Many poor mothers consider baby formula more modern and better for a baby—a view promoted at times by unethical MNCs eager to market formula to large developing countries. In the worst cases, salespeople dressed like nurses gave out free samples to new mothers. But once mothers started using formula, their own milk dried up and they had to continue with the costly formula, which is inferior to breast milk and can be dangerous when water supplies are unsafe and means of sterilization and refrigeration are lacking. After a consumer boycott of a well-known MNC (Nestlé), formula producers agreed in the 1980s to abide by WHO guidelines for selling formula in poor countries.

27 Bellamy, Carol. *The State of the World's Children 2005: Childhood Under Threat*. NY: UNICEF, 2004.

Preventing Malaria with Mosquito Nets

You Are an Advisor to the Leader of a Developing Country

Globally, the disparities in access to health care are striking. The 75 percent of the world's people living in the South have about 30 percent of the world's doctors and nurses. In medical research, less than 5 percent of world expenditures are directed at problems in developing countries, according to WHO. The biggest killers are AIDS, acute respiratory infections, diarrhea, TB, malaria, and hepatitis. More than 600 million people are infected with tropical diseases—300 to 500 million with malaria alone. Yet, because the people with such diseases are poor, there is often not a large enough market for drug companies (MNCs) in the industrialized world to invest in medicines for them. And when poor countries need medicines developed for rich markets, the drugs may be prohibitively expensive—as with the AIDS drugs discussed in Chapter 11 (see pp. 444–447).

In one case, the U.S. Army created a lotion that can protect against infection by snail-borne worms that carry schistosomiasis, which WHO considers the second-worst public health problem in the world. Soldiers who serve in tropical areas can now be protected, but the drug company that produces the lotion has no plans to make it available to ordinary people because the market cannot afford the product. In another case, a drug used against river blindness disease was profitably marketed by a drug company as a veterinary medicine in the United States, but was not profitable as a human medicine in the global South. After the company began donating the drug, an international campaign gave it annually to 25 million people and largely eliminated river blindness in West Africa.[28]

Safe water is another essential element of meeting basic human needs. In many rural locations, people must walk miles every day to fetch water. Access to water is not running water in every house, but a clean well or faucet for a village. Unfortunately, many third world people lack such access—half or more of the population in India, Bangladesh, and Pakistan; two-thirds in Nigeria and Indonesia; one-quarter in relatively well-off Brazil and Mexico. Even among those with access to safe drinking water, many lack sanitation facilities (such as sewers and sanitary latrines). Half the world's population does not have access to sanitation, and as a result suffers from recurrent epidemics and widespread diarrhea, which kill millions of children each year.

In theory, providing for basic needs should give poor people hope of progress and should ensure political stability. However, it is not always the result. In Sri Lanka, a progressive-minded government implemented one of the world's most successful basic needs strategies, addressing nutrition, health care, and literacy. The policy showed that even a very poor country could meet basic needs at low levels of per capita income. Then an ethnic civil war broke out. The war became more and more brutal—with death squads and indiscriminate reprisals on civilians—until it consumed the progress Sri Lanka had made.

War in the global South—both international and civil war—is a leading obstacle to the provision of basic needs and political stability.[29] War causes much greater damage to society than merely the direct deaths and injuries it inflicts. In war zones, economic infrastructure such as transportation is disrupted, as are government services such as health care and education. Wars drastically reduce the confidence in economic and political stability on which investment and trade depend.

Almost all the wars of the past 50 years have taken place in the global South (see p. 198). The shadow of war stretches from Central America through much of Africa, the Middle East, and South Asia. These wars may be the single greatest obstacle to economic development in the global South. War is often part of a vicious circle for states unable to rise out of poverty.

---

[28] *Science* 246, December 8, 1989: 1242. Brown, David. Blindness Prevention Expanded in Africa. *The Washington Post*, Dec. 15, 2001: A24.

[29] Dixon, William J., and Bruce E. Moon. Domestic Political Conflict and Basic Needs Outcomes: An Empirical Assessment. *Comparative Political Studies* 22 (2), 1989: 178–98.

In the 1990s, despite the daunting problems of war and the HIV/AIDS epidemic, public health in the global South registered some important gains. Infant tetanus deaths were halved and access to safe water extended to nearly a billion more people. Polio was nearly eliminated, but resistance to vaccination in parts of Nigeria let the disease begin to spread again, with four countries having indigenous virus populations as of 2006.[30]

The fragility of life in poor, developing countries was demonstrated all too starkly in December 2004, when a major underwater earthquake caused a deadly tsunami that struck Indonesia, Sri Lanka, India, Thailand, and other states in the region. The human cost of the natural disaster was horrific, as officials estimated more than 160,000 killed. Some coastal villages lost nearly 70 percent of their populations. The tsunami destroyed hundreds of coastal villages in the region, decimated fishing industries, and exacerbated poverty in the area.

The tsunami's effect on coastal areas was described by then U.S. Secretary of State Colin Powell as "similar to a nuclear weapon." The loss of villages, ports, and ships will mean dependence by tens of thousands on outside assistance. The already overburdened health infrastructure had to deal with immediate tsunami-related injuries, and also long-term threats of typhoid, cholera, and malaria due to contaminated water supplies, destruction of sanitation facilities, and the destruction of shelters to guard against insects. In addition, tourism income will suffer. These factors led the Asian Development Bank to predict that more than 2 million will be thrown into poverty by the tsunami.

The disaster also affected political violence in Sri Lanka and Indonesia, where victims were caught between their governments, rebel groups, and international aid organizations, which all brought different agendas to the relief effort. Although natural disasters are costly no matter where they occur, disasters in the developing world can make a difficult situation even worse—in the case of the tsunami, in a matter of hours. The international community began work on a tsunami warning system for the Indian Ocean similar to one already operating in the Pacific.

World Hunger

Of all the basic needs of people in the global South, the most central is *food*. **Malnutrition** (or malnourishment) refers to the lack of needed foods including protein and vitamins. The term *hunger* refers broadly to malnutrition or outright **undernourishment**—a lack of calories. Hunger does not usually kill people through outright starvation, but it weakens them and leaves them susceptible to infectious diseases that would not ordinarily be fatal.[31]

World Hunger

Some 850 million people—about one in eight worldwide—are chronically undernourished (see Table 12.2). Their potential contribution to economic accumulation is wasted because they cannot do even light work. And they are a potential source of political instability—including international instability—as long as they stay hungry. At the World Food Summit in 1996, world leaders adopted a goal to cut hunger in half by 2015. By 1999, with the number of undernourished people falling but only by 8 million a year

---

[30] Esman, Milton J., and Ronald J. Herring, eds. *Carrots, Sticks and Ethnic Conflict: Rethinking Development Assistance*. Michigan, 2001. Thomas, Caroline, and Paikiasothy Saravanamuttu, eds. *Conflict and Consensus in South/North Security*. Cambridge, 1989. World Health Organization. Polio Endemic Countries Hit All-Time Low of Four [News Release]. Geneva: Feb. 1, 2006.

[31] Leathers, Howard D. and Phillips Foster. *The World Food Problem: Tackling the Causes of Undernutrition in the Third World*. 3rd ed. Boulder: Rienner, 2004. Smil, Vaclav. *Feeding the World: A Challenge for the Twenty-First Century*. MIT, 2000. Dréze, Jean, Amartya Sen, and Athar Hussain, eds. *The Political Economy of Hunger: Selected Essays*. Oxford, 1995. Sen, Amartya. *Poverty and Famines: An Essay on Entitlement and Deprivation*. Oxford, 1981.

TABLE 12.2 ■ Who's Hungry?
Chronically Undernourished People by Region, c. 2002

Region	Number (millions)	Percentage of Population	10 Years Earlier
S. Asia	380	16%	20%
China	140	11%	16%
Africa	200	33%	36%
Latin America	50	10%	13%
Middle East	40	10%	8%
Russia/E. Europe	30	7%	6%
Industrialized Countries	10	n.a.	n.a.
Total World	850	13%	16%

Notes: Data are from 2000–2002 and 1990–1992. Chronic undernourishment means failing to consume enough food on average over a year to maintain body weight and support light activity.

Source: Based on Food and Agriculture Organization. *The State of Food Insecurity in the World 2004.* Rome: FAO, 2004, pp. 34–6.

and only in selected countries, the Food and Agriculture Organization (FAO) stated that "there is no hope of meeting that goal."[32]

The world has the potential to produce enough food to feed all the world's people. Indeed, just the food *thrown away* in the United States alone is equivalent to one pound per week for each of the world's billion hungriest people. The problem is not so much that there is an absolute shortage of food (though that condition does exist in some places) but that poor people do not have money to buy food.

Traditionally, rural communities have grown their own food—**subsistence farming.** Colonialism disrupted this pattern, and the disruption has continued in postcolonial times. Third world states have shifted from subsistence to commercial agriculture. Small plots have been merged into big plantations, often under the control of wealthy landlords. By concentrating capital and orienting the economy toward a niche in world trade, this process is consistent with liberal economics. But it displaces subsistence farmers from the land. Wars displace farmers even more quickly, with similar results.

Commercial agriculture relies on machinery, commercial fuels, and artificial fertilizers and pesticides, which must be bought with cash and often must be imported. To pay for these supplies, big farms grow **cash crops**—agricultural goods produced for export to world markets.[33] Such crops typically provide little nutrition to local peasants; examples include coffee, tea, and sugar cane. When a plantation is built or expanded, subsistence farmers end up working in the plantation at very low wages or migrating to cities in search of jobs. Often they end up hungry.

International food aid itself can sometimes contribute to these problems.[34] Agricultural assistance may favor mechanized commercial agriculture. And if an international agency floods an area with food, prices on local markets drop, which may force even more local farmers out of business and increase dependence on handouts from the government or international community. Also, people in a drought or famine often have to travel to feeding centers to receive the food, halting their work on their own land.

---

[32] Food and Agriculture Organization. *The State of Food Insecurity in the World 1999*. Rome: FAO, 1999.

[33] Barkin, David, Rosemary L. Batt, and Billie R. DeWatt. *Food Crops vs. Feed Crops: Global Substitution of Grains in Production*. Boulder, CO: Lynne Rienner, 1990.

[34] Uvin, Peter. Regime, Surplus, and Self-Interest: The International Politics of Food Aid. *International Studies Quarterly* 36 (3), 1992: 293–312.

Rural and Urban Populations

The displacement of peasants from subsistence farming contributes to a massive population shift that typically accompanies the demographic transition. More and more people move to the cities from the countryside—**urbanization.** This is hard to measure exactly; there is no standard definition of when a town is considered a city. But industrialized states report that about 70 to 90 percent of their populations live in cities. By contrast, China is only 20 percent urbanized—a level typical of Asia and Africa. Most Middle Eastern states are a bit more urban (40 to 50 percent), and South American ones are 70 to 85 percent urban.

LANDLESS

Subsistence farmers displaced from their land risk chronic hunger and sometimes starvation. In Sudan (1993), famine and war forced this starving girl to set out for a feeding center, stalked by a vulture at one point. She survived the incident, but the South African photographer committed suicide the next year, haunted by the photo (which had won a Pulitzer prize).

Urbanization is not caused by higher population growth in cities than in the countryside. In fact, the opposite is true. In cities, the people are generally better educated, with higher incomes. They are further along in the demographic transition, and have lower birth rates than people in the countryside. Rather, the growth of urban population is caused by people moving to the cities from the countryside. They do so because of the higher income levels in the cities—economic opportunity—and the hope of more chances for an exciting life. They also move because population growth in the countryside stretches available food, water, arable land, and other resources.

Capital accumulation is concentrated in cities. To some extent this makes urban dwellers more politically supportive of the status quo, especially if the city has a sizable middle class. Governments extend their influence more readily to cities than to the countryside—Chinese government policies adopted in Beijing often have little bearing on village life. But urban dwellers can also turn against a government: they are better educated and have rising expectations for their futures. Often rebellions arise from frustrated expectations rather than from poverty itself.

In many cities, the influx of people cannot be accommodated with jobs, housing, and services. In third world slums, basic human needs often go unmet. Many states have considered policies to break up large land holdings and redistribute land to poor peasants for use in subsistence farming—**land reform.**[35] Socialists almost always favor land reform, and many capitalists also favor it in moderation. The main opponents of land reform are large landowners, who often wield great political power because of their wealth and international connections to markets, MNCs, and other sources of hard currency. Landowners have great leverage in bargaining with peasants—from using the legal system to having virtual private armies.

[35] Dorner, Peter. *Latin American Land Reform in Theory and Practice*. Wisconsin, 1992. Deininger, Klaus W. *Land Policies for Growth and Poverty Reduction*. Oxford, 2003.

WOMEN'S POWER

The status of women in countries of the global South affects their prospects for economic development. Women are central to rural economies, to population strategies, and to the provision of basic human needs, including education. Here, a women's organization meets in a home in northern Pakistan, 1998.

Women in Development

Economic accumulation in poor countries is closely tied to the status of women in those societies.[36] This is a recent revelation; most attention in the past has focused on men as supposedly the main generators of capital. Governments and international reports concentrated on work performed by male wage earners. Women's work, by contrast, often is not paid for in money and does not show up in financial statistics. But women in much of the world work harder than men and contribute more to the economic well-being of their families and communities. Women are key to efforts to improve the lot of children and reduce birthrates. In nutrition, education, health care, and shelter, women are central to providing the basic needs of people in poor countries.

Yet women hold inferior social status to men in the countries of the South (even more so than in the North). For instance, when food is in short supply, men and boys often eat first, with women and girls getting what is left. Because of this practice, of the world's malnourished children 80 percent are female, according to Oxfam America.

WEB LINK

Women and Development

Discrimination against girls is widespread in education and literacy. Worldwide, nearly twice as many women as men are illiterate. Across the global South, only in Latin America do women's literacy rates approach those of men. In Pakistan, 50 percent of boys but fewer than 30 percent of girls receive primary education. Throughout Asia, Africa, and the Middle East (though not in Latin America), more boys receive education, especially at the secondary level. At university level, only 30 percent of students are women in China and the Middle East, a bit more than 20 percent in South Asia and Africa (but 45 percent in Latin America). The Taliban regime in Afghanistan (1996–2001) took extreme measures against women's education, banning all girls from school and all women from work.

States and international agencies have begun to pay attention to ending discrimination in schooling, assuring women's access to health care and birth control, educating mothers about prenatal and child health, and generally raising women's status in society (allowing them a greater voice in decisions). These issues occupied the 1995 UN women's conference in Beijing, China, attended by tens of thousands of state and NGO representatives.

---

36 Nussbaum, Martha, and Jonathan Glover, eds. *Women, Culture, and Development: A Study of Human Capabilities*. Oxford, 1996. Tinker, Irene, and Gale Summerfield, eds. *Women's Rights to House and Land: China, Laos, Vietnam*. Boulder: Lynne Rienner, 1999. Afshar, Haleh and Deborah Eade. *Development, Women, and War: Feminist Perspectives*. Oxford: Oxfam, 2004. Aguilar, Delia D., and Anne E. Lacsamana. *Women and Globalization*. Amherst, NY: Humanity Books, 2004. Rai, Shirin M. *Gender and the Political Economy of Development: From Nationalism to Globalization*. Malden, MA: Blackwell, 2002.

For example, international agencies help women organize small businesses, farms, and other income-producing activities. UNICEF has helped women get bank loans on favorable terms to start up small businesses in Egypt and Pakistan as well as cooperative farms in Indonesia. Women have organized cooperatives throughout the global South, often in rural areas, to produce income through weaving and other textile and clothing production, retail stores, agriculture, and so forth.[37] In the slums of Addis Ababa, Ethiopia, women heads of household with no land for subsistence farming had been forced into begging and prostitution. Women taking part in the Integrated Holistic Approach Urban Development Project organized income-producing businesses from food processing to cloth weaving and garment production. These profitable businesses earned income for the women and helped subsidize health and sanitation services in the slums.

Migration and Refugees

Refugees

The processes just outlined—basic-needs deprivation, displacement from land, urbanization—culminate in one of the biggest political issues affecting North-South relations—**migration** from poorer to richer states.[38] Millions of people from the global South have crossed international borders, often illegally, to reach the North.

Someone who moves to a new country in search of better economic opportunities, a better professional environment, or better access to their family, culture, or religion is engaging in migration (emigration from the old state and immigration to the new state). Such migration is considered voluntary. The home state is not under any obligation to let such people leave, and, more important, no state is obligated to receive migrants. As with any trade issue, migration creates complex patterns of winners and losers. Immigrants often provide cheap labor, benefiting the host economy overall, but also compete for jobs with (poor) citizens of the host country.

Most industrialized states try to limit immigration from the global South. Despite border guards and fences, many people migrate anyway, illegally. In the United States, such immigrants come from all over the world, but mostly from nearby Mexico, Central America, and the Caribbean. In Western Europe, they come largely from North Africa, Turkey, and (increasingly) Eastern Europe.[39] Some Western European leaders worry that the loosening of border controls under the process of integration (see pp. 385–387) will make it harder to keep out illegal immigrants. Indeed, fear of immigration is one reason why Swiss voters rejected membership in the EU. In 2004–2006, tens of thousands of migrants and refugees from sub-Saharan Africa came to Morocco and climbed over razor-wire fences to enter two tiny Spanish enclaves there. Once on Spanish soil, they could not be sent home if they kept authorities from determining their nationality. The increase in migrants trying to reach the enclaves in Morocco followed Spanish efforts to stem the flow of migrants crossing in boats from North Africa to Spain itself near the Gibraltar straits. In turn, when Spain cracked down on the crossings at the Morroco enclaves, Africans set out in boats and rafts to reach the Spanish-owned Canary Islands in the Atlantic off Morocco.

---

[37] Bystydzienski, Jill, ed. *Women Transforming Politics: Worldwide Strategies for Empowerment*. Indiana, 1992. Basu, Amrita. *Two Faces of Protest: Contrasting Modes of Women's Activism in India*. California, 1992. Todd, Helen. *Women at the Center: Grameen Bank Borrowers After One Decade*. Boulder, CO: Westview, 1996.
[38] Brettell, Caroline, and James Hollifield, eds. *Migration Theory: Talking Across Disciplines*. NY: Routledge, 2000. Stalker, Peter. *Workers Without Frontiers: The Impact of Globalization on International Migration*. Boulder, CO: Lynne Rienner, 2000. Meyers, Eytan. *International Immigration Policy: An Empirical and Theoretical Analysis*. NY: Palgrave, 2004.
[39] Aleinikoff, Alexander, and Douglas Klusmeyer, eds. *From Migrants to Citizens: Membership in a Changing World*. Washington: Carnegie Endowment for International Peace, 2000. Massey, Douglas S. and J. Edward Taylor. *International Migration: Prospects and Policies in a Global Market*. Oxford, 2004.

TABLE 12.3 ■ Refugee Populations, 2004

Region	Millions	Main Concentrations
Middle East and Asia	6	Afghanistan, Iran, Pakistan, and Sri Lanka
Africa	5	Tanzania, Liberia, Chad, Sudan
Latin America	2	Colombia
Western and Eastern Europe	6	Former Yugoslavia, Russia, Germany[a]
North America	1	United States[a]
World Total	20	

[a] Various regions of origin.

Note: Includes refugees, asylum-seekers, returned refugees, and internally displaced people. Excludes 4 million Palestinians under UN Relief and Works Agency (UNRWA).

Source: UN High Commissioner for Refugees (UNHCR).

International law and custom distinguish migrants from **refugees,** people fleeing to find refuge from war, natural disaster, or political persecution.[40] (Fleeing from chronic discrimination may or may not be grounds for refugee status.) International norms obligate countries to accept refugees who arrive at their borders. Refugees from wars or natural disasters are generally housed in refugee camps temporarily until they can return home (though their stay can drag on for years). Refugees from political persecution may be granted asylum to stay in the new state. Acceptance of refugees—and the question of which states must bear the costs—is a collective goods problem.

The number of international refugees in the world grew from 3 million in 1976 to 10 million in 2004. In addition, 7 million more people are currently displaced within their own countries. The majority of refugees and internally displaced people have been displaced by wars (see Table 12.3).

The political impact of refugees has been demonstrated repeatedly in recent years. After the Gulf War, Iraq's persecution of rebellious Iraqi Kurds sent large numbers of Kurdish refugees streaming to the Turkish border, where they threatened to become an economic burden to Turkey. Turkey closed its borders, and the hungry Iraqi Kurds were left stranded in the mountains. The United States and its allies then sent in military forces to protect the Kurds and return them to their homes in Iraq—violating Iraq's territorial integrity but upholding the Kurds' human rights. When the Kurdish-controlled area of Iraq became a base for Kurdish guerrillas operating in Turkey, the Turkish Army in 1995 invaded the area (another violation of Iraqi sovereignty). The close connection of economics and international security is clear from this episode—a security-related incident (the war) caused an economic condition (starving Kurds) that in turn led to other security ramifications (U.S. military protection of Kurdish areas of Iraq; Turkish invasion of the area).

The connection of economics and security appears in other refugee questions as well. The Palestinian refugees displaced in the 1948 and 1967 Arab-Israeli wars (and their children and grandchildren) live in "camps" that have become long-term neighborhoods, mainly in Jordan and Lebanon. Economic development is impeded in these camps because

[40] UN High Commissioner for Refugees. *The State of the World's Refugees* (annual). Oxford. Loescher, Gil. *The UNHCR and World Politics: A Perilous Path*. Oxford, 2001. Zolberg, Aristide, Astri Suhrke, and Sergio Aguayo. *Escape from Violence: Conflict and the Refugee Crisis in the Developing World*. Oxford, 1989. Gordenker, Leon. *Refugees in International Politics*. Columbia, 1987.

POLICY PERSPECTIVES

President of South Africa, Thabo Mbeki

PROBLEM *Confronting a regional humanitarian crisis without sacrificing the well-being of your own population.*

BACKGROUND Imagine that you are the president of South Africa. Your neighbor to the north, Zimbabwe, has recently experienced political instability. The president of Zimbabwe, Robert Mugabe, has clamped down on political opposition while undertaking a controversial land reform program. This reform program has redistributed large farms taken from white land owners. (Like South Africa, Zimbabwe was once ruled by a white-only government).

Not only has the redistribution led to accusations of corruption—wealthy elites received many of the best farms—but agricultural production in Zimbabwe has been paralyzed. Zimbabwe's economy has been nearing collapse for the past two years. There are massive food and fuel shortages; half of the population is estimated to be dependent on government food aid, and fuel is in such short supply that government buses rarely run. Inflation has recently run nearly 500 percent a year, while unemployment is nearly 70 percent in Zimbabwe.

You have supported your neighbor and ally, President Mugabe, in his land and economic reform program. You have personally pledged not to interfere with politics in Zimbabwe. More workers, however, are beginning to find their way into your country from Zimbabwe.

This is troubling since your own economic situation, while improved in the last five years, is still shaky. Your economy has grown at 3 to 5 percent recently and your export sector is doing well. Still, your unemployment rate is above 30 percent and your crime rate is very high. Many blame too many low-skilled and low-educated workers for both of these high rates.

Another concern for both your country and Zimbabwe is HIV/AIDS. South Africa's infection rate is near 22 percent of the adult population, while Zimbabwe's is 34 percent. Both states' health care systems are overburdened by the prevalence of this disease.

SCENARIO Now imagine that there is further political unrest in Zimbabwe. Along with further agricultural problems and food shortages, this leads to massive refugee flows into your country. The refugees begin setting up makeshift camps near the border while they look for jobs, food, and protection.

These camps are a potential problem for your government. Such refugee camps will certainly be a conduit for the transmission of HIV/AIDS. The refugees will be costly to feed and shelter, while some may attempt to migrate permanently into your country to find jobs.

From a humanitarian perspective, however, international norms oblige you to protect those fleeing from natural disasters (famines), political persecution, and conflict. Refusing to deal with the refugees will certainly bring tremendous international criticism of your government.

CHOOSE YOUR POLICY What do you do with the refugees? Do your forcefully repatriate them to Zimbabwe? This could add to the political and economic instability of Zimbabwe. Do you allow the refugees to stay? This could lead to resentment on the part of your own population if the refugees take jobs, drain food supplies, or burden your health care system. How do you balance humanitarian needs with a concern for your own people's economic well-being?

HUMAN CARGO

Refugees are both a result of international conflicts and a source of conflict. In addition to those fleeing war and repression, and those seeking economic opportunity, hundreds of thousands of people each year cross borders as sex and labor slaves. This truck x-rayed entering Mexico from Guatemala in 1999 may have held Central American migrants seeking work in Mexico or, equally well, sex slaves from Asia or Eastern Europe en route to the United States.

the host states and Palestinians insist that the arrangement is only temporary. The poverty of the refugees in turn fuels radical political movements among the camp inhabitants. The question of Palestinian refugees' right to return to what is now Israel was one of two issues that blocked agreement at the failed Camp David II summit in 2000.

It is not always easy to distinguish a refugee fleeing war or political persecution from a migrant seeking economic opportunity. Illegal immigrants may claim to be refugees in order to be allowed to stay, when really they are seeking better economic opportunities. In recent decades this issue has become a major one throughout the North.

In Germany, France, Austria, and elsewhere, resentment of foreign immigrants has fueled upsurges of right-wing nationalism in domestic politics. Germany, with lax regulations for asylum seekers (they could live for years at state expense while applications for refugee status were processed), became a favored destination for growing numbers of immigrants—most of whom were not political refugees. In 1999, Austria alarmed its EU partners by including a far-right party in a coalition government.

After a 1991 coup in Haiti deposed the elected president, tens of thousands of poor people set off for U.S. shores in small boats. Were they fleeing from persecution or just looking for better economic opportunities (especially plausible given the U.S.-led economic sanctions that had damaged Haiti's economy)? The U.S. government screened the Haitians, granted asylum to a few, and shipped most back to Haiti. As the numbers grew, the United States began intercepting boats on the high seas and returning them directly to Haiti—a practical response that nonetheless violated international law. Eventually, the United States ultimately intervened militarily to restore Haiti's president to power. Similarly, the problem of illegal immigration from Mexico seems to lack any real solution except to improve economic conditions in Mexico, which continues to be a slow task.

Trafficking In addition to migration and refugees, a growing number of persons—estimated at about 700,000 annually—are trafficked across international borders against their will. They include both sex slaves and labor slaves, with each category including both females and males, adults and children. Perhaps 20,000 of these people are trafficked to the United States annually. In 2005, the U.S. State Department listed 14 countries making insufficient efforts to stop human trafficking, including friends such as Kuwait and Jamaica.[41]

[41] U.S. Department of State. *Trafficking in Persons Report 2005*. Washington, DC: Dept. of State, 2005.

In general, South-North migration of all types creates problems for the industrialized states that, it seems, can only be solved by addressing the problems of the South itself. To the extent that the North does not help address those problems, people in the South may turn to other solutions, which often include revolutionary strategies.

Revolution

Poverty and lack of access to basic human needs are prime causes of revolutions, especially when poor people see others living much better.[42] Most revolutionary movements espouse egalitarian ideals—a more equal distribution of wealth and power. Political revolutions seek to change the form of government; social revolutions also seek changes in the structure of society, such as class relations. Most third world countries have had active revolutionary movements at some time since their independence.

Revolutionary Movements

During the Cold War years, the classic third world revolutionary movement was a communist insurgency based in the countryside. Such a revolution typically was organized by disenchanted students, professionals, and educated workers—usually committed to some variant of Marxist ideology—who won support from laborers and peasants. Its targets were the state, the military forces backing up the state, and the upper classes whose interests the state served. Usually "U.S. imperialism" or another such foreign presence was viewed as a friend of the state and an enemy of the revolution.[43]

Sometimes the U.S. government gave direct military aid to governments facing such revolutionary movements; in a number of countries, U.S. military advisers and even combat troops were sent to help put down the revolutions and keep communists from taking power. The United States often tried (but rarely with success) to find a third force, between repressive dictators and communist revolutionaries, that would be democratic, capitalist, and committed to peaceful reform. For its part, the Soviet Union often armed and helped train the revolutionaries. If a revolution won power, then it was the Soviet Union that armed the new government and sent military advisers, and the United States that supported antigovernment rebels.

Thus, the domestic politics of third world countries became intertwined with great-power politics in the context of the North-South gap. In reality, many of these governments and revolutions had little to do with global communism, capitalism, or imperialism. They were local power struggles—sometimes between the haves and the have-nots, sometimes between rival ethnic groups—into which great powers were drawn.

Some third world revolutions succeeded in taking power: they gained strength, captured some cities, and (often following the defection of part of the government army) marched on the capital city and took control. New foreign policies quickly followed (see "Postrevolutionary Governments" later in this chapter).

---

[42] Skocpol, Theda. *Social Revolutions in the Modern World*. Cambridge, 1994. Skocpol, Theda. *States and Social Revolutions: A Comparative Analysis of France, Russia, and China*. Cambridge, 1979. Gurr, Ted Robert. *Why Men Rebel*. Princeton, 1970. McAdam, Doug, Sidney Tarrow, and Charles Tilly. *Dynamics of Contention*. Cambridge, 2001.

[43] Parenti, Michael. *The Sword and the Dollar: Imperialism, Revolution, and the Arms Race*. NY: St. Martin's, 1988.

Elsewhere, and more frequently, revolutions failed: ever-smaller numbers of guerrillas were forced ever-farther into the countryside with dwindling popular support. A third outcome became more common in recent years—a stalemated revolution in which after ten or twenty years of guerrilla warfare neither the revolutionaries nor the government defeats the other. In these cases, the international community may step in to negotiate a cease-fire and the reincorporation of the revolutionaries, under some set of reforms in government practices, into peaceful political participation. This happened successfully in El Salvador, and elsewhere with varying degrees of success.

The Chinese revolution of the 1930s and 1940s was the model of a successful communist revolution for decades thereafter. In Southeast Asia, communist guerrillas ultimately took power in South Vietnam, Cambodia, and Laos, but lost in Thailand, Burma, and Malaysia. In Latin America, Fidel Castro's forces took power in Cuba in 1959 after years of guerrilla war. But when Castro's comrade-in-arms, Che Guevara, tried to replicate the feat in Bolivia, Guevara failed and was killed.[44]

By the early 1990s, these communist third world revolutions seemed to have played themselves out—winning in some places, losing in others, and coming to a stalemate in a few countries. The end of the Cold War removed superpower support from both sides, and the collapse of the Soviet Union and the adoption of capitalist-oriented economic reforms in China undercut the ideological appeal of communist revolutions.

Several Marxist revolutionary movements in Peru lingered after the Cold War, using brutal tactics of terrorism that were answered with harsh repression by Peru's government. One group seized the Japanese embassy during a reception in 1996, and held hundreds of foreign hostages for months until a military attack ended the occupation.[45]

Islamic Revolutions

Although third world revolutions almost always advocate for the poor versus the rich and for nationalism versus imperialism, the particular character of these movements varies across regions and time periods. In Africa, where colonialism left behind state boundaries at odds with ethnic divisions, many revolutionary movements have a strong tribal and provincial base; this may fuel secessionism by a province (such as Eritrea from Ethiopia). Asian revolutionary movements tapped into general anticolonial sentiments, as when Vietnamese communists fought to oust the French colonizers and then saw the war against the United States as a continuation of the same struggle. In Latin America, where national independence was won long ago, revolutions tended to be couched in terms of class struggle against rich elites and their foreign allies (states and MNCs).

In the post–Cold War era, some of the most potent revolutionary movements are Islamic, not communist. Islam is now a key focal point of global North-South conflict. Islamic political activists in Middle Eastern countries, like revolutionaries elsewhere, derive their main base of strength from championing the cause of the poor masses against rich elites. Like other revolutionaries throughout the global South, Islamic movements in countries such as Turkey and Egypt draw their base of support from poor slums, where the revolutionaries sometimes provide basic services unmet by the government. The Lebanese radical group Hezbollah (or Hizbollah)—included on the U.S. list of terrorist organizations after years of attacks on Israelis during the Israeli occupation of southern Lebanon—runs

---

[44] McClintock, Cynthia. *Revolutionary Movements in Latin America*. Washington, DC: U.S. Institute of Peace, 1998. Dominguez, Jorge. *To Make a World Safe for Revolution: Cuba's Foreign Policy*. Harvard, 1989. Colburn, Forrest D. *The Vogue of Revolution in Poor Countries*. Princeton, 1994.

[45] Stavig, Ward. *The World of Túpac Amaru: Conflict, Community, and Identity in Colonial Peru*. Nebraska, 1999. Gorriti, Ellenbogen Gustavo. *The Shining Path: A History of the Millenarian War in Peru*. North Carolina 1999.

hundreds of schools, hospitals, and other charities, and held eight seats in Lebanon's parliament as of 2005.[46]

Islamic revolutionary movements often criticize the Westernized ways of the ruling elite. For example, in Iran the Shah had been armed by the United States as a bulwark against Soviet expansion into the Middle East. The Islamic revolutionaries who overthrew him in 1979 (led by Ayatollah Khomeini) declared the United States, as the leading political and cultural force in the industrialized West, to be the world's "great Satan." (Later, reformers in Iran offered other, less confrontational, interpretations of Islam.)

Some Islamic perspectives reject the European-based cultural framework on which the modern international system rests. This rejection was dramatically illustrated when, after its revolution, Iran refused to protect the safety of U.S. diplomats and the territorial integrity of the U.S. embassy in Iran (see "Laws of Diplomacy" on pp. 281–283). Western values regarding human rights and women's roles have been similarly rejected, notably in the extreme policies of the Taliban movement in Afghanistan. Of course, Islam encompasses a broad spectrum of political practices and forms of government, mostly not revolutionary.

ISLAM AND THE WEST

In some Muslim-populated countries, Islam is a political rallying point with anti-Western connotations—especially in authoritarian countries in which the mosque is a permitted gathering point. Islamic radicals frequently attack Western concepts of politics and culture, including some of the underpinnings of the international system. Here, Pakistanis protest offensive cartoons depicting the prophet Mohammed in a Danish newspaper, 2006.

Whereas Iran's revolution was directed against a U.S.-backed leader, an Islamic guerrilla war in Afghanistan showed that similar ideas could prevail against a Soviet-backed leader. There it was communism and Soviet domination, rather than capitalism and Western domination, that Islamic revolutionaries overthrew. After a decade of destructive civil war (in which U.S. aid helped the revolutionaries), the Islamic forces took power in 1992. However, the Islamic factions then began fighting among themselves—based partly on ethnic and regional splits and partly on the different foreign allies of different factions. The fundamentalist Taliban faction (see pp. 194–195) seized control of the capital and most of Afghanistan in 1996, but the war continued. The al Qaeda terrorist network used Taliban-controlled territory as a global base until U.S. military intervention brought anti-Taliban leaders back into power in 2001.

The defeat of fundamentalists in Afghanistan, however, put pressure on its much larger next-door neighbor, nuclear-armed Pakistan, whose military ruler has tried, since 2001, to smother Islamic extremists and hold together a stable, relatively secular government. Radically anti-American Islamic parties in 2002 elections won control of Pakistan's two provinces bordering Afghanistan. Elsewhere in Asia, Islamic extremist

---

[46] Husain, Mir Zohair. *Global Islamic Politics*. 2nd ed. NY: Longman, 2003. Esposito, John L. *Unholy War: Terror in the Name of Islam*. Oxford, 2002. Lewis, Bernard. *The Crisis of Islam: Holy War and Unholy Terror*. NY: Modern Library Edition, 2003.

groups connected with al Qaeda continue to operate. Documents uncovered in the 2001 Afghanistan campaign thwarted a plot in Singapore to blow up the U.S. embassy. But in 2002 terrorists killed hundreds—mostly Australians—in a nightclub bombing in Bali, Indonesia. U.S. advisors meanwhile began helping to counter Islamic guerrillas on Philippine islands. In 2003, al Qaeda and related groups carried out terror bombings worldwide—in Morocco, Saudi Arabia, Russia, the Philippines, Indonesia, Iraq, and Turkey—and called on followers to go to Iraq to fight the Americans and their allies. In 2004, they bombed trains in Madrid, killing hundreds and apparently tipping an election against the pro-American Spanish government—and thus inducing Spain to pull its troops out of Iraq. In 2005 their followers bombed the London subway and bus system.

In Algeria, Islamic revolutionaries organized against the ruling party that itself had kicked out the French colonizers in 1962 but was now seen as corrupt, inept, and not revolutionary enough. The Islamic parties won preliminary parliamentary elections in 1991 and were assured of coming to power in the final elections. Instead, the military took over, canceled the elections, and touched off eight years of violence before a new president reached a peace agreement with the main rebel faction.

Engaging the South

Elsewhere in the Middle East, Islamic movements are active in Algeria, Tunisia, Jordan, and Tajikistan. In Jordan, Islamic parties for years controlled the largest bloc of seats in the parliament. In the former Soviet republic of Tajikistan they were a major faction in civil strife after the Soviet Union's demise. Middle Eastern Islamic revolutionaries also took a keen interest in the fate of Muslims targeted for genocide in Bosnia from 1992 on. They saw this conflict as part of a broad regional (or even global) struggle of Western, Christian imperialism against Islam—a struggle dating back to the Crusades almost a thousand years ago. In the 1990s, Muslim civilians were targeted by Christians in wars in Bosnia, Azerbaijan, and Chechnya.

The 2003 Iraq War inflamed anti-American feeling and helped radicalize politics across the Muslim world, especially in Arab countries that saw the U.S. invasion as a humiliation to Arab dignity and a parallel to Israel's occupation of Arab land. Turkey's government, newly led by an Islamic-rooted party, agreed to let U.S. troops move through Turkey en route to Iraq, but Turkey's parliament refused to allow it, and U.S. forces had to make do without a northern front.

Postrevolutionary Governments

When revolutionaries succeed in taking power, their state's domestic and international politics alike are affected. This effect occurred in China in 1949; Cuba in 1959; Algeria in 1962; South Vietnam, Cambodia, Angola, and Mozambique in 1975; Nicaragua and Iran in 1979; and Afghanistan in 1992.

Even though revolutionaries advocate the broad distribution of wealth, they tend to find after taking power that centralizing accumulation is more practical: it gives the state more control of wealth and power (with which to meet the needs of the masses, or line the pockets of the new leaders, as the case may be). Over time, the new elite may come to resemble the old one, although individuals change places. Similarly, revolutionaries often advocate improving women's status, but after taking power male revolutionaries have tended to push aside their female comrades, and traditional gender roles have reappeared.[47]

[47] Urdang, Stephanie. *And Still They Dance: Women, War and the Struggle for Change in Mozambique*. NY: Monthly Review Press, 1989.

After many revolutions, the meeting of basic human needs has been severely impeded by continuing political violence and even civil war. For example, the socialist government that took power in Angola in 1975 wanted to improve the lot of poor people, but instead civil war ravaged the country for more than 15 years and the poor ended up much hungrier than ever. The communist Khmer Rouge faction that took power in Cambodia in 1975 sought to radically alter the society by destroying economic classes, destroying concentrations of capital, destroying ideas that ran contrary to the revolution, abolishing money, and rebuilding the entire nation in the image of their own ideology. They executed almost everyone associated with government, business, or universities, or who had independent ideas. They then evacuated the populations of cities into the countryside, where hundreds of thousands starved to death. Clearly, destroying capital does not help meet poor people's basic needs.

RARE SUCCESS

South Africa's former president, Nelson Mandela, (here shown at a march of the African National Congress in Boipatong, 1992), had unusual success in making the difficult transition from revolutionary to state leader, and then leaving office peacefully. He had the advantage of coming to power nonviolently (relatively speaking), enjoying tremendous world respect, and leading a country that is relatively prosperous (though with huge inequalities) in a very poor continent.

Violence and war—both international and civil war—are tremendous obstacles to economic accumulation and the provision of basic human needs. It is a great contradiction of violent revolutions that they rely on the methods of war to gain power, supposedly to redistribute wealth and meet people's basic needs. Yet rich and poor alike are often caught in a downward spiral of indiscriminate violence and destruction. And after taking power, violent revolutionaries often face continuing civil or international war in the struggle to keep power. Successful revolutions often induce neighboring states either to contain the revolution or to take advantage of the new government's instability. For example, within a year of the 1979 revolution in Iran, Iraq had attacked in hopes of conquering Iran while it was weak. (European states did much the same to France after the French Revolution of 1789.)

In foreign policy, revolutionary governments often start out planning radically different relationships with neighbors and great powers. The pattern of international alliances often shifts after revolutions, as when a Cold War client of one superpower shifted to the other after a change of government. But the new government usually discovers that, once that it holds power, it has the same interest as other states in promoting national sovereignty and territorial integrity. The rules of the international system now work for the revolutionaries instead of against them, once they control a state. Their state also has the same geographical location as before, the same historical conflicts with its neighbors, and the same ethnic ties. So it is not unusual over time to find similar foreign policies emanating from a revolutionary government as from its predecessor.

After revolutionaries have been in power for a decade or two, they tend to become less revolutionary. Power tends to corrupt or co-opt even the best-intentioned socialists, and officials find some of the same opportunities for corruption as those in the previous government did. Even for the most honest leaders, the need to develop the economy often creates pressures to build up new concentrations of capital. Perhaps these are now owned by the state, rather than by private banks or landowners. But hierarchies tend to reappear. Furthermore, violent revolutions most often lead to authoritarian rule (for fear that counterrevolutionaries will retake power), not to multiparty democracy. Thus the revolutionary party has a monopoly on power, year after year, which leads to a certain conservatism.

These tendencies are illustrated in the experiences of Algeria and China. The young revolutionaries of the National Liberation Front drove the French colonialists out of Algeria in 1962. Twenty years later, these revolutionaries were moderate enough to be intermediaries between revolutionary Iran and the United States in the hostage crisis of 1980. And ten years later, the old revolutionaries were the entrenched rulers against whom young Islamic revolutionaries rose up. Similarly, in China the revolutionaries who took power in 1949 were able to make common cause with the U.S. imperialists by 1971, and by 1989 they were the conservative rulers shooting down student protesters in the streets of Beijing.

Thus, although revolutions create short-term shifts in foreign policy, over the longer term the rules of international relations have tended to triumph over revolutionary challenges. Likewise, though revolutions promise great economic change, the overall state of economic conditions and relations—especially between North and South—has been resistant to change.

Overall, North-South relations show how difficult it has become to separate political economy from international security. The original political relations contained in European imperialism led to economic conditions in the South—from high population growth to urbanization and concentrations of wealth—that in turn led to political movements for independence, and later to revolutions. The various aspects of the North-South gap considered in this chapter—from hunger and refugees to the structure of commodity exports—all contain both economic and political-military aspects.

Marxists emphasize that the economic realities of accumulation, or the lack of accumulation, lie beneath all the political struggles related to global North-South relations. But Marxists' strategies—from armed revolutions to self-reliance to state ownership—have not been very successful at changing those realities. Chapter 13 therefore turns in depth to the question of how economies in the South can develop the accumulation process and what role the North can play in that process.

THINKING CRITICALLY

1. In what ways does the North American Free Trade Agreement (NAFTA) discussed in Chapter 8 reflect the overall state of North-South relations as described in this chapter? How would capitalism and socialism as general approaches to the theory of wealth accumulation differ in their views of the agreement?
2. The zones of the world economy as described by world-system theorists treat the North as a core and the South as largely a periphery. Can you think of exceptions to this formula? How seriously do such exceptions challenge the overall concept as applied to North-South relations generally? Be specific about why the exceptions do not fit the theory.

3. In North and South America, independence from colonialism was won by descendants of the colonists themselves. In Asia and Africa, it was won mainly by local populations with a long history of their own. How do you think this aspect has affected the postcolonial history of one or more specific countries from each group?
4. Suppose you lived in an extremely poor slum in the global South and had no money or job—but retained all the knowledge you now have. What strategy would you adopt for your own survival and well-being? What strategies would you reject as infeasible? Would you adopt or reject the idea of revolution? Why?
5. Suppose that Islamic revolutions succeeded in taking power throughout most of the Middle East. How, if at all, might this change the relations of states in that region with states in the North? What historical precedents or other evidence supports your view?

CHAPTER SUMMARY

- Most of the world's people live in poverty in the global South. About a billion live in extreme poverty, without access to adequate food, water, and other necessities.
- Moving from poverty to well-being requires the accumulation of capital. Capitalism and socialism take different views on this process. Capitalism emphasizes overall growth with considerable concentration of wealth, whereas socialism emphasizes a fair distribution of wealth.
- Most states have a mixed economy with some degree of private ownership of capital and some degree of state ownership. However, state ownership has not been very successful in accumulating wealth. Consequently, many states have been selling off state-owned enterprises (privatization), especially in Russia and Eastern Europe.
- Marxists view international relations, including global North-South relations, in terms of a struggle between economic classes (especially workers and owners) that have different roles in society and different access to power.
- Since Lenin's time, many Marxists have attributed poverty in the South to the concentration of wealth in the North. In this theory, capitalists in the North exploit the South economically and use the wealth thus generated to buy off workers in the North. Revolutions thus occur in the South and are ultimately directed against the North.
- IR scholars in the world-system school argue that the North is a core region specializing in producing manufactured goods and the South is a periphery specializing in extracting raw materials through agriculture and mining. Between these are semiperiphery states with light manufacturing.
- Today's North-South gap traces its roots to the colonization of the Southern world regions by Europe over the past several centuries. This colonization occurred at different times in different parts of the world, as did decolonization.
- Because of the negative impact of colonialism on local populations, anticolonial movements arose throughout the global South at various times and using various methods. These culminated in a wave of successful independence movements after World War II in Asia and Africa. (Latin American states gained independence much earlier.)
- Following independence, third world states were left with legacies of colonialism, including their basic economic infrastructures, that made wealth accumulation difficult in certain ways. These problems still remain in many countries.

- Wealth accumulation (including the demographic transition discussed in Chapter 11) depends on the meeting of basic human needs such as access to food, water, education, shelter, and health care. Third world states have had mixed success in meeting their populations' basic needs.
- War has been a major impediment to meeting basic needs, and to wealth accumulation generally, in poor countries. Almost all the wars of the past 50 years have been fought in the global South.
- Hunger and malnutrition are rampant in the global South. The most important cause is the displacement of subsistence farmers from their land because of war, population pressures, and the conversion of agricultural land into plantations growing export crops to earn hard currency.
- Urbanization is increasing throughout the global South as more people move from the countryside to cities. Huge slums have grown in the cities as poor people arrive and cannot find jobs.
- Women's central role in the process of accumulation has begun to be recognized. International agencies based in the North have started taking women's contributions into account in analyzing economic development in the South.
- Poverty in the South has led huge numbers of migrants to seek a better life in the North; this has created international political frictions. War and repression in the South have generated millions of refugees seeking safe haven. Under international law and norms, states are generally supposed to accept refugees but do not have to accept migrants.
- Many people throughout the global South have turned to political revolution as a strategy for changing economic inequality and poverty. Often, especially during the Cold War, states in the North were drawn into supporting one side or the other during such revolutions.
- Today the most potent third world revolutions are the Islamic revolutions in the Middle East. Even more than the communist revolutions of the past, Islamic revolutions are directed against the North and reject the Western values on which the international system is based. Like communist ones, Islamic revolutions draw support and legitimacy from the plight of poor people.
- When revolutionaries succeed in taking power, they usually change their state's foreign policy. Over time, however, old national interests and strategies tend to reappear. After several decades in power, revolutionaries usually become conservative and in particular come to support the norms and rules of the international system (which are favorable to them as state leaders).
- North-South relations, although rooted in a basic economic reality—the huge gap in accumulated wealth—reflect the close connections of economics with international security.

KEY TERMS

less-developed countries (LDCs) 455
developing countries 455
capital accumulation 458
economic surplus 458
consumption goods vs. investment 459
capitalism vs. socialism 459, 460
Marxism 460
Stalinism 461
economic class/class struggle 461
bourgeoisie vs. proletariat 461, 462
superstructure and economic base 462
imperialism 463
world-system theory 464
core, periphery, semi-periphery 464, 465
neocolonialism 472
dependency theory 472
enclave economy 472
basic human needs 474
malnutrition and undernourishment 477
subsistence farming 478
cash crop 478
urbanization 479
land reform 479
migration 481
refugees 481

ONLINE PRACTICE TEST

Take an online practice test at
www.internationalrelations.net

❑ A
❑ B
☑ C
❑ D

LET'S DEBATE THE ISSUE

Poverty and Inequality in the South: Should the Developed North Increase Aid to the Developing South?[a]

by Mir Zohair Husain

Overview Throughout the developing world, the poor endure unimaginable suffering on a daily basis. As many as 12 million people in the South die each year from treatable infectious diseases—malaria alone has cut the economic strength of Africa by half.[b] Disease and malnourishment contribute to the region's present average annual per capita income being lower than it was in the 1960s, with nearly half the population surviving on less than 65 cents a day.[c]

The extreme poverty in the South (Latin America, Asia, and Africa) contrasts with the wealth of the developed countries of the North (North America, Europe, Japan/Pacific, and Russia). Yet the mass media and governments of developed countries focus on sensational issues, such as war and terrorism, while ignoring the pressing realities of poverty and inequality that plague the South.

The chronic poverty in the South raises two pressing questions: What are the consequences if the world fails to significantly reduce poverty and inequality in the South? Should the North increase its economic and humanitarian aid to the South?

Argument 1 The North Must Help the South

Poverty in the South can no longer be ignored. The South's mediocre leadership, misallocation of its limited resources, rapid population growth, and sluggish economic growth are contributing to more poverty.

> . . . 1.2 billion people live on less than what $1 a day will buy in America. And 2.8 billion live on less than $2 . . . [which means that today] only 23 percent of the global population lives on less than $1 a day, compared with 30 percent in 1990. . . . In absolute numbers, more people are now extremely poor than in 1990 if China is excluded. . . . [In fact,] 54 countries are poorer, as measured by per capita GDP. Sub-Saharan Africa is worst off, with a per-capita GDP. falling in 20 nations. (Jeff Madrick. "Grim Facts on Global Poverty." *The New York Times,* August 7, 2003.)

Developed countries perpetuate poverty in developing countries. The North talks about increasing aid to alleviate poverty in the South. However, the North's crippling tariffs and subsidies to its own producers vastly reduce the benefits of financial and humanitarian assistance to the South. *These subsidies and tariffs end up costing developing countries five times more in lost markets than what is received through aid.*[d]

> . . . Britain, the United States and European nations should abolish the huge agricultural subsidies that give their farmers an unfair advantage over Africans. The amount that rich countries spent on such subsidies in 2002 was the equivalent of the income of all the people in sub-Saharan Africa combined. (Celia W. Dugger. "Commission on Poverty in Africa Seeks a Doubling of Aid. *The New York Times,* March 12, 2005.)

The increasing poverty and inequality in the South contribute to terrorism. President Bush connects poverty with terrorism. In 2002, he pledged to increase U.S. foreign aid by 50 percent within five years, saying, "We fight against poverty because hope is an answer to terror."

[a]This debate builds upon concepts covered within Chapter 12 and introduces the issue of foreign aid, which is discussed further in Chapter 13.

[b]"The Plagues of Poverty." *The New York Times,* March 19, 2002.

[c]Barry Bearak. "Why People Still Starve." *The New York Times,* July 13, 2003.

[d]Tim Winer. "More Aid, More Need: Pledges Still Falling Short." *The New York Times,* March 24, 2002.

Moreover, because of mass communications, a sense of deprivation pervades the masses in the South as they envy and resent the lives lived by the majority in the North.

> Half of the world's inhabitants are in poverty, millions without jobs, without adequate food or clean water, without decent homes, without much if any education, without health or dental care, without a political voice and without hope for the future. None of this can ever justify the mass killing of innocent people. But the stubborn realities of global hunger and poverty that help fuel hatred exist. . . .
>
> Modern communications have spread the word to these masses that the privileged few who rule them are living in luxury that exceeds all measure. Across the seas, the poor observe others with wealth, military might, comfort and pleasure that overwhelm the imagination. . . .
>
> For half a century, . . . [many have predicted that] the world's poor would one day explode out of their misery. The technological and communications revolutions will aid that explosion. (George McGovern. "The Healing in Helping the World's Poor." *The New York Times,* January 1, 2002.)

Argument 2 The North's Increasing Aid Will Not End the South's Poverty

The South's poverty is already decreasing, so increasing aid is not necessary. Most studies look at poverty in terms of countries, rather than in terms of individuals. The numbers skew the fact that more people are better off and greater efforts by developed countries are not necessary.

> [Professor Sala-i-Martin, an economist at Columbia University, points out], "Treating countries like China and Grenada as two data points with equal weight does not seem reasonable because there are about 12,000 Chinese citizens for each person living in Grenada."
>
> Over the last three decades, and especially since the 1980s, the world's two largest countries, China and India, have raced ahead economically. So have other Asian countries with relatively large populations. . . . The result is that 2.5 billion people have seen their standards of living rise toward those of the billion people in the already developed countries—decreasing global poverty and increasing global equality. From the point of view of individuals, economic liberalization has been a huge success. (Virginia Postrel. "The Rich Get Rich and Poor Get Poorer. Right? Let's Take Another Look." *The New York Times,* August 15, 2002.)

Increasing foreign aid will not reduce the South's poverty and inequality. Historically, the North provided assistance to the South, but many countries in the South remained poor because of incompetent, autocratic, and corrupt leaders. Therefore, more economic aid will not improve conditions in the South.

> Nigeria's economy has actually shrunk over the last three decades, and the absolute poverty rate—the percentage of the population living on less than $1 a day in 1985 dollars—skyrocketed to 46 percent in 1998 from 9 percent in 1970. . . . While most Nigerians were falling further into destitution, the political and economic elite grew richer. [The problem is a politicized economy with widespread corruption and a failure to liberalize their market.]
>
> [Nigeria] is typical of Africa, which is growing ever poorer. Fully 95 percent of the world's 'one-dollar poor' live in Africa, and in many countries they make up the vast majority of the population. (Virginia Postrel. "The Rich Get Rich and Poor Get Poorer. Right? Let's Take Another Look." *The New York Times,* August 15, 2002.)

The form in which economic assistance is given will reduce poverty. Currently, most affluent states and international financial institutions, such as the World Bank and the International Monetary Fund (IMF), give economic assistance to developing countries in the form of loans, not grants. Furthermore, the timely repayment of these loans is expected. This only heightens the debt burden of cash-strapped developing countries and weakens their ability to alleviate poverty. Therefore, debt relief is needed as much as economic assistance.

> Over the last several years, private aid groups as well as governments have championed debt forgiveness for poor countries, especially in sub-Saharan Africa, which often have to spend more money to service their debts than to provide essential services that would help their citizens climb out of poverty. (Elizabeth Becker. "Wealthiest Nations to Increase Aid to Poorest." *The New York Times,* February 23, 2005.)

WEB LINK

Poverty and Inequality in the South

Questions

1. What are the major reasons for poverty and inequality in developing countries?
2. What will happen in the medium to long term if the North does not increase its economic and humanitarian assistance to the South? Explain.

Selected Readings

Stephen Smith. *Ending Global Poverty: A Guide to What Works.* NY: Palgrave Macmillan, 2005.

William R. Cline. *Trade Policy and Global Poverty.* Washington, DC: Institute for International Economics, 2004.

New Delhi bus stop, 2000.

CHAPTER 13

International Development

What Is Development?

Economic development refers to the combined processes of capital accumulation, rising per capita incomes (with consequent falling birthrates), increasing skills in the population, adoption of new technological styles, and other related social and economic changes.[1] The most central aspect is the accumulation of capital (with its ongoing wealth-generating potential). The concept of development has a subjective side that cannot be measured statistically—the judgment of whether a certain pattern of wealth creation and distribution is good for a state and its people. But one simple measure of economic development is the per capita GDP—the amount of economic activity per person.

By this measure, most of the global South made progress on economic development in the 1970s, with real per capita GDP growth of almost 3 percent annually. This rate was a bit higher than in the global North (despite the higher population growth in the South, which pulls down per capita GDP). However, in the 1980s this economic development came to a halt except in Asia. Per capita GDP *decreased* from 1981 to 1991 in Latin America, Africa, and the Middle East.[2] By contrast, China had 7.5 percent annual growth. In the 1990s, real economic growth returned across much of the South—about 5 to 6 percent annual growth for the South as a whole, and even higher for China, compared to 2 to 3 percent in the global North. China stands out among the regions of the South as making rapid progress toward economic development. All the other regions of the global South showed much slower progress, if any, and faced serious problems moving development forward.

Growth varies greatly across regions and countries, as well as within countries. The gap between rich and poor—both within countries and globally—is apparently widening over the years. In the decade of the 1990s, so prosperous for much of the North, 21 countries experienced declines in the UN's Human Development Index; half of Latin America either stagnated or declined over the decade. In 2003, declines occurred in Eastern Europe and Central Asia, especially Russia, Ukraine, Moldova, and Tajikistan.

---

[1] Stiglitz, Joseph, and Gerald Meier. *Frontiers in Development*. Oxford, 2000. Stone, Diane. *Banking on Knowledge: The Genesis of the Global Development Network*. NY: Routledge, 2001. Bates, Robert H. *Prosperity and Violence: The Political Economy of Development*. NY: Norton, 2001. Kothari, Uma, and Martin Minogue, eds. *Development Theory and Practice: Critical Perspectives*. NY: Palgrave, 2002. Helpman, Elhanan. *The Mystery of Economic Growth*. Cambridge: Belknap, 2004.

[2] South and East Asia here includes South Korea, Taiwan, and Hong Kong. United Nations. *World Economic and Social Survey* [annual].

These conditions lead some observers to wonder if the global South is dividing into two parts, one moving forward (especially China) and one stalled or sliding backwards (especially Africa).[3]

Regarding how income is distributed and spent, the perspectives and prescriptions of capitalism and socialism again diverge (see pp. 459–461). Capitalists tend to favor the concentration of capital as a way to spur investment rather than consumption (and to realize economies of scale and specialization). In line with liberalism, capitalists favor development paths that tie third world states closely to the world economy and international trade.[4] They argue that although they defer equity, such development strategies maximize efficiency. Once a third world state has a self-sustaining cycle of accumulation under way, it can better redress poverty in the broad population. To do so too early would choke off economic growth, in this view.

The same concept applies broadly to the world's development as a whole. From a capitalist perspective, the North-South gap is a stage of world development in which capital accumulation is concentrated in the North. This unequal concentration creates faster economic growth, which ultimately will bring more wealth to the South as well (a "trickle-down" approach). There is no practical way, in this view, to shift wealth from the North to the South without undermining the free market economics responsible for global economic growth.

Socialists, by contrast, argue that meaningful third world development should improve the position of the whole population and of the poor—sooner rather than later. Thus, socialists tend to advocate a more equitable distribution of wealth; they dispute the idea that greater equity will impede efficiency or slow down economic growth. Rather, by raising incomes among the poorer people, a strategy based on equity will speed up the demographic transition and lead more quickly to sustained accumulation. Such a strategy seeks to develop a state's economy from the bottom up instead of the top down.

On a global level, socialists do not see the North-South disparities as justified by global growth benefits. They favor political actions to shift income from North to South in order to foster economic growth in the South. Such a redistribution, in this view, would create faster, not slower, global economic growth—as well as more balanced and stable growth.

In reality, most states in the South use a mix of the two strategies in their economic policies, as do the industrialized states in shaping their roles in third world development. Welfare capitalism, such as most industrialized states practice, distributes enough wealth to meet the basic needs of almost everyone while letting most wealth move freely in capitalist markets. Such a mix is harder to achieve in a third world state where the smaller total amount of wealth may force a choice between welfare and capitalism.

The capitalist theory that unequal income distributions are related to higher economic growth is only weakly supported by empirical evidence. Many states with fairly equitable income distributions have high growth rates (including South Korea, Taiwan, Singapore, and Hong Kong); many with unequal distributions have grown slowly if at all (Zambia, Argentina, and Ghana). But there are also cases of relatively equitable countries that grow slowly (India) and inequitable ones that grow rapidly (Malaysia).

---

[3] United Nations. *Human Development Report 2004*. NY: United Nations, 2004. Kennedy, Paul. *Preparing for the Twenty-First Century*. NY: Random House, 1993.

[4] Easterly, William R. *The Elusive Quest for Growth: Economists' Adventures and Misadventures in the Tropics*. MIT, 2001. McEwan, Arthur. *Neo-Liberalism or Democracy? Economic Strategy, Markets, and Alternatives for the 21st Century*. NY: Zed/St. Martin's, 1999.

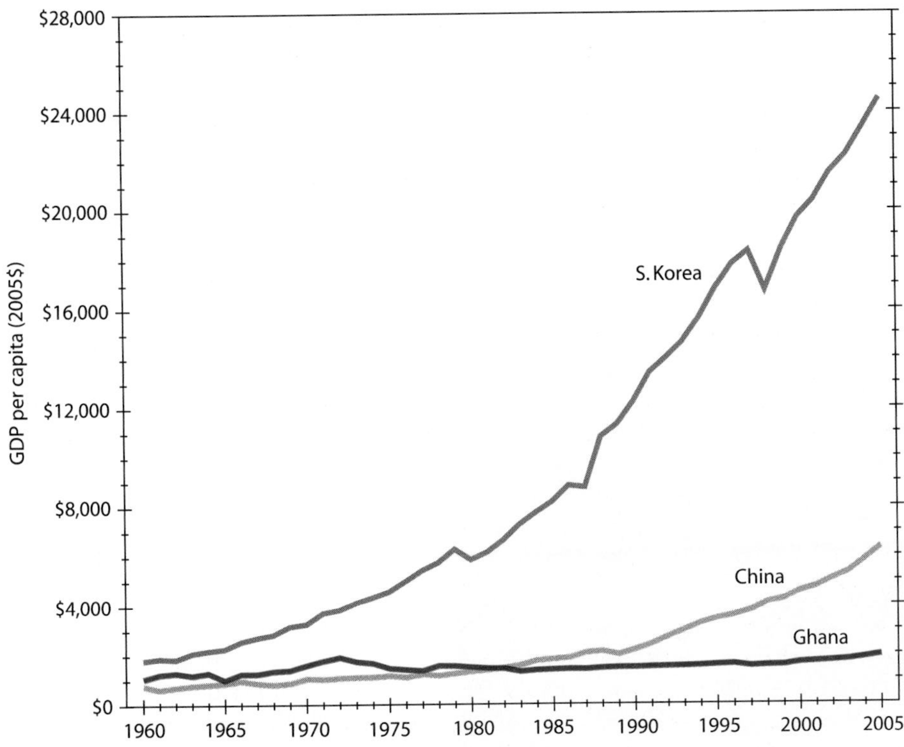

FIGURE 13.1 ■ Per Capita GDP of South Korea, China, and Ghana

Source: Based on Penn World Tables and World Bank and IMF data.

Experiences

Although much of the global South went backward in the 1980s, some Asian states continued to develop and China began to raise its GDP per capita rapidly, though from a low starting level (see Figure 13.1). This difference indicates that a single, simplified model of the South does not apply to all third world countries. One must consider the various experiences of different countries as they try different approaches to development.[5]

The Newly Industrializing Countries

Given the extent of poverty in the global South, is it even possible for a third world country to lift itself out of poverty? The answer is "yes," at least for some countries. A handful of poor states—called the **newly industrializing countries (NICs)**—have achieved self-sustaining capital accumulation, with impressive economic growth.[6] These semiperiphery states, which export light manufactured goods, posted strong economic growth in the

---

[5] Arnold, Guy. *The End of the Third World*. NY: St. Martin's, 1993.

[6] Amsden, Alice. *The Rise of the 'Rest': Challenges to the West from Late-Industrializing Economies*. Oxford, 2001. Haggard, Stephan. *Developing Nations and the Politics of Global Integration*. Washington, DC: Brookings, 1995. Kohli, Atul. *State-Directed Development: Political Power and Industrialization in the Global Periphery*. Cambridge, 2004.

A "TIGER"

Singapore is one of the "four tigers" (with Hong Kong, Taiwan, and South Korea). Even after the setback of a 1997 financial crisis, their growth has made them prosperous by the standards of the global South. Other countries are trying to emulate the success of these NICs. But no single, simple lesson applicable to other states emerges from the NICs.

1980s and early 1990s (see "The World-System" on pp. 464–466). They suffered a setback in the late 1990s, because growth had been too fast, with overly idealistic loans, speculative investments, and corrupt deals (see pp. 359–362). Notwithstanding these setbacks, the NICs resumed growth and have developed much further and faster than most of the global South.

The most successful NICs are the **"four tigers"** or **"four dragons"** of East Asia: South Korea, Taiwan, Hong Kong, and Singapore. Each has succeeded in developing particular sectors and industries that are competitive on world markets.[7] These sectors and industries can create enough capital accumulation within the country to raise income levels not just among the small elite but across the population more broadly.

Many third world countries are trying to apply the model of the NICs, but so far few have succeeded. Most poor states remained mired in poverty, with as many failures as successes. Scholars do not know whether the NICs are just the lucky few that have moved from the periphery to the semiperiphery of the world-system (see p. 464), or whether their success can eventually be replicated throughout the world.

South Korean Development

South Korea, with iron and coal resources, developed competitive steel and automobile industries that export globally, creating a trade surplus (see "Balance of Trade" on pp. 310–311). For example, Hyundai cars and trucks, sold in the United States and other countries, are produced by the giant South Korean MNC, Hyundai. The state has been strongly involved in industrial policy, trying to promote and protect such industries. By the mid-1990s, South Korea had an income level per capita equivalent to that of Spain; Korean companies began to move manufacturing operations to Britain where production costs were lower. In this century, South Korean income has continued to rise impressively.

Taiwan too has a strong state industrial policy. It specializes in the electronics and computer industries, where Taiwanese products are very successful worldwide, and in other light manufacturing. Taiwan holds one of the world's largest hard-currency reserves.

Hong Kong—controlled by China since 1997—also has world-competitive electronics and other light industries, but its greatest strengths are in banking and trade—especially trade between southern China and the rest of the world. Hong Kong is a small territory

[7] Minami, Ryoshin, Kwan S. Kim, and Malcolm Falkus, eds. *Growth, Distribution, and Political Change: Asia and the Wider World*. NY: St. Martin's, 1999. Berger, Mark T. *The Battle for Asia: From Decolonization to Globalization*. NY: RoutledgeCurzon, 2004.

with some of the world's highest real estate prices, and great internal disparities of wealth. Its rich neighborhoods are jammed with high-rise office buildings and expensive apartments, and Hong Kong is a financial center for much of Asia.

Singapore is a trading city located at the tip of the Malaysian peninsula—convenient to the South China Sea, the Indian Ocean, and Australia. Singapore has developed niches in light manufacturing and has (like Hong Kong) attracted MNCs to locate headquarters there.

For different reasons, each of these states holds a somewhat unusual political status in the international system. South Korea and Taiwan are hot spots of international conflict. South Korea and North Korea are separate states and have never formally ended the Korean War (fought in 1950–1953). Taiwan is formally part of China, but in practice operates independently. Both South Korea and Taiwan came under the U.S. security umbrella during the Cold War. Both were militarized, authoritarian states intolerant of dissent then, although they later became democratic. U.S. spending in East Asia during the Cold War benefited South Korea and Taiwan. In these cases military conflict did not impede development.

Hong Kong and Singapore have a different political profile. They are both former British colonies. They are more city-states than nation-states, and their cities are trading ports and financial centers. Although not as repressive or as militarized as South Korea and Taiwan during the Cold War era, Hong Kong and Singapore were not democracies either. Hong Kong was ruled by a British governor (and since 1997 by the government in Beijing), Singapore by a dominant individual (who once banned sales of the *Asian Wall Street Journal* after it criticized him).

Thailand has been suggested as a potential "fifth tiger." It received enormous foreign investment in the 1980s (mostly from Japan) and created a sizable middle class. But its growth masked serious problems that put Thailand at the center of the 1997 financial crisis in Asia. Nonetheless, Thailand recovered and posted strong growth (until the 2001 world recession), despite continuing problems with bad loans.

Malaysia is also trying to follow closely in the footsteps of the tigers. Again, it is too soon to say whether this will succeed. *Indonesia* set a goal in 1969 to become an NIC by 1994. It fell short of that goal, but has made some progress in attracting foreign investment. With 200 million people, Indonesia's major assets are cheap labor (an average wage of about 25 cents per hour) and exportable natural resources, including oil. All of these Asian countries were caught in the 1997 financial downturn, which slowed their growth. Since 2001 several countries have also had to address problems of terrorism within their borders, and Indonesia faced simmering ethnic unrest in several islands. These factors dimmed the economic prospects of the would-be NICs of Southeast Asia.

Israel has developed economically in an unusual manner. It received sustained infusions of outside capital from several sources—German reparations, U.S. foreign aid, and contributions from Zionists in foreign countries. This outside assistance was particular to the history of German genocide against Jews during World War II and the efforts of Jews worldwide to help build a Jewish state afterward. Few if any developing countries could hope to receive such outside assistance (relative to Israel's small size). In common with the other NICs, however, Israel has a strong state involvement in key industries, and it has carved out a few niches for itself in world markets (notably in cut diamonds and military technology).

Thus, it is unclear whether there are general lessons to be learned from the success of the "four tigers." Hong Kong and Singapore are small trading cities located at the intersection of industrialized and third world regions (Japan/Pacific, South Asia, and China). There are no equivalents elsewhere in the global South. South Korea and Taiwan came of age while enmeshed in security relationships with the United States that no longer apply to most third world countries, if they ever did.

The Chinese Experience

Very few of the global South's people live in NICs. The largest, South Korea, has fewer than 50 million. China is more than 20 times its size. Size alone makes China's efforts to generate self-sustaining accumulation worthy of study. But China has also had one of the fastest-growing economies in recent years.

Mao Zedong

Between the communist victory of 1949 and the Cultural Revolution of the late 1960s, in the era of Chairman Mao Zedong, Chinese economic policy emphasized national self-sufficiency and communist ideology. The state controlled all economic activity through central planning and state ownership. An "iron rice bowl" policy guaranteed basic food needs to all Chinese citizens (at least in theory).

After Mao died in 1976, China under Deng Xiaoping instituted economic reforms and transformed its southern coastal provinces (near Hong Kong and Taiwan) into **free economic zones** open to foreign investment and run on capitalist principles. Peasants work their own fields, instead of collective farms, and get rich (by Chinese standards) if they do well. Entrepreneurs start companies, hire workers, and generate profits. Foreign investment has flooded into southern China, taking advantage of its location, cheap labor, and relative political stability. Other areas of China have gradually opened up to capitalist principles as well. The state now requires more industries to turn a profit and gives more initiative to managers to run their own companies and spend the profits as they see fit. Economic growth has been rapid since these policies were instituted. Standards of living are rising substantially.

However, China is also recreating some of the features of capitalism that Mao's revolutionaries had overturned. New class disparities are emerging, with rich entrepreneurs driving fancy imported cars while poor workers find themselves unemployed (earlier, socialism guaranteed everyone employment despite reduced efficiency). Unprofitable state-owned industries laid off 10 million workers in the 1990s, with more coming each year. In the countryside, areas bypassed by development still contain 200 million desperately poor Chinese peasants. Social problems such as prostitution returned, as did economic problems such as inflation (since tamed). Most frustrating for ordinary Chinese is the widespread official corruption accompanying the get-rich atmosphere.

Popular resentment over such problems as inflation and corruption led industrial workers and even government officials to join students in antigovernment protests at Beijing's Tiananmen Square in 1989. Authorities used the military to violently suppress the protests, killing hundreds of people and signaling its determination to maintain tight political control while economic reform proceeded. This policy of combining eco-

START YOUR ENGINES

China's rapid economic growth has raised incomes dramatically, especially for a growing middle class. These successes followed China's opening to the world economy and adoption of market-oriented reforms. China is emerging as a major producer and consumer of automobiles, and even luxury imported sports cars like these in 2003 are finding buyers among China's newly rich.

nomic reform with political orthodoxy was reaffirmed at the Party Congress in 1992 and again in 1997 and 2002.

China's leaders felt vindicated by subsequent economic performance. Foreign investors returned quickly after the political disruption of 1989, and economic growth roared ahead at 12 percent per year in 1992–1994. Inflation returned, however, reaching 22 percent in 1994 as a result of what the government called "mistakes." The government then devalued the Chinese currency and successfully tamed inflation by trimming growth back to 10 percent annually—a difficult task requiring both economic skill and political will. By 1997, with inflation in check and growth proceeding rapidly, Shanghai's mayor estimated that his city alone was using 18 percent of the world's construction cranes.[8]

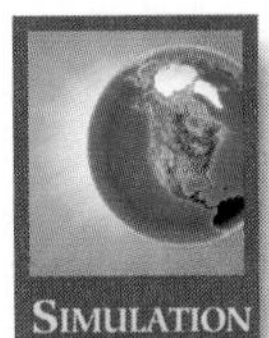
SIMULATION
You Are a Member of the Chinese Government

Since its currency was not convertible, China weathered the 1997 Asian financial crisis despite its widespread problems with bad bank loans, money-losing state industries, and corruption.

MNCs continue to shift production to China year by year because China's labor force is vast, low-paid, and disciplined (strikes are not allowed). Of the $700 billion in foreign direct investment (see pp. 364–365) in Asia in 1990–2000, nearly half was in mainland China. The largest investor, Motorola, put in more than $3 billion, and General Motors built a $1.5 billion plant near Shanghai. Some 40,000 Taiwanese companies invested $60 billion. These foreign investments primed rapid growth in Chinese exports—to $250 billion in 2000 and over $750 billion in 2005. In the next few years, China is poised to join the United States, Japan, and Germany as a major automobile exporter. China's car production quadrupled from 2001 to 2004. China's relatively new WTO membership is accelerating these trends.[9]

By 2005, with a new generation of Chinese leaders in charge—led by President Hu Jintao—China had continued rapid economic growth (close to 10 percent annually) year after year, with the help of large government infrastructure expenditures. President Hu consolidated his position in 2004 as his predecessor relinquished control of the military. Hu's stated top priority is to address the growing inequality between the country's newly rich strata and the hundreds of millions left in poverty in the countryside or laid off from jobs in state-owned industries in the cities (along with migrants from the countryside who cannot find work in the cities). In rural villages, hundreds of "mass incidents of unrest" took place each day in 2004, ranging from protests to full-scale riots put down by lethal force, as peasants reacted to land seizures, taxes, pollution, and corruption by local officials. The government suppressed news of these protests, in mass media and over the internet.

VIDEO
China Rising: The Boom

China's recent membership in the WTO raises new questions about how the ongoing Chinese opening of its economy to the world can coexist with continued political authoritarianism under communist rule. For example, 110 million Chinese are Internet users, and hundreds of millions more may join them within a few years. (China also has 300 million cell phone subscribers.) They will be able to communicate with overseas partners, monitor shipments, and follow economic trends globally. They will also be able to bypass government-controlled sources of political information. Some observers expect economic integration in an information era to inexorably open up China's political system and lead to democratization, whereas other experts think that as long as Chinese leaders deliver economic growth, the population will have little appetite for political change.

INFOREV
China and the Internet

China's economic success has given it both more prestige in the international system and a more global perspective on international relations far from China's borders. In late 2004, President Hu visited Latin America, making large-scale deals for resources to fuel

[8] Lardy, Nicholas R. *China's Unfinished Economic Revolution*. Washington, DC: Brookings Institution, 1998. Lieberthal, Kenneth. *Governing China*. 2nd ed. NY: W. W. Norton, 2004. Kaiser, Robert G. China Rising: Is America Paying Attention? *The Washington Post*, Oct. 26, 1997: C1.

[9] Chandler, Clay. A Factory to the World. *The Washington Post*, Nov. 25, 2001: A1, A30.

China's Neighborhood

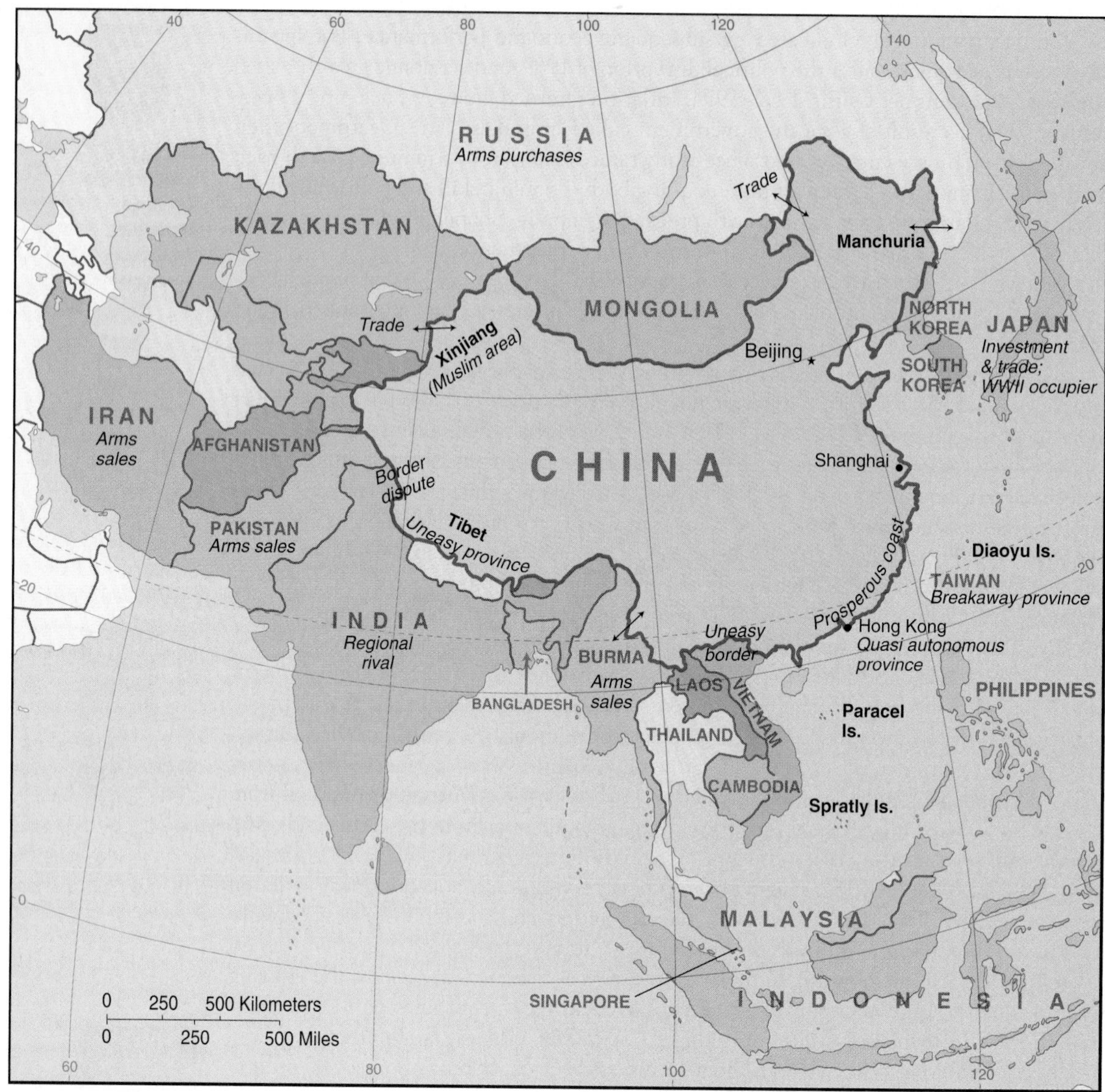

China's continuing growth is the leading success of economic development in the global South. China's future path will affect all of Asia.

China's growth—copper from Chile, tin from Bolivia, and soybeans from Brazil. China's need to import energy, meanwhile, gave it new interest in the politics of the Middle East, Central Asia, and Russia. In recognition of China's new importance in the world economy, the G7 leading economies invited China to meet with them—a possible first step toward membership in the G7. China's rising international standing is also reflected in the selection of Beijing to host the 2008 Olympics.

It is unclear what lessons China's economic success over the past decade holds for the rest of the global South. The shift away from central planning and toward private ownership was clearly a key factor in its success, yet the state continued to play a central role in

THINKING THEORETICALLY

Why Is China So Successful?

China's economic growth in the 1980s and 1990s stands out (along with a few other East Asian countries) from the pattern of sluggish development (if any) elsewhere in the global South. Several different explanations can be offered for China's success. One explanation rooted in a conservative world view is that China's traditional Confucian culture (shared to some extent by its East Asian neighbors) provides the discipline and social cohesion that allow rapid economic development and relative political stability. (China's path, then, would not apply to other areas of the global South.) The trouble with this explanation is that China's cultural traditions have been fairly fixed from decade to decade, yet China's politics have careened from civil war to totalitarian stability to Cultural Revolution to reformism, and its economic development has varied from the disaster of the Great Leap Forward in the 1950s to the success of market socialism since the 1980s. A theoretical explanation in which the outcome varies so much while the hypothesized cause remains fixed is not very appealing.

A more liberal approach—and the dominant one now for explaining China's success—emphasizes the effect of market-oriented reforms in opening the way for rapid growth and rising incomes. Since liberals tend to favor open economies and free trade, they make much of the fact that when China moved its economic system in these directions, growth picked up rapidly. This explanation is appealing in that it can be applied widely to other countries of the South. However, the evidence that it actually works well across the board is not very strong. After all, economic reforms similar to China's have been implemented in many other countries, yet China's performance far exceeds most of those other cases. This line of thinking then suggests avenues for further refinement of this theoretical approach. For example, one could tease apart the various elements of China's economic reforms—ranging from agricultural reforms to privatization to allowing foreign investment and so forth—and see which ones coincide with other successful cases in the global South.

A different explanation can be found in world-system theory (a more revolutionary approach). China can be seen as moving from the periphery zone of the world economy to the semiperiphery (along with some East Asian neighbors). As we have seen, China's exports of light-industrial products support this characterization. In this theory, however, such a movement between zones does not change the overall structure of the world-system. Some regions such as China move up a zone; others such as Russia and Eastern Europe move down a zone (from core to semiperiphery). But the periphery itself must remain, and only a small part of the world can ever belong to the core. Thus, China's economic rise does not provide lessons or a viable path for states elsewhere in the global South. This theoretical approach, as compared to the liberal one, is a bit vague on its predictions ("some move up, some move down") and thus hard to test. But its main conclusion—that the success of one region does not indicate any overall convergence of the South with the North—is borne out by the data in Chapter 12. China is, so far, the exception to a persistent (even growing) North-South gap.

overseeing the economy (even more than in the NICs). These topics are being debated vigorously as China navigates its new era of rising prosperity and rising expectation, and as other poor states look to China's experience for lessons.

Other Experiments

Other sizable third world states have pursued various development strategies, with mixed successes and failures. *India*, like China, deserves special attention because of its size. Its economy was until recently based loosely on socialism and state control of large industries but on private capitalism in agriculture and consumer goods. The state subsidizes basic goods and gives special treatment to farmers. Unlike China, India has a relatively democratic government, but a fractious one, with various autonomy movements and ethnic conflicts. India's government is corrupt from top to bottom, and corruption has held back accumulation.

Indian state-owned industries, like those elsewhere, are largely unprofitable. To take an extreme example, 12 years after a fertilizer plant was built, it employed 3,000 workers but had not produced any fertilizer. India's socialist philosophy and widespread poverty also limit the growth of a middle class to support capital accumulation and state revenue: less than 1 percent of the population pays any income tax. Furthermore, bureaucracy in India has discouraged foreign investment. In the 1990s, China received many times the foreign investment that India did. The 1991 collapse of the Soviet Union—India's major trading partner—threw India into a severe economic crisis that nearly caused it to default on its international debts. India sought help from the IMF and the World Bank and committed itself to far-reaching economic reforms such as reducing bureaucracy and selling money-losing state-owned industries (see "IMF Conditionality," pp. 520–522). Although reforms have been imperfectly carried out, India saw robust economic growth in the late 1990s and early 2000s, and developed special strength in the export of computer software services. Like China, India is a huge country now rising steadily out of extreme poverty, though at somewhat slower growth rates than China's.

Other large Asian states—*Bangladesh*, *Pakistan*, *Vietnam*, and the *Philippines*—are more deeply mired in poverty and have dimmer prospects for capital accumulation in the coming years. All have problems with state bureaucracies and corruption. Vietnam is a communist state trying to follow a reform model parallel to China's. The Philippines is trying to overcome a rebellion in the countryside and a history of political instability that discourages foreign investment. It has not fully recovered from the looting of its economy and treasury under the Marcos dictatorship in the 1970s and early 1980s. Pakistan also faces political instability and a chronic danger of war with India. Bangladesh is extremely poor, with no apparent foothold to get accumulation started.

Brazil and *Mexico* are the largest third world states in the Western hemisphere. Brazil built up a sizable internal market by concentrating income in a growing middle and upper class, especially after a military coup in 1964. However, its cities are still ringed with huge slums filled with desperately poor people. In the 1980s, Brazil returned to democratic civilian rule and began economic reforms such as selling off unprofitable state-owned enterprises, promoting free markets, and encouraging foreign investment. Nonetheless, by the early 1990s, Brazil remained well more than $100 billion in debt (the largest foreign debt in the global South). It had annual inflation of 200 percent and more, causing the currency's value to fall drastically. The president was impeached in a corruption scandal. The positive side of this embarrassing episode for Brazil was a constitutional, civilian transfer of power. With faster economic growth and foreign investment, a bigger grain harvest, and a substantial trade surplus, Brazil's main problem by 1993 was inflation. The anti-inflation plan of finance minister Fernando Cardoso was so successful that he was elected president in 1995, and other countries tried to copy his methods. In the 1997 currency crisis, Cardoso was able to scare off currency speculators, though at the cost of a dramatic slowdown in Brazil's economy. Brazil received a $41 billion IMF package in 1998, devalued its currency in 1999, and felt heat from next-door Argentina's financial meltdown in 2001. In 2002, the IMF gave Brazil a $30 billion bailout loan, with few requirements for domestic reform, because of worries that a financial collapse in Brazil would damage the world economy in a way that Argentina could not.

The election of a leftist president, Lula da Silva, raised fears that free spending on social programs would undermine Brazil's financial position, but instead he reined in spending, brought down inflation, and stabilized Brazil's financial position in 2003, at the short-term cost of economic recession—proving that in Brazil, as in China, socialists can make pretty good capitalists. By early 2005, this belt-tightening had lowered da Silva's popularity but improved Brazil's economic situation and avoided a debt default.

Mexico's Economy

In Mexico, similar economic reforms were undertaken in the 1980s. Like Brazil, Mexico had pockets of deep poverty and a sizable foreign debt. Unlike Brazil, Mexico had oil to export (a good source of hard currency, despite low world prices). Mexico has also enjoyed relative political stability, though corruption was a problem. Leaders hoped the NAFTA free trade agreement would accelerate foreign investment, creating jobs and export opportunities. Mexico also sold off more than $20 billion of state-owned companies (sparing the strategic oil industry) to help lower its debt and bring down inflation. But assassinations and other political upheaval, including an armed rebellion in the South that broke out in response to the NAFTA accord, complicated Mexico's development problems. In 1994–1995, Mexico's currency collapsed and standards of living for many consumers took a sharp drop. With help from the United States, Mexico undertook new economic reforms and began to rebuild the economy and restore international and domestic confidence. A reformist president from outside the long-standing ruling party, Vicente Fox, was elected in 2000.[10] By NAFTA's tenth anniversary in 2003, these upheavals had brought Mexico neither a breakthrough nor a disaster. Mexico's economic growth has picked up since 2003 after several years of sluggish growth in 2000–2003.

In Africa, *Nigeria* is the largest country and, with oil to export, one of the less impoverished. In 1980, when oil prices were high, Nigeria began building a huge, Soviet-style steel plant, which leaders hoped would serve as the cornerstone of Nigerian economic development. Twelve years and $5 billion later, the plant was ready to start producing steel, in theory. It is the biggest industrial project in sub-Saharan Africa. By 2003, with the steel complex still not producing steel (but the government paying workers there to do nothing), the Nigerian government signed an agreement with an American company to take over management and provide billions of dollars in new foreign investment. The government brought in hundreds of Russian and Ukrainian experts to help. But the prospects for competitive steel production look doubtful.

Meanwhile, as world oil prices fell drastically in the 1980s, Nigeria went in debt by $35 billion. Corruption took a steady toll on the economy. This pattern of centralized industrialization under Nigeria's military government faces uncertain prospects at best, although oil exports provide continuing income.[11] Nigeria canceled a planned experiment in democracy in the early 1990s, and a military dictatorship continued in power. African Americans began an unusual campaign to press for democracy in Nigeria, in order to move Africa's largest country forward in both human rights and overall development. Finally, elections were held in 1999. Nigeria has enjoyed some political stability since then, but new ethnic conflicts broke into violence in 2001. Nigeria's condition remains fragile.

In the Middle East, the small countries with large oil exports—such as *Saudi Arabia*, *Kuwait*, and *Bahrain*—have done well economically. But they are in a special class; their experience is not one that third world states without oil can follow. *Iran* and *Iraq* are somewhat larger countries that have also benefited from oil exports. After the Iran-Iraq War ended in 1988, Iran began to grow robustly and to attract foreign investment. However, its Islamic radicalism creates frictions with Western powers and makes some investors wary. A reformist president of Iran opened new avenues to Western powers and

[10] Auerbach, Nancy Neiman. *States, Banks, Markets: Mexico's Path to Financial Liberalization in Comparative Perspective*. Boulder, CO: Westview, 2000.

[11] Noble, Kenneth B. Nigeria's Monumental Steel Plant: Nationalist Mission or Colossal Mistake? *The New York Times*, July 11, 1992: 3.

their investment capital, but his side lost a power struggle and U.S. sanctions remain. Meanwhile, Iraq squandered oil revenues on military adventures in Iran and Kuwait; its economic development was set back enormously by the bombing of its infrastructure during the Gulf War and by looting and ongoing violence after the 2003 Iraq War.

Turkey was somewhat successful in developing its economy without oil revenues, a rare case. Like South Korea and Taiwan, Turkey was an authoritarian state for many years but has allowed political liberalization since the 1990s. It has developed under a U.S. security umbrella (NATO) and has received considerable U.S. foreign aid. Like Mexico, Turkey is trying to join its richer neighbors—the EU (see p. 390). Turkey also hopes to develop strong ties with the five former Soviet Asian republics. Unlike Iran, Turkey formally espouses secular politics, with Islam relegated to the religious and cultural sphere. A small but growing minority of Turks favors a more explicitly Islamic, less secular basis for Turkish society. A long-standing violent conflict hinders development in Turkey's Kurdish region. Turkey suffered recession in 2000–2001 and received a $30 billion IMF bailout. In 2003–2004, Turkey's economy grew solidly and its debt position improved as a result of low interest rates.

Egypt is mired in poverty despite substantial U.S. aid since the late 1970s. The state owns 70 percent of industry, operates the economy centrally, imposes high import tariffs, and provides patronage jobs and subsidized prices in order to maintain political power. A major portion of Egypt's foreign debt was forgiven after it helped the anti-Iraq coalition in the Gulf War, but Egypt remains about $30 billion in debt. Reforms in the 1990s brought economic growth, but remaining problems include high unemployment, a trade deficit, and widespread corruption. Islamic militants disrupted Egypt's economy (especially tourism) and politics in the past decade.

These examples from all the regions of the global South illustrate the many approaches toward economic development that states have tried and the mixed success they have met.

Lessons

Clearly, the largest developing countries are following somewhat different strategies with somewhat different results. But several common themes recur. These themes concern trade, the concentration of capital, authoritarianism, and corruption.

Import Substitution and Export-Led Growth

Throughout the global South, states are trying to use international trade as the basis of accumulation. For the reasons discussed in Chapter 8, a policy of self-reliance or autarky is at best an extremely slow way to build up wealth. But through the creation of a trade surplus, a state can accumulate hard currency and build industry and infrastructure.

One way to try to create a trade surplus, used frequently a few decades ago, is through **import substitution**—the development of local industries to produce items that a country had been importing. These industries may receive state subsidies or tariff protection. This might seem to be a good policy for reducing dependency—especially on the former colonial master—while shrinking a trade deficit or building a trade surplus. But it is against the principle of comparative advantage and has not proven effective in most cases. Some scholars think that import substitution is a policy useful only at a very early phase of economic development, after which it becomes counterproductive. Others think it is never useful.

More and more states have shifted to a strategy of **export-led growth,** a strategy used by the NICs. This strategy seeks to develop industries that can compete in specific niches in the world economy. These industries may receive special treatment such as subsidies and protected access to local markets. Exports from these industries generate hard currency and create a favorable trade balance. The state can then spend part of its money on imports of commodities produced more cheaply elsewhere.

Such a strategy has risks, especially when a state specializes in the export of a few raw materials (see "Postcolonial Dependency" on pp. 470–472). It leaves poor countries vulnerable to sudden price fluctuations for their exports. For example, when world copper prices fell from $3,000 to $1,300 per ton in 1974, income fell accordingly in Zambia, which got 94 percent of export earnings from copper. It had to cut back imports of needed goods drastically and suffered a 15 percent decline in its (already low) GDP.[12]

The overall relationship between the prices of exported and imported goods—called the **terms of trade**—affects an export strategy based on raw materials. There is some evidence that in the 1950s and 1960s, and again in the 1980s, the terms of trade eroded the value of raw materials. A state trying to create trade benefits by exporting such goods would have to export more and more over time in order to import the same manufactured goods—a major obstacle to accumulation.

Because of both terms of trade and price fluctuations, states have looked to exporting manufactured goods, rather than raw materials, as the key to export-led growth. However, in seeking a niche for manufactured goods, a third world state must compete against industrialized countries with better technology, more educated work forces, and much more capital. For example, Nigeria's steel exports are unlikely to provide the desired trade surplus (although South Korean steel did so). Thus, third world countries need to be selective in developing export-oriented industrial strategies. It is not enough to subsidize and protect an industry until it grows in size; someday it has to be able to stand its own ground in a competitive world or it will not bring in a trade surplus.

Concentrating Capital for Manufacturing

Manufacturing emerges as a key factor in both export-led growth and self-sustaining industrialization (home production for home markets). It is not surprising that third world states want to increase their own manufacturing base and change the global division of labor based on manufacturing in the core and resource extraction in the periphery. One great difficulty in getting manufacturing started is that capital is required to build factories. Competitive factories in technologically advanced industries can require large amounts of capital. Most third world states lack a source of funds.

To invest in manufacturing, these countries must *concentrate* what surplus their economies produce. They face the familiar trade-off between short-term consumption and long-term investment. Money spent building factories cannot be spent subsidizing food prices or building better schools. Thus the concentration of capital for manufacturing can sharpen disparities in income. A political price must often be paid in the short term for reducing public consumption, even in industrialized states. In third world states there is little margin for reducing consumption without causing extreme hardship. The result may be crowds rioting in the streets or guerrillas taking over the countryside.

The problem is compounded by the need to create domestic markets for manufactured goods. Because it is unlikely that a manufacturing industry in a poor country will be immediately competitive on world markets, one common strategy is to build up the industry with sales to the home market (protected by tariffs and subsidies) before pursuing world markets. But home markets for manufactured goods do not come from poor peasants in the

[12] Brandt, Willy, et al. *North-South: A Programme for Survival*. MIT, 1980, p. 145.

CAPITAL INVESTMENT

Foreign investment, international debt, and domestic inequality all can help concentrate the necessary capital for manufacturing. In recent years, microcredit—very small loans made directly to very poor people—provides a way to use capital more diffusely. These women in Bangladesh (1997) bought a cell phone with a loan and rented time on it to villagers.

countryside or the unemployed youth in city slums. Rather, wealth must be concentrated in a *middle class* that has the income to buy manufactured goods.

The growing disparity of income in such a situation often triggers intense frustration on the part of poorer people, even those whose income is rising. (Political rebellion is fueled by relative deprivation as much as by absolute poverty.) A common way states respond to such problems is to crack down hard with force to stamp out the protests of the poor and of other political opponents of the government (see the next section).

Such problems might be minimized by reducing the amount of capital that needs to be squeezed from a third world state's domestic economy. Capital for manufacturing can come from foreign investment or foreign loans, for instance. This strategy reduces short-term pain, but it also reduces the amount of surplus (profit) available to the state in the long term. Another way to minimize the capital needs of manufacturing is to start out in low-capital industries. These industries can begin generating capital, which can in turn be used to move into somewhat more technologically demanding and capital-intensive kinds of manufacturing. A favorite starter industry is *textiles*. The industry is fairly labor-intensive, giving an advantage to countries with cheap labor, and does not require huge investments of capital to get started. Many third world states have built their own textile industries as a step toward industrialization. For this reason, many states imposed high tariffs on textiles, making them among the least freely traded commodities. But starting in 2005, textile tariffs have been removed worldwide, and textile exporters in developing countries will now find both greater access to Western markets and intensified competition from China.

There are some problems with concentrating capital for manufacturing. One is that it creates conditions ripe for corruption (discussed shortly). The problem is especially severe when authoritarian political control is used to enforce compliance with hardships that may accompany the concentration of wealth—an issue currently for China.

An approach that received international attention in the 1980s is based on a Peruvian entrepreneur's analysis of the **informal sector** in Lima's economy—black markets, street vendors, and other private arrangements.[13] These modes of business are often beyond state control and may not even show up in state-compiled economic statistics. Markets operate rather freely, and some scholars have begun to see such markets, rather than large manufacturing industries, as the core of a new development strategy.

WEB LINK

Microlending

A related approach to capitalization in very poor countries, growing in popularity in recent years, is **microcredit** (or *microlending*). Based on a successful model in Bangladesh (the Grameen Bank), microcredit uses small loans to poor people, especially women, to

[13] De Soto, Hernando. *The Other Path: The Invisible Revolution in the Third World*. NY: HarperCollins, 1989.

support economic self-sufficiency. The borrowers are organized into small groups, and take responsibility for each other's success, including repaying the loans. Repayment rates have been high, and the idea is spreading rapidly in several regions. In one high-tech twist, village women have begun using small loans to start businesses renting cellular phone time to make domestic or international calls. Rural farmers used the phone time to find out market conditions before making a long trek to sell their products. Thus, bringing the information revolution to isolated villages raised incomes for the farmers and the women alike, and the bank got its loans repaid. Microcredit is now being applied on a macroscale. By 2002, 40 million families had received loans from 2,500 institutions worldwide. Microcredit is the opposite of a trickle-down approach, instead injecting capital at the bottom of the economic hierarchy. A loan to buy a goat or cell phone may do more good, dollar for dollar, than a loan to build a dam.[14]

Authoritarianism and Democracy

Several decades ago, many scholars expected that third world states would follow the European and North American states in economic and political development. The gradual accumulation of capital would be accompanied by the gradual extension of literacy and education, the reduction of class and gender disparities, and the strengthening of democracy and political participation. The United States could be a model for third world development in this view. It had gone from poor colony to industrializing state to rich superpower. Political rights (including the vote) had been steadily extended to more segments of the population.[15]

In reality, democracy has not accompanied economic development in a systematic or general way. In fact, the fastest-growing states have generally been authoritarian states, not democracies. This observation has led to the theory that economic development is incompatible with democracy. Accordingly, political repression and the concentration of political control are necessary to maintain order during the process of concentrating capital and to start accumulation. Demands by poor people for greater short-term consumption must be refused. Class disparities must be sharpened. Labor discipline must be enforced at extremely low wage levels. Foreign investors must be assured of political stability—above all, that radicals will not take power and that foreign assets will not be nationalized in a revolution. A democracy may be inherently incapable of accomplishing these difficult and painful tasks, according to this theory.[16]

The NICs did not achieve their success through free and open democratic politics, but through firm state rule permitting little dissent. Chinese leaders, for example, contrast their recent economic successes, achieved under tight political control, with the failed Soviet efforts under Gorbachev to promote economic reform by first loosening political control.

Innovation and Political Reform in China

It has been suggested that a strong state facilitates capital accumulation.[17] Only a strong state in this view has the power to enforce and coordinate the allocations of wealth required to start accumulation going. But scholars do not agree on the definition of a strong state; some refer to the size of the state bureaucracy or its ability to extract taxes, others to its

---

[14] Gender and Microlending: Diversity of Experience. Special issue of *Critical Half: Annual Journal of Women for Women International*, vol. 2, 2004.

[15] Huntington, Samuel P. *The Third Wave: Democratization in the Late Twentieth Century*. Oklahoma, 1991. Robinson, William I. *Promoting Polyarchy: Globalization, U.S. Intervention, and Hegemony*. Cambridge, 1996.

[16] Chua, Amy. *World on Fire: How Exporting Free Market Democracy Breeds Ethnic Hatred and Global Instability*. NY: Doubleday, 2002. Zakaria, Fareed. *The Future of Freedom: Illiberal Democracy at Home and Abroad*. NY: W. W. Norton, 2003.

[17] Evans, Peter B., Dietrich Rueschemeyer, and Theda Skocpol, eds. *Bringing the State Back In*. Cambridge, 1985. Krasner, Stephen D. *Structural Conflict: The Third World Against Global Liberalism*. California, 1985.

legitimacy or its ability to enforce its will on the population. The idea of a strong state is often connected with economic nationalism (see p. 313), and sometimes with socialism (using the state for downward rather than upward wealth distribution, see pp. 460–461).

In reality, the theory that authoritarianism leads to economic development does not hold up, just as the theory that democracy automatically accompanies economic development does not hold up. Many authoritarian states have achieved neither political stability nor economic development. Others have realized political stability but have failed at economic accumulation. The many military dictatorships in Africa are among the least successful models in the global South. In Latin America, the poorest country, Haiti, had the most authoritarian government for decades.

Furthermore, authoritarian states can lead to greater political instability, not less. The harder the state cracks down, the more resentment the population feels. Instead of peaceful protests, violent insurgencies often grow out of such resentments. In Guatemala, a military government harshly repressed rural revolutionaries and their peasant sympathizers for decades until a peace agreement was reached in 1996. Since the 1960s, in this country of 9 million, repression and war killed 100,000 people, and another 45,000 "disappeared"; most were killed and buried in mass graves.[18] Guatemala's government at times received substantial U.S. aid (based on "anticommunism") and at other times was banned from receiving such aid (based on violations of human rights). But its decades of authoritarian rule did not stop dissent, bring political stability, attract much foreign investment, or create much economic accumulation.

Meanwhile, elsewhere in Latin America a wave of civilian governments replaced military ones in the late 1980s.[19] Economic conditions there have improved, not worsened, as a result. In states such as South Korea and Taiwan, which began industrializing under authoritarianism but have since shifted toward democracy, economic progress was not harmed. Relatively free elections and some tolerance of dissent signaled greater stability and maturity, and did not discourage investment or slow economic growth.

It has been suggested that authoritarian rule and the concentration of income in few hands represent a phase in the development process. First, capital must be concentrated to get accumulation started, and tight political control must be maintained during this painful phase. Later, more wealth is generated, income spreads to more people, the middle class expands, and political controls can be relaxed.

But again, the empirical reality does not support such a theory as a general rule. There is no guarantee that, even in early phases of accumulation, authoritarian control leads to economic development. In fact, flagrant human rights abuses seem to cause political instability at any stage of economic development. Some successful accumulators, such as Singapore, have maintained tight political control throughout the process. Others, such as South Korea and Turkey, have started with authoritarian rule and evolved into democracies. Still others, such as Costa Rica and Malaysia, have achieved good economic results while maintaining relative democracy and little repression. Similarly, among the countries that have done poorly in economic accumulation are both authoritarian regimes and democratic ones. Therefore, a state's form of political governance does not seem to determine its success in economic development. Future years will show whether China follows South Korea's example, gradually democratizing after decades of successful economic development.

---

[18] Human Rights Watch World Report 1990. Cited in *Science* 257, July 24, 1992: 479.

[19] Linz, Juan J., and Alfred Stepan. *Problems of Democratic Transition and Consolidation: Southern Europe, South America, and Post-Communist Europe*. Johns Hopkins, 1996. Przeworski, Adam. *Democracy and the Market: Political and Economic Reforms in Eastern Europe and Latin America*. Cambridge, 1991.

Corruption

Corruption

Corruption is an important negative factor in economic development in many states; corruption also plays a role in some of the theories just discussed about various strategies for using trade, industry, and government to promote economic development. In the past decade, high-level corruption cases have become high-profile international news, knocking governments from power in Brazil, Italy, Pakistan, Indonesia, and elsewhere, and sending two former South Korean presidents to jail.

Corruption centers on the government as the central actor in economic development, especially in its international aspects. Through foreign policy, the government mediates the national economy's relationship to the world economy. It regulates the conditions under which MNCs operate in the country. It enforces worker discipline—calling out the army if necessary to break strikes or suppress revolutions. It sets tax rates and wields other macroeconomic levers of control over the economy. And in most third world states it owns a sizable stake in major industries—a monopoly in some cases.

State officials will decide whether to let the MNC into the country, which MNC to give the drilling rights to, and what terms to insist on (leasing fees, percentages of sales, etc.). These are complex deals struck after long negotiations. Corruption merely adds another player, the corrupt official, to share the benefits. For instance, a foreign oil company can pay off an official to award a favorable contract, and both can profit. In 2003, U.S. prosecutors indicted a Mobil Oil executive and a New York banker for paying $78 million to two senior officials in Kazakhstan—with a kickback of $2 million for the Mobil executive—to secure Mobil's billion-dollar stake in a huge oil field there. He pleaded guilty to tax evasion, received a prison sentence, and had to pay taxes on the $2 million.

ADDITIONAL CHARGES MAY APPLY

Corruption is a major impediment to economic development in both rich and poor countries but more devastating to economies in the global South and to transitional former communist economies. In 2005, Ukraine's new reformist president disbanded the entire 23,000-member traffic police force to break up widespread corruption in its ranks. Here, a driver gets towed in the capital, 2005.

Corruption is by no means limited to the global South. But for several reasons corruption has a deeper effect in poor countries. First, there is simply less surplus to keep economic growth going; accumulation is fragile. Another difference is that in those developing countries dependent on exporting a few products, the revenue arrives in a very concentrated form—large payments in hard currency. This presents a greater opportunity for corruption than in a more diversified economy with more (smaller) deals. Furthermore, in third world countries incomes are often so low that corrupt officials are more tempted to accept payments.

Corruption in the global South presents a collective goods problem for states and MNCs in the global North: individually MNCs and their home states can profit by clinching a deal with a private payoff, but collectively the MNCs and states of the North lose money by having to make these payoffs. Therefore, there is an incentive to clamp down on corruption only if other industrialized states do likewise. The United States in recent decades has barred U.S. companies from making corrupt deals abroad, but other countries of the North had not done so until recently. Germany and Canada even allowed their companies to deduct foreign bribes on their taxes.

Transparency helps solve collective goods problems (see pp. 103–104). A Berlin-based NGO called Transparency International pushed successfully for action to stem corruption in international business deals. The group publishes annual surveys showing the countries that business executives considered most corrupt. The top five on the list in 2005 were Chad, Bangladesh, Turkmenistan, Burma, and Haiti. In 1997, the world's 29 leading industrialized states agreed to forbid their companies from bribing foreign officials.

Developing Chad's Oil

In Chad in 1999, a consortium led by Exxon Mobil and backed by World Bank loans struck a deal to build a $4 billion oil pipeline from the land-locked country, with oil revenues going through a Citibank account in London to avoid corruption. Chad promised to use 72 percent of the money to reduce poverty. But in 2005, as the oil money flowed in, Chad's government—under attack by rebels based in Sudan—pulled out of the deal to use the money for its military, and the World Bank suspended its loans.

Occasionally, government officials serve not their own private interests but those of a foreign state. Such a government is called a *puppet government*. The officials of such a government are bought off to serve the interests of a more powerful state (which may have installed the government through military conquest). For example, during the Cold War, both superpowers justified installing friendly governments by reference to global power politics. Critics, however, believed the puppet governments served business interests of the controlling state, not security interests. This and other issues concern the role of international business in third world accumulation.

North-South Business

Given the importance of international trade and investment to third world economic development, not only governments but private banks and MNCs from the North are also major participants in the economies of the South. Several large third world states have also created their own MNCs, though these play a fairly minor role compared to MNCs from the North.

Foreign Investment

Poor countries have little money available to invest in new factories, farms, mines, or oil wells. Foreign investment—investment in such capital goods by foreigners (most often MNCs)—is one way to get accumulation started (see "Foreign Direct Investment" on pp. 364–365). Foreign investment has been crucial to the success of China and other Asian developing countries. Overall, private capital flows to the global South totaled more than $150 billion in 2003—triple the amount given in official development assistance.[20]

Foreigners who invest in a country then own the facilities; the investor by virtue of its ownership can control decisions about how many people to employ, whether to expand or shut down, what products to make, and how to market them. Also, the foreign investor can usually take the profits from the operation out of the country (repatriation of profits).

[20] World Bank. *Global Economic Prospects and the Developing Countries 2004*. Washington: World Bank.

However, the host government can share in the wealth by charging fees and taxes, or by leasing land or drilling rights (see "Host and Home Government Relations" on pp. 365–368).

Because of past colonial experiences, many governments in the global South have feared the loss of control that comes with foreign investments by MNCs. Sometimes the presence of MNCs was associated with the painful process of concentrating capital and the sharpening of class disparities in the host state. Although such fears remain, they are counterbalanced by the ability of foreign investors to infuse capital and generate more surplus. By the 1980s and 1990s, as models based on autarky or state ownership were discredited and the NICs gained success, many poor states rushed to embrace foreign investment. China has been the most successful of these by far.

GM MOVES IN

Foreign investment is an important source of capital for economic development in the global South. The relationship of foreign investors and host countries transcends economics and draws in culture, politics, and identity. General Motors built this $1.5 billion Buick assembly line in Shanghai, the historical (and perhaps future) center of foreign economic penetration in China, 1998.

One way in which states have sought to soften the loss of control is through *joint ventures*, companies owned partly by a foreign MNC and partly by a local firm or the host government itself. Sometimes foreign ownership in joint ventures is limited to some percentage (often 49 percent), to ensure that ultimate control rests with the host country even though a large share of the profits go to the MNC. The percentage of ownership is usually proportional to the amount of capital invested; if a host government wants more control it must put up more of the money. Joint ventures work well for MNCs because they help ensure the host government's cooperation in reducing bureaucratic hassles and ensuring success (by giving the host government a direct stake in the outcome).

MNCs invest in a country because of some advantage of doing business there. In some cases, it is the presence of natural resources. Sometimes it is cheap labor. Sometimes geographical location is a factor. Some states have better *absorptive capacity* than others—the ability to put investments to productive use—because of more highly developed infrastructure and a higher level of skills among workers or managers. As these are most often middle-income states, the funneling of investments to states with high absorptive capacity tends to sharpen disparities *within* the global South.

MNCs also look for a favorable *regulatory environment* in which a host state will facilitate, rather than impede, the MNC's business. For example, Motorola had decided to invest more than $1 billion in new facilities in India in the 1990s, but changed its mind after encountering India's bureaucracy and shifted its investments toward China instead.[21]

MNC decisions about foreign investment also depend on prospects for *financial stability*, especially for low inflation and stable currency exchange rates. If a currency is not con-

[21] Gargan, Edward A. India's Rush to a Free Market Economy Stumbles. *The New York Times*, Aug. 15, 1992: 2.

vertible into hard currency, an MNC will not be able to take profits back to its home state or reinvest them elsewhere. Of equal importance in attracting investment is *political stability* (see pp. 368–370). Banks and MNCs conduct *political risk analyses* to assess the risks of political disturbances in third world states in which they might invest.

Beyond these financial considerations, a foreign investor producing for local markets wants to know that the host country's *economic growth* will sustain demand for the goods being produced. Similarly, whether producing for local consumption or export, the MNC wants the local *labor supply*—whether semiskilled labor or just cheap—to be stable. Foreign investors often look to international financial institutions, such as the World Bank and the IMF, and to private analyses, to judge a state's economic stability before investing in it.

MNCs and Third World Labor

Beyond their usual role in providing foreign investment, technology transfer, and loans (in the case of banks), MNCs also sometimes participate in more broadly conceived development projects in a host state. Such participation is a way of investing in political goodwill as well as helping provide political stability by improving the condition of the population. The attitude of the government and the goodwill of the population affect the overall business prospects of the MNC. In the long run, blatant exploitation is not the most profitable way to do business.

Technology Transfer

The productive investment of capital depends on the knowledge and skills—business management, technical training, higher education, as well as basic literacy and education—of workers and managers. Of special importance are the management and technical skills related to the key industries in a state's economy. In many former colonies, Europeans with such skills left after independence (see "Postcolonial Dependency" on pp. 470–474). In other states, the skills needed to develop new industries have never existed. A few states in the Persian Gulf with large incomes and small populations have imported a whole work force from foreign countries. But this practice is rare.

Most poor states seek to build up their own educated elite with knowledge and skills to run the national economy. One way to do so is to send students to industrialized states for higher education. This entails some risks, however. Students may enjoy life in the North and fail to return home. In most third world countries, every student talented enough to study abroad represents a national resource and usually a long investment in primary and secondary education, which is lost if the student does not return. The same applies to professionals (for example, doctors) who emigrate later in their careers. The problem of losing skilled workers to richer countries, called the **brain drain,** has impeded economic development in states such as India, Pakistan, and the Philippines (where more nurses emigrated than graduated nursing school in 2000-2004). At the extreme, more than 80 percent of Haiti's and Jamaica's college-educated citizens live abroad.

Technology transfer refers to a third world state's acquisition of technology (knowledge, skills, methods, designs, and specialized equipment) from foreign sources, usually in conjunction with foreign direct investment or similar business operations. A third world state may allow an MNC to produce certain goods in the country under favorable conditions, provided the MNC shares knowledge of the technology and design behind the product. The state may try to get its own citizens into the management and professional work force of factories or facilities created by foreign investment. Not only can physical capital accumulate in the country, so can the related technological base for further development. But MNCs are sometimes reluctant to share proprietary technology.

Technology transfer sometimes encounters difficulty when the technological style of the source country does not fit the needs of the recipient country. A good fit has been called *appropriate technology*.[22] In particular, the Soviet Union was fond of creating the "world's largest" factory of some type, and it tended to apply the same overly centralized approach to its investments and development projects in the global South—such as the huge Nigerian steel plant mentioned earlier. Furthermore, technology that seemed useful to bureaucrats in Moscow might not be appropriate to a recipient country; in 1960 the Soviets sent snowplows to the tropical country of Guinea.[23]

The **green revolution**—a massive transfer of agricultural technology coordinated through international agencies—deserves special mention.[24] This effort, which began in the 1960s, transplanted a range of agricultural technologies from rich countries to poor ones—new seed strains, fertilizers, tractors to replace oxen, and so forth. (Today genetically modified crops are high on the agenda.) The green revolution increased crop yields in a number of states, especially in Asia, and helped food supplies keep up with growing populations.

However, it did have drawbacks. Critics said the green revolution made recipients dependent on imported technologies such as tractors and oil, that it damaged the environment with commercial pesticides and fertilizers, and that it disrupted traditional agriculture (driving more people off the land and into cities). Environmental reactions to the green revolution—including the emergence of pesticide resistance in insect populations—have led to recent declines in crop yields, forcing changes.[25] For example, in Indonesia pesticides introduced in the green revolution created resistant strains of a rice parasite and killed off the parasite's natural predators. The pesticides also polluted water supplies. Recognizing the need to adapt imported technologies to local needs, the Indonesian government banned most pesticides in 1986 and adopted organic methods instead. In recent years, the Food and Agriculture Organization (FAO) has spread information about organic pest control through traditional village theater plays. Pesticide usage has declined sharply while rice production has increased.

Meanwhile, on the Indonesian island of Bali, "water priests" traditionally controlled the allocation of scarce water resources to agriculture. In the green revolution, such practices were often dismissed as superstitious nonsense and replaced with modern water-allocation schemes. But the water priests actually had more experience with local conditions over many years, and more legitimacy with the local farmers, than did the foreign experts. A U.S. anthropologist developed graphical software that the water priests could use to gain access to technical information about water supplies without sacrificing their own experience and authority.

Since the 1990s, states in the North have focused on technology transfer that promotes *environmentally sustainable development* (see pp. 415–417). Japan's MITI-funded International Center for Environmental Technology Transfer geared up to train 10,000 people from third world countries, over ten years, in energy conservation, pollution control, and other environmental technologies. Japan also hosts the International Environmental Technology Center, a project of the UN Environment Program (UNEP). Among other motives, Japan hopes these projects will encourage developing countries to choose Japanese technology and products.[26]

[22] Betz, Matthew J., Pat McGowan, and Rolf T. Wigand, eds. *Appropriate Technology: Choice and Development*. Duke, 1984. Willoughby, Kelvin W. *Technology Choice: A Critique of the Appropriate Technology Movement*. Boulder, CO: Westview, 1990.

[23] Legvold, Robert. *Soviet Policy in West Africa*. Harvard, 1970, p. 124.

[24] Alauddin, Mohammed, and Clement Tisdell. *The "Green Revolution" and Economic Development: The Process and Its Development in Bangladesh*. NY: St. Martin's, 1991. Perkins, John H. *Geopolitics and the Green Revolution: Wheat, Genes, and the Cold War*. Oxford, 1997.

[25] *Science* 256, May 22, 1992: 1140. *Science* 256, May 29, 1992: 1272.

[26] *Science* 256, May 22, 1992: 1145.

North-South Debt

Borrowing money is an alternative to foreign investment as a way of obtaining funds to prime a cycle of economic accumulation. If accumulation succeeds, it produces enough surplus to repay the loan and still make a profit. Borrowing has several advantages. It keeps control in the hands of the state (or other local borrower) and does not impose painful sacrifices on local citizens, at least in the short term.

Debt has disadvantages too. The borrower must service the debt—making regular payments of interest and repaying the principal according to the terms of the loan. **Debt service** is a constant drain on whatever surplus is generated by investment of the money. With foreign direct investment, a money-losing venture is the problem of the foreign MNC; with debt, it is the problem of the borrowing state, which must find the money elsewhere. Often, a debtor must borrow new funds to service old loans, slipping further into debt. Debt service has created a net financial outflow from South to North in recent years, as the South has paid billions more in interest to banks and governments in the North than it has received in foreign investment or development aid.

Debt Forgiveness

The failure to make scheduled payments, called a **default,** is considered a drastic action because it destroys lenders' confidence and results in cutoff of future loans. Rather than defaulting, borrowers attempt **debt renegotiation**—a reworking of the terms on which a loan will be repaid. By renegotiating their debts with lenders, borrowers seek a mutually acceptable payment scheme to keep at least some money flowing to the lender. If interest rates have fallen since a loan was first taken out, the borrower can refinance. Borrowers and lenders can also negotiate to restructure a debt by changing the length of the loan (usually to a longer payback period) or the other terms. Occasionally state-to-state loans are written off altogether—forgiven—for political reasons, as happened with U.S. loans to Egypt after the Gulf War.

Third world debt encompasses several types of lending relationships, all of which are influenced by international politics. The *borrower* may be a private firm or bank in a third world country, or it may be the government itself. Loans to the government are somewhat more common because lenders consider the government less likely to default than a private borrower. The *lender* may be a private bank or company, or a state (both are important). Usually banks are more insistent on receiving timely payments and firmer in renegotiating debts than are states. Some state-to-state loans are made on artificially favorable *concessionary* terms, in effect subsidizing economic development in the borrowing state.

In the 1970s and 1980s, many states in the South borrowed heavily from banks and states in the North, which encouraged the borrowing. The anticipated growth often did not materialize. In oil-exporting states such as Venezuela and Mexico, for instance, price declines reduced export earnings with which states planned to repay the loans. Other exporting states found that protectionist measures in the North, combined with a global economic slowdown, limited their ability to export. Sometimes borrowed funds were simply not spent wisely and produced too little surplus to service the debt.

As a result, by the 1980s a *third world debt crisis* had developed, particularly in Latin America.[27] Many third world states could not generate enough export earnings to service their debts, much less to repay them—not to speak of retaining some surplus to generate sustained local accumulation. Major states of the global South such as Brazil, Mexico, and

[27] Jorge, Antonio, and Jorge Salazar-Carrillo, eds. *The Latin American Debt*. NY: St. Martin's, 1992. Frieden, Jeffry A. *Debt, Development, and Democracy: Modern Political Economy and Latin America, 1965–1985*. Princeton, 1992. Kahler, Miles, ed. *The Politics of International Debt*. Cornell, 1986. Bradshaw, York W., and Ana-Maria Wahl. Foreign Debt Expansion, the International Monetary Fund, and Regional Variation in Third World Poverty. *International Studies Quarterly* 35 (3), 1991: 251–72.

India found foreign debt a tremendous weight on economic development. Although the "crisis" passed, and many debts were renegotiated to a longer-term basis, the weight of debt remains (see Table 13.1).

Debt renegotiation has become a perennial occupation of third world states. Such renegotiations are complex international bargaining situations, like international trade or arms control negotiations but with more parties. The various lenders—private banks and states—try to extract as much as they can, and the borrower tries to hold out for more favorable terms. If a borrowing government accepts terms that are too burdensome, it may lose popularity at home; the local population and opposition politicians may accuse it of selling out to foreigners, neocolonialists, and so on. But if the borrowing state does not give enough to gain the agreement of the lenders, it might have to default and lose out on future loans and investments, which could greatly impede economic growth.

GLOBALIZE THIS

Globalization is creating winners and losers while sharpening income disparities. Debt, currency crises, IMF conditionality, and the privatization of state-owned enterprises are among the sources of upheaval and poverty in many third world countries. This beggar was caught in Argentina's financial collapse in 2001.

For the lenders, debt renegotiations involve a collective goods problem: all of them have to agree on the conditions of the renegotiation but each really cares only about getting its own money back. To solve this problem, state creditors meet together periodically as the **Paris Club,** and private creditors as the **London Club,** to work out their terms. In January 2005, the Paris Club offered a debt freeze (a temporary stoppage of payments) to countries affected by the deadly tsunami in December 2004.

Through such renegotiations and the corresponding write-offs of debts by banks, third world states have largely avoided defaulting on their debts. Some large states threatened to default—or even to lead a coalition of third world states all defaulting at once—but backed off from such threats. However, in 2001, Argentina in effect defaulted on its debts. By then, financial institutions had adjusted psychologically to the reality that Argentina

TABLE 13.1 ■ Debt in the Global South, 2005

	Foreign Debt		Annual Debt Service	
Region	**Billion $**	**% of GDP[a]**	**Billion $**	**% of Exports**
Latin America	800	36%	140	26%
Asia	800	23	100	7
Africa	300	39	30	11
Middle East	300	34	40	7
Total "South"	2,200	33	310	13

[a]GDP not calculated at purchasing-power parity.

Notes: Regions do not exactly match those used elsewhere in this book. Africa here includes North Africa. Asia includes China.

Source: IMF. *Statistical Appendix to World Economic Outlook,* September 2005, pp. 266–7.

could not pay its debt, so the default did not cause a wider panic. Indeed, Argentina recovered—growing 9 percent a year since 2001—and in 2005 offered its creditors a take-it-or-leave-it deal for repayment of less than 30 cents on the dollar. Most took it, showing Argentina's strong position despite the default. Still, default is a risky course because of the integrated nature of the world economy, the need for foreign investment and foreign trade to accumulate wealth, and the risks of provoking international confrontations. Lenders too have generally proven willing to absorb losses rather than push a borrower over the edge and risk financial instability.

Despite stabilization, third world states have not yet solved the debt problem. As shown in Table 13.1, the South owes $2 trillion in foreign debt, and pays about $300 billion a year to service that debt. The debt service (in hard currency) absorbs more than a third of the entire hard-currency export earnings in Latin America—the region most affected. Africa's debt is equal to 40 percent of the annual GDP of the region. Some states in Asia are vulnerable to debt problems as well.

In recent years, activists and NGOs have called for extensive debt forgiveness for the poorest countries, most of which are in Africa. Critics say such cancellations just put more money in the hands of corrupt, inept governments. But in 2004, Britain promised nearly $200 million a year for debt relief and urged other Western countries to contribute. Under this prodding, and with a history of successful bilateral debt forgiveness totaling tens of billions of dollars in recent years, G7 members in 2005 agreed to eliminate all debts owed by 37 very poor countries to the World Bank and IMF—cutting almost in half the poorest countries' estimated $200 billion in debt. The first $40 billion, owed by 18 countries, began to be written off in 2006. The IMF was considering a controversial plan to revalue its gold holdings (currently valued at $8 billion but worth ten times that at market prices) as a source of finance for this debt relief.

IMF Conditionality

The International Monetary Fund (IMF) and the World Bank have a large supply of capital from their member states (see "The World Bank and the IMF" on pp. 349–352). This capital plays an important role in funding early stages of accumulation in third world states and in helping developing countries get through short periods of great difficulty. And, as a political entity rather than a bank, the IMF can make funds available on favorable terms.

The IMF does not give away money indiscriminately. Indeed, it scrutinizes third world states' economic plans and policies, withholding loans until it is satisfied that the right policies are in place. Then it makes loans to help states through the transitional process of implementing the IMF-approved policies. The IMF also sends important signals to private lenders and investors. Its approval of a state's economic plans is a "seal of approval" bankers and MNCs use to assess the wisdom of investing in that state. Thus, the IMF wields great power to influence the economic policies of third world states.

An agreement to loan IMF funds on the condition that certain government policies are adopted is called an **IMF conditionality** agreement; implementation of these conditions is referred to as a *structural adjustment program*.[28] Dozens of third world states have entered into such agreements with the IMF in the past two decades. The terms insisted on by the IMF are usually painful for the citizens (and hence for national politicians). The IMF

[28] Dasgupta, Biplab. *Structural Adjustment, Global Trade, and the New Political Economy of Development*. NY: Zed/St. Martin's, 1999. Sahn, David E., Paul A. Dorosh, and Stephen D. Younger. *Structural Adjustment Reconsidered: Economic Policy and Poverty in Africa*. Cambridge, 1997. Peet, Richard. *Unholy Trinity: The IMF, World Bank and WTO*. NY: Zed Books, 2003. Fischer, Stanley. *IMF Essays in a Time of Crisis: The International Financial System, Stabilization, and Development*. MIT, 2004. Vines, David and Christopher L. Gilber. *The IMF and its Critics: Reform of Global Finance Architecture*. Cambridge, 2004.

POLICY PERSPECTIVES

President of Egypt, Hosni Mubarak

PROBLEM *How to balance the demands of domestic actors and international financial institutions.*

BACKGROUND Imagine that you are the president of Egypt. Your economy is not in the healthiest of shape. Unemployment is high, running around 10 percent. Economic growth has been steady but slow, hovering around 3 percent for several years. Given your large and growing population, many believe this rate is far too low. Your country is saddled with a large debt burden—as of 2003, nearly $30 billion.

Recently, however, your government has begun to undertake new economic reforms. Led by a new group of young leaders (including your son), the government is selling several large state-owned industries to private investors. In particular, large state-owned banks are being privatized. In addition, rules governing who can own industries have been relaxed to allow international MNCs to invest in Egypt.

International actors have praised these moves toward reform. The International Monetary Fund (IMF) and the World Bank have extolled your economic plans and suggested an accelerated pace for reform.

In the past, you have been far more cautious in your approach to economic reform. State-owned industries are politically important for you because they employ large numbers of Egyptians. If not for state-owned industries, unemployment would be much higher than at present. When these industries are privatized, it is likely that many employees will be fired.

Already, the privatization that has occurred has been unpopular. To make up for the new waves of unemployed, you increased food subsidies. These increases led to more public debt, however, as they cost your government billions of dollars. In 2004, your budget deficit ran over $8 billion, which necessitated new loans from the IMF.

Still, you view these subsidies and state-owned industries as an important political tool for ensuring political stability for your government. You are increasingly challenged with calls for political reform, including holding elections and allowing Islamic parties (which you have outlawed in the past) to participate in politics. In the past, IMF-related programs have led to riots and civil unrest in your country.

SCENARIO Now imagine that after a particularly difficult year economically (because of a world economic downturn), you must return to the IMF for more loans. The IMF, however, demands even further economic reform as a condition for the new loans. While they praise your efforts so far, IMF negotiators push you to go further. They demand more privatization and the slashing of food subsidies.

Rejecting the IMF demands risks a cut in loans that would threaten your economic stability and frighten foreign investors away. The privatization and reform does seem to be improving the investment environment in your country, which is boosting your economy.

Acquiescing to the IMF conditions carries a large political risk, however. Privatization will lead to unemployment, while a cut in food subsidies will increase hunger, not to mention strengthening disenchantment with your regime.

CHOOSE YOUR POLICY Do you adopt further reforms, hoping to blame the IMF for your economic troubles with your public? Do you refuse the IMF loans and search for alternate sources of loans? How do you balance your domestic political needs with the demands of international economic institutions and investors?

demands that inflation be brought under control, which requires reducing state spending and closing budget deficits. These measures often spur unemployment and require that subsidies of food and basic goods be reduced or eliminated. Short-term consumption is curtailed in favor of longer-term investment. Surplus must be concentrated to service debt and invest in new capital accumulation. The IMF wants to ensure that money lent to a country is not spent for politically popular but economically unprofitable purposes (such as subsidizing food). It wants to ensure that inflation does not eat away all progress and that the economy is stable enough to attract investment. In addition, it demands steps to curtail corruption.

Because of the pain inflicted by a conditionality agreement—and to some extent by any debt renegotiation agreement—such agreements are often politically unpopular in the global South.[29] On quite a few occasions, a conditionality agreement has brought rioters into the streets demanding the restoration of subsidies for food, gasoline, and other essential goods. Sometimes governments have backed out of the agreement or have broken their promises under such pressure. Occasionally, governments have been toppled. In a country such as Peru, which in the early 1990s faced a violent leftist guerrilla war that fed on mass poverty, such a choice was especially difficult.

In Egypt, where the same word is used for bread as for life, cheap bread is vital to political stability, at least in the government's view. State-owned flour mills, and an annual subsidy of $750 million, ensure a supply of bread at one-third its real cost, for Egypt's large and poor population. These costs distort the free market, encouraging Egyptians to eat (and waste) more bread than they otherwise would, and driving the need for imported wheat to more than $1 billion per year. But when the government tried to raise the price of bread in 1977, street riots forced a reversal. Instead, the government has subtly changed the size and composition of loaves, and in 1996 began secretly mixing cheaper corn flour into state-milled wheat flour.

The IMF formula for stability and success is remarkably universal from one country to the next. When the IMF negotiated terms for economic assistance to Russia and the former Soviet republics in the early 1990s, the terms were similar to those for any third world state: cut inflation, cut government spending, cut subsidies, crack down on corruption. Critics of the IMF argue that it does not adapt its program adequately to account for differences in the local cultural and economic conditions in different states. (The United States would not qualify for IMF assistance because of government deficits.)

MIRACLE OF LOAVES

IMF conditionality agreements often called for reducing subsidies for food, transportation, and other basic needs. In Egypt, bread prices are heavily subsidized, forcing the government to use hard currency to import wheat. But public resistance to bread price increases is so strong that the government has not brought itself to cut the subsidy. Here, bread is delivered by bicycle in Cairo, 1996.

---

[29] Haggard, Stephan, and Robert R. Kaufman, eds. *The Politics of Economic Adjustment: International Constraints, Distributive Conflicts, and the State*. Princeton, 1992. Vreeland, James R. *The IMF and Economic Development*. Cambridge, 2003.

The South in International Economic Regimes

Because of the need for capital and the wealth created by international trade, most states of the global South see their future economic development as resting on a close interconnection with the world economy, not on national autarky or regional economic communities. Thus poor states must play by the rules embedded in international economic regimes (see Chapters 8 and 9).

The WTO trading regime tends to work against poor states relative to industrialized ones. A free trade regime makes it harder for poor states to protect infant industries in order to build self-sufficient capital accumulation. It forces competition with more technologically advanced states. A poor state can be competitive only in low-wage, low-capital niches—especially those using natural resources that are scarce in the North, such as tropical agriculture, extractive (mining and drilling) industries, and textiles.

Yet just these economic sectors in which third world states have comparative advantages on world markets—agriculture and textiles in particular—were largely excluded from the free trade rules of the GATT (see pp. 322–324). The GATT instead concentrated on free trade in manufactured goods, in which states in the North have comparative advantages. As a result, some third world states found that they were expected to open their home markets to foreign products, against which home industries are not competitive, yet see their own export products shut out of foreign markets. Current WTO negotiations are attempting to remedy this inequity.

Another criticism leveled at the WTO centers on the trade dispute system, where states may bring complaints of unfair trading practices. Such legal disputes can cost millions of dollars to litigate, requiring expensive lawyers and a large staff at WTO headquarters in Geneva. Few states in the global South can afford this legal process and therefore few use it to help their own industries knock down unfair barriers to trade. Recall that even if a state wins a WTO dispute, it gains only the right to place tariffs on the offending country's goods in an equal amount. For small states, this retaliation can inflict as much damage on their own economy as on the economy of the offending state.

To compensate for these inequities and to help third world states use trade to boost their economic growth, the WTO has a Generalized System of Preferences (see p. 323). These and other measures—such as the Lomé conventions in which EU states relaxed tariffs on third world goods—are exceptions to the overall rules of trade, intended to ensure that participation in world trade advances rather than impedes third world development.[30] Nonetheless, critics claim that third world states are the losers in the overall world trading regime.

In the past decade, a coalition of U.S. activist groups has accused the World Bank of supporting authoritarian regimes and underwriting huge infrastructure projects that displaced poor people. Critics allege that the Bank's portfolio of loans in the global South, totaling more than $100 billion, is more a hindrance than a help to true development. Bank officials respond that despite a few mistakes, the Bank and its mission are sound.

The tenuous position of the global South in international economic regimes reflects the role of power in IR. The global North, with nearly two-thirds of the world's wealth, clearly has more power—more effective leverage—than the South. The global disparity of power is accentuated by the fact that the South is split up into more than a hundred actors whereas the North's power is concentrated in eight large states (the G8 members). Thus, when the rules of the world economy were created after World War II, and as they

---

[30] Tussie, Diana, and David J. Glover, eds. *The Developing Countries in World Trade: Policies and Bargaining Strategies*. Boulder, CO: Lynne Rienner, 1993. Ravenhill, John. *Collective Clientelism: The Lomé Conventions and North-South Relations*. Columbia, 1985.

have been rewritten and adjusted over the years, the main actors shaping the outcome have been a handful of large industrialized states.

Countries in the South have responded in several ways to these problems with world economic regimes. In the 1970s, OPEC shifted the terms of trade for oil—bringing huge amounts of capital into the oil-exporting countries. Some third world states hoped such successes could be repeated for other commodities, resulting in broad gains for the global South, but these did not occur (see "Cartels" on pp. 330–332, and "Minerals, Land, Water" on pp. 435–437).

Also in the 1970s, many poor and middle-income states tried to form a broad political coalition to push for restructuring the world economy so as to make North-South economic transactions more favorable to the South. A summit meeting of the nonaligned movement (see pp. 92–93) in 1973 first called for a **New International Economic Order (NIEO)**.[31] Central to the NIEO was a shift in the terms of trade to favor primary commodities relative to manufactured goods. The NIEO proposal also called for the promotion of industrialization in the global South, and for increased development assistance from the North.

The NIEO never became much more than a rallying cry for the global South, partly because of the South's lack of power and partly because disparities within the South created divergent interests among states there. In the 1980s, the terms of trade further deteriorated for raw material exporters, and economic development slowed down in much of the global South. But in China and some other Asian countries, development accelerated.

UNCTAD

Countries in the South continue to pursue proposals to restructure world trade to benefit the South. These efforts now take place mainly through the *UN Conference on Trade and Development (UNCTAD)*, which meets periodically but lacks power to implement major changes in North-South economic relations.[32] Attempts to promote South-South trade (reducing dependence on the North) have proven largely impractical. However, recently Brazil's President, visiting China in 2004, referred to Brazil-China trade, which quadrupled in 1999–2003, as "a paradigm for South-South cooperation."[33] And efforts continue to boost cooperation and solidarity in the global South through a variety of groups such as the nonaligned movement and the UN.[34] Nonetheless, such efforts have done little to change the South's reliance on assistance from the North.

Foreign Assistance

Foreign assistance (or *overseas development assistance*) is money or other aid made available to third world states to help them speed up economic development or simply meet basic humanitarian needs.[35] Along with the commercial economic activities just discussed (in-

---

[31] Murphy, Craig N. *The Emergence of the NIEO Ideology*. Boulder, CO: Westview, 1984. Galtung, Johan. *The North/South Debate: Technology, Basic Human Needs, and the New International Economic Order*. NY: Institute for World Order, 1980.

[32] Williams, Marc. *Third World Cooperation: The Group of 77 in UNCTAD*. NY: St. Martin's, 1991. Weiss, Thomas G. *Multilateral Development Diplomacy in UNCTAD*. NY: St. Martin's, 1986.

[33] Rohter, Larry. China Widens Economic Role in Latin America. *The New York Times*, Nov. 20, 2004: A1.

[34] Page, Shelia. *Regionalism Among Developing Countries*. NY: Palgrave, 2000. Folke, Steen, Niels Fold, and Thyge Enevoldsen. *South-South Trade and Development: Manufacturers in the New International Division of Labour*. NY: St. Martin's, 1993. Erisman, H. Michael. *Pursuing Postdependency Politics: South-South Relations in the Caribbean*. Boulder, CO: Lynne Rienner, 1992.

[35] O'Hanlon, Michael, and Carol Graham. *A Half Penny on the Federal Dollar: The Future of Development Aid*. Washington, DC: Brookings, 1997. Hook, Steven W. *National Interest and Foreign Aid*. Boulder, CO: Lynne Rienner, 1995. Lumsdaine, David H. *Moral Vision in International Politics: The Foreign Aid Regime, 1949–1989*. Princeton, 1993.

vestments and loans), foreign assistance is a second major source of money for third world development. It covers a variety of programs—from individual volunteers lending a hand to massive government packages.

Different kinds of development assistance have different purposes. Some are humanitarian, some are political, and others are intended to create future economic advantages for the giver (these purposes often overlap). The state or organization that gives assistance is called a *donor;* the state or organization receiving the aid is the *recipient.* Foreign assistance creates, or extends, a relationship between donor and recipient that is simultaneously political and cultural as well as economic.[36] Foreign assistance can be a form of power in which the donor seeks to influence the recipient, or it can be a form of interdependence in which the donor and recipient create a mutually beneficial exchange.

Patterns of Foreign Assistance

The majority of foreign assistance comes from governments in the North. Private donations provide a smaller amount, although sometimes a significant one. In 1997, for instance, Ted Turner pledged $1 billion for UN programs, George Soros contributed or pledged nearly $2 billion in aid to Russia and other countries (see p. 344), and Bill Gates's foundation contributes hundred of millions annually to world health campaigns.

Table 13.2 lists the major donors toward the $80 billion in governmental foreign assistance provided in 2004. More than 90 percent of government assistance comes from members of the **Development Assistance Committee (DAC),** consisting of states from Western Europe, North America, and Japan/Pacific. Several oil-exporting Arab countries provide some foreign development assistance and in 2003, transition economies became a net "exporter" of financial aid. Three-quarters of the DAC countries' government assistance goes directly to governments in the global South as state-to-state **bilateral aid;** the rest goes through the UN or other agencies as **multilateral aid.**

Taking on Global Poverty

The DAC countries have set themselves a goal to contribute 0.7 percent of their GNPs in foreign aid. But overall they give less than half this amount. Only Norway, Sweden, Denmark, the Netherlands, and Luxembourg meet the target. In fact, Oxfam International recently reported that industrialized countries' aid dropped from 0.48 percent of income in 1960–65 to 0.34 percent in 1980–85 and then to 0.24 percent in 2003.[37]

The United States gives the lowest percentage of GNP—less than two-tenths of 1 percent—of any of the 30 states of the industrialized West that make up the OECD. In total economic aid given (nearly $20 billion), the United States has recently regained the lead over Japan (which cut foreign aid sharply to below $9 billion). Germany, Britain, and France each give about $8 billion. U.S. foreign assistance dropped by nearly half from 1992 to 1995 though it has since grown back. This and other decreases brought the world total in foreign assistance down substantially in the 1990s. After the 2001 terrorist attacks, Britain proposed a $50 billion increase in foreign aid, nearly doubling current levels, to tackle poverty that breeds extremism, and the United States raised its aid budget sharply. In 2002, rock star Bono took U.S. Treasury Secretary Paul O'Neill on a two-week tour through Africa to argue for increased U.S. foreign assistance. O'Neill lost his job later that year, but the U.S. foreign aid budget rose by more than 15 percent a year in 2003–2005.

Foreign Aid

[36] Ensign, Margee M. *Doing Good or Doing Well? Japan's Foreign Aid Program.* Columbia, 1992. Bobrow, Davis B., and Mark A. Boyer. Bilateral and Multilateral Foreign Aid: Japan's Approach in Comparative Perspective. *Review of International Political Economy* 3 (1), 1996: 95–121.

[37] Oxfam International. *Paying the Price: Why Rich Countries Must Invest Now in a War on Poverty.* Oxford, UK, 2005, p.6.

TABLE 13.2 ■ Who's Helping?
Foreign Assistance, 2004

Donor	Assistance Given: Billion $	Assistance Given: % of GNP[a]
World total	80.0	0.2%
Total G7	57.6	0.2%
United States	19.7	0.2%
Japan	8.9	0.2%
France	8.5	0.4%
Germany	7.5	0.3%
Britain	7.9	0.4%
Italy	2.5	0.2%
Canada	2.6	0.3%
Netherlands	4.2	0.7%
Sweden	2.7	0.8%
Denmark	2.0	0.9%
Norway	2.2	0.9%
Other "North"	9.2	
Arab Countries	2.0	

[a]GNP not calculated at purchasing-power parity.

Source: United Nations, *World Economic Situation and Prospects 2005.* NY: United Nations, 2005. p. 160. UN estimates based on OECD data; governmental aid only.

Types of Aid Bilateral aid takes a variety of forms. *Grants* are funds given free to a recipient state, usually for some stated purpose. *Technical cooperation* refers to grants given in the form of expert assistance in some project rather than just money or goods. *Credits* are grants that can be used to buy certain products from the donor state. For instance, the United States regularly gives credits that can be used for purchases of U.S. grain. If people in a recipient country become accustomed to products from the donor state, they are likely to buy those same products in the future.

Loans are funds given to help in economic development, which must be repaid in the future out of the surplus generated by the development process (they too are often tied to the purchase of products from the donor state). Unlike commercial loans, government-to-government development loans are often on concessionary terms, with long repayment times and low interest rates. Although still an obligation for the recipient country, such loans are relatively easy to service.

Loan guarantees, which are used only occasionally, are promises by the donor state to back up commercial loans to the recipient. If the recipient state services such debts and ultimately repays them, there is no cost to the donor. But if the recipient cannot make the payments, the donor has to step in and cover the debts. A loan guarantee allows the recipient state to borrow money at lower interest from commercial banks (because the risk to the bank is much lower).

Military aid is not normally included in development assistance, but in a broad sense belongs there. It is money that flows from North to South, from government to government, and it does bring a certain amount of value into the economies of the global South. If a country is going to have a certain size army with certain weapons, getting them free from a donor state frees up money that can be used elsewhere in the economy. However, of all the forms of development assistance, military aid is certainly one of the least efficient and most prone to impede rather than help economic development. It is also geared almost exclusively to political alliances rather than actual development needs.

The main agency dispensing U.S. foreign economic assistance (but not military aid) is the State Department's *Agency for International Development (USAID)*, which works mainly through the U.S. embassy in each recipient country. Major recipients of U.S. foreign aid include Israel, Egypt, and Turkey—all important strategic allies in the volatile Middle East. Like other great powers, the United States uses the promise of foreign aid, or the threat of cutting it off, as a leverage in political bargaining with recipients. For example, when Pakistan proceeded in the late 1980s with a nuclear weapons program, despite U.S. warnings, a sizable flow of U.S. aid was terminated. Then when Pakistan supported U.S. military action in next-door Afghanistan in 2001, U.S. aid was restored. The United States has sometimes cut off foreign aid to protest human rights violations by the military.

SEND HELP!

Governments provide more than $50 billion annually in foreign assistance, and private donors more than $10 billion more. In the West, the United States gives the least foreign aid as a percentage of GDP, despite recent increases. Governments' efforts over years to better coordinate their aid contributions allowed an unprecedented outpouring of relief—billions of dollars—to reach the survivors of the December 2004 tsunami in the Indian Ocean. Experts hoped aid efforts would continue long-term after the crisis disappeared from the headlines. Here, fishermen in Sri Lanka assess the tsunami damage.

The U.S. **Peace Corps** provides U.S. volunteers for technical development assistance in third world states. They work at the request and under the direction of the host state but are paid an allowance by the U.S. government. Started by President Kennedy in 1961, the Peace Corps now sends about 7,700 volunteers to 72 countries, where they participate in projects affecting about a million people. It is a small-scale program, but one that increases person-to-person contacts.

WEB LINK

Peace Corps

In foreign aid, the donor must have the permission of the recipient government to operate in the country. This goes back to the principle of national sovereignty and the history of colonialism. National governments have the right to control the distribution of aid and the presence of foreign workers on their soil. Only occasionally is this principle violated, as when the United States and its allies provided assistance to Iraqi Kurds against the wishes of the Iraqi government following the Gulf War. International norms may be starting to change in this regard, with short-term humanitarian assistance starting to be seen as a human right that should not be subject to government veto.

UN Programs Most of the multilateral development aid goes through *UN programs*. The place of these programs in the UN structure is described in Chapter 7 (see pp. 257–259). The overall flow of assistance through the UN is coordinated by the **UN Development Program (UNDP),** which manages 5,000 projects at once around the world (focusing especially on technical development assistance). Other UN programs focus on concentrating capital, transferring technology, and developing work force skills for manufacturing. UNIDO works on industrialization, UNITAR on training and research. But most UN programs—such as UNICEF, UNFPA, UNESCO, WHO, and others—focus on meeting basic needs.

UN programs have three advantages in promoting economic development. One is that governments and citizens tend to perceive the UN as a friend of the global South, not an alien force, a threat to sovereignty, or a reminder of colonialism. The UN can sometimes mobilize technical experts and volunteers from other third world countries so that people who arrive to help do not look like white European colonialists. A team of Egyptian medical workers under a UN program may be more easily accepted in an African country than French or British workers, however well intentioned.

Second, UN workers may be more likely to make appropriate decisions because of their backgrounds. UN workers who come from the global South or have worked in other poor countries in a region may be more sensitive to local conditions and to the pitfalls of development assistance than are aid workers from rich countries.

A third advantage is that the UN can organize its assistance on a global scale, giving priority to projects and avoiding duplication and the reinvention of the wheel in each state. For some issues—such as the fight against AIDS or the integration of development objectives with environmental preservation—there is no substitute for global organization.

A major disadvantage faced by UN development programs is that they are funded largely through voluntary contributions by rich states. Each program has to solicit contributions to carry on its activities, so the contributions can be abruptly cut off if the program displeases a donor government (see p. 443). Also, governments that pledge aid may not follow through. For instance, the UN complained in early 2005 that only 5 percent of the $500 million pledged for southern Sudan by the international community five months earlier had actually been paid. A second major disadvantage of UN programs is their reputation for operating in an inefficient, bureaucratic manner, without the cohesion and the resources that governments and MNCs in the North take for granted.

The Disaster Relief Model

The remainder of this chapter discusses three models of development assistance, distinguished by the type of assistance rather than the type of donor (all three models encompass both government and private aid). The three overlap in real life.

UN ReliefWeb

First is the disaster relief model. It is the kind of foreign assistance given when poor people are afflicted by famine, drought, earthquakes, flooding, or other such natural disasters. (War is also a disaster and can compound naturally occurring disasters.) When disaster strikes a poor state, many people are left with no means of subsistence and often without their homes. **Disaster relief** is the provision of short-term relief to such people in the form of food, water, shelter, clothing, and other essentials.

Disaster relief is very important because disasters can wipe out years of progress in economic development in a single blow. Generally, the international community tries to respond with enough assistance to get people back on their feet. The costs of such assistance are relatively modest, the benefits visible and dramatic. Having a system of disaster relief in place provides the global South with a kind of insurance against sudden losses that could otherwise destabilize economic accumulation.

Disasters generally occur quickly and without much warning. Rapid response is difficult to coordinate. International disaster relief has become more organized and better coordinated in the past decade but is still a complex process that varies somewhat from one situation to the next. Contributions of governments, private charitable organizations, and other groups and agencies are coordinated through the *UN Office of the Disaster Relief Coordinator (UNDRO)* in Geneva. In 2006, the UN set up a $500 million fund to enable it to respond quickly to disasters without waiting to raise funds first each time disaster strikes. Typically, international contributions make up no more than about one-third of the total relief effort, the remainder coming from local communities and national governments in the affected states. The U.S. government's contributions are coordinated by the *Office of Foreign Disaster Assistance (OFDA)*, which is part of USAID.

Disaster relief is something of a collective good because the states of the North do not benefit individually by contributing, yet they benefit in the long run from greater stability in the South. Despite this problem and the large number of actors, disaster relief is generally a positive example of international cooperation to get a job done. Food donated by the World Council of Churches may be carried to the scene in U.S. military aircraft and then distributed by the *International Committee of the Red Cross (ICRC)*. Embarrassing failures in the past—of underresponse or overresponse, of duplication of efforts or agencies working at cross-purposes—became rarer in the 1990s, and in the new century groups coordinate their actions effectively.[38]

The newfound success of the international community in coordinating relief efforts was evident after the December 2004 tsunami disaster in Asia. Within hours, millions lost family members, homes, possessions, safe drinking water, and ways of life. The World Health Organization estimated that 5 million people lacked basic supplies. The world community's response began quite modestly, but after the full extent of the disaster was beamed around the globe and the death toll climbed to staggering numbers, aid poured in to the region. More than $7 billion was pledged by states, IOs, and private citizens across the globe.

Both IOs and NGOs quickly mobilized to carry out what has been termed the "largest relief effort in human history." The efforts by these organizations were coordinated through a variety of relief agencies, including the International Committee of the Red Cross, the International Organization for Migration, the UNHCR, and Oxfam. Initially, it appeared as though the United States would coordinate its own relief efforts apart from the UN. President Bush reconsidered this position, however, and the United States ceded the lead role in relief to the UN. This somewhat spontaneous coordination of states, IOs, and NGOs seems contrary to the anarchical international system. Whether the cooperation between these actors will extend beyond the tsunami relief effort remains to be seen.

The relationship of disasters with economic development is complex, and appropriate responses vary according to location, type and size of disaster, and phase of recovery.[39] For instance, refugees displaced from their home communities have different needs from those of earthquake or hurricane victims whose entire communities have been damaged. Different resources are needed in the emergency phase (for example, food and medical supplies) than in the reconstruction phase (for example, earthquake-resistant housing designs). Responses that are too small in scale or too short-term may fail to meet critical needs, but those that are too large or prolonged can overwhelm the local economy and create dependency (reducing incentives for self-help). Thus, appropriate disaster relief can

---

[38] Maynard, Kimberly A. *Healing Communities in Conflict: International Assistance in Complex Emergencies*. Columbia, 1999.

[39] Anderson, Mary B., and Peter J. Woodrow. *Rising from the Ashes: Development Strategies in Times of Disaster*. Boulder, CO: Westview, 1989. Cuny, Frederick C. *Disasters and Development*. Oxford, 1983.

promote local economic development, whereas inappropriate responses can distort or impede such development.

International norms regarding states' legal obligations to assist others in time of natural disaster and to accept such assistance if needed are changing.[40] In the 1990s—designated by the UN as the International Decade for Natural Disaster Reduction—a new international regime in this area began solidifying, and it passed its biggest test with the tsunami of 2004.

The Missionary Model

Beyond disaster relief, many governments and private organizations provide ongoing development assistance in the form of projects administered by agencies from the North in local communities in the South to help meet basic needs. Although such efforts vary, one could call the approach a *missionary* model because it reflects the kind of charitable work long performed by missionaries in poor countries. In fact, many private programs are still funded by churches and carried out by missionaries. Often such assistance is considered "God's work." In contrast to the disaster relief model, "missionary" relief tends to be more sustained, not just rushing in to respond and then jumping out again (as inevitably happens in disaster relief mode). Most foreign aid falls into this category, since it includes typical ongoing government-to-government assistance. The government form however has its own strengths (large sums of money) and weaknesses (politicization of aid; corruption).

Such charitable programs are helpful though not without problems. They are a useful means by which people in the North funnel resources to people in the South. Even during the colonial era, missionaries did much good despite sometimes perpetuating stereotypes of European superiority and native inferiority. Today's efforts to help poor people in third world states give local individuals and communities, as well as governments, resources with which they may better contribute to national economic development. However, many handout programs provide only short-term assistance and do not create sustained local economic development. They do not address the causes of poverty, the position of poor countries in the world economy, or the local political conditions such as military rule or corruption. For example, one version of "missionary" assistance—advertised widely in the United States—lets citizens in rich countries "adopt" poor children in the global South. Photos of a hungry child stare at the reader from a magazine page while the accompanying text notes that a few cents a day can "save" the child. Although such programs raise awareness in the North of the extent of poverty in the South, at worst they tend to be exploitive and to reinforce racist and paternalistic stereotypes of the helplessness of people in the global South.

Such problems were evident in the political fight in the United States in 2005 over how to get food aid to hungry people in Africa. U.S. law requires that such food be grown in the United States and shipped to Africa in U.S. vessels. The Bush Administration proposed using U.S. funds to buy food locally in Africa, which would save a lot of money, get aid to the hungry months faster, and help African farmers. But the proposal was opposed by the so-called Iron Triangle of food aid—U.S. agribusiness that profits from selling the food to the government, U.S. shipping companies that profit from shipping it, and U.S. charities (including CARE and Catholic Relief Services) that fund a

[40] Toman, Jiri. Towards a Disaster Relief Law: Legal Aspects of Disaster Relief Operations. In Frits Kalshoven, ed. *Assisting the Victims of Armed Conflict and Other Disasters*. Dordrecht, Netherlands: Martinus Nijhoff, 1989.

healthy fraction of their budgets by selling in Africa some of the grain they ship from the United States. The charities, by becoming international grain merchants and flooding local markets with cheap food (both sold and given away), compete with local farmers and drive down local prices, harming long-term recovery. Yet, because of the Iron Triangle's lobbying power, Congress killed off the proposal to allow purchase of food locally in Africa.

There is a danger in the missionary model—including in large-scale governmental aid—that people from the North may provide assistance inappropriate for a third world state's local conditions and culture. This danger is illustrated by an experience in Kenya in the 1970s. Nomadic herders in the area of Lake Turkana near the Sahara desert—the Turkana tribe—were poor and vulnerable to periodic droughts. Western aid donors and the Kenyan government decided that the herders' traditional way of life was not environmentally sustainable and should be replaced by commercial fishing of the abundant tilapia fish in Lake Turkana. Norway, with long experience in fishing, was asked to teach fishing and boat-building methods to the Turkana. To create a commercially viable local economy, Norwegian consultants recommended marketing frozen fish fillets to Kenya and the world. Thus in 1981 Norway finished building a $2 million, state-of-the-art fish freezing plant on the shores of Lake Turkana and a $20 million road connecting the plant to Kenya's transportation system.

MOUTHWASH FOR MAURITANIA

The missionary model of foreign assistance contributes goods to third world economies, but often with little understanding of local needs or long-term strategies. Here, free supplies including cartons of mouthwash are delivered by the U.S. ambassador and the captain of a U.S. Navy ship participating in Project Handclasp, 1989.

There were only three problems. First, with temperatures of 100 degrees outside (a contrast with Norway!), the cost of operating the freezers exceeded the income from the fillets. So after a few days the freezers were turned off and the facility became a dried-fish warehouse. Second, Turkana culture viewed fishing as the lowest-status profession, suitable only for those incompetent at herding. Third, every few decades Lake Turkana shrinks as drought reduces the inflow of water. Such a drought in 1984–1985 eliminated the gulf where the fishing operations were based. The Norwegians might have foreseen these problems by doing more homework instead of just transplanting what worked in Norway. When the drought hit, the 20,000 herders who had been brought to the lake to learn fishing were left in an overcrowded, overgrazed environment in which every tree was cut for firewood and most cattle died. Instead of becoming self-sufficient, the Turkana people became totally dependent on outside aid.[41]

[41] Harden, Blaine. *Africa: Dispatches from a Fragile Continent*. NY: Norton, 1990.

The Oxfam Model

WEB LINK

Oxfam

A third model of development assistance can be found in the approach taken by the private charitable group **Oxfam America** (one of seven groups worldwide descended from the Oxford Committee for Famine Relief, founded in 1942 in Britain). Originally devoted to short-term aid to famine victims, and still active in that effort, Oxfam America realized that over the longer term people needed not just handouts of food but the means to feed themselves—land, water, seed, tools, and technical training.

The distinctive aspect of the Oxfam model is that it relies on local communities to determine the needs of their own people and to carry out development projects. Oxfam does not operate projects itself but provides funding to local organizations. Nor does Oxfam call itself a donor and these organizations recipients. Rather, it calls both sides "project partners"—working together to accomplish a task. In this model, a little outside money can go a long way toward building sustained local economic development. Furthermore, projects help participants empower themselves by organizing to meet their own needs.

For example, Oxfam America helped the Ethiopian women's cooperative mentioned on p. 481. Oxfam did not design or organize the project; women in Addis Ababa did. But when their garment-making workshop became profitable and was ready to expand and employ twice as many women, Oxfam gave the group a $15,000 grant to build a new building. This small grant helped to consolidate a new center of accumulation in one of the world's poorest neighborhoods.

The relationship between North and South—groups such as Oxfam and their project partners—is likened to a good marriage where decisions are made jointly and dependency does not develop. In this model, third world economic development is not charity; it is in the interests of people in the rich countries as well as the poor. A cooperative relationship between North and South is essential for a peaceful and prosperous world. Even in a narrow economic sense, development in the global South creates new markets and new products that will enrich the industrialized countries as well. In economics, the creation of wealth is a positive-sum game.

PARTNER IN DEVELOPMENT

The Oxfam model of foreign assistance emphasizes support for local groups that can stimulate self-sustaining economic development at a local level. A mutually beneficial North-South partnership is the global goal of such projects. These women show off a mill they purchased with microcredit from an Oxfam-affiliated group in Gambia, 2001.

The Oxfam approach seeks to reconceptualize development assistance to focus on long-term development through a bottom-up basic needs strategy. "Genuine development," in Oxfam's view, "enables people to meet their essential needs; extends beyond food aid and emergency relief; reverses the process of impoverishment; enhances democracy; makes possible a balance between populations and resources; improves the well-being and status of women; respects local cultures; sustains the natural environment; measures progress in human, not just monetary terms; involves change, not just charity; requires the empowerment of the poor;

and promotes the interests of the majority of people worldwide, in the global North as well as the South."[42]

To promote its approach to North-South relations (and to raise funds for its project partners), Oxfam America carries on education and action programs in the United States. The most prominent is an annual Fast for a World Harvest, a week before Thanksgiving, that raises awareness among U.S. citizens about the extent and causes of third world hunger. Participants at "hunger banquets" are assigned randomly to one of three groups: 15 percent eat an elaborate gourmet meal, 25 percent get a modest meal of rice and beans, and 60 percent eat a small portion of rice and water. Thanks to the information revolution (see Chapter 10), information about third world poverty and economic development is now more widely available to people in industrialized countries.

Because of disappointment with the political uses of foreign aid in the past, Oxfam has tried to minimize the role in its projects of governments in both the North and South. For instance, Oxfam does not accept government funds nor does it make grants to governments.

The general goals of the Oxfam model of foreign aid are consistent with a broader movement in the global South toward grassroots **empowerment.** Efforts such as those of Oxfam partners are organized by poor people to gain some power over their situation and meet their basic needs—not by seizing control of the state in a revolution but by means that are more direct, more local, and less violent. The key to success is getting organized, finding information, gaining self-confidence, and obtaining needed resources to implement action plans.

For example, women in Bangladesh have a very low status in rural society (see "Women in Development" on pp. 480–481). Often they cannot own property, participate in politics, or even leave their houses without their husbands' permission. Now some women in rural Bangladesh have organized women's groups to raise self-esteem, promote their rights, and mobilize them to change conditions. One woman reported: "Our husbands used to beat us—now they don't. They used to not let us in the fields—now we go with them. They used to not help us at home—now they do. . . . We now can do all this thanks to the group and the support it has given us."[43] In this example, economic development and the satisfaction of basic needs have been furthered not by violence or revolution, nor by the actions of the state, foreign governments, or international agencies, but directly at the community level.

In India, local women's groups using only the power of persuasion and logic have convinced some landowners to give them land for cooperative income-generating projects such as vegetable farming and raising silkworms. Elsewhere in India, women working as gatherers of wood and other forest products got organized to win the legal minimum wage for 250,000 female forest workers—three times what they had been paid before. In this case, government action was necessary, but the pressure for such action came from local organizing. The women took their case to the public and the press, staging protest marches and getting an art exhibit relating to their cause displayed in the provincial capital.

Such examples do not mean that national and foreign governments are unimportant. On the contrary, government policies affect millions of people more quickly and more widely than do grassroots efforts. Indeed, grassroots organizing often has as an ultimate goal the restructuring of national political and social life so that policies reflect the needs of poor people. But the successes of grassroots empowerment show that poor communities can be more than victims of poverty waiting to be saved or passive bystanders in North-South

---

[42] *Oxfam America News* [quarterly]. Boston: Oxfam America.

[43] Oxfam America. *Community* [video]. Boston: Oxfam, 1995.

relations. Nor do poor people need to place their hopes for change in violent revolutions aimed at toppling national governments—revolutions that lead to greater suffering more often than to stable economic development.

The Oxfam model has the advantage of promoting this trend toward grassroots empowerment, thereby overcoming the dangers of externally run programs under the disaster relief and missionary models. Also, Oxfam's building of long-term local partnerships paid off after the 2004 tsunami when these relationships let Oxfam effectively use $12 million in Internet contributions that materialized in two weeks.

However, the Oxfam model to date has been tested on only a very small scale. Although the model may be effective in the local communities it reaches, it would have to be adopted widely and replicated on a much larger scale in order to influence the overall prospects for development. In the case of both short- and long-term assistance to survivors of the 2004 tsunami, Oxfam's $12 million compares with about fifty times that amount pledged by the U.S. government. It is unclear whether the principles the model embodies, from a reliance on local community organizers to an avoidance of government involvement, would work on a massive scale. A model that bypasses governments also bypasses the majority of money spent for foreign aid globally.

Confronting the North-South Gap All three models of development assistance have contributions to make. Given the extent of its poverty, the global South needs all the help from the North that it can get. Perhaps the most important point is that people in the North become aware of the tremendous gap between North and South and try to address the problem. Third world poverty can seem so overwhelming that citizens in rich countries can easily turn their backs and just try to live their own lives.

But in today's interdependent world this really is not possible. North-South relations have become a part of everyday life. The integrated global economy brings to the North products and people from the South. The information revolution puts images of third world poverty on TV sets in comfortable living rooms. The growing role of the UN brings North and South together in a worldwide community. Security relations and political economy alike have shifted in the post–Cold War era to give new prominence to the global South.

THINKING CRITICALLY

1. How might the strong economic growth of the Asian NICs and of China affect proposals for an Asian free trade area similar to NAFTA and the EU? What would be the interests and worries of Japan, of China and the NICs, and of the poor states of the region, in such an arrangement?
2. Past successes in economic development have depended heavily on developing a manufacturing base, which requires access to scarce capital. How do you think the information revolution and the increasing role of services in the world economy might change this pattern? Might any countries in the global South find a niche in these growing sectors of the world economy and bypass manufacturing? What states or regions might be candidates for such an approach, and why?
3. How does the global South's debt problem compare with the U.S. debt, discussed in Chapter 9, in magnitude and effect? Do the two debt problems arise from similar causes? Which of them do you consider the more serious problem, and why?

4. Some scholars criticize the IMF for imposing harsh terms in its conditionality agreements with poor states. Others applaud the IMF for demanding serious reforms before providing financial resources. If you were a leader negotiating with the IMF, what kinds of terms would you be willing to agree to and what terms would you resist? Why?
5. If the states in North America, Western Europe, and Japan/Pacific all met the target of providing 0.7 percent of GNP in foreign assistance, what might the effects be? How much additional aid would be made available? To whom would it likely go? What effects might it have on the recipient states and on third world economic development overall?

CHAPTER SUMMARY

- Economic development in the global South has been uneven; per capita GDP increased in the 1970s but, except in Asia, decreased in the 1980s. Growth in the 1990s was brisk in Asia but slow elsewhere, with parts of Africa sliding backwards. The 2001 recession created further obstacles for development, but robust growth has returned since 2003.
- Evidence does not support a strong association of economic growth either with internal equality of wealth distribution or with internal inequality.
- The newly industrializing countries (NICs) in Asia—South Korea, Taiwan, Hong Kong, and Singapore—show that it is possible to rise out of poverty into sustained economic accumulation. Other third world states are trying to emulate these successes, but it is unclear whether these experiences can apply elsewhere.
- China has registered strong economic growth in the past 25 years of market-oriented economic reforms. Though still poor, China is the leading success story in economic development.
- Economic development in other large third world countries such as India, Brazil, and Nigeria has been slowed by the inefficiency of state-owned enterprises, by corruption, and by debt.
- Import substitution has been largely rejected as a development strategy in favor of export-led growth. This reflects both the experiences of the NICs and the theory of comparative advantage.
- Most poor states want to develop a manufacturing base, but this is a difficult thing to do. Even when focused on low-capital industries, states have generally had to sharpen income disparities in the process of concentrating capital for manufacturing.
- The theory that democratization would accompany and strengthen economic development has not been supported by the actual experiences of third world countries. But the opposite theory—that authoritarian government is necessary to maintain control while concentrating capital for industrialization—has also not been supported.
- Government corruption is a major obstacle to development throughout the global South.
- Given the shortage of local capital in most poor states, foreign investment by MNCs is often courted as a means of stimulating economic growth. MNCs look for favorable local conditions, including political and economic stability, in deciding where to invest.
- States in the global South seek the transfer of technology to support their future economic development. Technology transfer can be appropriate or inappropriate to local needs depending on the circumstances of each case.

- The green revolution of the 1960s was a massive North-South transfer of agricultural technology, which had both good and bad effects. Today's "green" technologies being transferred to the global South are techniques for environmentally sustainable development.
- Third world debt, resulting largely from overborrowing in the 1970s and early 1980s, is a major problem. Through renegotiations and other debt management efforts, the North and South have improved the debt situation in recent years. However, the South remains almost $2 trillion in debt to the North, and annual debt service consumes about one-sixth of all hard-currency earnings from exports of the South (much more in some regions and states).
- The IMF makes loans to states in the South conditional on economic and governmental reforms. These conditionality agreements often necessitate politically unpopular measures such as cutting food subsidies.
- The WTO trading regime works against the global South by allowing richer nations to protect sectors in which the global South has advantages—notably agriculture and textiles. The Generalized System of Preferences (GSP) tries to compensate by lowering barriers to third world exports.
- Efforts to improve the South's solidarity, cooperation, and bargaining position relative to the North—such as the New International Economic Order (NIEO)—have had little success.
- Foreign assistance, most of it from governments in the North, plays an important part in the economic development plans of the poorer states of the South.
- Only a few states in the North meet the goal of contributing 0.7 percent of their GNPs as foreign assistance to the South. The United States, at 0.1 percent of its GNP, contributes the smallest share of any industrialized state, and its contributions decreased sharply in the past decade.
- Most foreign aid consists of bilateral grants and loans from governments in the North to specific governments in the South. Such aid is often used for political leverage, and promotes the export of products from the donor state.
- About one-fifth of foreign aid is not bilateral but is funneled through multilateral agencies—mostly UN programs.
- Disaster relief provides short-term aid to prevent a natural disaster from reversing a poor state's economic development efforts. Disaster relief generally involves cooperation by various donor governments, local governments, the UN, and private agencies.
- Handouts to poor communities to meet immediate needs for food and supplies outside times of disaster—here called the missionary model—can be helpful but also have several drawbacks. Such aid can be inappropriate to local needs and can encourage dependence.
- Efforts to support local organizations working to empower poor people and generate community economic development—here called the Oxfam model—are promising but have been tried only on a small scale.

KEY TERMS

economic development 497
newly industrializing countries (NICs) 499
"four tigers"/"four dragons" 500
free economic zone 502
import substitution vs. export-led growth 508
terms of trade 509
informal sector 510
microcredit 510
brain drain 516
technology transfer 516
green revolution 517
debt service 518
default vs. debt renegotiation 518
Paris Club, London Club 519
IMF conditionality 520
New International Economic Order (NIEO) 524
foreign assistance 524
Development Assistance Committee (DAC) 525
bilateral and multilateral aid 525
Peace Corps 527
UN Development Program (UNDP) 528
disaster relief 528
Oxfam America 532
empowerment 533

ONLINE PRACTICE TEST

Take an online practice test at
www.internationalrelations.net

❑ A
❑ B
☑ C
❑ D

LET'S DEBATE THE ISSUE

Capitalism and Democracy in the Developing World: Do They Facilitate or Undermine Development?

by Mir Zohair Husain

Overview Following the collapse of the Soviet Union, Francis Fukuyama, a senior analyst in the U.S. State Department, announced the triumph of capitalism and democracy over all other economic and political systems. Economically, capitalism promotes private ownership of the means of production, distribution, and exchange; is profit oriented; and discourages governmental control or interference in the economy. Politically, democracy emphasizes leaders elected by the citizens; civil liberties (such as freedom of speech, assembly, and religion); civil rights (equal opportunities and justice); majority rule; and minority rights.

Proponents believe that capitalism creates economic growth to combat poverty, while democracy ends oppression suffering and the need for war by facilitating an open exchange of ideas. Countries such as the United States, South Korea, India, and Taiwan demonstrate the successful socioeconomic and political development possible through capitalism and democracy.

However, many economists contend that lifting protectionist policies will actually hurt the economies of developing countries. Furthermore, they argue that rising capitalist countries, such as Mexico and South Korea, are succeeding precisely because they protected their domestic industries in their infant stages. Moreover, absolute majority rule would be politically destabilizing to the South. In these situations, the poor majority might wield the political power, but remain economically deprived, resulting in the majority resenting a wealthy minority (often an ethnic minority) that dominates the country's economy. Such situations often result in conflict, instability, and bloodshed, rather than peace, liberty, and justice.

These issues continue to dominate the world stage. Following his reelection in November 2004, U.S. President George W. Bush has periodically reiterated America's commitment to promoting economic and political freedom. Will developing countries adopt capitalism and democracy only to find a hollow promise filled with more misery? Or will capitalism and democracy allow the South to share in the good fortune enjoyed by much of the West?

Argument 1 Capitalism and Democracy Create Progress and Prosperity

Capitalism promotes stability and progress through economic modernization. Globalization contributes to the spread of capitalism and democracy. These Western ideas promote a more peaceful and prosperous world.

> No two countries that both had McDonald's had fought a war against each other since each got its McDonald's. . . . [However,] globalization does not end geopolitics.
>
> Today's version of globalization—with its economic integration, digital integration, its ever-widening connectivity of individuals and nations, its spreading of capitalist values and networks to the remotest corners of the world. . . . increases the incentives for not making war and increases the costs of going to war in more ways than in any previous era in modern history. (Thomas L. Friedman. *The Lexus and the Olive Tree*, 1999. pp. 383, 387–8.)

Democracy offers a nonviolent political alternative. Many citizens of nondemocratic governments who lack a voice in their own country's determination become frustrated with their government's failure to meet their fundamental needs. Consequently, they find extremist groups appealing. Democracy, however, provides the institutions and values essential to people suffering from relative deprivation and humiliation.

[D]emocracy is no panacea, nor is anything else . . .

"Democratic governments in the Middle East are going to be much more difficult for the United States to handle because there will be more direct expression of sentiment, much of it hostile," said Rashid Khalidi, a professor of Middle Eastern studies at Columbia University. "But in the end it will be healthier and, yes, democracy could provide an outlet for the frustration that drives people to jihadism."

For many years, Islamism seemed the only such outlet. (Roger Cohen. "What's in It for America?" *The New York Times*, March 6, 2005.)

Even if capitalism and democracy are flawed, the alternatives are much worse. Critics of capitalism and democracy have not offered an alternative solution to the South's ills that simultaneously reaps the same rewards obtained now. Despite any shortcomings, capitalism and democracy are the best solutions that we have.

> . . . three big ideas now dominate global politics: The first is peace as a way of organizing international relations. The second idea that has triumphed is the notion that free markets are the best way for nations to grow from poverty to prosperity. And the third is that democracy is the ideal form of political organization. . . . To be sure, these ideas are not practiced everywhere, but they are far more powerful and attractive than any other ideas and have no serious rivals today. (Thomas L. Friedman. "Going Our Way." *The New York Times*, September 15, 2002.)

Argument 2 Capitalism and Democracy: Greed and Disorder

Capitalism institutionalizes economic inequality. Countries in the South converting to laissez-faire capitalism typically are unable to compete with developed countries, resulting in increasing inequality. Moreover, capitalist principles do not drive the more resourceful countries of the North to increase foreign assistance, both of which would help alleviate poverty in the South. Therefore, capitalism fosters an international indifference to the economically disadvantaged.

> Economic globalization [, the current form of capitalism,] has thus become a formidable cause of inequality among and within states, and the concern for global competitiveness limits the aptitude of states and other actors to address this problem. (Stanley Hoffmann. "Clash of Globalizations." *Foreign Affairs*, 81 (4) July/August 2003, pp. 107–8).

Democracy cannot guarantee freedom and prosperity for all developing countries. Democracy cannot be simply exported to the South. Indeed, democracy does have some prerequisites: Western democratic states had some distinct advantages, such as the Renaissance and the Reformation, established infrastructures, high literacy rates, and no population problems. In addition to countless democratic failures in the South, democracies in some states would actually make those countries even more unstable.

> Mr. Zakaria, the editor of *Newsweek International*, [writes] democracy can sometimes mean the accumulation of [power] by an electorate that is little more than a mob. An example is his native India, where Hindu politicians pursue the "rhetoric of hatred," which has led to "the ethnic cleansing of tens of thousands" simply because it appeals to so many anti-Muslim voters. He provides this cautionary note: "The Arab rulers of the Middle East are autocratic, corrupt and heavy-handed. But they are still more liberal, tolerant and pluralistic than what would likely replace them. Elections in many Arab countries would produce politicians who espouse views that are closer to Osama bin Laden's than those of Jordan's liberal monarch, King Abdullah." (Robert D. Kaplan. "Here's Your Vote; Liberty Can Wait." *The New York Times*, April 10, 2003.)

Developing countries with capitalism and genuine democracy breed ethnic conflicts. Promoting capitalism and democracy in the South may increase market-dominant minorities, which allow a minority ethnic group—not just an economic class—to gain disproportionately more than the poorer, majority ethnic group. Hence, capitalism and democracy create "an engine of ethnic nationalism, pitting a frustrated indigenous majority, easily aroused by demagogic politicians, against a resented, wealthy ethnic minority."[a]

> . . . democratization, by increasing the political voice and power of the "indigenous" majority, has fostered the emergence of demagogues—like Zimbabwe's Mugabe, Serbia's Milosevic, Russia's Zyuganov, Bolivia's Great Condor, and Rwanda's Hutu Power leaders—who opportunistically whip up mass hatred against the resented [market-dominant] minority, demanding that the country's wealth be returned to the "true owners of the nation." As a result, . . . [the West's global promotion of] free market democracy [has led] to ethnic confiscation, authoritarian backlash, and mass killing. (Amy Chua. *World on Fire*, NY: Doubleday. 2003, pp. 187–8.)

Questions

WEB LINK

Capitalism and Democracy

1. Should countries in the South embrace capitalism and democracy? Explain. What alternate system(s) would you suggest? Why?
2. Are the political and economic systems of a country given too much credit or blame, respectively, for the status of their country and people? What other features of a society could explain the level of success a country experiences?

Selected Readings

Amy Chua. *World on Fire.* NY: Doubleday, 2003.

Michael Mandelbaum. *The Ideas That Conquered the World: Peace, Democracy, and Free Markets in the Twenty-First Century.* NY: Public Affairs/Perseus, 2003.

---

[a]Amy Chua. "Power to the Privileged." *The New York Times*, January 7, 2003.

■ Soldier and child, Sarajevo, 1993.

CHAPTER 14

Postscript

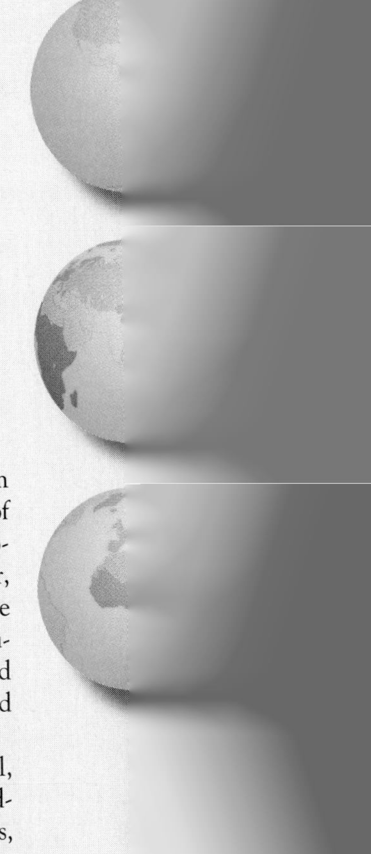

Ultimately the conflicts and dramas of international relations are little different from those of other spheres of political and social life. The problems of IR are the problems of human society—struggles for power and wealth, efforts to cooperate despite differences, social dilemmas and collective goods problems, the balance between freedom and order, trade-offs of equity versus efficiency and of long-term versus short-term outcomes. These themes are inescapable in human society, from the smallest groups to the world community. The subject of international relations is in this sense an extension of everyday life and a reflection of the choices of individual human beings. IR belongs to all of us—North and South, women and men, citizens and leaders—who live together on this planet.

Technological development is just one aspect of the profound, yet incremental, changes taking place in international relations. New actors are gaining power, longstanding principles are becoming less effective, and new challenges are arising for states, groups, and individuals alike. The post–Cold War era, a little more than a decade old, remains undefined. Will it, like past postwar eras, lapse slowly into the next prewar era, or will it lead to a robust and lasting "permanent peace"?

Consider a few aspects of these changes that this book has discussed. One major theme of the book was the nature of the international system as a well-developed set of rules based on state sovereignty, territoriality, and "anarchy"—a lack of central government. Yet, the international system is becoming more complex, more nuanced, and more interconnected with other aspects of planetary society. State sovereignty is now challenged by the principle of self-determination. International norms have begun to limit the right of government to rule a population by force against its will and to violate human rights. Territorial integrity is also problematical, since national borders do not stop information, environmental changes, or missiles. Information allows actors—state, substate, and supranational—to know what is going on everywhere in the world to coordinate actions globally.

Technology is also profoundly changing the utility and role of military force. The power of defensive weaponry makes successful attacks more difficult, and the power of offensive weaponry makes retaliation an extremely potent threat to deter an attack. The twentieth-century superpowers could not attack each other without destroying themselves, and a large force cannot reliably defeat a small one (or, to be more accurate, the costs of doing so are too high), as demonstrated by the United States in Vietnam and the Soviets in Afghanistan. Nonmilitary forms of leverage, particularly economic rewards, have become much more important power capabilities.

In IPE, we see simultaneous trends toward integration and disintegration among states. People continue to speak their own language, to fly their own flag, to use their own currency with its pictures and emblems. Nationalism continues to be an important force. At the same time, however, although people identify with their state, they also now hold competing identities based on ethnic ties, gender, and (in the case of Europe) region. In international trade, liberal economics prevails because it works so well. States have learned that in order to survive they must help, not impede, the creation of wealth by MNCs and other economic actors.

Environmental damage may become the single greatest obstacle to sustained economic growth in both the North and South (a trend presaged by Soviet-bloc environmental degradation, which contributed to that region's economic stagnation and collapse.) Because of high costs, the large number of actors, and collective goods problems, international bargaining over the environment is difficult. However, the 1992 Earth Summit's call for sustainable economic growth that does not deplete resources and destroy ecosystems may be supported by new technology that moves information, instead of materials, to accomplish the same goals. The traditional technological style of industrialization cannot be sustained environmentally on the giant scale of countries like China and India.

North-South relations meanwhile are moving to the center of world politics. Demographic and economic trends are sharpening the global North-South gap, with the North continuing to accumulate wealth while much of the South lingers in great poverty. Ultimately, the North will bear a high cost for failing to address the economic development of the South. Perhaps, by using computerization and biotechnology innovations, poor states can develop their economies much more efficiently than did Europe or North America.

The future is unknowable now, but as it unfolds you can compare it—at mileposts along the way—to the worlds that you desire and expect. The comparison of alternative futures may be facilitated by examining a variety of possible branch points where alternative paths diverge. For example, you could ask questions such as the following (asking yourself, for each one, why you answer the way you do for your desired future and expected future):

1. Will state sovereignty be eroded by supranational authority?
2. Will norms of human rights and democracy become global?
3. Will the UN evolve into a quasi-government for the world?
4. Will the UN be restructured?
5. Will World Court judgments become enforceable?
6. Will the number of states increase?
7. Will China become democratic? Will it become rich?
8. What effects will information technologies have on IR?
9. Will weapons of mass destruction proliferate?
10. Will military leverage become obsolete?
11. Will disarmament occur?
12. Will women participate more fully in IR? With what effect?
13. Will there be a single world currency?
14. Will there be a global free trade regime?
15. Will nationalism fade out or continue to be strong?
16. Will many people develop a global identity?
17. Will world culture become more homogeneous or more pluralistic?
18. Will the EU or other regional IOs achieve political union?
19. Will global environmental destruction be severe? How soon?
20. Will new technologies avert environmental constraints?
21. Will global problems create stronger or weaker world order?
22. Will population growth level out? If so, when and at what level?
23. Will the poorest countries accumulate wealth? How soon?
24. What role will the North play in the South's development?

The choices you make and actions you take will ultimately affect, in some way, the world you live in. You cannot opt out of involvement in international relations. You are involved, and year by year the information revolution and other aspects of interdependence are drawing you more closely into contact with the rest of the world. You can act in many ways, large and small, to bring the world you expect more into line with the world you desire. You can empower yourself by finding the actions and choices that define your place in international relations.

Now that you have completed the studies covered in this book, don't stop here. Keep learning about the world beyond your country's borders. Keep thinking about the world that might exist. Be a part of the changes that will carry this world through the coming decades. It's your world: study it, care for it, make it your own.

Glossary

acid rain Caused by air pollution, it damages trees and often crosses borders. Limiting acid rain (via limiting nitrogen oxide emissions) has been the subject of several regional agreements. (p. 429)

airspace The space above a state that is considered its territory, in contrast to outer space, which is considered international territory. (p. 180)

alliance cohesion The ease with which the members hold together an alliance; it tends to be high when national interests converge and when cooperation among allies becomes institutionalized. (p. 86)

Amnesty International An influential nongovernmental organization that operates globally to monitor and try to rectify glaring abuses of political (not economic or social) human rights. (p. 289)

anarchy In IR theory, the term implies not complete chaos but the lack of a central government that can enforce rules. (p. 73)

Antarctic Treaty (1959) One of the first multilateral treaties concerning the environment, it forbids military activity in Antarctica as well as the presence of nuclear weapons or the dumping of nuclear waste there, sets aside territorial claims on the continent for future resolution, and establishes a regime for the conduct of scientific research. (p. 429)

Antiballistic Missile (ABM) Treaty (1972) It prohibited either the United States or the Soviet Union from using a ballistic missile defense as a shield, which would have undermined mutually assured destruction and the basis of deterrence. (p. 244) See also *mutually assured destruction (MAD)* and *Strategic Defense Initiative (SDI)*.

arms race A reciprocal process in which two (or more) states build up military capabilities in response to each other. (p. 68)

autarky (self-reliance) A policy of avoiding or minimizing trade and trying to produce everything one needs (or the most vital things) by oneself. (p. 313)

balance of payments A summary of all the flows of money in and out of a country. It includes three types of international transactions: the current account (including the merchandise trade balance), flows of capital, and changes in reserves. (p. 352)

balance of power The general concept of one or more states' power being used to balance that of another state or group of states. The term can refer to (1) any ratio of power capabilities between states or alliances, (2) a relatively equal ratio, or (3) the process by which counterbalancing coalitions have repeatedly formed to prevent one state from conquering an entire region. (p. 76)

balance of trade The value of a state's exports relative to its imports. (p. 310)

ballistic missiles The major strategic delivery vehicles for nuclear weapons; they carry a warhead along a trajectory (typically rising at least 50 miles high) and let it drop on the target. (p. 233) See also *intercontinental ballistic missiles (ICBMs)*.

bargaining Tacit or direct communication that is used in an attempt to reach agreement on an exchange of value. (p. 62)

basic human needs The fundamental needs of people for adequate food, shelter, health care, sanitation, and education. Meeting such needs may be thought of as both a moral imperative and a form of investment in "human capital" essential for economic growth. (p. 474)

bilateral aid Government assistance that goes directly to the third world governments as state-to-state aid. (p. 525)

biodiversity The tremendous diversity of plant and animal species making up the earth's (global, regional, and local) ecosystems. (p. 422)

Biological Weapons Convention (1972) It prohibits the development, production, and possession of biological weapons, but makes no provision for inspections. (p. 237)

blue helmets The UN peacekeeping forces, so called because they wear helmets or berets in the UN color, blue, with UN insignia. (p. 266)

bourgeoisie In Marxist terminology, the class of owners of capital—people who make money from their investments rather than from their labor. (p. 461) See also *proletariat*.

brain drain Poor countries' loss of skilled workers to rich countries. (p. 516)

Bretton Woods system A post–World War II arrangement for managing the world economy, established at a meeting in Bretton Woods, New Hampshire, in 1944. Its main institutional components are the World Bank and the International Monetary Fund (IMF). (p. 349)

burden sharing The distribution of the costs of an alliance among members; the term also refers to the conflicts that may arise over such distribution. (p. 86)

capital accumulation The creation of standing wealth (capital) such as buildings, roads, factories, and so forth; such accumulation depends on investment and the creation of an economic surplus. (p. 458)

capitalism An economic system based on private ownership of capital and the means of production (standing wealth and other forms of property). (p. 459) See also *socialism*.

carrying capacity The limits of the planetary ecosystem's ability to absorb continual growth of population, industry, energy use, and extraction of natural resources. (p. 416)

cartel An association of producers or consumers (or both) of a certain product, formed for the purpose of manipulating its price on the world market. (p. 330)

cash crops Agricultural goods produced as commodities for export to world markets. (p. 478)

central bank An institution common in industrialized countries whose major tasks are to maintain the value of the state's currency and to control inflation. (p. 348)

centrally planned (command) economy An economy in which political authorities set prices and decide on quotas for production and consumption of each commodity according to a long-term plan. (p. 306)

chain of command A hierarchy of officials (often civilian as well as military) through which states control military forces. (p. 220)

Chemical Weapons Convention (1992) It bans the production and possession of chemical weapons, and includes strict verification provisions and the threat of sanctions against violators and against nonparticipants in the treaty. (p. 237)

Chernobyl A city in Ukraine that was the site of a 1986 meltdown at a Soviet nuclear power plant. (p. 431)

civil war A war between factions within a state trying to create, or prevent, a new government for the entire state or some territorial part of it. (p. 201)

class struggle The process in which the more powerful classes oppress and exploit the less powerful by denying them their fair share of the surplus they create. The oppressed classes try to gain power, to rebel, and to organize in order to seize more of the wealth for themselves. (p. 461)

Cold War The hostile relations—punctuated by occasional periods of improvement, or détente—between the two superpowers, the United States and the U.S.S.R., from 1945 to 1990. (p. 41)

collective goods problem A collective good is a tangible or intangible good, created by the members of a group, that is available to all group members regardless of their individual contributions; participants can gain by lowering their own contribution to the collective good, yet if too many participants do so, the good cannot be provided. (p. 103) See also *free riders*.

collective security The formation of a broad alliance of most major actors in an international system for the purpose of jointly opposing aggression by any actor; sometimes seen as presupposing the existence of a universal organization (such as the United Nations) to which both the aggressor and its opponents belong. (p. 106) See also *League of Nations*.

Commission on Sustainable Development An organization established at the 1992 UN Earth Summit that monitors states' compliance with their promises and hears evidence from environmental nongovernmental organizations (NGOs). (p. 417)

Common Agricultural Policy (CAP) A European Union policy based on the principle that a subsidy extended to farmers in any member country should be extended to farmers in all member countries. (p. 382)

common market A zone in which labor and capital (as well as goods) flow freely across borders. (p. 382)

Commonwealth of Independent States (CIS) The loose coordinating structure linking the former republics of the Soviet Union (except the Baltic states) since 1991. (p. 44)

comparative advantage The principle that says states should specialize in trading those goods that they produce with the greatest relative efficiency and at the lowest relative cost (relative, that is, to other goods produced by the same state). (p. 303)

compellence The use of force to make another actor take some action (rather than, as in deterrence, refrain from taking an action). (p. 67)

Comprehensive Test Ban Treaty (CTBT) (1996) It bans all nuclear weapons testing, thereby broadening the ban on atmospheric testing negotiated in 1963. (p. 245)

conditionality See *IMF conditionality*.

conflict A difference in preferred outcomes in a bargaining situation. (p. 169)

conflict and cooperation The types of actions that states take toward each other through time. (p. 5)

conflict resolution The development and implementation of peaceful strategies for settling conflicts. (p. 125)

constructivism A movement in IR theory that examines how changing international norms and actor's identities help shape the content of state interests. (p. 119)

consumption goods Goods whose consumption does not contribute directly to production of other goods and services, unlike some forms of investment. (p. 459)

containment A policy adopted in the late 1940s by which the United States sought to halt the global expansion of Soviet influence on several levels—military, political, ideological, and economic. (p. 41)

convertible currency The guarantee that the holder of a particular currency can exchange it for another currency. Some states' currencies are nonconvertible. (p. 341) See also *hard currency*.

core The manufacturing regions of the world-system. (p. 464)

cost-benefit analysis A calculation of the costs incurred by a possible action and the benefits it is likely to bring. (p. 68)

Council of Ministers A European Union institution in which the relevant ministers (foreign, economic, agriculture, finance, etc.) of each member state meet to enact legislation and reconcile national interests. When the meeting takes place among the state leaders it is called the "European Council." (p. 384) See also *European Commission*.

counterinsurgency An effort to combat guerrilla armies, often including programs to "win the hearts and minds" of rural populations so that they stop sheltering guerrillas. (p. 202)

coup d'état French for "blow against the state," it refers to the seizure of political power by domestic military forces—that is, a change of political power outside the state's constitutional order. (p. 222)

crimes against humanity A category of legal offenses created at the Nuremberg trials after World War II to encompass genocide and other acts committed by the political and military leaders of the Third Reich (Nazi Germany). (p. 288) See also *dehumanization* and *genocide*.

cruise missile A small winged missile that can navigate across thousands of miles of previously mapped terrain to reach a particular target; it can carry either a nuclear or a conventional warhead. (p. 234)

Cuban Missile Crisis (1962) A superpower crisis, sparked by the Soviet Union's installation of medium-range nuclear missiles in Cuba, that marks the moment when the United States and the Soviet Union came closest to nuclear war. (p. 42)

cultural imperialism A critical term for U.S. dominance of the emerging global culture. (p. 401)

customs union A common external tariff adopted by members of a free trade area; that is, participating states adopt a unified set of tariffs with regard to goods coming in from outside. (p. 382) See also *free trade area.*

cycle theories An effort to explain tendencies toward war in the international system as cyclical; for example, by linking wars with long waves in the world economy (Kondratieff cycles). (p. 172)

debt renegotiation A reworking of the terms on which a loan will be repaid; frequently negotiated by third world debtor governments in order to avoid default. (p. 518)

debt service An obligation to make regular interest payments and repay the principal of a loan according to its terms, which is a drain on many third world economies. (p. 518)

default The failure to make scheduled debt payments. (p. 518)

dehumanization Stigmatization of enemies as subhuman or nonhuman, leading frequently to widespread massacres or worse. (p. 190) See also *crimes against humanity* and *genocide.*

democracy A government of "the people," usually through elected representatives, and usually with a respect for individual rights in society (especially rights to hold political ideas differing from those of the government). (p. 160)

democratic peace The proposition, strongly supported by empirical evidence, that democracies almost never fight wars against each other (although they do fight against authoritarian states). (p. 161)

demographic transition The pattern of falling death rates, followed by falling birthrates, that generally accompanies industrialization and economic development. (p. 440)

dependency theory A Marxist-oriented theory that explains the lack of capital accumulation in the third world as a result of the interplay between domestic class relations and the forces of foreign capital. (p. 472) See also *enclave economy.*

deterrence The threat to punish another actor if it takes a certain negative action (especially attacking one's own state or one's allies). (p. 67) See also *mutually assured destruction (MAD).*

devaluation A unilateral move to reduce the value of a currency by changing a fixed or official exchange rate. (p. 347) See also *exchange rate.*

developing countries States in the global South, the poorest regions of the world—also called third world countries, less-developed countries, and undeveloped countries. (p. 455)

Development Assistance Committee (DAC) A committee whose members—consisting of states from Western Europe, North America, and Japan/Pacific—provide 95 percent of official development assistance to countries of the global South. (p. 525) See also *foreign assistance.*

difference feminism A strand of feminism that believes gender differences are not just socially constructed and that views women as inherently less warlike than men (on average). (p. 110)

diplomatic immunity Refers to diplomats' activity being outside the jurisdiction of the host country's national courts. (p. 282)

diplomatic recognition The process by which the status of embassies and that of an ambassador as an official state representative are explicitly defined. (p. 281)

direct foreign investment See *foreign direct investment.*

disaster relief The provision of short-term relief in the form of food, water, shelter, clothing, and other essentials to people facing natural disasters. (p. 528)

discount rate The interest rate charged by governments when they lend money to private banks. The discount rate is set by countries' central banks. (p. 348)

Doha Round A series of negotiations under the World Trade Organization that began in Doha, Qatar in 2001. It followed the *Uruguay Round* and focused on agricultural subsidies, intellectual property, and other issues. (p. 324)

dumping The sale of products in foreign markets at prices below the minimum level necessary to make a profit (or below cost). (p. 315)

economic base A society's mode of production, such as slavery, feudalism, or capitalism. (p. 462)

economic class A categorization of individuals based on economic status. (p. 461)

economic conversion The use of former military facilities and industries for new civilian production. (p. 215)

economic development The combined processes of capital accumulation, rising per capita incomes (with consequent falling birthrates), the increasing of skills in the population, the adoption of new technological styles, and other related social and economic changes. (p. 497)

economic surplus Made by investing money in productive capital rather than using it for consumption. (p. 458)

electronic warfare The use of the electromagnetic spectrum (radio waves, radar, infrared, etc.) in war, such as employing electromagnetic signals for one's own benefit while denying their use to an enemy. (p. 229)

empowerment In the development context, it refers to the grassroots efforts of poor people to gain power over their situation and meet their basic needs. (p. 533)

enclave economy An historically important form of dependency in which foreign capital is invested in a third world country to extract a particular raw material in a particular place—usually a mine, oil well, or plantation. (p. 472) See also *dependency theory*.

enclosure (of the commons) The splitting of a common area or good into privately owned pieces, giving individual owners an incentive to manage resources responsibly. (p. 414)

epistemic communities Transnational communities of experts who help structure the way states manage environmental and other issues. (p. 415)

ethnic cleansing Forced displacement of an ethnic group or groups from a particular territory, accompanied by massacres and other human rights violations; it has occurred after the breakup of multinational states, notably in the former Yugoslavia. (p. 176)

ethnic groups Large groups of people who share ancestral, language, cultural, or religious ties and a common identity. (p. 185)

ethnocentrism (in-group bias) The tendency to see one's own group (in-group) in favorable terms and an out-group in unfavorable terms. (p. 190)

Euratom Created in the Treaty of Rome in 1957 to coordinate nuclear power development by pooling research, investment, and management. (p. 381)

euro Also called the ECU (European currency unit), the euro is a single European currency used by 12 members of the European Union (EU). (p. 387)

European Commission A European Union body whose members, while appointed by states, are supposed to represent EU interests. Supported by a multinational civil service in Brussels, the Commission's role is to identify problems and propose solutions to the Council of Ministers. (p. 383) See also *Council of Ministers*.

European Court of Justice A judicial arm of the European Union, based in Luxembourg. The Court has actively established its jurisdiction and its right to overrule national law when it conflicts with EU law. (p. 384)

European Parliament A quasi-legislative body of the European Union that operates as a watchdog over the European Commission and has limited legislative power. (p. 384)

European Union (EU) The official term for the European Community (formerly the European Economic Community) and associated treaty organizations. The EU has 25 member states and is negotiating with other states that have applied for membership. (p. 380) See also *Maastricht Treaty*.

exchange rate The rate at which one state's currency can be exchanged for the currency of another state. Since 1973, the international monetary system has depended mainly on floating rather than fixed exchange rates. (p. 340) See also *convertibility*; *fixed exchange rates*; *Exchange Rate Mechanism (ERM)*; and *managed float*.

Exchange Rate Mechanism (ERM) A system that establishes nearly fixed exchange rates among European currencies while letting them all float freely relative to the rest of the world. (p. 343)

export-led growth An economic development strategy that seeks to develop industries capable of competing in specific niches in the world economy. (p. 508)

fiscal policy A government's decisions about spending and taxation, and one of the two major tools of macroeconomic policy making (the other being monetary policy). (p. 354)

fissionable material The elements uranium-235 and plutonium, whose atoms split apart and release energy via a chain reaction when an atomic bomb explodes. (p. 231)

fixed exchange rates The official rates of exchange for currencies set by governments; not a dominant mechanism in the international monetary system since 1973. (p. 342) See also *floating exchange rates.*

floating exchange rates The rates determined by global currency markets in which private investors and governments alike buy and sell currencies. (p. 342) See also *fixed exchange rates.*

foreign assistance Money or other aid made available to third world states to help them speed up economic development or meet humanitarian needs. Most foreign assistance is provided by governments and is called official development assistance (ODA). (p. 524) See also *Development Assistance Committee (DAC).*

foreign direct investment The acquisition by residents of one country of control over a new or existing business in another country. Also called *direct foreign investment.* (p. 352)

foreign policy process The process by which foreign policies are arrived at and implemented. (p. 139)

fossil fuels Oil, coal, and natural gas, burnt to run factories, cars, tractors, furnaces, electrical generating plants, and other things that drive an industrial economy. (p. 419)

"four tigers"/"four dragons" The most successful newly industrialized areas of East Asia: South Korea, Taiwan, Hong Kong, and Singapore. (p. 500)

free economic zones The southern coastal provinces of China that were opened to foreign investment and run on capitalist principles with export-oriented industries, in the 1980s and 1990s. (p. 502)

free riders Those who benefit from someone else's provision of a collective good without paying their share of costs. (p. 103) See also *collective goods problem.*

free trade The flow of goods and services across national boundaries unimpeded by tariffs or other restrictions; in principle (if not always in practice), free trade was a key aspect of Britain's policy after 1846 and of U.S. policy after 1945. (p. 35)

free trade area A zone in which there are no tariffs or other restrictions on the movement of goods and services across borders. (p. 381) See also *customs union.*

game theory A branch of mathematics concerned with predicting bargaining outcomes. Games such as Prisoner's Dilemma and Chicken have been used to analyze various sorts of international interactions. (p. 70)

gender gap Refers to polls showing women lower than men on average in their support for military actions, as well as for various other issues and candidates. (p. 114)

General Agreement on Tariffs and Trade (GATT) A world organization established in 1947 to work for freer trade on a multilateral basis; the GATT has been more of a negotiating framework than an administrative institution. It became the World Trade Organization (WTO) in 1995. (p. 322)

General Assembly See *UN General Assembly.*

Generalized System of Preferences (GSP) A mechanism by which some industrialized states began in the 1970s to give tariff concessions to third world states on certain imports; an exception to the most-favored nation (MFN) principle. (p. 323) See also *most-favored nation (MFN) concept.*

genocide The intentional and systematic attempt to destroy a national, ethnic, racial, or religious group, in whole or part. It was confirmed as a crime under international law by the UN Genocide Convention (1948). (p. 39) See also *crimes against humanity* and *dehumanization.*

geopolitics The use of geography as an element of power, and the ideas about it held by political leaders and scholars. (p. 61)

global culture Worldwide cultural integration based on a massive increase in satellite television, radio, and Internet communication. (p. 400)

globalization The increasing integration of the world in terms of communications, culture, and economics; may also refer to changing subjective experiences of space and time accompanying this process. (p. 300)

global warming A slow, long-term rise in the average world temperature caused by the emission of greenhouse gases produced by burning fossil fuels—oil, coal, and natural gas. (p. 418) See also *greenhouse gases.*

gold standard A system in international monetary relations, prominent for a century before the 1970s, in which the value of national currencies was pegged to the value of gold or other precious metals. (p. 340)

government bargaining model It sees foreign policy decisions as flowing from a bargaining process among various government agencies that have somewhat divergent interests in the outcome ("where you stand depends on where you sit"). Also called the "bureaucratic politics model." (p. 142)

great powers Generally, the half dozen or so most powerful states; the great-power club was exclusively European until the twentieth century. (p. 77) See also *middle powers.*

greenhouse gases Carbon dioxide and other gases that, when concentrated in the atmosphere, act like the glass in a greenhouse, holding energy in and leading to global warming. (p. 419)

green revolution The massive transfer of agricultural technology, such as high-yield seeds and tractors, to third world countries that began in the 1960s. (p. 517)

Gross Domestic Product (GDP) The size of a state's total annual economic activity. (p. 12)

groupthink The tendency of groups to validate wrong decisions by becoming overconfident and underestimating risks. (p. 147)

guerrilla war Warfare without front lines and with irregular forces operating in the midst of, and often hidden or protected by, civilian populations. (p. 202)

hard currency Money that can be readily converted to leading world currencies. (p. 341) See also *convertible currency.*

hegemonic stability theory The argument that regimes are most effective when power in the international system is most concentrated. (p. 105) See also *hegemony.*

hegemonic war War for control of the entire world order—the rules of the international system as a whole. Also known as world war, global war, general war, or systemic war. (p. 199)

hegemony The holding by one state of a preponderance of power in the international system, so that it can single-handedly dominate the rules and arrangements by which international political and economic relations are conducted. (p. 82) See also *hegemonic stability theory.*

high seas That portion of the oceans considered common territory, not under any kind of exclusive state jurisdiction. (p. 426) See also *territorial waters.*

home country The state where a multinational corporation (MNC) has its headquarters. (p. 365) See also *host country.*

host country A state in which a foreign multinational corporation (MNC) operates. (p. 365) See also *home country.*

human rights Rights of all persons to be free from abuses such as torture or imprisonment for their political beliefs (political and civil rights), and to enjoy certain minimum economic and social protections (economic and social rights). (p. 287)

hyperinflation An extremely rapid, uncontrolled rise in prices, such as occurred in Germany in the 1920s and some third world countries more recently. (p. 341)

idealism An approach that emphasizes international law, morality, and international organization, rather than power alone, as key influences on international relations. (p. 55) See also *realism.*

IMF conditionality An agreement to loan IMF funds on the condition that certain government policies are adopted. Dozens of third world states have entered into such agreements with the IMF in the past two decades. (p. 520) See also *International Monetary Fund (IMF).*

immigration law National laws that establish the conditions under which foreigners may travel and visit within a state's territory, work within the state, and sometimes become citizens of the state (naturalization). (p. 280)

imperialism The acquisition of colonies by conquest or otherwise. Lenin's theory of imperialism argued that European capitalists were investing in colonies where they could earn big profits, and then using part of those profits to buy off portions of the working class at home. (p. 463)

import substitution A strategy of developing local industries, often conducted behind protectionist barriers, to produce items that a country had been importing. (p. 508)

industrialization The use of fossil-fuel energy to drive machinery and the accumulation of such machinery along with the products created by it. (p. 35)

industrial policy The strategies by which a government works actively with industries to promote their growth and tailor trade policy to their needs. (p. 317)

infant mortality rate The proportion of babies who die within their first year of life. (p. 443)

infantry Foot soldiers who use assault rifles and other light weapons (mines, machine guns, and the like). (p. 225)

informal sector Those modes of business, such as black markets and street vendors, operating beyond state control; some scholars see this sector as the core of a new development strategy. (p. 510)

information screens The subconscious or unconscious filters through which people put the information coming in about the world around them. (p. 145) See also *misperceptions and selective perceptions*.

intellectual property rights The legal protection of the original works of inventors, authors, creators, and performers under patent, copyright, and trademark law. Such rights became a contentious area of trade negotiations in the 1990s. (p. 318)

intercontinental ballistic missiles (ICBMs) The longest-range ballistic missiles, able to travel 5,000 miles. (p. 233) See also *ballistic missiles*.

interdependence A political and economic situation in which two states are simultaneously dependent on each other for their well-being. The degree of interdependence is sometimes designated in terms of "sensitivity" or "vulnerability." (p. 311)

interest groups Coalitions of people who share a common interest in the outcome of some political issue and who organize themselves to try to influence the outcome. (p. 153)

intergovernmental organizations (IGOs) Organizations (such as the United Nations and its agencies) whose members are state governments. (p. 14)

International Committee of the Red Cross (ICRC) A nongovernmental organization (NGO) that provides practical support, such as medical care, food, and letters from home, to civilians caught in wars and to prisoners of war (POWs). Exchanges of POWs are usually negotiated through the ICRC. (p. 285)

International Court of Justice See *World Court*.

International Criminal Court (ICC) Permanent tribunal for war crimes and crimes against humanity. (p. 284)

international integration The process by which supranational institutions come to replace national ones; the gradual shifting upward of some sovereignty from the state to regional or global structures. (p. 377)

International Monetary Fund (IMF) An intergovernmental organization (IGO) that coordinates international currency exchange, the balance of international payments, and national accounts. Along with the World Bank, it is a pillar of the international financial system. (p. 349) See also *conditionality*.

international norms The expectations held by participants about normal relations among states. (p. 252)

international organizations (IOs) They include intergovernmental organizations (IGOs) such as the UN, and nongovernmental organizations (NGOs) such as the International Committee of the Red Cross (ICRC). (p. 254)

international political economy (IPE) The study of the politics of trade, monetary, and other economic relations among nations, and their connection to other transnational forces. (p. 5)

international regime A set of rules, norms, and procedures around which the expectations of actors converge in a certain international issue area (such as oceans or monetary policy). (p. 104)

international relations (IR) The relationships among the world's state governments and the connection of those relationships with other actors (such as the United Nations, multinational corporations, and individuals), with other social relationships (including economics, culture, and domestic politics), and with geographic and historical influences. (p. 3)

international security A subfield of international relations (IR) that focuses on questions of war and peace. (p. 5)

international system The set of relationships among the world's states, structured by certain rules and patterns of interaction. (p. 11)

International Whaling Commission An intergovernmental organization (IGO) that sets quotas for hunting certain whale species; states' participation is voluntary. (p. 423)

investment Putting surplus wealth into capital-producing activities rather than consuming it, to produce long-term benefits. (p. 459)

Iran-Contra scandal An episode in which the Reagan administration secretly sold weapons to Iran in exchange for the freedom of U.S. hostages held in Lebanon, and then used the Iranian payments to illegally fund Nicaraguan Contra rebels. (p. 148)

irredentism A form of nationalism whose goal is the regaining of territory lost to another state; it can lead directly to violent interstate conflicts. (p. 174)

Islam, Muslims A broad and diverse world religion whose divergent populations include Sunni Muslims, Shi'ite Muslims, and many smaller branches and sects, practiced by Muslims, from Nigeria to Indonesia, centered in the Middle East. (p. 192)

issue areas Distinct spheres of international activity (such as global trade negotiations) within which policy makers of various states face conflicts and sometimes achieve cooperation. (p. 4)

just war doctrine A branch of international law and political theory that defines when wars can be justly started (*jus ad bellum*) and how they can be justly fought (*jus in bello*). (p. 286) See also *war crimes*.

Keynesian economics The principles articulated by British economist John Maynard Keynes, used successfully in the Great Depression of the 1930s, including the view that governments should sometimes use deficit spending to stimulate economic growth. (p. 354)

land mines Concealed explosive devices, often left behind by irregular armies, which kill or maim civilians after wars end. Such mines number more than 100 million, primarily in Angola, Bosnia, Afghanistan, and Cambodia. A movement to ban land mines is underway; nearly 100 states have agreed to do so. (p. 225)

land reform Policies that aim to break up large land holdings and redistribute land to poor peasants for use in subsistence farming. (p. 479)

lateral pressure (theory of) It holds that the economic and population growth of states fuels geographic expansion as they seek natural resources beyond their borders, which in turn leads to conflicts and sometimes to war. (p. 182)

League of Nations Established after World War I and a forerunner of today's United Nations, the organization achieved certain humanitarian and other successes but was weakened by the absence of U.S. membership and by its own lack of effectiveness in ensuring collective security. (p. 37) See also *collective security*.

less-developed countries (LDCs) The world's poorest regions—the global South—where most people live; are also called underdeveloped countries, or developing countries. (p. 455)

liberal feminism A strand of feminism that emphasizes gender equality and views the "essential" differences in men's and women's abilities or perspectives as trivial or nonexistent. (p. 110)

liberalism (economic liberalism) In the context of IPE, an approach that generally shares the assumption of anarchy (the lack of a world government) but does not see this condition as precluding extensive cooperation to realize common gains from economic exchanges. It emphasizes absolute over relative gains and, in practice, a commitment to free trade, free capital flows, and an "open" world economy. (p. 298) See also *mercantilism* and *neoliberalism*.

limited war Military actions that seek objectives short of the surrender and occupation of the enemy. (p. 201)

London Club See *Paris Club*.

Maastricht Treaty Signed in the Dutch city of Maastricht and ratified in 1992, the treaty commits the European Union to monetary union (a single currency and European Central Bank) and to a common foreign policy. (p. 385) See also *European Union (EU)*.

malnutrition The lack of needed foods including protein and vitamins; about 10 million children die each year from malnutrition-related causes. (p. 477) See also *undernourishment*.

managed float A system of occasional multinational government interventions in currency markets to manage otherwise free-floating currency rates. (p. 343)

Marxism A branch of socialism that emphasizes exploitation and class struggle and includes both communism and other approaches. (p. 460) See also *socialism*.

mediation The use of a third party (or parties) in conflict resolution. (p. 125)

mercantilism An economic theory and a political ideology opposed to free trade; it shares with realism the belief that each state must protect its own interests without seeking mutual gains through international organizations. (p. 298) See also *liberalism*.

microcredit The use of very small loans to small groups of individuals, often women, to stimulate economic development. (p. 510)

middle powers States that rank somewhat below the great powers in terms of their influence on world affairs (for example, Brazil and India). (p. 79) See also *great powers*.

migration Movement between states, usually emigration from the old state and immigration to the new state. (p. 481)

militarism The glorification of war, military force, and violence. (p. 127)

military governments States in which military forces control the government; most common in third world countries, where the military may be the only large modern institution. (p. 222)

military-industrial complex A huge interlocking network of governmental agencies, industrial corporations, and research institutes, all working together to promote and benefit from military spending. (p. 154)

misperceptions and selective perceptions The selective or mistaken processing of the available information about a decision; one of several ways—along with affective and cognitive bias—in which individual decision making diverges from the rational model. (p. 145) See also *information screens*.

Missile Technology Control Regime A set of agreements through which industrialized states try to limit the flow of missile-relevant technology to third world states. (p. 236)

mixed economies Economies such as those in the industrialized West that contain both some government control and some private ownership. (p. 308)

monetary policy A government's decisions about printing and circulating money, and one of the two major tools of macroeconomic policy making (the other being fiscal policy). (p. 354)

Montreal Protocol (1987) An agreement on protection of the ozone layer in which states pledged to reduce and then eliminate use of chlorofluorocarbons (CFCs). It is the most successful environmental treaty to date. (p. 422)

most-favored nation (MFN) concept The principle that one state, by granting another state MFN status, promises to give it the same treatment given to the first state's most-favored trading partner. (p. 323) See also *Generalized System of Preferences (GSP)*.

multilateral aid Government foreign aid from several states that goes through a third party, such as the UN or another agency. (p. 525)

multinational corporations (MNCs) Companies based in one state with affiliated branches or subsidiaries operating in other states. (p. 362) See also *home country* and *host country*.

multipolar system An international system with typically five or six centers of power that are not grouped into alliances. (p. 80)

Munich Agreement A symbol of the failed policy of appeasement, this agreement, signed in 1938, allowed Nazi Germany to occupy a part of Czechoslovakia. Rather than appease German aspirations, it was followed by further German expansions, which triggered World War II. (p. 37)

mutually assured destruction (MAD) The possession of second-strike nuclear capabilities, which ensures that neither of two adversaries could prevent the other from destroying it in an all-out war. (p. 242) See also *deterrence*.

national debt The amount a government owes in debt as a result of deficit spending. (p. 356)

national interest The interests of a state overall (as opposed to particular parties or factions within the state). (p. 68)

nationalism The identification with and devotion to the interests of one's nation. It usually involves a large group of people who share a national identity and often a language, culture, or ancestry. (p. 32)

nation-states States whose populations share a sense of national identity, usually including a language and culture. (p. 11)

negotiation The process of formal bargaining, usually with the parties talking back and forth across a table. (p. 63)

neocolonialism The continuation, in a former colony, of colonial exploitation without formal political control. (p. 472)

neofunctionalism The theory which holds that economic integration (functionalism) generates a "spillover" effect, resulting in increased political integration. (p. 379)

neoliberalism Shorthand for "neoliberal institutionalism," an approach that stresses the importance of international institutions in reducing the inherent conflict that realists assume in an international system; the reasoning is based on the core liberal idea that seeking long-term mutual gains is often more rational than maximizing individual short-term gains. (p. 135) See also *liberalism*.

neorealism A version of realist theory that emphasizes the influence on state behavior of the system's structure, especially the international distribution of power. (p. 80) See also *realism*.

New International Economic Order (NIEO) A third world effort begun in the mid-1970s, mainly conducted in UN forums, to advocate restructuring of the world economy so as to make North-South economic transactions less unfavorable to the South. (p. 524)

newly industrializing countries (NICs) Third world states that have achieved self-sustaining capital accumulation, with impressive economic growth. The most successful are the "four tigers" or "four dragons" of East Asia: South Korea, Taiwan, Hong Kong, and Singapore. (p. 499)

nonaligned movement Movement of third world states, led by India and Yugoslavia, that attempted to stand apart from the U.S.-Soviet rivalry during the Cold War. (p. 92)

nongovernmental organizations (NGOs) Transnational groups or entities (such as the Catholic Church, Greenpeace, and the International Olympic Committee) that interact with states, multinational corporations (MNCs), other NGOs and intergovernmental organizations (IGOs). (p. 13)

Non-Proliferation Treaty (NPT) (1968) It created a framework for controlling the spread of nuclear materials and expertise, including the International Atomic Energy Agency (IAEA), a UN agency based in Vienna that is charged with inspecting the nuclear power industry in NPT member states to prevent secret military diversions of nuclear materials. (p. 240)

nonstate actors Actors other than state governments that operate either below the level of the state (that is, within states) or across state borders. (p. 13)

nontariff barriers Forms of restricting imports other than tariffs, such as quotas (ceilings on how many goods of a certain kind can be imported). (p. 315)

nonviolence/pacifism A philosophy based on a unilateral commitment to refrain from using any violent forms of leverage. More specifically, pacifism refers to a principled opposition to war in general rather than simply to particular wars. (p. 132)

normative bias The personal norms and values that IR scholars bring to their studies, such as a preference for peace rather than war. (p. 125)

norms (of behavior) The shared expectations about what behavior is considered proper. (p. 74)

North American Free Trade Agreement (NAFTA) A free trade zone encompassing the United States, Canada, and Mexico since 1994. (p. 327)

North Atlantic Treaty Organization (NATO) A U.S.-led military alliance, formed in 1949 with mainly West European members, to oppose and deter Soviet power in Europe. It is currently expanding into the former Soviet bloc. (p. 87) See also *Warsaw Pact*.

North-South gap The disparity in resources (income, wealth, and power) between the industrialized, relatively rich countries of the West (and the former East) and the poorer countries of Africa, the Middle East, and much of Asia and Latin America. (p. 17)

oil shocks The two sharp rises in the world price of oil that occurred in 1973–1974 and 1979. (p. 433)

optimizing Picking the very best option; contrasts with satisficing, or finding a satisfactory but less than best solution to a problem. The model of "bounded rationality" postulates that decision makers generally "satisfice" rather than optimize. (p. 146)

organizational process model A decision-making model in which policy makers or lower-level officials rely largely on standardized responses or standard operating procedures. (p. 142)

Organization of Petroleum Exporting Countries (OPEC) The most prominent cartel in the international economy; its members control about half the world's total oil exports, enough to significantly affect the world price of oil. (p. 330)

Oxfam America A private charitable group that works with local third world communities to determine the needs of their own people and to carry out development projects. Oxfam does not operate the projects but provides funding to local organizations to carry them out. (p. 532)

ozone layer The part of the atmosphere that screens out harmful ultraviolet rays from the sun. Certain chemicals used in industrial economies break the ozone layer down. (p. 421)

Paris Club A group of first world governments that have loaned money to third world governments; it meets periodically to work out terms of debt renegotiations. Private creditors meet as the London Club. (p. 519)

Peace Corps Started by President John Kennedy in 1961, it provides U.S. volunteers for technical development assistance in third world states. (p. 527)

peace movements Movements against specific wars or against war and militarism in general, usually involving large numbers of people and forms of direct action such as street protests. (p. 131)

periphery The third world regions of the world-system that mostly extract raw materials from their area. (p. 464)

positive peace A peace that resolves the underlying reasons for war; not just a cease-fire but a transformation of relationships, including elimination or reduction of economic exploitation and political oppression. (p. 130) See also *structural violence*.

postmodern feminism An effort to combine feminist and postmodernist perspectives with the aim of uncovering the hidden influences of gender in IR and showing how arbitrary the construction of gender roles is. (p. 110)

postmodernism An approach that denies the existence of a single fixed reality, and pays special attention to texts and to discourses—that is, to how people talk and write about a subject. (p. 121)

power The ability or potential to influence others' behavior, as measured by the possession of certain tangible and intangible characteristics. (p. 57)

power projection The ability to use military force in areas far from a country's region or sphere of influence. (p. 226)

prisoners of war (POWs) Soldiers who have surrendered (and who thereby receive special status under the laws of war). (p. 285)

proletariat In Marxist terminology, the class of workers who must sell their labor power to capitalists in order to survive and whose labor is needed to produce surplus value; more specifically, industrial factory workers. It was considered the class that would spearhead the socialist revolution. (p. 462) See also *bourgeoisie*.

proliferation The spread of weapons of mass destruction (nuclear, chemical, or biological weapons) into the hands of more actors. (p. 238)

pronatalist policy A government policy that encourages or forces childbearing, and outlaws or limits access to contraception. (p. 442)

prospect theory A decision-making theory that holds that options are assessed by comparison to a reference point, which is often the status quo but might be some past or expected situation. The model also holds that decision makers fear losses more than they value gains. (p. 147)

protectionism The protection of domestic industries against international competition, by trade tariffs and other means. (p. 314)

proxy wars Wars in the third world—often civil wars—in which the United States and the Soviet Union jockeyed for position by supplying and advising opposing factions. (p. 42)

public opinion In IR, the range of views on foreign policy issues held by the citizens of a state. (p. 156)

rally 'round the flag syndrome The public's increased support for government leaders during wartime, at least in the short term. (p. 159)

rational actors Actors conceived as single entities that can "think" about their actions coherently, make choices, identify their interests, and rank the interests in terms of priority. (p. 68)

rational model (of decision making) A model in which decision makers calculate the costs and benefits of each possible course of action, then choose the one with the highest benefits and lowest costs. (p. 141)

realism (political realism) A broad intellectual tradition that explains international relations mainly in terms of power. (p. 55) See also *idealism* and *neorealism*.

reciprocity A response in kind to another's actions; a strategy of reciprocity uses positive forms of leverage to promise rewards and negative forms of leverage to threaten punishment. (p. 66)

refugees People fleeing their countries to find refuge from war, natural disaster, or political persecution. International law distinguishes them from migrants. (p. 481)

reserves Hard-currency stockpiles kept by states. (p. 342)

risk assessment The preinvestment efforts by corporations (especially banks) to determine how likely it is that future political conditions in the target country will change so radically as to disrupt the flow of income. (p. 369)

satisficing The act of finding a satisfactory or "good enough" solution to a problem. (p. 146)

Secretariat See *UN Secretariat*.

secular (state) A state created apart from religious establishments and in which there is a high degree of separation between religious and political organizations. (p. 192)

security community A situation in which low expectations of interstate violence permit a high degree of political cooperation—as, for example, among NATO members. (p. 379)

Security Council See *UN Security Council*.

security dilemma A situation in which states' actions taken to assure their own security (such as deploying more military forces) are perceived as threats to the security of other states. (p. 75)

semiperiphery The area in the world-system in which some manufacturing occurs and some capital concentrates, but not to the extent of the core areas. (p. 465)

service sector The part of an economy that concerns services (as opposed to the production of tangible goods); the key focus in international trade negotiations is on banking, insurance, and related financial services. (p. 319)

settlement The outcome of a bargaining process. (p. 169)

Single European Act (1985) It set a target date of the end of 1992 for the creation of a true common market (free cross-border movement of goods, capital, people, and services) in the European Community (EC). (p. 385)

Sino-Soviet split A rift in the 1960s between the communist powers of the Soviet Union and China, fueled by China's opposition to Soviet moves toward peaceful coexistence with the United States. (p. 41)

socialism A term encompassing many political movements, parties, economic theories, and ideologies, historical and present-day. With its idea that workers should have political power (or a larger share of power), socialism favors the redistribution of wealth toward the workers who produce it. In economic policy, socialists have favored different combinations of planning and reliance on market forces, as well as various patterns of ownership. (p. 460) See also *capitalism* and *Marxism*.

sovereignty A state's right, at least in principle, to do whatever it wants within its own territory; traditionally sovereignty is the most important international norm. (p. 74)

Special Drawing Right (SDR) A world currency created by the International Monetary Fund (IMF) to replace gold as a world standard. Valued by a "basket" of national currencies, the SDR has been called "paper gold." (p. 351)

Stalinism The system that prevailed during Stalin's rule in the Soviet Union (1924–1953), which was marked by totalitarian state control under the Communist party and the ruthless elimination of the regime's opponents on a massive scale. (p. 461)

state An inhabited territorial entity controlled by a government that exercises sovereignty on its territory. (p. 10)

state-owned industries Industries such as oil-production companies and airlines that are owned wholly or partly by the state because they are thought to be vital to the national economy. (p. 308)

state-sponsored terrorism The use of terrorist groups by states, usually under control of a state's intelligence agency, to achieve political aims. (p. 204)

stealth technology The use of special radar-absorbent materials and unusual shapes in the design of aircraft, missiles, and ships to scatter enemy radar. (p. 230)

Strategic Arms Limitation Treaties (SALT) SALT I (1972) and SALT II (1979) put formal ceilings on the growth of U.S. and Soviet strategic weapons. SALT II was never ratified by the U.S. Senate (due to the subsequent Soviet invasion of Afghanistan). (p. 245)

Strategic Defense Initiative (SDI) A U.S. effort, also known as "star wars," to develop defenses that could shoot down incoming ballistic missiles, spurred by President Ronald Reagan in 1983. Critics call it an expensive failure that will likely be ineffective. (p. 243) See also *Antiballistic Missile (ABM) Treaty*.

structural violence A term used by some scholars to refer to poverty, hunger, oppression, and other social and economic sources of conflict. (p. 130) See also *positive peace*.

subsistence farming Rural communities growing food mainly for their own consumption rather than for sale in local or world markets. (p. 478)

subtext Meanings that are implicit or hidden in a text rather than explicitly addressed. (p. 122) See also *postmodernism*.

summit meeting A meeting between heads of state, often referring to leaders of great powers, as in the Cold War superpower summits between the United States and the Soviet Union or today's meetings of the Group of Eight on economic coordination. (p. 42)

superstructure In Marxist terminology, the forms of politics and culture that are shaped by the economic base or mode of production (slavery, feudalism, capitalism). (p. 462)

supranationalism The subordination of state authority or national identity to larger institutions and groupings such as the European Union. (p. 377)

tariff A duty or tax levied on certain types of imports (usually as a percentage of their value) as they enter a country. (p. 315)

technology transfer Third world states' acquisition of technology (knowledge, skills, methods, designs, specialized equipment, etc.) from foreign sources, usually in conjunction with direct foreign investment or similar business operations. (p. 516)

terms of trade The overall relationship between prices of imported and exported goods. (p. 509)

territorial waters The waters near states' shores generally treated as part of national territory. The UN Convention on the Law of the Sea provides for a 12-mile territorial sea (exclusive national jurisdiction over shipping and navigation) and a 200-mile exclusive economic zone (EEZ) covering exclusive fishing and mineral rights (but allowing for free navigation by all). (p. 179) See also *high seas* and *UN Convention on the Law of the Sea (UNCLOS)*.

third-world countries See *less-developed countries*.

tit for tat A strategy of strict reciprocity (matching the other player's response) after an initial cooperative move; it can bring about mutual cooperation in a repeated Prisoner's Dilemma game, since it ensures that defection will not pay. (p. 135)

total war Warfare by one state waged to conquer and occupy another; modern total war originated in the Napoleonic Wars, which relied upon conscription on a mass scale. (p. 199)

tragedy of the commons A collective goods dilemma that is created when common environmental assets (such as the world's fisheries) are depleted or degraded through the failure of states to cooperate effectively. One solution is to "enclose" the commons (split them into individually owned pieces); international regimes can also be a (partial) solution. (p. 414)

transitional economies Countries in Russia and Eastern Europe that are trying to convert from communism to capitalism, with various degrees of success. (p. 307)

Treaty of Rome (1957) The founding document of the European Economic Community (EEC) or Common Market, now subsumed by the European Union. (p. 381)

United Nations (UN) An organization of nearly all world states, created after World War II to promote collective security. (p. 10)

UN Charter The founding document of the United Nations; it is based on the principles that states are equal, have sovereignty over their own affairs, enjoy independence and territorial integrity, and must fulfill international obligations. The Charter also lays out the structure and methods of the UN. (p. 257)

UN Convention on the Law of the Sea (UNCLOS) A world treaty (1982) governing use of the oceans. The UNCLOS treaty established rules on territorial waters and a 200-mile exclusive economic zone (EEZ). (p. 426) See also *territorial waters*.

UN Conference on Trade and Development (UNCTAD) A structure established in 1964 to promote third world development through various trade proposals. (p. 272)

UN Development Program (UNDP) It coordinates the flow of multilateral development assistance and manages 5,000 projects at once around the world (focusing especially on technical development assistance). (p. 528)

UN Environment Program (UNEP) It monitors environmental conditions and, among other activities, works with the World Meteorological Organization to measure changes in global climate. (p. 421)

UN General Assembly Comprised of representatives of all states, it allocates UN funds, passes nonbinding resolutions, and coordinates third world development programs and various autonomous agencies through the Economic and Social Council (ECOSOC). (p. 257)

UN Secretariat The UN's executive branch, led by the secretary-general. (p. 257)

UN Security Council A body of five great powers (which can veto resolutions) and ten rotating member states, which makes decisions about international peace and security including the dispatch of UN peacekeeping forces. (p. 257)

undernourishment The lack of needed foods; a lack of calories. (p. 477)

urbanization A shift of population from the countryside to the cities that typically accompanies economic development and is augmented by displacement of peasants from subsistence farming. (p. 479)

Uruguay Round A series of negotiations under the General Agreement on Tariffs and Trade (GATT) that began in Uruguay in 1986, and concluded in 1994 with agreement to create the World Trade Organization. The Uruguay Round followed earlier GATT negotiations such as the Kennedy Round and the Tokyo Round. (p. 324) See also *World Trade Organization (WTO)*.

U.S.-Japanese Security Treaty A bilateral alliance between the United States and Japan, created in 1951 against the potential Soviet threat to Japan. The United States maintains troops in Japan and is committed to defend Japan if attacked, and Japan pays the United States to offset about half the cost of maintaining the troops. (p. 88)

war crimes Violations of the law governing the conduct of warfare, such as by mistreating prisoners of war or unnecessarily targeting civilians. (p. 283) See also *just war doctrine*.

Warsaw Pact A Soviet-led Eastern European military alliance, founded in 1955 and disbanded in 1991. It opposed the NATO alliance. See also *North Atlantic Treaty Organization (NATO)*. (p. 87)

weapons of mass destruction Nuclear, chemical, and biological weapons, all distinguished from conventional weapons by their enormous potential lethality, and by their relative lack of discrimination in whom they kill. (p. 231)

World Bank Formally the International Bank for Reconstruction and Development (IBRD), it was established in 1944 as a source of loans to help reconstruct the European economies. Later, the main borrowers were third world countries and, in the 1990s, Eastern European ones. (p. 349)

World Court (International Court of Justice) The judicial arm of the UN; located in The Hague, it hears only cases between states. (p. 276)

world government A centralized world governing body with strong enforcement powers. (p. 131)

World Health Organization (WHO) Based in Geneva, it provides technical assistance to improve health conditions in the third world and conducts major immunization campaigns. (p. 273)

world-system theory A view of the world in terms of regional class divisions, with industrialized countries as the core, poorest third world countries as the periphery, and other areas (for example, some of the newly industrializing countries) as the semiperiphery. (p. 464)

World Trade Organization (WTO) An organization begun in 1995 that expanded the GATT's traditional focus on manufactured goods, and created monitoring and enforcement mechanisms. (p. 322) See also *General Agreement on Tariffs and Trade (GATT)* and *Uruguay Round*.

zero-sum games A situation in which one actor's gain is by definition equal to the other's loss, as opposed to a non-zero-sum game, in which it is possible for both actors to gain (or lose). (p. 71)

Credits

Page 2: Reuters NewMedia, Inc./Corbis; **4:** Defense Visual Information Center; **11:** Ken Cedeno/Corbis; **13:** Patrick Hertzog/Pool/Reuters/Corbis; **44:** Emmanual Dunand/AFP/Getty Images; **54:** Franco Pagetti/Polaris; **58:** Abedin Taherkenareh/epa/epa/Corbis; **60:** Kevork Djansezian/AP/Wide World Photos; **63:** Reuters New Media/Corbis; **64:** AP/Wide World Photos; **70:** Mohammed Ameen/Reuters/Landov; **74:** Mike Theiler/Getty Images; **78:** China Newsphoto/Reuters/Corbis; **83:** AP/Wide World Photos; **85:** Chris Hondros/Getty Images; **88:** National Archives and Records Administration; **91:** AP/Wide World Photos; **98:** Caren Firouz/Landov; **101:** NASA TV/Reuters/Corbis; **103:** AP/Wide World Photos; **109:** Kevin Coombs/Reuters/Corbis; **111:** Chris Pfuhl/AFP/Getty Images; **113:** Max Montecinos/Reuters/Landov; **115:** AP/Wide World Photos; **117:** Corbis; **124:** AP/Wide World Photos; **126:** LUC GNAGO/Reuters/Corbis; **128:** David Silverman/Getty Images; **129:** AP/Wide World Photos; **132:** Jason Reed/Reuters/Corbis; **138:** Ken Cedono/Corbis; **140:** AP/Wide World Photos; **144:** AP/Wide World Photos; **148:** Brooks Kraft/Corbis; **150:** Alexandra Avajuab/Contact Press Images; **153:** Edgar Schoepal/AP/Wide World Photos; **155:** AP/Wide World Photos; **157:** Cheryl Ravelo/Reuters/Landov; **162:** Alaa Badarneh/epa/Corbis; **164:** AP/Wide World Photos; **168:** Haley/Sipa Press; **172:** Ria/Novosti/Sovfoto/Eastfoto; **176:** Jhai Jeumpa/Reuters/Corbis; **180:** Kyodo/Landov; **184:** Defense Visual Information Center; **186:** Adam Nadel/Polaris; **189:** Candace Feit/epa/Corbis; **193:** Reuters/Corbis; **197:** Reuters/Landov; **203:** Masatomo Kuriya; **211:** Bernard Bisson/Corbis Sygma; **212:** Laurent Van Der Stockt/Getty Images; **215:** Alex Maclean/Landslides; **221:** AP/Wide World Photos; **223:** AFP/Getty Images; **225:** AP/Wide World Photos; **227:** Department of Defense; **230:** AFP/Getty Images; **232:** Joe Raedle/Getty Images; **237:** Rina Castelnuovo/Contact Press Images; **239:** AP/Wide World Photos; **241:** Reuters/Corbis; **243:** AP/Wide World Photos; **250:** Justin Lane/epa/Corbis; **253:** Luc Gnago/Reuters/Corbis; **259:** Richard Perry/The New York Times; **262:** AFP Photo/Timothy A. Clary/Getty Images; **269:** AP/Wide World Photos; **272:** Reuters/Landov; **277:** AP/Wide World Photos; **279:** AP/Wide World Photos; **281:** Bettmann/Corbis; **283:** George Osodi/AFP/Getty Images; **288:** Koichi Kamoshida/Getty Images; **295:** Roger Ressmeyer/Corbis; **296:** Eliseo Fernandez/Reuters/Corbis; **301:** EPA/Landov; **307:** Deutsche Presse Agentur GMBH; **309:** Lucy Nicholson/Reuters/Corbis; **312:** T. Haley/Sipa Press; **315:** AP/Wide World Photos; **319:** Jamil Bittar/Reuters/Landov; **320:** AP/Wide World Photos; **325:** Paul Yeung/Reuters/Corbis; **326:** Pallava Bagla/Corbis Sygma; **329:** AP/Wide World Photos; **337:** Andersen-Ross/Brand X/PictureQuest.com; **338:** Zhang Heping/Kyodo/Landov; **341:** Paulo Whitaker/Reuters/Getty Images; **344:** EPA/Landov; **345:** AP/Wide World Photos; **347:** Greg Davis/TimePix/Getty Images; **349:** AFP/Getty Images; **358:** AP/Wide World Photos; **362:** Getty Images; **366:** Robin Moyer/Getty Images; **369:** Smock John/Sipa Press; **376:** James Hill/New York Times; **378:** Patrice Habans/Corbis Sygma; **382:** Frank Fournier/Contact Press Images; **386:** Reuters/Corbis; **389:** Virginia Mayo-Pool/Getty Images; **391:** AP/Wide World Photos; **395:** Andre Gamasore/Galbe.com; **397:** AFP/Getty Images; **399:** Document France 2/The New Yorker Magazine; **403:** Jeffrey Aaronson/Network Aspen; **412:** Michael Yamashita/Corbis; **414:** Reuters/Corbis; **416:** Josef Polleros/The Image Works; **419:** AP/Wide World Photos; **424:** Suzanne Opton/Timepix/Getty Images; **425:** AP/Wide World Photos; **430:** Fred Greaves/Reuters Newmedia Inc/Corbis; **436:** Stanton R. Winter/The New York Times ; **438:** Sa'ad Mohammed/EPA/Landov; **444:** AFPGetty Images; **447:** Sebastian D'Souza/AFP/Getty Images; **454:** © Tore Bergsaker/Dagbladet/All Over Press Norway/Retna; **456:** Olivier Matthys/epa/Corbis; **458:** Mufty Munir/epa/Corbis; **462:** AP/Wide World Photos; **468:** AP/Wide World Photos;; **472:** Vera Lentz; **475:** AP/Wide World Photos; **479:** Kevin Carter/Corbis Sygma; **480:** Ed Kashi/IPN/Aurora; **483:** AP/Wide World Photos; **484:** AP/Wide World Photos; **487:** Musa Farman/epa/Landov; **489:** Juhan Kuus/Sipa Press; **496:** Arko Datta/AFP/Getty Images; **500:** Steve Vidler/e-stock Photography, LLC; **502:** STR/AFP/Getty Images; **510:** AP/Wide World Photos; **513:** Gleb Garanich/Reuters/Corbis; **515:** AFP/Getty Images; **519:** AFP/Getty Images; **521:** AP/Wide World Photos; **522:** Josef Polleross; **527:** Sena Vidanagama/AFP/Getty Images; **531:** Defense Visual Information Center; **532:** Oxfam America; **540:** Unicef/HQ93-1149/Senad Gubelic

Icon credits: Video icon: Eric Curry/© Tecmap Corporation, © Royalty-Free/Corbis; **Web Link icon:** © W. Cody/Corbis; **Changing World Order icon:** © Dave Teel/Corbis; **Simulation icon:** © Matthias Kulka/Corbis; **InfoRev icon:** © John Gillmoure/Corbis

Author Index

Note: Entry format is page number followed by footnote number; 144n52 refers to page 144, footnote 52.

Subject Index

Note: **Boldface** entries and page numbers indicate key terms. Entries for tables and figures are followed by "*(table)*" and "*(fig.)*" respectively.